Socio-Economic Rights

ADJUDICATION UNDER
A TRANSFORMATIVE CONSTITUTION

Socio-Economic Rights

ADJUDICATION UNDER A TRANSFORMATIVE CONSTITUTION

SANDRA LIEBENBERG

BA LLB (UCT), LLM (Essex)
Attorney of the High Court of South Africa
HF Oppenheimer Professor of Human Rights Law,
Stellenbosch University

JUTA

First published in 2010
by
Juta & Co, Ltd
First Floor, Sunclare Building
21 Dreyer Street
Claremont
7708

ISBN 978 0 7021 8480 2

Set in 11/13 pt Bembo by GJ du Toit, Cape Town
Cover design by Drag and Drop
Print management by Print Communications

This book was peer reviewed prior to publication by two independent academic specialists in the field of socio-economic rights.

For Jan

COVER PHOTOGRAPH

The photograph on the cover is by Brenton Geach and first appeared on the front page of the *Cape Times* of 11 June 2009. It is reproduced with the kind permission of Independent Newspapers. The photograph shows members of the Joe Slovo community outside Cape Town receiving a report-back from community leaders and lawyers on the outcome of their appeal to the Constitutional Court against their eviction and relocation to Delft. This case is discussed in chapter 6 of the book. Thank you to Mzwanele Zulu, a community leader in the Joe Slovo informal settlement and a leading figure in the litigation, for the information he provided to me on the circumstances in which this photograph was taken.

Acknowledgments

This book has been written over a period of three and a half years, but it is the product of a much longer engagement in the relationship between law and social justice. My interest in the contribution of law to the struggles of impoverished communities developed whilst working as a fellow at the Legal Resources Centre in 1988, and as a lawyer in the public interest department of the law firm, Bernard Vukic and Potash from 1989 to 1993. During this period I was involved in various cases defending communities against forced removals in terms of apartheid laws, and representing them in their struggles for security of tenure and basic services.

Studying for my LLM degree in international human rights law at the University of Essex in 1993–1994, I first began to take seriously the idea that socio-economic rights were an integral component of human rights law and deserved more concerted attention from scholars and activists for social change. My friend, Catarina Krause of the Åbo Institute for Human Rights, Åbo Akademi University, Finland must bear the major responsibility for this. I am grateful to her for ongoing support, and for the opportunity to teach annually on a ground-breaking course on the justiciability of economic, social and cultural rights presented by the Institute.

I have benefited in the writing of this book from a vibrant and supportive community of scholars and activists working in the field of socio-economic rights both in South Africa and abroad. They are too numerous to record here, but their influence on the development of my thinking on various themes is apparent from the citations in the book. A few exceptions must, however, be made.

I have been deeply inspired by the groundbreaking work on transformative constitutionalism by Karl Klare, School of Law, Northeastern University (Boston). I have derived similar inspiration from the scholarship on legal responses to poverty by Lucy Williams of the Northeastern University School of Law. I am honoured that they agreed to read the manuscript and write the foreword.

Frank Michelman of Harvard University Law School, and the students in his seminar on 'Constitutions and Property' generously read and provided me with comments on chapter 7 of this book. His extensive scholarship has had a significant influence on my thinking and research.

My colleague, Geo Quinot similarly read and provided comments on chapter 8 and the section of the postscript (chapter 10) dealing with the Constitutional Court judgment in *Mazibuko* case. He was also a sounding-board for the ideas in this book over numerous cups of coffee.

I received invaluable advice and guidance from Iain Currie of the Wits Law School, from the inception of this book project. I am indebted to him for sharing his considerable experience with me and providing calm advice through the ups and downs of writing.

My gratitude also goes to the two academic peer-reviewers who took time out of their busy schedules to review the manuscript prior to its publication.

For the opportunity to be involved to be involved in socio-economic rights litigation, advocacy and educational initiatives in the area of socio-economic rights, I particularly thank my former colleagues and the current staff at the Socio-Economic Rights Project, Community Law Centre (UWC).

A number of practitioners and researchers working at the coalface of socio-economic rights litigation in South Africa and abroad were extremely helpful in supplying me with copies of unreported cases, court orders, settlement agreements as well as updating me on developments in their various socio-economic rights cases. I am grateful for their patience and generosity in responding to my persistent queries and requests for information, and for involving me in some of the litigation. In particular, my thanks go to Geoff Budlender, Jonathan Berger, Jackie Dugard, Beth Goldblatt, Adila Hassim, Steve Kahanovitz, Malcolm Langford, Bruce Porter, Sarah Sephton, Adila Hassim, Stuart Wilson, and the staff of the Black Sash, the Children's Institute (UCT) and the Alliance for Children's Entitlement to Social Security Rights (ACESS).

The research and writing of this book were supported by a generous grant from the National Research Foundation (NRF) under a focus area project on law and socio-economic transformation in South Africa. Further funding to support research on this project was provided through the University of Stellenbosch's overarching strategic research and outreach project on *Combating Poverty, Homelessness and Socio-Economic Vulnerability under the Constitution*, and the Claude Leon Foundation. My appreciation goes to these institutions for their support. Any opinion, findings and conclusions or recommendations expressed in this book are my own and the relevant institutions do not accept any liability in regard thereto.

I have been fortunate to enjoy the generous support of the Dean of the Stellenbosch Law Faculty, Gerhard Lubbe. Prof Lubbe and my colleagues in the Law Faculty provided an intellectually challenging and conducive environment in which to research and write this book. I am also grateful for the encouragement received throughout this project from Justice Laurie Ackermann.

At various periods during the writing of this manuscript I received excellent research assistance from various postgraduate law students. Special thanks are due in this context to Sharon Brink and Barbara Loots. Khulekani Moyo assisted me with the preparation of the index in the final stages. Gustav Muller made a substantial contribution through being a critical reader of the manuscript and was assiduous in his checking of sources and references. He has been an outstanding research assistant.

Martin Rollo rendered professional, meticulous proof-reading assistance. This book would not have seen the light of day without the gracious encouragement and expert management of Ute Kuhlmann of Juta & Co. It was a privilege and pleasure to work with her.

Naturally, I am solely responsible for all shortcomings and inadequacies in this work.

Any attempt to express the depth of my gratitude to my family can only be partial and inadequate. So I will simply record my appreciation of my late parents, Avril and Rudy, for giving me the support and space to be my own person and for encouraging me to read widely. Thank you to my son, Sam, for the patience and humour with which he endured my long hours behind the computer; to my stepson, Leif, for friendship; and, above all, to Jan whose love has made the dream of writing this book possible in every way.

Sandra Liebenberg
Stellenbosch, December 2009

Contents

Chapter 3

Chapter 4

Foreword

South Africa's negotiated transition to democracy—one of the great, liberating events of our times—will also be remembered for fostering an exceptional burst of legal creativity and innovation. The ingenious, two-stage constitution-making process presided over by a Constitutional Court led in 1996 to the adoption of a visionary text. The South African Constitution contains justiciable socio-economic, as well as civil and political, rights. It imposes a positive obligation on the state 'to promote and fulfill the rights in the Bill of Rights'. It subjects private as well as public power to democratic norms and calls for an interrogation and renovation of the private-law infrastructure of economic and social life. It is thoroughly egalitarian, and at the same time sensitive to social diversity and difference. It envisions a participatory, engaged, and transparent form of democracy.

Other legal systems have some of these features, including socio-economic rights. But South Africans combined these elements and added some inventions of their own to create something new in legal culture—transformative constitutionalism. The Constitutional Court has affirmed that 'a commitment ... to transform society ... lies at the heart of our new constitutional order'.[1] The Preamble announces that the people adopt the Constitution so as to 'establish a society based on democratic values, social justice and fundamental human rights' and to '[i]mprove the quality of life of all citizens and free the potential of each person.' The Constitution is meant not just to celebrate on paper the participatory democracy it envisions and the rights it guarantees, but, over time, to bring into being political and social conditions that will allow all who live in South Africa to actually experience self-determination and human fulfilment.

Socio-Economic Rights: Adjudication Under a Transformative Constitution is a comprehensive examination of this new conception of legality, South Africa's transformative constitutionalism. Liebenberg first reconstructs the ethical vision and political aspirations that inspired the Constitution and then provides a step-by-step account of the South African courts' journey into unknown territory as they commenced adjudication with respect to socio-economic rights during the first 15 years of the new dispensation. South Africa's transformative constitutionalism is by now a diffuse mass of doctrinal experimentation, intellectual creativity, concrete problem-solving, ambiguity, uncertainty, false starts, and, frankly, more than a few hopes and prayers. Liebenberg's great achievement is to pull all of these legal materials together and fuse them into a coherent whole. This book establishes South African socio-economic rights jurisprudence as an academic discipline. Confidently and with technical

[1] *Soobramoney v Minister of Health (KwaZulu-Natal)* 1998 1 SA 765 (CC); 1997 (12) BCLR 1696 (CC) (Chaskalson P) para 8.

sophistication, she demonstrates that judicial enforcement of socio-economic rights can be structured, principled, and appropriately respectful of, without being slavishly beholden to, the representative branches of government.

Sandra Liebenberg is eminently qualified to undertake this challenge. An internationally admired scholar in the field of socio-economic rights, she has been a close observer of and prolific commentator on every aspect of South Africa's unfolding socio-economic rights jurisprudence since the Constitution was entrenched. She played a role in the constitutional drafting process; her talents, insight, and sense of judgment were recognized when, as a relatively junior lawyer, she was appointed as one of the technical advisors to the Constitutional Assembly's 'Theme Committee' on Fundamental Rights. She was involved in preparing *amici curiae* submissions in several of the leading cases discussed in this study. She reads voraciously and views the subject through a wide-angle lens. Her doctrinal arguments are grounded in a carefully constructed theoretical framework and supplemented by up-to-the-minute comparative references.

The overriding argument of the book may be summarized thus. The inclusion of socio-economic rights in the final text is central to the Constitutional vision, which cannot be understood without perceiving that the socio-economic rights provisions are the platform upon which the distinctly South African conception of democracy is constructed. The Constitution seeks to entrench an 'empowered' or 'substantive,' not merely formal, understanding of democracy. This is intended to be a deliberative political and social system, inviting popular participation at all levels of decision making. In saying that the democratic aspiration is *substantive*, Liebenberg means that the South African Constitution contemplates that government will gradually, but steadily, take redistributive and institutional measures to insure that all people have the social and economic resources necessary for authentic participation in the democratic process and genuine experiences of self-determination and self-realization. Put another way, it is a foundational tenet of this Constitution that law and the State must pay attention to poverty and do what can be done to eradicate it.

But strong currents in South African legal culture reinforce a traditional and formalistic conception of rights. Liebenberg fears that this bias may block fulfillment of the constitutional dream and instead preserve the existing social order (albeit with the worst injustices of apartheid removed). Therefore, in addition to pressing forward for the realization of socio-economic rights, advocates and scholars must task themselves to unearth, criticize, re-imagine the assumptions and intellectual habits characteristic of the prevailing legal culture. This requires the development of a 'new interpretive approach',[2] the contours of which are outlined in this book.

The core of the project is the development of a normative account of socio-economic rights, their role in fostering deliberative democracy, and their interaction with the equality guarantee. 'This task should be approached by considering the purposes and values which the[se] rights seek to promote in light of their his-

[2] Page 77.

torical and current socio-economic context'.[3] This is not a request for a blueprint or a grand narrative. Quite the opposite, Liebenberg's refreshing approach conceives constitutionalism as an invitation to ever-evolving conversation and dialogue. The constitutional narrative should be an 'open fabric' with 'loose weave'.[4] Constitutional solutions are always provisional. '[T]he normative content of socio-economic rights should always remain contingent and incomplete, allowing space for the evolution of new meanings in response to changing contexts and forms of injustice'.[5]

To be sure, Liebenberg urges unwavering fidelity to the Constitution's transformative aspirations and unflagging attention to its commitment to the poor and marginalized groups in society. She provides several 'normative guidelines' to steer the project, including a holistic conception of human well being, a conception of the interdependence of all people, a focus on material disadvantage, an understanding of the interdependence of the rights in the Constitution, and a rich, dialogic, and empowering understanding of democracy. Beyond this, she is comfortable with a fluid understanding of the relationship of competing rights and calls for contingent, context-based solutions designed to solve real problems for real people. She is interested in constitutional principles, of course, but also very much in micro-level justice for the parties in their lived situation.[6]

A normative account of socio-economic rights is indispensable, but Liebenberg also emphasizes the need for a new understanding of separation of powers, new systems of remedies, and reconstruction of private law in the spirit of the Bill of Rights. Throughout the book, Liebenberg highlights what is surely one of the most pressing problems of 21st century constitutionalism, viz., to sketch out a deliberative, dialogic, and consultative understanding of the relationship between the coordinate branches of government, and particularly between the judiciary and the legislature. South Africans—and other peoples—have chosen to adopt the legal practice of socio-economic rights-based judicial review of legislative and executive action. The question now is how to adjust and calibrate the interactions between the branches so as to respect the democratic underpinnings of legislative primacy while affording ample scope for courts to infuse the socio-economic rights on paper with meaningful, enforceable content. Liebenberg cuts right through the shibboleths and mantras of school-book teaching on separation-of-powers to offer new ideas.

Perhaps the most important achievement of this book is her exhaustive, fine-grained, nuanced analysis of existing technologies of judicial review, particularly in her lengthy meditation on the medley of approaches thus far deployed by the Constitutional Court in socio-economic rights cases under the deceptively simple heading of 'reasonableness review'. This is accompanied by a precise but also

---

[3] Page 179.

[4] Page 48.

[5] Page 180.

[6] Pp. 278–79 (citing *Port Elizabeth Municipality v Various Occupiers* 2005 (1) SA 217 (CC); 2004 (12) BCLR 1268 (CC) para 38 (Sachs J)).

imaginative effort to refine the techniques of judicial review so as to make them more consonant with the Constitution's egalitarian, participatory, and deliberative values and aspirations. Similarly, she painstakingly develops why traditional, zero-sum, and monetary-oriented remedies must give way to new, more flexible, participatory remedial conceptions calculated to address complex, multi-valent social problems by drawing upon local knowledge and engaging the parties' problem-solving capacities.

Finally, Liebenberg reviews South African courts' performance thus far in fulfilling the mandate, imposed by Constitution's common- and customary-law development clauses,[7] to reconsider the private-law underpinnings of social and economic life and reconstruct them in light of the Constitutional ethos. Here she highlights both achievements, e.g., in the law of residential eviction, as well as fields in which she argues, correctly in our view, that more progress is needed (e.g., contracts).

This book should be read and studied by all who share the hope that legal practices can contribute to social transformation and social justice. We are honored to have this opportunity to take part in its launch.

Karl Klare
Lucy Williams

Program on Human Rights & the Global Economy
School of Law, Northeastern University, Boston, USA

[7] Constitution ss 8(3) & 39(2).

Preface

As a white South African who was born and grew up in the apartheid era, I was privileged to live in a decent house with good services in white suburbia, to go to a decent school and to have access to decent health care whenever I needed it. The vast majority of my fellow citizens were not. They were deprived of the right to vote, subjected to political repression, and suffered under the daily, soul-destroying indignities of apartheid. They were also subject to systemic deprivation and discrimination in their access to housing, land, health care, food, water, social security and education. The results of these policies are still manifest after 15 years of constitutional democracy. Large classes of people are marginalised from active participation in all spheres of South African society by a complex web of poverty, inequality and social subordination.

My research career has focused primarily on the question of how the judicial interpretation and enforcement of the socio-economic rights can be more responsive to conditions of systemic poverty and inequality in South African society. I have been particularly interested in how the influence of classic liberal legal culture in adjudication constrains the development of a more substantive jurisprudence on socio-economic rights. By this I mean a jurisprudence which opens up a sustained and serious engagement with the normative purposes and values which socio-economic rights should advance within the historical and social context of South African society.

The failure to take these purposes and values seriously in constitutional interpretation perpetuates legal doctrines which are blind to the experiences and consequences of poverty and inequality. The marginalisation of issues of social class within legal doctrine has implications for broader political discourses. This book explores these themes through an analysis and evaluation of the socio-economic rights jurisprudence which has developed since the coming into force of the 1996 Constitution on 4 February 1997.

The first chapter consists of a historical overview of the socio-economic injustices of the colonial and apartheid period. It then traces the major political struggles, intellectual debates and civil society processes which led to the inclusion of socio-economic rights as justiciable rights in the Bill of Rights in the 1996 Constitution.

The Constitution seeks to create an enabling legal framework for redressing the injustices of the past and creating a transformed society 'based on democratic values, social justice and fundamental human rights'. A fundamental feature of this Constitution is a holistic Bill of Rights which integrates civil and political rights with socio-economic and cultural rights. All of these rights are enforceable by the courts, which have a broad discretion to grant just and equitable remedies. Provision is also made for the application of the rights in the Bill of Rights to private actors, and for constitutional rights to influence the development of all areas of law.

The courts constitute important institutions for deliberation and judgment on the normative values and purposes that should shape and guide transformation in post-apartheid South Africa. Values such as respect for human dignity, non-discrimination on grounds such as race, gender and sexual orientation, freedom of religion, and rights supporting democratic participation have wrought far-reaching changes in several areas of public and private law. The various socio-economic rights in the Bill of Rights present the courts with an important opportunity to develop our legal system to be more attuned and responsive to poverty and social marginalisation in South African society. This conception of the role of the courts in promoting social and economic transformation is developed in the first part of chapter 2.

However, it is argued that there are deeply entrenched features of South Africa's legal and interpretative culture which constrain the potential of socio-economic rights to contribute to the transformation of the legal system. These facets of South African legal culture have their roots in classic liberal conceptions of law, rights and politics. Their tendency is to reproduce the binary oppositions of law/politics, negative/positive rights, civil and political rights/socio-economic rights, and public/private law. In addition, they favour rigid, territorial models of the separation of powers doctrine over more flexible, dialogic models.

The latter half of chapter 2 examines the implications of these and other features of classic liberal constitutionalism for the adjudication of socio-economic rights. It explores alternative approaches to the adjudication of socio-economic rights which can support the restructuring of institutions and systems that perpetuate poverty and starkly unequal participation in all spheres of society. Such endeavours go to the heart of the Constitution's aspiration to found a society based on social justice, the improvement in the quality of life of all and the freeing of the potential of each person.[8]

Chapter 3 situates the socio-economic rights in the Constitution within the overall context of the Bill of Rights. It examines the relevance of various features of the Bill of Rights to the adjudication of socio-economic rights. These include the State's overarching duties 'to respect, protect, promote and fulfil' rights, the provisions and jurisprudence on legal standing, and the limitation of rights. Finally, it considers the significance of the interpretative injunctions in s 39 of the Constitution. The latter provision expressly requires the courts to promote the constitutional values of human dignity, equality and freedom, and to consider international and foreign law sources when interpreting the Bill of Rights.

The remaining chapters of the book examine the jurisprudence on socio-economic rights which has developed since the coming into force of the 1996 Constitution. The focus is on the socio-economic rights entrenched in ss 26 (housing), 27 (health care, food, water and social security), 28(1)(*c*) (children's socio-economic rights), 29

[8] See the Preamble to the Constitution.

(education) and 35(2)(*e*) (the socio-economic rights of persons deprived of their liberty).[9]

A substantial jurisprudence has developed on these rights, which provides a solid basis for examining how the South African courts have responded to issues of socio-economic deprivation. The analysis seeks to identify the interpretative and remedial approaches in the jurisprudence which run counter to, or support, the transformative approaches identified in chapter 2. It also seeks to identify how the jurisprudence could be developed in various ways to support the transformative purposes of the Constitution.

Chapter 4 examines the model of reasonableness review developed by the Constitutional Court for evaluating the State's compliance with the positive duties imposed by ss 26 and 27 of the Constitution. It also examines the model of review applied to the negative duty to refrain from depriving people of their existing access to the socio-economic rights protected in ss 26 and 27.

Chapter 5 focuses on the jurisprudence which has developed pertaining to children's socio-economic rights, the right to education, and the socio-economic rights of persons deprived of their liberty. These rights are drafted differently to the cluster of socio-economic rights in ss 26 and 27 and are concerned with the rights of groups who are in particularly vulnerable situations.

The impact of s 26(3) of the Constitution on various aspects of evictions law in South Africa is examined in chapter 6. This chapter seeks to demonstrate how the housing rights in s 26 have created a fundamentally new paradigm for adjudicating disputes concerning the eviction of people from their homes. These developments within eviction law illustrate the potential of socio-economic rights to produce far-reaching changes in the legal concepts and frameworks governing disputes which affect people's socio-economic welfare.

Chapter 7 explores the normative framework and methodologies for applying the Bill of Rights in disputes between private parties in the specific context of socio-economic rights. The second half of the chapter examines the effect of socio-economic rights in selected areas of private law. It identifies substantive developments brought about by constitutional housing rights in the sphere of property law. In contrast, it is argued that socio-economic rights have had a minimal influence on the development of contract law. This is ascribed to the narrow and formalistic interpretation accorded to socio-economic rights in this area, as well as the methodological

[9] Although this book focuses on these rights, there are many other rights in the Bill of Rights which have significant socio-economic dimensions. These include labour rights (s 23), environmental rights (s 24), property and land rights (s 25), and cultural rights (ss 30 and 31). Moreover, as this book emphasises at several points, there is a close interrelationship between socio-economic rights and rights which are traditionally classified as civil or political rights, such as the rights to equality (s 9), human dignity (s 10), life (s 11), and administrative justice (s 33).

and ideological constraints on the development of the common law of contract to give full effect to constitutional rights and values.

The remedial jurisprudence of the courts pertaining to socio-economic rights is examined in chapter 8. This chapter covers the range of remedies available to redress various types of socio-economic rights violations. It shows how the remedial tools available to the courts can stimulate innovative, participatory forms of redress for socio-economic rights violations. Particular attention is paid to the potential of structural interdicts to facilitate participatory resolutions to complex, multifaceted socio-economic deprivations. Deprivations of this nature are deeply embedded in various political, economic and social institutions, and cannot be remedied by the traditional, 'once-off' court orders. Instead they require a broad range of affected groups and institutions to engage meaningfully with each other on a series of reforms to be adopted over a period of time. The court retains supervision over the agreed reforms and their implementation to ensure that they comply with the normative goals and values required to give effect to the constitutional rights at stake.

The penultimate chapter of the book is a postscript which considers the following three constitutional judgments which were handed down after this book's cut-off date for the consideration of new judgments: *Head of Department: Mpumalanga Department of Education v Hoërskool Ermelo*,[10] *Nokotyana v Ekurhuleni Metropolitan Municipality*,[11] and *Mazibuko v City of Johannesburg*.[12] Particular attention is paid to the *Mazibuko* judgment as it illustrates many of the weaknesses of the existing model of reasonableness review for adjudicating positive socio-economic claims. It also represents a failure by the Court to apply basic rights of procedural fairness to protect a poor community's access to a socio-economic right such as water.

The concluding chapter identifies the main themes and challenges emerging from the analysis of the jurisprudence. The decisions of the courts have serious and far-reaching consequences for the parties to a case, as well as for other groups and communities in similar situations. However, constitutional adjudication also has a broader significance. It helps shape the public discourse on the normative and ethical values in the Bill of Rights and their implications for processes of transformation. The inclusion of socio-economic rights in the Bill of Rights signals the need to expose the rules which create and regulate the social and economic institutions of our society to critical examination and revision. A failure to accept this challenge limits substantially the relevance of the constitutional project for those who are economically and socially oppressed.

The limits of socio-economic rights litigation in bringing about far-reaching social change are acknowledged. However, the book ultimately insists on the responsibility of the courts to interpret the socio-economic rights in the Constitution in ways which promote more just economic and social relationships in South Africa.

---

[10] [2009] ZACC 32.
[11] [2009] ZACC 33.
[12] [2009] ZACC 28.

The cut-off date for a substantive examination of relevant socio-economic rights jurisprudence and academic material was 31 August 2009. However, as noted above, a postscript is incorporated which discusses three significant Constitutional Court judgments handed down subsequent to this date. These cases have been selected on the basis that the court *a quo* judgments in the relevant cases have been considered in the text. In addition, where relevant, reference is made in footnotes to decisions handed down in the period 1 September 2009 to 30 November 2009.

In the interests of convenience and not overburdening the text, details of additional parties, joined matters and the like have been omitted from case names in the text and footnotes. The full case citations are provided in the table of cases.

CHAPTER 1

The Struggle for Recognition

Including Socio-Economic Rights in the Constitution

In this chapter *Page*

1.1 INTRODUCTION

The inclusion of socio-economic rights in the Constitution must be viewed in the context of the fundamental changes to South Africa's legal system which facilitated the transition to democracy. The major structural and normative change in South Africa's legal system was the shift from a system of parliamentary sovereignty which existed under apartheid[1] to a system of constitutional democracy with an entrenched and justiciable Bill of Rights.[2] The Constitution with its justiciable Bill of Rights

[1] For descriptions of the role of the system of parliamentary sovereignty in facilitating the apartheid political order in South Africa, see J Dugard *Human Rights and the South African Legal Order* (1978); and R L Abel *Politics by Other Means: Law in the Struggle Against Apartheid, 1980–1994* (1995).

[2] Section 2 of the 1996 Constitution of the Republic of South Africa (hereafter generally referred to as 'the Constitution') reads: 'This Constitution is the supreme law of the Republic; law or conduct inconsistent with it is invalid, and the obligations imposed by it must be fulfilled.' Section 74 of the Constitution stipulates the majorities required and procedures to be followed for amending various sections of the Constitution. Amendments to chapter 2 containing the Bill of Rights require the supporting vote of at least two thirds of the members of the National Assembly, and at least six provinces in the National Council of Provinces. Provision is also made for publication and public comment on proposed constitutional amendments. According to s 38 of the Constitution, all the rights in the Bill of Rights are enforceable by the courts. Competent courts must declare that 'any law or conduct that is inconsistent with the Constitution is invalid to the extent of its inconsistency'. In addition, the courts have wide powers to make 'any order that is just and equitable' to remedy constitutional infringements (s 172(1)).

created the legal foundations for the establishment of democracy in South Africa and the building of a new post-apartheid society.

This chapter commences with a broad overview of the systemic violations of socio-economic rights that occurred during the apartheid era. It examines the role of the apartheid legal order in engineering these inequalities and the limited possibilities which existed within the legal system to challenge these violations. It proceeds to analyse the proposals and debates concerning socio-economic rights emerging from the political parties and civil society during the constitutional negotiations leading up to the adoption of the 1993 ('interim') Constitution. Thereafter, the processes through which socio-economic rights were included in the 1996 Constitution are examined. The chapter concludes with a consideration of the Constitutional Court's response to the objections lodged against the socio-economic rights provisions in the Bill of Rights during the certification process.

1.2 THE APARTHEID ERA

Apartheid represented not only the disenfranchisement of the black population of South Africa, but also an institutionalised system which maintained white domination and privilege in the political, economic, social and cultural spheres. This was achieved at the expense of the black population who were deprived of access to land, subjected to underdevelopment in economically marginal reserves and 'homelands', and systemically discriminated against in their access to a range of social services and resources.

Although apartheid as a political ideology is mainly associated with the period of National Party rule from 1948 to 1994, it has deep roots in the prior colonial and post-Union period.[3] For example, pass laws were introduced during the 19th century in the Cape Colony and Natal Colony, and the Black Land Act 27 of 1913 prohibited Africans from owning or renting land outside the designated reserves. The reserves formed the basis of the Bantustans and 'independent' homelands during the era of 'Grand Apartheid' under National Party rule. The Black Land Act and the Development Trust and Land Act 18 of 1936 restricted the African population to 13% of the total land area of South Africa.[4] Africans who remained on the farms in white areas were reduced to the status of labour tenants or squatters.[5]

The Black (Urban Areas) Act 21 of 1923 extended segregation to urban areas. It laid the groundwork for the establishment of 'locations' on the peripheries of white towns and cities for the accommodation of black people who were functional to the labour needs of the white-dominated economy, and enabled local authorities to administer

[3] See in this regard S Terreblanche *A History of Inequality in South Africa 1652–2002* (2002), particularly chapters 5 to 8.

[4] See M Robertson 'Dividing the land: An introduction to apartheid land law' in C Murray & C O'Regan (eds) *No Place to Rest: Forced Removals and the Law in South Africa* (1990) 122–136 at 128–129.

[5] On the history of land dispossession in South Africa, see further, chapter 6, part 6.1.

stricter pass laws and control of black urban dwellers. The Mines and Works Act 12 of 1911 legislated job reservation policies which excluded black persons from a range of skilled jobs on the mines and railways. Far-reaching political, social and economic control over the black population was entrenched through legislation such as the Black Administration Act 38 of 1927.[6] Policies of influx control were rigorously pursued through legislation such as the Black (Urban Areas) Consolidation Act 25 of 1945.

When the National Party came to power in 1948, it entrenched and deepened the system of systemic racial segregation and 'separate development' through a range of legislation enacted by the white minority Parliament. Such legislation included the Population Registration Act 30 of 1950, Group Areas Act 41 of 1950 and its successor legislation, the Black Education Act 47 of 1953, the Reservation of Separate Amenities Act 49 of 1953, the Group Areas Act 36 of 1966, the Black Local Authorities Act 102 of 1982, and the Black Communities Development Act 4 of 1984. Racial inequalities were entrenched through a myriad of political, legal, social and cultural institutions.[7] The remaining rights in land, such as labour tenancy, which black people had in areas reserved for white ownership and occupation, were eroded through a series of policy and legislative measures.[8]

In the economic sphere, the apartheid regime provided full employment to white people through a combination of discriminatory labour market and educational policies, 'while channeling cheap African labour to unskilled jobs on the mines and on farms'.[9] As Jeremy Seekings and Nicoli Nattrass observe:

> [N]o other capitalist state (in either the North or the South) has sought to structure income inequalities as systematically and brutally as did South Africa under apartheid.[10]

Race and class intersected, and racial discrimination deepened the class divisions in South African society.[11] The effect of these deep class divisions was that the deracialisation of public policy in the late and post-apartheid periods had a limited impact on inequality.[12]

The apartheid-era legal system provided scant legal tools which could be used to resist these large-scale violations of a range of internationally recognised civil and

---

[6] For a description of the purpose and functions of these legislated 'building blocks of segregation' after Union in 1910 and prior to 1948, see D Oakes *Illustrated History of South Africa: The Real Story* (1988) 315–318.

[7] For an overview, see Terreblanche (note 3 above) 334–339.

[8] For a description of the legal and institutional mechanisms through which this dispossession was effected, see the judgment of Moseneke DCJ in *Department of Land Affairs v Goedgelegen Tropical Fruits (Pty) Ltd* 2007 (6) SA 199 (CC), 2007 (10) BCLR 1027 (CC).

[9] J Seekings & N Nattrass *Class, Race and Inequality in South Africa* (2005) 6.

[10] Ibid 2.

[11] Seekings and Nattrass observe: '[U]nder apartheid, discrimination within classes (by race) exaggerated the effect of inequalities between classes' (ibid 4). See also R Davies, D O'Meara & S Dlamini *The Struggle for South Africa: A Reference Guide Vol 1* (1985) 1–3.

[12] Ibid 4. See further the discussion in chapter 2, part 2.2.2 at notes 6–14 and accompanying text.

political rights, as well as economic, social and cultural rights.[13] The system of parliamentary sovereignty under the apartheid-era Constitutions did not allow for judicial review of legislation for consistency with human rights norms.[14] As described above, the pervasive system of racial segregation was instituted through a barrage of legislative measures.

There was also limited scope for challenging the systemic injustices of the apartheid era through the common law. The common law had no tradition of recognising entitlements to social and economic resources and services on the basis of need. The closest that the pre-constitutional common law comes to protecting people's access to social benefits and resources is within the context of administrative law. This could arise, for example, when people are deprived of access, or denied access to a social benefit through procedurally unfair or unreasonable administrative action.[15]

Practically all socio-economic benefits such as social security, education and health care were regulated by statute on a racially discriminatory basis.[16] Black people generally derived marginal benefit from whatever liberal rights and values were protected in the common-law tradition. Their lives were governed through an elaborate system of proclamations, administrative regulations and codified versions of African customary law embodied in legislation such as the Black Administration Act. As Langa DCJ (as he then was) observed, this Act became 'a cornerstone of racial oppression, division and conflict in South Africa, the legacy of which will still take years to completely

---

[13] In 1973, the UN General Assembly adopted the International Convention on the Suppression and Punishment of the Crime of Apartheid. In terms of this Convention, apartheid was declared as a crime against humanity (art I). The definition of the crime of apartheid included the following 'inhuman acts':

> Any legislative measures and other measures calculated to prevent a racial group or groups from participation in the political, social, economic and cultural life of the country and the deliberate creation of conditions preventing the full development of such a group or groups, in particular by denying to members of a racial group or groups basic human rights and freedoms, including the right to work, the right to form recognized trade unions, the right to education, the right to leave and to return to their country, the right to a nationality, the right to freedom of movement and residence, the right to freedom of opinion and expression, and the right to freedom of peaceful assembly and association. (art II (*c*))

[14] The three main South African Constitutions prior to 1994 were: the South Africa Act 1 of 1909; the Republic of South Africa Constitution Act 32 of 1961; and the Republic of South Africa Constitution Act 110 of 1983.

[15] For a discussion of the doctrine of legitimate expectation in South African pre-constitutional administrative law and its possible application to social benefits, see A J van der Walt 'A South African reading of Frank Michelman's theory of social justice' in H Botha, A J van der Walt & J van der Walt (eds) *Rights and Democracy in a Transformative Constitution* (2004) 163–211 at 171–174; and C Hoexter *Administrative Law in South Africa* (2007) 350–357.

[16] On the racialised basis of social security provisioning in South Africa, see H Bhorat 'The South African social safety net: Past, present and future' (1995) 12 *Development Southern Africa* 595–604; and S van der Berg 'South African social security under apartheid and beyond' (1997) 14 *Development Southern Africa* 485–503.

eradicate'.[17] Ngcobo J (as he then was) describes the role of this legislation in facilitating the forced removals and geographical segregation of the apartheid era:

> The Native Administration Act 38 of 1927 appointed the Governor-General (later referred to as the State President) as 'supreme chief' of all Africans. It gave him power to govern Africans by proclamation. The powers given to him were virtually absolute. He could order the removal of an entire African community from one place to another. The Native Administration Act became the most powerful tool in the implementation of forced removals of Africans from the so-called 'white areas' into the areas reserved for them. These removals resulted in untold suffering. This geographical plan of segregation was described as forming part of 'a colossal social experiment and a long term policy'.[18]

In the context of employment, labour rights were gradually extended to black workers through statutory reforms to the Labour Relations Act 1 of 1956 as a result of the struggles of the trade union movement.[19]

The codification of African customary law impeded its development so that it no longer evolved in accordance with the changing needs and mores of the communities it was meant to serve.[20] African women were most disadvantaged by the application of patriarchal norms such as the rule of primogeniture, which excluded women from inheriting property in intestate estates,[21] and their status as perpetual minors under the tutelage of their fathers or husbands.[22] This was aggravated by the breakdown of traditional family and community support systems in rural areas as a result of forced removals, urbanisation and the migrant labour system.[23] Moreover, the Roman-Dutch and English common law developed without dialogic engagement with the many positive values and rights embodied in African customary law, such as its flexibility, the settling of disputes through meetings and consensus-seeking, the fostering of family

---

[17] *Bhe v Magistrate Khayelitsha; Shibi v Sithole; South African Human Rights Commission v President of the Republic of South Africa* 2005 (1) SA 580 (CC), 2005 (1) BCLR 1 (CC) para 61 ('*Bhe*').

[18] *Western Cape Provincial Government: In re DVB Behuising (Pty) Ltd v North West Provincial Government* 2001 (1) SA 500 (CC), 2000 (4) BCLR 347 (CC) para 41 (footnotes omitted).

[19] See S Friedman *Building Tomorrow Today: African Workers in Trade Unions 1970–1984* (1987); J Baskin *Striking Back: A History of COSATU* (1991).

[20] See the discussion in *Bhe* (note 17 above) paras 80–82.

[21] The rule of male primogeniture as it applies in African customary law to the inheritance of property was declared unconstitutional by the Constitutional Court in the *Bhe* decision ibid.

[22] See T Nhlapo 'African customary law in the interim Constitution' in S Liebenberg (ed) *The Constitution of South Africa from a Gender Perspective* (1995) 157–166, 162.

[23] M Chanock *The Making of South African Legal Culture 1902–1936: Fear, Favour and Prejudice* (2001) 34.

and community responsibility and co-operation and the philosophy of *ubuntu*.[24] Its main reference points were Europe, and not Africa or African institutions.[25]

Given this context, public interest lawyering under apartheid consisted mainly of exploiting loopholes in racially discriminatory legislation in spheres such as land and housing or in repressive security legislation, or utilising the principles of administrative law to mitigate the worst excesses of apartheid legality.[26]

Within the liberation struggle, there existed some tradition of recognising economic, social and cultural rights. Thus the Freedom Charter adopted by the Congress of the People in 1955 contained a number of clauses proclaiming people's entitlement to social and economic resources and services. The Freedom Charter was a manifesto which sought to reflect people's vision and aspirations for a future non-racial, democratic society, and to serve as a mobilising platform.[27] It did not make any concrete proposals regarding the constitutional entrenchment or enforcement mechanisms for its contents.

It is beyond the scope of this book to examine how the idea of a justiciable Bill of Rights gained acceptance within the liberation movements.[28] However, in 1989, the *Constitutional Guidelines for a Democratic South Africa* adopted by the ANC[29] supported the inclusion of 'a Bill of Rights based on the Freedom Charter' in a new constitutional dispensation.[30] In addition to civil and political rights, the democratic State would be under a duty 'to protect the right to work, and guarantee education and social security'.[31] In addition, 'the state and all social institutions' would be under 'a constitutional duty to take active steps to eradicate, speedily, the economic and social inequalities produced by racial discrimination'.[32] The Guidelines also contained

[24] See *Bhe* (note 17 above) para 45. On *ubuntu*, see further chapter 3, part 3.3.1 at notes 92–94 and accompanying text.

[25] Chanock (note 23 above) 33–34.

[26] See Abel (note 1 above). The Constitutional Court describes how the courts under apartheid had to 'claim space and push boundaries to find means of controlling public power'. *Pharmaceutical Manufacturers Association of SA; In re: Ex Parte President of the Republic of South Africa* 2000 (2) SA 674 (CC), 2000 (3) BCLR 241 (CC) para 45.

[27] See V Taylor *Social Mobilisation: Lessons from the Mass Democratic Movement* (1997) 48–50.

[28] For an account of the concerns and debates about a Bill of Rights for a democratic South Africa within the African National Congress (ANC), see A Sachs 'South Africa's unconstitutional constitution: The transition from power to lawful power' (1997) 41 *St Louis LJ* 1249–1257.

[29] Reproduced in (1989) 5 *SAJHR* 129–132. Available at http://www.anc.org.za/ancdocs/policy/guidelines.htm (accessed on 7 July 2009).

[30] Ibid para (*h*). According to the Guidelines, the 'success of the constitution, will be, to a large extent, determined by the degree to which it promotes conditions for the active involvement of all sectors of the population at all levels in government and in the economic and cultural life'.

[31] Ibid para (*l*).

[32] Ibid para (*j*).

express clauses dealing with land reform, workers' rights, the rights of women and the protection of '[t]he family, parenthood and children's rights'.[33]

1.3 THE CONSTITUTIONAL NEGOTIATIONS

The unbanning of the liberation movements and the release of political prisoners set in motion the process of negotiations towards a political settlement and new constitutional dispensation for South Africa.[34] A two-phase constitution-making process was agreed to. This entailed the adoption of a negotiated transitional or 'interim' Constitution by the old order Parliament.[35] The first democratic elections were held in South Africa from 26 to 28 April 1994 under this interim Constitution. The second phase involved the negotiation and adoption of the 1996 Constitution by the democratically elected members of the Constitutional Assembly.

In the lead-up to the constitutional negotiations, most of the major political parties released their proposals for a future South African Constitution and Bill of Rights. The question of the inclusion of socio-economic rights in the Bill of Rights emerged as a major issue of debate among political parties, civil society organisations and constitutional scholars.

In 1990, the ANC's Constitutional Committee published its working document for the constitutional negotiations, *A Bill of Rights for a Democratic South Africa*.[36] This draft Bill of Rights included both civil and political rights as well as economic, social and cultural rights. Article 10 was entitled 'Social, Educational, Economic and Welfare Rights'.[37] It contained a general section placing a duty on the State, 'to the maximum of its available resources', to undertake 'appropriate legislative and executive action in order to achieve the progressive realisation of basic social, educational, economic and welfare rights for the whole population'.[38] The formulation of the relevant clause suggests that 'a floor of enforceable minimum rights' would be estab-

---

[33] Ibid paras (*u*), (*v*), (*w*) and (*x*) respectively. See in this regard, A Sachs 'A Bill of Rights for South Africa: Areas of agreement and disagreement' (1989) 21 *Colum Hum Rts L Rev* 13–44 at 23–26.

[34] On the background of the constitutional negotiations and process which facilitated the transition to democracy in South Africa, see generally L M du Plessis & H Corder *Understanding South Africa's Transitional Bill of Rights* (1994) chapter 1; H Ebrahim *The Soul of a Nation: Constitution-making in South Africa* (1998); R Spitz with M Chaskalson *The Politics of Transition: A Hidden History of South Africa's Negotiated Settlement* (2000); P Andrews & S Ellmann (eds) *The Post-Apartheid Constitutions: Perspectives on South Africa's Basic Law* (2001) and I Currie & J de Waal *The Bill of Rights Handbook* 5 ed (2005) 1–7.

[35] Constitution of the Republic of South Africa Act 200 of 1993 ('the interim Constitution').

[36] ANC *A Bill of Rights for a Democratic South Africa: Working Draft for Consultation* reproduced in (1991) 7 *SAJHR* 110–123.

[37] Ibid art 10.

[38] Ibid arts 10(1) and 10(2).

lished which could be expanded upon in legislative and policy measures.[39] Moreover, art 10 incorporates extensive provisions relating to 'freedom from hunger', 'the right to shelter', 'the right to education', 'the right to health', 'the right to work', and 'the right to a minimum income and welfare rights'. The drafting of certain of these specific rights suggests that they were envisaged as directly enforceable, immediate entitlements. These included the right to free and compulsory primary school education for all, and the prohibition on the eviction of people from their homes or from land 'without the order of a competent court which shall have regard to the availability of alternative accommodation'.[40] Apart from the article protecting 'social, educational, economic and welfare rights', there were separate articles protecting the rights of particular groups, such as workers,[41] women,[42] disabled persons,[43] and children.[44] There was also a separate clause dealing with environmental rights.[45] The ANC's proposals explicitly envisaged civil society participation and the responsibility of private actors in the realisation of socio-economic rights.[46] All the rights are subject to judicial enforcement.[47]

In his opening address to an ANC Conference on a Bill of Rights for a democratic South Africa, the then President of the ANC, Nelson Mandela, expressed his faith in the judiciary in relation to the enforcement of socio-economic rights:

> We leave it to the judiciary to determine which rights are directly enforceable at the instance of individuals. We shall be surprised if such rights as the right to clean water, to minimum nutrition and to adult education cannot be enforced by courts.[48]

---

[39] Ibid art 10(3).

[40] Ibid art 10(10) and 10(11). See further the analysis by N Haysom 'Constitutionalism, majoritarian democracy and socio-economic rights' (1992) 8 *SAJHR* 451–463 at 453.

[41] Ibid art 6. This article essentially protects the organisational rights of workers and trade unions. The right to work which places a duty on the State to facilitate increased employment is incorporated in art 10(13).

[42] Ibid art 7.

[43] Ibid art 8.

[44] Ibid art 9.

[45] Ibid art 12.

[46] Thus art 10(5) provides: 'The State may collaborate with non-governmental organisations and the private sector in achieving these goals, and may impose appropriate responsibilities on all social and economic bodies with a view to their materialisation.'

[47] Ibid art 16.

[48] N R Mandela 'Address: On the occasion of the ANC's Bill of Rights conference' in *A Bill of Rights for a Democratic South Africa: Papers and Report of a Conference Convened by the ANC Constitutional Committee, May 1991* (1991) 9–14 at 12. Albie Sachs mooted the idea of a 'Social Rights Commission' to complement the judicial enforcement of socio-economic rights. See, for example, A Sachs 'Towards a Bill of Rights in a democratic South Africa' (1990) 6 *SAJHR* 1–24 at 15–17. The ANC's Working Draft Bill of Rights (note 36 above) stated that the fundamental rights and freedoms contained therein 'shall be guaranteed by the courts' (art 16(1)). Parliament was expressly given 'a special responsibility for ensuring that the basic social, educational, economic and welfare rights set out in this Bill of Rights

Some insight into the ANC's motivations for supporting the inclusion of socio-economic rights is provided in a paper delivered by Dullah Omar, a member of the ANC's Constitutional Committee.[49] He argued that a failure to incorporate socio-economic rights in a Bill of Rights for a future democratic South Africa would have the effect, not only of making social and economic transformation impossible, but 'in reality actually nullify[ing] first generation rights, *inter alia*, equality and democracy, for the vast majority of South Africans'.[50] He identified two major objectives that a future constitutional framework for South Africa should promote. First, such a framework 'should not prevent social and economic transformation and the achievement of social and economic rights'. Second, it must 'create mechanisms and structures which will empower the people of our country to achieve and defend such rights through the Constitution and their own organizations'.[51]

Albie Sachs similarly argued in favour of including socio-economic rights, on the basis that it would promote the substantive enjoyment of all rights, and make the transition to democracy meaningful to people, not only in a formal sense, but also in facilitating an improved quality of life.[52] The same idea is captured powerfully by Nelson Mandela:

> A simple vote, without food, shelter and health care is to use first generation rights as a smokescreen to obscure the deep underlying forces which dehumanise people. It is to create an appearance of equality and justice, while by implication socio-economic inequality is entrenched. We do not want freedom without bread, nor do we want bread without freedom. We must provide for all the fundamental rights and freedoms associated with a democratic society.[53]

These views by leading figures within the ANC suggest that the inclusion of socio-economic rights in the Bill of Rights was perceived to be fundamental to the transformation of South African society in two interrelated ways. First, it promoted a substantive vision of human rights which would be responsive to all forms of subordination and injustice. In this regard, the ANC was clearly acutely conscious of the need for the post-apartheid legal system to facilitate the redress of the socio-economic legacy of apartheid. Second, it envisaged a constitutionally grounded process of transformation in which the citizenry is empowered to play an active role. The ability of ordinary people to invoke civil and political rights such as the right of freedom of association and speech as well as socio-economic rights was seen as integral to their active participation in the processes of reconstruction and development.

---

are respected' (art 16(6)). It also envisaged the establishment of a Human Rights Commission 'to promote observance of the Bill of Rights' (art 16(7)–(9)).

49 D Omar 'Enforcement of social and economic rights' in *A Bill of Rights for A Democratic South Africa* (1991) 106–114.

50 Ibid 112.

51 Ibid.

52 A Sachs (note 48 above) 4–6.

53 N R Mandela (note 48 above) 12.

Although the ANC's 1990 draft Bill of Rights was subsequently revised, it provided the substantive foundation of the party's position in the multi-party negotiations regarding a future constitutional dispensation for South Africa. The ANC's various draft proposals for a Bill of Rights incorporated socio-economic rights largely in the form discussed above.[54]

Between 1992 and 1993 the other major political parties released their proposals for a Constitution and Bill of Rights for South Africa as a basis for the multi-party constitutional negotiations. Most of these documents recognised socio-economic rights in some form. However, there are significant differences in the role envisaged for the courts in the enforcement of these rights.

The Democratic Party (DP) published its proposals in a document entitled *Freedom under the Rule of Law: Advancing Liberty in the New South Africa* (May 1993). Article 11 of this document entitled citizens to the essentials of life such as food and water necessary for survival, shelter from the elements, basic health care, basic education, and a clean and healthy environment. However, these rights were subject to legislative and executive discretion in the form and manner of their realisation. Thus art 11(2) provided:

> It is the province of Parliament, and of any other authority lawfully exercising power for the purpose to decide how these entitlements are to be realized. A decision which is reasonable and practicable and which respects the limitations on the resources available to realize the relevant entitlement shall be considered justifiable.

Legislation and administrative action would thus be subject to review for their 'justifiability' given the constitutional commitment to socio-economic rights. This evaluation would be guided by the criteria of reasonableness, practicability and respect for resource limitations.

In this respect, the DP proposal resembles the approach advocated by Etienne Mureinik in an influential article arguing in favour of the inclusion of socio-economic rights as justiciable rights in a future Bill of Rights on the grounds that it would deepen a culture of justification.[55] He essentially argued that there was no justification for excluding the socio-economic sphere from accountability to constitutional norms and values. He suggested that legislative and executive action or inaction impinging on socio-economic rights could be reviewed for 'sincerity' and

---

[54] See, for example, ANC *Bill of Rights for a New South Africa* (May 1992), arts 11 and 12; ANC *Draft Bill of Rights, Preliminary Revised Version* (February 1993), arts 11, 12 and 17(1). The major trade union federation, COSATU, also endorsed the inclusion of socio-economic rights in the Bill of Rights, particularly labour rights. See *The Workers' Charter* (COSATU, 1992); E Patel 'The right to work' in *A Bill of Rights for A Democratic South Africa* (1991) 85–95.

[55] E Mureinik 'Beyond a charter of luxuries: Economic rights in the Constitution' (1992) 8 *SAJHR* 464–474.

'rationality'.[56] He also proposed that review for government omissions in relation to socio-economic rights should be developed in South African law:

> Review of government inaction, though developing abroad, is virtually non-existent in this country. Now may be the time to develop it here. One way would be to ask the court to declare the government in dereliction of its duty to make an honest and reasonable effort to realize an economic right.[57]

In 1992 the Legislative Assembly of KwaZulu-Natal approved a *Constitution for the State of KwaZulu-Natal* which contained a Bill of Rights with civil and political rights as well as a number of 'social rights' such as a right to education, the right to work, the rights of senior citizens, a right to health care, and housing rights.[58] In addition, certain 'economic rights' are recognised such as 'the right to free economic initiative and enterprise'[59] and the right to property.[60] However, whereas the economic rights are directly justiciable in the same manner as civil and political rights, the positive action imposed by the social rights is expressly made dependent upon legislative action. This document largely formed the basis of the Inkatha Freedom Party (IFP) proposals on the Bill of Rights.

In 1986, the South African Law Commission (SALC) was tasked with investigating and making recommendations on group and human rights in South Africa. The SALC produced three reports, culminating in its *Final Report on Group and Human Rights* in 1994.[61] In its initial report, the SALC asserted that a 'Bill of Rights is not the place for enforcing positive obligations against the State'.[62] In its interim report, the SALC incorporated arguments against the inclusion of socio-economic rights as justiciable rights in the Bill of Rights. Its objections were based on a vision of a Bill of Rights as a protective device against the power of the State,[63] the fear that these rights would impose costs on the State that were beyond its available resources, and that these rights would force the judiciary to intrude on the legitimate terrain of the legislature.[64]

---

[56] Ibid 471–474.

[57] Ibid 473.

[58] Articles 42, 43, 45, 49 and 51.

[59] Article 30.

[60] Article 34.

[61] SALC, Working Paper 25 *Group and Human Rights* (1989); SALC, Interim Report: Project 58 *Group and Human Rights* (1991); SALC, Final Report: Project 58 *Group and Human Rights* (1994).

[62] SALC, Working Paper 25 *Group and Human Rights* ibid para 14.30.

[63] On the influence of 'negative constitutionalism' on the interpretation of the Bill of Rights, see further chapter 2, part 2.4.4.

[64] See SALC, Interim Report: Project 58 *Group and Human Rights* (note 61 above) 533–537. The SALC also argued against the inclusion of socio-economic rights in the Bill of Rights as directive principles of state policy on the basis that such directives would be of 'little legal significance' (536).

In its final report the SALC modified its position, conceding that the various categories of rights are interdependent.[65] After reviewing the academic contributions for and against the inclusion of socio-economic rights as justiciable rights,[66] it concluded that these rights should receive protection, either in the form of directive principles of state policy or through specific tailor-made legislation.[67] According to the SALC, considerable consensus existed that the 'entitlements to the essentials of life'[68] should receive constitutional acknowledgment in the form of directive principles of state policy. These directives should be made subject to the physical and financial capabilities of the State.[69] In cases where the content of various rights have crystallised sufficiently, these could be incorporated as directly enforceable rights in the Bill of Rights.[70] Finally, the Commission proposed an active role for the Human Rights Commission in gathering information from government departments and other organs of state on socio-economic programmes, making inputs on proposed legislation where socio-economic rights are affected, and making recommendations to the legislature and executive on the protection of these rights in the form of draft legislation.[71]

An influential contribution to the Bill of Rights debate emerged from a group of academics and public interest law practitioners. Entitled *A Charter for Social Justice*,[72] this document also proposed the inclusion of socio-economic rights in the Bill of Rights in the form of directives of state policy. The authors argued against the inclusion of socio-economic rights as directly justiciable rights in the Bill of Rights primarily on the grounds that they would force the courts to dictate on budgetary questions to the executive and legislative branches of government. In addition, it was argued that socio-economic rights entailed polycentric questions which courts were institutionally ill-suited to determine.[73]

The Charter envisaged the directives functioning as guidelines for the State in the formulation and implementation of policy, and as interpretive principles guiding the

---

65 SALC, Final Report: Project 58 *Group and Human Rights* (note 61 above) 185, 193.

66 Ibid 186–193.

67 Ibid 193.

68 This phrase is adopted from art 11 of the DP's Draft Bill of Rights. According to the SALC they included: just conditions of work; adequate health services; access to education; an adequate standard of living, in particular, housing and shelter, nutrition, and social security for those in need; and a clean and healthy environment for the present and future generations. SALC, Final Report: Project 58 *Group and Human Rights* (note 61 above) 193–194.

69 Ibid 194.

70 For example, that the right to free primary education could be enforced by means of a mandamus. Ibid 194–195.

71 Ibid 195–196.

72 H Corder, S Kahanovitz, J Murphy, C Murray, C O'Regan, J Sarkin, H Smith & N Steyter *A Charter for Social Justice: A Contribution to the South African Bill of Rights Debate* (1992).

73 Ibid 20–22. On the problem of polycentricity in adjudication, see chapter 2, part 2.4.8 at notes 230–244 and accompanying text.

courts in interpreting legislation and reviewing executive action.[74] It is noteworthy that the authors of the Charter proposed a justiciable guarantee against the removal of people from their homes without an order of court. A duty was imposed on the courts to take into account the existence of 'appropriate alternative accommodation' before making such an order.[75]

Another academic contribution to the Bill of Rights debate by Dennis Davis supported the inclusion of socio-economic rights in the Bill of Rights in the form of directive principles of state policy. Such directives would not be directly enforceable by the courts, but could indirectly influence constitutional jurisprudence, as has occurred in India.[76] However, unlike the authors of the *Charter for Social Justice*, Davis focused more on the politics of adjudicating socio-economic rights claims, rather than on the institutional competence of the judiciary to enforce these rights. His main argument against the inclusion of socio-economic rights as fully justiciable rights was that there was no guarantee that judges would interpret these highly indeterminate rights in ways which will promote a social democratic reading of the Constitution.[77] Entrusting the enforcement of socio-economic rights to an unelected, unaccountable judiciary would give the judiciary too much power and erode both representative and participatory democracy. Thus Davis argued:

> It elevates judges to the role of social engineers, concentrates power at the centre of the state and consequently erodes the influence of civil society.[78]

In other words, the inclusion of socio-economic rights as directly justiciable rights would undermine, rather than facilitate the project of democratic transformation.

---

[74] Ibid 22, and preamble to the Directives of State Policy at 65. The *Charter* also incorporates the principle of social democracy inspired by the 'social state principle' (*Sozialstaatsprinzip*) in art 20 of the German Constitution. Ibid 28. Thus the *Charter* proposed that limitations to rights must be 'demonstrably justified in a free and open social democracy' (art 1), and the rights must be interpreted 'to promote the values which underlie a free and open social democracy'. (art 26(2)). On the 'social state principle', see further chapter 3, part 3.3.3(*b*)(ii).

[75] Ibid art 21.

[76] D M Davis 'The case against the inclusion of socio-economic demands in a Bill of Rights except as directive principles' (1992) 8 *SAJHR* 475–490 at 486. See in this regard, chapter 3, part 3.3.3(*b*) (ii). For a later argument by Davis in support of a robust judicial role in the enforcement of the socio-economic rights in the Constitution, see D M Davis 'Adjudicating socio-economic rights in the South African Constitution: Towards "deference lite"?' (2006) 22 *SAJHR* 301–327.

[77] In this regard, Davis applies Dworkin's distinction between 'choice sensitive' issues, which are policy choices dependent on political preferences, and 'choice insensitive' issues, which are matters of principle and which should not be the subject of political choice. Socio-economic rights fall into the former category, while civil and political rights are in the latter. Ibid 478–479 (referring to R Dworkin 'What is equality? Part 4: Political equality' (1987) 22 *USF L Rev* 1–30 at 24).

[78] Ibid 489.

The proposals which the political parties placed on the table for the purposes of the multi-party constitutional negotiations, as well as those emanating from civil society, illustrate the tension between negative and preservative constitutionalism, on the one hand, and positive and transformation-orientated constitutionalism, on the other.[79] The DP proposals, although making some provision for socio-economic rights, were primarily orientated towards the protection of individual rights and liberties from state interference.[80] The National Party proposals for a Bill of Rights expressly stated that they are based on the principle of 'negative enforcement'.[81] Moreover, certain parties, such as the IFP and the National Party, sought to include clauses guaranteeing the free functioning of market institutions without making any explicit provision for the redress of the social and economic legacy of apartheid.[82]

In contrast, the ANC's constitutional proposals clearly envisaged an active role for the State in redistributing and promoting access to socio-economic resources and services by all. Nicolas Haysom argued that the ANC's commitment to constitutionalism was founded on a recognition 'of the centrality of a participatory democracy for a thorough transformation of South Africa'.[83] Together with civil and political rights, socio-economic rights were viewed as essential to facilitating this process of democratic transformation.[84]

1.4 THE 1993 CONSTITUTION

As noted above, the interim Constitution was intended to facilitate the transition to full democracy in South Africa with a democratically elected Constitutional Assembly being ultimately responsible for the drafting and adoption of the 'final' Constitution. The interim Constitution was the product of the multi-party negotiating process and was adopted by the old order Parliament.

There was a debate among the parties about how extensive the list of rights guaranteed in the chapter of fundamental rights in the interim Constitution should be.[85] Lourens du Plessis and Hugh Corder (who both served on the Technical Committee responsible for drafting the chapter on fundamental rights) describe the debate process as 'a tug of war between *minimalists* and *optimalists* which, in the end, resulted

---

[79] Du Plessis & Corder (note 34 above) 23–35 characterise these different approaches in terms of a libertarianism versus a liberationism. See also B de Villiers 'Social and economic rights' in D van Wyk, J Dugard, B de Villiers & D Davis (eds) *Rights and Constitutionalism: The New South African Legal Order* (1994) 599–628 at 621–628.

[80] See Du Plessis & Corder ibid 26.

[81] Article 15 of the South African Government *Charter of Fundamental Rights* (1993).

[82] See art 30 of the *Constitution for the State of KwaZulu-Natal* and art 15 of the South African Government's *Charter of Fundamental Rights*.

[83] N Haysom 'Democracy, constitutionalism and the ANC's Bill of Rights for a New South Africa' (1991) 7 *SAJHR* 102–109 at 108.

[84] See, for example, the analysis by Haysom ibid 106–107.

[85] Chapter 3 of the interim Constitution.

in a compromise'.[86] The SA Government/NP as well as the IFP and the governments of some of the homelands such as Ciskei and Bophuthatswana generally supported the optimalist approach with the maximum possible constraint on the parameters within which the democratically elected Constitutional Assembly would ultimately be able to operate. The liberation parties such as the ANC favoured a more minimalist approach which would constrain the scope of the final constitutional dispensation as little as possible. As Du Plessis and Corder observe, these positions were informed by the politics of the transition.[87]

Ultimately, chapter 3 of the interim Constitution included the traditional civil and political rights and a small but significant group of socio-economic rights. The socio-economic rights included were the following: the right of detained persons, including sentenced prisoners, 'to be detained under conditions consonant with human dignity, which shall include at least the provision of adequate nutrition, reading material and medical treatment at state expense';[88] labour rights;[89] the right of every person 'to an environment which is not detrimental to his or her health or well-being':[90] the right of children 'to security, basic nutrition and basic health and social services':[91] educational rights, including the right 'to basic education' and 'to instruction in the language of his or her choice where this is reasonably practicable'.[92] Other rights of an economic character included in the interim Constitution were the right to engage freely in economic activity[93] and property rights.[94] The latter clause was particularly controversial given the fears of the liberation parties and NGOs working in the land sector about its potential impact on land reform and resource redistribution.[95] In addition, the interim Constitution entrenches the right of every person 'to use the language and to participate in the cultural life of his or her choice'.[96]

None of these rights of a socio-economic character can be regarded as crucial to facilitating free and fair elections and the transition to democracy in South Africa. Du Plessis and Corder's account of the drafting process suggests that the presence of

---

[86] Du Plessis & Corder (note 34 above) 40.

[87] Ibid 41.

[88] Section 25(1)(*b*).

[89] Section 27.

[90] Section 29.

[91] Section 30(1)(*c*).

[92] Section 32.

[93] Section 26. This right was internally limited so as not to preclude measures aimed at socio-economic redistribution and equity: s 26(2).

[94] Section 28.

[95] For an account of the controversy surrounding the property clause in the interim Constitution, see M Chaskalson 'Stumbling towards section 28: Negotiations over the protection of property rights in the interim Constitution' (1995) 11 *SAJHR* 222–241; R Spitz with M Chaskalson (note 34) 313–329.

[96] Section 31. The rights of access to information (s 23), and the right to administrative justice (s 24) are also protected in the interim Constitution.

a number of the socio-economic rights in the interim Constitution were the result of civil society advocacy. Thus s 30(1)(*c*), entrenching children's socio-economic rights, was informed by 'helpful submissions' from the National Children's Rights Commission.[97] In addition, the bold step of including environmental rights in chapter 3 (s 29) was facilitated by 'several cogent submissions' by bodies concerned with conservation.[98]

All the rights in chapter 3 were subject to judicial enforcement by the provincial divisions of the Supreme Court[99] and the Constitutional Court as the court of final instance over 'any alleged violation or threatened violation of any fundamental right entrenched in Chapter 3'.[100]

Although limited in scope, the socio-economic rights incorporated in chapter 3 of the interim Constitution provided the foundation for the development of the expansive set of socio-economic rights in the 1996 Constitution.

1.5 THE 1996 CONSTITUTION

The 1996 Constitution was negotiated and adopted by the Constitutional Assembly comprising the two houses of the democratically elected Parliament (the National Assembly and the Senate) sitting jointly.[101] The 1996 Constitution had to comply with the Constitutional Principles contained in sched 4 to the interim Constitution and could not come into force until the Constitutional Court had certified that all the provisions of the text complied with these Principles.[102] The primary Principle relevant to the drafting of the Bill of Rights in the 1996 Constitution was Constitutional Principle II which read:

> Everyone shall enjoy all universally accepted fundamental rights, freedoms and civil liberties, which shall be provided for and protected by entrenched and justiciable provisions in

---

[97] Du Plessis & Corder (note 34 above) 46. See also Spitz with Chaskalson (note 34 above) 364–366. The National Party was particularly interested in obtaining guarantees of language and cultural rights, including the right to establish educational institutions based on a common culture, language and religion. See Du Plessis & Corder ibid 187–188.

[98] See Du Plessis & Corder ibid 184; Spitz with Chaskalson ibid 362–363.

[99] Section 101(3)(*a*) of the interim Constitution.

[100] Section 98(2)(*a*) of the interim Constitution. The Appellate Division had no direct constitutional jurisdiction under the interim Constitution (s 101(5)).

[101] Section 68 of the interim Constitution.

[102] Section 71 of the interim Constitution. The Constitutional Court refused to certify the first draft of the Constitution: see *Ex parte Chairperson of the Constitutional Assembly: In re Certification of the Constitution of the Republic of South Africa 1996* 1996 (4) SA 744 (CC), 1996 (10) BCLR 1253 (CC) ('*First Certification* judgment'). The Constitutional Assembly reconvened and amended the text of the Constitution, which was re-submitted to the Court on 11 October 1996. This amended text was certified by the Court as being in compliance with the Constitutional Principles: *Certification of the Amended Text of the Constitution of the Republic of South Africa, 1996* 1997 (2) SA 97 (CC), 1997 (1) BCLR 1 (CC) ('*Second Certification* judgment'). The Constitution entered into force on 4 February 1997.

> the Constitution, which shall be drafted after having given due consideration to *inter alia* the fundamental rights contained in Chapter 3 of the Constitution.

The first major issue to be determined in relation to whether socio-economic rights should be included as justiciable rights in the Constitution was whether Constitutional Principle II obliged their inclusion. This depended on whether these rights could be classified as 'universally accepted fundamental rights'. The Technical Committee advising the Theme Committee of the Constitutional Assembly charged with the drafting of the Bill of Rights was asked to provide an opinion on the meaning of this phrase.[103] Based on a survey of international and comparative law, the Technical Committee concluded that socio-economic rights were 'universally accepted fundamental rights', and recommended their inclusion as justiciable rights in the Constitution.[104]

During the drafting process, the major political parties and the public were invited to make submissions on the content of the Bill of Rights. The Technical Committee was given the mandate to synthesise these submissions, conduct international and comparative law research on the various proposals and to recommend draft formulations of the relevant clauses.[105] Most of the political parties represented in the Constitutional Assembly were in favour of the recognition of socio-economic rights in some form.[106]

In addition, there was strong civil society support for the inclusion of socio-economic rights as fully justiciable rights in the Bill of Rights. An alliance of human rights and development NGOs, academics, trade unions, women's organisations and church groups was formed to campaign for the inclusion of this group of rights in the Constitution. This alliance, the *Ad Hoc Campaign for Social and Economic Rights*,

---

[103] The members of the Technical Committee were Professors John Dugard, Ignatius Rautenbach, Halton Cheadle and the author. This committee remained actively involved until the adoption of the Constitution in conducting background research and draft proposals on the formulation of the various provisions in the Bill of Rights (chapter 2). The committee was also charged with evaluating and making recommendations on the submissions of civil society concerning the content of the Bill of Rights. The relevant Theme Committee of the Constitutional Assembly dealing with the Bill of Rights was known as Theme Committee 4.

[104] Technical Committee (Theme Committee 4) *The meaning of 'universally accepted fundamental rights' in Constitutional Principle II, Schedule 4 to the Constitution of the Republic of South Africa Act 200 of 1993* (1995) para 12 (document on file with author).

[105] See, for example, Constitutional Assembly, Constitutional Committee Sub-Committee *Draft Bill of Rights, volume 1, Explanatory Memoranda*, 9 October 1995, 1–285 (document on file with author).

[106] See Constitutional Assembly, Theme Committee 4, Fundamental Rights *Party Submissions: Socio-Economic rights* (14 August 1995) (document on file with author). The National Party expressed the most ambivalence in this regard, but given their support for language and cultural rights in general, and educational institutions based on a common language and culture in particular, they could not object strenuously to the inclusion of other rights with a socio-economic character.

presented a petition to the Constitutional Assembly in which they argued that the struggle for democratisation of South African society included both the franchise as well as the recognition of social and economic rights. They argued that socio-economic rights were critical to the reconstruction and development of South African society, and that disadvantaged groups 'should be granted every available means to protect and progressively realise these individual and collective human rights in South Africa'.[107]

The Alliance further contended that the courts needed a holistic framework of rights in order to avoid interpretations that were skewed towards the protection of vested property rights and negative liberties. Socio-economic rights could provide significant mechanisms for disadvantaged groups to hold the State accountable should it disregard their fundamental needs. However, these rights could also assist the State in defending redistributive social legislation and programmes against constitutional challenges brought by private parties.

On the symbolic importance of including socio-economic rights in the Bill of Rights, the petition stated:

> [I]t is useful to see the constitution as a mirror. ... If this mirror does not show protection from shelters being demolished, does not show protection from being chased out of school or hospital queues, then it does not reflect the lives to which we aspire for all South Africans. If it is only a mirror that reflects the image of a more privileged sector of society then it is a constitution for only those people and not all the people.[108]

While there was broad-ranging support for the inclusion of socio-economic rights in the Constitution, it is also important to note that a number of powerful constituencies in civil society were opposed to the inclusion of socio-economic rights in the Bill of Rights.[109]

According to an analysis of the party submissions by the Technical Committee, there was general consensus that socio-economic rights should be drafted in such a way that:

> (*a*) they do not place an obligation on the state which cannot be fulfilled in terms of its resources and capacity;

---

[107] *Petition to the Constitutional Assembly by the Ad Hoc Campaign for Social and Economic Rights* (19 July 1995) (document on file with author). Extracts of this petition are published in S Liebenberg & K Pillay (eds) *Socio-Economic Rights in South Africa: A Resource Book* (2000) 19–20. This petition was endorsed by 55 leading civil society organisations in South Africa. Many of the submissions made at a public hearing on the theme of 'social and economic rights in the Bill of Rights' hosted by the Constitutional Assembly on 1 August 1995 also supported the inclusion of these rights as justiciable entitlements.

[108] *Petition to the Constitutional Assembly* ibid 3–4.

[109] For example, the Chamber of Mines and Institute of Race Relations made submissions opposing the inclusion of these rights: see Technical Committee Memorandum to Theme Committee IV *Matters arising from the public submissions* (7 March 1996) (document on file with author).

(*b*) they preserve the distinction between the roles of the judiciary and the legislature. This entails ensuring that the legislature is given the main responsibility for elaborating and implementing the rights, with the courts possessing the necessary powers of review;

(*c*) the main duty on the State is to provide opportunities and remove constraints which prevent access to social and economic rights in South Africa.[110]

The strong influence of international law, particularly the International Covenant on Economic, Social and Cultural Rights (1966), is evident from the formulation of the relevant socio-economic rights provisions. Thus the qualified positive duty on the State to take 'reasonable legislative and other measures within its available resources' and the concept of 'progressive realisation' is based on art 2 of the International Covenant on Economic, Social and Cultural Rights.[111] According to the Technical Committee, this formulation had the advantage of facilitating consistency between South Africa's domestic policies and laws and its international human rights law, and pointed the courts in the direction of an important international law resource to guide the interpretation of the rights.[112] The preparatory documents also reflect an ongoing concern that the content and design of the Bill of Rights should give effect to the interdependence between all human rights.[113]

1.6 THE CERTIFICATION PROCESS

During the certification process, objections were raised against the inclusion of socio-economic rights in the Bill of Rights.[114] The objections were threefold. First,

---

[110] Constitutional Assembly, Constitutional Committee Sub-Committee *Draft Bill of Rights, volume 1, Explanatory Memoranda* 9 October 1995, 1–285 at 154. See also 141–177, dealing with the sections on housing, health care, food, water and social assistance, children's rights and the right to education.

[111] Article 2(1) of the International Covenant on Economic, Social and Cultural Rights reads as follows:

> Each State Party to the present Covenant undertakes to take steps, individually and through international assistance and co-operation, especially economic and technical, to the maximum of its available resources, with a view to achieving progressively the full realization of the rights recognized in the present Covenant by all appropriate means, including particularly the adoption of legislative measures.

See *Memorandum of the Panel of Constitutional Experts on the meaning of 'progressive realization'* (6 February 1996); Technical Committee IV *Memorandum on sections 25 and 26 of the Working Draft of the Constitution* (14 February 1996) (document on file with author).

[112] Technical Committee IV *Memorandum on sections 25 and 26 of the Working Draft of the Constitution* (14 February 1996) (document on file with author).

[113] *Memorandum of the Panel of Constitutional Experts on the meaning of 'progressive realization'* (6 February 1996) para 2; Technical Committee IV *Supplementary memorandum on Bill of Rights and Party Submissions*, commenting on proposals to group socio-economic rights together in a single clause (1995), 13 (documents on file with author).

[114] See *First Certification* judgment (note 102 above) paras 76–78. The main objectors were the SA Institute of Race Relations, the Free Market Foundation and the Gauteng Association of Chambers of Commerce and Industry. The Legal Resources Centre, the Centre

it was argued that socio-economic rights were not 'universally accepted fundamental rights' for the purposes of Constitutional Principle II. Second, the inclusion of socio-economic rights was inconsistent with the doctrine of separation of powers which was required in terms of Constitutional Principle VI.[115] Third, it was argued that these rights were not justiciable.

The Constitutional Court disposed of the first objection on the basis that Constitutional Principle II 'permits the CA (Constitutional Assembly) to supplement the universally accepted fundamental rights with other rights not universally accepted'.[116]

The separation of powers objection was based on the argument that socio-economic rights would compel the judiciary 'to encroach upon the proper terrain of the legislature and executive', particularly by 'dictating to the government how the budget should be allocated'.[117] The Court conceded that socio-economic rights may result in courts making orders which have direct implications for budgetary matters. However, the Court pointed out that the enforcement of many civil and political rights such as equality, freedom of speech and right to a fair trial will also often have such implications. It concluded that the inclusion of socio-economic rights within a Bill of Rights did not confer upon the courts a task 'so different from that ordinarily conferred upon them by a bill of rights that it results in a breach of the separation of powers'.[118]

Finally, in response to the justiciability objection, the Court held that, given its view that socio-economic rights were not 'universally accepted fundamental rights', their justiciability was not required by Constitutional Principle II. Nevertheless, the fact that socio-economic rights have budgetary implications is not an automatic bar to their justiciability. The Court observed, at the 'very minimum, socio-economic rights can be negatively protected from improper invasion'.[119]

Thus the socio-economic rights in ss 26, 27, 28(1)(*c*) and 29 survived the certification process. A number of observations can be made in relation to the Court's response to the objections to the inclusion of socio-economic rights as justiciable rights in the Constitution. First, the Court provides no analysis of comparative or international law, nor any reasoning, to support its view that socio-economic rights

---

for Applied Legal Studies and the Community Law Centre (UWC) argued in favour of the inclusion of socio-economic rights at the certification hearing (annexure 3 to the judgment). See also A Jeffrey 'The new Constitution: A triumph for liberalism? Some doubts' in R W Johnson & D Welsh with the assistance of L Husemeyer (eds) *Ironic Victory: Liberalism in Post-Liberation South Africa* (1998) 31–44 at 35–38.

[115] Constitutional Principle VI provides: 'There shall be a separation of powers between the legislature, executive and judiciary, with appropriate checks and balances to ensure accountability, responsiveness and openness.' Schedule 4 to the interim Constitution.

[116] *First Certification* judgment (note 102 above) para 76.

[117] Ibid para 77.

[118] Ibid.

[119] Ibid para 78.

are not 'universally accepted fundamental rights'. However, this was not fatal, given the political support for their inclusion in the Bill of Rights and the view taken by the Court on the broad latitude afforded by Constitutional Principle II to the Constitutional Assembly in supplementing universally accepted rights with other rights.

Second, the Court's refusal to draw a categorical distinction between civil and political rights, on the one hand, and socio-economic rights, on the other, supports a vision of the Bill of Rights which is not based on rigid hierarchies and distinctions between different types of rights.[120] Thus the Court acknowledged that both socio-economic rights and civil and political rights entail positive obligations and can have implications for the budget without resulting in a breach of the separation of powers doctrine.[121] This suggests a more flexible model of the separation of powers doctrine which is not premised on a rigid demarcation between the roles and functions of the three branches of government.[122]

Finally, although the judgment can be read to prefer a model of judicial enforcement of socio-economic rights premised on negative constitutionalism,[123] it is clear that the Court viewed negative protection from 'improper invasion' as the minimum dimension of the justiciability of socio-economic rights. The enforcement of positive duties is not precluded.

1.7 CONCLUSION

The inclusion of socio-economic rights as justiciable rights in the Constitution represented the culmination of a process of struggle to recognise the socio-economic dimensions of human dignity, freedom and equality. This struggle had deep roots in the anti-apartheid struggle, and was carried forward in the negotiating process primarily by the liberation movements in conjunction with a vibrant civil society campaign.

Socio-economic rights were regarded as crucial to an integrated, holistic Bill of Rights which would reflect the needs and aspirations of all groups in South Africa. It was hoped that these rights would enrich participatory democracy by enabling persons marginalised by poverty to challenge decisions and omissions which have an impact on socio-economic well-being. Moreover, these rights would give the state

---

[120] On the interdependence between rights as a feature of transformative adjudication of the Bill of Rights, see chapter 2, part 2.4.3.

[121] The Court pointed out in relation to civil and political rights such as fair trial rights and equality rights, that a court 'may require the provision of legal aid, or the extension of state benefits to a class of people who formerly were not beneficiaries of such benefits'. *First Certification* judgment (note 102 above) para 77.

[122] On the implications of this model of the separation of powers doctrine for transformative adjudication, see chapter 2, part 2.4.7.

[123] *First Certification* judgment (note 102 above) para 78. On 'negative constitutionalism' and its implications for transformative adjudication, see chapter 2, part 2.4.4.

an express mandate to adopt legislation and programmes aimed at achieving a more equitable distribution of social and economic resources and services, particularly by extending access to excluded and marginalised communities. At the same time, while constitutionally mandated, social reforms should be undertaken in a manner which respects the other rights in the Constitution, such as the right to just administrative action (s 33). As the Constitutional Court has underscored, this is an essential requirement of processes of transformation which are grounded in respect for the rule of law.[124]

In conclusion, socio-economic rights were regarded as crucial to facilitating the fundamental transformation of South African society. The following chapter examines the implications of the transformative nature of the South African Constitution for the adjudication of socio-economic rights.

[124] *Bel Porto School Governing Body v Premier of the Province, Western Cape,* 2002 (3) SA 265 (CC), 2002 (9) BCLR 891 (CC) para 7; *Bato Star Fishing (Pty) Ltd v Minister of Environmental Affairs and Tourism* 2004 (4) SA 490 (CC), 2004 (7) BCLR 687 (CC) para 76.

CHAPTER 2

A Transformative Jurisprudence on Socio-Economic Rights

In this chapter *Page*

2.1 INTRODUCTION

This chapter examines the implications of a transformative conception of the South African Constitution for the adjudication of socio-economic rights claims. It considers the nature and implications of transformative constitutionalism against the backdrop of the deep patterns of poverty and inequality that characterise South African society.

The transformative potential of entrenching socio-economic rights as justiciable rights in the Bill of Rights is explored through examining the challenges they pose to classic liberal conceptions of constitutional rights. These include challenging formal conceptions of rights and remedies, and the construction of rigid dichotomies between negative and positive rights, the public and private spheres, and between rights and democracy. They further call into question understandings of the separation of powers doctrine premised on inflexible functional demarcations between the three branches of government.

It is argued that there are strong currents within South Africa's legal culture that reinforce these classic liberal views of constitutional rights and judicial review. Until judges, lawyers and NGOs involved in socio-economic rights litigation are conscious of the strictures and dichotomies that pervade classic liberal constitutional theory and are able to imagine alternative conceptions, the transformative potential of socio-economic rights will not be realised.

Alternative approaches to the judicial review of a Bill of Rights which incorporates socio-economic rights as justiciable human rights are explored. By seeking to facilitate deep changes in South Africa's legal and political culture, these approaches advance the transformative ethos of the Constitution. The theoretical understanding of the judicial role in adjudicating socio-economic rights claims developed in this chapter provides the basis for evaluating South Africa's evolving jurisprudence on socio-economic rights in subsequent chapters.

2.2 A TRANSFORMATIVE CONSTITUTION

2.2.1 Klare's concept of transformation grounded in law

In a seminal article published in 1998, Karl Klare described the South African Constitution as entailing a project of 'transformative constitutionalism'. He described this project as:

> [A] long-term project of constitutional enactment, interpretation and enforcement committed (not in isolation, of course, but in a historical context of conducive political developments) to transforming a country's political and social institutions and power relationships in a democratic, participatory, and egalitarian direction. Transformative constitutionalism connotes an enterprise of inducing large-scale social change through nonviolent political processes grounded in law.[1]

[1] K Klare 'Legal culture and transformative constitutionalism' (1998) 14 *SAJHR* 146–188 at 150.

The notion of 'transformative constitutionalism' has found a deep resonance in academic literature,[2] the jurisprudence of the courts,[3] and civil society campaigns for social justice.

Like other constitutions adopted during periods of political transition, the Constitution is 'simultaneously backward- and forward-looking'.[4] It provides a legal framework within which to redress the injustices of the past as well as to facilitate the creation of a more just society in the future. The following part of the chapter explores the implications of a Constitution which is committed to redressing past injustices and guiding the creation of a transformed society.

2.2.2 Redressing the legacy of the past

In its backward-looking aspect, the Constitution aims to facilitate the transformation of society by setting right the wrongs of the past. Thus one of the purposes which the preamble of the Constitution proclaims is the healing of the divisions of the past.

---

[2] Scholars, judges and lawyers have elaborated on and explored the implications of 'transformative constitutionalism' in various areas of constitutional law. See, for example, C Albertyn & B Goldblatt 'Facing the challenges of transformation: Difficulties in the development of an indigenous jurisprudence of equality' (1998) 14 *SAJHR* 248–275; A J van der Walt 'Tentative urgency: Sensitivity for the paradoxes of stability and change in the social transformation decisions of the Constitutional Court' (2001) 16 *SAPR/PL* 1–27; D Moseneke 'The fourth Bram Fischer memorial lecture: Transformative adjudication' (2002) 18 *SAJHR* 309–319; H Botha, A J van der Walt & J van der Walt (eds) *Rights and Democracy in a Transformative Constitution* (2004); H Botha 'Metaphoric reasoning and transformative constitutionalism (part 2)' (2003) 1 *TSAR* 20–36; M Pieterse 'What do we mean when we talk about transformative constitutionalism?' (2005) 20 *SAPL* 155–166; A J van der Walt 'Legal history, legal culture and transformation in a constitutional democracy' (2006) 12 *Fundamina* 1–47; S Liebenberg 'Needs, rights and transformation: Adjudicating social rights' (2006) 1 *Stell LR* 5–36; P Langa 'Transformative constitutionalism' (2006) 17(3) *Stell LR* 351–360.

[3] See *S v Makwanyane* 1995 (3) SA 391 (CC), 1995 (6) BCLR 665 (CC) para 262; *Du Plessis v De Klerk* 1996 (3) SA 850 (CC), 1996 (5) BCLR 658 (CC) para 157; *Bato Star Fishing (Pty) Ltd v Minister of Environmental Affairs and Tourism* 2004 (4) SA 490 (CC), 2004 (7) BCLR 687 (CC) paras 73–74; *Minister of Finance v Van Heerden* 2004 (6) SA 121 (CC), 2004 (11) BCLR 1125 (CC) para 142; *City of Johannesburg v Rand Properties (Pty) Ltd* 2007 (1) SA 78 (W), 2006 (6) BCLR 728 (W) paras 51–52; *Rates Action Group v City of Cape Town* 2004 (5) SA 545 (C), 2004 (12) BCLR 1328 (C) para 100.

[4] Ruti Teitel *Transitional Justice* (2000) 191. Teitel's study shows that:

> While the rule of law in established democracies is forward-looking and continuous in its directionality, law in transitional periods is backward-looking and forward-looking, retrospective and prospective, continuous and discontinuous (215).

See also R Teitel 'Transitional jurisprudence: The role of law in political transformation' (1997) 106 *Yale LJ* 2009–2080 at 2014.

These divisions must be understood in terms of the complex interaction of colonialism, apartheid and capitalism over four centuries.[5]

Racial inequalities are the most apparent and publicised marker of disadvantage in our society. This is the product of South Africa's history of institutionalised racial domination described in chapter 1. However, the intersection of race and class and the persistence of deep class-based divisions in the late and post-apartheid periods have resulted in a post-apartheid society which is formally deracialised, but which has one of the highest levels of income inequality in the world.[6]

The legacy of apartheid's social and economic policies is still deeply inscribed on the landscape of South African society. The unemployment rate in post-apartheid South Africa is in the region of 40% on the expanded definition of unemployment which includes discouraged work-seekers.[7] It is estimated that 19,2 million people in South Africa, representing 48% of the population, live below the poverty line, according to an absolute measure of poverty pegged at an income per adult of R322 per month.[8] Poverty and income inequality has strong racial,[9] gender[10] and spatial[11] (rural/urban as well as provincial) dimensions.[12] Despite achievements of the democratic government in extending access to basic services such as health care, water,

---

[5] For an account of the impact of colonialism, apartheid and capitalism on generating the current inequalities in South African society, see S Terreblanche *A History of Inequality in South Africa: 1652–2002* (2002).

[6] J Seekings & N Nattrass *Class, Race and Inequality in South Africa* (2005) at 3 highlight the fact that 'South Africa's poor … are unusually poor (relative to the rich, that is): average household incomes in the bottom income decile were just one-hundredth of the average household incomes in the top decile. This is a larger ratio than that of Brazil, where the ratio stood at "only" 1:50.' They observe further that 'income inequality in South Africa is proving resistant to change and may in fact have worsened since the end of apartheid'. (3–4; see also chapter 9). See further H Bhorat & R Kanbur 'Introduction: Poverty and well-being in post apartheid South Africa' in H Bhorat & R Kanbur (eds) *Poverty and Policy in Post-apartheid South Africa* (2006) 1–14 at 5.

[7] The official unemployment statistics (as of March 2009) put the official national rate of unemployment at 21,9%. According to the expanded definition (which incorporates all non-economically active people between the ages of 15 and 64), the unemployment rate rises to 42,65%: Statistics SA, *Statistical Release P0211, Quarterly Labour Force Survey, Quarter 4 2008* (2 March 2009). Available at http://www.statssa.gov.za/Publications/P0211/P02114thQuarter2008.pdf (accessed on 7 March 2009).

[8] H Bhorat & C van der Westhuizen *Economic Growth, Poverty and Inequality in South Africa: The First Decade of Democracy* (2008) 4. Available at http://www.thepresidency.gov.za/docs/reports/15year_review/social/economic_growth.pdf (accessed on 7 March 2009).

[9] Bhorat & Van der Westhuizen ibid, table 1 at 3 and accompanying text at 3–4 (poverty) and table 4 at 12 and accompanying text (inequality of income distribution).

[10] Ibid table 3 at 7 and accompanying text at 7.

[11] Ibid table 2 at 6 and accompanying text at 5–7 (poverty) and table 6 at 16 and accompanying text at 15–16.

[12] See also United Nations Development Programme (UNDP) (principal author: V Taylor) *South Africa: Transformation for Human Development* (2000) 55.

education and electricity,[13] many, predominantly black, South Africans still lack access to affordable services of a decent quality.[14]

A further intersecting vector of disadvantage and inequality in South African society is that of gender. Patterns of gender equality are also deeply embedded in our social fabric, historically reinforced by a plethora of discriminatory customary, common-law and legislative provisions.[15] As Justice O'Regan of the Constitutional Court observed, '[t]hese patterns of discrimination are particularly acute in the case of black women, as race and gender discrimination overlap.'[16] Widespread structural unemployment and deep levels of poverty perpetuate the systemic marginalisation of black women in particular.[17]

Poverty and the multiple, intersecting forms of inequality in South Africa profoundly affect, not only peoples' survival, health and psychological well-being, but also their ability to participate on equal terms in the shaping of our new democracy.

2.2.3 Guiding a transforming society

The transformative character of the Constitution will be a limited one if it is defined solely by reference to the redress of apartheid wrongs. The South African Constitution is also 'forward-looking' in the sense that it aims at facilitating the construction[18] of a new political, social and economic order 'based on democratic values, social justice and fundamental human rights'.[19] This new order expressly envisages improving the quality of life and freeing the potential of each person.[20]

The constitutional commitment to work towards a society based on social justice implies not only the redressing of the outcomes of past injustice, but a deep restructuring of the underlying institutional arrangements which generate various forms of political, economic, social and cultural injustice.[21] A commitment to redress systemic

---

13 Bhorat & Kanbur (note 6 above) 6–7.

14 Ibid.

15 F Kaganas & C Murray 'Law and women's rights in South Africa: An overview' (1994) *AJ* 1–38; S Liebenberg & M O'Sullivan 'South Africa's new equality legislation: A tool for advancing women's socio-economic equality?' (2001) *AJ* 70–103 at 70–74; B Goldblatt 'Citizenship and the right to child care' in A Gouws (ed) *(Un)thinking Citizenship: Feminist Debates in Contemporary South Africa* (2005) 117–136.

16 *Brink v Kitshoff NO* 1996 (4) SA 197 (CC), 1996 (6) BCLR 752 (CC) para 44. For a discussion of the intersecting gender and race dimensions of poverty, see D Budlender *Women and Men in South Africa: Five Years On* (2002).

17 See D Budlender 'Women and poverty' (2005) 64 *Agenda* 30–36.

18 Ruti Teitel (2000, note 4 above) highlights this 'constructivist' role of constitutions in transitional societies. A constitution of this nature, 'explicitly reconstructs the political order associated with injustice' (197). She describes such constitutions as 'agents in the construction of the transformation' (200). See also R Teitel (1997, note 4 above) 2075–2080.

19 Preamble.

20 Preamble.

21 See Albertyn & Goldblatt (note 2 above) (the transformation project requires 'a complete reconstruction of the state and society, including a redistribution of power and resources

inequalities and social injustice arising from the past can therefore not be limited simply to the formal deracialisation of political, economic and social policy. Such a commitment will be a hollow one if it does not also seek to address the underlying causes of the persisting poverty and forms of inequality in our society.[22] Moreover, it requires openness to recognising and responding to both persisting and new forms of disadvantage and marginalisation that have emerged in post-apartheid South African society. These include the HIV/AIDS epidemic,[23] new categories of marginalised workers created by the changing nature of the post-apartheid labour market,[24] and the xenophobia and discrimination against the various categories of non-nationals in the country.[25] As Henk Botha observes:

> The Constitution, in this view, does not seek simply to consolidate and preserve the outcome of past constitutional struggles, but requires us to carry these struggles forward through political action and openness to new struggles for recognition.[26]

2.2.4 Transformative constitutionalism, democracy and rights

There is deep contestation and debate on what the underlying causes of poverty and inequality in South Africa are, as well as the nature and pace of the changes to the legal, political and economic system that are needed to give effect to the transformative goals of the Constitution. This is reflected, for example, in the heated debate concerning government's macroeconomic and distributional policies. Critical voices in civil society have argued that government has adopted an essentially neo-liberal

---

along egalitarian lines'); Liebenberg (note 2 above) (arguing for an interpretation of socio-economic rights that will advance fundamental reforms to the legal underpinnings of the current economic and social system).

22 Seekings & Nattrass (note 6 above) argue that inequality has persisted after 1994 because 'the distributional regime of the late apartheid period has been reformed (primarily through deracialisation) rather than transformed or rejected in favour of a more egalitarian one.' (6; see also chapters 10 to 11).

23 According to epidemiological data on HIV/AIDS in South Africa, it is estimated that 18% of South Africans between the ages of 15 and 49 years are living with HIV. Available at http://www.unaids.org/en/KnowledgeCentre/HIVData/Epidemiology/epifactsheets.asp#S (accessed on 11 February 2008).

24 Official unemployment statistics obscure significant aspects of the nature of employment in South Africa which include the related phenomena of the 'working poor' earning very low wages, the decline in formal sector employment, and the growth of non-standard forms of employment characterised by low wages, minimal benefits, and no security. See J Theron 'Employment is not what it used to be: The nature and impact of the restructuring of work in South Africa' in E Webster & K von Holdt (eds) *Beyond the Apartheid Workplace* (2005).

25 This was most graphically illustrated by the outbreak of xenophobic violence in South Africa in May 2008.

26 H Botha 'Freedom and constraint in constitutional adjudication' (2004) 20 *SAJHR* 249–283 at 277.

macroeconomic policy which has failed to prioritise the needs and interests of the poor or effect a fundamental redistribution of resources.[27]

The Constitution does not provide a comprehensive blueprint for a transformed society nor stipulate the precise processes for achieving it. Instead it provides a set of institutions, rights and values for guiding and constraining processes of social change. Active debate and contestation concerning the nature of social change, and the political and legal reforms necessary for achieving it, should not be viewed as antithetical to transformation, but rather as integral to its achievement. Chief Justice Langa describes the conception of transformation embraced by the Constitution as an open-ended process of ongoing dialogue and contestation in the quest for a more just society as follows:

> [T]ransformation is not a temporary phenomenon that ends when we all have equal access to resources and basic services and when lawyers and judges embrace a culture of justification. Transformation is a permanent ideal, a way of looking at the world that creates a space in which dialogue and contestation are truly possible, in which new ways of being are constantly explored and created, accepted and rejected and in which change is unpredictable but the idea of change is constant. This is perhaps the ultimate vision of a transformative, rather than a transitional Constitution. This is the perspective that sees the Constitution as not transformative because of its peculiar historical position or its particular socio-economic goals but because it envisions a society that will always be open to change and contestation, a society that will always be defined by transformation.[28]

This understanding of transformation affirms the centrality of democratic deliberation in the ongoing processes of transforming the current status quo.[29] It resonates with South Africa's history of a negotiated political settlement, and enriches and deepens the participatory, democratic culture which lies at the heart of South Africa's

[27] See, for example, The Congress of South African Trade Unions (COSATU) *Accelerating Transformation: COSATU's Engagement with Policy and Legislative Processes during South Africa's First Term of Democratic Governance* (2000) 83; H Marais *South Africa: Limits to Change – The Political Economy of Transformation* (1998); S Liebenberg 'Making a difference: Human rights and development – reflecting on the South African experience' in B Andreassen & S P Marks *Development as a Human Right: Legal, Political and Economic Dimensions* (2006) 167–195 at 171.

[28] Langa (note 2 above) 354.

[29] On deliberative democracy, See generally J Habermas *Between Facts and Norms: Contributions to a Discourse Theory of Law and Democracy* (trans W Rehg, 1996); A Gutmann & D Thompson *Democracy and Disagreement* (1996); T Roux 'Democracy' in S Woolman et al (eds) *Constitutional Law of South Africa* 2 ed (Original Service, September 2006) chapter 10 at 15–18; S Benhabib 'Toward a deliberative model of democratic legitimacy' in S Benhabib *Democracy and Difference: Contesting the Boundaries of the Political* (1996); I M Young *Inclusion and Democracy* (2000) 16–51. For a reading of the Constitution in terms of a deliberative model of democracy, see D Davis *Democracy and Deliberation* (1999).

transformative Constitution.[30] As Sachs J writes in *Minister of Health NO v New Clicks South Africa (Pty) Ltd (Treatment Action Campaign as Amicus Curiae)*:

> The right to speak and to be listened to is part of the right to be a citizen in the full sense of the word. In a constitutional democracy dialogue and the right to have a voice on public affairs is constitutive of dignity. Indeed, in a society like ours, where the majority were for centuries denied the right to influence those who ruled over them, the right 'to be present' when laws are being made has deep significance. [31]

Deliberative and participatory democracy coexist with the mechanisms for citizen participation in the institutions and processes of representative democracy.[32] However, they enrich and deepen representative democracy by expanding the opportunities for people's active participation in decision-making processes. They thus represent a more substantive conception of democracy than participating in periodic elections and in the formal mechanisms created for allowing citizens input in the institutions of representative democracy. Through creating multiple sites of dialogue and avenues of participation, their aim is to encourage greater participation in the public and private institutions which affect various aspects of people's lives. These include institutions such as community policing forums, traditional councils, communal property associations, workplaces, various professional bodies, non-governmental organisations and economic institutions.[33]

---

[30] One of the founding constitutional values is a multi-party system of democratic government based on accountability, responsiveness and openness (s 1(*d*)). The Constitution also expressly provides for public access to and participation in legislative processes: see ss 59, 72 and 118. Among the 'basic values and principles governing public administration' is that '[p]eople's needs must be responded to, and the public must be encouraged to participate in policy-making' (s 195(1)(*e*)).

[31] 2006 (2) SA 311 (CC), 2006 (1) BCLR 1 (CC) para 627.

[32] I Currie & J de Waal *The Bill of Rights Handbook* 5 ed (2005) 13–18 argue that the Constitution recognises three forms of democracy: representative democracy, participatory democracy and direct democracy. For a discussion of how the democratic provisions of the Constitution relate to contemporary accounts of democracy, see Roux (note 29 above) chapter 10. See particularly Roux's explanation of the distinction between deliberative democracy and participatory democracy (ibid 15–16).

[33] Iris Marion Young advocates a 'decentred model of deliberative democracy' (note 29 above) 44–47. According to this model,

> [T]he democratic process cannot be identified with one institution or set of institutions – the state, or legislative bodies, or courts, etc. Rather the processes of communication that give normative and rational meaning to democracy occur as flows and exchanges among various social sectors not brought together under a unifying principle. ... On this conception, democratic communication and influence flows between non-state institutions of civil society and state institutions (ibid 46, footnotes omitted).

Nancy Fraser also conceives of deliberative democracy as consisting of a diverse, dispersed network of public sites which include 'opinion-making' bodies such as NGOs, social movements and the media, and 'policy/legislation-making' public bodies such as legislatures and executives. See N Fraser 'Rethinking the public sphere: A contribution to the

Deliberative democracy represents a particular form of participatory democracy which is grounded in a belief that participation in public debate and dialogue can transform people's initial views and preferences, thereby laying the basis for reaching agreements.[34] An important requirement of deliberative democracy is that all participants retain an open mind and a willingness to transform their own initial perceptions of their interests and preferences in the deliberative process. This implies, as Iris Young states, that participants 'cannot come to the discussion of a collective problem with commitments that bind them to the authority of prior norms or unquestionable beliefs'.[35] Participants should also be accountable for the positions they articulate in various deliberative forums.[36] Furthermore, deliberation should not seek to evade the reality of deep structural inequalities on the assumption of a commonality of interests or to reach an easy consensus.[37] As Young points out, '[w]here there are structural

critique of actually existing democracy' in C Calhoun (ed) *Habermas and the Public Sphere* (1991) 109–142.

34 For an influential account of deliberative democracy, see Gutmann & Thompson (note 29 above). A central feature of dialogic politics is that it is an activity of public reasoning aimed at establishing normative values. As such, it is distinct from pluralist politics characterised by bargaining or exerting pressure to obtain an advantage in satisfying citizens' self-interests or preferences. According to Frank Michelman dialogic politics 'envisions politics as a process of reason not just of will, of persuasion not just of power, directed toward agreement regarding a good or just, or at any rate acceptable, way to order those aspects of life that involve people's social relations and social natures'. F I Michelman 'Bringing the law to life: A plea for disenchantment' (1989) 74(2) *Cornell L Rev* 256–269 at 257.

35 I M Young (note 29 above) 24.

36 Ibid 24–26.

37 A criticism of deliberative democracy is that it assumes a closed community of dialogic participants engaged in relatively harmonious deliberation concerning commonly held ends. See, for example, A Boshoff 'Law as dialogic politics' in H Botha, A J van der Walt & J van der Walt (eds) *Rights and Democracy in a Transformative Constitution* 1–12. Young points out that an emphasis on reasoned, dispassionate deliberation, and the assumption of a unity of ends, values and interests among participants, particularly under circumstances of social inequality, 'sometimes excludes the expression of some needs, interests, and suffering of injustice, because these cannot be voiced within the operative premises and frameworks' (ibid 37). She thus argues for a model of deliberative democracy which does not assume, or even aim at, a commonality of ends or interests, but seeks the more modest goal of reaching 'situation-specific agreements' which are always 'provisional and renewable' (ibid 43). This resonates with Tshepo Madlingozi's advocacy of alliances among post-apartheid social movements based on a contingent 'commonality' as opposed to an enforced unity of purposes: T Madlingozi 'Post-apartheid social movements and the quest for the elusive "new" South Africa' (2007) 34 *J of Law & Soc* 77–98 at 95–96. In the context of 'a highly differentiated and marginalised polity' in post-apartheid South Africa, Bettina von Lieres warns of the limitations of the 'politics of consensus' and deliberative forms of democracy based on the assumption of 'a single community held together by an ever growing general commitment to the "common good"'. See B van Lieres 'Marginalisation and citizenship in post-apartheid South Africa' in S L Robins (ed) *Limits to Liberation after Apartheid: Citizenship, Governance and Culture* (2005) 22–32 at 30–31.

conflicts of interest generating deep conflicts of interest, processes of political communication are more about struggle than agreement'.[38]

In order to approximate the ideals of fairness and justice, deliberative processes and forums should be open to a plurality of interests and reflect the full diversity of groups and communities in a society.[39] In addition, all groups should be able to participate in deliberative processes as peers or political equals.[40] This requires more than a formal opportunity to participate, but that all in society, particularly disadvantaged groups, have the substantive means of participating effectively.[41] Ensuring the substantive conditions for equal participation, in turn requires that attention be paid to the institutional obstacles impeding parity of participation for certain groups.[42]

As discussed above,[43] poverty and multiple forms of inequality marginalise large sections of South African society. Systemic forms of discrimination on grounds such as race, gender, sexual orientation and HIV status exist alongside inequality in people's access to social services and economic resources. The various forms of discrimination on the basis of people's status intersect with poverty to create new, invidious forms of systemic disadvantage. It is evident that we are far from creating the more equitable distribution of resources necessary to facilitate parity of participation in a range of public and private institutions. A commitment to a process of transformation that values equitable participation in the shaping of our new democracy cannot therefore fail to address the material conditions that impede such participation.

Many tenets of deliberative democracy, such as the creation of opportunities for transparent, accountable dialogue and debate on public values affecting key policy choices, align well with a constitutional democracy which requires significant decisions to be weighed and evaluated in the light of certain fundamental norms and

---

[38] I M Young (note 29 above) 44.

[39] Ibid 23.

[40] See Nancy Fraser's notion of 'participatory parity' developed in 'Social justice in the age of identity politics: Redistribution, recognition, and participation' in N Fraser & A Honneth *Redistribution or Recognition? A Political-Philosophical Exchange* (2003) 7–109.

[41] J Cohen 'The economic basis of deliberative democracy' (1989) 6 *Soc Philos Policy* 25–50. See also J Cohen 'Procedure and substance in deliberative democracy' in S Benhabib (ed) *Democracy and Difference: Contesting the Boundaries of the Political* (1996) 95–119.

[42] Fraser argues that fair democratic deliberation 'requires parity of participation for all actual and possible deliberators'. This in turn implies just distribution and reciprocal recognition. In other words, she rejects formal notions of democracy and equal autonomy as inadequate for ensuring that all groups have a substantively fair chance of influencing public deliberation around social policy. While she acknowledges that this reflects the circularity of democratic justice, she argues that this circularity is not vicious. Instead 'it faithfully expresses the reflexive character of justice as understood from the democratic perspective'. According to Fraser, the solution to this circularity is not to seek to abolish it in theory, but 'rather to work to abolish it in practice by changing social reality'. Fraser (note 40 above) 44. On the circularity problem in deliberative democracy, See further S Benhabib (note 29 above) 78–79; T Roux (note 29 above) 18 (and sources cited by him in note 2).

[43] See parts 2.2.2 and 2.2.3 above.

values.[44] Moreover, constitutional guarantees of both civil and political rights as well as economic, social and cultural rights are consistent with the commitment of deliberative democracy to substantively equal participation in deliberation.[45]

The adjudication of human rights norms may be seen as a significant forum for deliberation on whether the outcomes of formal democratic processes are consistent with these norms. Within this conception, courts are significant components of deliberative democracy,[46] instead of being perceived solely as 'counter-majoritarian' institutions requiring justification as exceptions to democratic institutions.[47] It is significant in this regard, that the Bill of Rights is described in the South African Constitution, as 'a cornerstone of democracy in South Africa' which 'enshrines the rights of all people in our country and affirms the democratic values of human dignity, equality and freedom'.[48]

However, as argued below,[49] this does not imply that the adjudication of human rights norms may not in fact operate to undermine deliberative and participatory democracy. There is clearly a tension between adjudication as a forum for authoritative decision-making according to binding legal norms,[50] and its potential to serve as

---

[44] On law as a site of dialogic politics, see F I Michelman 'Law's republic' (1988) 97(8) *Yale LJ* 1493–1537; C Bateup 'The dialogic promise: Assessing the normative potential of theories of constitutional dialogue' (2005–2006) 71(3) *Brook L Rev* 1109–1180; S Fredman *Human Rights Transformed: Positive Rights and Positive Duties* (2008) 105–113.

[45] Joshua Cohen observes that civil and political liberties 'help to comprise a system of institutional conditions in which free deliberation among equals can proceed in the first place'. Cohen 'The economic basis of deliberative democracy' (note 41 above) 38. In relation to economic rights, he observes: 'The deliberative conception requires … that citizens have equal standing in deliberative arenas, and that material inequalities should not fix their access to or influence in deliberative arenas' (ibid 47). For an argument that constitutionalising a right of 'social citizenship' will enrich democratic deliberation, see F I Michelman 'The constitution, social rights, and liberal political justification' (2003) 1 *I. Con* 13–34.

[46] More specifically, Michelman describes adjudication as 'one institutionally specialized form' of dialogical politics (note 34) n 44. In *S v Mhlungu* 1995 (3) SA 867 (CC), 1995 (7) BCLR 793 (CC) para 129, Sachs J characterised constitutional interpretation as 'a principled judicial dialogue, in the first place between members of this Court, then between our Court and other courts, the legal profession, law schools, Parliament, and indirectly, with the public at large'.

[47] There is an extensive literature seeking to explain and justify the judicial review of human rights norms in democratic societies. For a brief discussion of contemporary approaches in constitutional theory to this debate, see Roux (note 29 above) 18–22.

[48] Section 7(1).

[49] See parts 2.3.1 and 2.3.2 below.

[50] As Henk Botha observes, while reforms to the litigation process can enhance the diversity of voices able to participate in litigation, the court ultimately has the power 'to privilege some interpretations over others'. H Botha 'Democracy and rights: Constitutional interpretation in a postrealist world' (2000) 63 *THRHR* 561–581 at 573. For further critiques of civic republic constitutional theories, see K van Marle 'Communitarian and civic republican theories' in C Roederer & D Moellendorf *Jurisprudence* (2004) 412–437 at 428–436.

a forum for deliberation over the meaning and implications of the normative commitments in a Constitution.

Nevertheless, I contend that developing an understanding of law and legal processes as a particular form of dialogic politics can assist in countering or mitigating the law's tendency towards authority and closure. The interpretation of open-textured human rights norms provides particular scope for developing interpretations of rights which are as responsive as possible to the disjuncture between lived experiences of poverty and deep power imbalances and the constitutional ideal of social justice. The balance of this chapter examines the changes in legal and interpretive style and method which are required to enable socio-economic rights norms to contribute meaningfully to democratic transformation of the aforementioned conditions.

In summary, I have argued that, in addition to recognising and regulating representative democracy, the Constitution promotes a participatory, deliberative conception of democratic transformation. This model supports robust contestation, debate and struggle in the process of transforming society. While not prescribing a comprehensive vision of a just society, it is responsive to the inequalities and material deprivations which prevent certain groups from participating as equals in the creation of a new society. The specific role of the judiciary is examined in the next part, focusing particularly on the adjudication of socio-economic rights claims.

2.3 SOCIO-ECONOMIC RIGHTS AND TRANSFORMATIVE CONSTITUTIONALISM

2.3.1 Socio-economic rights as justiciable human rights

Transformative constitutionalism implies that the project of social transformation must be guided by and take place within the normative and institutional framework of the Constitution.

Although all the constitutional provisions are relevant to the achievement of these purposes, the Bill of Rights is particularly significant as it creates the possibility for ordinary people to challenge exercises of public or private power that undermine the rights underpinning this constitutional vision.

The mechanisms created for the enforcement of the Bill of Rights enable individuals and groups to obtain a hearing on the impact of policies and legislation on the fundamental interests protected by the various rights. These procedures are usually invoked when affected groups believe that their rights have been violated or disregarded in the representative democratic processes. Apart from the danger of legislators and policy-makers being subject to 'capture' by powerful business and interest groups in society,[51] they function under the constraints of limited time, resources and

[51] Martha Jackman observes: 'Modern parliamentary government concentrates power in the executive branch of government, to which cohesive, well-organized producer interests have been the most successful in gaining access.' M Jackman 'Constitutional contact with

bureaucratic pressures.[52] As a result, the official avenues of political representation and participation frequently fail to provide effective protection for the rights of marginalised groups in society.

The Bill of Rights guarantees a full set of universally recognised civil and political rights,[53] substantive equality guarantees,[54] rights to just administrative action[55] and access to information,[56] a property clause,[57] environmental rights,[58] as well as an array of economic, social and cultural rights.[59] The borders between the various categories of rights are porous[60] and their classification into these groups represents a construct of human rights law.[61] Nevertheless, the historic privileging of civil and political rights within human rights law has resulted in the interests and values protected by economic, social and cultural rights being marginalised within both international

---

the disparities of the world: Poverty as a prohibited ground of discrimination under the Canadian *Charter* and human rights law' (1994) II *RCS* 76–122 at 97.

52 For a description of the blockages in legislative processes arising from 'blind spots' and 'burdens of inertia', see R Dixon 'Creating dialogue about socio-economic rights: Strong-form versus weak-form judicial review revisited' (2007) 5(3) *I. Con* 391–418 at 402–403.

53 See s 10 (human dignity), s 11 (the right to life), s 12 (freedom and security of the person), s 13 (the right against slavery, servitude and forced labour), s 14 (the right to privacy), s 15 (freedom of religion, belief and opinion), s 16 (freedom of expression), ss 17–18 (rights of free assembly and association), ss 19–20 (political and citizenship rights), s 21 (freedom of movement and residence), s 34 (the right of access to courts), and s 35 (the rights of arrested, detained and accused persons).

54 Section 9. Substantive equality signifies an attempt by the law to address the real conditions of institutional and material inequalities that impede certain groups from participating as equals in all spheres of social life. See C Albertyn 'Equality' in H Cheadle, D Davis & N Haysom (eds) *South African Constitutional Law: The Bill of Rights* 1–65 at 4–7; See also *Minister of Finance v Van Heerden* 2004 (6) SA 121 (CC), 2004 (11) BCLR 1125 (CC) paras 26–27.

55 Section 33.

56 Section 32.

57 Section 25.

58 Section 24. The precursor of this clause was s 29 of the interim Constitution.

59 In fact, there is no universally accepted classification of rights. Rights which can be regarded as having a broadly social, economic or cultural character in the South African Bill of Rights are: s 22 (freedom of trade, occupation and profession); s 23 (labour relations); s 26 (housing); s 27 (health care, food, water and social security); s 28(1)(*c*) (children's socio-economic rights); s 29 (education); ss 30–31 (language and cultural rights); and s 35(2)(*e*) (the socio-economic rights of detained persons).

60 On the interdependence between the various 'categories' of rights, see further part 2.4.3 below.

61 For an overview of the historical development of economic, social and cultural rights as human rights within international human rights law, see A Eide 'Economic, social and cultural rights as human rights' in A Eide, C Krause & A Rosas (eds) *Economic, Social and Cultural Rights: A Textbook* 2 ed revised (2001) 9–28.

human rights law and comparative constitutional law.[62] The recognition of socio-economic rights represents an attempt to redress the tendency within liberal human rights discourse to exclude issues of impoverishment and material disadvantage from its referential framework.

The Bill of Rights in the South African Constitution seeks to respond in a holistic manner to a broad spectrum of interests that are fundamental to people's functioning in a democratic society committed to the values of human dignity, equality and freedom. The recognition of poverty and economic marginalisation as human rights issues has significant potential to contribute to the transformation of the South African legal system, its rules, institutions and traditions. In turn, the recognition and promotion of the values and purposes underpinning these rights in the legal system has the potential to facilitate corresponding social policy developments within the broader political culture in South Africa. Craig Scott and Patrick Macklem argued at the time of the drafting of the 1996 Constitution that a decision by the South African constitution-makers to include civil and political rights in the Bill of Rights but to treat social rights as non-justiciable would create the danger that 'the values underpinning social rights would be devalued as a result of selective constitutionalization'.[63] They go on to observe:

> In the absence of entrenched social rights, it would be unwise to expect that values left unconstitutionalized (and thus not reinforced by the continuing processes of constitutional interpretation) could hold their own in wider political discourse. ... A constitutional vision that includes only traditional civil liberties within its interpretive horizon fails to recognize the realities of life for certain members of society who cannot see themselves in the constitutional mirror. Instead, they will see the constitutional construction and legitimation of a legal self for whom social rights are either unimportant or taken for granted. With the passage of time and absent important countervailing factors, this normative vision will help to confirm the very reality that it posits. [64] (Footnotes omitted.)

2.3.2 Democratic transformation: The potential and limits of socio-economic rights litigation

The South African Constitution creates various mechanisms for holding the State and private actors accountable for violations of socio-economic rights. State

---

[62] In particular, this has resulted in weaker enforcement mechanisms for economic, social and cultural rights in both international law and comparative constitutional law. On socio-economic rights in international and foreign law jurisdictions, see chapter 3, parts 3.3.2 and 3.3.3.

[63] C Scott & P Macklem 'Constitutional ropes of sand or justiciable guarantees? Social rights in a new South African Constitution' (1992) 141 *U Pa L Rev* 1–148 at 27.

[64] Ibid 35–36. See J F Handler 'Constructing the political spectacle: The interpretation of entitlements, legalization and obligations in social welfare history' (1990) 56 *Brook L Rev* 899–974 for an analysis of the possibilities that rights created in the United States for disadvantaged groups to politicise and publicise issues such as systemic race and gender discrimination and poverty.

institutions supporting constitutional democracy, such as the South African Human Rights Commission, the Commission for Gender Equality and the Commission for the Promotion and Protection of the Rights of Cultural, Religious and Linguistic Communities, are given particular constitutional obligations in relation to promoting, monitoring, investigating and reporting on human rights.[65] The Human Rights Commission is given a specific constitutional mandate to monitor socio-economic rights.[66] Other institutions such as the Commission for Gender Equality, the Public Protector and the Commission for the Promotion and Protection of the Rights of Cultural, Religious and Linguistic Communities all have distinctive roles to play in relation to constitutionally protected rights.[67]

The status of socio-economic rights as *justiciable* rights in the South African Constitution vests in the judiciary an important role in interpreting these rights. The judiciary as an institution is constitutionally obliged to consider claims based on these rights seriously and to develop new and innovative remedies if a breach of the relevant provisions in the Bill of Rights is established.[68]

Through their interpretation of socio-economic rights, courts have a limited, but nevertheless significant role to play in facilitating democratic transformation. Primarily, they serve as an influential forum where the multifaceted dimensions of poverty and the social responses to it can be evaluated in the light of constitutional rights and values. The adjudication of socio-economic rights claims can enrich South Africa's democracy in a number of ways. First, it can provide a forum where the impact of legislation and policies on the lives of the poor receives serious and reasoned consideration in the light of the values and commitments of the Constitution.

---

[65] These institutions are created in chapter 9 of the Constitution and are regulated by specific statutes such as the Human Rights Commission Act 54 of 1994, the Commission on Gender Equality Act 39 of 1996, and the Commission for the Promotion and Protection of the Rights of Cultural, Religious and Linguistic Communities Act 19 of 2002.

[66] Thus s 184(3) provides: 'Each year, the South African Human Rights Commission must require relevant organs of state to provide the Commission with information on the measures that they have taken towards the realisation of the rights in the Bill of Rights concerning housing, health care, food, water, social security, education and the environment.' See D G Newman 'Institutional monitoring of social and economic rights: A South African case study and a new research agenda' (2003) 19 *SAJHR* 189–216; C Heyns 'Taking socio-economic rights seriously: The "domestic reporting procedure" and the role of the South African Human Rights Commission in terms of the new Constitution' (1999) *DJ* 1–32; J Klaaren 'A remedial interpretation of the *Treatment Action Campaign* decision' (2003) 19 *SAJHR* 455–468. The Commission must also integrate socio-economic rights within its other functions and powers such as the investigation of human rights abuses, the carrying out of research and human rights education. See ss 184(1) and (2) of the Constitution read together with the Human Rights Commission Act 54 of 1994.

[67] K Pillay 'The Commission for Gender Equality: What is its role?' (1998) 1 *ESR Review* 13–15.

[68] The Constitution vests in competent courts a broad discretion to grant 'just and equitable' remedies for breaches of the Constitution (see s 172(1)(*b*)). See further chapter 8.

Second, it can facilitate meaningful participation by civil society and communities in the formulation and implementation of social programmes by requiring such participation as a component of the relevant rights,[69] and by requiring transparency in the formulation of social policies and programmes.[70] Third, it can develop the normative basis of those parts of our legal system that regulate traditionally private relations in ways that protect and facilitate poor people's access to socio-economic resources. Finally, it can prod our polity as a whole to be more responsive to systemic socio-economic inequalities and deprivations.[71]

However, there are a number of institutional and political factors which determine whether the courts can play an effective role in processes of social transformation. For example, Siri Gloppen has developed a theoretical framework which examines the efficacy of social rights litigation in providing an institutional voice for the poor. She identifies four major stages relevant to the impact of public interest litigation: 'voice', 'responsiveness', 'capability', and 'compliance'. She explains these stages as follows:

> *Voice* concerns the ability of marginalised groups effectively to voice their claims or have them voiced on their behalf. Court *responsiveness* refers to the willingness of the courts to respond to the concerns of marginalised groups. *Capability* refers to judges' ability to give legal effect to social (and other) rights in ways that significantly affect the situation of marginalised groups, while *compliance* concerns the extent to which these judgments are politically authoritative, and whether the political branches comply with them and implement and reflect them in legislation and policies. [72]

I focus in this work on issues of legal interpretation and culture in the judicial enforcement of human rights norms in both public and private law under the South African

[69] See, for example, the discussion of the eviction cases in chapter 6, parts 6.4 and 6.5.

[70] See the discussion of *Minister of Health v Treatment Action Campaign (No 2)* 2002 (5) SA 721 (CC), 2002 (10) BCLR 1033 (CC) in chapter 4, part 4.3.

[71] On the discursive political effect of socio-economic rights adjudication, see for example: D Brand 'The "politics of need interpretation" and the adjudication of socio-economic rights claims in South Africa' in A J van der Walt (ed) *Theories of Social and Economic Justice* (2005) 17–36 at 24; Scott & Macklem (note 63 above) 27–31; Liebenberg (note 2 above) 17–19; 34–35. On the use of social rights discourse by non-governmental organisations in advocacy around law and policy reforms, see S Wilson 'Taming the Constitution: Rights and reform in the South African education system' 20 (2004) *SAJHR* 418–447; M Heywood 'Preventing mother-to-child HIV transmission in South Africa: Background, strategies and outcomes of the Treatment Action Campaign Case against the Minister of Health' (2003) 19 *SAJHR* 278–315; M Heywood 'Shaping, making and breaking the law in the campaign for a National HIV/AIDS Treatment Plan' in P Jones & K Stokke (eds) *Democratising Development: The Politics of Socio-Economic Rights in South Africa* (2005) 181–212.

[72] S Gloppen 'Courts and social transformation: An analytical framework' in R Gargarella, P Domingo & T Roux (eds) *Courts and Social Transformation in New Democracies* (2006) 35–59 at 37.

Constitution. These are specifically relevant to the stages of judicial responsiveness and capability identified by Gloppen.[73]

Despite this potential, the adjudication of socio-economic norms as a significant institutional site for promoting democratic transformation has limitations and potentially regressive tendencies.[74] While the adjudication of socio-economic rights claims can enhance deliberative democracy in the ways set out above, it also has the potential to undermine the participatory, deliberative model of democratic transformation promoted by the Constitution.[75] This occurs in a number of ways.

First, by interpreting socio-economic rights narrowly and excluding certain needs from the scope of the relevant provisions, the judiciary can undermine popular struggles to have these needs recognised and affirmed in broader political discourse.[76] A related danger is that adjudicative culture and practices operate to reinforce the public/private dichotomy by imposing strong duties of accountability on public actors for meeting socio-economic rights claims, while imposing weak or non-existent standards of accountability on private institutions.[77] The appearance of inevitability and normality generated by such interpretations[78] can divert attention from the limited range of meanings generated by legal processes and interpretive communities with the result that judicial interpretations of the rights are insulated from a broader transformative critique.[79] Adjudication can thus operate to prevent a serious consideration

---

73 Gloppen ibid 51–52.

74 See notes 49–50 above and accompanying text.

75 For an early critique of the potential of justiciable socio-economic rights to undermine participatory democracy, see D M Davis 'The case against the inclusion of socio-economic demands in a Bill of Rights except as directive principles' (1992) 8 *SAJHR* 475–490. See also chapter 1, notes 76–78 and accompanying text. As Martha Minow observes: 'Rights discourse, like any language, may mislead, seduce, falsely console or wrongly inflame.' M Minow 'Interpreting rights: An essay for Robert Cover' (1987) 96 *Yale LJ* 1860–1915 at 1910.

76 See M Pieterse 'Eating socioeconomic rights: The usefulness of rights talk in alleviating social hardship revisited' (2007) 29 *HRQ* 796–822. Pieterse draws particularly on Peter Gabel's work on the limitations of rights discourse in supporting the struggle of social movements to achieve transformative social change. See P Gabel 'Symposium: A critique of rights: The phenomenology of rights-consciousness and the pact of the withdrawn selves' (1984) 62 *Texas L Rev* 1563–1599.

77 See further chapter 2, part 2.4.5 below and chapter 7.

78 As P Lenta 'Democracy, rights disagreements and judicial review' (2004) 20 *SAJHR* 1–31 at 29 observes: 'Judges most often write in a monological voice that effaces the appearance of freedom of choice, and presents the verdict as forced by the logic of the situation itself.'

79 The legal community represents only one, albeit an authoritative and dominant, source for generating interpretations of the socio-economic rights provisions in the Constitution. For a discussion within the South African legal tradition of Peter Häberle's concept of an 'open community of constitutional interpreters', see L M du Plessis 'Legal academics and the open community of constitutional interpreters' (1996) 12 *SAJHR* 214–229. The danger is that judicial interpretations are powerful and their power lies in persuading the

of alternative interpretations of socio-economic rights in wider political discourse that may better advance the transformative purposes of the Constitution.

At the other end of the spectrum, courts can be insufficiently responsive to the legitimate diversity of ways in which socio-economic rights can be interpreted and realised in practice. An approach premised on the courts possessing all the answers on how best to realise socio-economic rights, can also have negative repercussions for democratic transformation. The likely effect is to induce legislative and executive lethargy, and an abdication of the primary role of these branches under the Constitution to give effect to the socio-economic rights guaranteed by formulating and implementing social legislation and programmes through broadly participative processes.[80] Similarly such an approach is disempowering to civil society movements who have a crucial role in advocating for particular interpretations of social rights and programmes to give effect to them.[81]

It does not follow that the courts should avoid developing a substantive interpretation of socio-economic rights. On the contrary, as argued below, a substantive interpretation of rights is central to transformative adjudication under the South African Constitution.[82] Elaborating on the normative commitments and purposes of these rights is not inconsistent with exercising restraint at the review or remedial stage of litigation when the evidence indicates that a court-imposed solution or remedy will not constitute the most fair or effective way of realising the particular right.[83] On the other hand, when there are systemic blockages in the political processes pertaining to a particular right, and an immediate remedy is required to prevent

---

polity that the interpretation accorded to particular rights are the normal or inevitable meaning that these rights have. As Rosemary Coombe '"Same as it ever was": Rethinking the politics of legal interpretation' (1989) 34 *McGill LJ* 603–652 at 636 observes, the fact that the conventions of the legal community constrain the meanings of legal text, and that they make such interpretations seem determinate 'or so completely cast in stone that they have (or seem to have) the character of bedrock, should give us less cause for complacency than it does for alarm'.

[80] For accounts of the reduction in 'democratic responsiveness' resulting from strong forms of judicial review of socio-economic rights claims, see M Tushnet 'New forms of judicial review and the persistence of rights- and democracy-based worries' (2003) 38 *Wake Forest L Rev* 813–838; Dixon (note 52 above); C Steinberg 'Can reasonableness protect the poor? A review of South Africa's socio-economic rights jurisprudence' (2006) 123 *SALJ* 264–284; M S Kende *Constitutional Rights in Two Worlds* (2008) 272–274.

[81] The Treatment Action Campaign has been successful in advocating, both outside and inside the courts, for an acceptance of antiretroviral therapy as an integral component of the right of access to health care services in s 27 of the Constitution. For a richly textured account of the strategies employed by the TAC, see Heywood (note 71 above).

[82] See part 2.4.2 below.

[83] On the possibilities of 'weak remedies' for strong substantive rights in the context of socio-economic rights adjudication, see M Tushnet 'Social welfare rights and forms of judicial review' (2003–2004) 82 *Texas L Rev* 1895–1919; M Tushnet 'Enforcing socio-economic rights: Lessons from South Africa' (2005) 6 *ESR Review* 2–6.

serious harm to claimant groups, robust judicial intervention is required. This can take the form of a stringent scrutiny of government's justificatory arguments combined with an immediate remedy, such as ordering the provision of a particular service to the claimants, or reading a particular group into benefit-conferring legislation.[84] Enforcing constitutional rights in ways which promote democratic transformation is an exacting task which requires acute sensitivity to the dynamic interaction between legal and broader political processes. In this context, general and abstract prescriptions about the degree of deference a court should apply at the review or remedial stage in enforcing constitutional socio-economic rights are unhelpful. Wherever possible, courts should seek to stimulate participatory strategies by government and civil society to give effect to constitutional rights, without abdicating their constitutional role to critically assess compliance with the normative standards these rights impose.

Another way in which the adjudication of socio-economic rights claims can undermine transformative politics is to reinforce negative cultural stereotypes concerning claimant groups. Judicial pronouncements can position claimants as passive beneficiaries of social goods and services, instead of active agents entitled to participate in the defining and meeting of their needs.[85] Edgar Pieterse and Mirjam van Donk argue that an empowering conception of socio-economic rights requires that the State and powerful private institutions fulfil their responsibilities 'in a way that recognises its citizens and their representative organisations as "rights holders" and active agents in the realisation of human rights and development'.[86] The danger of promoting a conception of socio-economic rights as commodities conferred on passive beneficiaries by a benevolent State is that it deflects attention away from the more fundamental reforms required to the underlying institutions and structures that

[84] See, for example, the high level of scrutiny and strong remedies applied in cases such as *Minister of Health v Treatment Action Campaign (No 2)* (note 70 above) and *Khosa v Minister of Social Development; Mahlaule v Minister of Social Development* 2004 (6) SA 505 (CC), 2004 (6) BCLR 569 (CC). See the discussion of these cases in chapter 4, part 4.3.

[85] See, for example, N Fraser *Unruly Practices: Power, Discourse and Gender in Contemporary Social Theory* (1989) 161–187 at 174 (analysing the dynamics of disempowerment that take place within expert needs discourses); J Nedelsky 'Reconceiving autonomy: Sources, thoughts and possibilities' (1989) 1 *Yale J of Law and Feminism* 7–36 (exploring the potential of the administration of welfare benefits in modern bureaucratic states to undermine the autonomy of the recipients of benefits and ways of countering this tendency through administrative justice rights); Scott & Macklem (note 63 above) 33–35 (referring to the dangers of social rights adjudication slipping into a 'protectionist paternalism that risks treating civil liberties as trade-offs for the satisfaction of social need claimed as right' (34)).

[86] E Pieterse & M van Donk 'The politics of socio-economic rights in South Africa ten years after apartheid' (2004) 5 *ESR Review* 12–15 at 12.

generate poverty and systemic social inequalities,[87] and the primacy of social mobilisation and struggle in achieving these changes.[88]

The tensions between the transformative and regressive potential of socio-economic rights litigation cannot be wished away. Our best chance of placing social rights litigation on a transformative trajectory is to be conscious of its regressive potential, and to develop creative ways of enhancing its potential to deepen a rights-based democracy.[89] As Joel Handler observes:

> Rights talk can change beliefs and expectations, but this may or may not lead to concrete change, or change in the desired direction. Rights consciousness has constitutive and transformative possibilities, but they are possibilities only.[90]

There are choices to be made when the judiciary interprets the rights guarantees in the Constitution. And these choices have very real consequences for those who are homeless, hungry, illiterate or suffering ill health.[91] The challenge for South African courts is to develop a substantive account of the values and purposes which the socio-economic rights protect, coupled with adjudicative strategies which are attuned to the complex institutional environment and social power relations which determine their concrete realisation.[92]

---

[87] For a discussion of this tendency in the adjudication of socio-economic rights claims, see S Liebenberg (note 2 above) 8–10; 17–19.

[88] For an analysis of the dynamics of social movements in South Africa in challenging the neo-liberal tendencies of the post-apartheid macroeconomic paradigm, manifested particularly in models of service delivery based on cost-recovery to impoverished communities, see T Madlingozi (note 37 above); R Greenstein 'Socio-economic rights, radical democracy and power: South Africa as a case study' in N Gordon (ed) *From the Margins of Globalization: Critical Perspectives on Human Rights* (2004) 87–126.

[89] See, for example, the discussion of the potential of structural interdicts to enhance institutional and public collaboration and participation in programmatic measures to give effect to socio-economic rights: chapter 8, part 8.6.

[90] J F Handler (note 64 above) 968. On the possibility of critical revision within the legal form and transformative legal interpretation, see F I Michelman (note 34 above) 258; D Cornell 'Institutionalization of meaning, recollective imagination and the potential for transformative legal interpretation' (1988) 136 *U Pa L Rev* 1135–1229.

[91] Joan Williams 'Critical legal studies: The death of transcendence and the rise of the new langdells' (1987) 62 *NYULR* 429–496 at 494–495 points out that the choices we make about our legal doctrine are important as they 'constrain the scope of our conversations about vital issues, and delimit future sense and nonsense':

> For example, do we want to choose a legal system in which our pain at seeing poor people homeless has no voice? Do we want a law in which our sharp concern over environmental degradation is discussed largely in terms of whether bureaucrats have followed the correct procedures in enforcing often unsatisfactory statutes? Do we want a law blind to the important differences between a huge commercial supply contract and an arrangement by which an elderly worker has earned his living for his entire working life?

[92] See further part 2.4.2 below.

2.4 DEVELOPING THE JURISPRUDENCE: TRANSFORMATIVE APPROACHES

2.4.1 The influence of classic liberal legal culture

South African legal culture[93] has a number of features which constrain the development of a transformative jurisprudence on socio-economic rights.[94] In particular, it contains strong traces of classic liberal legal culture such as formalism, deference to legislative choices,[95] and dichotomous conceptions of negative and positive rights, public and private law, law and politics. Karl Klare describes the key political and philosophical underpinnings of 'liberal legalism' in the following terms:

> Liberal legalist jurisprudence and its institutions are closely related to the classical liberal political tradition, exemplified in the work of Hobbes, Locke and Hume. The metaphysical underpinnings of liberal legalism are supplied by the central themes of that tradition: the notion that values are subjective and derive from personal desire, and that therefore ethical discourse is conducted profitably only in instrumental terms; the view that society is an artificial aggregation of autonomous individuals; the separation in political philosophy between public and private interest, between state and civil society; and a commitment to a formal or procedural rather than a substantive conception of justice.[96]

The fulfilment of the transformative potential of socio-economic rights will depend in part on the willingness of South African judges, practitioners and other participants in socio-economic rights litigation to revisit and refashion many traditional concepts of liberal legalism that inhibit creative, innovative responses to socio-economic rights claims.[97] This part considers the major conceptions of rights and adjudication

---

[93] Karl Klare' (note 1 above) 166–167 notes that legal culture encompasses the 'enduring political and ethical commitments [that] influence professional discourse' as well as the '"inarticulate premises, culturally and historically ingrained" in the professional discourse and outlook'. (Citation to Kriegler J in *Du Plessis v De Klerk* 1996 (3) SA 850 (CC), 1996 (5) BCLR 658 (CC) para 19.)

[94] For an analysis of the constraints imposed by judicial culture on developing a transformative interpretation of the Constitution in general, see Klare (note 1 above). For an analysis of the constraints posed by legal culture and ideology in the particular context of socio-economic rights adjudication in South Africa, see M Pieterse 'Coming to terms with the judicial enforcement of socio-economic rights' (2004) 20 *SAJHR* 383–417 at 396–399.

[95] As Pieterse (ibid) 398 observes, the culture of deference in the South African context was 'cultivated over the decades-long ascendancy of parliamentary sovereignty'. See also J Dugard 'The judicial process, positivism and civil liberty (1971) 88 *SAJHR* 181–200.

[96] Karl Klare 'Law-making as praxis' (1979) *Telos* 123–135 at 132, n 28.

[97] André van der Walt (2006, note 2 above) 18 notes the implications of a hegemonic legal tradition and culture such as one based on 'a liberalist view of society and a positivist view of law' for excluding alternative perspectives, different arguments and innovative solutions. Klare (note 1 above) 169-171 observes that a progressive or transformative approach to adjudication, which 'pushes on the law/politics boundary and invites reference to social realities outside and beyond legal practices', does not guarantee politically and socially

in classic liberal legalism that must be revisited in order to open up transformative possibilities in socio-economic rights litigation.

2.4.2 Transforming formal rights into substantive rights

The classic liberal tradition of rights tends to rely on formal rights and formal legal reasoning.[98] According to the formal conception, rights are regarded as having an objective, value-free and fixed meaning. It is the role of judges to discern this meaning and to apply it as neutrally and objectively[99] as possible to the facts of the specific cases before them.[100] Rights are abstracted from their social context, and the real world consequences flowing from the enforcement of these abstract rules and principles are deemed irrelevant. Despite sustained critiques by the legal realists and critical legal theorists,[101] formalism has a powerful traction in South African legal culture.[102]

---

transformative outcomes. However, he gives two reasons why he believes that a progressive legal culture is a necessary condition for the long-term success of transformative constitutionalism. First, 'expressions of faith in the constraining power of legal texts and ritual invocation of the law/politics boundary obscure and mystify the choices judges and advocates routinely make in their interpretive work. This reduces the transparency of the legal process, thereby undermining its contribution to deepening democratic culture.' Second, a conservative jurisprudential approach (in the aforementioned sense) 'may induce a kind of intellectual caution that discourages appropriate constitutional innovation and leads to less generous or innovative interpretations and application of the Constitution than are permitted by the text and drafting history'.

98 For a discussion of the formal conception of rights in the liberal traditions, see generally J Singer 'Legal realism now' (1988) 76 *CLR* 465–544 at 519–522; H Botha (note 50 above) 563–567; J M Woods 'Justiciable social rights as a critique of the liberal paradigm' (2003) 38 *Tex Int L J* 763–794.

99 For an example of attempts to develop objective and neutral standards of adjudication, see H Wechsler 'Towards neutral principles of constitutional law' (1959) 73 *Harvard LR* 1–35; K R Greenawalt 'The enduring significance of neutral principles' (1978) 78 *Columbia LR* 982–1021.

100 J Singer (note 98 above) 497 describes formalism in legal reasoning as the belief that the legal system can be categorized into general principles 'composed of rigidly defined concepts'. These principles were thought capable of generating 'specific legal conclusions by a logical, objective, and scientific process of deduction'. Accordingly, '[h]ighly abstract concepts were thought to be operative or capable of generating specific consequences by their very nature'.

101 J Singer (note 98 above); M V Tushnet 'Following the rules laid down: A critique of interpretivism and neutral principles' (1983) 96 *Harvard LR* 781–821; R M Unger 'The critical legal studies movement' (1983) 96 *Harvard* LR 561–675; M Minow (note 75 above) D Kennedy *A Critique of Adjudication {fin de siècle}* (1997); L M Seidman 'Critical constitutionalism now' (2006) 75 *Fordham L Rev* 575–592. On the implications of the 'interpretive turn' in the social sciences for legal interpretation, see R Coombe (note 79 above).

102 On the formalism of South African legal culture, See generally A Cockrell 'Rainbow jurisprudence' (1996) 12 *SAJHR* 1–38, particularly at 7–8; A Cockrell 'Adjudication styles in South African private law' (1993) 56 *THRHR* 590–607; A J van der Walt 'Tradition

The socio-economic rights in South Africa's Constitution have the potential to contribute to the transformation of our legal and political culture by inviting recourse to a set of values and social and material realities which have hitherto been suppressed in our legal culture. The conditions of social and economic deprivation in which many people in South Africa live their lives are rendered important subjects of constitutional concern. However, their potential to contribute to the transformation of South African legal culture will be constrained if their interpretation is controlled by formalism.

Developing the normative content of socio-economic rights and elucidating the nature of the duties they impose on public and private actors are fundamental responsibilities of the courts under South Africa's transformative Constitution. A substantive interpretation of socio-economic rights is central to promoting the transformative purposes of the South African Constitution for a number of reasons.

First, as argued above, where people lack access to important socio-economic needs, the deliberative and participatory purposes of the Constitution are undermined.[103]

Second, the courts are accorded a significant role under South Africa's Constitution to uphold and enforce the rights and values entrenched in the Bill of Rights, of which socio-economic rights are an integral component. The South African courts are therefore important institutions where deliberation and accountability for the fundamental normative commitments of South Africa's constitutional order are fostered. There is no other institution with both the authority and responsibility to make final binding pronouncements on the nature and scope of the rights in the Bill of Rights. If the courts adopt formalistic or overly narrow interpretations of the rights in the Bill of Rights, the normative force of human rights guarantees in governance and society as a whole will be diminished. This is contrary to the constitutional conception of the Bill of Rights as 'a cornerstone of democracy in South Africa'.[104]

Third, although all the rights in the Bill of Rights are deeply relevant to the struggles of poor and marginalised groups, socio-economic rights speak directly to the material conditions of their lives. The relevance of the courts as guardians of this particular set of normative commitments will be eroded if they fail to give meaning to the socio-economic rights in the Constitution. The responsibility becomes even more significant in contexts where state institutions are failing to integrate a rights-based approach in their developmental practices and policies.[105] In the absence of a

---

on trial: A critical analysis of the civil law tradition in South African property law' (1995) 11 *SAJHR* 169–206; J Froneman 'Legal reasoning and legal culture: Our "vision" of law' (2005) 1 *Stell LR* 3–20; M Chanock *The Making of South African Legal Culture 1902–1936: Fear, Favour and Prejudice* (2001) 36.

[103] See Cohen (note 41 above) and the discussion of socio-economic rights as a floor for participatory/deliberative democracy in part 2.2.4 above at notes 41–42 above and accompanying text.

[104] Section 7(1) of the Constitution.

[105] On rights-based approaches to development, see J K Hansen & H Sano 'The implications and value added of a rights-based approach' in B A Andreassen & S P Marks (eds) *Development as a Human Right* (2006) 36–56.

robust affirmation by the courts of socio-economic rights as fundamental human rights commitments, a general 'culture of justification'[106] in respect of the realisation of socio-economic rights in South Africa will be unattainable.

Moreover, there are features of adjudication which make it well suited to developing the normative content of human rights guarantees. Thus the judiciary are trained to interpret the nature and scope of rights, to systematically analyse evidence, to listen carefully to all the parties to the litigation, to explore the implications of their arguments with them, to research relevant precedent, academic literature, international and foreign law, and ultimately to write a judgment which provides transparent, comprehensive reasons for the conclusions reached.[107] Litigants, whose voices may be marginalised in the broader society and political processes, have at least formal equality of voice in the litigation process.[108] However, as Gloppen's analytical framework indicates, whether disadvantaged groups are able to effectively voice their claims through litigation and whether courts will be responsive to their concerns, depends on a myriad of legal, institutional, social, political and economic factors.[109] If disadvantaged litigants do succeed, against the odds, in marshalling the substantial resources of money, time, energy and emotional commitment entailed in bringing a case to the courts, the least they can expect is a judgment which engages seriously with the normative commitments underlying the particular rights invoked.

Developing the normative commitments of the socio-economic rights provisions in the Constitution also increases the transparency of judicial interpretation of the Bill of Rights. If 'judicial avoidance' or minimalism[110] as a 'reflex, an

---

106 Etienne Mureinik powerfully described South Africa's constitutional dispensation as representing a shift from a 'culture of authority' to a 'culture of justification': E Mureinik 'A bridge to where?: Introducing the interim Bill of Rights' (1994) 10 *SAJHR* 31–48. Establishing a 'culture of justification' for the exercise of all forms of power (whether public or private) is consistent with the culture of reason-giving which is required for deliberative democracy to flourish.

107 See in this regard Marius Pieterse (note 94 above) 395.

108 As Pieterse ibid 392 observes, one of the factors which make courts suited as a forum for deliberation in rights disputes is that 'the individual rights-bearer is given a direct voice' in the process of mediating such disputes between the citizenry and elected representatives.

109 Gloppen (note 72 above) and accompanying text. For an account of the factors affecting the South African Constitutional Court's ability to provide an effective 'institutional voice for the poor', see J Dugard & T Roux 'The record of the South African Constitutional Court in providing an institutional voice for the poor: 1995–2004' in R Gargarella, P Domingo & T Roux (eds) *Courts and Social Transformation in New Democracies: An Institutional Voice for the Poor?* (2006) 107–125.

110 For a defence of judicial minimalism as a significant and valuable strategy for constitutional adjudication in South Africa, see I Currie 'Judicious avoidance' (1999) 15 *SAJHR* 138–165. Currie draws on the work of Cass Sunstein in defence of judicial minimalism or 'incompletely theorized agreements' in constitutional law. See C R Sunstein 'Foreword: Leaving things undecided' (1996) 110 *Harvard LR* 4–101; C R Sunstein 'Incompletely

adjudicative habit, inclination, style or strategy'[111] becomes entrenched in South African adjudicative culture, many of the theoretical and value-based premises underpinning all judicial decision-making will remain unarticulated. As such, the premises and values which determine the outcomes of litigation will be opaque and inaccessible for critical public scrutiny and debate. This will negate the contribution of adjudication as a site of deliberation and engagement regarding the fundamental norms and values animating our constitutional democracy. As Justice O'Regan observes:

> Lawyers are often tempted to leave unexplored fundamental assumptions ... . Leaving such assumptions unspoken may be tempting but it is dangerous. Our most deep assumptions remain unexpressed and unacknowledged: they may not be challenged or endorsed. A constitutional order requiring openness and accountability in relation to the exercise of public power cannot tolerate judicial avoidance of reasoning on fundamental constitutional values.[112]

Developing the legal and institutional meaning of socio-economic rights requires engagement with the values and purposes which these rights protect and promote.[113] It also requires judicial sensitivity and understanding of the historical and current social and economic context as well as the range of impacts which poverty and inequality has on the lives of disadvantaged groups. In this enterprise, theoretical inquiry into the values and purposes of socio-economic rights occurs in dynamic interaction with the evolving public understanding of the historical and social context of systemic poverty, inequality and complex forms of marginalisation of various groups in South Africa.[114] This constant dialogue between theoretical understandings and social contexts is necessary if the constitutional meanings which socio-

---

theorized agreements in constitutional law' (2007) 74 *Social Research* 1–24. For a critique of judicial minimalism 'as either an accurate description of or a desirable prescription for our Bill of Rights jurisprudence', see S Woolman 'The amazing, vanishing Bill of Rights' (2007) 124 *SALJ* 762–794 at 764–765.

[111] Currie ibid 159.

[112] C O'Regan 'From form to substance: The constitutional jurisprudence of Laurie Ackermann' in A J Barnard-Naudé, D Cornell & F du Bois (eds) *Dignity, Freedom and the Post-Apartheid Legal Order: The Critical Jurisprudence of Laurie Ackermann* (2008) 1–17 at 16.

[113] This accords with the overall orientation of substantive legal reasoning towards the underlying justification for rules in relation to their justness and the consequences they have for society, as opposed to their formal authority. See A Cockrell 1996 (note 102 above) 5; Froneman (note 102 above) 4–7.

[114] The Constitutional Court in *Government of the Republic of South Africa v Grootboom* 2001 (1) SA 46 (CC), 2000 (11) BCLR 1169 (CC) ('*Grootboom*') para 21 noted that both the textual setting as well as the social and historical context were relevant to the interpretation of the rights in the Bill of Rights. For an explicit reliance on the historical and social context in interpreting the provisions in the Bill of Rights, see *Port Elizabeth Municipality v Various Occupiers* 2005 (1) SA 217 (CC), 2004 (12) BCLR 1268 (CC) paras 8–13. However, even references to broader historical, political and social contexts can constrain the development of transformative interpretations of socio-economic rights when there

economic rights acquire over time are to be maximally responsive to the multiple forms of deprivation experienced by various groups in South Africa, and their own articulations of their needs.[115]

Developing a substantive interpretation of the socio-economic rights in the Bill of Rights should not imply that courts are obliged to develop a 'grand narrative' or a fixed, comprehensive theory of socio-economic rights. An evolving narrative on the ethical values and purposes of these rights is no less substantive for its lack of completeness and closure. It is the open fabric of the narrative, its loose weave, which makes possible ongoing renewal and responsiveness to changing conditions in South Africa's socio-economic rights jurisprudence. Nevertheless, if judicially enforceable socio-economic rights are to have any influence on legal and political culture in South Africa, we cannot do without a narrative about what these constitutional rights mean. The unfolding of this narrative must be guided by the various signposts contained in the Constitution.

The Constitution expressly enjoins the courts to develop interpretations of the Bill of Rights which 'promote the values that underlie an open and democratic society based on human dignity, equality and freedom'.[116] In order to do so, courts must have regard to the diverse accounts of the justifications and purposes of socio-economic rights[117] and their relationship with the values[118] of democracy,[119]

---

is an uncritical reliance on fixed and exclusive understandings of contexts. As Coombe (note 79 above) 633–634 cautions:

> Accounts of legal interpretation which point to contexts, however defined, as stable referents which constrain practice, misunderstand the dynamic *process* whereby context or culture is both reproduced and transformed by the practices it enables.

On the dangers of a 'grand narrative' approach to South Africa's history in constitutional interpretation, see P de Vos 'A bridge too far? History as context in the interpretation of the South African Constitution' (2001) 17 *SAJHR* 1–33.

[115] On the processes by which expert needs discourses such as legal discourses recast social struggles around needs into bureaucratic or 'administerable needs', see Nancy Fraser 'Talking about needs: Interpretive contests as political contests in welfare-state societies' (1989) 99 *Ethics* 291–313, particularly at 306–307. See also Brand (note 71 above) 21.

[116] Section 39(1)(*a*) of the Constitution.

[117] This will require engagement with the diverse disciplines of philosophy, political theory and economic theory from which many of these justifications emanate. As Karl Klare observes, it is necessary 'to step outside of' rights discourse in order to fill rights with legal and institutional meaning'. K Klare 'Legal theory and democratic reconstruction: Reflections on 1989' (1991) 25 *UBC* 69–103 at 101.

[118] The foundational values of the Constitution are explicitly set out in s 1 of the Constitution.

[119] See, for example, the theoretical work on the role of socio-economic rights in promoting participatory and deliberative democracy cited in 2.2.4 above, particularly at notes 41–45 above. See also Frank Michelman's application of John Ely Hart's principle of 'representation reinforcement' to argue for the recognition of welfare rights in American constitutional jurisprudence on the basis that these rights guarantee the economic basis for effective participation in the political process by all in society. F I Michelman 'Welfare

dignity,[120] equality,[121] and freedom.[122] Such an approach represents a fundamental departure from a formalist interpretation of these rights premised on 'neutral', 'value-free' adjudication of the relevant legal texts.

---

rights in a constitutional democracy' (1979) 3 *Wash Univ LQ* 659–693. For an analysis and evaluation of Michelman's theories on welfare rights, see A J van der Walt 'A South African reading of Frank Michelman's theory of social justice' in H Botha, A J van der Walt & J van der Walt (eds) *Rights and Democracy in a Transformative Constitution* (2004) 163–211.

120 Frank Michelman has also developed a theory of justification for the recognition of socio-economic rights derived from the moral duty that society owes to all its members to ensure that they can enjoy human dignity understood as self-respect. F I Michelman 'The Supreme Court, 1968 term: On protecting the poor through the fourteenth amendment' (1969) 83 *Harvard LR* 7–59; F Michelman 'In pursuit of constitutional welfare rights: One view of Rawls' theory of justice' (1973) 121 *U Pa L Rev* 962–1091. For an account of the role of dignity in the adjudication of socio-economic rights in the context of the South African Constitution, see S Liebenberg 'The value of human dignity in interpreting socio-economic rights' (2005) 21 *SAJHR* 1–31.

121 For examples of scholarship developing the interlinkages between socio-economic rights and equality as a value and right, see chapter 4, part 4.5, particularly at notes 415–418.

122 Amartya Sen argues that freedom lies at the heart of the concept of human rights. Sen identifies two distinctive dimensions of freedom that demand special acknowledgment – substantive opportunities and freedom of processes. The idea of human capabilities is of special relevance to the opportunity aspect of freedom, in that it allows an appropriate distinction between '(1) what a person values *doing* or *being*, and (2) the *means* she has to achieve what she values'. See A Sen 'Elements of a theory of human rights' (2004) 32 *Philosophy and Public Affairs* 315–356 at 328–332. An integrated set of human rights norms, incorporating both civil and political rights and economic, social and cultural rights, helps guarantee the value combinations of human functionings or capabilities needed to achieve substantive freedom (ibid 332). See also A Sen *Development as Freedom* (2001). Martha Nussbaum has attempted to derive a universal list of human rights norms from the capabilities approach. See, for example, M C Nussbaum *Women and Human Development: The Capabilities Approach* (2000) 74–75; M C Nussbaum 'Capabilities, human rights, and the Universal Declaration' in B H Weston & S P Marks (eds) *The Future of International Human Rights* (1999) 25–64. For discussions of the relevance of the capabilities approach to socio-economic rights in the South African context, see J C Froneman 'Enforcing socio-economic rights under a transformative constitution: The role of the courts' (2007) 8 *ESR Review* 20–25; S Liebenberg 'The value of freedom in interpreting socio-economic rights' in A J Barnard-Naudé, D Cornell & F du Bois (eds) *Dignity, Freedom and the Post-Apartheid Legal Order* (2008) 149–196. Although not explicitly articulated in terms of the constitutional value of freedom, David Bilchitz's philosophical justification for socio-economic rights centres on the general capabilities and resources required to enable human beings to have and realise a diversity of purposes: *Poverty and Fundamental Rights: The Justification and Enforcement of Socio-Economic Rights* (2007) 3–4, 40–46. For a different argument, which grounds social rights in the value of autonomy, see C Fabre 'Constitutionalising social rights' (1998) 6 *The Journal of Political Philosophy* 263–284.

Each of these values and theoretical approaches offers valuable insights and perspectives on the purposes which socio-economic rights advance in a constitutional democracy. Different values and purposes will be implicated depending on the nature and context of particular cases. Thus a case involving a claim for the provision or protection of state-provided shelters on behalf of women in abusive relationships entails understanding the right of access to adequate housing in terms of its interrelationship with the value of autonomy, and the related right to freedom and security of the person.[123] A claim by Hindu prisoners for the provision of vegetarian food implicates the right of persons deprived of their liberty to adequate nutrition,[124] as well as respect for diverse religious and cultural beliefs.[125] A claim by parents for public and private childcare facilities is located at the intersection of fair labour practices, social security and the advancement of gender equality as a right and fundamental value of our constitutional democracy. Given deeply inscribed gender roles, the failure of state and communal support for care-giving roles entrenches and deepens patterns of gender inequality and disadvantage.[126] Instituting eviction proceedings against a homeless community who have resided on land for a substantial period of time without any attempt to engage with them, implicates the housing rights entrenched in s 26 of the Constitution interpreted in the light of the constitutional values of dignity and participatory democracy.[127]

A substantive approach to the interpretation of socio-economic rights is sensitive to contextual variations in which socio-economic rights violations occur and the wide range of interdependent rights and values which are implicated.[128] Moreover, an approach which is categorically wedded to a single value or set of interests to justify the constitutional protection of socio-economic rights may have the effect of foreclosing dialogue and debate on the different values and interests which are at stake in particular socio-economic rights claims.[129]

---

[123] Section 12(1)(*c*) of the Constitution.

[124] Section 35(2)(*e*) of the Constitution.

[125] Freedom of conscience, religion, thought, belief and opinion are protected in s 15 of the Bill of Rights. The Constitutional Court has emphasised the value of diversity in South Africa's constitutional project: See, for example, *Minister of Home Affairs v Fourie; Lesbian and Gay Equality Project v Minister of Home Affairs* 2006 (1) SA 524 (CC), 2006 (3) BCLR 355 (CC) para 60; *MEC for Education: KwaZulu-Natal v Pillay* 2008 (1) SA 474 (CC), 2008 (2) BCLR 99 (CC) para 65.

[126] See B Goldblatt 'Citizenship and the right to child care' in A Gouws (ed) *(Un)thinking Citizenship: Feminist Debates in Contemporary South Africa* (2005) 117–136.

[127] See the discussion of *Occupiers of 51 Olivia Road, Berea Township and 197 Main Street, Johannesburg v City of Johannesburg* 2008 (3) SA 208 (CC), 2008 (5) BCLR 475 (CC) in chapter 6, part 6.4.

[128] A J van der Walt (note 119 above) 204–211 argues in favour of 'a multistranded or pluriform rather than a uniform theoretical approach to the protection of socio-economic rights'.

[129] Dixon (note 52 above) 417.

The value of a substantive approach to the interpretation of socio-economic rights is that it brings to the surface the theoretical understandings and values informing particular interpretations of the relevant rights. This enhances the transparency of judicial decision-making, making it more accessible to public scrutiny and evaluation. In this manner, socio-economic rights adjudication has the potential to enrich deliberation in the broader political culture over the meaning and implications of constitutional rights and values. The 'feedback loop' thus created enables an iterative process of reflection, critique and learning. This process creates the most favourable conditions for developing a jurisprudence on socio-economic rights which is responsive to the multifarious forms of social and economic deprivation and marginalisation in South Africa, and to the voices of those marginalised by these conditions. Similarly, requiring the State in the context of socio-economic rights litigation to present fully elaborated arguments and evidence of its policy or resource justifications promotes transparency and accountability to constitutional rights and values in social policy formulation and implementation.

2.4.3 An interdependent conception of human rights

A further feature of the formalist approach to rights is the tendency to view the various rights protected in bills of rights as protecting mutually discrete values and interests. This approach fails to recognise that the most invidious and entrenched forms of disadvantage involve multiple, interlinked forms of subordination which implicate a number of interrelated rights. A substantive approach to human rights interpretation is concerned with the social and economic conditions and relationships which are needed to ensure the full and effective enjoyment of various rights.[130]

The inclusion of socio-economic rights as justiciable rights in the South African Bill of Rights render conditions of social and economic disadvantage important subjects of constitutional concern. This enables a more integrated approach to the adjudication of human rights claims in which close attention is paid to the interrelationship between civil and political rights and economic, social and cultural rights.[131] It is

[130] In the context of equality rights, Cathi Albertyn describes a substantive approach to equality as one which is concerned with remedying systemic and entrenched forms of inequalities. She observes that 'this requires that judges and lawyers understand the context in which inequality occurs, and identify the social and economic conditions that structure action and create unequal and exclusionary consequences for groups and individuals'. See C Albertyn 'Substantive equality and transformation in South Africa' (2007) 23 *SAJHR* 253–276 at 259.

[131] It is a fundamental tenet of international human rights law, that human rights are indivisible, interdependent and interrelated: *The Proclamation of Tehran, 1968,* Final Act of the International Conference on Human Rights, Tehran, UN doc A/CONF. 32/41 art 13; Vienna Declaration and Programme of Action adopted by the World Conference on Human Rights, 25 June 1993, UN doc A/CONF. 157/24 para 5, Part I. For an account of the theoretical and practical implications of 'interdependence', see C Scott 'The interdependence and permeability of human rights norms: Towards a partial fusion of the international

frequently difficult to guarantee one set of rights fully and effectively without also protecting other rights.[132] For example, without an education, the right to freedom of expression, while not meaningless, cannot fulfil many of its fundamental purposes in an open and democratic society. In contemporary societies, people's ability to communicate their positions effectively in public forums such as the media and to organs of state such as the parliament and the executive depends on both literacy and an understanding of the content of competing opinions and policy proposals. Conversely, the right to an education is impoverished, if freedom of expression and association is not guaranteed in a society.

The Constitutional Court has affirmed the interdependence and interrelatedness of all rights. Yacoob J explains the implications of this interrelationship between civil and political rights and social and economic rights as follows:

> Our Constitution entrenches both civil and political rights and social and economic rights. All the rights in our Bill of Rights are inter-related and mutually supporting. There can be no doubt that human dignity, freedom and equality, the foundational values of our society, are denied those who have no food, clothing and shelter. Affording socio-economic rights to all people therefore enables them to enjoy the other rights in chapter 2. The realisation of these rights is also key to the advancement of race and gender equality and the evolution of a society in which men and women are equally able to achieve their full potential.[133]

An approach to interpretation that takes seriously the interdependence between all the rights in the Bill of Rights entails recognising that other civil and political rights, such as the right to life (s 11)[134] and the right to freedom and security of the person

---

covenants on human rights' (1989) 27 *OHLJ* 769–878. See also chapter 3, part 3.3.3(b)(ii), note 216. See also the discussion by S Liebenberg & B Goldblatt (2007) 'The interrelationship between equality and socio-economic rights under South Africa's transformative Constitution' 23 *SAJHR* 335–361 at 338–341.

[132] As Craig Scott ibid 786 observes, the concept of interdependence in human rights law is derived from the insight that 'values seen as directly related to the full development of personhood cannot be protected and nurtured in isolation'.

[133] *Grootboom* (note 114 above) paras 23 and 83. See also *Khosa v Minister of Social Development* (note 84 above) para 40; *Kaunda v President of the RSA* 2005 (4) SA 235 (CC), 2004 (10) BCLR 1009 (CC) para 274; *Union of Refugee Women v Private Security Industry Regulatory Authority* 2007 (4) SA 395 (CC), 2007 (4) BCLR 339 (CC) para 111.

[134] See M Pieterse 'A different shade of red: Socio-economic dimensions of the right to life in South Africa' (1999) 15 *SAJHR* 372–385. In *S v Makwanyane* 1995 (3) SA 391 (CC), 1995 (6) BCLR 665 (CC) paras 326–7, O'Regan J writes that it 'is not life as mere organic matter that the Constitution cherishes, but the right to human life: the right to live as a human being, to be part of a broader community, to share in the experience of humanity'. Chaskalson P (as he then was) affirmed in *Soobramoney v Minister of Health (KwaZulu-Natal)* 1998 (1) SA 765 (CC), 1997 (12) BCLR 1696 (CC) para 31 that access to housing, food and water, employment opportunities, and social security are aspects of the right to human life.

(s 12),[135] should also be interpreted in ways that diminish disadvantage and facilitate their full and equal enjoyment. It is significant, for example, that the equality clause in the Bill of Rights expressly indicates that equality 'includes the full and equal enjoyment of all rights and freedoms'.[136] This implies that the right to equality must be interpreted in ways that promote greater equality in people's access to the resources and services protected in the socio-economic rights provisions in the Bill of Rights. As stated by Moseneke J (as he then was) in *Minister of Finance v Van Heerden*:[137]

> Absent a positive commitment progressively to eradicate socially constructed barriers to equality and to root out systematic or institutionalised under-privilege, the constitutional promise of equality must, in the context of our country, ring hollow.

In the same way that the adjudication of civil and political rights claims such as the right to life and equality should include a consideration of the interests underpinning socio-economic rights claims, so the interpretation of socio-economic rights should also reflect the values of freedom and dignity underpinning many civil and political rights. The courts should avoid interpreting socio-economic rights in ways that position claimants as passive objects of state bureaucracy. Instead they should develop a notion of rights that is empowering and recognises people's agency in relation to the definition and meeting of their needs.[138] Sachs J recognises this when he warns against regarding those who are landless and poor 'as helpless victims, lacking the possibilities of personal moral agency'.[139] In this context, the rights of access to information (s 32) and administrative justice (s 33) can play a significant role in facilitating poor people's right to be heard and to participate in socio-economic decision-making that affects their rights.

There are no watertight divisions between the different rights in the Bill of Rights, nor a universally accepted method of classification.[140] A substantive interpretation of

---

[135] In *Rail Commuters Action Group v Transnet Ltd t/a Metrorail* 2005 (2) SA 359 (CC), 2005 (4) BCLR 301 (CC), the Constitutional Court held that Metrorail and the Commuter Corporation were under a duty to ensure that reasonable measures were taken to provide for the security of rail commuters while they were making use of rail transport services. The relevant legislation regulating the provision of rail transportation services had to be interpreted in the light of the constitutional rights to human dignity (s 10), life (s 11) and to freedom and security of the person (s 12) (see particularly para 82).

[136] Section 9(2).

[137] *Van Heerden* (note 3 above) para 31. The Constitutional Court has recognised an affirmative duty on public and private institutions to take reasonable positive measures to accommodate and enable the equal participation of marginalised and vulnerable groups. See *MEC for Education: KwaZulu-Natal v Pillay* (note 125 above) para 72. See also ss 1 and 15(2)(*c*) of the Employment Equity Act 55 of 1998; ss 14(3)(i) and (ii) of the Promotion of Equality and Prevention of Unfair Discrimination Act 4 of 2000.

[138] See the discussion at notes 85–88 above and accompanying text.

[139] *Port Elizabeth Municipality* (note 114 above) para 41. See further chapter 6, part 6.2.2.

[140] For example, labour rights are protected in International Covenant on Civil and Political Rights, 1966 (art 22), as well as in International Covenant on Economic, Social and Cul-

human rights norms recognises how various forms of social injustice overlap and interact with each other to create new forms of disadvantage and marginalisation.[141] Instead of insisting on rigid boundaries between rights, it seeks to uncover the fluid interrelationships between rights and to develop their content and scope in a way which does justice to the holistic concept of human well-being endorsed by our Bill of Rights.

2.4.4 Transcending the negative/positive rights dichotomy

The distinction between civil and political rights on the one hand, and economic, social and cultural rights on the other, has traditionally been premised on the fiction that civil and political rights exclusively impose obligations of restraint and non-interference with people's liberties on the State (so-called 'negative' obligations) while economic, social and cultural rights impose 'positive' duties on the State to secure the necessities of life for all.[142] The perception that civil and political rights impose only duties of restraint on the State gave rise to the notion that they are politically neutral, since their enforcement does not require the judiciary to make policy choices with distributional implications.[143] By contrast, economic and social rights have traditionally been perceived to require judges to encroach on the terrains of the democratically elected legislature and the executive by prescribing to them on matters of social and economic policy. They have therefore been characterised as policy goals or aspi-

---

tural Rights, 1966 (art 8). Property rights are not recognised in either of these major international human rights treaties, but are recognised in certain regional human rights treaties, for example, the European Convention for the Protection of Human Rights and Fundamental Freedoms, 1950 (art 1, Protocol 1), the American Convention on Human Rights, 1969 (art 21), and the African Charter on Human and Peoples' Rights, 1981 (art 14).

[141] Many of the insights of the way in which various processes and relations of subordination interact with each other to create entrenched forms of disadvantage are derived from feminist legal theory in the context of equality rights. See, for example, K Crenshaw 'Demarginalizing the intersection between race and sex: A black feminist critique of anti-discrimination doctrine, feminist theory, and antiracist politics' (1989) *Univ of Chicago Legal Forum* 139–168; D Hutchinson 'Identity crisis: "Intersectionality", "multidimensionality", and the development of an adequate theory of subordination' (2001) 6 *Michigan J of Race and Law* 285–317. For an insightful account of the contribution and limitations of intersectionality in the context of non-discrimination law, see J Conaghan 'Intersectionality and UK equality initiatives' (2007) 23 *SAJHR* 317–334.

[142] See, for example, E G Vierdag 'The legal nature of the rights granted by the International Covenant on Economic, Social and Cultural Rights' (1978) 9 *Netherlands Yearbook of International Law* 69–103.

[143] K D Ewing 'Social rights and constitutional law' 1999 *Public Law* 104–123 at 112–113. See, further, the discussion by Marius Pieterse (note 94 above) 389 of traditional characterisations of the different 'nature' of civil and political rights on the one hand, and economic, social and cultural rights on the other.

rations, which should not be enforced through adjudication mechanisms in constitutional or international law.[144]

However, the privileging of negative duties fails to recognise that policy choices are made when judges elect to protect only negative liberties, and fail to respond to the claims of those who lack the resources to participate as equals in society. In other words, enforcement of only negative duties is not an ideologically neutral adjudicative approach. An approach which privileges negative duties, furthermore, fails to interrogate the way in which existing legal rules operate to reinforce poverty and social marginalisation.[145]

Scholars have consistently demonstrated that the classic distinctions between civil and political rights on the one hand, and economic, social and cultural rights on the other, are based on a fiction.[146] Civil and political rights such as the right to vote, the right to a fair trial and equality rights have resource and policy implications for the State. This was expressly acknowledged by the Constitutional Court in the first Certification judgment.[147] The resource implications of the right to a fair trial, a classic civil and political right, were highlighted by the Constitutional Court in *S v Jaipal* in the following terms:

> For the State to respect, protect, promote and fulfil the rights in the Bill of Rights, resources are required. The same applies to the State's obligation to assist and protect the courts to ensure their independence, impartiality, dignity, accessibility and effectiveness. The right

[144] See, for example, M J Dennis & D P Stewart 'Justiciability of economic, social and cultural rights: Should there be an international complaints mechanism to adjudicate the rights to food, water, housing, and health?' (2004) 98 *AJIL* 462–515. The distinction between 'negative' civil and political rights as legitimate, judicially enforceable rights and 'positive' economic, social and cultural rights as policy goals or aspirations not giving rise to legal recourse, tracks the classic liberal tradition's insistence on an impenetrable boundary between politics and law. See the analysis in A Barber 'Fallacies of negative constitutionalism' (2007) 75 *Fordham LR* 651–668.

[145] For an account of the role of law in the United States in reinforcing economic marginalisation, see L A Williams 'Welfare and legal entitlements: The social roots of poverty' in D Kairys (ed) *The Politics of Law: A Progressive Critique* (1998) 569–590. See further Fredman's analysis (note 44 above) 96–98 of the privileging of duties of restraint in comparative jurisprudence.

[146] See, for example, P Alston & G Quinn 'The nature and scope of states parties' obligations under the International Covenant on Economic, Social and Cultural Rights' (1987) 9 *HRQ* 156–229; Scott & Macklem (note 63 above) 45–84; P de Vos 'Pious wishes or directly enforceable human rights? Social and economic rights in South Africa's 1996 Constitution' (1997) 13 *SAJHR* 67–101 at 78–91; S Liebenberg 'Identifying violations of socio-economic rights: The role of the South African Human Rights Commission' (1997) 1 *Law, Democracy and Development* 161–191; S Fredman 'Human rights transformed: Positive duties and positive rights' (2006) 3 *Public Law* 498–520.

[147] *Ex parte Chairperson of the Constitutional Assembly: In re Certification of the Constitution of the Republic of South Africa 1996* 1996 (4) SA 744 (CC), 1996 (10) BCLR 1253 (CC) para 76 (*First Certification* judgment).

> to a fair trial requires considerable resources in order to provide for buildings with court rooms, offices and libraries, recording facilities and security measures and for adequately trained and salaried judicial officers, prosecutors, interpreters and administrative staff.[148]

The Court went on to hold that the fact that the optimum fulfilment of fair trial rights is resource dependent means that 'all those concerned with and involved in the administration of justice – including administrative officials, judges, magistrates, assessors and prosecutors – must purposefully take *all reasonable steps* to ensure maximum compliance with constitutional obligations, even under difficult circumstances'.[149] (Emphasis added.)

Conversely, the Court has also held that the effective protection of socio-economic rights sometimes entails imposing a duty on the State to refrain from interfering in people's existing access to socio-economic resources.[150]

Characterising particular rights as inherently 'negative' or 'positive' is problematic in both theory and practice. In the first place it is arbitrary and difficult to apply in practice, as the realisation of all rights requires an interlocking combination of positive and negative conduct, frequently from more than one actor.[151] Framing a claim in terms of a negative or a positive duty is contingent on the stage at which a legal challenge is brought, and how the issues are framed in the pleadings. For example, had the *Grootboom* community challenged their eviction from the land earmarked for low-cost housing development, the case would have proceeded on the basis of a breach of the negative duty to refrain from interfering unjustifiably in existing access to housing.[152] However, the eviction itself was not challenged and the case proceeded on the basis of the positive duties on the State to provide access to shelter to people who are homeless.

The second problematic aspect of the distinction is that it fails to acknowledge the far-reaching positive measures required to maintain the status quo. As Matthew Craven points out:

> [T]he belief that the fact of homelessness or poverty invokes an obligation to provide housing or food, and is therefore subject only to progressive achievement, obscures the possibility of any responsibility for the structures and processes that were themselves productive of those conditions.[153]

---

[148] 2005 (4) SA 581 (CC), 2005 (5) BCLR 423 (CC) paras 55–56.

[149] Ibid (footnotes omitted). The reference to the concept of reasonableness in relation to the State's positive obligations in respect of fair trial rights is noteworthy.

[150] See, for example, *First Certification* judgment (note 147 above) para 78; *Residents of Bon Vista Mansions v Southern Metropolitan Local Council* 2002 (6) BCLR 625 (W); *Jaftha v Schoeman; Van Rooyen v Stoltz* 2005 (2) SA 140 (CC), 2005 (1) BCLR 78 (CC). See further chapter 4, part 4.6.

[151] For a discussion of the difficulties of applying the distinction between duties of restraint and positive duties, see Fredman (note 44 above) 98–100.

[152] See in this regard, the comments of the Constitutional Court in *Grootboom* (note 114 above) para 88. See further the discussion of the case in chapter 4, part 4.3 above.

[153] M Craven 'Assessment of the progress on adjudication of economic, social and cultural rights' in J Squires, M Langford & B Thiele (eds) *The Road to a Remedy: Current Issues in*

Existing entitlements or access to resources are subject to robust judicial enforcement, whereas positive claims to resources or social services are frequently treated as aspirational,[154] and subject to weaker forms of judicial review and enforcement. This tends to legitimise existing resource distributions and reinforce the marginalised position of those who cannot gain access to resources and services through market mechanisms and the network of legal rules and institutions that underpin them.[155]

The Constitution places an overarching set of obligations on the State to 'respect, protect, promote and fulfil the rights in the Bill of Rights'.[156] The State is thus both constrained and mandated by a combination of negative and positive duties to secure the rights in the Bill of Rights.[157] The Court has recognised that ss 26 and 27 of the Constitution impose both negative and positive obligations on the State and, in the case of the negative duties, on 'all other entities and persons'.[158] As will be seen, the Court has developed a different model of review depending on whether it sees the case as involving a breach of the negative or positive duties imposed by the relevant rights. Thus, where a breach of the negative duty 'to desist from preventing or impairing' existing access to rights is found, any justifications by the State must be evaluated in terms of the stringent requirements of s 36 (the general limitations clause).[159] Where the case is found to implicate the positive duty on the State in terms of ss 26(2) and 27(2), the reasonableness of any justifications raised by the State is largely determined with reference to the internal criteria contained in ss 26(2) and 27(2): (*a*) the duty 'to take reasonable legislative and other measures'; (*b*) 'to achieve

---

the Litigation of Economic, Social and Cultural Rights (2005) 27–42 at 34–35. Scott & Macklem (note 63 above) 46–47 observe:

> In North America, judges have tended to take traditional private law entitlements as the essential components of a largely unarticulated normative baseline. What goes unsaid in the invocating of such a baseline is the fact that property and the right to contract require extensive positive state action to be effective legal institutions, and can in fact be seen as the state structure upon which modern industrial society emerged. (Footnotes omitted.)

For further critiques of the negative/positive rights dichotomy, see B Porter 'The crisis of ESC rights and strategies for addressing it' in J Squires et al (eds) *The Road to a Remedy: Current Issues in the Litigation of Economic, Social and Cultural Rights* (2005) 43–69 at 55–58; D Brand 'Introduction to socio-economic rights in the South African Constitution' in D Brand & C H Heyns (eds) *Socio-Economic Rights in South Africa* (2005) 1–56 at 10–12; D M Davis 'Adjudicating the socio-economic rights in the South African Constitution: Towards "deference lite"?' (2006) 22 *SAJHR* 301–327 at 305.

[154] See, for example, the observations of Madala J characterising socio-economic rights as 'ideals' in *Soobramoney* (note 134 above) para 42.

[155] See Craven (note 153 above) 36.

[156] Section 7(2).

[157] On the origins and interpretation of this typology, and its application in the context of socio-economic rights, see chapter 3, part 3.2.2.

[158] *Grootboom* (note 114 above) paras 34 and 46.

[159] See *Jaftha* (note 150 above) paras 31–33. See further chapter 4, part 4.6.2.

the progressive realisation' of the right; and (*c*) 'within its available resources'.[160] The implications of this differential model of review applied respectively to the negative and positive duties imposed by socio-economic rights are explored in chapter 4, parts 4.6–4.7.

Despite its qualified nature, the affirmation by the Constitutional Court of a justiciable positive duty on the State to adopt comprehensive programmes that are 'capable of facilitating the realisation'[161] of the relevant socio-economic rights is significant. The Court hereby requires the State to play an active role in ensuring access to the social services and economic resources protected by the various socio-economic rights.[162]

However, the judicial enforcement of these positive duties poses a number of challenges to cherished liberal ideals of a strict separation between law and politics, clearly defined boundaries between the roles and functions of the three branches of government, and a judiciary that is deferential to the political branches. Transformative adjudication in cases such as these requires new ways of thinking about the relationship between the judiciary and the other branches of government, as well as about the role of the judiciary in protecting the interests of those who are marginalised from participation in our society by structural impoverishment.[163]

A good start can be made by interrogating critically the dichotomy between negative and positive rights which underpins the ideology of negative constitutionalism in classic liberalism.[164] In the context of real-world structural inequalities with its interlocking forms of subordination,[165] transformative adjudication should strive for the most effective and substantive vindication of the values and interests protected by the relevant rights. Such an approach recognises that all rights generate a combination of negative and positive duties on the State and private actors. Whether, in the circumstances of a particular case, the right implicated requires restraint or positive

---

[160] *Grootboom* (note 114 above) para 38. The socio-economic rights of children in s 28(1)(*c*) and of detained persons in s 35(2)(*e*) are formulated without reference to the qualifiers of 'reasonable measures', 'progressive realisation', and 'within available resources' contained in ss 26(2) and 27(2). These rights are discussed further in chapter 5, part 5.2.

[161] *Grootboom* (note 114 above) para 41.

[162] On the need for positive measures to redress the legacy of 'decades of systematic racial discrimination', see *Bato Star* (note 3 above) para 74. Similarly, Kriegler J observes in *Du Plessis v De Klerk* (note 3 above) para 147:

> We do not operate under a Constitution in which the avowed purpose of the drafters was to place limits on governmental control. Our Constitution aims at establishing freedom and equality in a grossly disparate society.

[163] Henk Botha (2003, note 2 above) 20–21 argues that transformative constitutionalism requires a reconsideration of the dichotomies 'in terms of which apartheid law was structured' and a reconceiving 'of legal concepts and categories in *relational* terms'.

[164] See Barber (note 144 above).

[165] The term 'interlocking subordination' is derived from Joanne Conaghan (note 141 above) 328 who credits the work of Patricia Hill Collins *Black Feminist Thought: Knowledge, Consciousness and the Politics of Empowerment* (1990) (see n 50, 328).

action, or a combination, should not depend on an abstract analysis of the essential nature of the relevant right and the duties it imposes. Instead what is required is a contextual evaluation of the measures required from the parties to generate outcomes most consonant with the values and interests promoted by the relevant right.

The degree of deference which it is appropriate to accord to other branches of government should be guided by pragmatic considerations concerning the institution which is best placed to ensure its effective and equitable realisation. This inquiry must be informed by the background and unique factual matrix of the particular case and its social and historical context.

2.4.5 Deconstructing the public/private divide

Classic liberal conceptions of law are premised on a rigid demarcation between 'public' and 'private' spheres.[166] The private sphere is associated with domestic institutions such as the family and with economic institutions such as the marketplace in modern capitalist societies, in which the assumption is that equal, autonomous individuals transact freely with each other.[167] Traditionally these 'private' institutions such as the family and marketplace are regarded in liberal theory as the 'natural' institutions for distributing social and economic resources. The State's role in these zones of freedom and privacy should be minimised and restricted to facilitating the unimpeded functioning of these institutions.[168] Within this paradigm, the function of bills of rights in national constitutions is to shield citizens against unwarranted State intrusions in their 'natural' rights and liberties.[169] The unarticulated baseline of 'natural' rights and liberties is largely common-law entitlements of property and contract.[170]

---

[166] On the philosophical and historical origins of the liberal distinction between private and public, see D Gobetti 'Humankind as a system: Private and public agency at the origins of modern liberalism' in J Weintraub & K Kumar (eds) *Public and Private in Thought and Practice: Perspectives on a Grand Dichotomy* (1997) 103–132.

[167] For an analysis of the multiple and shifting meanings and configurations of the public/private distinction, see J Weintraub 'The theory and politics of the public/private distinction' in Weintraub & Kumar ibid 1–42.

[168] See, for example, R Nozick *Anarchy, State and Utopia* (1974); F A Hayek *The Constitution of Liberty* (1960).

[169] Thus Randy Barnett *Restoring the Lost Constitution: The Presumption of Liberty* (2004) 263 argues that the United State's Constitution should be interpreted on the basis of a 'Presumption of Liberty', which he describes in the following terms:

> The freedom to act within the boundaries provided by one's common law or 'civil' rights may be viewed as a central background presumption of the Constitution … . There is no constitutional privilege to commit a tort or breach of contract; but so long as one is acting rightfully, one should presumptively be immune from government interference.

See the critique by Barber (note 144 above) of this conception. For an account of the function of rights in liberal political theory, see generally L Hamilton 'The context and argument of *The Political Philosophy of Needs*' (2006) 25(3) *SA J Philos* 224–232 at 225–226.

[170] See Scott & Macklem (note 63 above) 46–47; L A Williams 'Beyond labour law's parochialism: A re-envisioning of the discourse of redistribution' in J Conaghan, R M Fischl &

Nancy Fraser argues that the effect of relegating the meeting of needs to domestic or market institutions has a depoliticising effect in social discourses on needs:

> Domestic institutions depoliticize certain matters by personalizing and/or familializing them; they cast these as private-domestic or personal-familial matters in contradistinction to public, political matters. Official economic capitalist system institutions, on the other hand, depoliticize certain matters by economizing them; the issues in question are cast as impersonal market imperatives, or as 'private' ownership prerogatives, or as technical problems for managers and planners, all in contradistinction to political matters.[171]

According to classical liberal political ideology, the main threat to freedom is the power of the State. However, this fails to account for the relative weakness of many States in the globalised economy and the relative power of large national and transnational private institutions such as corporations.[172] In an age where many formerly public services are being outsourced to private companies and public utilities are being privatised,[173] the effect of a formalist application of the public/private divide is to extend immunity from the norms and values of human rights law to many actors performing critical public functions.

The consequence is that the economic and social relationships which are structured by these private law norms and institutions are hidden from public scrutiny. They are thus insulated from critical scrutiny and evaluation for their consistency with the normative public values and ethical commitments embodied in modern bills of rights.[174] Seidman describes how classical liberal rights served to obscure the extent to which public and private power are intertwined:

K Klare (eds) *Labour Law in an Era of Globalization: Transformative Practices and Possibilities* (2002) 96–97.

171 N Fraser (note 85 above) 168.

172 N Fraser 'Reframing justice in a globalizing world' (2005) 36 *New Left Review* 1–19 at 9–10. See further D M Chirwa 'Towards binding economic, social and cultural rights obligations of non-state actors in international and domestic law: A critical survey of emerging norms' (2005, unpublished LLD thesis, UWC); C Scott 'Multinational enterprises and emergent jurisprudence on violations of economic, social and cultural rights' in A Eide, C Krause & A Rosas (eds) *Economic, Social and Cultural Rights: A Textbook* 2 ed revised (2001) 563–595 at 566–567.

173 See generally K De Feyter & F Gómez Isa (eds) *Privatisation and Human Rights in the Age of Globalisation* (2005); A Kok & M Langford 'Water' in S Woolman et al (eds) *Constitutional Law of South Africa* 2 ed (original service, 2004), chapter 56B, 21–28 on the privatization of water services; M Pieterse 'Beyond the welfare state: Globalisation of neo-liberal culture and the constitutional protection of socio-economic rights in South Africa (2003) 14 *Stell LR* 3–28 at 26.

174 André van der Walt (note 102 above) 184 discusses how private law rights such as property rights in the South African context have traditionally been 'valued and protected as trumps which insulate the individual from all but the most limited unavoidable state actions'. The effect has been to insulate these interests from public law norms of accountability. See also L A Williams (note 170 above) 96; H Botha (note 50 above) 567.

> Liberal rights both grew out of, and reinforced, the public-private distinction as the core of Liberal legal ideology. Liberal rights were almost always conceptualized as claims by private persons against the state, rather than as claims to state resources to combat private oppression. Claims to Liberal rights therefore both ignored and obfuscated the extent to which the private sphere was, itself, constructed by public decisions. The failure to detect state responsibility had the effect of taking off the table constitutional claims to radical redistribution of 'private' resources and power.[175]

The civil law (Roman-Dutch) tradition of South African law is premised on a clear dichotomy between private and public spheres.[176] The express provision made in the South African Bill of Rights for the application of human rights norms in private relations ('horizontal application')[177] challenges this public/private dichotomy in our legal history and tradition. These provisions in the South African Constitution require the law to be developed so that private entities are accountable to the rights and values in the Bill of Rights.

The controversy which accompanies the horizontal application of human rights norms in general,[178] is intensified in the context of the application of socio-economic rights to private relations. As noted above, classic liberalism seeks to preserve maximum freedom from interference in the 'private' spheres of the family and marketplace. Any redistributive measures in favour of the poor are to emanate from state-provided benefits and services. The notion that, in certain circumstances, some of the negative or positive duties imposed by socio-economic rights may bind private parties poses a direct challenge to the mythology of a private sphere free of state influence and a public sphere in which the role of a Bill of Rights is to restrain an over-zealous State.

There has been a gradual recognition of the implications of socio-economic rights in the sphere of private law.[179] Despite these developments in South African

---

175 Seidman (note 101 above) 578.

176 See, for example, A J van der Walt (note 102 above) 180–181. Alfred Cockrell describes the purpose of clear distinction drawn between public and private law thus:

> [T]he in-built presumption that law should be apolitical and not highly regulatory gives way only in a distinct sphere which is labelled 'public law'. By clearly bifurcating the two realms, the Romanist distinction seeks to preserve the juristic integrity of private law from the pollutionist tendency of public law.

See A Cockrell 'Can you paradigm?' – Another perspective on the public law/private law divide' (1993) *AJ* 227–247 at 228.

177 Section 8(2) provides that: 'A provision of the Bill of Rights binds a natural or juristic person if, and to the extent that, it is applicable, taking into account the nature of the right and the nature of any duty imposed by the right.' Furthermore, s 39(2) enjoins every court, tribunal or forum to 'promote the spirit, purport and objects of the Bill of Rights' when developing the common law or customary law. See further chapter 7, parts 7.2.1–7.2.4.

178 For a discussion of this controversy in the context of South African constitutional law, see S Woolman & D Davis 'The last laugh: *Du Plessis v De Klerk*, classic liberalism, creole liberalism, and the application of fundamental rights under the interim and final constitutions' (1996) 12 *SAJHR* 361–404.

179 These developments are discussed in chapter 7.

constitutional law, the naturalised baseline of private entitlements in classic liberal theory has the potential to exercise a restraining influence in a number of respects on the influence of socio-economic rights on private law rights and doctrines.

The judiciary is generally reluctant to undertake any major doctrinal reforms of common-law institutions in order to give effect to constitutional rights and values, preferring to view this as a prerogative of the democratically elected legislature.[180] Furthermore, legislative interferences in existing common-law rights have to be clear and unambiguous,[181] and are sometimes interpreted to restrict the clearly pro-reform purposes of particular legislation.[182] However, there is also an important line of cases in which legislation enacted to give effect to socio-economic rights in the land and housing sphere has been interpreted generously, despite the impact of this legislation on common-law entitlements.[183] This illustrates the potentially transformative impact of socio-economic rights on private law rules. In the sphere of contract law, the courts have been far less willing to allow socio-economic rights to exert a substantive influence on legal doctrine.[184]

Finally, there is the danger that constitutional rights such as the right to freedom of the person and privacy, will be interpreted to invalidate social legislation which interferes with private law entitlements.[185]

---

180 See also chapter 7, part 7.2.6.

181 See the discussion and evaluation of this presumption of statutory interpretation in the light of the Constitution by L M du Plessis *Re-interpretation of Statutes* (2002) 177–181.

182 See the discussion of this tendency in the context of land reform legislation in: A J van der Walt, (2006, note 2 above) 12–13; A J van der Walt *Constitutional Property Law* (2005) 419–424.

183 See, for example, the cases of *Ndlovu v Ngcobo; Bekker v Jika* 2003 (1) SA 113 (SCA), [2002] 4 All SA 384 (SCA) (holding that the Prevention of Illegal Eviction from and Unlawful Occupation of Land Act 19 of 1998 (PIE) applied to a tenant who is holding over subsequent to the lawful termination of his lease); *Port Elizabeth Municipality* (note 114 above) (interpreting PIE to require a balancing of the rights of ownership and the housing rights of occupiers in eviction situations). See further chapter 6, parts 6.2.2–6.2.3.

184 See further chapter 7, part 7.4.

185 The notorious example in the US context is *Lochner v New York* 198 US 45 (1905) overturning regulatory labour legislation on grounds of its interference with contractual liberty. In the South African context, Isaiah Berlin's concept of negative liberty ('Two concepts of liberty' *Four Essays on Liberty* (1969)) was referred to by Ackermann J in his minority judgment in *Ferreira v Levin NO* 1996 (1) SA 984 (CC), 1996 (1) BCLR 1 (CC) para 69 in support of his argument that the right to freedom protected in s 11 of the interim Constitution should be interpreted as 'the right of individuals not to have obstacles to possible choices and activities placed in their way by … the State'. Chaskalson P (as he then was) for the majority rejected this interpretation of the right to freedom, holding that it would place an obligation on the State to justify all regulatory actions which infringe on this broad concept of non-interference in individual freedom (see in particular para 54). See Liebenberg (note 122 above).

The possibility of the horizontal application of the socio-economic rights provisions in the Bill of Rights invites a critical re-examination of the network of private law rules and doctrines. It invites the judiciary to participate, along with the legislature, in the transformation of common-law institutions such as property and contract, by considering the needs of those who are without access to basic resources, who are homeless and who lack bargaining power. In this way, fundamental concepts of our common law, such as the exclusivity of ownership and the role of doctrines such as good faith, reasonableness and public policy in contract law, are subject to re-evaluation and development to give effect to 'the spirit, purport and objects' of socio-economic rights.[186]

2.4.6 Rights and democracy: A creative tension

Justiciable socio-economic rights pose a particular challenge to another dilemma that has long plagued political and constitutional theorists – the tension between democracy and rights in countries with supreme constitutions and justiciable bills of rights. This tension finds expression in its classic form in the 'countermajoritarian dilemma'. According to this dilemma there is a fundamental difficulty with reconciling the power of judicial review vested in unelected judges to enforce constitutional rights with the will of the democratically elected majority.

Constitutional theory based on classic liberal approaches responds to this tension by insisting on clearly defined boundaries between the role and functions of the three branches of government (a strict 'separation of powers' doctrine),[187] by viewing legislative interferences in the 'private' sphere as suspect and therefore requiring justification, and by seeking to deny or minimise the role of politics in adjudication by asserting 'a neutral and objective' legal method.[188] As Henk Botha observes, the 'traditional, liberal view of the counter-majoritarian difficulty uncritically equates democracy with the representative institutions found in modern Western states, and thus blinds theorists to the often tenuous link between these institutions and the people'.[189] Furthermore, he argues, 'the attempt to ground adjudication in a neutral

---

186 In the context of property rights, see A J van der Walt 'Exclusivity of ownership, security of tenure, and eviction orders: A critical evaluation of recent case law' (2002) 18 *SAJHR* 371–419; A J van der Walt 'Ownership and eviction: Constitutional rights in private law' (2005) 9 *Edin LR* 32–64. For accounts of the need to develop contractual doctrines to bring them into alignment with constitutional values, see D Bhana & M Pieterse 'Towards a reconciliation of contract law and constitutional values: *Brisley* and *Afrox* revisited' (2005) 122 *SALJ* 865–895; D Moseneke 'Transformative constitutionalism: Its implications for the law of contract' (2009) 1 *Stell LR* 1–13.

187 See, generally S Seedorf & S Sibanda 'Separation of powers' in S Woolman et al (eds) *Constitutional Law of South Africa* 2 ed (Original Service, June 2008) chapter 12.

188 For a discussion of the liberal response to the tension between democracy and rights, see Botha (note 50 above) 562 and 563–567; Seidman (note 101) above.

189 Botha ibid 563.

and objective method fails to come to terms with the realist insight that judges do make law, and inevitably rely on ethical and political considerations in doing so'.[190]

The South African Constitution is premised on an interrelationship between the Bill of Rights and the democratic values on which the Constitution is founded. Section 7(1) signals this interdependence between rights and democracy in the following terms:

> This Bill of Rights is a cornerstone of democracy in South Africa. It enshrines the rights of all people in our country and affirms the democratic values of human dignity, equality and freedom.

This provision signals a departure from classic liberal conceptions of bills of rights which view rights as enclaves of freedom, protected and separated from democratic politics.

The South African Constitution endorses a richer, more multilayered conception of both democracy and rights. Democracy encompasses, but transcends, simple majoritarian politics conducted through the institutions of representative democracy. I have argued above that it embraces a multiplicity of forums through which public discourse and justification take place on the substantive meaning of the normative commitments and values of the Constitution. Similarly, the concept of rights under the South African Constitution resonates with the relational, dialogic model.[191] This contrasts with conceptions of rights as 'trumps' over communal interests,[192] or protecting strict boundaries between the individual and the collective.[193]

There are a number of features of the South African Bill of Rights that suggest that it is best conceived as an instrument for facilitating dialogue in a variety of institutional sites on the social relationships and institutions that are consonant with the fundamental rights and foundational constitutional values.[194] These include the express duty on the State to 'respect, protect, promote and fulfil the rights in the Bill of Rights'[195] as well as its expansive application provisions.[196] The general limitations clause, in particular, establishes that the justifiability of limitations to rights must be

---

190 Ibid.

191 On the concept of rights as means to structure conversations about the relationships between individuals and between individuals and communities, See further E M Schneider 'The dialectic of rights and politics: Perspectives from the women's movement' (1986) *NYULR* 589–652; M Minow (note 75 above); J Nedelsky 'Reconstructing rights as relationship' (1993) 1 *RCS* 1–26; H Botha (2003, note 2 above).

192 The notion of 'rights as trumps' derives from the work of Ronald Dworkin *Taking Rights Seriously* (1977) xi.

193 On the metaphor of rights as boundaries and its limitations, see J Nedelsky (note 191 above) 5–11; H Botha (2003, note 2 above).

194 As Nedelsky (note 191 above) 8 observes, according to this concept of rights, 'interdependence becomes the central fact of political life, not an issue to be shunted to the periphery'.

195 Section 7(2).

196 Sections 8 and 39(2).

considered against the yardstick of 'an open and democratic society based on human dignity, equality and freedom'.[197] This evaluation can only properly occur following a rigorous conversation which traverses the nature and purposes of the rights and the justifications for failing to achieve their realisation within existing institutional constraints and socio-economic circumstances.

In the context of the adjudication of socio-economic rights, the Constitutional Court has developed a model of reasonableness review for assessing compliance with the positive duties imposed by these rights. Reasonableness is assessed in the light of a number of interrelated and open criteria.[198] The best reading of this model requires the courts to undertake a rigorous evaluation of the State's acts or omissions in relation to the normative commitments and purposes promoted by these rights. However, as is argued in chapter 4, a major shortcoming of the reasonableness model of review is its failure to develop a substantive interpretation of the various socio-economic rights. The effect of this failure is that the evaluation of the reasonableness of the State's conduct occurs without a proper consideration of the purposes, values and interests that the relevant rights should protect in our young democracy. The focus of the analysis thus tends to fall disproportionately on the justifications of the State as opposed to the normative commitments protected by the relevant right and its application to the circumstances and needs of the beneficiaries. This inhibits the potential of adjudication to serve as a forum of transformative dialogue on the realisation of socio-economic rights in South Africa.

In the end, the judicial enforcement of socio-economic rights represents an inevitably imperfect and flawed 'attempt to synchronise the real world with the ideal construct of a constitutional world'.[199] However, the bounds of possibility in this endeavour should never be glibly assumed. A transformative approach to the adjudication of socio-economic rights requires that these bounds are determined only after a searching scrutiny of the content and scope of the relevant rights and the public or private justifications offered for our collective failure to achieve their realisation. If the judicial role in enforcing socio-economic rights is understood in this manner, their adjudication can become a significant institutional space for evaluating the impact of policies and legislation as well as private power on the constitutional rights of disadvantaged groups. It has the further potential of enhancing the transparency and accountability of social policy-making by requiring the State and private actors to justify their decisions in the light of the purposes of socio-economic rights.[200] In

---

[197] Section 36(1).

[198] On the criteria informing reasonableness review, see chapter 4, part 4.3.3.

[199] I borrow here from Kriegler J's evocative description of the remedial role of the courts in constitutional adjudication. See *Fose v Minister of Safety and Security* 1997 (3) SA 786 (CC), 1997 (7) BCLR 851 (CC) para 94.

[200] See in this regard, Etienne Mureinik's perceptive analysis of the potential of socio-economic rights to broaden the culture of reasoned justification in South Africa's nascent constitutional democracy: E Mureinik 'Beyond a charter of luxuries: Economic rights in the Constitution' (1992) 8 *SAJHR* 464–474. See further E Mureinik (note 106 above) 32.

this manner adjudication can contribute to the deliberative and participatory dimensions of South Africa's constitutional democracy.

Finally, the status of socio-economic rights as justiciable rights in the South African Bill of Rights means that successful litigants can invoke the power of the courts to order 'just and equitable' remedies.[201] This is one of the key features distinguishing adjudication from other deliberative forums in democratic societies. The significance of the courts' remedial jurisdiction is that successful litigants can expect some concrete measures aimed at aligning social realities with constitutional rights and values. The fact that this will constitute an imperfect endeavour does not detract from its significance, even if all it achieves is a mitigation of the harshness and deprivation of people's lives.[202] Apart from the power to order immediate measures of relief, the South African courts have remedial mechanisms at their disposal to facilitate active participation by beneficiary communities in the remedying of socio-economic rights violations.[203] Through their remedial jurisprudence the courts can enhance democratic participation in the remedying of rights violations.

In this process of interpreting and enforcing socio-economic rights there will be an inevitable tension between the role of the judiciary and the role of the elected branches of government. However, this need not be a destructive tension, but rather one which deepens our understanding of both democracy and rights.[204] The following section examines this tension in the context of the judicial review of human rights norms and the separation of powers doctrine.

2.4.7 Reconceptualising the separation of powers doctrine

One of the responses of classic liberal constitutional theory to the tension between democracy and rights is to construct strict boundaries between the role and functions of the legislative, executive and judicial branches of government. The legislative branch is responsible for making law in the form of legislation, the executive branch is responsible for developing and implementing policy and legislation, and the judiciary is responsible for interpreting and enforcing the law. A system of mutual control and accountability control is established through a system of checks and balances of which the institution of judicial review is an important component in many contemporary democracies.[205]

---

[201] Section 172(1)(*b*). See further chapter 8, part 8.2.

[202] See, for example, the Constitutional Court's description in *Port Elizabeth Municipality* (note 114 above) para 38 of the role courts can play in achieving 'micro-justice' in the context of the conflict between property and housing rights which frequently occurs when people are evicted from their homes.

[203] See, for example, the discussion of structural remedies in chapter 8, part 8.6.

[204] See Botha (note 50 above) 581.

[205] See generally I Currie & J de Waal (note 32 above); M Pieterse (note 94 above) 385–386; PB Kurland 'The rise and fall of the "doctrine" of separation of powers' (1986) 85 *Michigan LR* 592–613.

The purpose of separation of powers doctrine in liberal democracies is primarily twofold. First, it enables the complex tasks of governance, law-making and law-enforcement to be performed by the institution that is best placed to perform these functions. Second, by dividing power and creating systems of mutual control, it militates against an excessive concentration of power in any one branch of government.[206] These aspects of the doctrine are integral to the transformative ethos of the Constitution in that they allocate functions to the branch of government most institutionally equipped to perform that function, and encourage a relationship of mutual accountability, responsiveness and openness between the three branches, and between government and the public.[207]

However, the doctrine also has the potential to frustrate transformation when it assumes an idealised form of strictly demarcated separate spheres, instead of a functional and pragmatic device to facilitate responsive, accountable governance. In its idealised, static form, the separation of powers doctrine may be ritually invoked by the courts as a way of avoiding their constitutional mandate to interpret and enforce constitutionally guaranteed rights.

This is particularly the case in relation to the adjudication of socio-economic rights claims. Socio-economic rights challenge many of the fundamental tenets of classic liberal constitutional theory by requiring active involvement of the State in the redistribution of resources. Their status as justiciable rights requires the judiciary to scrutinise, evaluate and, if necessary, order changes to social and economic policy, or the reshaping of private law rights and doctrines to extend access to resources to socio-economically marginalised groups. These functions have traditionally been regarded as the preserves of the executive and legislative branches of government.[208] The role of bills of rights has been to guard against social reforms which may impinge on individual liberties. As has been argued, the judicial enforcement of civil and political rights also has budgetary and policy implications.[209] However, civil and political

---

[206] In *Glenister v President of the Republic of South Africa* 2009 (1) SA 287 (CC), 2009 (2) BCLR 136 (CC) para 35 the Constitutional Court observed that the principle of checks and balances 'focuses on the desirability that the constitutional order, as a totality, prevents the branches of government from usurping power from one another. The system of checks and balances operates as a safeguard to ensure that each branch of government performs its constitutionally allocated function and that it does so consistently with the Constitution'.

[207] The values of accountability, responsiveness and openness in governance are among the foundational values recognised in s 1(*d*) of the Constitution.

[208] One of the grounds on which the objectors challenged the inclusion of socio-economic rights in the Constitution in the certification process was that they breached the separation of powers doctrine because they required courts to prescribe to the legislature and executive on policy and budgetary matters. See *First Certification* judgment (note 147 above) para 77.

[209] See *First Certification* judgment ibid. See also the discussion of this judgment in chapter 1, part 1.6.

rights are viewed as less problematic in liberal constitutional theory. This is probably at least partially due to the fact that they protect core institutions and tenets of liberal democracies, such as the right to vote, fair trial rights, and freedom of expression and association.

The bounded, static concept of the separation of powers doctrine has a number of limitations. In the first place, it does not reflect the realities of the contextual and shifting nature of the functions and relationships between the three branches in modern democracies. As Richard Calland and Mandy Taylor point out, modern government simply does not conform to the clear-cut conception of the roles of the three branches as outlined above:

> Many of the decisions about the use of public power occur by way of delegated legislation, regulation or *ad hoc* policy. Policy is determined extensively by the executive branch of government, with the legislature in reality confined to the task of scrutinizing policy and making recommendations to the government on policy. In reality, moreover, the executive is the initiator of changes in law and policy, the legislature merely the respondent. This reflects a wider reality: that the executive arm of government holds most of the cards – the expertise, the resources, the experience in technocrats. In most government systems the world over, but especially in Westminster systems, there is a relative imbalance of power between the two arms of government. [210]

Furthermore, this model is also particularly ill-suited to a transformative constitution such as South Africa's in which co-operation between the three branches of government is essential for empowering government to take the necessary developmental and redistributive measures envisaged by the Constitution, particularly in relation to socio-economic rights.[211]

The Constitutional Court has generally emphasised that the Constitution does not envisage bright-line boundaries or a competitive model of relations between the three spheres of government.[212] Instead it values a flexible and co-operative model

---

[210] R Calland & M Taylor 'Parliament and the socio-economic imperative – what is the role of the national legislature?' (1997) 1 *LDD* 193–220 at 198. The accuracy of this assessment in the context of the functioning of Parliament in South Africa is borne out by many of the conclusions and recommendations of the *Report of the Independent Panel Assessment of Parliament* (2009). Available at http://www.parliament.gov.za/content/The%20Panel%20for%20Assessment%20of%20Parliament%20Report_Final4_mail~1.pdf (accessed on 7 March 2009). Of particular concern is the impact of South Africa's party list system of electoral representation on the fulfilment of parliament's oversight mandate in respect of the Executive (see particularly chapter 3 of the report). See further Pieterse (note 94 above) 388 and the various sources cited there.

[211] In *De Lange v Smuts NO* 1998 (3) SA 785 (CC), 1998 (7) BCLR 779 (CC) para 60, the Constitutional Court held that a balance must be developed between 'the need, on the one hand, to control government by separating powers and enforcing checks and balances, and, on the other, to avoid diffusing power so completely that the government is unable to take timely measures in the public interest'.

[212] Thus in the *First Certification* judgment (note 147 above) para 111 the Constitutional Court held that the doctrine of separation of powers is not 'a fixed or rigid constitutional doc-

of relations between the three branches of government, as well as between the three spheres of national, provincial and local government.[213] The three spheres of government as well as the branches of government within each sphere are constituted as distinctive, but also interdependent and interrelated.[214] A relationship of 'accountability, responsiveness and openness' is envisaged.[215] This is more akin to a flexible, dialogic model of the separation of powers doctrine which entails, in Martha Minow's words, 'a continual process of mutual action and interaction' in which context plays a crucial role.[216]

In this model, the focus is not so much on whether one branch of government has transgressed the boundaries of the other, but rather on 'whether the branches all remain able to participate in the process of mutually defining their boundaries.'[217] This is consistent with the central purpose of the doctrine of separation of powers, which is to prevent a concentration of power in any one branch of government. In other words, no one branch should monopolise all the power and dominate the conversation and processes of transformation.

Scholars sympathetic to the dialogic conception of adjudication characterise this process of mutual interaction as a 'constitutional dialogue' between the different

---

trine' and that 'it is given expression in many different forms and made subject to checks and balances of many kinds'. However, on occasion, the Court has tended to revert to the more traditional metaphor of the separation of powers doctrine as constituting separate 'terrains', whose functions may overlap but which 'are in the main separate, and should be kept separate'. Per Chaskalson P (as he then was) in *Ferreira v Levin NO* 1996 (1) SA 984 (CC) para 183. See also the recent description by Ngcobo J in *Director of Public Prosecutions, Transvaal v Minister for Justice and Constitutional Development* 2009 (4) SA 222 (CC), 2009 (7) BCLR 637 (CC) para 183 of the boundaries of judicial review:

> Under our constitutional democracy, courts have no power to supervise or interfere with the exercise by the executive or legislature of its functions unless the circumstances amount to a clear disregard by the executive of the powers and duties conferred upon it by the Constitution. Where there is such a disregard, courts are not only entitled but obliged to intervene. But judicial review under our constitutional democracy does not give courts the power to exercise executive or legislative functions. It permits courts to call upon the executive and legislature to observe the limits of their powers but does not permit courts to exercise those powers themselves. Courts therefore have the duty to patrol the constitutional borders defined by the Constitution. They cannot, therefore, cross those borders.

On bounded notions of the separation of powers doctrine, see, generally, H Botha (note 26 above) 277–278.

213 See chapter 3 of the Constitution.

214 See ss 40 and 41.

215 See s 1(*d*). Constitutional Principle VI to the interim Constitution required the Constitution to have 'a separation of power between the legislature, the executive and the judiciary, with appropriate checks and balances to ensure accountability, responsiveness and openness'.

216 M Minow *Making all the Difference: Inclusion, Exclusion and American Law* (1990) 361.

217 Ibid.

branches of government.[218] Dialogic engagement in this context will frequently be characterised by disharmony and mutual resistance to an over-assertion of power by one branch.[219] What is important, however, is that the branches of government remain engaged with each other in a manner which is open and respectful of the institutional strengths and weaknesses of each other.[220] Through this process the limits of each branch's institutional power will be continually defined and redefined as they respond to the multifarious challenges of South Africa's evolving constitutional democracy.

Critically, this 'constitutional dialogue' should not be conceived as an exclusively institutional dialogue between the branches and various spheres of government. It should incorporate the state institutions supporting constitutional democracy such as the Human Rights Commission and the Commission for Gender Equality, but more importantly, the rich diversity of civil society and communities in South Africa. This is necessary to counter the domination of institutionalised politics,[221] and to facilitate participatory democracy in which marginalised and alternative voices are heard and receive considered responses.[222] The possibility of fundamental changes to dominant paradigms and prevailing power relations is enhanced when courts, parliament and the executive are responsive to these voices.

A dialogic, dynamic model of the separation of powers doctrine implies a nuanced role for the judiciary in the enforcement of socio-economic rights. Socio-economic rights adjudication has a particular contribution to make in requiring government and powerful private actors to give serious and reasoned consideration to the claims of those who lack access to the economic and social resources. These groups usually resort to litigation because their claims have not been recognised or pursued in the formal political processes. If judges are to play this role effectively they will, in appropriate cases, be required to make decisions with significant policy and budgetary implications. However, in other cases, they may be required to exercise restraint and deference to the institutional strengths and skills of the other branches. For example, the facts of the particular case may demonstrate that a decision requires a delicate

---

218 C Scott & J Nedelsky 'Constitutional dialogue' in J Bakan & D Schneiderman (eds) *Social Justice and the Constitution: Perspectives on a Social Union for Canada* (1992) 59–83 at 59; K Roach 'Constitutional, remedial and international dialogues about rights: The Canadian experience' (2005) 40 *Texas Int L J* 537–576.

219 Scott & Macklem (note 63 above) 42.

220 See also A Sachs 'The judicial enforcement of socio-economic rights: The *Grootboom* case' (2003) 56 *Current Legal Problems* 579–601 at 599.

221 On the limitations of institutional politics in realising the Constitution's transformative commitments, see D Brand (note 71 above).

222 The Constitutional Court has underscored the centrality of participatory democracy to the achievement of constitutional goals and values, and affirmed the duty of the State to take positive measures to ensure that the public has the effective capacity and opportunity to participate in decision-making processes. See *Doctors for Life International v Speaker of the National Assembly* 2006 (6) SA 416 (CC), 2006 (12) BCLR 1399 (CC) paras 108, 112–117.

balancing of the rights and needs of a number of social groups who are not represented by any of the parties to the litigation. In these circumstances, one of the other branches of government may be better placed to undertake this balancing and reconciliation of competing rights and interests after hearing submissions from all affected groups. In other cases, it may be evident that unless a particular service or resource is granted to the applicants, the consequences will be severe and a balancing of competing rights and public purposes is not required. In such a case a more searching scrutiny of the policy justifications for the denial of access to the service in question and a stronger remedy will be appropriate.

A fluid, dialogic model of the separation of powers doctrine is best suited to promoting a transformative jurisprudence on socio-economic rights. As the Constitutional Court has reiterated, the courts are required by the Constitution 'to ensure that all branches of government act within the law and fulfil their constitutional obligations'.[223] However, they must do so in a way which respects[224] the particular institutional role and competencies of the other branches.[225] This implies that the decision by a court to apply a more or less robust standard of review and remedial approach in a particular socio-economic rights case should be substantively and transparently justified in the light of the purposes and values protected by the rights at stake, and after a careful consideration of the institutions and processes which are most capable of advancing their realisation. Where the legislative and executive branches are failing to fulfil their constitutional responsibilities in relation to socio-economic rights, the courts should be consistently prompting them to give effect to these rights through comprehensive, participatory social programmes and legislation.

Ultimately, the appropriate institutional role for the courts in social rights litigation should depend on a contextual evaluation of the most effective means of vindicating the relevant rights in the light of the particular facts and circumstances in a case.

2.4.8 Institutional competence revisited

A further obstacle frequently raised against the justiciability of socio-economic rights is the institutional competence of the judiciary to make complex economic and

---

223 *Doctors for Life International* ibid, citing *President of the Republic of South Africa v United Democratic Movement (African Christian Democratic Party Intervening; Institute for Democracy in South Africa as Amici Curiae)* 2003 (1) SA 472 (CC), 2002 (11) BCLR 1164 (CC) para 25.

224 As O'Regan J observes in her judgment in *Bato Star* (note 3 above) paras 46–48 that the notion of 'respect' for the roles and functions of the other branches of government is a more apt description than 'deference' for the stance of courts in judicial review. Although this judgment concerned the judicial review of administrative action, O'Regan J's observations are equally apposite to judicial review of fundamental rights norms in a constitutional democracy.

225 *Glenister v President of the Republic of South Africa* (note 206 above) para 33.

social policy decisions.[226] The issue of institutional competence in this area has two distinct dimensions.

The first concerns the competence of the judiciary to make decisions which entail specialised expertise in matters of social policy and public finance. It is argued that judges lack the special training to make sensible decisions in these spheres.[227] However, commercial litigation, delictual claims, the review of administrative action, and tax disputes all entail judges assessing evidence and arguments in a range of specialist fields. The special expertise of decision-makers in the area of social or economic policy warrants an appropriate degree of respect from judicial officers.[228] However, the mere fact that the subject matter of a case is complex and entails specialised knowledge does not absolve a judge from responsibility for adjudicating the dispute in the light of the normative requirements of the applicable constitutional right and the evidence presented. As O'Regan J observes in the context of the judicial review of administrative decisions:

> A court should not rubber-stamp an unreasonable decision simply because of the complexity of the decision or the identity of the decision-maker.[229]

The second dimension of institutional competence concerns the unforeseeable ramifications of socio-economic rights adjudication. In litigation, a court is restricted to a limited spectrum of facts and arguments relevant to the particular dispute between the parties. However, a judicial decision enforcing human rights could have 'knock-on' effects causing budgetary and policy distortions and affecting a range of rights and interests of parties who are not before the court. Lon Fuller coined the term 'polycentric disputes' to describe disputes arising in litigation which give rise to many diverging issues, each of which is linked to the other in a complex web of interdependent relationships.[230] He likens polycentric disputes to a spider's web:

> A pull on one strand will distribute tensions after a complicated pattern throughout the web as a whole. Doubling the original pull will, in all likelihood, not simply double each of the resulting tensions but will rather create a different complicated pattern of tensions. This would certainly occur, for example, if the doubled pull caused one or more of the

[226] See further in this regard Scott & Macklem (note 63 above) 43–84; S Liebenberg 'Socio-economic rights' in M Chaskalson et al (eds) *Constitutional Law of South Africa* (Revision service 3, 1998), chapter 41 at 10–11; Pieterse (note 94 above) 392–396.

[227] Justice Albie Sachs argues that the main difficulty entailed in the judicial enforcement of socio-economic rights is one of judicial capacity, rather than institutional legitimacy. See Sachs (note 220 above) 588–589.

[228] See note 224 above.

[229] *Bato Star* (note 3 above) para 48.

[230] Lon Fuller derives the concept from M Polanyi's book, *The Logic of Liberty: Reflections and Rejoinders* (1951): Fuller 'The forms and limits of adjudication' (1978) 92 *Harvard LR* 353–409 at 394.

> weaker strands to snap. This is a 'polycentric' situation because it is 'many centered' – each crossing of strands is a distinct center for distributing tensions.[231]

The first observation to make in relation to the problem of polycentricity is that it is not restricted to adjudication in the field of social and economic rights. The enforcement of most, if not all, rights have polycentric implications. For example, a decision that the right to life requires the abolition of the death penalty[232] requires provision for the re-sentencing of prisoners currently sentenced to death,[233] as well as for the construction and maintenance of high security imprisonment facilities for those convicted of serious crimes. This has implications for the justice system, for penal policy and for the State's budget.[234]

The second observation is that the fact that a decision has polycentric implications does not necessarily render it unsuitable for adjudication. In fact, Lon Fuller concedes that 'there is no better illustration of a polycentric relationship than an economic market'.[235] However, he holds that 'the laying down of rules that will make a market function properly is one for which adjudication is generally well suited'.[236] These views are revealing in that they illustrate that, for Fuller, it is not polycentricity per se that is problematic in adjudication, but rather polycentric decision-making in areas such as social welfare. This reflects the general bias in classic liberal legal theory against the judicial enforcement of welfare rights.

A less intrusive standard of scrutiny of the State's justifications for failing to provide a certain social service may be undertaken in circumstances where a court does not have information or evidence relating to the manifestly far-reaching consequences of its order for other rights and State responsibilities.[237] However, where a court does have a factual basis for reasonably predicting the consequences of the relief claimed and assessing its justifiability in the light of the constitutional requirements, institu-

---

231 Ibid 395. For a classic example of the Constitutional Court's reluctance to interfere in medical and political decisions with extensive polycentric implications, see *Soobramoney* (note 134 above). See further the discussion of *Soobramoney* in chapter 4, 4.2.2.

232 As was decided by the Constitutional Court in *S v Makwanyane* (note 3 above).

233 The administrative and systemic problems encountered in re-sentencing condemned prisoners in the aftermath of the Constitutional Court's decision in *S v Makwanyane* (note 3 above) is well illustrated by the Court's decision to assume a supervisory jurisdiction over this process after lengthy delays. See *Sibiya v Director of Public Prosecutions, Johannesburg* 2005 (5) SA 315 (CC), 2005 (8) BCLR 812 (CC). See further the discussion of these cases in chapter 8, part 8.6.2.

234 Similar considerations apply to decisions based on the right to equality in s 9, as the Constitutional Court observed in the *First Certification* judgment (note 147 above). See also the Court's decision in *Khosa* (note 84 above).

235 Fuller (note 230 above) 403.

236 Ibid 403–404.

237 The minimally intrusive rationality standard of scrutiny adopted by the Court in the *Soobramoney* decision (note 134 above) was clearly motivated by the polycentric implications of interfering with the budgetary and rationing decisions applicable to kidney dialysis treatment.

tional competence does not represent a barrier to the enforcement of the relevant right. Not to do so in such a case would represent an abdication of its duty to adjudicate and grant appropriate relief for violations of rights in the Bill of Rights.

It should also be borne in mind that it is the State's responsibility to respond appropriately and make the necessary adjustments to social and economic policy in the light of judicial decisions. This is an integral component of the institutional dialogue between the judiciary and the legislative and executive branches of government in the context of fundamental rights adjudication.

Polycentricity as a barrier to the enforcement of socio-economic rights is frequently overstated. It is premised on the existence of a rational, comprehensive and carefully calibrated social and economic programme designed by the executive and legislative branches of government – the 'perfect spider web'. It does not allow for the reality that executives and legislatures in contemporary democratic societies may either be hostile or indifferent to the interests of poor communities or may also be subject to 'blind spots' due to a lack of information, expertise or capacity in formulating and implementing social policy.[238]

While courts and litigation have institutional disadvantages, they also have certain advantages.[239] For example, judges are well placed to consider in a reasoned, impartial manner the impact of policies and legislation on the constitutional rights of particularly vulnerable groups. They may be able to cut through bureaucratic red tape[240] when this is obstructing the realisation of the rights concerned. In addition, they are able to provide both individualised and systemic remedies that are carefully tailored to redress the particular circumstances of a rights violation. The more comprehensive and thorough the evidence and argument placed before the courts by the parties in litigation, the more confident a court will feel about making a responsible decision.[241]

---

[238] On the concept of 'blind spots' in legislative processes, see Dixon (note 52 above) 402.

[239] See, further, Pieterse (note 94 above) 394.

[240] On 'burdens of inertia' in legislative processes, see Dixon (note 52 above) 402–403.

[241] *Amicus curiae* briefs can play an important role in this context by presenting the courts with different perspectives and possible solutions to the legal disputes in a particular case. See, for example, the important role played by the *amici curiae* in *Grootboom* (note 114 above), acknowledged by the Court at paras 17–18. See further M Heywood 'Debunking "conglomo-talk": A case study of the *amicus curiae* as an instrument for advocacy, investigation and mobilization' (2001) 5 *LDD* 133–162. For suggestions of reforms to the processes of social rights litigation that can contribute to ameliorating the institutional disadvantages of the courts, see M Pieterse (note 94 above) 395–396. A fruitful area for further research and comparative study is the type of reforms to human rights litigation that will enable a broader range of information and perspectives to be placed before the courts. These could include, for example, studying the experience of the Indian courts in relation to judicially appointed fact-finding and remedial committees. See in this regard, S Shankar & P B Mehta 'Courts and socioeconomic rights in India' in V Gauri & D M Brinks (eds) *Courting Social Justice: Judicial Enforcement of Social and Economic Rights in the Developing World* (2008) 174–176.

It is certainly appropriate for courts to consider the limitations of their own institutional position and capabilities in adjudicating rights. However, as Marius Pieterse argues, respect for the institutional competencies of the other branches of government and taking seriously the judicial mandate to enforce socio-economic rights should not be cast as '"either/or" counterpoles'.[242] In a similar vein, Craig Scott and Philip Alston note that 'judicial involvement is not an on-off switch: just because a court cannot legitimately or competently deal with all – or even many – aspects of a case does not mean it should deal with none'.[243]

A substantive and transparent evaluation of the rights and values at stake and the facts placed before the court in a particular case is required to determine the nature and degree of judicial intervention that is appropriate. The fact that a decision is complex or has policy and resource implications is not a sufficient justification for the judiciary to abdicate their responsibility to interpret and enforce socio-economic rights.[244]

2.4.9 Innovative remedies

Classic liberal constitutionalism is premised on a model of negative review in terms of which legislation or conduct is declared invalid when it infringes constitutional rights.[245] However, the enforcement of socio-economic rights frequently requires the imposition of positive duties on the State, and sometimes on private parties, to extend access to social and economic resources to those who currently lack such access. Effective redress for systemic deprivations of access to socio-economic rights will frequently require a complex series of structural and institutional reforms adopted over a period of time. The types of positive remedies required to realise socio-economic

242 Pieterse (note 94 above) 394.

243 C Scott & P Alston 'Adjudicating constitutional priorities in a transnational content: A comment on *Soobramoney's* legacy and *Grootboom*'s promise' (2000) 16 *SAJHR* 206–268 at 242–243.

244 *Manqele v Durban Transitional Metropolitan Council* 2002 (6) SA 423 (D), [2002] 2 All SA 39 (D) is an illustration of a court's failure to engage with the substantive content of the right of access to sufficient water in the Constitution (s 27(1)(*b*) read with (2)) in interpreting s 3 of the Water Services Act 108 of 1997. At the stage of this litigation, the Act had been passed but no regulations had been promulgated defining the right of access to basic water supply and basic sanitation enacted in s 3 of the Act. Niles-Dunér J held that he could not give content to the right to a basic water supply in s 3 of the Act and it was accordingly unenforceable (427 F–G). The court failed to interpret s 3 of the Act in the light of s 27 of the Constitution (as required by s 39(2)), adopting the view that '[t]hese are policy matters which fall outside the purview of my role and function, and are inextricably linked to the availability of resources' (427 E–F). See also the discussion of *Mazibuko v City of Johannesburg* [2009] ZACC 28 in chapter 9 (Postscript), part 9.4.

245 This is a consequence of the bias in favour of negative over positive rights discussed in part 2.4.4 above.

rights are not easily accommodated within the model of negative review premised on a 'once and for all' judicial order, striking down a particular law or policy.[246]

The enforcement of socio-economic rights may require mandatory orders against the executive,[247] and even in appropriate cases, structural interdicts involving ongoing judicial supervision of their implementation.[248] However, where legislation or policy deprives people of their existing access to socio-economic rights, many of the traditional remedies for rights violations may be usefully deployed to provide effective relief.[249]

The broad powers of the courts to grant 'just and equitable' remedies to remedy constitutional defects provide ample scope for innovative remedies in the context of socio-economic rights litigation. Courts are required to evaluate in the circumstances of each socio-economic rights case which type of remedy will be most effective in protecting the rights and values at stake. However, unless the courts transcend the model of negative review and final, 'once-and-for-all' court orders, their ability to craft transformative remedies will be constrained.[250]

2.5 CONCLUSION

The Constitution creates a legal framework for the fundamental transformation of unjust political, social, economic and cultural relations in South African society. It envisages a process of active deliberation concerning the nature and processes of a transforming society. This deliberation must be open to a diversity of voices, and enable all groups, particularly those experiencing systemic disadvantage, to participate as equals in formal and informal deliberative institutions. This requires far-reaching positive measures to redress various forms of social, economic and cultural marginalisation prevalent in South African society.

The inclusion of socio-economic rights in the Bill of Rights represents a commitment in the country's highest law to ensuring that all have access to the social services and economic resources necessary for participation as equals. The transformative potential of socio-economic rights lies in the extent to which these rights can stimulate the redress of the underlying conditions and structures that generate systemic impoverishment and social marginalisation for certain groups. In the first place this 'calls for a concerted, co-ordinated and co-operative national effort in which gov-

---

[246] See in this regard W Trengove 'Judicial remedies for violations of socio-economic rights' (1999) 1 *ESR Review* 8–11 at 9. See further the discussion in chapter 8, part 8.6.1.

[247] On mandatory orders in the context of socio-economic rights litigation, see chapter 8, part 8.5.3.

[248] On structural interdicts and supervisory orders in the context of socio-economic rights litigation, see chapter 8, part 8.6.

[249] See chapter 8, part 8.3.

[250] See chapter 8, parts 8.6.3 and 8.11.

ernment in each of its three spheres and panoply of resources and the skills of civil society are marshalled, inspired and led'.[251]

However, socio-economic rights are also justiciable rights under the South African Constitution. The judiciary thus has an important responsibility to promote their transformative potential through interpretation and enforcement. Interpretation is central to all legal texts, particularly broadly formulated constitutional rights guarantees.[252] The mere presence of these rights in the Bill of Rights does not guarantee that they will be interpreted in ways that challenge systemic forms of disadvantage and disempowerment.[253]

There are strong strands of classic liberal political theory running through South Africa's legal tradition and culture. Their influence has considerable potential to restrain the development of a transformative jurisprudence on socio-economic rights. The transformative challenge posed by socio-economic rights can only be met by developing new interpretive approaches in response to the core dichotomies and dilemmas of classic liberal constitutionalism.

This chapter has explored various interpretive approaches and strategies that can facilitate a transformative jurisprudence on socio-economic rights. Perhaps the most significant of these is the need for the South African courts to develop a substantive account of the normative commitments underpinning the various socio-economic rights in the Bill of Rights. This requires elaborating on the values and purposes which these rights protect and their implications in ways which are responsive to the relevant historical and social context and the voices of marginalised groups.

At its best, socio-economic rights litigation can help bring about fundamental reforms to the legal system to make it more responsive to the claims of impoverished groups in both public and private law.[254] However, the limits of social rights litigation in advancing democratic transformation must also be acknowledged. Unless all participants in socio-economic rights litigation are conscious of the institutional lim-

---

[251] I use the words of Chaskalson CJ in *Treatment Action Campaign* (note 84 above) para 123.

[252] Elizabeth Mensch 'The history of mainstream legal thought' in D Kairys (ed) *The Politics of Law: A Progressive Critique* 3 ed (1998) 23–53 at 34 describes the centrality of interpretation and ethical choice in adjudication:

> Words are created by people in history, and their definition inevitably varies with particular context and with the meaning brought to them by the judges who are asked to interpret them. That act of interpretation is, in every instance, an act of social choice.

[253] As Scott & Macklem (note 63 above) 33 observe:

> All legal texts possess regressive potential. The entrenchment of social rights provides a boost to certain kinds of arguments aimed at combating disadvantage, but entrenchment alone does not ensure that such arguments will prevail.

[254] In this respect, winning social benefits through litigation can be likened to Nancy Fraser's concept of 'non-reformist reforms'. These reforms, although they do not in themselves change the underlying structural causes of inequality and poverty, can, if strategically pursued, cumulatively create the conditions in which deeper changes become possible. See N Fraser (note 40 above) 78–82. For an application in the context of socio-economic rights litigation in South Africa, see Liebenberg (note 2 above).

itations of the courts and consider the possibility that the particular claim may be more effectively addressed through another forum such as advocacy or community mobilisation, there will be the ever-present danger of untimely or inappropriate resort to litigation, and judgments that impede rather than facilitate transformation.[255] On the other hand, without a full appreciation of the transformative potential of socio-economic rights litigation, there will be many missed opportunities to improve the lives of the poor and to keep alive the constitutional vision of a more just society.

The following chapters analyse and evaluate South Africa's evolving jurisprudence on socio-economic rights in the light of the theoretical understanding of transformative approaches to the adjudication of these rights developed in this chapter.

---

[255] Jonathan Berger underscores the critical importance of embedding social rights litigation in broader strategies of civil society mobilisation, organisation and advocacy if social rights litigation is to have a meaningful impact. He goes on to observe:

> Although litigation remains an indispensable tool, without which the inertia of a flawed political process may never be broken, it becomes most effective when its use is limited and targeted. Simply put, broad social change will not be won in the courts alone.

See J Berger 'Litigating for social justice in post-apartheid South Africa: A focus on health and education' in V Gauri & D M Brinks (eds) *Courting Social Justice: Judicial Enforcement of Social and Economic Rights in the Developing World* (2008) 38–99 at 95.

CHAPTER 3

Socio-Economic Rights in the Context of the Bill of Rights

In this chapter *Page*

3.1 INTRODUCTION

A central feature of transformative adjudication identified in the previous chapter is a substantive approach to the interpretation of the rights in the Bill of Rights. A substantive approach to the interpretation of socio-economic rights entails engaging with the real life impact of social and economic deprivation of disadvantaged groups, and considering its implications in the light of the values and interests underpinning these rights.[1] This requires a consideration of the context both of the rights themselves and the circumstances in which particular groups allege a violation of their rights. The textual setting of the relevant rights within the framework of the Constitution, as well as their historical, political, economic and social context, must be taken into account.[2]

This chapter locates socio-economic rights within the broader context of the Bill of Rights. It focuses on provisions and relevant jurisprudence which are significant for the development of a transformative jurisprudence on socio-economic rights. In the first part an overview is provided of the relevant socio-economic rights provisions. Thereafter the significance of the overall framework of state duties pertaining to the Bill of Rights in s 7(2) is explored, as well as the provisions governing legal standing, *amicus curiae* interventions, and limitations of rights.[3]

The second part of the chapter focuses on the implications of s 39(1) of the Constitution for the interpretation of the socio-economic rights provisions in the Bill of Rights. This section requires the courts, when interpreting the Bill of Rights, to promote the values of human dignity, equality and freedom. It also requires them to consider international law and permits them to consider foreign law. The previous chapter argued that transformative adjudication implies a willingness to explore new approaches to the interpretation of rights that promote the foundational constitutional values of human dignity, equality and freedom. I argue that this openness should extend to international and foreign jurisprudence on socio-economic rights which can open up innovative interpretative possibilities.

3.2 SIGNIFICANT PROVISIONS IN THE BILL OF RIGHTS

3.2.1 Socio-economic rights: Textual formulation

The core set of socio-economic rights which are the primary focus of this book are those protected in ss 26, 27, 28(1)(*c*), 29(1) and (2) and 35(2)(*e*) of the Constitution. Section 26(1) entrenches the right of everyone 'to have access to adequate housing', and s 27(1) the right of everyone 'to have access to (*a*) health care services, including reproductive health care; (*b*) sufficient food and water; and (*c*) social security, including, if they are unable to support themselves and their dependants, appropriate social assistance'. These first sections are qualified by a second subsection, which reads:

---

[1] On a substantive approach to the adjudication of socio-economic rights, see chapter 2, part 2.4.2.

[2] See *Government of the Republic of South Africa v Grootboom* 2001 (1) SA 46 (CC), 2000 (11) BCLR 1169 (CC) ('*Grootboom*') para 22. On aspects of the historical and social context within which socio-economic rights must be considered, see chapter 1, part 1.2; and chapter 2, part 2.2.

[3] The relevant provisions and jurisprudence on the application of the rights in the Bill of Rights are considered in chapter 7. Remedies for socio-economic rights violations are considered in chapter 8.

> The state must take reasonable legislative and other measures, within its available resources, to achieve the progressive realisation of each of these rights.

Section 26(3) reads as follows:

> No one may be evicted from their home, or have their home demolished, without an order of court made after considering all the relevant circumstances. No legislation may permit arbitrary evictions.

Section 27(3) provides that:

> No one may be refused emergency medical treatment.[4]

In addition, the Constitution entrenches a set of basic socio-economic rights for children within the context of s 28, a special clause devoted to children's rights.[5] Section 28(1)(*c*) confers upon every child the right 'to basic nutrition, shelter, basic health care services and social services'.[6]

Section 29(1) protects educational rights by conferring on 'everyone' the right (*a*) 'to a basic education, including adult basic education; and (*b*) to a further education, which the state, through reasonable measures, must make progressively available and accessible'. Section 29(2) gives everyone the 'right to receive education in the official languages of their choice in public educational institutions where that education is reasonably practicable'. All 'reasonable educational alternatives, including single medium institutions' must be considered in order 'to ensure the effective access to, and implementation of, this right'. The factors which must be taken into account in considering these alternatives are '(*a*) equity; (*b*) practicability; and (*c*) the need to redress the results of past racially discriminatory laws and practices'.[7] Section 29(3) gives everyone a qualified right to 'establish and maintain, at their own expense, independent educational institutions that (*a*) do not discriminate on the basis of race; (*b*) are registered with the state; and (*c*) maintain standards that are not inferior to standards at comparable public educational institutions'. Finally, s 29(4) expressly states that the previous subsection 'does not preclude state subsidies for independent educational institutions'. This is essentially a 'liberty' right which expressly entitles private actors, subject to certain conditions, to establish institutions for realising the par-

---

[4] The rights in ss 26 and 27 are the focus of chapter 4, while chapter 6 considers the implications of s 26(3) for evictions law in South Africa.

[5] A child is defined in s 28(3) as a person under the age of 18 years.

[6] Children's socio-economic rights are discussed in chapter 5, part 5.2. Other important rights with a socio-economic character guaranteed to children are the right to be protected from 'maltreatment, neglect, abuse or degradation' (s 28(1)(*d*)), and from 'exploitative labour practices' (s 28(1)(*e*)). See also s 28(1)(*f*), which prohibits requiring a child to perform work or provide services that 'are inappropriate for a person of that child's age', or 'place at risk the child's well-being, education, physical or mental health or spiritual, moral or social development'.

[7] Section 29(2)(*a*)–(*c*) of the Constitution.

ticular right. It does not impose a positive duty on the State to support such private institutions.[8]

Persons who are deprived of their liberty are guaranteed a special set of socio-economic rights. Thus s 35(2)(*e*) provides that everyone 'who is detained, including every sentenced prisoner' has the right 'to conditions of detention that are consistent with human dignity, including at least exercise and the provision, at state expense, of adequate accommodation, nutrition, reading material and medical treatment'.[9]

As can be observed, there are three basic formulations used in these socio-economic rights provisions. The rights in the first two subsections of ss 26 and 27 are defined in terms of a right of 'access to' the relevant socio-economic goods and services. Furthermore, the duty on the State to realise these rights is expressly qualified by the phrases, 'reasonable legislative and other measures', 'available resources', and 'progressive realisation'. The right to 'further education' is not phrased as an 'access' right, but is qualified in terms similar to the latter rights. The right to receive education in the official language of one's choice is qualified according to the criterion of reasonable practicability. Second, certain socio-economic rights are formulated as direct entitlements without the internal qualifying phrases encountered in ss 26 and 27. These provisions pertain to the right to basic education, and the socio-economic rights of children and persons deprived of their liberty. The third type of formulation takes the form of prohibitions on arbitrary evictions and demolitions and the refusal of emergency medical treatment respectively. The way in which these rights have been interpreted in the jurisprudence is analysed in the following three chapters.

3.2.2 The duty of the State 'to respect, protect, promote and fulfil' rights

Section 7(1) which introduces the Bill of Rights affirms that it is 'a cornerstone of democracy in South Africa and affirms the democratic values of human dignity, equality and freedom'. As argued previously, this establishes a synergy, instead of an opposition, between the democratic ethos of the Constitution and the rights and values underpinning them in the Bill of Rights.[10]

Section 7(2) places a duty on the State to 'respect, protect, promote and fulfil the rights in the Bill of Rights.' The Constitutional Assembly preparatory documents indicate that the inclusion of this overarching framework of duties was recommended by the Technical Committee after receiving public submissions in support of its

---

[8] Educational rights are discussed in chapter 5, part 5.3.

[9] The socio-economic rights of persons deprived of their liberty are discussed in chapter 5, part 5.4. See also s 35(2)(*f*) which confers the right on every detained person to be visited by that person's spouse or partner, next of kin, chosen religious counsellor and chosen medical practitioner.

[10] Chapter 2, part 2.4.6.

inclusion.[11] Its origins lie in the analysis by the scholar Henry Shue of the nature of the obligations imposed on States by human rights.[12] Shue argued that the effective guarantee of all human rights – whether classified as civil and political, or economic, social or cultural – requires a combination of negative duties of restraint on the State, and positive duties to protect and ensure the rights.[13]

International human rights law recognises that the effective guarantee of human rights depends on a combination of negative and positive duties. Thus art 2(1) of the International Covenant on Civil and Political Rights (1966) requires States Parties 'to respect and to ensure' the rights in the Covenant to all individuals within their territory. Moreover, States Parties are required in terms of art 2(2) to undertake 'to take the necessary steps ... to adopt such legislative or other measures as may be necessary to give effect to the rights recognized' in the Covenant. In terms of art 1 of the African Charter on Human and Peoples' Rights (1981), States Parties 'recognize the rights, duties and freedoms enshrined in this Charter and shall undertake to adopt legislative or other measures to give effect to them'. Even the right against torture which is traditionally conceived as placing a duty on State officials to refrain from conduct amounting to torture, requires far-reaching positive measures to secure effective guarantees against torture taking place within a State's territory. Thus art 2 of the Convention against Torture and Other Cruel, Inhuman or Degrading Treatment or Punishment (1984) requires States Parties to 'take effective legislative, administrative, judicial or other measures to prevent acts of torture in any territory under [their] jurisdiction'.[14]

A number of international human rights courts and commissions have also highlighted the combination of negative and positive duties imposed by various human rights treaty provisions. For example, in The *Mayagna (Sumo) Indigenous Community*

---

[11] Technical Committee IV, *Memorandum: Section 7: The State must respect, protect, promote and fulfil the rights in this Bill of Rights* (8 March 1996) (document on file with author).

[12] H Shue *Basic Rights: Subsistence, Affluence, and US Foreign Policy* (1980). For a discussion of this typology of duties in the context of socio-economic rights in South Africa, see S Liebenberg 'Violations of socio-economic rights: The role of the South African Human Rights Commission' in P Andrews and S Ellman (eds) *The Post-Apartheid Constitutions: Perspectives on South Africa's Basic Law* (2001) 405–443; P de Vos 'Pious wishes or directly enforceable human rights? Social and economic rights in South Africa's 1996 Constitution' (1997) 13 *SAJHR* 67–101.

[13] Thus he argued that rights impose duties 'to avoid' depriving people of their rights, to 'protect' them from deprivation, and 'to aid' the deprived. H Shue ibid at 52–53.

[14] The Inter-American Court of Human Rights has held in the *Velásquez Rodriguez Case*, Judgment of July 29, 1988 (Ser. C) No 4 para 172 that States are under a duty to exercise 'due diligence' in acting to prevent violations of the rights in the American Convention on Human Rights (1969). The Court elaborates on this duty as follows:

> The State has a legal duty to take *reasonable steps* to prevent human rights violations and to use the means at its disposal to carry out a serious investigation of violations committed within its jurisdiction, to identify those responsible, to impose the appropriate punishment and to ensure the victim adequate compensation. (para 174) (emphasis added)

of Awas Tingni Case,[15] the Inter-American Court of Human Rights found that the Nicaraguan government had violated the property rights of the Awas Tingni indigenous community protected in art 21 of the American Convention on Human Rights (1969) through a combination of actions and omissions in granting a concession to a foreign corporation to undertake logging on untitled land which included the ancestral lands of the Awas Tingni, as well as through its failure to demarcate and title the territory in question.[16]

The typology of 'respect, protect, promote and fulfil' has been increasingly adopted as a framework for analysis by the supervisory bodies under international human rights treaties, particularly the UN Committee on Economic, Social and Cultural Rights, which supervises States Parties' obligations under the International Covenant on Economic, Social and Cultural Rights (1966).[17] It analyses States Parties' duties in relation to these rights in terms of a duty to refrain from interfering directly or indirectly with people's enjoyment of the relevant rights (the duty 'to respect'), a duty to prevent private parties from interfering with the enjoyment of the relevant rights through the adoption of legislative and other regulatory measures (the duty 'to protect'),[18] and the duty to take positive measures that assist individuals and communities to gain access to and enjoy the full realisation of the relevant rights (the duty

---

[15] Inter-American Court of Human Rights, Judgment of August 31, 2001 (Ser. C) No 79.

[16] For an analysis of the significance of this case, see T J Melish 'The Inter-American Court of Human Rights: Beyond progressivity' in M Langford (ed) *Social Rights Jurisprudence: Emerging Trends in International and Comparative Law* (2008) 372–408 at 392–395. The European Court of Human Rights has also recognised the need for positive measures to protect the various rights in the European Convention on Human Rights (1950). See, for example, *Airey v Ireland* (1979) 2 EHRR 305 (the right to a fair hearing in art 6(1) of the Convention requires the provision of free legal assistance in certain circumstances); *X & Y v The Netherlands* (1986) 8 EHRR 235 para 23 (respect for the right to family or private life in art 8 of the Convention entails positive duties on the State to protect individuals against abuses of their rights by other individuals); *Plattform Arzte für Das Leben v Austria* 139 ECHR (Series A) (1988) (effective enjoyment of the right to peaceful assembly in art 11 of the Convention sometimes requires positive measures to be taken, even in the sphere of private relations); *López Ostra v Spain* (1995) 20 EHRR 277 (the state is under a positive duty to take reasonable and appropriate measures to protect the applicant's right to respect for their home and family life under art 8(1) of the Convention; this requires regulatory measures to be adopted to prevent environmental pollution by industries in their vicinity).

[17] See also *The Maastricht Guidelines on Violations of Economic, Social and Cultural Rights* reprinted in (1998) 20 *HRQ* 691–705. The Maastricht Guidelines were adopted in 1997 by a group of international law experts to elaborate on the obligations of States Parties to the International Covenant on Economic, Social and Cultural Rights (1966). They are the successor to *The Limburg Principles on the Implementation of the International Covenant on Economic, Social and Cultural Rights* reprinted in (1987) 9 *HRQ* 122–135. The *Limburg Principles* were also adopted by a group of international law experts in 1996.

[18] Where services, such as water services, are privatised, the Committee requires States Parties 'to prevent [water services providers] from compromising equal, affordable, and

'to fulfil'). The Committee disaggregates the latter duty into obligations 'to facilitate and provide'. The duty 'to facilitate' is understood in terms of providing a framework of laws and policies that assist individuals and groups to enjoy the rights. The duty 'to provide' arises when individuals or a group are unable to realise the right themselves by the means at their disposal.[19] The duty 'to promote' is perhaps least well-developed in the General Comments. From later General Comments, it can be inferred that it encompasses educational and informational programmes that promote awareness of the relevant rights and the mechanisms in place to access them.[20]

The African Commission on Human and Peoples' Rights has recently adopted this typology of obligations in its landmark socio-economic rights decision in *The Social and Economic Rights Action Centre (SERAC) and the Centre for Economic and Social Rights v Nigeria*[21] ('*SERAC*'). The case concerned the actions of the then military government of Nigeria in facilitating and failing to protect the Ogoni communities against the environmental pollution of their lands, and the destruction of their food sources and homes by the Shell Petroleum Development Corporation in a consortium with the state oil company, the Nigerian National Petroleum Company. The Commission found violations of a number of articles of the African Charter on Human and Peoples' Rights (1981), including the right to health (art 16), the right of peoples to freely dispose of their wealth and natural resources (art 21), environment rights (art 24), the right to housing or shelter,[22] and the right to food.[23]

---

physical access to sufficient, safe and acceptable water'. The Committee elaborates on this protective duty of the State as follows:

> To prevent such abuses an effective regulatory system must be established, in conformity with the Covenant and this General Comment, which includes independent monitoring, genuine public participation and imposition of penalties for non-compliance.

General Comment No 15 (Twenty-ninth sess, 2002) *The right to water (arts 11 and 12 of the Covenant)* UN doc. E/C.12/2002/11 para 24.

[19] UN Committee on Economic, Social and Cultural Rights, General Comment No 12 (Twentieth sess, 1999) *The right to adequate food (art 11 of the Covenant)*, UN doc. E/2000/22 para 15; General Comment No 14 (Twenty-second sess, 2000) *The right to the highest attainable standard of health (art 12 of the Covenant)* UN doc. E/C.12/2000/4 paras 34–37; General Comment No 15 ibid paras 20–29; General Comment No 18 (Thirty-fifth sess, 2005) *The right to work (art 6 of the Covenant)*, UN doc. E/C.12/GC/18 paras 23–28; General Comment No 19 (Thirty-ninth sess, 2007) *The right to social security (art 9)*, UN doc. E/C.12/GC/19 paras 43–51.

[20] See General Comment No 15 (note 18 above) para 25; General Comment No 18 ibid para 28; General Comment No 19 ibid para 49.

[21] Communication no. 155/96 (2001) AHRLR 51 (ACHPR 2001) paras 44–48.

[22] Although this right is not expressly protected in the African Charter, the Commission derived it from a joint reading of the rights to property (art 21), the right to health (art 16), and the right to protection of the family (art 18(1)). *SERAC* ibid para 60.

[23] The right to food is also not expressly protected in the African Charter, but the Commission held that it was implicit in the right to life (art 4), the right to health (art 16) and the right to economic, social and cultural development (art 22). *SERAC* ibid para 64.

The Commission held that the government had directly violated the rights of the Ogoni peoples by placing its legal and military powers at the disposal of the oil companies. It had, moreover, failed to take reasonable measures to protect the communities against the violations perpetrated by the oil companies.[24] A noteworthy feature of the Commission's decision is the emphasis placed on the State's duty to 'provide meaningful opportunities for individuals to be heard and to participate in development decisions affecting their communities'.[25] Facilitating participation in public and private decision-making which affects people's economic and social rights is thus regarded as integral to the State's protective duties.

To date, the Constitutional Court has not explicitly relied on this typology. However, it has recognised, in a range of judgments, the negative and positive duties imposed in different contexts by both civil and political rights as well as economic, social and cultural rights.[26]

Despite this recognition, South African jurisprudence must still contend with the traditional bias in liberal legalism towards negative constitutionalism. The enforcement of positive duties by courts is controversial in liberal constitutional theory. Because of their more manifest budgetary and policy implications, these duties are perceived to pose a direct threat to the doctrine of separation of powers.[27]

Thus courts generally tend either to deny relief or to apply a more deferential standard of scrutiny where positive measures are at issue in a particular case.[28] In chapter 2, it was argued that the distinction between negative and positive duties is not a static or immutable quality of rights. Bruce Porter gives the example of the positive measures required to secure equality of participation in society by people with disabilities such as the installation of wheelchair ramps and elevators in public buildings. Such positive measures are only necessary because these buildings were designed without any consideration for the access needs of people with disabilities. As Porter observes:

---

[24] Ibid paras 52, 55 and 57–58.

[25] Ibid paras 53 and 55.

[26] For example, the positive duties imposed by the right to vote in s 19 of the Constitution were recognised in the 'prisoners' right to vote' cases: *August v Electoral Commission* 1999 (3) SA 1 (CC), 1999 (4) BCLR 363 (CC) ('*August*'); *Minister of Home Affairs v National Institute for Crime Prevention and Reintegration of Offenders (NICRO)* 2005 (3) SA 280 (CC), 2004 (5) BCLR (CC) ('*NICRO*'). Conversely, the negative duties imposed by socio-economic rights were recognised in *Jaftha v Schoeman; Van Rooyen v Stoltz* 2005 (2) SA 140 (CC), 2005 (1) BCLR 78 (CC) ('*Jaftha*') paras 31–34. See further the discussion of *Jaftha* in chapter 4, part 4.6.2. See also the High Court judgments in *Residents of Bon Vista Mansions v Southern Metropolitan Local Council* 2002 (6) BCLR 625 (W) para 19, and *City of Cape Town v Rudolph* 2004 (5) SA 39 (C), 2003 (11) BCLR 1236 (C) 74H–75D.

[27] See further chapter 2, parts 2.4.4 and 2.4.7.

[28] For example, in *Deshaney v Winnebago County Department of Social Services* 489 US 189 (1989), the United States Supreme Court rejected arguments that the due process clause of the American Constitution imposed positive duties on State agencies to guarantee certain minimal levels of safety and security to its citizens.

> Defining the right only in terms of the nature of the state obligation to provide does not challenge the pattern of social exclusion that lies behind the need for positive measures to provide. [29]

Categorising a case in terms of the duty to respect, protect, promote or fulfil rights should not determine the appropriate interpretative approach to the rights at issue.[30] Whether restraint or positive measures are required from the respondents in a particular case will depend on a contextual evaluation of what types of actions or omissions are needed in the particular circumstances to secure the effective enjoyment of the relevant rights.[31] Such a decision cannot be determined by some kind of *a priori* analysis of where the claim fits in the matrix of duties.

The value of the holistic framework of duties recognised in s 7(2) lies primarily in its potential to facilitate a substantive and contextual approach to the adjudication of human rights. It embraces a form of positive constitutionalism which aims to secure the full and effective enjoyment of the rights in the Bill of Rights. In order to reach this goal, s 7(2) recognises that a combination of negative and positive duties may be required, depending on the relevant context. The courts thus have an express constitutional mandate to enforce, not only negative duties of restraint, but also positive duties of protection, promotion and fulfilment of rights. This assists in overcoming the bias towards negative constitutionalism which restrains the development of a transformative jurisprudence on socio-economic rights.

3.2.3 Legal standing, *amici curiae* interventions and access to legal services

The expansive and generous provisions on legal standing (*locus standi*) contained in the Bill of Rights are of particular importance for the practical justiciability of socio-economic rights. Section 38 confers standing on a broad category of persons who allege that a right in the Bill of Rights has been infringed or threatened to approach a competent court for appropriate relief. This includes anyone acting in their own interest or on behalf of persons who cannot act in their own name, class actions, actions in the public interest, and associations acting in the interest of their members.[32]

The Constitutional Court has given a broad interpretation to the standing provisions in s 38 requiring only an allegation that, objectively speaking, a right in the

---

[29] B Porter 'The crisis of ESC rights and strategies for addressing it' in J Squires, M Langford & B Thiele (eds) *The Road to a Remedy: Current Issues in the Litigation of Economic, Social and Cultural Rights* (2005) 43–69 at 55–56.

[30] See also I E Koch 'Dichotomies, trichotomies or waves of duties?' (2005) 5 *HRLR* 81–103.

[31] See further the critique of the differential model of review developed by the Constitutional Court for the negative and positive duties imposed by socio-economic rights in chapter 4, part 4.7.

[32] Section 38(*a*)–(*e*) of the Constitution.

Bill of Rights has been infringed or threatened, and that the parties seeking relief have a sufficient interest in obtaining the remedy they seek.[33] A broad and generous approach to legal standing is essential to facilitate the ability of communities and groups living in poverty to vindicate their socio-economic rights in circumstances where they have been unable to do so through other democratic means and processes.[34] However, at the same time, it is also important that the rules pertaining to legal standing prevent abuse of the generous standing provisions by legal practitioners and civil society organisations that are not genuinely acting in the interests of the relevant communities or act in ways that marginalise the participation of affected communities in such litigation.[35]

The jurisprudence on *locus standi* developed thus far by the courts has sought to reconcile these two concerns by incorporating safeguards to ensure proper representation of litigants. As Froneman J observed in *Ngxuza v Secretary, Dept of Welfare, Eastern Cape Provincial Government* [36] ('*Ngxuza*'):

> It is true that the nature of public law litigation creates problems of its own, namely that of proper representation. The kinds of problems that may arise are those associated with ensuring:
> (1) that only those who wish to be involved in the case are;
> (2) that those who wish to be involved are given the chance to make the representations they may wish to make; and
> (3) that the party presenting the case adequately represents future interests.
>
> These problems are, however, not factors that militate against a broad view of standing. At most they require safeguards to ensure the broadest and most effective representation in and presentation of public interest litigation.[37]

Ngxuza is the leading case on class actions. It concerned an application for the reinstatement of the disability grants of tens of thousands of social grant recipients that had been unlawfully terminated by the Eastern Cape provincial government. In the Court *a quo* the applicants, assisted by the Legal Resources Centre, were granted leave to act as representatives on behalf of all people in the Eastern Cape Province

---

[33] *Ferreira v Levin NO; Vryenhoek v Powell NO* 1996 (1) SA 984 (CC), 1996 (1) BCLR 1 (CC) ('*Ferreira*') paras 165–167. See also I Currie & J de Waal *The Bill of Rights Handbook* 5 ed (2005) 82–84.

[34] In *Ngxuza v Secretary, Department of Welfare, Eastern Cape Provincial Government* 2001 (2) SA 609 (E), 2000 (12) BCLR 1322 (E) Froneman J observed: 'Particularly in relation to so-called public interest litigation there can be no justification of a restrictive approach' (at 619 B–D). Similarly, in *Ferreira* ibid para 230, O'Regan J noted that 'it is important that it is not only those with vested interests who should be afforded standing in constitutional challenges, where remedies may have a wide impact'.

[35] For a description and attempt at remedying some of the abuses associated with the representation of applicants for social security grants, see the judgment of Wallis AJ in *Cele v The South African Social Security Agency* 2009 (5) SA 105 (D), 2008 (7) BCLR 734 (D).

[36] Note 34 above.

[37] Ibid 619 E–F.

whose disability grants had been suspended or cancelled within the relevant period. Provision was made in the Court's order for notice and publication of the action, for procedures allowing members of the class to opt out of the litigation, and for the Department of Welfare's assistance in identifying the members of the class.[38]

On appeal, Cameron JA (as he then was) held that the case was well suited to class action proceedings in that those affected by the arbitrary administrative action of the provincial government were a large and disparate group of claimants, all poor and 'lacking in protective and assertive armour', and each with a small monetary claim unsuited for individual enforcement.[39] The Supreme Court of Appeal upheld the order of Froneman J in the High Court. The outcome of *Ngxuza* was thus the development of the common law to make provision for class actions in accordance with s 38(*c*) of the Constitution.[40]

Public interest actions are an important mechanism through which systemic violations of socio-economic rights affecting a large section of the public can be challenged. They are particularly useful when the affected groups are disadvantaged and do not have access to legal services. Permitting legal standing on this basis enables violations of socio-economic rights to be redressed which could not otherwise be brought because of the financial and practical difficulties associated with the joinder of a large and disparate affected group or the complexity of class action proceedings.[41] Public interest actions are also well suited, not only to the redress of past wrongs, but also to deter and prevent future rights violations.[42] The disadvantage of public interest actions is that they may be abused by 'busybodies' who do not genuinely represent the interests and concerns of the affected communities. In these circumstances, the potential of public interest litigation to enhance participatory democracy is undermined.

The Constitutional Court has thus developed certain broad criteria to guide it in determining whether a person or organisation is genuinely acting in the public interest. Thus in *Ferreira,* O'Regan J held that a court should have regard to –

> whether there is another reasonable and effective manner in which the challenge can be brought; the nature of the relief sought, and the extent to which it is of general and prospective application; and the range of persons or groups who may be directly or indirectly affected by any order made by the court and the opportunity that those persons or groups have had to present evidence and argument to the court. [43]

---

[38] *Ngxuza* (note 34 above) 629I-631D. The practical difficulties associated with class actions and the devices available to deal with these difficulties are discussed at 623H–625B.

[39] *Permanent Secretary, Department Welfare, E Cape Provincial Government v Ngxuza* 2001 (4) SA 1184, 2001 (10) BCLR 1039 (SCA) ('*Ngxuza (SCA)*') para 12.

[40] Ibid.

[41] See the discussion by Cameron JA in *Ngxuza (SCA)* (note 39 above) paras 4–6.

[42] See the observations of O'Regan J in *Ferreira* (note 33 above) para 229.

[43] Ibid para 234. These criteria were formulated in O'Regan J's separate judgment in *Ferreira* on the interpretation of s 7(4)(*b*) of the interim Constitution.

The Court endorsed this approach in relation to s 38(*d*) of the Constitution in *Lawyers for Human Rights v Minister of Home Affairs*.[44] It held that the list of factors to be considered by a court before authorising an individual or organisation to act in the public interest was not closed. Additional factors to be considered included the degree of vulnerability of the affected group, the nature of the right alleged to be infringed, and the consequences of the infringement of the right.[45]

In the context of socio-economic rights, the Treatment Action Campaign[46] and other members of civil society brought the litigation which led to the celebrated judgment in *Minister of Health v Treatment Action Campaign (No 2)*[47] ('*Treatment Action Campaign*') as a public interest challenge to government's restrictive programme to reduce mother-to-child transmission of HIV.[48] Although the High Court described it as a class action,[49] it is more accurately an illustration of an action brought in the public interest.

A further illustration of the flexible approach taken to legal standing by the courts in litigation aimed at enforcing the rights in the Bill of Rights is the case of *Highveldridge Residents Concerned Party v Highveldridge TLC*,[50] which concerned a challenge by a residents' voluntary association to the disconnection of the water supply to households in a township by the local authority. Section 38(*e*) of the Constitution permits an association to act in the interests of its members in seeking relief for a violation of the rights in the Bill of Rights. The applicant's *locus standi* was challenged on the basis that it appeared from the applicant's constitution that it did not possess legal personality and was not authorised by its constitution to institute action in its own name. It was alleged that the applicant accordingly did not comply with the common-law requirements for legal standing by voluntary associations.[51]

Kruger J held that the restrictions placed by the common law on the legal standing of voluntary associations should not be allowed to constitute an 'impenetrable

---

44 2004 (4) SA 125 (CC), 2004 (7) BCLR 775 (CC).

45 Ibid para 18. See also *Kiliko v Minister of Home Affairs* 2006 (4) SA 114 (C), 2007 (4) BCLR 416 (C) para 12. The applicants had been issued with the asylum-seeker permits sought by them subsequent to the institution of the legal proceedings in this case. The Court held that they nevertheless had standing on a public interest basis to challenge the practices and policy of the respondents pertaining to the manner in which they accepted applications for asylum and issued permits in terms of s 22 of the Refugees Act 130 of 1998.

46 The Treatment Action Campaign is an organisation with the primary objective of campaigning for equitable access to affordable treatment for all people with HIV/AIDS, and supporting the prevention and elimination of all new HIV infections.

47 2002 (5) SA 721(CC), 2002 (10) BCLR 1033 (CC).

48 Ibid paras 2–3. For an analysis of the *Treatment Action Campaign* case, see chapter 4, part 4.3.

49 *Treatment Action Campaign v Minister of Health* 2002 (4) BCLR 356 (T) 359A–B.

50 2002 (6) SA 66 (T), 2003 (1) BCLR 72 (T).

51 Kruger J observed that, '[f]rom the wording and tenor of the applicant's constitution it is evident that the applicant reflects the spirit of a popular movement, rather than the characteristics ordinarily shown by an "orthodox" voluntary association' (ibid para 10).

obstacle'[52] to their seeking redress on behalf of their members for an alleged infringement of the Bill of Rights, as this would be incompatible with various constitutional principles. According to the Court:

> Those principles include, *inter alia*, the constitutional norms of accountability, responsiveness and openness on which the constitutional State is founded. It would equally be contrary to the ideal of a vibrant and thriving civil society which actively participates in the evolvement and development of a rights culture pursuant to the rights enshrined in the Bill of Rights. To hold otherwise would, in my view, be to disregard the interests of 'the poorest in our society' who are often not in a position where legal advice is readily accessible and who are more often than not, dependent upon action taken by informally structured associations of civil society so that legitimate issues may be addressed on their behalf. It will also be contrary to the basic values of human dignity, equality and freedom which underlie the spirit, purport and objects of the Bill of Rights.[53]

The Court proceeded to develop the common law to facilitate actions brought by voluntary associations on behalf of their members in litigation aimed at vindicating their constitutional rights. It observed that the practical difficulties associated with representative actions could be overcome by crafting an appropriate order that provided for the identification and participation by individuals who wished to associate themselves with the action.[54] This was necessary to maintain a 'proper balance' between 'granting access to organisations of civil society in matters where rights enshrined in the Bill of Rights are at stake on the one hand, and the proper and efficient running of the public administration on the other'.[55] This is another illustration of an enabling, pragmatic approach towards legal standing in the context of human rights litigation brought on behalf of disadvantaged claimants.

It is also possible for individuals and organisations to participate in human rights litigation through *amicus curiae* ('friend of the court') interventions. In order to be admitted as an *amicus* to litigation, an applicant must demonstrate that their submissions will be useful to the Court and different from those of the parties to the litigation.[56] *Amici* interventions offer an important opportunity for non-governmental organisations and others with experience and expertise in the field to contribute to the development of South Africa's socio-economic rights jurisprudence.[57] They have

52 Ibid para 25.

53 Ibid para 24.

54 Ibid para 40.

55 Ibid para 36.

56 Rule 10 of the Rules of the Constitutional Court, Government Notice R1675, *Government Gazette* 25726, 31 October 2003. Similar provisions exist with regard to *amici* interventions in the High Courts and the Supreme Court of Appeal.

57 For example, the Community Law Centre (University of the Western Cape) and the South African Human Rights Commission intervened as joint *amici curiae* in the *Grootboom* (note 2 above) case, and contributed to developing the arguments in relation to s 26 of the Constitution. See also M Heywood 'Debunking "conglomo talk": A case study of the amicus curiae as an instrument for advocacy, investigation and mobilization' (2001) 5 *LDD*

the potential to enrich our socio-economic rights jurisprudence by presenting alternative arguments and perspectives.[58]

A major problem in the South African context remains the problem of access to legal services for the poor. As Cameron JA pointed out in the *Ngxuza* decision, '[t]he law is a scarce resource in South Africa'.[59] Section 35(3) of the Constitution expressly guarantees the right to legal representation at state expense in criminal trials 'if substantial injustice would otherwise result'.[60] However, s 34, which guarantees a right of access to courts, does not expressly confer a right to legal representation. Nevertheless, a substantive interpretation of this right would require that the State take positive financial and administrative measures to ensure equal and effective access to the courts by all. Without such access, the role of Courts as important deliberative forums on the meaning and implications of constitutional rights is seriously devalued. As Geoff Budlender has argued:

> Access to justice should be a core concern of the courts, for it goes to the very essence of their function. If people in need are not able to bring their cases to court and present them effectively, then the courts cannot satisfactorily perform the function entrusted to them by the Constitution. [61]

A system of State legal aid for indigent persons in criminal and civil cases is provided through the Legal Aid Board. The Board has converted from a *judicare* system (state funding for private attorneys and advocates) to the establishment of Justice Centres envisaged as 'one-stop legal aid shops'. However, this system still excludes a large proportion of the population due to the strict financial means test, lack of physical access to Justice Centres, particularly in rural areas, and the bias towards funding for criminal

133–162; L Chenwi 'Litigating socio-economic rights through *amicus briefs*' (2009) 10 *ESR Review* 7–10.

[58] See, for example, the acknowledgment in the various judgments of the usefulness of the *amici curiae* submissions in the recent judgment of the Constitutional Court in *Residents of Joe Slovo Community, Western Cape v Thubelisha Homes, Minister for Housing and Minister of Local Government and Housing, Western Cape (Centre on Housing Rights and Evictions and Community Law Centre, University of the Western Cape as amici curiae)* [2009] ZACC 16, 2009 (9) BCLR 847 (CC). This case is discussed in chapter 6, part 6.5.

[59] *Ngxuza (SCA)* (note 39 above) para 1. See also *Mohlomi v Minister of Defence* 1997 (1) SA 124 (CC), 1996 (12) BCLR 1559 (CC) para 14.

[60] Section 35(3)(*g*). Important guidelines on the interpretation of the phrase, 'substantial injustice' in this context were provided by the Constitutional Court in *S v Vermaas; S v Du Plessis* 1995 (3) SA 292 (CC), 1995 (7) BCLR 851 (CC). Didcott J for the Court also expressed concern regarding the apparent tardiness of the State to adopt the necessary financial and administrative measures to give effect to this right. He observed that the right to legal representation at State expense 'becomes an empty gesture and makes a mockery of the Constitution ... if it is not backed by mechanisms that are adequate for the enforcement of the right' (para 16). Subsequent to this judgment there has been some improvement in legal representation for persons facing criminal charges. See G Budlender 'Access to courts' (2004) 121 *SALJ* 339–358 at 351.

[61] Ibid 355.

over civil matters.[62] Most public interest socio-economic cases are run or supported by non-governmental organisations dependent on donor funding, such as the Legal Resources Centre, Lawyers for Human Rights, the Women's Legal Centre, the AIDS Law Project, the Centre for Applied Legal Studies, and the Community Law Centre. University law clinics play an important role in extending access to legal services, particularly in 'bread and butter' civil cases. There are also a number of grassroots organisations and social movements who do vital work in educating communities concerning their rights, and working jointly with them in deciding whether and under what conditions to pursue public interest litigation.[63]

Despite these initiatives, many people in South Africa experience violations of socio-economic rights, which go unchallenged due to a lack of access to legal services. A concerted multi-prong strategy is needed to ensure consistent access to good quality legal services for disadvantaged communities. This is a critical challenge if socio-economic rights are to play a meaningful role in facilitating transformation in South Africa.[64]

A generous and flexible approach to legal standing, *amicus curiae* interventions and substantially expanded access to legal services are vital to enabling a broader range of groups to enforce socio-economic rights. The direct participation by disadvantaged groups in socio-economic rights litigation is essential to conveying the impact and social consequences of poverty by those directly affected. This should in turn contribute to developing a jurisprudence on socio-economic rights which is more attuned to the needs and circumstances of these groups.[65]

3.2.4 Limitation of rights

Traditionally, constitutional analysis under the Bill of Rights entails a 'two-stage approach'. The first stage concerns the interpretation of the scope of the relevant right and whether the challenged law, conduct or omission amounts to a *prima facie*

---

62 See the analysis by M Heywood & A Hassim 'Remedying the maladies of "lesser men or women": The personal, political and constitutional imperatives for improved access to justice' (2008) 24 *SAJHR* 263–280 at 273–277. On proposals to extend access to legal services through pro bono and community service initiatives, see J Brickhill 'The right to a fair civil trial: The duties of lawyers and law students to act pro bono' (2005) 21 *SAJHR* 293–322.

63 For a perspective on the role of these movements and their engagement with the legal system in South Africa's constitutional democracy, see T Madlingozi 'The Constitutional Court, court watchers and the commons: A reply to Professor Michelman on constitutional dialogue, "interpretive charity" and the citizens as sangomas' (2008) 1 *CCR* 63–75.

64 See the analysis and proposals by J Dugard 'Courts and the poor in South Africa: A critique of systemic judicial failures to advance transformative justice' (2008) 24 *SAJHR* 214–238.

65 See the critique by Madlingozi (note 63 above) of the lack of engagement and responsiveness by legal elites to the realities and claims of social movements and community organisations.

breach of the right. The burden of adducing evidence and persuading the court at this first stage rests on the applicant. If an infringement of the relevant right is established, the burden shifts to the State (or private respondent) to persuade the court that the right has been justifiably limited in terms of the general limitations clause (s 36).[66]

Section 36(1) of the Constitution provides that the rights in the Bill of Rights may be limited 'only in terms of law of general application to the extent that the limitation is reasonable and justifiable in an open and democratic society based on human dignity, equality and freedom'. In order to determine whether a limitation is 'reasonable and justifiable' a court must consider 'all relevant factors, including –

(*a*) the nature of the right;
(*b*) the importance of the purpose of the limitation;
(*c*) the nature and extent of the limitation;
(*d*) the relation between the limitation and its purpose; and
(*e*) less restrictive means to achieve the purpose.

A precondition for invoking the general limitations clause is the existence of a law of general application. This incorporates all forms of legislation, as well as rules of the common law and customary law. Policies, practices and programmes do not generally constitute laws of general application.[67] In the context of socio-economic rights cases which often involve challenges to the State's failure to enact the necessary legislation or adopt comprehensive programmes,[68] the State will not be able to rely on the general limitations clause should it be found that the relevant right has been infringed.

The advantage of a law of general application in the form of parliamentary legislation is that the purpose, extent and means of restricting rights are publicly debated

[66] See Currie & De Waal (note 33 above) 165–168, and the jurisprudence cited by them here. However, as the authors point out, the Court does not always adhere to this two-stage process, and may conduct a limitations analysis on a 'hypothetical' assumption that a rights violation has occurred: see, for example, *Christian Education South Africa v Minister of Education* 2000 (4) SA 757 (CC), 2000 (10) BCLR 1051 (CC); *S v Jordan* 2002 (6) SA 642 (CC), 2002 (11) BCLR 1117 (CC) paras 28–29. See the criticism by Currie & De Waal of the elision of the first stage of constitutional analysis at 166 (footnote 11). For a recent affirmation of the importance of the 'two-stage approach', see *Director of Public Prosecutions, Transvaal v Minister for Justice and Constitutional Development* 2009 (4) SA 222 (CC), 2009 (7) BCLR 637 (CC) para 141.

[67] Currie & De Waal argue that '[a] mere policy or practice (even of an organ of state) cannot qualify as "law"' (note 33 above) 169. See *August* (note 26 above) para 23; *Hoffmann v South African Airways* 2001 (1) SA 1 (CC), 2000 (11) BCLR 1211 para 41. Compare the discussion by S Woolman & H Botha 'Limitations' in S Woolman *et al* (eds) *Constitutional Law of South Africa* 2 ed OS (2006) chapter 34 at 53, n 3 and the views of the authors cited there.

[68] See, for example, *Treatment Action Campaign* (note 47 above) which entailed a challenge, based on the right of access to health care services in s 27 of the Constitution, to government's refusal to adopt a comprehensive programme to reduce mother-to-child transmission of HIV.

and considered in terms of the democratic process. Parliament and provincial legislatures are constitutionally obliged to facilitate public participation in the legislative process.[69] Where rights are limited in terms of executive policy decisions and practices, there is less scope for democratic participation in these decisions both by legislatures and the general public. The lack of scope for public participation is compounded by the lack of transparency in the manner in which executive decision-making frequently occurs.

A limitation will only be considered 'reasonable and justifiable' if the purpose of the limitation is sufficiently important and consonant with an open and democratic society based on human dignity, equality and freedom. Moreover, the means selected to fulfil this purpose must be proportional to the purpose sought to be achieved. The factors listed in (*a*) to (*e*) of s 36(1) are important considerations for guiding the proportionality inquiry to be conducted by the courts. A crucial consideration is whether the purpose of the limitation could have been achieved through less restrictive means.

During the second stage the respondent must place before the court appropriate evidence regarding the purpose that is sought to be achieved by the limitation and the likelihood of the underlying policy advancing this purpose. This includes, for example, sociological or statistical data.[70] If the State fails to place such evidence and arguments before the court, it runs the risk of failing to persuade the court that the limitation is reasonable and justifiable.[71]

The general limitations inquiry institutes a relational approach to rights adjudication which is not premised on rigid boundaries between individual rights and collective interests. As Henk Botha notes, '[It] focuses on the relationship between a fundamental-rights limitation and its purpose and/or the comparative weight of competing rights and interests'.[72] It is also

---

[69] See ss 59, 72 and 118 of the Constitution; *Doctors for Life International v Speaker of the National Assembly* 2006 (6) SA 416 (CC), 2006 (12) BCLR 1399 (CC).

[70] Rule 31(1) of the Rules of the Constitutional Court (note 56 above) makes provision for the introduction of relevant factual material '[p]rovided that such facts: (*a*) are common cause or otherwise incontrovertible; or (*b*) are of an official, scientific, technical or statistical nature and capable of easy verification.'

[71] See *Moise v Greater Germiston Transitional Local Council* 2001 (4) SA 491 (CC), 2001 (8) BCLR 765 (CC) para 19. In *NICRO* (note 26 above), the Court held that it may not always be possible to prove that 'a policy directed to a particular concern will be effective' (para 35). In these circumstances, a court was entitled to evaluate the justification claim on the basis of 'common sense and judicial knowledge' (para 36). However, in this case which concerned the right of prisoners to vote, the Court refused to uphold the limitations argument as there was no clear evidence of the policy objectives which the State sought to achieve through disenfranchising prisoners (paras 65–67).

[72] H Botha 'Metaphoric reasoning and transformative constitutionalism (part 2)' (2003) 1 *TSAR* 20–36 at 26. He discusses the balancing metaphor in limitations analysis and its implications for transformative constitutionalism at 26–31.

> dialogic to the extent that it institutes a debate about the cogency of the justifications offered for the limitation of a fundamental right, and requires judges to articulate the substantive reasons for their decisions, rather than simply declare the case to fall within a particular category.[73]

Thus Botha describes the Constitutional Court's limitations jurisprudence as 'an attempt to place relationship and context at the centre of fundamental-rights litigation, and thus to avoid the rigidity of a categorisation approach'.[74]

In the context of an alleged breach of the positive duties imposed by ss 26 and 27, the entire justification argument will occur in the context of the internal 'reasonableness' test where there is no requirement of a law of general application. In chapter 4, the various factors which should inform the standard of scrutiny to be applied in the context of this internal reasonableness test are discussed.[75]

The reasonableness model of review developed by the Constitutional Court to assess compliance with the positive duties imposed by ss 26 and 27 also has the potential to facilitate a relational and dialogic approach to rights adjudication.[76] The reasonableness of the State's conduct or omissions should be assessed in the light of the values and interests which the rights protect, the impact of the deprivation on the claimant group, and the state's resource and other justifications for failing to extend access to the relevant rights.

However, it will be argued in the following chapter that reasonableness analysis in terms of ss 26 and 27 tends to elide the initial critical stage of engaging with the substantive content and implications of the particular socio-economic rights.[77] In addition, unlike the general limitations clause, reasonableness review in terms of ss 26(2) and 27(2) does not incorporate an express proportionality requirement. However, a proportionality analysis is arguably inherent in the criteria developed by the Court for evaluating the reasonableness of the State's conduct.[78] There is also a concern that justifications based on resource constraints will not be subject to the rigorous scrutiny to which they are subject in terms of the general limitations clause.[79] A consideration of resource constraints as a justification for failing to give effect to a socio-economic right must engage with the question whether the State's allocation decisions and prioritisation of resources are consistent with an open and democratic

---

[73] Ibid.

[74] Ibid 26.

[75] Chapter 4, part 4.4.5.

[76] The Court has expressly refrained from deciding whether 'reasonableness' in terms of ss 26(2) and 27(2) bears the same meaning as that in s 36. See *Khosa v Minister of Social Development; Mahlaule v Minister of Social Development* 2004 (6) SA 505 (CC), 2004 (6) BCLR 569 (CC) ('*Khosa*') paras 83–84. Reasonable review is analysed and evaluated in chapter 4, parts 4.3 and 4.4.

[77] See particularly the discussion in chapter 4, part 4.4.2.

[78] On the criteria for assessing reasonableness, see chapter 4, part 4.3.3.

[79] See in this regard *NICRO* (note 26 above) paras 47–51, and the discussion in chapter 4, parts 4.4.4 and 4.4.5.

society committed to the values of human dignity, equality and freedom.[80] Finally, there is no requirement in the internal 'reasonableness' test in terms of ss 26 and 27 that limitations may only be effected through a law of general application. It is thus incumbent on courts when scrutinising the reasonableness of the State's justifications in terms of ss 26 and 27 to be sensitive to the possibility that there has been a lack of democratic deliberation in making the relevant policy choices. A lack of meaningful engagement with affected communities should be an important fact weighing against finding a particular policy or measure reasonable in the context of socio-economic rights litigation.[81]

These difficulties arise only in the context of the positive duties imposed by the rights in ss 26 and 27. The Court has carved out a clear role for the general limitations clause where it identifies a breach of the negative duty in ss 26(1) and 27(1) not to deprive people of their existing access to the relevant rights.[82] However, this disjuncture in the way the Court treats negative and positive violations of socio-economic rights arguably perpetuates the classic liberal dichotomy between negative and positive rights.[83]

Interpreted substantively, both the internal reasonableness inquiry in ss 26 and 27 and the general limitations clause are capable of facilitating a transparent evaluation of the rights at stake for claimants, possible competing rights and countervailing public policy considerations. There can never be a perfect resolution of the tensions inherent in this exercise. Its value lies in exposing to reasoned deliberation and public scrutiny the constitutional issues at stake and the (inevitably imperfect) methods of their resolution. This is one of the important ways in which adjudication can promote the type of deliberation which animates transformative constitutionalism.

3.3 INTERPRETATION

3.3.1 The values of human dignity, equality and freedom

Section 39(1)(*a*) of the Constitution provides that when interpreting the Bill of Rights, a court, tribunal or forum 'must promote the values that underlie an open and democratic society based on human dignity, equality and freedom'.

This affirms the central role assigned by the Constitution to the values of democracy, human dignity, equality and freedom in the interpretation of the rights in the Bill of Rights. As expressed by Sachs J in *Sidumo v Rustenburg Platinum Mines Ltd* ('*Sidumo*')[84]

---

[80] See further chapter 4, part 4.4.4.

[81] See the discussion of the jurisprudence on 'meaningful engagement' in the context of eviction cases, in chapter 6, parts 6.4 and 6.5.

[82] *Jaftha* (note 26 above) para 34. See chapter 4, parts 4.6–4.7.

[83] See in this regard, chapter 2, part 2.4.4.

[84] 2008 (2) SA 24 (CC), 2008 (2) BCLR 158 (CC).

> The values of the Constitution are strong, explicit and clearly intended to be considered part of the very texture of the constitutional project. They are implicit in the very structure and design of the new democratic order. The letter and the spirit of the Constitution cannot be separated; just as the values are not free-floating, ready to alight as mere adornments on this or that provision, so is the text not self-supporting, awaiting occasional evocative enhancement. The role of constitutional values is certainly not to provide a patina of virtue to otherwise bald, neutral and discrete legal propositions. Text and values work together in integral fashion to provide the protections promised by the Constitution.[85]

Section 39(1)(*a*) also requires the court to actively *promote* these values in interpreting the rights. This underscores the important role which the Constitution gives the courts of safeguarding and promoting the founding values of our society. It also indicates that the primary orientation of the South African Constitution is towards positive as opposed to negative constitutionalism. Herein lies the major distinction between transformative as opposed to preservative constitutionalism. Transformative constitutionalism is committed to positive measures to redress both the legacy of the past as well as new and emerging forms of subordination that deny human dignity, equality and freedom to certain groups in our society.[86]

The Constitutional Court's equality jurisprudence, in particular, has generally evinced a substantive, as opposed to a formal, approach to these values. This entails a critical examination of economic and social institutions and relationships to ascertain their impact on the participation of disadvantaged groups in all spheres of our young democracy. As Cathi Albertyn observes:

> [T]he claim for substantive equality has emerged from the recognition that inequality not only emerges from irrational legal distinctions, but is often more deeply rooted in social and economic cleavages between groups in society. Such inequalities are referred to as 'systemic' as they are rooted in the structures, systems and institutions of society. Legal claims (usually of discrimination) that target such inequalities require an understanding of the underlying social and economic conditions that create and reinforce these inequalities, if such claims are to remedy inequality. [87]

Various theoretical attempts to explicate socio-economic rights in terms of the values of human dignity, equality and freedom have been discussed in chapter 2.[88] I have argued that each of these values illuminates important dimensions of socio-economic rights, and that it would be a mistake to attempt to justify socio-economic rights exclusively in terms of one or the other value. In any event these values are interlinked, and each expresses important dimensions of our lives as individual and social

[85] Ibid para 149 (footnotes omitted).

[86] See in this regard chapter 2, part 2.2.

[87] C Albertyn 'Equality' in H Cheadle, D Davis & N Haysom (eds) *South African Constitutional Law: The Bill of Rights* (2006) 1–65 at 5. See also chapter 2, part 2.4.3.

[88] Chapter 2, part 2.4.2.

beings. Kriegler J refers to human dignity, equality and freedom as 'conjoined, reciprocal and covalent values' which are 'foundational' to South Africa.[89]

However, if these values are to inform a transformative interpretation of socio-economic rights, we must draw on traditions of philosophy and social theory which support the positive, relational potential of these values. There is a tradition of scholarship which associates particularly the values of human dignity and freedom with 'negative' freedom and is based on a conception of individuals as isolated, atomistic beings.[90] This is at odds with both the positive, redistributive role envisaged for the State by various provisions of the Constitution and a socially interconnected and embodied concept of humanity.[91]

The interdependence between individuals and communities is captured in the South African context by the concept of *ubuntu,* explained as follows by Sachs J in *Port Elizabeth Municipality v Various Occupiers*[92] ('*Port Elizabeth Municipality*'):

> The spirit of *ubuntu*, part of the deep cultural heritage of the majority of the population, suffuses the whole constitutional order. It combines individual rights with a communitarian philosophy. It is a unifying motif of the Bill of Rights, which is nothing if not a structured, institutionalised and operational declaration in our evolving new society of the need for human interdependence, respect and concern.[93]

Mokgoro J gives content to this notion of interdependence and mutual responsibility when she observes:

> Sharing responsibility for the problems and consequences of poverty equally as a community represents the extent to which wealthier members of the community view the minimal well-being of the poor as connected with their personal well-being and the well-being of the community as a whole. In other words, decisions about the allocation

---

[89] *S v Mamabolo* 2001 (3) SA 409 (CC), 2001 (5) BCLR 449 (CC) para 41. In *Sidumo* (note 84 above) para 149 Sachs J observed that the constitutional values 'by their nature … resist compartmentalisation'. See also Ackermann J's comments on the interlinkages between dignity and freedom in *Ferreira* (note 33 above) para 49.

[90] See, for example, I Berlin 'Two concepts of liberty' in *Four Essays on Liberty* (1969) 118–172. See also the critiques of the Constitutional Court's deployment of human dignity as a value in its early equality jurisprudence: D Davis 'Equality: The majesty of legoland jurisprudence' (1999) 116 *SALJ* 398–414; C Albertyn & B Goldblatt 'Facing the challenge of transformation: Difficulties in the development of an indigenous jurisprudence of equality' (1998) 14 *SAJHR* 248–276. Attempts have also been made to demonstrate that human dignity as a value is capable of being interpreted in ways that are more consonant with the transformative ethos of the Constitution: see, for example, S Cowen 'Can "dignity" guide South Africa's equality jurisprudence?' (2001) 17 *SAJHR* 34–58; S Liebenberg 'The value of human dignity in interpreting socio-economic rights' (2005) 21 *SAJHR* 1–31; C Albertyn (note 87 above) 8–10.

[91] See in this regard *National Coalition for Gay and Lesbian Equality v Minister of Justice* 1999 (1) SA 6 (CC), 1998 (12) BCLR 1517 (CC) para 117; *Bernstein v Bester* 1996 (2) SA 751 (CC), 1996 (4) BCLR 449 (CC) para 67.

[92] 2005 (1) SA 217 (CC), 2004 (12) BCLR 1268 (CC).

[93] Ibid para 37 (footnotes omitted).

> of public benefits represent the extent to which poor people are treated as equal members of society.[94]

The Constitutional Court has held on a number of occasions that the core constitutional values of human dignity, equality and freedom are implicated in circumstances of material deprivation. In *Soobramoney v Minister of Health (KwaZulu-Natal)*,[95] Chaskalson P (as he then was) affirmed that the Constitution commits us to transforming the 'deplorable conditions' and 'great poverty' in which people live, in order to give effect to the values of human dignity, freedom and equality. He went on to observe that, '[f]or as long as these conditions continue to exist that aspiration will have a hollow ring'.[96] In *Grootboom*, the Court stated that the issues in the case were a reminder of the intolerable conditions under which many people in South Africa were still living. They brought home 'the harsh reality that the Constitution's promise of dignity and equality for all remains a distant dream'.[97] The Court draws particularly on the value of human dignity to justify the component of the reasonableness test which requires measures to respond to the needs of those most desperate.[98]

These are positive indications that the Court is promoting positive, relational interpretations of the foundational constitutional values of human dignity, equality and freedom in its evolving socio-economic rights jurisprudence. Giving meaning and substance to the foundational values in this manner is essential for the transformative trajectory of socio-economic rights jurisprudence.

Although not explicitly referred to in s 39(1), the commitment to a society based on 'social justice' in the preamble to the Constitution is also important in developing the substantive content of the founding constitutional values of human dignity, equality and freedom.[99] It signals our Constitution's commitment to creating political, economic and social institutions and relationships that enable people to develop in all dimensions of their humanity and participate as equals in our democracy. Social justice has particular resonance in socio-economic rights adjudication, as the deep

---

94 *Khosa* (note 76 above) para 74.

95 1998 (1) SA 765 (CC), 1997 (12) BCLR 1696 (CC) para 8.

96 Ibid.

97 *Grootboom* (note 2 above) para 2; *Khosa* (note 76 above) paras 40–44.

98 *Grootboom* (note 2 above) para 44; *Khosa* (note 76 above) paras 80–82. See also chapter 4, part 4.3.3 at note 114 and accompanying text.

99 In *S v Mhlungu* 1995 (3) SA 867 (CC), 1995 (7) BCLR 793 (CC) para 112 Sachs J makes the following observations concerning the significance of the preamble to the transitional Constitution:

> The preamble in particular should not be dismissed as a mere aspirational and throat-clearing exercise of little interpretive value. It connects up, reinforces and underlies all of the text that follows. It helps to establish the basic design of the Constitution and indicates its fundamental purposes.

See further the discussion in L M du Plessis *Re-Interpretation of Statutes* (2002) 239–242.

levels of poverty and socio-economic inequality represent stark manifestations of social injustice in South Africa.[100]

3.3.2 International law

(*a*) Broadening the dialogue

Section 39(1)(*b*) of the Constitution requires that, when interpreting the Bill of Rights, a court 'must consider international law'. This provision signals the Constitution's openness and receptiveness to the norms and values of the international community. It also resonates with the reciprocal way in which international law and institutions supported the struggle against apartheid, and were in turn influenced by this struggle. At the same time, it helps give effect to the constitutional commitment, as reflected in the preamble, to '[b]uild a united and democratic South Africa able to take its rightful place as a sovereign state in the family of nations'. This expresses South Africa's aspiration to be a part of the international community, to adhere to its normative standards, and to contribute to the development of international law based on our domestic experiences of human rights and democratic transformation.[101]

The deliberative vision of democracy and human rights supported by the Constitution extends beyond the boundaries of our nation state to incorporate the broader international community. The process of interpreting and giving meaning to human rights norms can be understood as a dialogic process which includes a range of national and international actors. This may be one of the more positive features of globalisation, where the meaning accorded to fundamental human rights norms can be influenced by a cross-cultural dialogue extending across national boundaries. As Kent Roach observes:

> A globalized world is one where people, including judges, engage in multiple and ongoing conversations that cross borders. It is hopefully a world characterized by a sense of openness, modesty, and willingness to learn from others.[102]

Roach characterises a dialogic conception of rights as involving 'an interaction of multiple sources of authority'. He contrasts it with 'a more monological and positivistic conception of authority and with judicial supremacy in enforcing constitutional rights and remedies'.[103] A dialogic conception of the interpretation of human rights is thus receptive to outside influence, and is more concerned with the persuasive force of legal arguments than their formal pedigree or binding character.

---

[100] On the possibility of social justice playing a similar role to the social state principle in German and Colombian constitutional law, see 3.3.3(*b*)(ii) below.

[101] O'Regan J notes in *Kaunda v President of the Republic of South Africa* 2005 (4) SA 235 (CC), 2004 (10) BCLR 1009 (CC) para 222 that 'our Constitution recognises and asserts that, after decades of isolation, South Africa is now a member of the community of nations, and a bearer of obligations and responsibilities in terms of international law'.

[102] K Roach 'Constitutional, remedial, and international dialogues about rights: The Canadian experience' (2004–2005) 40 *Texas Int L J* 537–576 at 538.

[103] Ibid 539.

The express openness of the Constitution to international and comparative law in the interpretation of the Bill of Rights supports this deliberative or dialogic conception of human rights. Engagement with both international and comparative law sources in adjudicating the rights in the Bill of Rights can generate new ways of understanding and interpreting these rights and thereby support transformative adjudication. It can also promote a greater awareness of the reality that South Africa is located in an increasingly interdependent world in which human rights are no longer viewed as exclusively matters of domestic concern.

(*b*) International law as interpretative guide and as binding law

In the context of using international law to interpret the rights in the Bill of Rights, the Court has held that reference may be had to both binding as well as non-binding international law.[104] The latter may include treaties to which South Africa is not a party[105] or those it is precluded from ratifying.[106] It may even include appropriate, 'soft' international law.[107] The latter are standards which have not yet crystallised into treaty provisions or norms of customary international law. They include resolutions adopted at international conferences organised under the auspices of the United Nations or regional bodies such as the African Union,[108] guidelines adopted by international organisations,[109] or reports and guidelines issued by special rapporteurs, working groups and other non-treaty based international mechanisms.[110] This is a powerful vindication of the notion that, in interpreting the rights in the Bill of

[104] *S v Makwanyane* 1995 (3) SA 391 (CC), 1995 (6) BCLR 665 (CC) para 35 ('*Makwanyane*').

[105] Such as, for example, the International Covenant on Economic, Social and Cultural Rights (1966), which is the only major international human rights treaty which South Africa has not yet ratified.

[106] Such as, for example, the European Convention for the Protection of Human Rights and Fundamental Freedoms (1950) and the American Convention on Human Rights (1969).

[107] An indication that 'soft' international law is included among the 'tools of interpretation' which the Court may consider is Chaskalson P's (as he then was) reference in *Makwanyane* (note 104 above) para 35 to 'reports of specialised agencies such as the International Labour Organisation'.

[108] For example, the *Vienna Declaration and Programme of Action* adopted in 1993 by UN World Conference on Human Rights, UN doc A/CONF. 157/23; the *Beijing Declaration and Platform for Action* adopted in 1995 by the Fourth World Conference on Women, UN doc A/CONF.177/20; and the *Johannesburg Declaration on Sustainable Development* (2002) A/CONF.199.L6.

[109] For example, the *Voluntary Guidelines to Support the Progressive Realisation of the Right to Adequate Food in the Context of National Food Security*, adopted by the 127th session of the Food and Agricultural Organisation (FAO) Council, 2004.

[110] For example, the *Basic Principles and Guidelines on Development-Based Evictions and Displacement* developed under the auspices of the UN Special Rapporteur on adequate housing as a component of the right to an adequate standard of living, Miloon Kothari, UN doc A/HRC/4/18, 5 February 2007 (Annex 1). On the relevance of the *Basic*

Rights, the South African courts are to have regard to the persuasive authority of a variety of international instruments on human rights without being limited to formally binding international law sources.[111] International law that is binding on South Africa includes primarily treaties to which it is a State party as well as norms of customary international law.[112]

The use of international law for the purposes of interpreting the Bill of Rights in terms of s 39(1)(*b*) must be distinguished from the binding status of international law in domestic law. Section 39(1)(*b*) refers to interpretative guides which the Court 'must consider', but is not bound to follow. As has been observed, the Court has adopted a flexible approach to the sources that may be referred to during the process of interpreting the Bill of Rights.

In contrast, international law becomes binding within South African domestic law through the provisions of ss 231 and 232 of the Constitution. In this regard, South Africa basically follows a dualist system regarding international treaties, requiring ratified treaties to be 'enacted into law' by national legislation before they acquire binding force in domestic law.[113] The only exception is in relation to 'self-executing' treaty provisions, which are law in the Republic unless inconsistent with the Constitution or an Act of Parliament.[114]

The question of what constitutes a self-executing treaty provision has been notoriously controversial and difficult to define. It is mainly understood to refer to provisions of a treaty that can be directly applied in municipal law without the need for legislative incorporation.[115] In an early General Comment, the UN Committee on Economic, Social and Cultural Rights[116] indicated that the following provisions of

Principles and Guidelines to South Africa's jurisprudence on evictions, see chapter 6, part 6.5 at note 248.

111 See also J Dugard *International Law: A South African Perspective* 3 ed (2005) 65–66.

112 Customary international law is one of the sources of international law described in art 38(1) of the Statute of the International Court of Justice as 'a general practice accepted as law'. A rule of customary international law generally binds all states in the international community unless a particular state can show that it is a persistent objector to an emerging rule of customary international law. However, certain norms of customary international law, such as the prohibition on torture, have the status of *ius cogens* from which no derogation is permitted (art 53, Vienna Convention on the Law of Treaties, 1969). See further in this regard Dugard ibid 29–34; 43–46.

113 Section 231(4) of the Constitution. The process for ratifying international agreements such as treaties are set out in ss 231(1)–(3) of the Constitution.

114 Section 231(4) of the Constitution.

115 See Dugard (note 111 above) 62. On self-executing treaty provisions in the context of socio-economic rights, see M Scheinin 'Direct applicability of economic, social and cultural rights: A critique of the doctrine of self-executing treaties' in K Drzewicki, C Krause & A Rosas (eds) *Social Rights as Human Rights: A European Challenge* (1994) 73–87.

116 On the International Covenant on Economic, Social and Cultural Rights (1966) and the legal status of the 'General Comments' issued by the UN Committee on Economic, Social and Cultural Rights, see note 132 below.

the International Covenant on Economic, Social and Cultural Rights are capable of immediate application by judicial and other organs in national legal systems: the right of men and women to the equal enjoyment of economic, social and cultural rights (art 3);[117] the right to fair wages and equal remuneration for work of equal value (art 7(*a*)(i)); trade union rights (art 8); special measures of protection and assistance to children (art 10(3)); the right to free and compulsory primary education (art 13(2)(*a*)); the right to establish and send one's children to private educational institutions subject to certain conditions (arts 13(3) and (4)); and respecting the freedom 'indispensable for scientific research and creative activity' (art 15(3)). The Committee comments that '[a]ny suggestion that these provisions are inherently non-self-executing would seem to be difficult to sustain'.[118] In its later General Comment on the domestic application of the Covenant[119] the Committee commented that it is especially important 'to avoid any *a priori* assumption' that the norms in the Covenant should be considered to be non-self-executing. It goes on to observe that many of these norms 'are stated in terms which are at least as clear and specific as those in other human rights treaties, the provisions of which are regularly deemed by courts to be self-executing'.[120]

In contrast to treaty provisions, customary international law is part of South African domestic law 'unless it is inconsistent with the Constitution or an Act of Parliament'.[121] The question whether any socio-economic or cultural right forms part of customary international law is a difficult one. These rights are included in the Universal Declaration of Human Rights (1948),[122] and a range of international and regional human rights treaties. However, the question is whether there is sufficient state practice (*usus*) and the opinion on the part of states that a particular socio-economic right is legally binding (*opinio juris*) to support its status as a customary law norm. Undoubtedly, in certain contexts some of the rights have attained the status of customary international law, or are in the process of crystallising as norms of customary law. These include, for example, the intentional deprivation of food, potable water and medical care in respect of civilians and non-combatants in armed conflicts, or the mass forced eviction or displacement of groups without basic substantive and procedural safeguards.[123]

---

[117] See also UN Committee on Economic, Social and Cultural Rights, General Comment No 16 (Thirty-fourth sess, 2005) *Article 3: the equal right of men and women to the enjoyment of all economic, social and cultural rights*, UN doc E/C 12/2005/3.

[118] UN Committee on Economic, Social and Cultural Rights, General Comment No 3 (Fifth sess, 1990) *The nature of states parties obligations (art 2(1) of the Covenant)* UN doc E/1991/23 para 5.

[119] UN Committee on Economic, Social and Cultural Rights, General Comment No 9 (Nineteenth sess, 1998) *Domestic application of the Covenant* UN doc E/1999/22.

[120] Ibid para 11.

[121] Section 232 of the Constitution.

[122] On the legal status of the Universal Declaration of Human Rights, see note 126 below.

[123] For example, the definition of the crime of 'genocide' in The Statute of the International Criminal Court (1998) includes '[d]eliberately inflicting on the group conditions of life

Section 232 of the Constitution indicates that its provisions trump any conflicting customary international law norm.[124] Nevertheless, the relevant norm remains binding on South Africa as a matter of international law and South Africa will incur state responsibility under international law for breaches of these norms.

In addition, when interpreting any legislation, the courts are enjoined by the Constitution to 'prefer any reasonable interpretation of the legislation that is consistent with international law over any alternative interpretation that is inconsistent with international law'.[125] Thus legislation that affects people's socio-economic rights should be interpreted, as far as reasonably possible, to be in conformity with applicable international law. This provides additional impetus for the courts to interpret social and economic legislation in ways that take into account widely accepted international normative values. The full potential of s 233 has been largely unexplored to date in socio-economic rights advocacy and adjudication.

The following section focuses on the use of international law sources to interpret the socio-economic rights provisions in the Constitution.

(c) International law on socio-economic rights: Treaties and jurisprudence

Socio-economic rights are recognised in the Universal Declaration of Human Rights (1948),[126] and are protected in a wide range of international, regional and specialised human rights conventions.[127] This analysis will focus on the jurisprudence which

---

calculated to bring about its physical destruction in whole or in part' (art 6(*c*)). 'Crimes against humanity' are defined to include '[d]eportation or forcible transfer of population' (art 7(*d*)). The term, 'deportation or forcible transfer of population' is defined as the 'forced displacement of the persons concerned by expulsion or other coercive acts from the area in which they are lawfully present, without ground permitted under international law' (art 7(2)(*d*)). The definition of 'war crimes' includes '[i]ntentionally using starvation of civilians as a method of warfare by depriving them of objects indispensable to their survival, including wilfully impeding relief supplies as provided for under the Geneva Conventions' (art 8(2)(*b*)(xxv)).

124 See, for example, the decision in *Azanian People's Organisation (AZAPO) v President of the Republic of South Africa* 1996 (4) SA 671 (CC), 1996 (12) BCLR 1561 (CC) ('*AZAPO*'). For a critique of the reasoning in *AZAPO*, see Dugard (note 111 above) 67–69.

125 Section 233 of the Constitution.

126 See arts 22–26 of the Universal Declaration of Human Rights. The Declaration, as a resolution of the General Assembly, is not legally binding in its own right. Ian Brownlie and Guy S Goodwin-Gill *Basic Documents on Human Rights* 4 ed (2002) at 18 describe its status as follows:

> [S]ome of its provisions either constitute general principles of law (see the Statute of the International Court of Justice, Article 38(1)(*c*)), or represent elementary considerations of humanity. More important is its status as an authoritative guide, produced by the General Assembly, to the interpretation of the Charter [of the United Nations]. In this capacity the Declaration has considerable indirect legal effect, and is regarding by the Assembly and by some jurists as a part of the 'law of the United Nations'.

127 For an overview of the historical and normative development of international human rights law in relation to economic, social and cultural rights, see H J Steiner & P Alston

has emerged under the individual complaints procedures under the various treaties. However, it should be noted that the other major supervisory system, the periodic state reporting procedure, provided for under all the international and regional human rights treaties, also constitutes a significant source pertaining to the interpretation by the relevant treaty body of the rights protected under the treaty.

The major international convention protecting economic, social and cultural rights is the International Covenant on Economic, Social and Cultural Rights (1966) (ICESCR).[128] This is the sister Covenant to the International Covenant on Civil and Political Rights (1966) (ICCPR).[129] South Africa has ratified the ICCPR and its two Optional Protocols.[130] However, at the date of finalising this manuscript it had signed, but not ratified the ICESCR.[131]

Nevertheless, as noted in the previous section, non-binding international law can be used as a guide to interpreting the Bill of Rights in terms of s 39(1)(*b*). The main sources for interpreting the provisions of the ICESCR Covenant are accordingly the general comments adopted by the UN Committee on Economic, Social and

International Rights in Context: Law, Politics, Morals 3 ed (2000) 237–320.

[128] 993 UNTS 3. Adopted on 16 December 1966, and entered into force on 3 January 1976. As at 8 July 2009, there were 160 States Parties to ICESCR.

[129] 999 UNTS 171. Adopted on 16 December 1966, and entered into force on 23 March 1976. It has two Optional Protocols, the first concerning the right of individuals to submit 'communications' to the supervisory body under the Covenant, the Human Rights Committee, and the second concerning the abolition of the death penalty. As at 8 July 2009, there were 164 States Parties to the ICCPR. For the history behind the adoption of two separate Covenants, one protecting civil and political rights, the other economic, social and cultural rights, see M C R Craven *The International Covenant on Economic, Social and Cultural Rights: A Perspective on its Development* (1995) 16–22; C Scott 'The interdependence and permeability of human rights norms: Towards a partial fusion of the international covenants on human rights' (1989) 27 *OHLJ* 769–878 at 791–814; S Liebenberg 'The International Covenant on Economic, Social and Cultural Rights and its implications for South Africa' (1995) 11 *SAJHR* 359–378 at 360–362. A significant reason for their separation was the perception by States at the time that the nature of the obligations imposed by economic, social and cultural rights differed fundamentally from those imposed by civil and political rights. Consequently, States envisaged a different mechanism for the supervision of State parties' obligations under the two Covenants.

[130] South Africa ratified the ICCPR on 10 December 1998 and its two Optional Protocols on 28 August 2002. For an analysis of the significant indirect protection for social rights provided by the Human Rights Committee (the supervisory body under the ICCPR), see M Scheinin 'Human Rights Committee: Not only a committee on civil and political rights' in M Langford (ed) *Social Rights Jurisprudence: Emerging Trends in International and Comparative Law* (2008) 540–552.

[131] According to art 18 of the Vienna Convention on the Law of Treaties (1969) 8 ILM 679, although a State is not bound by a treaty that it has signed but not ratified, it is obliged to refrain from acts 'which would defeat the objects and purpose' of such a treaty.

Cultural Rights,[132] and the concluding observations of the Committee's review of States Parties' reports under the reporting mechanism in the Covenant.[133] This is due to the fact that the ICESCR has historically lacked an equivalent protocol to the first Optional Protocol to the ICCPR, providing for a right to submit individual communications to the treaty supervisory body.[134] This has now been rectified by the adoption of the Optional Protocol to the ICESCR by the General Assembly on 10 December 2008.[135]

The ICESCR is of particular relevance to the interpretation of ss 26, 27 and 29 because the Covenant was a major source of reference for the drafting of these provisions.[136] Both the ICESCR and the Constitution refer to the concepts of the taking of legislative measures, 'progressive realisation', and the limits of available resources.[137] However, the Court noted in *Grootboom* that there were differences in the formula-

---

[132] As at 30 November 2009, the Committee had adopted 21 general comments on various provisions of the ICESCR. The general comments are available at http://www2.ohchr.org/english/bodies/cescr/comments.htm (accessed on 25 July 2009). Although these comments are not legally binding, they carry persuasive weight as indications of how the primary supervisory organ in terms of the Covenant interprets its provisions. See in this regard Craven (note 129 above) 91–92.

[133] The reporting procedure is set out in arts 16–22 of the Covenant. See further M Craven 'Towards an unofficial petition procedure: A review on the role of the UN Committee on Economic, Social and Cultural Rights' in K Drzewicki, C Krause & A Rosas (eds) *Social Rights as Human Rights: A European Challenge* (1994) 91–113; P Alston 'Out of the abyss: The challenges confronting the new UN Committee on Economic, Social and Cultural Rights' (1987) 9 *HRQ* 332–381; M Langford & J King 'Committee on Economic, Social and Cultural Rights: Past, present and future' in M Langford (ed) *Social Rights Jurisprudence: Emerging Trends in International and Comparative Law* (2008) 477–516 at 479.

[134] See generally in this regard K Arambulo *Strengthening the Supervision of the International Covenant on Economic, Social and Cultural Rights: Theoretical and Procedural Aspects* (1999).

[135] Optional Protocol to the International Covenant on Economic, Social and Cultural Rights, UN doc resolution A/RES/63/117. For an overview of the history leading to the adoption of this Optional Protocol, see Langford & King (note 133 above) 514–516; L Chenwi 'Correcting the historical asymmetry between rights: The Optional Protocol to the International Covenant on Economic, Social and Cultural Rights' (2009) 9 *AHRLJ* 23–51.

[136] See chapter 1, part 1.5, notes 111–113 and accompanying text. See further J Fitzpatrick & R C Slye 'Economic and social rights – South Africa: Role of international standards in interpreting and implementing constitutionally guaranteed rights' (2003) 97 *AJIL* 669–680.

[137] Compare ss 26 and 27 with art 2(1) of the ICESCR which reads as follows:

> Each State Party to the present Covenant undertakes to take steps, individually and through international assistance and co-operation, especially economic and technical, to the maximum of its available resources, with a view to achieving progressively the full realization of the rights recognized in the present Covenant by all appropriate means, including particularly the adoption of legislative measures.

For an early but influential article on the nature of States Parties' obligations under the ICESCR, see P Alston & G Quinn 'The nature and scope of States Parties' obligations

tion of the relevant provisions, and that these were 'significant in determining the extent to which the provisions of the Covenant may be a guide to an interpretation of s 26'.[138] The Court highlighted the following differences in relation to the right to housing:[139]

(*a*) The Covenant provides for a *right to adequate housing* while s 26 provides for the *right of access* to adequate housing.

(*b*) The Covenant obliges states parties to take *appropriate* steps which must include legislation while the Constitution obliges the South African state to take *reasonable* legislative and other measures.

These differences were raised by the Court in the course of declining to accept the arguments of the *amici curiae* that s 26 should be interpreted to incorporate the concept of 'minimum core obligations' endorsed by the UN Committee on Economic, Social and Cultural Rights.[140] Nevertheless, the Court accepted the Committee's interpretation of the phrase, 'progressive realisation' as being 'in harmony with the context in which the phrase is used in our Constitution'.[141] It thus held that there 'is no reason not to accept that it bears the same meaning in the Constitution as in the document from which it was so clearly derived'.[142] As discussed in the following chapter, the Court raised a number of institutional, theoretical and practical concerns regarding the adoption of the concept of minimum core obligations in our constitutional jurisprudence on ss 26 and 27.[143] Ultimately, the Court should explain the particular interpretive approach it adopts on the basis of substantive considerations, rather than minor differences in the textual formulations between the Constitution and the ICESCR.

Economic, social and cultural rights are also protected in a range of specialised human rights treaties such as the International Convention on the Elimination of All Forms of Racial Discrimination (1966),[144] the Convention on the Elimination of All Forms of Discrimination against Women (1979),[145] the Convention on the Rights of the Child (1989),[146] and the Convention on the Rights of Persons with Disabilities (2006).[147] The race and women's conventions aim primarily at the elimination of discrimination on the grounds of race and sex respectively. However, they contain a number of provisions specifically relating to the equal enjoyment of economic,

---

under the International Covenant on Economic, Social and Cultural Rights' (1987) 9 *HRQ* 156–229.

[138] *Grootboom* (note 2 above) para 28.

[139] Ibid para 28.

[140] See further chapter 4, part 4.3.2.

[141] *Grootboom* (note 2 above) para 45.

[142] Ibid. See further chapter 4, part 4.4.3.

[143] Chapter 4, part 4.3.2.

[144] 660 UNTS 195 (ratified by South Africa on 10 December 1998).

[145] 1249 UNTS 13 (ratified by South Africa on 15 December 1995).

[146] 28 ILM 1456 (ratified by South Africa on 16 June 1995).

[147] UN doc A/61/611 (ratified by South Africa on 30 November 2007).

social and cultural rights. The race, women and disability conventions incorporate an optional individual petition procedure, thus generating jurisprudence on the interpretation of the protected rights in the context of concrete cases.[148] The children's rights convention contains a comprehensive range of economic, social and cultural rights pertaining to children. However, as it lacks an individual petition procedure, the interpretation of the convention rights must be derived from the review of States Parties' reports and from General Comments adopted by the Committee on the Rights of the Child.[149]

Socio-economic rights are also protected in various regional human rights instruments. The African Charter on Human and Peoples' Rights (1981) ('The African Charter')[150] contains a number of economic, social and cultural rights.[151] It also protects rights relating to self-determination, development, peace and security, and the

---

[148] Article 14 of the International Convention on the Elimination of All Forms of Racial Discrimination; Optional Protocol to the Convention on the Elimination of Discrimination Against Women (1999), 39 ILM 281. The latter Optional Protocol entered into force on 22 December 2000. South Africa has accepted the individual complaints procedure under both these treaties by making the necessary declaration in terms of art 14 of the race convention, and by acceding to the Optional Protocol to the women's convention on 18 October 2005. For an analysis of the jurisprudence pertaining to social rights by the treaty bodies under these conventions, see N Prouvez 'Committee on the Elimination of Racial Discrimination: Confronting racial discrimination and inequality in the enjoyment of economic, social and cultural rights' in M Langford (ed) *Social Rights Jurisprudence: Emerging Trends in International and Comparative Law* (2008) 517–539; L Farha 'Committee on the Elimination of Discrimination Against Women: Women claiming economic, social and cultural rights – The CEDAW potential' in M Langford (ed) *Social Rights Jurisprudence: Emerging Trends in International and Comparative Law* (2008) 553–568. See also the Optional Protocol to the Convention on the Rights of Persons with Disabilities (2007) (ratified by South Africa on 30 November 2007). On social rights of persons living with disabilities, see generally N Ziv 'The social rights of people with disabilities: Reconciling care and justice' in D Barak-Erez & A M Gross (eds) *Exploring Social Rights: Between Theory and Practice* (2007) 369–395.

[149] See G van Bueren 'Committee on the Rights of the Child: Overcoming inertia in this age of no alternatives' in M Langford (ed) *Social Rights Jurisprudence: Emerging Trends in International and Comparative Law* (2008) 569–587.

[150] 21 ILM 59 (1982) (as at 1 July 2009, 53 African States had ratified the African Charter).

[151] Articles 15–18. The African Charter was ratified by South Africa on 9 July 1996. See generally J Oloka-Onyango 'Beyond the rhetoric: Reinvigorating the struggle for economic, social and cultural rights in Africa' (1995) 26 *Cal W Int'l L J* 1–71; C A Odinkalu 'Implementing economic, social and cultural rights under the African Charter on Human and Peoples' Rights' in M Evans & R Murray (eds) *The African Charter on Human and Peoples' Rights: The System in Practice, 1986–2000* (2002) 178–218; D M Chirwa 'African regional human rights system: The promise of recent jurisprudence on social rights' in M Langford (ed) *Social Rights Jurisprudence: Emerging Trends in International and Comparative Law* (2008) 323–338.

environment.[152] Apart from a reporting mechanism, the Charter also provides for the submission of communications to the African Commission on Human and Peoples' Rights concerning violations of the Charter.[153] The African Charter thus contains a holistic set of human rights guarantees combined with an individual communications mechanism. As noted by Danwood Chirwa, the Commission's interpretative approach has also sought to reinforce the indivisibility and interdependence of the rights in the African Charter.[154]

Initially, there were few communications in which the Commission dealt specifically with the interpretation of the social and economic rights in the African Charter. However, in 2001, the Commission handed down its landmark decision on socio-economic rights in the *SERAC* case.[155] This was followed in 2003 by the Commission's decision concerning the interpretation of the right to health in art 16 of the Charter in *Purohit and Moore v The Gambia.*[156]

The Protocol to the African Charter on the establishment of an African Court on Human and Peoples' Rights (1998) came into force on 25 January 2004.[157] The establishment of a judicial body which can give legally binding judgments coupled with appropriate remedies[158] as well as advisory opinions[159] has the potential to provide substantial impetus to the developing body of jurisprudence on these rights in Africa. However, this potential is seriously curtailed by allowing States Parties to control

---

152 Articles 20–24.

153 Articles 55–59.

154 Chirwa (note 151 above) 324. A significant future source of guidance on the Commission's interpretation of the economic, social and cultural rights in the African Charter is the Draft Principles and Guidelines on the Economic, Social and Cultural Rights in the African Charter. At the date of finalising this manuscript, they had been published for public comment, but had not yet been adopted. Available at http://www.achpr.org/english/other/Draft_guideline_ESCR/Draft_Pcpl%20&%20Guidelines.pdf (accessed on 10 July 2009).

155 Note 21 above. See the discussion of this communication at notes 21–25 above and accompanying text. See further H O Yusuf 'Oil on troubled waters: Multi-national corporations and realizing human rights in the developing world, with specific reference to Nigeria' (2008) 8 *AHRLJ* 79–107.

156 Communication No 241/2001 (2003) *AHRLR* (ACHPR 2003). See also *Kevin Mgwanga Gunme v Cameroon* Communication No 266/2003, ACHPR, EX.CL/529(XV), Annex 4 concerning complaints of economic discrimination and marginalisation on behalf of the people of Southern Cameroon.

157 OAU doc CM/2051 (LXVII). South Africa ratified the Protocol on 3 July 2002. As at 1 November 2009 there were 25 ratifications of this Protocol. See generally J C Mubangizi & A O'Shea 'An African Court of Human and Peoples' Rights' (1999) 24 *SAYIL* 256–269.

158 See art 27 of the Protocol on the African Court on Human and Peoples' Rights. In terms of art 30 of the Protocol, States parties 'undertake to comply with the judgment in any case to which they are parties within the time stipulated by the Court and to guarantee its execution'.

159 Article 4 of the Protocol on the African Court on Human and Peoples' Rights.

direct access to the Court by individuals and NGOs.[160] Shortly after the coming into force of the aforementioned Protocol, the African Union resolved to merge the African Court on Human and Peoples' Rights and the African Court of Justice (created in terms of the Constitutive Act of the African Union),[161] into a single Court. The Protocol on the Statute of the African Court of Justice and Human Rights was opened for signature and ratification on 1 July 2008, but has not yet entered into force.[162] Subject to certain transitional provisions it will replace the 1998 Protocol on the African Court on Human and Peoples' Rights. The implications of this merger for the development of a coherent and substantive body of jurisprudence on human rights in Africa remain to be seen.[163]

Two further regional human rights instruments that incorporate economic, social and cultural rights are the African Charter on the Rights and Welfare of the Child (1990),[164] and the Protocol to the African Charter on Human and Peoples' Rights on the Rights of Women in Africa (2003).[165] There are rich opportunities for a reciprocal interchange between South Africa's evolving jurisprudence on socio-economic rights, and that emerging from the African regional human rights system. The advantage of being part of a regional system is that there are similarities in the broader context. In particular, African countries face the common challenge in the post-colonial era of achieving sustainable development and equitable resource redistribution.

---

[160] In order for individuals and NGOs within a State party's jurisdiction to be permitted to institute cases directly before the Court, a declaration by that State party is required. See art 5(3) read with art 34(6) of the Protocol. As at the date of finalising this manuscript only two States Parties, Mali and Burkino Faso, had made declarations accepting the competence of the Court to receive individual and NGO petitions. See further the commentary by M du Plessis in Dugard (note 111 above) 566–568.

[161] Constitutive Act of the African Union (2000), and the Protocol of the Court of Justice of the African Union (2003).

[162] In terms of art 9, this Protocol will enter into force 30 days after the deposit of the 15th instrument of ratification. As at 30 November 2009 only Libya and Mali had ratified the Protocol.

[163] The 2003 'merger Protocol' contains similar provisions limiting access by individuals and NGOs: see art 8(3) read with art 30(*f*).

[164] Ratified by South Africa on 7 January 2000. The African Children's Charter has its own supervisory body, the Committee of Experts on the Rights and Welfare of the Child. It has the power to examine state reports, to receive individual and interstate communications and to conduct investigations (see arts 43–45). See generally Chirwa (note 151 above) 333–334 and D M Chirwa 'The merits and demerits of the African Charter on the Rights and Welfare of the Child' (2002) 10 *Int J of Child Rights* 157–177.

[165] Ratified by South Africa on 17 December 2004. The Women's Protocol is subject to the same supervisory mechanisms available under the African Charter. The extensive socio-economic rights in this Protocol can therefore by litigated before both the African Commission and Court on Human and Peoples' Rights. On the Women's Protocol, see generally Chirwa (note 151 above) 333.

The Inter-American regional human rights system under the auspices of the Organisation of American States (OAS) also protects economic, social and cultural rights in a range of instruments, primarily the American Declaration of the Rights and Duties of Man (1948),[166] the American Convention on Human Rights (1969),[167] and the Additional Protocol to the American Convention on Human Rights in the Area of Economic, Social and Cultural Rights (1988) ('Protocol of San Salvador').[168]

The Inter-American Commission on Human Rights[169] and the Inter-American Court of Human Rights[170] have both developed an extensive jurisprudence on socio-economic rights.[171] Of particular significance is the willingness of the Commission and Court to develop standards relating to the positive duties of the State to protect and ensure the realisation of various rights.[172]

In addition, they have adopted an innovative remedial jurisprudence geared towards the redress of systemic violations of human rights, and the prevention of future violations. Thus the Inter-American Commission on Human Rights has, for example, required the State to ensure participation by the victims and their legal

---

166 OAS doc. OEA/Ser.L/V/II.65, Doc 6.

167 1144 UNTS 123. Art 26 of the Convention reads:

> The States Parties undertake to adopt measures, both internally and through international cooperation, especially those of an economic and technical nature, with a view to achieving progressively, by legislation or other appropriate means, the full realization of the rights implicit in the economic, social, educational, scientific, and cultural standards set forth in the Charter of the Organization of American States as amended by the Protocol of Buenos Aires.

However, the Commission and Court have developed the socio-economic dimensions of many other rights in the American Convention on Human Rights, such as the right to life (art 4), rights of the child (art 19), and the right to property (art 21). The latter right has been particularly significant in the context of the protection of the land and self-determination rights of indigenous communities within the jurisdiction of the OAS.

168 28 ILM 156.

169 The Commission, an organ of the OAS, has both a mandate to promote human rights as well as to consider petitions concerning the violation of human rights. See arts 41–51 of the American Convention on Human Rights.

170 The Court was established in 1979 as 'an autonomous judicial institution' of the OAS. It has both a contentious (arts 61–63), and advisory jurisdiction (art 64) under the American Convention on Human Rights.

171 For a comprehensive analysis and critique of this jurisprudence of the Commission and Court in the sphere of economic, social and cultural rights, see T J Melish 'The Inter-American Commission on Human Rights: Defending social rights through case-based petitions' in M Langford (ed) *Social Rights Jurisprudence: Emerging Trends in International and Comparative Law* (2008) 339–371; T J Melish (note 16 above) 372–408.

172 The most significant jurisprudence of the Inter-American Commission and Court has developed in relation to a range of rights in the American Convention on Human Rights (1969), even though the Protocol of San Salvador contains a more comprehensive range of economic, social and cultural rights. The reason for this is that the system of individual petitions established by the Protocol is restricted to only two rights, namely trade union rights in art 8(*a*), and the right to education in art 13. See art 19(6) of the Protocol of San Salvador.

representatives in the crafting of an appropriate remedy and has been prepared to assume a supervisory jurisdiction over its implementation.[173] According to Tara Melish, this proactive, 'hands-on' approach by the Commission to the implementation of its formal recommendations has promoted 'a dynamic process of local-level reform that continues at the domestic level, long after its final report is issued'.[174]

The Inter-American Court of Human Rights has sought to prevent future violations of rights for the applicants and similarly situated groups through 'guarantees of non-repetition'.[175] This entails far-reaching positive orders involving the adoption of new legislation, policies, plans of actions and development programmes.[176] The Court has also been emphatic in affirming its 'inherent and non-discretional' competence to monitor compliance with its decisions through the exercise of a supervisory jurisdiction. Tara Melish comments that:

> [T]he Court's supervisory jurisdiction has proved vital not only for ensuring the fullest possible State compliance with Court orders – 'the materialization of justice for the specific case'[177] – but also for giving victims and their representatives a direct voice in holding governments accountable for responding effectively to human rights violations.[178]

The major human rights treaty in the European regional human rights system is the European Convention for the Protection of Human Rights and Fundamental Freedoms (1950).[179] The only socio-economic right expressly protected in the Convention is the right to education in art 2, Protocol No 1.[180] Nevertheless, the European Commission and Court of Human Rights[181] have provided significant protection to socio-economic interests through an application of norms traditionally associated with civil and political rights.[182] The prohibition on inhuman or degrading

---

[173] See Melish 'The Inter-American Commission on Human Rights' (note 171 above).

[174] Ibid 371.

[175] See the jurisprudence described by Melish 'The Inter-American Court of Human Rights' (note 16 above) 402–404.

[176] Ibid.

[177] *Baena Ricardo et al. Case*, Supervisory Jurisdiction, Judgment of Nov. 28, 2003, Inter-Am Ct HR (Ser.C) No 104 para. 72.

[178] Melish 'The Inter-American Court of Human Rights' (note 16 above) 405.

[179] ETS No. 5.

[180] A significant case on this right is the *Case Relating to Certain Aspects of the Laws on the Use of Languages in Education in Belgium ('Belgian Linguistics* cases' *(No 2))* (1979) 1 EHRR 252. See also the commentary on the further jurisprudence on this right by L Clements & A Simmons 'European Court of Human Rights: Sympathetic unease' in M Langford (ed) *Social Rights Jurisprudence: Emerging Trends in International and Comparative Law* (2008) 409–427 at 424–425.

[181] With the entry into force of Protocol No 11 to the Convention (on 1 November 1998), the enforcement mechanisms for the Convention were amended to provide for the exclusive jurisdiction of the European Court of Human Rights in relation to violations of the Convention.

[182] For recent analyses of the jurisprudence of the European Court of Human Rights in relation to social rights, see Clements & Simmons (note 180 above); E Brems 'Indirect

treatment,[183] the right to a fair criminal and civil trial,[184] the right to respect for one's private and family life, home and correspondence,[185] the prohibition on discrimination,[186] and the right to peaceful enjoyment of one's possessions have been of particular importance in the latter development.[187] Another development which has significant potential to provide enhanced protection against discrimination in socio-economic spheres is the coming into force on 1 April 2005 of Protocol No 12 to the European Convention for the Protection of Human Rights and Fundamental Freedoms providing for a general prohibition of discrimination.[188]

protection of social rights by the European Court of Human Rights' in D Barak-Erez & A M Gross *Exploring Social Rights: Between Theory and Practice* (2007) 135–167.

183 Article 3. See, for example *Dulas v Turkey* Application no 25801/94, judgment of 30 January 2001 (destruction of the applicant's home in circumstances causing severe personal suffering); *Moldovan v Romania (no 2)* (2007) 44 EHRR 16 (destruction of homes of Roma families by a pogrom in their village resulting in appalling living conditions); *D v United Kingdom* (1997) 24 EHRR 423 (the deportation of a person in the advanced stage of AIDS to his state of origin where he would not have access to appropriate medical care and would die destitute); *Keenan v United Kingdom* (2001) 33 EHRR 38 (art 3 violated by a failure to provide appropriate medical treatment to a detainee suffering from a mental illness).

184 Article 6. The procedural protections in art 6 have been particularly applied to protect social security entitlements. See, for example *Feldbrugge v Netherlands* (1986) 8 EHRR 425; *Schuler-Zgraggen v Switzerland* (1993) 16 EHRR 405; *Salesi v Italy* (1993) 26 EHRR 187; *Kerojavi v Finland* (1996) EHRLR 66. See also the discussion by M Scheinin 'Economic and social rights as legal rights' in A Eide, C Krause & A Rosas (eds) *Economic, Social and Cultural Rights: A Textbook* 2 ed (2001) 29–54 at 34–38.

185 Article 8. The Court has gradually extended the reach of art 8 to encompass various procedural and proportionality protections for people facing eviction from their homes. See, for example *Buckley v United Kingdom* (1996) 23 EHRR 101; *Chapman v United Kingdom* (2001) 33 EHRR 18; *Connors v United Kingdom* (2004) 40 EHRR 189; *Moldovan* (note 183 above). See the analysis by Clements & Simmons (note 180 above) 414–416. See also the discussion of *Connors* in chapter 4, part 4.6.2 at notes 469–473 and accompanying text.

186 Article 14 and Protocol No 12 (2000) to the Convention.

187 Article 1, Protocol 1. In a number of cases, the Court has held that social welfare benefits and entitlements may constitute 'possessions' or 'property' in terms of this article. See, for example *Gaygusuz v Austria* (1997) 23 EHRR 364. This provision has also provided some indirect protection for housing-related interests. See, for example *James v the United Kingdom* (1986) ECHR Ser A, No 98; *Blečič v Croatia* Application no 59532/00, judgment of 29 July 2004; *Mellacher v Austria* (1989) 12 EHRR 391. Compare *Hutten-Czapska v Poland* (2006) 42 EHRR 15. See also the analysis by Clements & Simons (note 180 above) 416–417.

188 See art 1 of the Protocol. On international law jurisprudence pertaining to non-discrimination in the field of social rights, see generally C Krause & M Scheinin 'The right not to be discriminated against: The case of social security' in T Orlin, A Rosas & M Scheinin (eds) *The Jurisprudence of Human Rights Law: A Comparative Interpretive Approach* (2000) 253–286.

The European Court on Human Rights has rejected a strict conceptual divide between civil and political rights and socio-economic rights. Thus in *Airey v Ireland* it stated that:

> [T]he mere fact that an interpretation of the Convention may extend into the sphere of social and economic rights should not be a decisive factor against such an interpretation; there is no water-tight division separating that sphere from the field covered by the Convention.[189]

In their analysis of the jurisprudence of the European Court of Human Rights relating to the protection of socio-economic interests, Luke Clements and Alan Simmons argue that the Court has interpreted the Convention to protect social and economic interests at least in the context where the state is directly or indirectly complicit in depriving applicants of these necessities.[190] However, in the absence of a clear textual mandate in the Convention, it has been reluctant to impose far-reaching positive duties on States to provide access to housing, health care, social security and other socio-economic rights. It has generally invoked the 'margin of appreciation' doctrine to accord a measure of deference to the judgments of national authorities who are considered to be more attuned to the needs and circumstances of national circumstances.[191] Particularly where the claim requires an extensive resource allocation by national authorities, the Court has held that national authorities are better placed to achieve an appropriate balance between individual and communal interests. In this respect, its orientation is primarily towards the protection of individuals and groups against negative violations of their rights.[192]

With regard to remedies, the Court is confined to identifying specific defects in the State's laws or administrative arrangements and compensating victims for violations of their rights. This constitutes a very limited remedial framework compared to that of the Inter-American Commission and Court on Human Rights. It is clearly not well suited to dealing with systemic violations of socio-economic rights which may require a set of structural reforms over a period of time to remedy and prevent future violations of the relevant rights.[193]

The incorporation of the European Convention on Human Rights in United Kingdom law through the Human Rights Act of 1998 has provided an important opportunity for the rights to be interpreted and developed by national courts. Thus, for example, courts in the United Kingdom have held that the failure to provide

---

189 *Airey v Ireland* (note 16 above) para 26. In this case, the Court derived the right to legal representation from the right to a fair trial in art 6 of the Convention.

190 Clements & Simmons (note 180 above) 410.

191 See *Handyside v United Kingdom* (1979) EHRR 737 para 49.

192 See also the analysis and conclusions of Brems (note 182 above) 163 and 167.

193 On structural remedies, see further chapter 8, part 8.6.

welfare assistance to asylum seekers amounted to degrading treatment in terms of art 3 of the European Convention on Human Rights.[194]

A further European human rights treaty, the European Social Charter, focuses expressly on economic and social rights.[195] States Parties' obligations under the Charter are supervised through a reporting system, and an optional collective complaints system which came into force in 1998.[196] The European Committee of Social Rights is the body primarily responsible for interpreting the Charter in the context of the reporting and complaints procedure.[197] However, it is subordinate to the Committee of Ministers of the Council of Europe, a political body, which is solely responsible for addressing recommendations to States Parties.[198] To date, the European Committee

---

[194] *R (on the application of Q) v Secretary of State for the Home Department* [2003] EWCA Civ 364; *Ex p Adam, Limbuela and Tesema* [2005] UKHL 66. Lord Bingham held in the latter case that treatment is 'inhuman or degrading if, to a seriously detrimental extent, it denies the most basic needs of any human being' (para 6). See the analysis in S Fredman 'Human rights transformed: Positive duties and positive rights' (2006) 3 *Public Law* 498–520; J A King 'United Kingdom: 'Asserting social rights in a multi-layered system' in Langford (ed) *Social Rights Jurisprudence: Emerging Trends in International and Comparative Law* (2008) 276–294 at 286–287. See generally R Burchill, D Harris and A Owers (eds) *Economic, Social and Cultural Rights: Their Implementation in United Kingdom Law* (1999).

[195] The original Social Charter was adopted in 1961, 529 UNTS, 35 ETS. It has been substantially revised and updated with the inclusion of a number of additional rights in a new treaty, the Revised European Social Charter (1996), ETS No. 163.

[196] Additional Protocol to the European Social Charter providing for a System of Collective Complaints (1995), ETS No. 158, and Part IV, Art D of the Revised European Social Charter. Collective complaints can be brought by three major categories of organisations: International organisations of employers, trade unions and international NGOs which have consultative status with the Council of Europe.

[197] For an analysis of the jurisprudence of the Committee, see U Khaliq & R Churchill 'The European Committee of Social Rights: Putting flesh on the bare bones of the European Social Charter' in M Langford (ed) *Social Rights Jurisprudence: Emerging Trends in International and Comparative Law* (2008) 428–452. Significant decisions on the merits of the Committee under the Collective Complaints procedure include: *International Association Autism-Europe v France* Complaint No 13/2003 (right to equality in education for children with autism); *International Federation of Human Rights Leagues (FIDH) v France* Complaint No 14/2003 (entitlement of illegal immigrants to medical assistance); *European Roma Rights Centre v Greece* Complaint No 15/2003; *European Roma Rights Centre v Italy* Complaint No 27/2004; *European Roma Rights Centre v Bulgaria* Complaint No 31/2005 (housing and eviction-related rights of Roma communities in various European countries); *European Federation of National Organisations Working with the Homeless (FEANTSA) v France* Complaint No 39/2006. The text of these and other decisions of the Committee are available on the Council of Europe's website at http://www.coe.int/t/dghl/monitoring/socialcharter/Complaints/Complaints_en.asp (accessed on 25 July 2009).

[198] This is the major drawback of the supervisory system of the European Social Charter in that the Committee of Ministers has generally been reluctant to address recommendations to non-complying States in both the reporting and collective complaints procedure. See Khaliq & Churchill ibid 451–452.

of Social Rights has decided a number of complaints concerning unsatisfactory application of the European Social Charter by States Parties. Despite the unsatisfactory enforcement mechanisms of the European Charter, the jurisprudence of the European Committee of Social Rights is developing into a significant international resource on the interpretation of economic and social rights.

(*d*) International law and constitutional law: A dialectic relationship

Although international human rights law has recognised economic, social and cultural rights as human rights norms since the adoption of the Universal Declaration of Human Rights in 1948, the enforcement mechanisms for this group of rights has generally been inferior to that available under instruments protecting civil and political rights. However, as the above analysis has shown, this trend is gradually being reversed in international and regional human rights treaties. The ability of individuals, groups and NGOs to submit petitions alleging violations of socio-economic rights to international and regional human rights supervisory bodies enables international jurisprudence on these rights to develop in the context of concrete cases. This affords a more useful resource for consideration in developing South African's own constitutional jurisprudence on socio-economic rights.

International human rights law represents the fundamental normative values and commitments of the international community of States. Along with internationally recognised civil and political rights, socio-economic rights are regarded as central to the protection of human dignity.[199] It is thus fitting that the Constitution imposes a mandatory duty on the courts to consider international law in interpreting the Bill of Rights. International human rights law also provides a rich resource for communities and civil society organisations to challenge the erosion of human rights standards that can occur in domestic contexts due to political or economic factors.

This process of considering international law standards promotes the kind of critical self-reflection which should underpin the development of a transformative jurisprudence on socio-economic rights. O'Regan J observes that the foundational constitutional value of promoting and protecting human rights –

> is to be understood in the context of a growing international consensus that the promotion and protection of human rights is part of the responsibility of both the global community and individual States, and there is a need to take steps to ensure that those fundamental human rights recognised in international law are not infringed or impaired.[200]

In turn, South Africa's evolving jurisprudence on socio-economic rights can influence the development of international law pertaining to these rights. It is noteworthy, for example, that the draft Optional Protocol to the International Covenant on

---

199 The first preambular paragraph of the Universal Declaration of Human Rights (1948) proclaims:

> Whereas recognition of the inherent dignity and of the equal and inalienable rights of all members of the human family is the foundation of freedom, justice and peace in the world.

200 *Kaunda* (note 101 above) para 221.

Economic, Social and Cultural Rights provides for a form of reasonableness review in examining communications.[201] This probably owes much to the influence of the South African jurisprudence on socio-economic rights.[202] This exemplifies the dialogic understanding of the development of human rights jurisprudence. This dialogue can no longer be confined to national boundaries and must incorporate the normative and institutional developments within international human rights law.

3.3.3 Foreign law

(*a*) Deepening the substantive interpretation of constitutional rights

Section 39(1)(*c*) of the Constitution permits the courts to consider foreign law when interpreting the Bill of Rights. The difficulties of drawing on comparative constitutional law for the interpretation of a national constitution are well known.[203] Apart from practical difficulties relating to language differences and the differing legal systems of various jurisdictions, constitutional provisions acquire a distinctive meaning through their operation in concrete political, economic and social contexts. Thus it is very difficult, if not impossible, to understand the true import and implications of comparative constitutional law and jurisprudence without a deep understanding of the relevant contexts.[204] References to comparative constitutional law in the interpretation of a national constitution are thus susceptible to two main criticisms: arbitrariness, in the sense that judges frequently only draw from jurisdictions whose language and legal traditions are familiar to them; and superficiality, in that they suffer from the inevitable lack of in-depth knowledge of the relevant historical, social and legal contexts.

On the other hand, openness to learning from other constitutional cultures and traditions constitutes a major resource for transformative critique and development of our own constitutional culture. A willingness to consider alternative interpretations generated by other legal cultures and traditions destabilises the sense of naturalness and inevitability of the interpretations generated by our own legal culture and tradition. It may be that a judge concludes, after a consideration of the interpretative approaches of other jurisdictions, that a particular solution or interpretation is uniquely 'right' (at least for now) in our current South African circumstances. This

---

201 See note 135 above. For the text of art 8(4) of the Optional Protocol, see ch 4, part 4.3.3, note 100.

202 See, for example, B Porter 'The reasonableness of article 8(4) of the Optional Protocol: Adjudicating claims from the margins' (2009) 27 *NJHR* 39–53.

203 See, for example, M Tushnet 'The possibilities of comparative constitutional law' (1999) 108 *Yale LJ* 1225–1309; S Choudhry 'Globalization in search of justification: Towards a theory of comparative constitutional interpretation' (1999) 74 *Ind LJ* 819–892.

204 As Tushnet (ibid) at 1307 observes:

> Particular institutions serve complex functions in each constitutional system, and there is little reason to think that directly appropriating an institution that functions well in one system will produce the same beneficial effect when it is inserted into another.

enhances the value of considering comparative constitutional law. By doing so, judges are continually challenged to refine their justification for a particular interpretation.[205] Consideration of comparative law thus has the potential to deepen substantive legal reasoning.[206] Choudhry describes this dialogic engagement with comparative sources in constitutional interpretation as follows:

> In … dialogic interpretation, courts identify the normative and factual assumptions underlying their own constitutional jurisprudence by engaging with comparable jurisprudence of other jurisdictions. Through a process of interpretive self-reflection, courts may conclude that domestic and foreign assumptions are sufficiently similar to one another to warrant the use of comparative law. Conversely, courts may conclude that comparative jurisprudence has emerged from a fundamentally different constitutional order; this realization may sharpen an awareness of constitutional difference or distinctiveness.[207]

A constitutional culture that is relatively closed to learning from other cultures and experiences is inevitably an insular and limited one. Thus, for example, Cathy Albisa and Jessica Schultz argue that one of the obstacles to the emergence of a more robust jurisprudence protecting socio-economic interests and values in the United States is 'a lack of awareness about alternative legal systems that can offer compelling analyses to support economic and social rights'.[208]

From this perspective the consideration of comparative constitutional law, however imperfect and inevitably selective, offers many opportunities to deepen and enrich our own constitutional jurisprudence. Our jurisprudence will be the poorer for not accepting the Constitution's invitation to be open to the experiences – both negative and positive – of other jurisdictions.

---

205 Tushnet (note 203 above) at 1307 describes the process of critical self-reflection generated by the use of comparative materials in constitutional interpretation as follows:

> In thinking about a particular domestic institution or rule, we may discover that as we consider new details about another system's institution or rule and ignore others we have previously thought important, we refine our understanding of the domestic institution or rule.

206 On the relationship between a substantive interpretation of rights and transformative constitutionalism, see also chapter 2, part 2.4.2.

207 S Choudhry (note 203 above) 825. Froneman J expresses a similar insight in *Ngxuza* (note 34 above) 623C when he observes that foreign law sources 'are instructive not because we should slavishly do what others have done or are doing, but because we might learn something from them to assist us in our quest for democracy'. See also L M Du Plessis 'Interpretation' in S Woolman et al (eds) *Constitutional Law of South Africa* 2 ed (Original Service 2008) chapter 32, 183–191.

208 C Albisa & J Schultz 'The United States: A ragged patchwork' in M Langford (ed) *Social Rights Jurisprudence: Emerging Trends in International and Comparative Law* (2008) 230–249, 247. See also M H Marshall '"Wise parents do not hesitate to learn from their children": Interpreting state constitutions in an age of global jurisprudence' (2004) 79 *NYULR* 1641–1656.

The following part examines the broad modalities through which socio-economic interests are protected, together with illustrative examples.[209]

(*b*) Socio-economic rights: Models of protection

(i) *Direct protection*

There are relatively few national constitutions that are comparable, in the extent of their commitment to the judicial enforcement of socio-economic rights, with the South African Constitution. The South African Constitution incorporates not only a broad range of express socio-economic rights, but also subjects these rights to the same forms of judicial protection and remedies available in respect of the civil and political rights in the Bill of Rights.

Constitutions which expressly incorporate a range of socio-economic rights and provide for judicial enforcement can be found mainly in Central and Eastern Europe[210] and South America. The literature dealing with the jurisprudence of these countries reveals that the courts are willing to impose, at times far-reaching, positive duties on the State to protect and advance access to socio-economic rights. Particularly in many South American jurisdictions, the courts are clearly playing an important role in protecting vulnerable and disadvantaged groups such as indigenous communities against violations of their socio-economic rights by public and private actors.[211]

---

209 See generally S Liebenberg 'The protection of economic and social rights in domestic legal systems' in A Eide, C Krause & A Rosas (eds) *Economic, Social and Cultural Rights: A Textbook* 2 ed (2001) 55–84.

210 A number of post-communist states in Eastern and Central Europe incorporate socio-economic rights and make no distinction between the enforceability of civil and political rights, and socio-economic rights. See W Sadurski *Rights before Courts: A Study of Constitutional Courts in Post-Communist States of Central and Eastern Europe* (2005) 177–179. The jurisprudence of the Hungarian Constitutional Court on socio-economic rights is perhaps best known given its controversial role in welfare reforms undertaken by Hungary in the post-communist period: see A Sajó 'How the rule of law killed Hungarian welfare reform' (1996) 5 *EECR* 31–41; M Langford 'Hungary: Social rights or market redivivus?' in M Langford (ed) *Social Rights Jurisprudence: Emerging Trends in International and Comparative Law* (2008) 250–266; A Sajó 'Social rights as middle class entitlements in Hungary: The role of the Constitutional Court' in R Gargarella, P Domingo & T Roux (eds) *Courts and Social Transformation in New Democracies: An Institutional Voice for the Poor?* (2006) 83–105.

211 See, for example, the discussion by the following authors of the jurisprudence on socio-economic rights in various South American jurisdictions: In R Gargarella, P Domingo & T Roux (eds) *Courts and Social Transformation in New Democracies: An Institutional Voice for the Poor?* (2006): R U Yepes 'The enforcement of social rights by the Colombian Constitutional Court: Cases and debates' 127–151; C Courtis 'Judicial enforcement of social rights: Perspectives from Latin America' 169–180; J Reinaldo de Lima Lopes 'Brazilian courts and social rights: A case study revisited' 185–211. In M Langford (ed) *Social Rights Jurisprudence: Emerging Trends in International and Comparative Law*: M Sepúlveda 'Colombia: The Constitutional Court's role in addressing social injustice' 144–162; C Courtis 'Argentina: Some

More common are constitutions which make provision for one or two justiciable socio-economic rights such as the right to education and protection of children,[212] or minority language and educational rights.[213] In giving effect to s 23 of the Canadian Charter of Rights and Freedoms, the Supreme Court of Canada ruled in *Doucet-Boudreau v Nova Scotia (Minister of Education)*[214] that the government of Nova Scotia was under an obligation to build minority language schools within certain time limits, and made a supervisory order requiring the government to report back to the Court on its progress in implementing the order.

(ii) *Protection through directive principles of state policy, civil and political rights, and the 'social state principle'*

Particularly in countries where there are no express provisions relating to socio-economic rights, the values and interests underlying these rights are frequently protected through civil and political rights. This occurs mainly in two ways. The first is when civil and political rights, such as the rights to life, human dignity and security of the person, are interpreted expansively so as to incorporate economic and social rights. This development can be facilitated in the context of constitutions where socio-economic rights are incorporated in the form of directive principles of state policy.[215] The second situation entails the application of rights such as equality rights or administrative justice rights to protect socio-economic interests.[216] These two ways

promising signs' 163–181; F Piovesan 'Brazil: Impact and challenges of social rights in the courts' 182–191; E Gonzalez 'Venezuela: A distinct path towards social justice' 192–208.

[212] See, for example, art 7 of the German Basic Law. Article 6 of the German Basic Law requires special state protection for marriage and the family, as well as imposing a duty on the state to pass legislation giving 'illegitimate' children the same opportunities for their physical and mental development and for their place in society as are enjoyed by 'legitimate' children. On the enforceability of constitutional commands directed to the legislature such as these in German constitutional law, see E de Wet 'The enforceability of socio-economic directive principles/legislative commands with special reference to Constitutional Principle XI of the South African Transitional Constitution' (1995) 112 *SALJ* 462–480. In the United States, many state constitutions contain rights relating to the establishment of an educational system and equal access to education. See Albisa & Schultz (note 208 above) 240–243.

[213] For example, s 23 of the Canadian Charter of Rights and Freedoms.

[214] [2003] 3 SCR 3. See M Jackman & B Porter 'Socio-economic rights under the Canadian Constitution in M Langford (ed) *Social Rights Jurisprudence: Emerging Trends in International and Comparative Law* (2008) 226–228.

[215] This is not always the case. Thus, in contrast to the Indian courts, the Irish courts have been far less bold in drawing on the Directive Principles in the Irish Constitution to protect socio-economic values and interests. See in this regard, A Nolan 'The separation of powers doctrine vs. socio-economic rights' in M Langford (ed) *Social Rights Jurisprudence: Emerging Trends in International and Comparative Law* (2008) 295–319.

[216] Craig Scott 'The interdependence and permeability of human rights norms: Towards a partial fusion of the International Covenants on Human Rights' (1989) 27 *OHLJ* 769–878 at 779–786 distinguishes between the concepts of 'organic interdependence' and 'related

of protecting socio-economic rights in national constitutions will be discussed in turn.

Perhaps the pre-eminent example of the first type of situation is the Indian constitutional jurisprudence. The Indian Supreme Court has drawn on the formally unenforceable Directive Principles in Part IV of the Indian Constitution[217] to infuse the right to life in art 21 of the Indian Constitution with substantive content. Thus the right to life has been interpreted to incorporate the basic necessities of life such as adequate nutrition, clothing, reading facilities,[218] the right to a livelihood,[219] the right to shelter,[220] the right to health care,[221] and the right to education.[222] These developments occurred in the context of renewed judicial activism following the internal state of emergency in India between 1975 and 1977, and the crisis of legitimacy experienced by the judiciary. In order to facilitate greater access to justice by disadvantaged and marginalised groups the judiciary developed the mechanism of public interest litigation. The rules of standing and procedure were substantially relaxed and 'litigants were freed from the stranglehold of formal law and lawyering'.[223] The major developments in socio-economic rights jurisprudence in India have occurred through public interest litigation.[224]

---

interdependence' between civil and political rights, and socio-economic rights. 'Organic interdependence' refers to the situation when one right is interpreted to incorporate another right, for example, when the right to life is interpreted to include a right to an adequate standard of living or livelihood. Related interdependence involves the question whether a civil and political right, for example, the right to a fair hearing, applies to a socio-economic right such as social security. In this case, the two sets of rights are treated as equally important and complementary, but autonomous.

[217] Section 37 of the Indian Constitution reads: 'The provisions contained in this part shall not be enforceable by any court, but the principles laid down are nevertheless fundamental in the governance of the country and it shall be the duty of the state to apply these principles in making laws.'

[218] *Francis Coralie Mullin v The Administrator* (1981) 1 SCC 608.

[219] *Olga Tellis v Bombay Municipal Corporation* (1985) 3 SCC 545.

[220] *Shanti Star Builders v Narayan K. Totame* (1990) 1 SCC 520; *Ahmedabad Municipal Corporation v Nawab Khan Gulab Khan* (1997) 11 SCC 123.

[221] *Paramanand Katara v Union of India* (1989) 4 SCC 286; *Paschim Banga Khet Majoor Samity v State of West Bengal* (1996) 4 SCC 37.

[222] *Unnikrishnan J P v State of Andhra Pradesh* (1993) 1 SCC 645.

[223] S Muralidhar 'India: The expectations and challenges of judicial enforcement of social rights' in M Langford (ed) *Social Rights Jurisprudence: Emerging Trends in International and Comparative Law* (2008) 102–124 at 109.

[224] See generally Muralidhar ibid; R Sudarshan 'Courts and social transformation in India' in Gargarella R, Domingo P & Roux T (eds) *Courts and Social Transformation in New Democracies: An Institutional Voice for the Poor?* (2006) 153–168; J Kothari 'Social rights in India: Developments of the last decade' in D Barak-Erez & A M Gross *Exploring Social Rights: Between Theory and Practice* (2007) 171–192; S Shankar & P B Mehta 'Courts and socio-economic rights in India' in V Gauri & D M Brinks (eds) *Courting Social Justice: Judicial Enforcement of Social and Economic Rights in the Developing World* (2008) 146–182.

The Indian Supreme Court has not always been consistent in imposing positive duties on the State to provide or to facilitate access to the various socio-economic rights it has incorporated within the scope of the right to life. Thus in the celebrated 'pavement-dwellers' case of *Olga Tellis v Bombay Municipal Corporation*,[225] the Court held that the eviction of impoverished pavement dwellers by the Bombay Municipal Corporation would have the effect of depriving them of their right to a livelihood. The latter was recognised in the Directive Principles of State Policy in arts 39(*a*) and 41,[226] and these Directives informed the interpretation of the right to life in art 21.

However, the Court held that this did not imply that the State could be positively compelled to provide an adequate means of livelihood or work to its citizens. Instead it created a basis for negative review in the sense that persons could not be deprived of their livelihoods without a just and fair procedure established by law. The Court interpreted the relevant statutory provisions, authorising the municipal Commissioner to remove encroachments on pavements, to require the provision of a hearing to the pavement dwellers even though the relevant statutory provision expressly authorised the removal of encroachments without notice.[227] Although the Court ultimately upheld the right of the Commissioner to remove the pavement dwellers, it gave positive directions regarding the postponement of the evictions until after the monsoon season, and the relocation of those pavement dwellers in respect of whom there had been a previous undertaking to provide alternative accommodation.[228]

The courts have been more willing to impose positive duties on the State in cases where social justice legislation has been enacted, but it had not being properly implemented.[229]

In other cases, particularly in the context of health rights, the right to education, and the right to food, the Indian courts have been more willing to impose far-reaching positive duties on the State even in the absence of legislative and executive measures.[230] In the context of educational rights, the Supreme Court took the significant step of declaring that the passage of time and the non-compliance by the State with the Directive Principle concerning education had converted the latter into an enforceable right. Article 45 requires the State 'to endeavour to provide, within a period of ten years from the commencement of this Constitution, for free and com-

---

225 Note 219 above.

226 These Directive Principles respectively oblige the state to direct its policy towards securing the right to an adequate means of livelihood, and the right to work.

227 *Olga Tellis v Bombay Municipal Corporation* (note 219 above) 79F–81A.

228 Ibid 98D–H. See also *Ahmedabad Municipal Corporation* (note 220 above).

229 See, for example, *Bandhua Mukti Morcha v Union of India* (1984) 3 SCC 161 concerning the non-implementation of legislation designed to terminate the system of bonded labour.

230 See, for example, *Paschim Banga Khet Majoor Samity* (note 221 above) cited in *Soobramoney* (note 95 above) paras 18–20. For criticism of the Constitutional Court's restrictive interpretation of this case, see C Scott & P Alston 'Adjudicating constitutional priorities in a transnational context: A comment on *Soobramoney's* legacy and *Grootboom*'s promise' (2000) 16 *SAJHR* 206–268 at 237, 245–248.

pulsory education for all children until they complete the age of 14 years'. The Court observed that this obligation had not been complied with during a passage of 44 years – more than four times the period stipulated in art 45.[231] Judicial pronouncements to this effect led in 2002 to the insertion of a directly enforceable right to education for all children between the ages of 6 and 14 in the fundamental rights chapter of the Indian Constitution.[232]

The Supreme Court has given innovative and far-reaching positive orders in the context of a series of public interest petitions concerning the right to food brought by the People's Union for Civil Liberties. The initial petition was brought after several states faced successive years of drought. Despite large stockpiles of grain in state granaries, many Indian families faced starvation. Various orders were made by the Court in successive petitions arising from these circumstances. These orders directed the affected states to ensure the provision of food to especially vulnerable groups, the proper functioning of the ration shops under the public distribution system, the recognition of the benefits available under various nutritional schemes of the State as entitlements, the provision of a cooked midday meal for all children in government and government-assisted schools,[233] and the adoption of special measures to ensure transparency, public awareness and local participation in the distribution of food supplies. The Court has also maintained a supervisory jurisdiction of the implementation of its directions.[234]

The Directive Principles have also played a role in requiring the State to regulate private institutions to ensure that their fees do not exclude disadvantaged groups.[235] Finally, the Directive Principles have been invoked to uphold statutes that impose limitations on certain of the fundamental rights where the purpose of the legislation is to give effect to the relevant Directive Principle.[236]

While the Indian judiciary has certainly exhibited boldness and creativity in responding to the needs of the poor, its track record has been more ambiguous in

---

[231] *Unnikrishnan J P* (note 222 above) paras 171, 181, and 183. See the discussion of these developments by Muralidhar (note 223 above) 115–116.

[232] Article 21-A, Part III.

[233] With the assistance of the public health expert evidence placed before it, the Court was able to specify the minimum nutritional requirements that had to be met in respect of different groups of children.

[234] For a discussion of these petitions, see Muralidhar (note 223 above) 116–117; C Gonsalves, P R Kumar & A K Srivastava (eds) *Right to Food* 2 ed (2005).

[235] In the context of private educational institutions, see the cases of *Jain v State of Karnataka* (1992) 3 SCC 666; *Unnikrishnan J P* (note 222 above). See the discussion of these decisions in S Liebenberg 'Socio-economic rights' in M Chaskalson et al *Constitutional Law of South Africa* (Revision Service 3, 1998), chapter 41 at 23–24.

[236] For a discussion of this jurisprudence, see B de Villiers 'The socio-economic consequences of directive principles of state policy: Limitations on fundamental rights' (1992) 8 *SAJHR* 188–199; B de Villiers 'Social and economic rights' in D van Wyk, J Dugard, B de Villiers & D Davis (eds) *Rights and Constitutionalism: The New South African Legal Order* 599–628 at 618–621.

recent times. In the context of the right to work and 'rights in work', Muralidhar observes that 'the trend of judicial decisions has witnessed a moving away from recognition and enforcement of such rights and toward deferring to executive policy that has progressively denuded those rights'.[237] A similar trend can be discerned in relation to the displacement of communities as a result of major development projects such as dam construction or for environmental reasons. [238] In these cases, the right of disadvantaged groups to be heard and to participate in decisions which have a fundamental effect on their rights has been subordinated to considerations of economic efficiency and environmental considerations.

While the Indian courts are generally willing to uphold a duty on the State to provide a basic minimum of the necessities of life, they are reluctant to make decisions which may disrupt the *status quo* in areas such as economic development and the functioning of private market institutions in an era of increasing liberalisation.[239]

The second form of indirect protection of socio-economic rights identified involves cases where traditional civil and political rights are applied to protect socio-economic interests. Thus, equality rights can protect equal access to welfare and other socio-economic benefits by disadvantaged groups. This development requires courts to adopt a substantive interpretation of equality which is responsive to socio-economic disadvantage. It also requires the imposition of duties on organs of State and private parties to take positive measures to enable marginalised groups to enjoy full and equal access to social benefits.[240] In this context poverty often overlaps with other grounds of discrimination such as race, gender and disability.

The Canadian Supreme Court has, for example, applied s 15 (the equality provision) of the Canadian Charter on Rights and Freedoms to social benefits.[241] In *Eldridge v British Columbia (Attorney General)*,[242] the Court rejected the contention that governments should be entitled to provide benefits to the general population without ensuring that disadvantaged members of the society have the resources to take full advantage of those benefits. It held that this approach 'bespeaks a thin and impoverished version of s 15(1)' of the Charter.[243] It elaborated on this substantive, positive concept of equality by holding that 'discrimination can accrue from a failure to take positive steps to ensure that disadvantaged groups benefit equally from services offered to the general public'.[244] Accordingly, the failure of the Medical Services Commission and hospitals of British Columbia to provide sign language interpre-

[237] Muralidhar (note 223 above) 112.

[238] *Narmada Bachao Andolan v Union of India* (2000) 10 SCC 664; *N D Jayal v Union of India* (2004) 9 SCC 362. See the discussion by Muralidhar ibid 118–120.

[239] Muralidhar ibid 123.

[240] See also the discussion on the interdependence of rights in chapter 2, part 2.4.3.

[241] *Tetrault-Gadoury v Canada (Employment and Immigration Commission)* [1991] 2 SCR 22; *Schacter v Canada* [1992] 2 SCR 679.

[242] [1997] 3 SCR 624 paras 72–73.

[243] Ibid paras 72–73.

[244] Ibid para 78.

tation for deaf patients as part of the publicly funded scheme for the provision of medical care violated s 15(1) of the Charter, and could not be saved under s 1 (the general limitations clause).[245]

Another area where social benefits have received protection has been through the application of the principles of procedural fairness.[246] For example, in *Goldberg v Kelly*[247] ('*Goldberg*') the US Supreme Court held that procedural due process under the Fourteenth Amendment required that welfare recipients be afforded an evidentiary hearing to determine eligibility before social security benefits were terminated by welfare authorities. Welfare payments were likened to 'property interests', thus triggering due process protections.[248] The Court held that the interest of the eligible recipient in the uninterrupted receipt of public assistance coupled with the State's interest that his or her payments not be erroneously terminated clearly outweighs the State's competing concern to prevent any increase in its fiscal and administrative burdens.[249] Justice Brennan described the important constitutional values promoted by the provision of welfare assistance in the following terms:

> Welfare, by meeting the basic demands of subsistence, can help bring within the reach of the poor the same opportunities that are available to others to participate meaningfully in the life of the community … . Public assistance, then, is not mere charity, but a means to 'promote the general Welfare, and secure the Blessings of Liberty to ourselves and our Posterity.'[250]

---

[245] See B Porter 'Beyond Andrews: Substantive equality and positive obligations after *Eldridge* and *Vriend*' (1998) 9 *Constitutional Forum* 71–82. A subsequent case that has been criticised for its failure to protect young people's access to social security benefits is *Gosselin v Québec (Attorney-General)* 2002 SCR 84. See G Brodsky '*Gosselin v Québec (Attorney-General)*: Autonomy with a vengeance' (2003) 15 *CJWL* 194–214; S Liebenberg 'The value of human dignity in interpreting socio-economic rights' (2005) 21 *SAJHR* 1–31 at 18–21; S Fredman 'Providing equality: Substantive equality and the positive duty to provide' (2005) 21 *SAJHR* 163–190 at 177–180. See also the United States cases of *Brown v Board of Education* 347 US 483 (1954) (racially segregated public schools system held to be unconstitutional), and *Plyler v Doe* 257 US 202 (1982) (a Texas statute withholding from local school districts any state funds for the education of children who were illegal aliens, and authorising local districts to deny enrolment to such children, violated the Fourteenth Amendment). The Federal Constitutional Court of Germany held in the *Numerus Clausus I Case* (1072) 33 *BVerfGE* 303 that fair and equitable admission criteria were required to guarantee equal participation rights in educational institutions.

[246] See also the cases under the European Convention on Human Rights (1950) cited at note 184 above.

[247] 397 US 254 (1970).

[248] Ibid. For a critique on the reliance of a private law model of property rights to trigger due process safeguards for welfare benefits, see J Nedelsky 'Reconceiving autonomy: Sources, thoughts and possibilities' (1989) 1 *Yale J of Law and Feminism* 7–36 at 32.

[249] *Goldberg* (note 247 above) 265–266.

[250] Ibid 264–265.

Although the Court has subsequently retreated from the status and protection it accorded welfare rights in *Goldberg*,[251] the rule remains that welfare benefits cannot be arbitrarily terminated. Lawrence Tribe observes that such a rule is 'explicable only in terms of an underlying right to subsistence at least when a welfare program has been established'.[252]

The third mechanism through which the socio-economic interests receive indirect protection is through the incorporation of some form of 'social state principle' in certain constitutions. The most well-known example is that of the German Federal Constitution ('Basic Law'). The Basic Law does not incorporate a range of express socio-economic rights, but refers to Germany as a social, law-based State ('*Sozialer Rechtsstaat*').[253] This constitutional norm constitutes a directive to the State to orientate its policies and legislation towards the protection and promotion of people's social and economic welfare. It also provides an interpretative guideline for the judiciary and executive. However, as Erika de Wet points out, the social state principle does not confer any subjective rights on individuals. These are derived indirectly when the legislature enacts social legislation in conformity with the social state principle.[254]

The German Constitutional Court has expressly linked the social state principle with human dignity, requiring the State to take positive action in the spheres of social security, health care and education to ensure living conditions consistent with human dignity.[255] The social state principle has also served to justify regulatory measures taken by the State in relation to the provision of essential services, the prices of essential goods, and the protection of key industries. The Court has generally rejected challenges to these measures based on property rights and freedom of competition on the basis that the social state principle compels the State to combat excessive prices and costs of basic goods such as essential foodstuffs, medicines and housing. These measures are deemed to be in the general interest of the community as a

---

[251] *Dandridge v Williams* 397 US 471 (1970); *Jefferson v Hackney* 406 US 535 (1972); *Mathews v Eldridge* 424 US 319 (1976).

[252] L Tribe *American Constitutional Law* (1978) 1644. For an analysis and assessment of the United States jurisprudence on welfare rights, see L A Williams 'Issues and challenges in addressing poverty and legal rights: A comparative United States/South African analysis' (2005) 21 *SAJHR* 436–472 at 440–446. See also the scholarship of Frank Michelman referred to in chapter 2, notes 119–120. For a comparison between South African and United States jurisprudence on socio-economic rights, see M S Kende *Constitutional Rights in Two Worlds: South Africa and the United States* (2009) 243–285.

[253] Articles 20 and 28. Its origins appear to have been inspired partially by the social insurance programmes established by Bismarck under the German Empire of 1871. However, the social state principle also had a forward-looking dimension in that it signalled the extensive social reconstruction needed in Germany after the War. See E de Wet 'Can the social state principle in Germany guide state action in South Africa in the field of social and economic rights?' (1995) 11 *SAJHR* 30–49 at 32–34.

[254] De Wet ibid 32.

[255] See the jurisprudence discussed by De Wet ibid 35–37.

whole, as they guard against poverty.[256] State intervention in market, employment and family relationships has also been justified on the basis that the social state principle mandates the protection of disadvantaged and vulnerable groups against exploitative social relationships.[257]

Erika de Wet describes the departure represented by the social state principle from classic liberal legal theory as follows:

> The social state principle, in order to secure social justice, is thus required to counterbalance the consequences of the Classic-Liberal philosophy according to which the state is only obliged to protect individual freedom against the abuse of state power. The Classical-Liberal position leaves socio-economic relationships to self-regulation by the community (free market). [258]

The social state has to be reconciled with the concept of the 'law-based state' ('*Rechtsstaat*') which is characterised by legal certainty, the separation of powers doctrine and respect for individual liberties.[259] Thus, although the State is mandated to take positive action to promote greater social justice, these measures must respect the individual rights and freedoms in the Basic Law, and be proportional to their objective.[260]

In German constitutional law, the social state principle thus plays an indispensable role in protecting the values and interests underpinning socio-economic rights. It thereby assists in counteracting the bias towards individual liberty and negative constitutionalism in classic liberal legal theory.[261]

Another constitution which is described as a 'social state' (*'estado social')* is the 1991 Colombian Constitution.[262] Magdalena Sepúlveda summarises the Colombian Constitutional Court's interpretation of this principle as follows:

> According to the Court, respect for this principle imposes on all authorities the duty to take steps to address social inequalities, to facilitate the inclusion and participation of the population in the economic and social life of the nation and to stimulate the progressive improvement of the material conditions of existence of marginalised sectors of society. [263]

The social state principle in conjunction with a range of explicitly protected social and economic rights[264] has given rise to a remarkably rich jurisprudence on socio-economic rights by the Colombian Constitutional Court.[265] A literal interpretation of the Constitution would suggest recourse to the Courts only in respect of the tradi-

---

[256] See the jurisprudence discussed by De Wet ibid 37–38.
[257] Ibid 39–42.
[258] Ibid 39.
[259] Ibid 44–45.
[260] Ibid 45–46.
[261] See generally chapter 2, part 2.4.4.
[262] Article 1 of the 1991 Colombian Constitution.
[263] M Sepúlveda (note 211 above) 162.
[264] Articles 42–77.
[265] Sepúlveda (note 211 above).

tional civil and political rights in the Constitution. However, the Court has drawn on the social state principle and a purposive interpretation of the relevant provisions to grant relief in respect of socio-economic rights through the writ of protection ('*acción de tutela*') mechanism in art 86 of the Constitution. Thus the Court has granted relief in cases where the violation of socio-economic rights will affect the enjoyment of fundamental civil and political rights such as the right to life, personal integrity or dignity,[266] when groups do not experience the minimum conditions for a dignified life,[267] or when it identifies a so-called 'unconstitutional state of affairs'. The latter situation arises when, through its consideration of individual cases, the Court identifies a pattern of systemic violations of human rights. In these circumstances, the Court does not confine its relief to the individual petitioners, but orders State authorities to take comprehensive measures to redress the violations, including the adoption and implementation of plans of action.[268]

The social state principle plays a significant role in both German and Colombian constitutional law in promoting and protecting social values and interests. There is significant scope for the principle of 'social justice' in the preamble to the South African Constitution to play an enhanced role as a guiding principle in our constitutional rights jurisprudence. It should facilitate a jurisprudence which is attuned and responsive to systemic inequalities and socio-economic deprivations. The transformative goals of the Constitution will be enhanced by allowing the principle of social justice to play a more active role in the interpretation of the Bill of Rights.

The above analysis shows that even when socio-economic rights are not directly protected in national constitutions, courts have nevertheless adopted interpretive methods which provide significant protection for the values and interests underlying these rights in a number of jurisdictions. This occurs through an expansive interpretation of civil and political rights, gradually extending the justiciable scope of directive principles of state policy, applying rights such as equality and procedural fairness to social benefits, and allowing principles such as the social state to play an active role in interpreting rights.

Nevertheless, the direct protection of socio-economic rights as justiciable entitlements offers the best opportunity to develop a jurisprudence which engages seriously with the content of these rights and the nature and scope of the obligations they impose. Whether socio-economic rights are directly or indirectly protected, the key issues at the heart of their adjudication remain. These concern the willingness of courts to undertake a substantive evaluation of social rights claims within their historical and social contexts, the degree of deference shown to political or private actors, and the crafting of innovative and effective remedies.

---

266 In these situations, socio-economic rights are referred to as 'fundamental rights by connection' ('*derecho fundamental por conexidad*'). See Sepúlveda (note 211 above) 147.

267 Ibid 147–148.

268 Ibid 148–149.

3.4 CONCLUSION

This chapter has considered the location of the socio-economic rights provisions within the broader context of the Bill of Rights. It has examined the overall framework of duties imposed by the Constitution as well as the provisions and jurisprudence relating to legal standing, the limitation and interpretation of rights. These provisions provide crucial support to the emergence of a transformative jurisprudence on socio-economic rights.

The duties imposed on the State in s 7(2) 'to respect, protect, promote and fulfil' the rights in the Bill of Rights signal a sharp departure from the model of negative constitutionalism favoured by classic liberal constitutional theory. Rights must not only be respected, they must be actively promoted, protected and fulfilled. The generous provisions in the Bill of Rights on legal standing indicate that their purpose is to promote effective access to relief by individuals and groups who experience a violation of their rights. The jurisprudence which has developed thus far on representative actions such as class actions, actions in the public interest, and actions by associations on behalf of their members, facilitates the redress of systemic violations of socio-economic rights. The general limitations clause in the Bill of Rights institutionalises a relational concept of rights. A consideration of the justifiability of limitations to rights requires an open and transparent evaluation of the appropriate relationship between the rights of individuals, and between individual rights and communal interests.

Section 39 mandates an explicit value-orientated approach in the interpretation of the various rights in the Bill of Rights. There are political and philosophical traditions associated with the founding constitutional values of human dignity, equality and freedom which call attention to and elucidate human interdependence and social responsibility. These traditions provide support for the far-reaching institutional and social reforms needed to enable everyone to participate as equals in society. Drawing on these traditions in adjudication can help realise the transformative potential of socio-economic rights. Similarly the commitment to social justice in the preamble of the Constitution can provide an important interpretive guide for the entire Bill of Rights. It can support interpretations of rights that challenge systemic patterns of subordination in social relationships.

The receptiveness of the South African Constitution to international and foreign sources enriches the dialogical interaction which informs the interpretation of human rights norms. The value of considering international and foreign jurisprudence is not that it will yield perfect solutions to the problems of the judicial enforcement of socio-economic rights. Rather, these sources expand the range of jurisprudential approaches available for critical reflection in developing our own jurisprudence on these rights. This openness to deliberative dialogue and ongoing self-examination and renewal is an important aspect of South Africa's transformative Constitution.

The remainder of the book analyses and evaluates the South African jurisprudence on socio-economic rights within the theoretical and contextual framework which has been developed.

CHAPTER 4

Reconceiving Reasonableness Review

Sections 26 and 27

In this chapter *Page*

4.1 INTRODUCTION

In the period since the adoption of the 1996 Constitution, the High Courts, the Supreme Court of Appeal and the Constitutional Court have developed a substantial body of jurisprudence on socio-economic rights.[1] The landmark Constitutional Court cases in which the foundations of the jurisprudence on socio-economic rights have been laid are: *Soobramoney v Minister of Health, KwaZulu-Natal* [2] ('*Soobramoney*'), *Government of the Republic of South Africa v Grootboom*[3] ('*Grootboom*'), *Minister of Public Works v Kyalami Ridge Environmental Association*[4] ('*Kyalami Ridge*'), *Minister of Health v Treatment Action Campaign*[5] ('*Treatment Action Campaign*'), *Khosa v Minister of Social Development; Mahlaule v Minister of Social Development*[6] ('*Khosa*'), *Port Elizabeth Municipality v Various Occupiers*[7] ('*Port Elizabeth Municipality*'), *Jaftha v Schoeman; Van Rooyen v Stoltz*[8] ('*Jaftha*'), *President of the Republic of South Africa v Modderklip Boerdery (Pty) Ltd* [9] ('*Modderklip*'), *Occupiers of 51 Olivia Road v City of Johannesburg*[10] ('*Olivia Road*'), *Residents of Joe Slovo Community, Western Cape v Thubelisha Homes*[11] ('*Joe Slovo*').

---

[1] The High Courts and Supreme Court of Appeal all have jurisdiction in constitutional matters (for example, Bill of Rights litigation) with the exception of a limited number of constitutional matters that fall within the exclusive jurisdiction of the Constitutional Court (s 167(4) of the Constitution). It is a requirement that the Constitutional Court confirm any order of constitutional invalidity in respect of an Act of Parliament, a provincial Act or any conduct of the President made by the High Courts or Supreme Court of Appeal before that order has any force (s 167(5) read with s 172(2)(*a*)).

[2] *Soobramoney v Minister of Health (KwaZulu-Natal)* 1998 (1) SA 765 (CC), 1997 (12) BCLR 1696 (CC).

[3] *Government of the RSA v Grootboom* 2001 (1) SA 46 (CC), 2000 (11) BCLR 1169 (CC).

[4] *Minister of Public Works v Kyalami Ridge Environmental Association (Mukhwevho Intervening)* 2001 (3) SA 1151 (CC), 2001 (7) BCLR 652 (CC).

[5] *Minister of Health v Treatment Action Campaign (No 2)* 2002 (5) SA 721 (CC), 2002 (10) BCLR 1033 (CC).

[6] *Khosa v Minister of Social Development; Mahlaule v Minister of Social Development* 2004 (6) SA 505 (CC), 2004 (6) BCLR 569 (CC).

[7] *Port Elizabeth Municipality v Various Occupiers* 2005 (1) SA 217 (CC), 2004 (12) BCLR 1268 (CC).

[8] *Jaftha v Schoeman; Van Rooyen v Stoltz* 2005 (2) SA 140 (CC), 2005 (1) BCLR 78 (CC).

[9] *President of the Republic of South Africa v Modderklip Boerdery (Pty) Ltd (Agri SA, Amici Curiae)* 2005 (5) SA 3 (CC), 2005 (8) BCLR 786 (CC).

[10] *Occupiers of 51 Olivia Road, Berea Township and 197 Main Street, Johannesburg v City of Johannesburg* 2008 (3) SA 208 (CC), 2008 (5) BCLR 475 (CC).

[11] *Residents of Joe Slovo Community, Western Cape v Thubelisha Homes* [2009] ZACC 16, 2009 (9) BCLR 847 (CC).

These cases have primarily dealt with housing, health care services and social security rights. Administrative justice rights have also constituted an important vehicle for protecting socio-economic rights. Particularly in the field of social security rights, the High Courts have relied extensively on the right to administrative justice to protect people against unreasonable or procedurally unfair administrative action in relation to accessing social assistance grants, and the termination or suspension of these grants.[12]

This chapter focuses on the constitutional jurisprudence which has developed in litigation against the State based on ss 26 and 27 of the Constitution. The first part traces the emergence and development of the model of reasonableness review for assessing compliance with the positive duties imposed by the socio-economic rights in ss 26 and 27 through the leading cases of *Soobramoney*,[13] *Grootboom*,[14] *Treatment Action Campaign*,[15] and *Khosa*.[16] The Court has not provided a detailed explanation of what it understands by the positive duties imposed by socio-economic rights. However, the aforementioned cases have generally involved two kinds of situations. The first is that the State has failed to formulate or implement a programme to give effect to the socio-economic rights of a section of the population. The second scenario involves an allegation of unreasonable exclusion from an existing legislative or other programme giving effect to socio-economic rights. Both of these situations raise the question of the interrelationship between socio-economic rights and the right to equality in s 9 of the Constitution.[17]

The following part evaluates the model of reasonableness review developed by the Constitutional Court as well as an approach founded on the recognition of minimum core obligations in the light of the transformative approaches to the adjudication

---

[12] See, for example, *Bushula v Permanent Secretary, Department of Welfare, Eastern Cape Provincial Government* 2000 (2) SA 849 (E), 2000 (7) BCLR 728 (E); *Mahambehlala v MEC for Welfare, Eastern Cape* 2002 (1) SA 342 (SE), 2001 (9) BCLR 890 (SE); *Vumazonke v MEC for Social Development, Eastern Cape, and Three Similar Cases* 2005 (6) SA 229 (SE); *MEC, Department of Welfare, Eastern Cape v Kate* 2006 (4) SA 478 (SCA). For a discussion of these developments, see N de Villiers 'Social grants and the Promotion of Administrative Justice Act' (2002) 18 *SAJHR* 320–349; C Plasket 'Administrative justice and social assistance' (2003) 120 *SALJ* 494–524; S Liebenberg 'The judicial enforcement of social security rights in South Africa: Enhancing accountability for the basic needs of the poor' in E Riedel (ed) *Social Security as a Human Right: Drafting a General Comment on Article 9 ICESCR* (2006) 69–90.

[13] Note 2 above.

[14] Note 3 above.

[15] Note 5 above.

[16] Note 6 above.

[17] The overlap between equality rights and socio-economic rights was expressly dealt with in the *Khosa* case (note 6 above). However, there has also been significant scholarship highlighting the relevance of viewing the *Grootboom* (note 3 above) and *Treatment Action Campaign* (note 5 above) cases through the interrelated paradigms of equality and socio-economic rights. See parts 4.3.4 and 4.5 below.

of socio-economic rights discussed in chapter 2.[18] I argue for a reconceived model of reasonableness review which is grounded in a substantive interpretation of the socio-economic rights protected in ss 26 and 27. The implications of this approach are explored in relation to various aspects of socio-economic rights adjudication. These include the interpretation of the concept of 'progressive realisation', evaluating justifications based on resource constraints, whether direct benefits can be claimed through socio-economic rights litigation, the relationship between ss 26 and 27 and the general limitations clause, and the burden of proof in socio-economic rights litigation.

The second part of the chapter analyses the approach developed by the Court to the review of the negative duties imposed by socio-economic rights. The Court's conception of these negative duties as well as the distinctive model of review applied to these duties is examined through a discussion of the leading Constitutional Court decision in *Jaftha*.[19] This section concludes with a critical evaluation of the bifurcated model of review developed in respect of the negative and positive duties imposed by ss 26 and 27.[20]

The last substantive theme examined in this chapter is the role that socio-economic rights can play in assisting the State to defend legislation and programmes aimed at extending these rights to disadvantaged groups. The chapter concludes with proposals for the key directions in which South Africa's socio-economic jurisprudence should develop so as to better advance the transformative purposes of the Constitution.

4.2 THE EMERGENCE OF REASONABLENESS REVIEW: *SOOBRAMONEY*

4.2.1 The judgment

Soobramoney was the first major Constitutional Court case in which the interpretation of the socio-economic rights in the Constitution was considered. The major question which the Court was called upon to decide was whether the health rights in s 27 of the Constitution entitled a chronically ill man in the final stages of renal failure to an order obliging a public hospital to admit him to the renal dialysis programme of the hospital. Because the need for kidney dialysis treatment far outstripped the limited number of dialysis machines available at the public hospital, the renal unit had developed a set of guidelines for rationing access to dialysis treatment. According to these guidelines, the primary requirement for admission to the dialysis programme was that a patient must be eligible for a kidney transplant.[21] Eligibility for a transplant requires the patient to be 'free of significant vascular or cardiac disease'. Mr Soobramoney did not qualify for the treatment in terms of these guidelines as he was a diabetic who

[18] Chapter 2, part 2.4.

[19] Note 8 above.

[20] On the theoretical and practical difficulties in sustaining a conceptual distinction between positive and negative rights in human rights law, see chapter 2, part 2.4.4.

[21] *Soobramoney* (note 2 above) para 3.

suffered from ischaemic heart and cerebro-vascular disease. Kidney dialysis treatment would prolong his life but, given his general health condition, there was no reasonable prospect of a cure.[22] He had procured kidney dialysis treatment from private hospitals, but had run out of funds to continue such treatment. His death was imminent should he not receive kidney dialysis treatment. An urgent application was launched in the High Court for an order requiring Addington Hospital to admit him to the dialysis programme. This application was dismissed, and was appealed to the Constitutional Court.

The Constitutional Court considered the claim on the basis of three rights: the right to life (s 11), the right against the refusal of emergency medical treatment (s 27(3)), and the right to have access to health care services (ss 27(1) and (2)). Although the appellant relied on the former two rights, the Constitutional Court also considered the applicability of the latter right.

With respect to the claim based on the right to life, the Court held that an unqualified positive obligation to provide access to life-prolonging medical treatment should not be inferred from the right to life in the context of the South African Constitution where a qualified right of access to health care services is expressly entrenched in s 27.[23] In other words, the right to life should not be relied upon to impose obligations on the State which were inconsistent with the more limited obligations expressly conferred in s 27. It contrasted the South African Constitution to the Indian Constitution where various socio-economic entitlements have been derived from the right to life in art 21 of the Indian Constitution.[24] The Court held that such an approach would be inconsistent with a purposive approach to constitutional interpretation which required specific attention to the Bill of Rights and Constitution as a holistic document considered in the light of its particular history and background. Although a purposive approach would sometimes require a generous interpretation to be given to particular rights, the context of a particular provision may require that it be given 'a narrower or specific meaning'.[25]

The Court also dismissed the appellant's argument that s 27(3) should be construed consistently with the right to life so as to encompass a right to life-saving treatment at state expense where a patient is unable to afford private treatment. It held that the effect of such an interpretation would be to prioritise tertiary health care treatments of terminal illnesses over preventative health care and treatment of non-life-threatening conditions. This would be inconsistent with the obligations imposed upon the State under ss 27(1) and (2).[26]

---

22 Ibid para 1.

23 Ibid para 15.

24 Ibid. On the development of the Indian jurisprudence in relation to socio-economic rights, see chapter 3, part 3.3.3.(*b*)(ii).

25 Ibid paras 16–17 (citing *S v Makwanyane* 1995 (3) SA 391 (CC), 1995 (6) BCLR 665 (CC) para 325).

26 Ibid para 19.

Turning to the specific scope of s 27(3), the Court held that it was reserved for situations of 'sudden catastrophes' requiring immediate medical attention and not to the ongoing treatment of chronic illnesses for the purposes of prolonging life.[27] It observed that the right is 'couched in negative terms – it is a right not to be refused emergency medical treatment'.[28] It inferred from this formulation that its purpose 'seems to be to ensure that treatment be given in an emergency, and is not frustrated by reason of bureaucratic requirements or other formalities'.[29] The Court also suggested that the right to emergency medical treatment was restricted to currently available emergency medical facilities:

> What the section requires is that remedial treatment that is necessary *and available* be given immediately to avert that harm.[30] (Emphasis added.)

Mr Soobramoney was thus held to have no cause of action in terms of either s 11 or s 27(3) of the Constitution. Instead the Court held that his claim fell to be determined in terms of ss 27(1) and (2) of the Constitution – the qualified right of access to health care services.[31] Two primary questions had to be answered in determining whether the refusal of Addington Hospital to admit Mr Soobramoney to the dialysis treatment programme constituted an infringement of these provisions. The first was whether it was necessary to ration access to kidney dialysis treatment to patients such as the applicant. Secondly, if such rationing was necessary, whether the guidelines adopted by the renal unit of Addington Hospital complied with the constitutional requirements imposed by ss 27(1) and (2) and, if so, whether they were applied 'fairly and rationally' to the applicant's case.

The first issue essentially concerns whether and under what conditions limited resources constitute a valid basis for limiting access to medical treatment for patients in the situation of the applicant. The Court commenced by noting that the court *a quo* had found that the provincial ministry of health in KwaZulu-Natal had 'conclusively proved that there are no funds available to provide patients such as the applicant with the necessary treatment'.[32] The appellant had not disputed this finding, but argued that the State could provide additional funding for kidney dialysis treatment for patients such as himself who were suffering from chronic renal failure.[33] In response, the Court referred to the budgetary constraints facing provincial health departments in general, including the year-on-year overspending by KwaZulu-Natal Department of Health.[34] The scarcity of resources meant that the need for access to kidney dialysis treatment greatly exceeded the number of available dialysis machines.

---

27 Ibid paras 13, 20–22.
28 Ibid para 20.
29 Ibid.
30 Ibid para 20.
31 Ibid para 22.
32 Ibid para 23.
33 Ibid.
34 Ibid paras 24–26.

The Court noted that this was a national problem extending to all renal clinics.[35] The diversion of additional resources to the renal dialysis programme and similar tertiary health care interventions from within the health budget would prejudice other important health programmes.[36] If the overall health budget was substantially increased to fund all health care programmes this would diminish the resources available to the State to meet other social needs in the spheres of access to housing, food and water, employment opportunities, and social security.[37]

Ultimately the Court was not persuaded that it was reasonable to require the State to divert additional resources to the renal dialysis programme in order to cater for all patients in his situation. This inevitably implied that it was necessary for health authorities to ration access to certain forms of medical treatments. The appellant had not suggested that the relevant guidelines established by the hospital were unreasonable. Neither had he argued that they were not applied 'fairly and rationally' when the decision was taken that he did not qualify for dialysis treatment.[38] Accordingly, no breach of s 27(1)(*a*) read with (2) had been established.

As the above analysis demonstrates, the primary basis for evaluating a claim that the State has failed to fulfil a duty imposed on it by s 27 is whether the conduct and decisions of the relevant organs of State are reasonable in the circumstances. Moreover, the Court indicated that a significant measure of deference would be accorded to the decisions of the legislative and executive organs of state in fixing the health budget, and to the medical authorities in devising and applying the criteria for making the 'agonising choices'[39] as to who should and should not receive medical treatment. Thus it held that courts 'will be slow to interfere with rational decisions taken in good faith by the political organs and medical authorities whose responsibility it is to deal with such matters'.[40]

4.2.2 Evaluating *Soobramoney*

(*a*) Emergency medical treatment: section 27(3)

The first aspect of the *Soobramoney* judgment which requires critical scrutiny is the Court's construction of the right against the refusal of emergency medical treatment in s 27(3) of the Constitution. In order to justify its finding that the appellant's claim fell outside the scope of s 27(3), the Court was obliged to provide some interpretation of the nature and ambit of the entitlement contained in this subsection. As will

---

[35] Ibid para 24.

[36] Ibid paras 27–28, 30.

[37] Ibid paras 28, 31. This is a classic illustration of the difficulty of 'polycentricity' in adjudication. See further in this regard chapter 2, part 2.4.8 at notes 230–244 and accompanying text.

[38] Ibid paras 25.

[39] Ibid paras 24, 30.

[40] Ibid para 29.

be seen, this is in marked contrast to the absence of almost any engagement with the content and scope of the right of access to health care services in s 27(1)(*a*).

The Court is careful to interpret s 27(3) so as to distinguish it from the general right of access to health care services in s 27(1)(*a*). Thus s 27(3) applies only to sudden medical emergencies as opposed to, for example, the ongoing treatment of chronic illnesses. This distinction is understandable given the formulation of s 27(3) and its location within the overall structure of s 27. The right against the refusal of emergency medical treatment is protected in a separate subsection located after the description of the nature of the State's positive obligations in relation to the realisation of the various rights listed in s 27(1). Section 27(3) is clearly designed to carve out a specific aspect of the general right of health care services, emergency medical treatment, which gives rise to special obligations. Thus this right is not subject to the qualifications in s 27(2) relating to reasonable measures, progressive realisation or resource availability. Its purpose is to ensure that every person is able to receive the treatment which is deemed medically necessary in a health emergency. The latter could be due to an accident or to a crisis such as a heart attack or stroke. Any limitations to this right would be subject to the stringent requirements of the general limitations clause, including the requirement of a law of general application in s 36(1).[41]

A problematic feature of the judgment is the suggestion that the scope of the right is confined to the denial of access to *existing* facilities, thus curtailing the potential positive dimensions of this right. The positive duties which s 27(3) imposes on the State could include the expansion of emergency medical services in certain areas where there are no or inadequate facilities, or increasing the number of ambulances in a particular region where current services are patently inadequate to cope with emergency health needs. It could further support a challenge to the closure of existing emergency services due to, for example, budgetary cut-backs. The consequence of an inadequate provision of emergency health care services is that people who are faced with 'sudden catastrophes' are in effect refused emergency health care. There is no textual or purposive justification for the limited, negative construction which the Court appears to give to this right.[42] On the contrary, as Scott and Alston point out, the purely negative interpretation given to s 27(3) would appear to make it a redundant right in the light of the negative duty on the State under s 27(1) to desist from prevention or impairing the right of access to health care services.[43]

The following observations by Sachs J in his concurring judgment suggest a more expansive interpretation of s 27(3) in the light of its underlying values and purposes:

---

[41] On the role of the general limitations clause in socio-economic rights adjudication, see 4.4.5 below.

[42] See the critique by C Scott & P Alston 'Adjudicating constitutional priorities in a transnational context: A comment on *Soobramoney's* legacy and *Grootboom's* promise' (2000) 16 *SAJHR* 206–268.

[43] Ibid 245–248.

> The special attention given by s 27(3) to non-refusal of emergency medical treatment relates to the particular sense of shock to our notions of human solidarity occasioned by the turning away from hospital of people battered and bleeding or of those who fall victim to sudden and unexpected collapse. It provides reassurance to all members of society *that accident and emergency departments will be available* to deal with unforeseeable catastrophes which could befall any person, *anywhere at any time*.[44] (Footnotes omitted, emphasis added.)

It is instructive in this context to compare the approach adopted by the Indian Supreme Court in the case of *Paschim Banga Khet Mazdoor Samity v State of West Bengal*.[45] This case, cited by the Constitutional Court, in support of its interpretation of s 27(3),[46] concerned the victim of a train accident who sustained serious injuries. He was turned away from various hospitals on the grounds that ranged from a lack of room to accommodate him to a lack of facilities to provide the necessary emergency treatment. Eventually he was forced to secure the necessary treatment at a private hospital. The Supreme Court derived the right to emergency medical treatment from the right to life protected in art 21 of the Indian Constitution. However, the judgment did not confine itself to ordering compensation to the victim for the negative violation of his right. It also focused on the positive measures needed to ensure 'that proper medical facilities are available for dealing with emergency cases'.[47] The Court's order entailed placing extensive positive duties on the State to improve emergency health care infrastructure and services, including the formulation and implementation of 'a time-bound plan' for providing these services.[48] This illustrates how an entitlement to emergency medical treatment can give rise to positive orders to remedy institutional and systemic deficiencies in the provision of emergency health care services.

(*b*) Sections 27(1) and (2)

The second significant aspect of the *Soobramoney* judgment concerns the Court's approach to the interpretation of ss 27(1) and (2). Negligible attention is devoted to the substantive content of the right of everyone 'to have access to health care services' in s 27(1)(*a*). Instead, after having determined that the appellant's claim falls to be decided in terms of ss 27(1) and (2),[49] the Court proceeds immediately to discuss the budgetary limitations and polycentric implications of the appellant's claim.[50] The implication is that the right in s 27(1)(*a*) is both defined and limited by reference to the State's available resources. This is reinforced by the observation that ss 27(1) and (2) 'entitle everyone to have access to health care services provided by the

---

44 *Soobramoney* (note 2 above) para 51.
45 (1996) 4 SCC 37.
46 *Soobramoney* (note 2 above) paras 18–20.
47 *Paschim Banga Khet Majoor Samity v State of West Bengal* (note 45 above) para 15.
48 Ibid para 16.
49 *Soobramoney* (note 2 above) para 22.
50 Ibid paras 23–31.

State "within its available resources"'.[51] An implied reasonableness standard is used to assess justifiability of the appellant's claim. *Soobramoney* thus established, in Danie Brand's terminology, a 'means-end justificatory model'.[52] According to this model, the Court asks the basic question whether a particular policy or programme is 'reasonably related to the constitutionally prescribed goal of providing access to' the relevant socio-economic right.[53] Within this justificatory model, the Court can vary the standard of scrutiny applied to interrogate the link between the relevant programme and the constitutional goal.[54]

Soobramoney could be read to suggest that the Court was committed to a deferential rationality standard of scrutiny in evaluating socio-economic rights claims in terms of ss 26 and 27.[55] It has also been read to suggest that the Court will confine its scrutiny of resource-based justifications for not providing access to socio-economic rights to existing budgetary allocations.[56] However, the standard of scrutiny adopted in this case must be viewed in the light of the nature of the health care intervention at issue in the case. Kidney dialysis treatment constitutes a relatively expensive, tertiary health care programme. The principle would have to be extended to all those in need of similar health care interventions. It was not seriously contested that ordering the extension of the programme to accommodate Mr Soobramoney and others in his situation would have spiralling repercussions for other health care programmes as well as social programmes outside the health care sector. Given the evidence of limited health care resources, rationing to certain kinds of tertiary health programmes was clearly necessary so as to ensure fairness to all those requiring treatment as well as obtaining maximum benefit from the available technology.[57] Furthermore, the Court did not exclude interrogating whether an increased allocation of resources to the health department for the purposes of kidney dialysis treatment for people with

---

[51] Ibid para 22.

[52] D Brand 'The proceduralisation of South African socio-economic rights jurisprudence or "What are socio-economic rights for?"' in H Botha, A J van der Walt & J van der Walt (eds) *Rights and Democracy in a Transformative Constitution* (2004) 33–56 at 40.

[53] Ibid.

[54] Ibid n 45.

[55] See, for example, C Steinberg 'Can reasonableness protect the poor? A review of South Africa's socio-economic rights jurisprudence' (2006) 123 *SALJ* 264–284 at 279.

[56] D Moellendorf 'Reasoning about resources: *Soobramoney* and the future of socio-economic rights claims' (1998) 14 *SAJHR* 327–333. As Moellendorf observes, the implication of confining the scope of right solely to existing budgetary allocations is that government's budgetary decisions will be allowed to determine the content of rights, instead of our constitutional commitment to human rights norms and values guiding economic policy (332).

[57] The Court stated:

> By using the available dialysis machines in accordance with the guidelines more patients are benefited than would be the case if they were used to keep alive persons with chronic renal failure, and the outcome of the treatment is also likely to be more beneficial because it is directed at curing patients, and not simply maintaining them in a chronically ill condition. (para 25)

chronic renal failure was justifiable. However, it was not presented with compelling arguments or evidence to justify making such an order. Moreover, the Court was not in a position to engage seriously with the latter argument as the respondent was the provincial Minister of Health and the national government had not been joined as a party.

However, the judgment provides the first indication that the Constitutional Court will depart from the traditional two-stage approach to Bill of Rights litigation in the context of claims implicating the positive duties imposed by the socio-economic rights in ss 26 and 27. The two-stage approach entails an initial principled focus on the nature and scope of the relevant right and whether the impugned legislation or conduct infringes the right. Thereafter the burden is placed on the respondent to establish that limitations to the right are reasonable and justifiable according to the stringent requirements of the general limitations clause (s 36).[58] Instead, the Court conflates both stages of the analysis in considering whether the denial of Mr Soobramoney's access to dialysis treatment is justifiable. The result is a disproportionate focus on the justifiability of the restriction, and an inadequate engagement with the purposes and values which s 27(1)(*a*) was intended to protect and the impact of its denial on the claimant. The Court's reasoning has a distinctly utilitarian flavour when it observes, for example:

> The State has to manage its limited resources in order to address all these claims. There will be times when this requires it to adopt a holistic approach to the larger needs of society rather than to focus on the specific needs of particular individuals within society.[59]

The result is that the Court's evaluation of the relevant budgetary allocation decisions and of the rationing criteria for kidney dialysis treatment accords minimal sufficient weight to the values and purposes of health care as a human right. There is almost no attempt to interpret access to health care services as a constitutionally protected right, or to refer to relevant international and comparative law. In assessing the budgetary limitations facing the health departments, no reference is made to the implications of a human rights-based approach to policy and budgetary decision-making.[60] The criteria established by Addington Hospital for rationing access to kidney dialysis treatment are evaluated according to the standards of reasonableness, rationality and fairness. However, these broad standards are not interrogated further to establish to what extent human rights values, particularly those relevant to health care rights, informed the design of the relevant rationing criteria.

In fairness to the Court, it was not presented with the evidence and arguments to support a more in-depth engagement with health care rights of the above-mentioned

---

[58] See also part 4.4.5 below.

[59] *Soobramoney* (note 2 above) para 31.

[60] For the implications of a human rights-based approach to developmental policies, see J K Hansen & H O Sano 'The implications and value added of a rights-based approach' in B A Andreassen & S P Marks (eds) *Development as a Human Right: Legal, Political and Economic Dimensions* (2006) 36–56.

nature. The appellant based his claim on the right to life and the guarantee against the refusal of emergency medical treatment in s 27(3), and did not develop an argument in terms of s 27(1)(*a*) read with (2). Nevertheless, the failure of the Court to accord substantive significance to s 27(1)(*a*), coupled with the focus of the inquiry falling almost entirely on the State's reasons for limiting access to kidney dialysis treatment divests socio-economic rights of their transformative potential. Without clear guidance being provided by the courts on the nature and scope of socio-economic rights such as health care, it is unlikely that they will exert a fundamental influence in the State's decision-making concerning social programmes and budgetary allocations. Moreover, if the traditional approach is followed where the burden to persuade a court on the justifiability of restrictions to rights rests on the respondents,[61] one could expect more from the State in justifying its budgetary allocation decisions and rationing criteria in terms of the interests and values protected by health rights. Even if this analysis does not take place in terms of the general limitations clause, it will be argued that a similar approach should be adopted in applying the criteria in ss 26(2) and 27(2) to the rights protected in ss 26(1) and (2).

(*c*) Interdependence

In chapter 2, it was argued that an interpretive approach which surfaces the interrelated values and rights at stake in particular cases promotes the transformative ethos of the Constitution.[62] Such an approach seeks to do justice to the complex experience and interrelated dimensions of poverty without reducing it to a single constitutional right or value in the name of promoting conceptual clarity in constitutional adjudication. The facts of the *Soobramoney* case provided an important early opportunity for the Court to develop the interrelationship between the rights to life and health care rights.

The Court held that the structure of the South African Bill of Rights with its express incorporation of a number of socio-economic rights militates against deriving positive socio-economic duties from the right to life as the Indian Supreme Court has done.[63] It can readily be accepted that it would be anomalous to derive more extensive obligations from a particular right in circumstances where the specific interests at stake are expressly protected in a more limited form by another set of rights.[64] Such an approach would be inconsistent with a contextual approach to the interpretation

---

[61] See further part 4.4.5 below.

[62] Chapter 2, part 2.4.2.

[63] See the discussion of the constitutional jurisprudence of the Indian Supreme Court pertaining to socio-economic rights in chapter 3, part 3.3.3 at notes 217–239 and accompanying text.

[64] Where a specific right, for example the right to marriage and family life, is not expressly protected in the Bill of Rights, the Court has been willing to derive such a right from a more general right such as the right to human dignity (s 10). See *Dawood v Minister of Home Affairs* 2000 (3) SA 936 (CC), 2000 (8) BCLR 837 (CC) paras 34–37.

of the Bill of Rights. However, this should not imply that the right to life and the right to health care are interpreted to protect mutually discrete interests and to suppress the significant interconnection between these two rights.[65]

This interdependence could have been developed in *Soobramoney* through a more substantive analysis of the role of the right to life and its underlying values in the interpretation of the health care rights entrenched in s 27. This occurs in a more satisfactory fashion in the separate concurring judgment of Sachs J where he points out that, although the primary functions of health care rights are to preserve and improve life, the inevitability of death must also be acknowledged. It is easy to lose sight of this basic fact of human existence in the context of proliferating technologies at the frontiers of medical science aiming to prolong life (usually at a substantial cost) in cases of terminal illness and old age.[66] These scientific advances and their implications for the fair distribution of health care resources must also incorporate an acceptance of the reality of our human mortality. As Sachs J points out:

> However the right to life may come to be defined in South Africa, there is in reality no meaningful way in which it can constitutionally be extended to encompass the right indefinitely to evade death. [67]

A consideration of the value of life in the rationing of scarce tertiary health care treatments would also require consideration for those whose lives could be saved or significantly improved by less resource-intensive forms of medical intervention such as immunisations or access to anti-retroviral therapy.[68] This is a function of an interdependent social existence where decisions regarding the allocation of health care resources affect others. This reality necessitates a transparent, fair and constitutionally consistent policy for allocating scarce health resources, and for guiding decisions in individual cases.[69]

The need to recognise our mortality and the health care rights of others is not an argument for the proposition that all forms of tertiary health care should be abandoned in favour of primary health care interventions. Public health specialists point out that the primary and tertiary health care sectors form an integrated, interdependent system. There are cogent public health and human rights arguments for

---

[65] Scott and Alston (note 42 above) 237 describe the type of reasoning where the inclusion of certain rights in the Constitution is used as a basis for narrowing the scope of other rights as 'negative inferentialism'. On the interconnections between the right to health and the right to life, see M Pieterse 'A different shade of red: Socio-economic dimensions of the right to life in South Africa' (1999) 15 *SAJHR* 372–385. See also the statement of Madala J in his concurring judgment in *Soobramoney* (note 2 above): 'The State undoubtedly has a strong interest in protecting and preserving the life and health of its citizens and to that end must do all in its power to protect and preserve life.' (para 39).

[66] *Soobramoney* (note 2 above) para 56.

[67] Ibid para 57.

[68] See in this regard the observation of Chaskalson P (as he then was) in *Soobramoney* (ibid) para 31.

[69] Ibid para 53.

ensuring a reasonable allocation of resources to tertiary health care institutions and interventions.[70] The State should therefore be placed under a burden to justify its allocations to the primary, secondary and tertiary health care sectors in the light of the interrelated norms and values underpinning the rights to life and health care services. Only once it is concluded that the overall allocation of resources to the tertiary health care sector is reasonable in the light of constitutional commitments, should the inevitability of rationing access to scarce, expensive medical interventions be accepted.[71] Here again, while a court should respect the particular experience and expertise of health authorities and professionals in designing rationing criteria, it is not absolved from its constitutional duty to scrutinise the relevant criteria for consistency with relevant constitutional rights. Thus both the budgetary and administrative decisions which establish the overall parameters within which medical rationing decisions are made, as well as the particular rationing criteria, should be closely scrutinised for consistency with the constitutionally protected interest of every person to gain access to the services which are necessary to preserve and protect their life and health. The State should have been required to demonstrate that all the decisions which resulted in Mr Soobramoney being denied access to kidney dialysis treatment were constitutionally compliant.

A consideration of the right to life and the values and interests underpinning it would not necessarily have changed the outcome of the *Soobramoney* judgment. However, a deeper analysis of the complex interrelationship between the rights to life and health care in the context of tertiary medical interventions would have provided a more substantive basis for justifying the refusal of Mr Soobramoney's claim to kidney dialysis treatment, even though it would prolong his life.[72]

(*d*) Public and private health care

A final aspect which the *Soobramoney* case highlights is the reality in South Africa that many are excluded from access to medical services which are available to those with access to sufficient resources. As the Court observed, it is a 'hard and unpalatable fact' that, had the appellant been a wealthy person, he would have been able to continue purchasing the kidney dialysis treatment from the private health care sector.[73] This suggests the Court's awareness of the social injustice implicit in a situation where the wealthy can purchase life-preserving health care services from which the poor

---

[70] See R Kirsch 'Poor people get cancer too' (2007) 97 *SAMJ* 471.

[71] Marius Pieterse 'Health care rights, resources and rationing' (2007) 124 *SALJ* 514–536 at 532 observes that the Court's scrutiny in the *Soobramoney* case arguably extended only to the parameters of the functional rationing decisions that were made in relation to access to dialysis treatment 'whereas the constitutional compliance of the legion of political, budgetary and administrative decisions that shaped the contours of this choice was either assumed or left unquestioned'.

[72] On the significance of substantive legal reasoning for transformative adjudication, see chapter 2, part 2.4.2.

[73] *Soobramoney* (note 2 above) para 31.

are excluded. This injustice is aggravated in the South African context, where there is a substantial gap between the well-resourced private health care sector and the under-resourced public health care sector, resulting in significantly unequal access to quality health care between rich and poor persons.[74] While wealth-based inequalities in access to social commodities are endemic to market societies, our Constitution accords health care the special status of a human rights norm. This has implications for the degree of inequality that is constitutionally tolerable in access to health care and the quality of the services received. Should a constitutional challenge be brought to the deeply inadequate state of health care services in the public sector,[75] it would be artificial and formalistic for litigants and the court to ignore the structural implications of South Africa's two-tier health system for the fulfilment of s 27 rights.

The large role of the private sector in delivering health care services in South Africa can be ameliorated through legislative interventions[76] and the development of the common law to facilitate greater access to such services.[77] However, in the longer term, fundamental reforms to the overall structure of the health care system in South

---

[74] According to a study of the South African health system, 'the public-private mix is undoubtedly the greatest equity challenge facing the South African health system'. The study reports widening disparities in the resources available to each sector, relative to the population that each serves, over the past decade. There are massive disparities in expenditure per patient in the public and private health care system respectively, as well as the human resources between the two sectors. Thus one specialist doctor serves fewer than 500 people on average in the private sector, but nearly 11 000 people in the public health sector. D McIntyre et al *SHIELD Work Package 1 Report: A Critical Analysis of the Current South African Health System* (2007) Health Economics Unit (University of Cape Town) and Centre for Health Policy (University of the Witwatersrand) v and 31. Available at http://web.uct.ac.za/depts/heu/SHIELD/reports/SouthAfrica1.pdf (accessed on 7 April 2009).

[75] See L Reynolds & D Sanders 'Our children are dying in droves – and this is why' *Cape Times* 22 August 2007, 9.

[76] For example, s 29(1)(*n*) of the Medical Schemes Act 131 of 1998 stipulates that the rules of a medical scheme shall not take into account grounds such as age, sex, and past or present state of health of applicants in determining admission to membership or the contributions payable. A further example of legislative regulation of the private health care sector to ensure compliance with constitutional obligations is s 5 of the National Health Act 61 of 2003 which provides that '[a] health care provider, health worker or health establishment may not refuse a person emergency medical treatment'. A 'health establishment' is defined to include public and private health care facilities (s 1). This provision thus gives horizontal effect to s 27(3) of the Constitution. In terms of s 90(1)(*m*) of the National Health Act, the Minister of Health is empowered to make regulations concerning emergency medical services and emergency medical treatment.

[77] For an analysis of how the common law should be developed to promote the health rights in the Constitution, see M Pieterse *A Benefit-Focused Analysis of Constitutional Health Rights* (2005) Unpublished PhD thesis, University of the Witwatersrand, 150–174; M Pieterse 'Indirect horizontal application of the right to have access to health care services' (2007) 23 *SAJHR* 157–179.

Africa and the disparities it generates will have be addressed if the constitutional promise of universal access to health care services is to be fulfilled.

(*e*) Conclusion

The *Soobramoney* judgment established the basic paradigm of reasonableness review for evaluating compliance with the positive duties imposed by the socio-economic rights in ss 26 and 27.

A major critique of the judgment from the perspective of developing a substantive interpretation of socio-economic rights is the lack of engagement with the purposes and values protected by the right of access to health care services in s 27(1)(*a*) of the Constitution. The failure to develop the normative content of health care rights, including its interrelationship with other rights such as the right to life, results in a disproportionate focus on the State's justificatory arguments. The assessment of such arguments also occurs in the absence of a normative framework which should have been supplied by an analysis of the content and scope of the right of access to health care services.[78]

As noted above, the outcome of the *Soobramoney* case would not necessarily have been different, but it would have led to a more satisfactory explanation of why upholding the refusal to admit Mr Soobramoney to kidney dialysis treatment was consistent with constitutional requirements. In addition, the entrenchment of socio-economic rights in the Constitution should lead to fundamental changes in both the manner and substance of government and expert decision-making which affects access to these rights. It is hard to imagine that legislators, state officials and medical personnel would be inspired by the *Soobramoney* judgment to take the human right to health care seriously in their budgeting and policy processes as well as the formulation of criteria for rationing access to medical interventions.

By failing to engage seriously with health care as a human right, the Constitutional Court missed an opportunity to promote the transformative potential of socio-economic rights.

4.3 DEVELOPING 'REASONABLENESS REVIEW': *GROOTBOOM, TREATMENT ACTION CAMPAIGN* AND *KHOSA*

4.3.1 Introduction

It was almost three years after the *Soobramoney* judgment that the next major test case on socio-economic rights reached the Constitutional Court. The *Grootboom* case concerned a group of adults and children who had moved onto private land from an

[78] As David Bilchitz *Poverty and Fundamental Rights: The Justification and Enforcement of Socio-Economic Rights* (2007) 143 argues, the '*measures* which the government adopts must be reasonable in relation to the objective it seeks to achieve. … This enquiry requires the specification of some content to the right, independently of the notion of reasonableness.'

informal settlement owing to the 'appalling conditions' in which they were living.[79] They were evicted from the private land. Following the eviction, they camped on a sports field in the area. However, they could not erect adequate shelters as most of their building materials had been destroyed during the eviction. Accordingly, they found themselves in a precarious position where they had neither security of tenure, nor adequate shelter from the elements.[80] They applied to the Western Cape High Court, Cape Town on an urgent basis for an order against all three spheres of government, requiring them to provide temporary shelter or housing until they obtained permanent accommodation. The High Court held that there was no violation of s 26 (the right of everyone to have access to housing), but found a violation of s 28(1)(*c*) (the right of children to shelter).[81] On appeal, the Constitutional Court declared that the State's housing programme fell short of compliance with s 26(1) and (2) (the qualified right of everyone to have access to adequate housing), but found no violation of the right of children to shelter under s 28(1)(*c*).

Almost two years after *Grootboom*, the Constitutional Court delivered judgment in the *Treatment Action Campaign* case which involved a challenge to the limited nature of the measures introduced by the State to prevent mother-to-child transmission of HIV. It was argued that the State unreasonably prohibited the administration of the antiretroviral drug, Nevirapine, at public hospitals and clinics outside a limited number of research and training sites.[82] This drug was of proven efficacy in reducing *intrapartum* mother-to-child transmission of HIV. It was further contended that the State had failed to produce and implement a comprehensive national programme for the prevention of mother-to-child transmission of HIV. According to the Treatment Action Campaign (TAC), the aforementioned conduct and omissions of the State constituted violations of the right of everyone to have access to health care services in s 27 of the Constitution as well as children's right to have access to basic health care services in s 28(1)(*c*). Both the High Court[83] and the Constitutional Court held that the State's programme to prevent mother-to-child transmission of HIV did not comply with its obligations in terms of ss 27(1) and (2) (the qualified right of everyone to have access to health care services). The Constitutional Court made both declaratory and mandatory orders against the Government.

---

79 *Grootboom* (note 3 above) para 3.

80 Ibid paras 9–11.

81 *Grootboom v Oostenberg Municipality* 2000 (3) BCLR 277 (C).

82 Nevirapine was available at two pilot sites per province. See *Treatment Action Campaign* (note 5 above) paras 10–11.

83 *Treatment Action Campaign v Minister of Health* 2002 (4) BCLR 356 (T).

4.3.2 Minimum core obligations

In both the *Grootboom* and *Treatment Action Campaign* cases, the Constitutional Court was urged by the *amici curiae* in these cases[84] to adopt the concept of a 'minimum core obligation' in assessing the State's compliance with the positive duties imposed by ss 26 and 27. This concept has been endorsed by the United Nations Committee on Economic, Social and Cultural Rights in interpreting States Parties' obligations under the International Covenant on Economic, Social and Cultural Rights.[85]

In *Grootboom*, although the parties had based their arguments on the right of children to shelter in terms of s 28(1)(*c*), the *amici* broadened the issues before the Court to include a consideration of s 26 of the Constitution.[86] They highlighted the unjust results of the reasoning of the court *a quo*, namely the exclusion of adults without children from shelter in crises while those with children were entitled to relief.[87] They argued that s 26(1) read with (2) imposes a minimum core obligation on the State to ensure that those who are truly homeless and in crises receive some rudimentary form of shelter. The State has a burden to demonstrate that it has prioritised its resources to satisfy this minimum core obligation. Section 28(1)(*c*) was a specific manifestation of this minimum core obligation, as it placed it beyond doubt that the basic socio-economic needs of children in especially vulnerable circumstances

---

[84] In *Grootboom*, the joint *amici* were the Community Law Centre (UWC) and the South African Human Rights Commission. In *Treatment Action Campaign*, the *amici* were the Community Law Centre (UWC) and IDASA. Copies of the *amici curiae's* submissions in both cases are on file with the author, who assisted in their preparation.

[85] The UN Committee on Economic, Social and Cultural Rights described the concept of minimum core obligations as follows:

> On the basis of the extensive experience gained by the Committee, as well as by the body that preceded it, over a period of more than a decade of examining States parties' reports the Committee is of the view that a minimum core obligation to ensure the satisfaction of, at the very least, minimum essential levels of each of the rights is incumbent upon every State Party. Thus, for example, a State Party in which any significant number of individuals is deprived of essential foodstuffs, of essential primary health care, of basic shelter and housing, or of the most basic forms of education is, *prima facie*, failing to discharge its obligations under the Covenant. … In order for a State Party to be able to attribute its failure to meet at least its minimum core obligations to a lack of available resources it must demonstrate that every effort has been made to use all resources at its disposition in an effort to satisfy, as a matter of priority, those minimum obligations.

General Comment No 3 (Fifth sess 1990), *The nature of States' parties obligations (art 2(1) of the Covenant)*, UN doc E/1991/23 para 10. See also chapter 3, part 3.3.2(*c*), notes 136–143 and accompanying text.

[86] *Grootboom* (note 3 above) para 18.

[87] The High Court in *Grootboom v Oostenberg Municipality* (note 81 above) 286H–187B applied a *Soobramoney*-style rationality test to find that the government housing programme did not infringe s 26 of the Constitution. However, it held that the situation of the *Grootboom* community which resulted in children being without shelter constituted an infringement of s 28(1)(*c*) of the Constitution. As it would not be in the best interests of the child (s 28(2)) for children to be separated from their parents, the parents of the child enjoyed a derivative right to shelter (288H-289D). See further chapter 5, part 5.2.3.

must be satisfied. The *amici* thus located the minimum core obligation at one end of a continuum of positive obligations imposed on the State by s 26(2) to realise progressively the right in s 26(1) of everyone to have access to 'adequate' housing.[88] The non-fulfilment of the minimum core could also be justified by resource constraints, but there would be a heavy burden of justification on the State to show that it had prioritised its resources to ensure the fulfilment of this core obligation.[89]

Following the Court's rejection of this approach in *Grootboom*, the *amici* in *Treatment Action Campaign* located the minimum core in the first subsection of s 27(1) (and by implication also s 26(1)). They argued that every individual is entitled to a basic core of health care services comprising the minimum necessary for a dignified human existence. This basic core right is not subject to the qualifications of resource constraints and progressive realisation in s 27(2). Over and above this minimum core entitlement, the State is obliged, in terms of s 27(2), to take reasonable measures within its available resources to achieve progressively *the full* realisation of the relevant duties. In other words, s 27(2) is not exhaustive of the State's positive duties. It supplements the unqualified core duty in terms of s 27(1) to ensure to everyone basic levels of the relevant rights with a qualified obligation to improve the nature of services and resources until the right is fully realised.[90] In the context of the *Treatment Action Campaign* case, it was argued that this minimum core should be interpreted in the light of the value of human dignity, and should include the provision of Nevirapine to pregnant women with HIV and their newborn babies.

In responding to the arguments of the *amici* in *Grootboom* and *Treatment Action Campaign*, the Court raised a number of principled, textual, pragmatic and institutional objections to the concept. The major principled objection raised by the Court to the concept of a minimum core obligation is the fact that groups are differently situated and their socio-economic needs vary according to their different contexts.[91] Thus in the context of the right to have access to adequate housing, the Court highlighted the fact that the needs and opportunities for the enjoyment of the rights were diverse:

---

[88] See Submissions on behalf of the *Amici Curiae*, 10 September 2002 (note 84 above) para 27.

[89] This is consistent with the approach adopted by the UN Committee on Economic, Social and Cultural Rights in General Comment No 3 (note 85 above). However, in later General Comments, the Committee has adopted a less flexible position by insisting that the non-fulfilment of core obligations cannot be justified under any circumstances: General Comment No 14 (Twenty-second sess, 2000) *The right to the highest attainable standard of health (art 12 of the International Covenant on Economic, Social and Cultural Rights)*, UN doc E/C.12/2000/4 para 47; General Comment No 15 (Twenty-ninth sess, 2002) *The right to water (arts. 11 and 12 of the International Covenant on Economic, Social and Cultural Rights)*, UN doc E/C. 12/2002/11 para 40.

[90] See Submissions on behalf of the *Amici Curiae*, April 2003 (note 84 above) paras 14 and 23.

[91] *Grootboom* (note 3 above) paras 32–33.

> [T]here are those who need land; others need both land and houses; yet others need financial assistance. There are difficult questions relating to the definition of the minimum core in the context of a right to have access to adequate housing, in particular whether the minimum core obligation should be defined generally or with regard to specific groups of people.[92]

The second objection raised by the Court relates to its lack of an adequate informational base to determine the content of minimum core obligations. The Court asserted that the UN Committee on Economic, Social and Cultural Rights developed the content of minimum core obligations on the basis of its extensive experience in scrutinising State reports under the International Covenant on Economic, Social and Cultural Rights, 1966. Given the diversity of the needs and circumstances of various groups, the Court held that it did not have 'sufficient information to enable it to determine what would comprise the minimum core obligation in the context of our Constitution'.[93]

Third, the Court held that the textual formulation of ss 26 and 27 did not support the interpretation advanced by the *amici* in the *Treatment Action Campaign* case. The obligations placed on the State by s 26(2) and 27(2) relate to the realisation of the rights in s 26(1) and 27(1). The rights in ss 26(1) and 27(1) are thus limited by considerations of resource constraints and progressive realisation. There is accordingly no unqualified duty on the State to provide access to the rights in ss 26 and 27 immediately and on demand.[94]

The fourth objection was of a pragmatic nature in that the Court was of the view that minimum core obligations impose unrealistic demands on the State in that it is 'impossible to give everyone access even to a "core" service immediately'.[95]

Finally, the Court held that the minimum core was incompatible with the institutional competencies and role of the courts. Thus it held that 'courts are not institutionally equipped to make the wide-ranging factual and political enquiries necessary for determining what the minimum core standards' should be.[96] The Court went on to comment:

> Courts are ill-suited to adjudicate upon issues where court orders could have multiple social and economic consequences for the community. The Constitution contemplates rather a restrained and focused role for the courts.[97]

---

92 Ibid para 33.

93 Ibid para 31. However, as Matthew Craven *The International Covenant on Economic, Social and Cultural Rights* (1995) 91 observes, the General Comments are not in fact based on the assessment of State reports, but are an assertion of the Committee's 'authority to exercise an interpretative function *in abstracto*'.

94 *Grootboom* (note 3 above) para 95; *Treatment Action Campaign* (note 5 above) para 32.

95 *Treatment Action Campaign* (note 5 above) para 35.

96 Ibid para 37.

97 Ibid para 38.

The Court thus rejected an interpretation of the socio-economic rights in ss 26 and 27 that would 'give rise to a self-standing and independent positive right enforceable irrespective of the considerations mentioned in s 27(2)'.[98] The core inquiry, according to the Court, was whether the measures taken by the State to realise the socio-economic rights in ss 26 and 27 were reasonable. However, it did indicate that the evidence in a particular case may show that there is a minimum core of a particular service that should be taken into account in determining whether the measures adopted by the State are reasonable.[99]

4.3.3 Criteria for assessing reasonableness

Having disposed of the arguments of the *amici* in favour of a minimum core obligation, the Court in *Grootboom* proceeded to develop a model of 'reasonableness review' for adjudicating the positive duties imposed by ss 26 and 27. In reviewing these positive duties, the central question that the Court asks is whether the means chosen are reasonably capable of facilitating the realisation of the socio-economic rights in question.[100] The Court's approach is designed to allow government a margin of discretion relating to the specific policy choices adopted to give effect to socio-economic rights:

> A Court considering reasonableness will not enquire whether other more desirable or favourable measures could have been adopted, or whether public money could have been better spent. The question would be whether the measures that have been adopted are

---

[98] Ibid para 39.

[99] *Grootboom* (note 3 above) para 33; *Treatment Action Campaign* (note 5 above) para 34.

[100] *Grootboom* (note 3 above) para 41. Reasonableness review has synergies with the approach of the UN Committee on Economic, Social and Cultural Rights to the interpretation of the obligations imposed upon States Parties by art 2 of the International Covenant on Economic, Social and Cultural Rights (1966). Thus it has held that States Parties are under an obligation to take steps that are 'deliberate, concrete and targeted as clearly as possible towards meeting the obligation recognized in the Covenant'. General Comment No 3 (note 85 above) para 2. Reasonableness review also approximates the description of 'obligations of conduct' imposed by economic, social and cultural rights according to *The Maastricht Guidelines on Violations of Economic, Social and Cultural Rights*. Thus an obligation of conduct 'requires action reasonably calculated to realize the enjoyment of a particular right'. 'The Maastricht Guidelines on Violations of Economic, Social and Cultural Rights' (1998) 20 *HRQ* 691–705 para 7. The Maastricht Guidelines were adopted by a group of international law experts as a contribution to understanding the obligations imposed by the International Covenant on Economic, Social and Cultural Rights. It is noteworthy that the standard of reasonableness review has also been explicitly incorporated in the recently adopted Optional Protocol to the International Covenant on Economic, Social and Cultural Rights, 2008, UN doc. A/HRC/8/L.2. Thus art 8(4) reads:

> When examining communications under the present Protocol, the Committee shall consider the reasonableness of the steps taken by the State Party in accordance with Part II of the Covenant. In doing so, the Committee shall bear in mind that the State Party may adopt a range of possible policy measures for the implementation of the rights set forth in the Covenant.

> reasonable. It is necessary to recognise that a wide range of possible measures could be adopted by the State to meet its obligations. Many of these would meet the requirement of reasonableness. Once it is shown that the measures do so, this requirement is met.[101]

The Court has indicated that it will assess the reasonableness of the State's conduct in the light of the social, economic and historical context, and consideration will be given to the capacity of institutions responsible for implementing the programme.[102] While *Soobramoney* raised the spectre of the adoption of a thin standard of rationality scrutiny for socio-economic rights claims, the Court in *Grootboom* and *Treatment Action Campaign* proceeded to develop a more substantive set of criteria for assessing the reasonableness of the State's acts or omissions.[103] Thus a reasonable government programme in the context of socio-economic rights will have the following features:[104]

- It must be capable of facilitating the realisation of the right;[105]
- It must be comprehensive, coherent, co-ordinated;[106]
- Appropriate financial and human resources must be made available for the programme;[107]
- It must be balanced and flexible[108] and make appropriate provision for short-, medium- and long-term needs;[109]
- It must be reasonably conceived and implemented;[110]

---

[101] Ibid. O'Regan J describes the purpose of the reasonableness standard as follows in *Rail Commuters Action Group v Transnet Ltd t/a Metrorail* 2005 (2) SA 359 (CC), 2005 (4) BCLR 301 (CC) para 87:

> In adopting this standard the Court requires the bearer of constitutional obligations to perform them in a manner which is reasonable. This standard strikes an appropriate balance between the need to ensure that constitutional obligations are met, on the one hand, and recognition for the fact that the bearers of those obligations should be given appropriate leeway to determine the best way to meet the obligations in all the circumstances.

In this case, the standard of reasonableness review was adopted for assessing the positive duties imposed by the South African Transport Services Act 9 of 1989 to secure the safety of commuters read in the light of ss 10 (human dignity), 11 (right to life) and 12 (the right to freedom and security of the person) of the Constitution.

[102] *Grootboom* (note 3 above) para 43.

[103] See *Bel Porto School Governing Body v Premier, Western Cape* 2002 (3) SA 265 (CC), 2002 (9) BCLR 891 (CC) para 46; *Khosa* (note 6 above) para 67.

[104] The Court noted in *Khosa* (note 6 above) para 44 that the factors identified in the assessment of reasonableness were not a closed list and that 'all relevant factors have to be taken into account'. The Court went on to observe that '[w]hat is relevant may vary from case to case depending on the particular facts and circumstances'.

[105] *Grootboom* (note 3 above) para 41.

[106] Ibid paras 39 and 40.

[107] Ibid para 39.

[108] Ibid paras 68, 78, 95.

[109] Ibid para 43.

[110] Ibid paras 40–43.

- It must be transparent, and its contents must be made known effectively to the public.[111]
- It must make short-term provision for those whose needs are urgent and who are living in intolerable conditions.[112]

The last element comes closest to a basic threshold that must be met for a government programme to pass muster in terms of the reasonableness inquiry. The Court elaborates on this element and its role in the assessment of the reasonableness of the government's measures in the following terms:

> To be reasonable, measures cannot leave out of account, the degree and extent of the denial of the right they endeavour to realise. Those whose needs are most urgent and whose ability to enjoy all rights is therefore most in peril, must not be ignored by the measures aimed at achieving realisation of the right. It may not be sufficient to meet the test of reasonableness to show that the measures are capable of achieving a statistical advance in the realisation of the right. Furthermore, the Constitution requires that everyone be treated with care and concern. If the measures, though statistically successful, fail to respond to the needs of those most desperate, they may not pass the test.[113]

The Court emphasises that human dignity is the animating value of the reasonableness standard of review in the context of socio-economic rights:

> It is fundamental to an evaluation of the reasonableness of State action that account be taken of the inherent dignity of human beings. The Constitution will be worth infinitely less than its paper if the reasonableness of State action concerned with housing is determined without regard to the fundamental constitutional value of human dignity. Section 26, read in the context of the Bill of Rights as a whole, must mean that the respondents have a right to reasonable action by the State in all circumstances and with particular regard to human dignity. In short, I emphasise that human beings are required to be treated as human beings.[114]

Although not as clearly and prominently stated as the other criteria for reasonableness review, there are indications in both *Grootboom* and *Treatment Action Campaign* that the Court will also have regard to government engagement with affected communities and civil society in realising socio-economic rights. In *Grootboom*, Yacoob J observed that when the occupation of the New Rust land (from which the Grootboom community had been evicted) had become evident, he would have 'expected officials of the municipality to engage' with the community, and attempt to achieve 'a case-

---

111 *Treatment Action Campaign* (note 5 above) para 123.

112 *Grootboom* (note 3 above) paras 44, 64, 68, 99; *Treatment Action Campaign* (note 5 above) para 78.

113 *Grootboom* (note 3 above) para 44. See A J van der Walt 'A South African reading of Frank Michelman's theory of social justice' in H Botha, A J van der Walt & J van der Walt (eds) *Rights and Democracy in a Transformative Constitution* (2004) 163–211 at 207.

114 *Grootboom* (note 3 above) para 83. See A Sachs 'The judicial enforcement of socio-economic rights' (2003) 56 *Current Legal Problems* 579–601 at 594–596; S Liebenberg 'The value of human dignity in interpreting socio-economic rights' (2005) 21 *SAJHR* 1–31.

by-case' resolution of the situation after investigation of the circumstances of the occupation.[115] In the *Treatment Action Campaign* case, the Court observed that the 'magnitude of the HIV/AIDS challenge facing the country calls for a concerted, co-ordinated national effort in which government in each of its three spheres and the panoply of resources and skills of civil society are marshalled, inspired and led'.[116] Transparency and effective communication by government were acknowledged as essential for promoting and enabling civil society participation in responding to this major public health threat.[117] The Court concluded that 'for a public programme such as this to meet the constitutional requirement of reasonableness, its contents must be made known appropriately'.[118] As will be seen, 'meaningful engagement' and the pursuit of mediated solutions are playing an increasingly important role in assessing the justice and equity of the eviction of people from their homes.[119]

The assessment of the reasonableness of government programmes is influenced by two further criteria derived from ss 26(2) and 27(2). The first is the concept of 'progressive realisation' which was interpreted as follows in *Grootboom*:

> The term 'progressive realisation' shows that it was contemplated that the right could not be realised immediately. But the goal of the Constitution is that the basic needs of all in our society be effectively met and the requirement of progressive realisation means that the State must take steps to achieve this goal. It means that accessibility should be progressively facilitated: legal, administrative, operational and financial hurdles should be examined and, where possible, lowered over time. Housing must be made more accessible not only to a larger number of people but to a wider range of people as time progresses.[120]

In this context, the Court also specifically endorsed the views of the UN Committee on Economic, Social and Cultural Rights that 'any deliberately retrogressive measures ... would require the most careful consideration and would need to be fully justified by reference to the totality of the rights provided for in the Covenant and in the context of the full use of the maximum available resources'.[121]

The second criterion is the availability of resources. In this regard, the Court held that 'both the content of the obligation in relation to the rate at which it is achieved as well as the reasonableness of the measures employed to achieve the result are governed by the availability of resources'.[122] This is a consequence of the Court's interpretation that the positive duties imposed by the socio-economic rights provisions are limited

---

115 Ibid para 87.

116 *Treatment Action Campaign* (note 5 above) para 123.

117 Responsiveness to people's needs, public participation in policy-making and transparency are among the basic values and principles governing public administration in terms of s 195(*e*) and (*g*) of the Constitution. This requires that the public be provided with 'timely, accessible and accurate information' (s 195(*g*)).

118 *Treatment Action Campaign* (note 5 above) para 123.

119 See the jurisprudence discussed in chapter 6, parts 6.4 and 6.5.

120 *Grootboom* (note 3 above) para 45.

121 Ibid para 45 citing General Comment No 3 (note 85 above) para 9.

122 Ibid para 46.

by the second subsection of ss 26 and 27.[123] Although the precise budget allocation for urgent needs was 'for national government to decide in the first instance',[124] it is obliged to allocate 'a reasonable part' of the national budget for this purpose.[125] In the *Treatment Action Campaign* case, the Court scrutinised and ultimately rejected the State's arguments that it did not have sufficient resources to provide Nevirapine throughout the public health sector.[126]

In *Grootboom*, the Court found that the government's housing programme, though in other respects rational and comprehensive,[127] was inconsistent with s 26 of the Constitution in that it failed 'to provide relief for people who have no access to land, no roof over their heads, and who are living in intolerable conditions or crisis situations'.[128] The Court did not specify what form this relief should take, but simply made a declaratory order to the effect that the State's housing programme should include 'reasonable measures' to provide relief for this group.[129] However, it indicated that these measures should be similar, 'but not necessarily limited to those contemplated in the Accelerated Managed Land Settlement Programme'.[130] This programme had been drafted by the local authority, but was not in force when the case commenced.[131]

In the *Treatment Action Campaign* case, the Government had defended its restrictive policy on mother-to-child transmission, raising concerns ranging from the efficacy and safety of Nevirapine to a lack of resources and capacity to roll out a comprehensive programme to prevent mother-to-child transmission of HIV throughout the public health sector. The Court closely scrutinised and ultimately rejected all of these justifications. An assessment of the medical and expert evidence showed 'that the provision of Nevirapine will save the lives of a significant number of infants even if it is administered without the full package and support services that are available at the research and training sites'.[132] Concerns regarding the development of resistance to the drugs were dismissed as 'likely to be transient' and outweighed by the benefits to be gained and the suffering to be avoided by the administration of Nevirapine.[133] The safety concerns of the government also lacked credibility given the fact that

---

[123] *Soobramoney* (note 2 above) paras 11, 28; *Grootboom* (note 3 above) para 38; *Treatment Action Campaign* (note 5 above) para 39.

[124] *Grootboom* (note 3 above) para 66.

[125] Ibid. See also para 68.

[126] See notes 136–140 below and accompanying text.

[127] See the observations of the Court in relation to this programme: *Grootboom* (note 3 above) paras 53–55 and 64.

[128] Ibid para 99.

[129] Ibid para 2(*b*) of the Order. On declaratory orders in the context of socio-economic rights, see generally chapter 8, part 8.4.

[130] Ibid.

[131] Ibid para 60.

[132] Ibid para 57.

[133] Ibid para 59.

Nevirapine was recommended for the purpose of reducing mother-to-child transmission of HIV by the World Health Organisation and endorsed by the South African Medicines Control Council.[134] Moreover, Nevirapine was government's own drug of choice in its research and training sites which catered for approximately 10% of all births in the public sector. It was 'unthinkable that government would gamble with the lives or health of thousands of mothers and infants'.[135]

The State's resource constraints arguments were evaluated in relation to the two legs of the challenge mounted by the TAC to the programme. The first leg of the challenge concerned the restriction placed on doctors from prescribing Nevirapine in facilities where testing and counselling facilities already existed. The administration of the drug is a relatively simple procedure, and the manufacturers had made a free offer of the drug to the South African government for a period of five years.[136] Accordingly the Court concluded that 'this aspect of the claim and the orders made will not attract any significant additional costs'.[137] As the Court observed:

> Where counselling and testing facilities exist, the administration of Nevirapine is well within the available resources of the State and, in such circumstances, the provision of a single dose of Nevirapine to mother and child where medically indicated is a simple, cheap and potentially lifesaving medical intervention.[138]

The second leg of the challenge concerned the extension of testing, counselling and treatment facilities to clinics that currently lack these facilities (the 'roll-out' of the programme). Regarding the capacity arguments of the government, particularly in relation to training for counselling on the use of Nevirapine, the Court found that this was 'not a complex task and it should not be difficult to equip existing counsellors with the necessary additional knowledge'.[139] After a close analysis, the Court concluded that the capacity and costs arguments did not have sufficient factual cogency to outweigh the impact on a particularly vulnerable group of the denial of a basic life-saving medical intervention.[140] It held that the failure to take measures without delay to permit and facilitate the use of the anti-retroviral drug, Nevirapine, throughout public health care facilities in South Africa for the purpose of preventing mother-to-child transmission of HIV was unreasonable. These omissions accordingly violated the right of access to health care services entrenched in s 27.

The Court granted mandatory orders relating to the provision of Nevirapine for the purpose of reducing the risk of mother-to-child transmission of HIV in public hospitals and clinics where medically indicated, and the extension of testing and counselling facilities throughout the public health sector 'to facilitate and expedite' the use

[134] Ibid paras 60–61.
[135] Ibid para 62.
[136] Ibid para 19.
[137] Ibid para 71.
[138] Ibid para 73.
[139] Ibid para 95.
[140] Ibid paras 90–92, 115–120.

of Nevirapine.[141] The Court was prepared to be specific regarding the nature of the service to be provided, namely the antiretroviral drug, Nevirapine, along with the necessary testing and counselling facilities. However, it made provision in its order for the government to adapt its policy 'if equally appropriate or better methods become available to it for the prevention of mother-to-child transmission of HIV'.[142]

Key factors accounting for the robust standard of scrutiny applied in this case were the lack of alternatives for achieving a substantial reduction in mother-to-child of HIV, the severe impact on poor mothers and children of the denial of antiretroviral treatment, and the high quality expert and other evidence TAC placed before the Court. This evidence enabled the Court to evaluate the various justifications raised by the State for its refusal to roll out the provision of Nevirapine throughout the public health sector.[143]

Although reasonableness review is intended to allow the State a margin of discretion regarding its precise policy choices in giving effect to socio-economic rights, the Court will, in appropriate cases, apply a stringent standard of scrutiny to the government's policy choices, and will be specific regarding the measures required to remedy infringements of the rights. This is well illustrated by the facts of the *Treatment Action Campaign* case where there could not be reasonable democratic disagreement about the type of service required to give effect to the right in question, and the impact of the denial of the service on a vulnerable beneficiary group was severe. In cases where there has been a failure to make provision for a particular group, but there are a range of reasonable policy options that could remedy the constitutional defect, the Court prefers remedies that allow the State a degree of latitude in designing an appropriate policy solution.[144]

4.3.4 Equality rights and socio-economic rights

The decision of the Constitutional Court in *Khosa*[145] is significant for illustrating how equality rights and socio-economic rights can mutually reinforce each other to support a finding that a government programme unfairly or unreasonably excludes a particular group. The effect of such a finding is that the programme must be expanded to include the excluded group with a corresponding increase in the budgetary allocations to the relevant programme.

---

[141] Ibid para 135. On mandatory orders in the context of socio-economic rights, see generally chapter 8, 8.5.3.

[142] Ibid para 135, Order para 4.

[143] See, for example, *Treatment Action Campaign* (note 5 above) para 90 on the nature of the expert evidence before the Court in relation to the extension of testing and counselling facilities throughout the public health sector.

[144] See, for example, the broad declaratory order made in the *Grootboom* case (note 3 above). See further chapter 8, part 8.4.2.

[145] *Khosa* (note 6 above).

Khosa involved an application for an order confirming the constitutional invalidity of certain provisions of the Social Assistance Act 59 of 1992 and the Welfare Laws Amendment Act 106 of 1997 which limited eligibility for non-contributory social assistance grants to South African citizens. The applicants were Mozambican citizens who had lived in South Africa since 1980, and had acquired permanent resident status in South Africa. This group was destitute and, but for their lack of South African citizenship, would otherwise have qualified for access to the various social assistance grants. It was primarily contended that these provisions infringed both the right of everyone to have access to social assistance (s 27(1)(*c*) read with (2)) and the right against unfair discrimination (s 9(3)).

The Court commenced by considering the reasonableness of the exclusion of permanent residents from the Social Assistance Act in terms of the right of access to social security in s 27(1)(*c*) read with (2) of the Constitution. It noted that the Constitution confers the right of access to social security on 'everyone'.[146] The following factors were identified as being relevant to the assessment of the reasonableness of the exclusion: 'the purpose served by social security, the impact of the exclusion on permanent residents and the relevance of the citizenship requirement to that purpose'.[147] Furthermore, it held that the assessment of the reasonableness of the exclusion must have regard to 'the impact that this has on other intersecting rights', for example, the equality rights entrenched in s 9 of the Constitution.[148]

According to the Court, the purpose of the right of access to social assistance for those unable to support themselves and their dependants is to ensure that the basic necessities of life are accessible to all. It is an expression of our foundational constitutional commitment to the values of human dignity, freedom and equality.[149] Given these purposes and the *prima facie* entitlement of 'everyone' to have access to social security, the Court held that differentiating on the basis of citizenship in relation to social grants 'must not be arbitrary or irrational nor must it manifest a naked preference'.[150] A differentiating law which did not meet the basic requirement of rationality constituted a violation of both s 9(1) and s 27(2) of the Constitution.[151]

The State sought to justify restricting social grants to citizens on the basis that their exclusion was temporary, as they could, after a period of five years, apply for citizenship by reason of naturalisation. Mokgoro J rejected this argument as a manifestation of the social contract assumption found in American jurisprudence whereby

---

[146] Section 27(1). See *Khosa* ibid paras 53–57.

[147] Ibid para 49.

[148] Ibid. See also para 45. In the subsequent Constitutional Court decision in *Mashavha v President of the Republic of South Africa* 2005 (2) SA 476 (CC), 2004 (12) BCLR 1243 (CC) para 51 the Court observed that social assistance was 'an area of governmental responsibility very closely related to human dignity'.

[149] *Khosa* (note 6 above) para 52.

[150] Ibid para 53.

[151] Ibid.

social benefits and entitlements are reserved for citizens.[152] She also pointed out that the grant of naturalisation was not a foregone conclusion for permanent residents and may well be subject to administrative discretion beyond their control.[153]

The Court next considered whether financial considerations could constitute a reasonable ground for limiting access to the benefits in question to citizens.[154] The State had argued that the extension of social grants to permanent residents would impose 'an impermissibly high financial burden on the state'.[155] In assessing the validity of this argument, the Court faced the difficulty of a lack of evidence as to 'the numbers of persons who hold permanent resident status, or who would qualify for social assistance if the citizenship barrier were to be removed'.[156] The State estimated that the additional annual cost of including permanent residents in the relevant grants 'could range between R243 million and R672 million'. The wide range of the possible increase indicated the speculative nature of the calculations. Even so, the Court deduced that the cost of including permanent residents in the system would be only a small proportion of the total cost of social grants.[157] Approximately one fifth of the projected expenditure on social grants for permanent residents was in respect of child grants. The unconstitutionality of the citizenship requirement in respect of the child support grant had been conceded by the State. As the Court observed, the remainder 'reflects an increase of less than 2% on the present cost of social grants (currently R26.2 billion) even on the higher estimate'.[158] Thus the State was unable to produce convincing evidence to support its argument that the costs of extending social grants to permanent residents would impose an excessively high financial burden on it.

The State further argued that the exclusion of permanent residents from social grants was reasonable in that it furthered the immigration policy of the State, which seeks to exclude persons who may become a burden on the State and thereby to encourage self-sufficiency among foreign nationals. The Court accepted that limiting the cost of social welfare was a legitimate government concern, and that it was also permissible to control applications for permanent residence by excluding those who may become a burden on the State. However, once a person was admitted as a permanent resident and later became 'a burden' on the State, it was not justifiable to exclude them from access to social assistance. The Court held that this 'may be a cost we have to pay for the constitutional commitment to developing a caring society, and granting access to socio-economic rights to all who make their homes here'.[159]

Examining the claim through the lens of equality rights, the Court inquired whether the exclusion of permanent residents from social grants amounted to 'unfair

[152] Ibid para 57.
[153] Ibid para 56.
[154] Ibid paras 45, 58.
[155] Ibid para 60.
[156] Ibid paras 61–62.
[157] Ibid para 62.
[158] Ibid.
[159] Ibid para 65.

discrimination' in terms of s 9(3) of the equality clause.[160] The test for unfair discrimination involves the consideration of a number of factors, particularly its impact on the group discriminated against.[161] As citizenship is not a listed prohibited ground of discrimination, the burden is on the applicants to prove that it is unfair.[162]

The Court noted that non-citizens were a vulnerable group in society.[163] Their exclusion from important statutory benefits has 'a strong stigmatising effect'.[164] Like citizens, permanent residents contribute to the welfare system through the payment of taxes. Consequently, 'the lack of congruence between benefits and burdens created by a law that denies benefits to permanent residents almost inevitably creates the impression that permanent residents are in some way inferior to citizens and less worthy of social assistance.'[165] Analysing the impact of the exclusion, the Court held that it not only places an undue burden on the families, friends or communities of the permanent residents, but 'is likely to have a serious impact on the dignity of

---

[160] Section 9 of the Constitution prohibits direct or indirect unfair discrimination on a range of listed grounds (including race, sex, gender, sexual orientation, age and disability.). These do not represent a closed list. Other unlisted grounds (e.g. citizenship and HIV-status) may be recognised as analogous grounds of differentiation if they have an adverse effect on the dignity of the individual, or some other comparable effect: *Harksen v Lane NO* 1998 (1) SA 300 (CC), 1997 (11) BCLR 1489 (CC) para 46 ('*Harksen*'). See, for example, *Hoffmann v South African Airways* 2001 (1) SA 1 (CC), 2000 (11) BCLR 1211 (CC) (HIV-positive status recognised as analogous ground of discrimination). Section 9(2) also provides expressly that restitutionary measures (affirmative action) may be taken '[t]o promote the achievement of equality'.

[161] In *Harksen* ibid para 51 the Court summarised the relevant considerations to be:

(*a*) the position of the complainants in society and whether they have suffered in the past from patterns of disadvantage, whether the discrimination in the case under consideration is on a specified ground or not;

(*b*) the nature of the provision or power and the purpose sought to be achieved by it. If its purpose is manifestly not directed, in the first instance, at impairing the complainants in the manner indicated above, but is aimed at achieving a worthy and important societal goal, such as, for example, the furthering of equality for all, this purpose may, depending on the facts of the particular case, have a significant bearing on the question whether complainants have in fact suffered the impairment in question;

(*c*) with due regard to (*a*) and (*b*) above, and any other relevant factors, the extent to which the discrimination has affected the rights or interests of the complainants and whether it has led to an impairment of their fundamental human dignity or constitutes an impairment of a comparably serious nature.

[162] Section 9(5) creates a rebuttable presumption that discrimination is unfair if it is based on one of the grounds listed in s 9(3).

[163] Foreign citizens are a minority in all countries and have little political muscle. Second, citizenship is a personal attribute which is difficult to change. *Khosa* (note 6 above) para 71. See also *Larbi-Odam v Member of the Executive Council for Education (North-West Province)* 1998 (1) SA 745 (CC), 1997 (12) BCLR 1655 (CC) in which the Court held that rendering permanent residents ineligible for employment as teaching staff in public schools constituted unfair discrimination on the ground of citizenship.

[164] Ibid para 74.

[165] Ibid.

the permanent residents concerned who are cast in the role of supplicants'.[166] The Court concluded that the total denial of access to a constitutionally protected socio-economic right also constituted unfair discrimination in terms of s 9(3). It relegated them 'to the margins of society' and deprived them 'of what may be essential to enable them to enjoy other rights vested in them under the Constitution'.[167]

The Court's assessment of the reasonableness of the exclusion of permanent residents in *Khosa* incorporates a proportionality analysis.[168] There were other less drastic methods for reducing the risk of permanent residents becoming 'a burden' to the State than excluding them from gaining access to social assistance.[169] Ultimately, the impact of the exclusion from social assistance on the life and dignity of permanent residents outweighed the financial and immigration considerations on which the State relied.[170] The stringent standard of review applied in this case should be understood in the context of the denial of a basic social benefit to a vulnerable group, and the intersecting breaches of a socio-economic right and the right against unfair discrimination.[171]

While the *Khosa* decision represents a welcome affirmation of the entitlement of non-citizens to socio-economic rights, concerns remain that the decision may have the effect of marginalising less privileged categories of non-citizens such as temporary residents and undocumented migrants.[172] The Court was careful to limit its extension of social security grants to the category of permanent residents 'who, like citizens have made South Africa their home'.[173] Moreover, it is disturbing that the Court suggested that a less restrictive way of achieving the purpose of limiting social security claims on the State was to adopt immigration policies controlling the entry of potential permanent residents who may become a burden on the State.[174] It remains to be seen whether the *Khosa* decision represents the first step in a gradual process of extending socio-economic rights to those marginalised by an intersection of poverty and nationality, or the outer limits of the Court's willingness to expand access to socio-economic rights to non-nationals.

---

[166] Ibid para 76.

[167] Ibid paras 77, 81.

[168] See the analysis by D Brand 'Introduction to socio-economic rights in the South African Constitution' in D Brand & C Heyns (eds) *Socio-Economic Rights in South Africa* (2005) 51.

[169] *Khosa* (note 6 above) paras 64–65.

[170] Ibid para 82.

[171] In addition to equality, the Court held that the rights to life and human dignity were also implicated by the social security scheme put in place by the State to meet its s 27 obligations. Ibid para 44.

[172] See the critique of this aspect of the judgment by L Williams 'Issues and challenges in addressing poverty and legal rights: A comparative United States/South African analysis' (2005) 21 *SAJHR* 436–472 at 463–471.

[173] *Khosa* (note 6 above) paras 58, 59.

[174] Ibid para 65.

The Court's subsequent decision in *Union of Refugee Women v Director, Private Security Industry Regulatory Authority*[175] suggests a more restrictive approach to extending entitlements of a socio-economic character to another category of non-nationals – refugees.[176] In this case, the Court held that the provisions of s 23(1)(*a*) of the Private Security Industry Regulation Act 56 of 2001, which makes South African citizenship or permanent residence a requirement for registration with the Private Security Industry Regulatory Authority, did not constitute unfair discrimination against refugees seeking employment in the private security industry in South Africa. The majority of the Court held that the discrimination was not unfair in that it did not place a blanket ban on refugees seeking employment, and was rationally related to a legitimate State purpose of regulating the powerful private security industry.[177]

A significant factor which influenced the Court's assessment that the discrimination was not unfair was the possibility for non-nationals such as refugees to apply for an exemption in terms of s 23(6) of the Act by showing 'good cause' for the Private Security Industry Regulatory Authority to depart from the strict requirements of citizenship or permanent residence as a precondition for registration.[178] The majority accordingly held that the discrimination in this matter, 'objectively determined, has very little, if any, potential to impair the essential content of the dignity of the applicants in any significant or substantial manner and is fair'.[179] However, the Regulatory Authority was ordered to communicate to applicants and potential applicants the nature of the information required to apply for an exemption in terms of s 23(6), and to exercise their discretion in terms of this subsection in line with the broad guidelines provided in the judgment.[180] The Court emphasised that providing the public with 'timely, accessible and accurate information' was necessary to foster transparency in public administration as required by s 195(1)(*g*) of the Constitution.[181]

In their dissenting judgment, Mokgoro J and O'Regan J[182] were of the view that both the social stigma and stereotypes promoted by the exclusion of refugees from registration as private security providers, as well as the material and financial impact of their exclusion from this form of employment rendered the discrimination unfair in terms of s 9(3) of the Constitution.[183] They held that the exemption provided for in terms of s 23(6) of the Act did not remove the discriminatory impact of the citizenship/permanent residence requirement in s 23(1)(*a*) of the Act. Once refugees complied with the other requirements of s 23(1) for establishing their suitability and

[175] 2007 (4) SA 395 (CC), 2007 (4) BCLR 339 (CC).

[176] See generally M Foster *International Refugee Law and Socio-Economic Rights: Refuge from Deprivation* (2007).

[177] Note 175 above, paras 61–67.

[178] Ibid paras 48, 67.

[179] Ibid para 66.

[180] Ibid 75–87.

[181] Ibid 83.

[182] Langa CJ and Van der Westhuizen J concurred in this judgment.

[183] Note 175 above, paras 115–122.

trustworthiness as private security providers, it was unreasonable to expect them to show further 'good cause' in terms of s 23(6).[184]

The right to equality has also influenced the interpretation of the administration of social assistance payments in terms of the Social Assistance Act 59 of 1992. Thus in *Mashavha v President of the RSA*,[185] the Constitutional Court declared the assignment of the administration of the Social Assistance Act to the provinces in terms of Proclamation R7 to be unconstitutional in that it fell within the ambit of s 126(3) of the Interim Constitution. The latter provision excludes from assignment to provincial level matters requiring uniform national norms and standards for their effective performance and minimum standards across the nation. The Court held that the delivery of social assistance grants was such a matter. In doing so, it emphasised the importance of the right and value of equality in the delivery of social assistance rights:

> The history of our country and the need for equality cannot be ignored in the interpretation and application of s 126(3). Equality is not only recognised as a fundamental right in both the interim and 1996 Constitutions, but is also a foundational value. To pay, for example, higher old age pensions in Johannesburg in Gauteng than in Bochum in Limpopo, or lower child benefits in Butterworth than in Cape Town, would offend the dignity of people, create different classes of citizenship and divide South Africa into favoured and disfavoured areas.[186]

4.4 TOWARDS SUBSTANTIVE REASONABLENESS

4.4.1 The 'minimum core' approach

(*a*) Core contestations

The Court's refusal to adopt the concept of minimum core obligations as a basic threshold in assessing compliance by the State with its positive duties in terms of ss 26 and 27[187] has attracted considerable criticism.[188] It has been questioned whether the

---

[184] Ibid 120.

[185] Note 148 above. In response, the State has established the Social Security Agency in terms of the Social Security Agency Act 9 of 2004 with primary responsibility for the administration of social assistance in terms of the Social Assistance Act.

[186] Ibid para 51.

[187] As noted above, the Court left open the possibility in both the *Grootboom* and *Treatment Action Campaign* cases that the minimum core obligation could play a role in the assessment of the reasonableness of government programmes. See note 99 above and accompanying text. According to Albie Sachs (note 114 above), the Court 'did not reject the minimum core notion', but rather implied 'that such minimum core obligation could be satisfied through broad governmental programmes aimed at meeting minimum needs and did not have to be met by acknowledging individual entitlements enforceable through the courts' (599).

[188] See, for example, Scott & Alston (note 42 above) 244–245, 250, 252; S Liebenberg 'South Africa's evolving jurisprudence on socio-economic rights: An effective tool in challenging poverty?' (2002) 6 *LDD* 159–191; D Bilchitz 'Giving socio-economic rights teeth: The

Court's 'reasonableness review' jurisprudence sufficiently defines the content of the relevant socio-economic rights,[189] and protects those who are experiencing a severe deprivation of minimum essential levels of basic socio-economic goods and services. This category of claimants is in danger of suffering irreparable harm to their lives, health and human dignity[190] if they do not receive urgent assistance.

David Bilchitz argues that the minimum core obligation protects people's urgent threshold interests in survival, 'as the inability to survive wipes out all possibility for realizing the sources of value in the life of a being'.[191] On this conception, the minimum core places an obligation on the State to ensure that individuals 'are not exposed to the general conditions that threaten their survival'.[192] Individuals also have a more maximal interest 'in the general conditions that are necessary for the fulfilment of a *diversity* of purposes'.[193] This would require a standard of socio-economic provisioning which allows them to flourish and achieve their goals. However, the meeting of minimum core obligations should enjoy prioritised consideration in social policymaking and in the judicial enforcement of these rights, due to the urgency of the interests they protect. Without the meeting of the minimum essential needs which people require to survive, the State's obligation to progressively achieve the full realisation of the rights becomes meaningless. In the context of adjudication, courts give effect to this prioritisation by requiring particularly weighty reasons by way of justification from the State for a failure to fulfil survival-related needs.[194]

---

minimum core and its importance' (2002) 118 *SALJ* 484–501; D Bilchitz 'Towards a reasonable approach to the minimum core: Laying the foundations for future socio-economic rights jurisprudence' (2003) 19 *SAJHR* 1–26; Bilchitz (note 78 above).

[189] See, for example M Pieterse 'Coming to terms with judicial enforcement of socio-economic rights' (2004) 20 *SAJHR* 383–417 at 410–411.

[190] The *amici* in the *Treatment Action Campaign* case (note 5 above) derived the standard for determining minimum core obligations from the value of human dignity. For an argument that human dignity requires taking account of the relative urgency of the needs of different individuals and groups and a corresponding urgent response, see Liebenberg (note 114 above) 15–18; 22–23.

[191] Bilchitz (note 78 above) 187.

[192] Ibid 40, 188.

[193] Ibid 41.

[194] The 'weighted priority' which must be accorded to core obligations in adjudication implies that such a core obligation can only be overridden by a reason of equivalent importance (ibid 210–213). Bilchitz identifies four such weighty reasons which can justify overriding core obligations: (1) scarcity of resources; (2) situations where the minimal interests of some individuals can only be met by dedicating a disproportionately vast amount of resources to them; (3) the need to preserve some space for individuals to pursue interests beyond the minimal interest in survival, such as 'opportunities to realise their goals and achieve positive experiences'; (4) situations when the realisation of the minimum core of a particular right would prevent the realisation of the minimum core of other rights and liberties. Ibid 212.

On the other hand, a number of academic commentators have contested the view that a model of review based on the concept of minimum core obligations is better suited to the judicial review of positive socio-economic rights claims.[195] They elaborate on many of the concerns articulated by the Court in relation to the minimum core concept.[196] The critiques which have the most serious implications for the transformative adjudication of socio-economic rights claims are considered here.

(*b*) The minimum core and democracy

The first set of critiques relate broadly to the impact of the minimum core concept on the functioning of democratic institutions and on democratic culture in South Africa.

The concept of minimum core obligations purportedly creates the danger that courts will transgress the boundaries of their institutional legitimacy and competence/capacity.[197] Through defining and enforcing minimum core obligations, courts may be tempted to usurp government's policy-making functions. However, the notion of bounded 'separate spheres' does not accord with the relational, dialogic character of the relationship between the different spheres of government under the South African Constitution.[198] Moreover, as the *Grootboom*, *Treatment Action Campaign* and *Khosa* cases illustrate, reasonableness review also results in the courts making orders which have specific implications for government policy. This is precisely the function of judicial review of fundamental rights entrenched in a supreme Constitution. Legislation or conduct inconsistent with the Constitution must be declared invalid and the State will be obliged to modify its policies accordingly. As the Court stated in the *Treatment Action Campaign* case:

> Where State policy is challenged as inconsistent with the Constitution, Courts have to consider whether in formulating and implementing such policy the State has given effect

---

[195] A Sachs (note 114 above); M Wesson '*Grootboom* and beyond: Reassessing the socio-economic rights jurisprudence of the South African Constitutional Court' (2004) 20 *SAJHR* 284–308; B Porter 'The crisis of economic, social and cultural rights and strategies for addressing it' in J Squires, M Langford & B Thiele (eds) *The Road to a Remedy: Current Issues in the Litigation of Economic, Social and Cultural Rights* (2005) 43–69 at 48–55; M S Kende 'The South African Constitutional Court's embrace of socio-economic rights: A comparative perspective' (2003) 6 *Chap L Rev* 137–160 at 153–154; M S Kende 'The South African Constitutional Court's construction of socio-economic rights: A response to the critics' (2003–2004) 19 *Conn J Int'l L* 617–629; C Steinberg (note 55 above); K Lehmann 'In defense of the Constitutional Court: Litigating socio-economic rights and the myth of the minimum core.' (2006) 22 *Am Univ Int Law Rev* 163–197.

[196] See in this regard part 4.3.2 above.

[197] See *Treatment Action* Campaign (note 5 above) paras 37–38. According to Albie Sachs (note 114 above) 588–589) the real difficulty for courts in setting concrete standards for the delivery of socio-economic rights is one of institutional capacity. See further Kende 2003–2004 (note 195 above) 624.

[198] Chapter 2, part 2.4.7.

> to its constitutional obligations. If it should hold in any given case that the State has failed to do so, it is obliged by the Constitution to say so. Insofar as that constitutes an intrusion into the domain of the Executive, that is an intrusion mandated by the Constitution itself.[199]

This is the case for all rights in the Bill of Rights, regardless of whether they are formally classified as civil, political, economic, social or cultural rights.

From the perspective of fostering the deliberative features of South Africa's constitutional democracy, a greater concern is that the enforcement of minimum core obligations by courts will undermine institutional and social dialogue in the process of realising socio-economic rights. Thus Carol Steinberg argues that the minimum core represents an 'intrusive rule-based' approach which is likely to stifle institutional conversation and collaboration between the three branches of government.[200] In contrast, she argues:

> [T]he abstract and open-ended nature of the reasonableness inquiry should be understood as a 'democracy-promoting' form of minimalism in which the court settles the case before it on narrow grounds, avoiding the laying down of clear rules and final resolutions that will inhibit the effective functioning of the other branches of government.[201]

She argues that the case-by-case evolution of standards on socio-economic rights promoted by reasonableness review is more likely to promote 'the kind of argumentative give-and-take, evolution, learning and compromise' which will produce wiser and more sustainable decisions in relation to these rights.[202]

While an institutional dialogue between the branches of government is to be encouraged, it constitutes an insufficient response to the ideal of democratic transformation entailing multiple sites of political mobilisation and participation in transforming social and economic power relations.[203] The institutional advantages of the legislature as the preeminent institution for realising socio-economic rights should not be overstated. However sound the theoretical justifications for preferring legislative measures for giving effect to socio-economic rights, they premised on a certain idealised understanding of the role and functioning of modern legislatures which does not reflect the reality in either South Africa or other jurisdictions. Most modern legislatures are subject to the constraints of time and resource pressures, are at a relative disadvantage to the executive in relation to technical expertise and resources, and are subject to capture by powerful business and other interest groups. In the South African context, Parliament is effectively dominated by a single party owing to its overwhelming electoral majority. These systemic defects in legislative

---

199 *Treatment Action Campaign* (note 5 above) para 99.
200 Steinberg (note 55 above) 274.
201 Ibid 276.
202 Ibid 272.
203 See the discussion in chapter 2, part 2.2.4.

processes result in legislation which neglects the rights of groups who are politically, economically and socially marginalised.[204]

Moreover, many of the decisions made in relation to socio-economic rights are policy and administrative decisions which do not enjoy the same democratic legitimacy as legislative decisions. As a consequence, in making and implementing socio-economic policy and programmes, the purposes and values which socio-economic rights are intended to promote may be overlooked or discounted. A preference for abstraction and minimalism in giving content to socio-economic rights may afford the legislature or executive more latitude in formulating and implementing socio-economic policies, but its effect may be to reinforce the marginalisation of groups whose rights are systemically neglected by the institutions of representative democracy. As Karl Klare observes, when courts act to fulfil constitutional rights, 'sometimes the net result in context is that the democracy-enlarging consequences of the court's decision outweigh its counter-majoritarian form'. He cites the *Treatment Action Campaign* case as an example.[205]

However, judicial definitions of the 'minimum core obligations' imposed by various socio-economic rights can have the effect of curtailing broader social dialogue concerning the conceptual and value-based underpinnings of socio-economic rights. This critique is based on the understanding that there is a legitimate diversity of views regarding the nature and role of socio-economic rights, how different socio-economic needs should be prioritised and ranked, and the measures through which these rights should be realised.[206] The minimum core concept seeks to establish a normative essence for socio-economic rights which is beyond contestation and debate. As such, it tends to promote closure in broader deliberative and discursive processes regarding the normative content, prioritisation and methods of realising

---

204 See also chapter 2, parts 2.4.6–2.4.7.

205 K Klare 'Legal subsidiarity and constitutional rights: A reply to André van der Walt' (2008) 1 *CCR* 129–154 at 136–137. Danie Brand argues that there is an overemphasis in the Court's socio-economic rights jurisprudence on the institutional relations between the different branches of government, and insufficient attention to promoting broader discursive engagement within civil society regarding socio-economic rights. See D Brand 'The "politics of need interpretation" and the adjudication of socio-economic rights in South Africa' in A J van der Walt (ed) *Theories of Social and Economic Justice* (2005) 17–36.

206 Dixon points out that while it may be possible 'as an abstract and theoretical matter' to formulate the morally and constitutionally correct grounding for these core obligations, it is also likely and reasonable that South Africans, with a variety of different life experiences and perspectives, will differ on these questions. See R Dixon 'Creating dialogue about socio-economic rights: strong-form versus weak-form judicial review revisited' (2007) 5 *I Con* 391 at 416–417. Dixon describes the various theoretical groundings which have been provided for the minimum core concept in constitutional scholarship, and the varying practical consequences which these approaches have for the interpretation of socio-economic rights claims (400–401). See also Steinberg (note 55 above) 275; Wesson (note 195 above) 304–305.

socio-economic rights.[207] This approach fails to acknowledge the socially and communally determined processes and values through which social needs are identified and validated.[208]

(c) The illusive content of the core

A second major critique of the minimum core concept concerns its linkage to survival needs. In the first instance, the survival standard does not guarantee the clarity and certainty which is claimed for it in defining priority claims in socio-economic rights adjudication. Given the fact that threats to life can be relatively short, medium or long term, the survival standard does not provide clear guidance as to which socio-economic interventions should be adopted or enjoy prioritised consideration in policymaking and adjudication. Health education measures concerning the dangers of smoking or the need for safe sex may not save lives in the short term, but may have a significant impact on long-term mortality rates. What relative priority should therefore be given to these measures as opposed to other interventions which have a more immediate impact in saving lives, for example, the expansion of emergency medical services in rural areas? There are no easy, incontrovertible answers. This suggests that the quest for an uncontested standard to guide prioritisation in the context of socio-economic rights is misplaced.

A further difficulty with the survival-based standard is that it results in either over- or under-inclusivity in the specification of core obligations. On the one hand, people can survive on very little which could give rise to a minimalist approach to socio-economic provisioning. Amartya Sen points out that people have been known to survive with incredibly little nutrition and that so-called '"minimum nutrition requirements" have an inherent arbitrariness that goes well beyond variations between groups and regions'.[209] On the other hand, in the context of health care rights, a survival-based standard supports the provision of expensive, tertiary health care interventions. Such interventions will, under conditions of scarcity, occur at the expense of less expensive preventative and primary health care interventions.[210] In the context

---

207 See in this regard K G Young 'The minimum core of economic and social rights: A concept in search of content' (2008) 33 *The Yale Journal of International Law* 112–175 at 138–140.

208 For a discussion of the way in which social needs are politically and discursively determined, see N Fraser *Unruly Practices: Power, Discourse and Gender in Contemporary Social Theory* (1989) 144–160 at 163–183; N Fraser 'Talking about needs: Interpretive contests as political conflicts in welfare-state societies' (1989) 99 *Ethics* 291–313. For applications of Fraser's theoretical perspectives on the struggle over needs in contemporary capitalist societies, see D Brand (note 205 above); S Liebenberg 'Needs, rights and transformation: Adjudicating social rights' (2006) 1 *Stell LR* 5–36.

209 A Sen *Poverty and Famines: An Essay on Entitlement and Deprivation* (1981) 12 (discussed by Young (note 207 above) 131).

210 The ethical and practical problems associated with the survival-based standard for determining minimum core obligations in the context of health rights impels Bilchitz to

of other socio-economic rights such as education, the focus on biological survival simply does not accord with the purposes and interests which this right is intended to protect and promote.

Grounding the concept of a minimum core obligation in the biological survival standard is also unduly reductionist in the context of a transformative constitution which seeks to promote the achievement of social justice. Thus Katharine Young argues that the emphasis on minimalism behind the core 'is suggestive, when attached to life, of a more scientific, needs-based assessment of the commodities necessary for biological survival'.[211] As O'Regan J observes in *S v Makwanyane*:

> It is not life as mere organic matter that the Constitution cherishes but the right to human life: the right to live as a human being, to be part of a broader community, to share in the experience of humanity … . The right to life is more than existence, it is a right to be treated as a human being with dignity.[212]

In striving to establish clear and judicially manageable standards for the adjudication of socio-economic rights claims, the minimum core approach is in danger of encouraging minimalism in social provisioning when the context may in fact render such minimalism unnecessary and inappropriate.

A related concern with an understanding of the minimum core concept linked to an inflexible standard such as survival is its lack of responsiveness to the diverse needs and circumstances of differently placed groups.[213] The underlying concern is that the concept of minimum core obligations may result in the exclusion or marginalisation of the needs of various groups that do not fit the background norms informing the definition of core obligations.

Attempting to ground core obligations in a single metric such as survival overlooks the fact that people have other important needs which warrant priority consideration in a constitutional order committed to the values of democracy, human dignity, equality and freedom.[214] For example, the provision of childcare facilities may not be crucial to survival, but given the gendered burden of care coupled with the

---

develop the notion of 'the pragmatic minimum threshold' in relation to health rights. The pragmatic minimum core represents a conglomeration of the principled survival-based standard together with a range of other theoretical and practical considerations such as the resources and capacity available in a particular society. See Bilchitz (note 78 above) 220–225.

211 Young (note 207 above) 131. See the similar concern expressed by Porter (note 195 above) 55.

212 *Makwanyane* (note 25 above) paras 326–327.

213 As will be recalled, the Court in *Grootboom* referred to the difficulty of defining minimum core obligations in the light of the diversity of needs and circumstances of different groups. See *Grootboom* (note 3 above) para 33.

214 See, for example, Dixon's argument that it is equally plausible to base a notion of minimum core obligations on the values of human dignity and equality (note 206 above) 399–401. For an argument that a heightened review standard should be applied to basic needs claims identified by reference to a dignity-standard, see Liebenberg (note 114 above).

conditions of socio-economic deprivation in which many women live, the provision of such facilities is critical to their ability to participate equally in employment, development programmes and other social institutions.[215] The exclusion of such gender-specific priorities simultaneously reinforces the marginalisation of women's needs as well as the needs of those men and women who undertake the burden of reproductive work in our society. Similarly, the provision of various forms of specially adapted housing and social services to people with disabilities may not be necessary for their survival, but is nonetheless crucial for their ability to participate as equals in society.[216]

A 'minimum core' approach grounded in biological survival is thus insufficiently responsive to the diversity of important needs faced by differently situated groups in our society. In respect of other socio-economic rights, such as the right to education, the focus on biological survival simply does not accord with the broader purposes and interests which this right protects.

(*d*) The interrelated character of needs

A third major critique of the minimum core approach is its dependence on a two-tiered approach to the adjudication of positive socio-economic rights claims. This approach requires distinguishing between core needs (those that implicate survival) and non-core needs (those that relate to fulfilling a range of purposes and flourishing as a human being).[217] However, the difficulty, as the aforementioned examples illustrate, is that social needs are interconnected and there is no clear-cut, generally agreed distinction between core and non-core needs.

Nancy Fraser describes needs-based claims as 'nested' in that they are 'connected to one another in ramified chains of "in order to" relations'.[218] It is generally possible to

---

[215] See B Goldblatt 'Citizenship and the right to child care' in A Gouws (ed) *(Un)thinking Citizenship: Feminist Debates in Contemporary South Africa* (2005) 117–136. Goldblatt argues that childcare rights can be derived from the right of everyone to social security (s 27(1)(*c*)), the right of children to social services (s 28(1)(*c*)), and the right to fair labour practices (s 23(1)). The African Charter on the Rights and Welfare of the Child (1990) (ratified by South Africa on 7 January 2000) places an obligation on States Parties to take all appropriate measures, in accordance with their means and national conditions, 'to assist parents and others responsible for the child in the performance of child-rearing and ensure the development of institutions responsible for providing care of children; and to ensure that the children of working parents are provided with care services and facilities'. See art 20(2)(*b*) and (*c*).

[216] See further S Liebenberg & B Goldblatt 'The interrelationship between equality and socio-economic rights under South Africa's transformative constitution' (2007) 23 *SAJHR* 335–361 at 339–341.

[217] Bilchitz (note 78 above) 202 argues that the 'two-tier structure' that he proposes 'has the benefit of offering a clear, structured way in which to approach the application of socio-economic rights to particular situations'.

[218] Fraser 1989 (note 208 above) 163.

reach consensus on what Fraser terms, 'thin needs' such as the need of people in non-tropical climates for shelter in order to survive.[219] However, as soon as one inquires into the detail of what precisely is required in order to provide shelter which can be sustained and fulfil its purposes, a diversity of views is encountered.[220] For example, ensuring that housing is located close to employment and livelihood opportunities is generally not defined as part of the minimum core obligations of the State.[221] Nevertheless, the location of housing is a crucial factor in the ability of low-income communities to pursue sustainable livelihood strategies.[222]

Taking location into account in fulfilling core obligations will usually require the State to purchase more expensive land closer to employment opportunities, thus increasing substantially the resource implications of providing basic shelter. However, this detracts from the clarity of definition and relatively low-cost implications which is an argument in favour of the minimum core as a manageable judicial standard for the enforcement of certain basic subsistence needs. On the other hand, excluding location from the ambit of core obligations in the sphere of housing will relegate a crucial dimension of the housing needs of the poor to lower down the hierarchy of judicial enforcement.

Determining whether factors such as location should be taken into account in a housing rights case cannot be satisfactorily resolved through resorting to the distinction between 'core' and 'non-core' obligations. As will be argued, courts should rather strive to develop an account of the purpose and values which the particular rights are intended to promote, paying careful attention to the relevant historical and social contexts and disadvantaged groups' articulations of their needs and the measures needed to fulfil them. The reasonableness of the State's acts or omissions should be assessed

---

219 Ibid.

220 Ibid.

221 The UN Committee on Economic, Social and Cultural Rights lists the 'location' of housing as one of the elements which must be taken into account in assessing the 'adequacy' of housing in terms of art 11 of the International Covenant on Economic, Social and Cultural Rights. Thus adequate housing 'must be in a location which allows access to employment options, health care services, schools, child-care centres and other social facilities. ... Similarly housing should not be built on polluted sites nor in immediate proximity to pollution sources that threaten the right to health of the inhabitants.' General Comment No 4 (Sixth sess, 1991) *The right to adequate housing (art 11(1) of the Covenant* UN doc E/1992/23 para 8(*f*). It is not mentioned as an element of the minimum core obligations of the State. Bilchitz argues that the general standard that constitutes the minimum core obligation of the State in relation to housing would be that everyone should have 'access to accommodation that involves, at least, protection from the elements in sanitary conditions with access to basic services, such as toilets and running water' (note 78 above) 198.

222 The issue of the location of alternative accommodation for those facing eviction from their homes was a major issue in *Occupiers of 51 Olivia Road* (note 10 above) and in the *Joe Slovo* case (note 11 above). See further chapter 6, parts 6.4 and 6.5.

in the light of a constantly evolving understanding of the normative commitments promoted by the various socio-economic rights provisions.

Another criticism which has been levelled against the two-tier approach to the adjudication of positive socio-economic rights claims is that the strong prioritisation of core needs is likely to be counterproductive to the goals of longer-term developmental programmes.[223] Murray Wesson argues that the effect of this adjudicative approach will be to encourage the diversion of State resources from longer-term, and often more efficient, investments, to temporary, emergency-type measures.[224] He argues for a more flexible, nuanced approach in the light of the 'spectrum of needs' faced by the State.[225] Such an approach does not prioritise one set of needs to the exclusion of others, and allows for a balance between short-, medium- and long-term goals.[226] This underscores the point made above that socio-economic needs are interconnected. Optimal developmental approaches aim to achieve synergy between measures designed to meet urgent needs and programmes geared to achieve the sustainable and adequate realisation of socio-economic rights in the long term.

However, the need for a nuanced and integrated approach should not detract from the importance of ensuring that basic socio-economic needs are met. As the Court noted in *Grootboom*, a general statistical improvement in access to socio-economic rights may nevertheless fail to meet the constitutional requirement that everyone must be treated 'with care and concern'.[227] Moreover, empirical evidence suggests that the meeting of social needs is frequently the prerequisite for sustainable economic and social development.[228] The fulfilment of people's immediate needs is therefore an important component of the positive duties imposed by socio-economic rights.

(*e*) Integrating the minimum core

The critiques of the minimum core concept discussed above do not necessarily require the concept to be jettisoned. It has the potential to play a valuable role in socio-economic rights adjudication by signalling the high priority which should be attached in social policy to ensuring that the urgent material needs of vulnerable and

---

[223] Wesson (note 195 above).

[224] Ibid 304.

[225] Ibid 303.

[226] Ibid 304. See also the similar argument by Dixon (note 206 above) 411.

[227] *Grootboom* (note 3 above) para 44.

[228] See, e.g., Committee of Inquiry into a Comprehensive System of Social Security for South Africa *Transforming the Present, Protecting the Future* (2002), available at http://www.welfare.gov.za/Documents/2002/2002.htm (accessed on 26 May 2009); Economic Policy Research Institute *The Social and Economic Impact of South Africa's Social Security System* (2004), available at http://www.sarpn.org.za/documents/d0001041/Full_Report.pdf (accessed on 26 May 2009). Children's development and future life prospects are particularly affected by a failure to ensure that their basic socio-economic needs are met. See, e.g., D Budlender & I Woolard *The Impact of the South African Child Support and Old Age Grants on Children's Schooling and Work* International Labour Organisation (ILO) (2006).

disadvantaged groups receive immediate attention.[229] A consideration of its shortcomings and pitfalls should rather invite a re-evaluation of its formulation and role in the context of socio-economic rights adjudication.

The minimum core concept need not be grounded exclusively in the survival-based standard, but can encompass other foundational constitutional values such as participatory democracy, equality, freedom and human dignity. Moreover, the minimum core concept need not be located within a rigid, two-tier approach to the adjudication of socio-economic rights but can, as will be discussed in the following part, play an important role in the evaluation of the reasonableness of the State's measures in realising socio-economic rights.

4.4.2 Reconceiving reasonableness

(*a*) Normative flexibility versus normative weakness

The model of 'reasonableness review' adopted by the Constitutional Court for adjudicating the positive duties imposed by socio-economic rights has been criticised for amounting to an administrative law model which does not engage in a sufficiently substantive analysis of the content of socio-economic rights and the obligations they impose.[230] It has been argued that the vagueness and openness of the reasonableness inquiry allow courts to avoid giving clear normative content to socio-economic rights.[231] In part, the notion of minimum core obligations constitutes an attempt to respond to this critique of reasonableness review by carving out a clear normative content for socio-economic rights.[232]

For other scholars, the major advantage of reasonableness review is that it enables courts to attain a skilful balance between 'displacing democratic judgments about how to set priorities' and abdicating any meaningful role in the judicial enforcement of socio-economic rights.[233] Reasonableness review, it is argued, places a burden of justification or explanation on government that it has engaged in reasonable priority-setting.[234]

---

[229] See Young (note 207 above) 172–174 on the critical analysis which is required to understand the usefulness of the minimum core concept in confronting dominant economic orthodoxies.

[230] See D Brand (note 52 above).

[231] Pieterse (note 189 above) 410–411. Dennis Davis observes that reasonableness review can easily degenerate into a highly deferential standard of review: D M Davis 'Socio-economic rights in South Africa: The record of the Constitutional Court after ten years' (2004) 5 *ESR Review* 3–5 at 5; D M Davis 'Adjudicating the socio-economic rights in the South African Constitution: Towards 'deference lite'? (2006) 22 *SAJHR* 301–327 at 311.

[232] Bilchitz 2003 (note 188 above) 9–10.

[233] C R Sunstein 'Social and economic rights? Lessons from South Africa' (2000–2001) 11(4) *Const Forum* 123–131 at 131.

[234] Ibid 130.

In many respects, reasonableness review provides the courts with a flexible and context-sensitive basis for evaluating socio-economic rights claims. It allows government the space to design and formulate appropriate policies to meet its socio-economic rights obligations. At the same time, it subjects government's choices to the requirements of reasonableness, inclusiveness, and particularly, the threshold requirement that all programmes must provide short-term measures of relief for those whose circumstances are urgent and intolerable.[235] Reasonableness review enables the Court to adjust the stringency of its review standard informed by factors such as the position of the claimant group in society,[236] the nature of the resource or service claimed,[237] and the impact of the denial of access on the claimant group.[238] The Court's jurisprudence suggests that the government's justifications will be subject to more stringent scrutiny when a disadvantaged sector of society is deprived of access to essential services and resources. In this regard, the Court has acknowledged the poor as a vulnerable group in society, whose needs require special attention.[239]

Thus the reasonableness inquiry takes into account a number of considerations relevant to the claimant group, the nature of the service or resource in question, as well as the historical, economic and social context[240] in which the claim arises. In these respects, 'reasonableness review' avoids closure and creates the ongoing possibility of challenging various forms of socio-economic deprivations in a wide range of different contexts. Through the jurisprudence, the courts have developed clear standards for holding the State accountable for its acts and omissions in the sphere of socio-economic rights. This, combined with the responsiveness of reasonableness review to diverse contexts, facilitates participation and dialogical interaction between the State, civil society and the courts in defining and adopting measures to give effect to socio-economic rights. This is exemplified by the way in which the TAC has been able to use reasonableness review to win a major victory in the provision

---

235 Carol Steinberg (note 55 above) 277 argues that 'the intense scrutiny' of government conduct, combined with the heavy weighting of the values of human dignity and equality in the proportionality assessment, gives the reasonableness inquiry in socio-economic rights cases a discrete character.

236 See, for example, the historical context and current socio-economic circumstances of the claimants sketched by the Court in its judgments in *Grootboom* (note 3 above) paras 2–11; *Treatment Action Campaign* (note 5 above) paras 78–79; *Khosa* (note 6 above) paras 71, 76–77, 80–81.

237 In *Soobramoney* (note 2 above), a more tertiary and expensive form of medical treatment was claimed and the Court applied an undemanding standard of rationality review. In contrast, in *Grootboom*, *Treatment Action Campaign* and *Khosa* the review standard was stricter and involved a more searching scrutiny of government's justifications for denying the applicants access to a basic level of service provision.

238 In the *Grootboom, Treatment Action Campaign* and *Khosa* cases, the lack of access to the socio-economic programme in question had a severe impact on the respective claimant groups.

239 *Grootboom* (note 3 above) para 36; *Treatment Action Campaign* (note 5 above) para 79.

240 *Grootboom* (note 3 above) paras 43–44, 92.

of appropriate medical treatment to reduce the risk of the transmission of HIV from mother to child.[241] This victory was a significant breakthrough in the broader transformative strategy of the TAC to achieve a general anti-retroviral programme for people living with HIV/AIDS. The TAC and other civil society organisations were able to use the criteria for a reasonable programme established in the *Grootboom* case and the mother-to-child transmission case in broad-based advocacy for a general anti-retroviral roll-out programme.[242]

However, a significant disadvantage of reasonableness review is that it conflates the two-stage approach to constitutional analysis with its initial principled focus on the scope of the right and the beneficiary group, and thereafter a consideration of possible justifications offered by the respondent for the infringement.[243] Woolman and Botha elucidate the differing nature of the inquiry which takes place during the first and second stages of constitutional analysis.[244] The first stage is concerned with developing the content of the relevant right and evaluating whether the respondent's conduct or omissions infringes the right. The second stage entails an inquiry into the respondent's purposes for limiting the right and an inquiry into the proportionality of the means chosen to achieve this purpose, including a consideration of 'less restrictive means'.[245] The limitations inquiry enables a relational dialogue between claimants, respondents and the court on the justifiability of the State's purposes and the particular means chosen to achieve these purposes.[246]

The reasonableness model of review offers no clear distinction between determining the scope of the right, whether it has been breached, and justifications for possible infringements.[247] This allows the courts to elide an initial principled engagement with the purpose and underlying values of the relevant rights and the impact of the deprivations on the claimant groups. The focus of the inquiry in socio-economic rights claims is on the justifiability of the State's policy choices without a sustained analysis of the substantive values and purposes which the relevant rights protect

---

241 See M Heywood 'Preventing mother-to-child HIV transmission in South Africa: Background, strategies and outcomes of the Treatment Action Campaign Case against the Minister of Health' (2003) 19 *SAJHR* 278–315.

242 This programme was announced by government in August 2003. See further the civil society submission on the operational plan for the roll-out of an antiretroviral programme entitled 'A People-Centred ARV Programme'. Available at http://www.tac.org.za/Documents/TreatmentPlan/FullFinalSubmissiontoARVTaskTeam.doc (accessed on 20 April 2009). See further M Heywood 'Shaping, making and breaking the law in the campaign for a national HIV/AIDS Treatment Plan' in P Jones & K Stokke (eds) *Democratising Development: The Politics of Socio-Economic Rights in South Africa* (2005) 181–212.

243 See further part 4.4.5 below.

244 On the distinct nature of the inquiry undertaken in relation to the first and second stages of constitutional analysis, see S Woolman & H Botha 'Limitations' in Woolman et al (eds) *Constitutional Law of South Africa* 2 ed OS (2006) chapter 34, 1–6;16–29.

245 Section 36(1)(*e*).

246 See generally chapter 3, part 3.2.4.

247 See further the discussion in part 4.4.5 below.

under South Africa's transformative constitution. In *Grootboom*, the Court held that the overarching obligation of the State in terms of s 26 (and, by implication, s 27) was the adoption of a comprehensive, co-ordinated programme which 'must be capable of facilitating the realisation of the right'.[248] However, as David Bilchitz points out, until some understanding is developed of the content of the right, the assessment of whether the measures adopted by the State are reasonably capable of facilitating its realisation takes place in a normative vacuum.[249]

There are a number of indications in the judgments that the scope and content of the rights referred to in ss 26(1) and 27(1) are defined by relying on the State's justifications in terms of ss 26(2) and 27(2) for failing to expand access to the claimant groups.[250] Thus in *Khosa*[251] the Court held:

> [S]ection 27(1) and section 27(2) cannot be viewed as separate or discrete rights creating entitlements and obligations independently of one another. Section 27(2) exists as an internal limitation on the content of section 27(1) and *the ambit* of the section 27(1) right can therefore not be determined without reference to the reasonableness of the measures adopted to fulfil the obligation towards those entitled to the right in section 27(1).[252]

In other words, the Court has failed to develop an independent interpretation of the rights in the first sub-sections of ss 26 and 27. This approach narrows the dialogic space in adjudication for these groups to attempt to persuade the courts to adopt particular interpretations of the content of relevant rights. This detracts significantly from the capacity of courts to serve as significant institutions where deliberation concerning the meaning and implications of constitutional rights and values occurs.[253] As Marius Pieterse observes:

> [W]hile the reasonableness approach shows some sensitivity to vulnerability and need, the Court's denial of enforceable entitlements inherent to socio-economic rights in its current application of the approach significantly restricts individuals in articulating their demands for need-satisfaction as rights-claims. As a result, the beneficiaries' voices are dampened specifically in relation to that aspect of the socio-economic rights dialogue (the identification and elaboration of need) to which they can most valuably contribute.[254]

A lack of engagement with the underlying values and purposes of socio-economic rights has the further consequence that these values and the impact of the depriva-

---

[248] *Grootboom* (note 3 above) para 41.

[249] Bilchitz (note 78 above) 143.

[250] See, for example, *Soobramoney* (note 2 above) paras 11, 54 (concurring judgment of Sachs J); *Treatment Action Campaign* (note 5 above) paras 23 and 39; and *Khosa* (note 6 above) para 43.

[251] Note 6 above.

[252] Ibid para 43 (footnotes omitted, emphasis added).

[253] See in this regard chapter 2, part 2.3.2.

[254] M Pieterse 'On "dialogue", "translation" and "voice": A reply to Sandra Liebenberg' in S Woolman & M Bishop (eds) *Constitutional Conversations* (2008) 331–347 at 343–347.

tion on the claimant group are accorded insufficient weight in the evaluation of the reasonableness of the State's acts or omissions.

An examination of the leading cases on socio-economic rights illustrates that the Court has not spent much interpretive energy in developing the substantive content of the various socio-economic rights. A promising start was made in *Grootboom* in which the Court held that 'access to adequate housing' implies a recognition that 'housing entails more than bricks and mortar':

> It requires available land, appropriate services such as the provision of water and the removal of sewage and the financing of all of these, including the building of the house itself. For a person to have access to adequate housing all of these conditions need to be met: there must be land, there must be services, there must be a dwelling.[255]

However, there is very little engagement with various important purposes and values protected by the right to housing. The Court's main engagement with constitutional values, particularly human dignity, is in the context of justifying the element of the reasonableness test which requires that the State provide short-term measures of relief for those in desperate need.[256] These values do not play any significant role in developing the substantive content of the rights protected in ss 26(1) and 27(1).

Socio-economic rights such as adequate and culturally appropriate housing are not simply commodities to meet basic material needs, but enable people to fulfil their potential and to participate as equals in society. Thus the right to housing is more than simply the provision of shelter against the elements, but enables people to fulfil a diverse range of psychological, social, cultural and economic needs.[257] The significance of the concept of a home will also vary for differently placed groups and this must also be taken into account in developing the meaning and purpose of housing as a human right.[258] Similarly, an understanding of the significance of housing as right requires a detailed and nuanced appreciation of the historical and social context of housing in South Africa.[259]

---

255 Ibid para 35.

256 *Grootboom* (note 3 above) para 44.

257 For an analysis of the meanings and values which have evolved in relation to the concept of 'home', see L Fox 'The meaning of home: A chimerical concept or a legal challenge?' (2002) 29 *J of Law & Soc* 580–610. See also L Fox *Conceptualising Home – Theories, Laws and Policies* (2007).

258 While for many groups a fixed place of abode connecting them to a settled community and network of social and economic relations will be significant, for other groups the concept of home is integrally connected to a travelling and itinerant lifestyle. See, for example, the Roma Rights cases referred to in chapter 3, note 197. See also C Goldie 'Living in Public Space: A Human Rights Wasteland?' (Unpublished PhD thesis, Faculty of Law, University of New South Wales, March 2008) (an exposition of the position in domestic and international law of indigenous people living in public space in and around Darwin, Australia).

259 Compare, for example, the detailed analysis of forced evictions in South Africa undertaken by Sachs J in developing the interpretation of s 26(3) of the Constitution and legislation

In the *Treatment Action Campaign* case, there is even less engagement with the scope and content of the right of access to 'health care services, including reproductive health care' in s 27(1).[260] The Court's main focus is to demonstrate that government's inflexible stance regarding the confining of Nevirapine to the nine research sites could not be justified in the light of the policy, capacity and resource arguments raised by the State. The Court briefly refers to the fact that the administration of Nevirapine to mother and child at the time of birth is a 'potentially lifesaving medical intervention'.[261] However, beyond this, the Court does not explain why the provision of antiretroviral drugs and attendant services to reduce the risk of HIV-transmission should form an integral part of health care services in the South African context.[262] For example, in addition to children's rights to life and basic health care services, access by poor, mainly black, women to Nevirapine in the public health sector to reduce the risk of mother-to-child transmission of HIV could be regarded as an integral component of the right to reproductive health care. Such treatment advances the constitutional values of human dignity and equality, particularly in the context of the gendered burden of child care.

Similarly, in the case of *Khosa v Minister of Social Development*,[263] while the Court emphasises the significance of the values of human dignity and equality in evaluating the reasonableness of the exclusion of permanent residents from the social assistance legislation, it engages only very superficially with the content or scope of the social security and assistance rights in s 27(1)(*c*).[264]

The Constitutional Court's engagement with relevant international human rights standards and comparative jurisprudence on socio-economic rights is also unsatisfactory. There is now a substantial body of international and comparative jurisprudence that the courts can consider in developing the normative content of socio-economic rights.[265] For example, the European Committee on Social Rights, which supervises

enacted to give effect to it in *Port Elizabeth Municipality* (note 7 above).

260 See also Bilchitz 2003 (note 188 above) 7–8.

261 *Treatment Action Campaign* (note 5 above) paras 72–73.

262 It is noteworthy in this regard that the UN Committee on Economic, Social and Cultural Rights regards the provision of 'essential drugs, as from time to time defined under the WHO Action Programme on Essential Drugs' as part of the core obligations imposed by the right to the highest attainable standard of health in art 12 of the International Covenant on Economic, Social and Cultural Rights. See General Comment No 14 (note 89 above) para 43(*d*). The Committee also regards the taking of measures 'to prevent, treat and control epidemic and endemic diseases' to be an obligation of 'comparable priority' (para 44(*c*)). On the right to health in international law, see generally B C A Toebes *The Right to Health as a Human Right in International Law* (1999).

263 Note 6 above.

264 See the very brief treatment of the ambit of the right of access to social security in terms of s 27(1)(*c*) in *Khosa* ibid paras 46–47.

265 See chapter 3, parts 3.3.2 and 3.3.3.

the obligations of States Parties to the European Social Charter,[266] has developed a sophisticated understanding of the housing rights in the Charter. Thus in the complaint of *European Roma Rights Centre v Greece*, the Committee held:

> The right to housing permits the exercise of many other rights – both civil and political as well as economic, social and cultural. It is also of central importance to the family. The Committee recalls its previous case law to the effect that in order to satisfy Article 16 states must promote the provision of an adequate supply of housing for families, take the needs of families into account in housing policies and ensure that existing housing be of an adequate standard and include essential services (such as heating and electricity). The Committee has stated that adequate housing refers not only to a dwelling which must not be sub-standard and must have essential amenities, but also to a dwelling of suitable size considering the composition of the family in residence. Furthermore the obligation to promote and provide housing extends to security from unlawful eviction.[267]

The purpose of considering international and comparative law sources is not to uncritically import interpretations of socio-economic rights developed in other jurisdictions. Ultimately the courts remain under a duty to consider which interpretations best advance the values and transformative commitments of the Constitution in the historical and current political, economic and social context of South Africa. However, a reflective and nuanced consideration of international standards and the jurisprudence of other democratic societies can generate new options and possibilities in considering our own jurisprudence.[268] This openness to deliberative dialogue and ongoing self-examination and renewal is essential if socio-economic rights are to fulfil their transformative potential under the Constitution. It also ensures that the courts give proper effect in developing their jurisprudence under the Bill of Rights to those international law standards that are binding on South Africa.[269]

(*b*) Developing the normative content of socio-economic rights

Given the Constitutional Court's commitment to the model of reasonableness review for evaluating compliance with the positive duties imposed by ss 26 and 27, the critical question is whether this model can be developed so as to ensure a more substantive engagement with the purposes and underlying values of socio-economic rights. Such an approach should aim at preserving the openness and sensitivity to context

---

[266] Housing rights are protected in art 16 of the European Social Charter (1961) and arts 16 and 31 of the European Social Charter (Revised), 1996. A system of collective complaints was instituted through the Additional Protocol to the European Social Charter Providing for a System of Collective Complaints, 1995.

[267] *European Roma Rights Centre v Greece,* Complaint No 15/2003 para 24. See also *European Roma Rights Centre v Italy*, Complaint No 27/2004; *European Roma Rights Centre v Bulgaria*, Complaint No 31/2005.

[268] On the contribution of foreign law to the Constitutional Court's jurisprudence on the Bill of Rights, see generally T Roux 'The dignity of comparative constitutional law' (2008) *AJ* 185–203.

[269] See chapter 3, part 3.3.2(*b*).

of reasonableness review so as to facilitate the participatory and deliberative values of the Constitution.

A textual analysis supports a more substantive consideration of the nature and scope of the rights protected in ss 26 and 27. As the Court observed in the *Treatment Action Campaign* case, sub-sections (1) and (2) of ss 26 and 27 are linked.[270] The description of the State's obligations in the second sub-sections refers back to the rights described in the first sub-section of ss 26 and 27.[271] Nevertheless, these rights are contained in a separate sub-section. The purpose of this textual separation can only be to direct attention in the first instance to the nature of the relevant socio-economic rights and their underlying purposes.[272] Only once this analysis has taken place, is it possible to assess whether the measures adopted by the State are reasonable in relation to the normative commitments fostered by the relevant rights. In the absence of a principled attempt to develop the content of the rights in the first sub-section, the criteria of reasonableness review amount to little more than a list of 'good governance' standards for the State as opposed to fundamental human rights analysis.[273]

This implies a modified approach to the interpretation of ss 26 and 27, requiring the courts to make a conscious effort to develop the normative content of the various socio-economic rights described in ss 26(1) and 27(1). This task should be approached by considering the purposes and values which the rights seek to promote in the light of their historical and current socio-economic context. Developing the substantive meanings of the rights in s 26(1) and 27(1) should not imply arriving at a comprehensive and final definition of the relevant rights. On the contrary, the normative content of socio-economic rights should always remain contingent and incomplete, allowing space for the evolution of new meanings in response to changing contexts and forms of injustice. The precise implications of the normative commitments of the rights in particular cases can also be explored at the remedial stage. The participatory structural interdicts discussed in chapter 8 offer rich opportunities to promote engagement between affected parties on the specific measures required to give effect to the relevant socio-economic rights.[274]

A promising recent illustration of how the normative content of socio-economic rights can be developed taking into account both the beneficiaries' articulation of their own needs, as well as expert evidence and relevant international standards is

[270] *Treatment Action Campaign* (note 5 above) para 29.

[271] Ibid para 30.

[272] In its Memorandum to the Chairpersons and Executive Director of the Constitutional Assembly (dated 14 February 1996), the Technical Committee to Theme Committee IV wrote that the socio-economic provisions 'have been framed to assert the right and then to specify certain dimensions of the right – for example, the nature of the positive duty on the State, and the protection against arbitrary evictions'. They go on to advise that 'these rights cannot *solely* be reduced to an obligation on the state to take positive steps to improve people's access to housing, health care etc'. (Document on file with author.)

[273] See Brand (note 52 above) 43–51.

[274] See further in this regard, chapter 8, part 8.6.

the judgment of Tsoka J in *Mazibuko v The City of Johannesburg (Centre on Housing Rights and Evictions as amicus curiae) ('Mazibuko')*.[275] The Court concluded that the City's free basic water policy of 25 litres per person per day (or 6 kiloliters per household per month) was insufficient to meet their basic needs, to live in dignity and to avoid threats to their lives and health. Fifty litres of free basic water per person per day was held to be consistent with the normative standards imposed by s 27(1)(*b*). Tsoka J further held that it was 'uncontested that the respondents have the financial resources' to increase the free basic water allocation to the Phiri residents.[276] In these circumstances, it was unreasonable for the City to limit its free basic water allocation to 25 litres per person per day when it is 'able to provide 50 litres per person per day without straining its capacity on water and its financial resources'.[277]

The City was accordingly ordered to provide 'each applicant and other similarly placed residents of Phiri Township with [a] free basic water supply of 50 litres per person per day'.[278] The Court furthermore found that the imposition of prepayment water meters on the Phiri community was unlawful and unconstitutional, and ordered the respondents to provide the residents with 'the option of a metered supply installed at the cost of the City of Johannesburg'.[279] A noteworthy feature of the judgment is its rich contextual analysis of the impact of an inadequate water supply and the prepayment meter system on people living with HIV/AIDS in the Phiri community, as well as in deepening racial and gender inequalities.[280]

On appeal, the Supreme Court of Appeal held that 42 litres was the quantum of water which constituted 'sufficient' water for the purposes of s 27(1)(*b*). In evaluating the sufficiency of the water supply the Court took into account the three interrelated standards of life, health and dignity.[281] It found support for these standards in international law, particularly the influential General Comment No 15 adopted in 2002 by the UN Committee on Economic, Social and Cultural Rights under the International Covenant on Economic, Social and Cultural Rights (1966).[282] Streicher JA for the Court held that assessing the quantity of water required for a dignified existence requires a context-sensitive evaluation which takes into account, for example, whether people need additional water as they rely on waterborne sanitation, as in the case of the Phiri residents. It found that the 25 litres standard could not have taken into account the water needs of communities relying on waterborne sanitation.[283] The Court arrived at 42 litres per person per day as a sufficient quantum of water by

---

275 [2008] 4 All SA 471 (W).
276 Ibid para 181.
277 Ibid.
278 Ibid para 183. Order para 183.5.1.
279 Ibid. Order para 183, 5.2.
280 See, for example, ibid paras 151–159; 169–179.
281 *City of Johannesburg v Mazibuko* 2009 (3) SA 592 (SCA); 2009 (8) BCLR 791 (SCA). para 17.
282 Note 89 above.
283 Ibid para 18.

taking into account the evidence presented by the experts on behalf of the appellants and respondents respectively on the quantity of water required for various household needs such as drinking, food preparation, bathing, and toilet flushing.[284]

The next major issue considered by the Court was whether the City was obliged to provide 42 litres (or a lesser quantity of water) free of charge. The City contended that there is nothing in the Water Services Act 108 of 1997 or Regulations which obliges them to provide 'free' water. In interpreting the phrase, 'access to' in s 27(1)(*b*), the Court endorsed the UN Committee on Economic, Social and Cultural Rights' stipulation that 'access to water entails both physical and financial access'.[285] In other words, water should be affordable for all 'and must be accessible to all including the most vulnerable or marginalized sections of the population, in law and in fact'.[286] The contention that the City was not obliged to provide at least some quantity of water free of charge was rejected on the basis of the Court's interpretation of the Water Services Act, the Free Basic Water Policy of Government and the City, as well as the obligation to ensure that water was economically accessible in terms of s 27(1) of the Constitution. In determining the extent of the obligation to provide water free to people living in poverty, the key criterion was what would be reasonable, taking into account the City's available resources and other competing claims. The Court took cognisance of the fact that the City had various other claims on its budget.[287]

It concluded, however, that the City's decision to provide only 6 kilolitres of water per household (or 25 litres per person per day) was 'materially influenced by an error of law and falls to be set aside on that basis'.[288] Essentially the City had failed to appreciate that it had both statutory and constitutional obligations to provide a sufficient amount of water, including reasonable provision of free water for those who could not afford to pay for it. [289] The prepayment water meters were also declared unlawful.[290]

A positive feature of the Supreme Court of Appeal's reasoning in relation to the free basic water entitlement of the Phiri community is its willingness to engage with the substantive interests and values of water as a human right, and to articulate normative standards against which the sufficiency of the water supply to an impoverished community must be measured. In addition, it is significant that the Court affirms that the right of 'access to' water is not equivalent to access through exclusively commercial mechanisms. It includes a constitutional obligation on the State to ensure that

---

284 Ibid paras 21–24.

285 General Comment No 15 (note 89 above) para 12(*c*).

286 *City of Johannesburg v Mazibuko* (note 281 above) para 28.

287 Ibid para 37.

288 Ibid para 38.

289 For a discussion of the remedy granted by the Supreme Court of Appeal in respect of the free basic water supply, see chapter 8, part 8.5.3(*a*) at notes 248–265 and accompanying text.

290 For a discussion of the suspended declaration of invalidity in respect of the prepayment water meters, see chapter 8, part 8.3.5 at notes 118–127 and accompanying text.

water is economically accessible to the poor, including an obligation to supply free water to meet basic needs. More problematic is the defining of 42 litres of water per person per day as 'sufficient water' for the purposes of s 27(1)(*b*) of the Constitution. This sets a normative 'ceiling' which allows no scope for progressive realisation in terms of s 27(2).[291]

The courts have a critical role and responsibility in terms of the Constitution to articulate the substantive commitments and values promoted by socio-economic rights. In so doing, they stimulate deliberative engagement with the constitutional commitments embodied in the socio-economic rights provisions by the other branches of government as well as society as a whole.[292]

Only once a focused and sustained effort to develop the values and purposes underpinning the socio-economic rights at stake in a particular case has occurred, can a proper assessment be made regarding whether the measures adopted by the State are reasonable given its obligations to 'respect, protect, promote and fulfil' the relevant rights.[293] Sections 26(2) and 27(2) describe the nature of the State's obligations in relation to the rights listed in the first sub-section. In this context, the criteria developed by the Court for a reasonable government programme are useful for assessing compliance by the State with these duties.[294] In considering whether the circumstances of a particular case are inconsistent with these values and purposes, careful attention should be paid to the impact of the State's acts or omissions on the claimant group as well as their own articulations of their needs and preferred solutions. In this way, the meaning of socio-economic rights emerges from a dynamic interaction between value-based reasoning and a striving to understand the complex historical and social matrix in which socio-economic rights claims are situated. This approach together with the initial engagement with the substance of the socio-economic rights in ss 26(1) and 27(1) militates against reasonableness review degenerating into an unprincipled and unduly deferential standard of review.

(*c*) Justification and basic needs

A further dimension of reasonableness review which requires development is the standard of justification which should be applied in various types of socio-economic

---

291 For a critique of this aspect and other aspects of the Supreme Court of Appeal's judgment, see J Dugard and S Liebenberg 'Muddying the waters: The Supreme Court of Appeal's judgment in the *Mazibuko* case' (2009) 10 *ESR Review* 11. For an analysis and critique of the Constitutional Court's judgment in the *Mazibuko* case, see chapter 9 (postscript), part 9.4.

292 Christine Bateup 'The dialogic promise: Assessing the normative potential of theories of constitutional dialogue' (2006) 71 *Brook L Rev* 1109–1180 at 1175 points out that 'judges can both facilitate constitutional discussion at a society-wide level and make unique institutional contributions to the consideration of constitutional values in the context of individual cases'.

293 Section 7(2) of the Constitution. See further chapter 3, part 3.2.2.

294 See footnotes 104–112 above and accompanying text.

rights cases. As noted above, one of the advantages of the minimum core approach is that it places a weighty burden of justification on the State in cases where people are deprived of their basic needs. This promotes social and economic policies which are responsive to people's needs.[295] When people's basic needs go unmet, they live in conditions which are inconsistent with human dignity and freedom, and are unable to participate as equals in society. Thus in *Grootboom*, the Court observed:

> The right of access to adequate housing is entrenched because we value human beings and want to ensure that they are afforded their basic human needs. A society must seek to ensure that the basic necessities of life are provided to all if it is to be a society based on human dignity, equality and freedom.[296]

As noted, the Court has acknowledged that there 'may be cases where it may be possible and appropriate to have regard to the content of a minimum core obligation to determine whether the measures taken by the State are reasonable'.[297] An example of the application of this approach is the High Court judgment in the *Mazibuko* case.[298] It assessed 50 litres of water per person per day to be the minimum essential level of free basic water required to meet the needs of the Phiri residents. This minimum quantum should be taken into account in assessing the reasonableness of the measures adopted by the State in terms of s 27.[299] The valuable contribution of the concept of minimum core obligations in directing priority attention to people's basic needs should be incorporated in the reasonableness analysis by placing a particularly heavy burden of justification on the State in circumstances where a person or group lacks access to a basic socio-economic service or resource corresponding to the rights in ss 26 and 27.[300]

---

[295] One of the basic values and principles governing public administration in South Africa is that '[p]eople's needs must be responded to, and the public must be encouraged to participate in policy-making. (s 195(1)(*e*) of the Constitution). See also s 153(*a*) of the Constitution, requiring a municipality to 'structure and manage its administration and budgeting and planning processes to give priority to the basic needs of the community, and to promote the social and economic development of the community'.

[296] *Grootboom* (note 3 above) para 44. See also *Khosa* (note 6 above) para 52.

[297] *Grootboom* ibid para 33; *Treatment Action Campaign* (note 5 above) para 34.

[298] See notes 275–280 above and accompanying text.

[299] See the Court's analysis at paras 127–134 and 181. In this regard, the Court relied on the possible role for minimum core obligations as a consideration in assessing the reasonableness of the measures adopted by the State contemplated in the *Grootboom* (note 3 above) and *Treatment Action Campaign* (note 5 above) cases.

[300] The adjustment of the reasonableness review standard in accordance with the severity of the rights deprivation was explicitly acknowledged by the Constitutional Court in *Rail Commuters Action Group v Transnet Ltd t/a Metrorail* (note 101 above). The Court held at para 88 that the assessment of reasonableness should include, among others factors, 'the extent of any threat to fundamental rights should the duty not be met as well as the intensity of any harm that may result. The more grave is the threat to fundamental rights, the greater is the responsibility on the duty-bearer'.

In determining what constitutes a basic social need or the necessities of life, the courts need not be guided by a single overarching standard such as biological survival. The inquiry should be primarily guided by a context-sensitive assessment of the impact of the deprivation on the particular group. In assessing the severity of the impact, the courts should consider the implications of the lack of access to the resource or service in question for other intersecting rights and values such as the rights to life, freedom and security of the person, equality and human dignity.[301] This accords with an interpretive approach which embraces the interdependence between various constitutional rights and values.[302] Courts should also be alert to the ways in which the denial of access to the particular right creates or reinforces patterns of inequality and marginalisation in our society.[303]

Further guidance can be sought from applicable international and comparative law. Thus consideration should be given to whether the service or resource at issue is regarded by the UN Committee on Economic, Social and Cultural Rights or other international human rights institutions as comprising part of the minimum core obligations of the State, or if it is a component of the public services generally provided by States in other democratic societies.[304]

A failure to ensure such basic social provisioning should only be justifiable when resources are demonstrably inadequate,[305] or other compelling justifications exist. The latter may include, for example, comparable urgent priorities which are justifiable in an open and democratic society based on human dignity, equality and freedom. The seriousness of the impact of the deprivation in question may warrant a strict proportionality requirement approximating the evaluation in terms of the general limitations clause (s 36).[306] A proportionality assessment also requires the State to consider

---

[301] In *Khosa* (note 6 above), Mokgoro J was at pains to emphasise the implications of socio-economic deprivation for other rights and values in the Bill of Rights. See, for example paras 40–45 and para 49.

[302] See generally chapter 2, part 2.4.3.

[303] On the interrelationship between socio-economic rights and the right and value of equality, see further Liebenberg & Goldblatt (note 216 above).

[304] On the role of international and comparative law in interpreting socio-economic rights in the Bill of Rights, see generally chapter 3, parts 3.3.2(*a*) and 3.3.3(*a*).

[305] In General Comment No 3 (note 85 above) para 10, the UN Committee on Economic, Social and Cultural Rights commented as follows:

> In order for a State party to be able to attribute its failure to meet at least its minimum core obligations to a lack of available resources it must demonstrate that every effort has been made to use all resources that are at its disposition in an effort to satisfy, as a matter of priority, those minimum obligations.

[306] The Court's 'hard look' at the State's policy and budgetary justifications in the *Khosa* case (note 6 above) essentially amounted to a proportionality assessment. The denial of access to basic social grants had devastating consequences for permanent residents who, as impoverished non-nationals, were a vulnerable and marginalised group in society. No policy measures, other than the inclusion of permanent residents within the scope of the

lesser forms of provisioning where it is not possible to meet everyone's basic needs within current resource constraints.[307]

This suggested approach to the review of positive socio-economic rights claims is not premised on a dichotomous distinction between core and non-core interests. Compliance with the obligations in the second sub-sections of ss 26 and 27 is assessed in terms of the single evaluative criterion of reasonableness. However, the standard of scrutiny is varied in accordance with the nature of the service or resource to which access is sought and the impact of its denial on the complainant group. A stringent standard of scrutiny, requiring weighty justifications from the State and incorporating a proportionality analysis, is apposite where a vulnerable group lacks access to a basic socio-economic service or resource. This deprivation implicates founding constitutional values and other intersecting rights such as a life, human dignity, democratic participation and freedom. Guidance regarding basic standards of social provisioning can also be obtained from relevant international standards as well as other open and democratic societies committed to the values of human dignity, equality and freedom.

Where the service in question is of a more tertiary nature, and the evidence reveals that ordering its provision will prejudice the realisation of other rights and legitimate state purposes, the standard of scrutiny can be relaxed.[308] However, the courts remain duty-bound to undertake a serious assessment of whether available resources in fact permit the State to provide the more extensive socio-economic resource or service. The purpose of the rights in ss 26 and 27 is to ensure the full realisation of the relevant rights to a constitutionally acceptable level of adequacy and sufficiency.[309] Although the State is afforded the latitude to achieve this 'progressively', this does not imply that the obligation to provide improved social services is deferred in circumstances where it has the capacity to ensure such access. The State should thus be required to place the necessary budgetary and policy information before the court to enable an assessment of its existing resources and capacity.[310]

Reconceiving reasonableness review along the lines proposed facilitates a relational and dialogic approach to interpreting the rights in the Bill of Rights. As argued in chapter 2, this approach is well suited to advancing the constitutional commitment to democratic, rights-based transformation.[311]

---

social grants scheme established by the Social Assistance Act, would suffice to comply with the State's obligations in terms of ss 27 and 9. See further part 4.3.4 above.

307 This argument is developed in Liebenberg (note 114 above) 21–29.

308 This is illustrated by the *Soobramoney* case (note 2 above). See 4.2.2 above.

309 These are the phrases generally used to describe the rights in ss 26(1) and 27(1).

310 See further part 4.4.4 below.

311 See chapter 2, part 2.4.6.

4.4.3 Progressive realisation and retrogressive measures

The Court interprets 'progressive realisation' to mean the dismantling of a range of legal, administrative, operational and financial obstacles which impede access to the rights, and the expansion over time of such access, to a larger number and broader range of people.[312] However, if ss 26 and 27 are interpreted to place a strong obligation on the State to ensure that everyone has access to at least a basic level of the relevant socio-economic rights, 'progressive realisation' would refer primarily to the State's obligation to gradually improve the quality of the goods and services to which people have access until the goal of the full realisation of the rights is achieved.[313] As David Bilchitz argues in the context of the right to adequate housing in s 26:

> Progressive realization involves an improvement in the adequacy of housing for the meeting of human interests. It does not mean that some receive housing now, and others receive it later; rather, it means that each is entitled as a matter of priority to basic housing provision, which the government is required to improve gradually over time.[314]

The approach to reasonableness review for which I have argued requires the State to act with due diligence and without delay[315] to extend access to basic services to all groups in need thereof.[316] The fact that the State is unable to ensure the full realisation of the rights in the short term, does not absolve it from the obligation to take immediate steps to provide relief to those in urgent socio-economic need to avoid them suffering irreparable harm.[317] This approach is supported in the socio-

---

[312] *Grootboom* (note 3 above) para 45. See further note 120 above and accompanying text.

[313] This is also consistent with the approach of the UN Committee on Economic, Social and Cultural Rights to the interpretation of 'progressive realisation' in General Comment 3 (note 85 above) which incorporates the notion of a 'minimum core obligation'. The Court in *Grootboom* (ibid) referred with approval to the Committee's views on 'progressive realisation' as being 'in harmony with the context in which the phrase is used in our own Constitution'. See also note 121 above.

[314] Bilchitz (note 78 above) 193.

[315] For a discussion of the 'due diligence' standard and jurisprudence in international law in relation to the positive duties imposed by civil and political rights such as the rights to life, liberty and security of the person, see C Scott & P Macklem 'Constitutional ropes of sand or justiciable guarantees? Social rights in a new South African Constitution' (1992) 141 *U Pa L Rev* 1–148 at 53–57. They note as follows:

> While the due diligence standard allows for adjustments to be made according to the availability of state resources, lack of resources is not an automatically dispositive defense. On the contrary, the duty to protect is so important that states are required to give a certain priority of resources to police and related means of protection such as the court system. (53, footnotes omitted.)

[316] Section 237 of the Constitution requires that '[a]ll constitutional obligations must be performed diligently and without delay'.

[317] The *Maastricht Guidelines on Economic, Social and Cultural Rights* (note 100 above) para 8 state:

> The fact that the full realization of most economic, social and cultural rights can only be achieved progressively, which in fact also applies to most civil and political rights, does not alter the nature of the legal obligation of States which requires that certain steps be taken immediately and others

economic jurisprudence of the Court by the requirement that a reasonable government programme must provide for those in urgent need and living in 'intolerable conditions'.[318] The provision of a basic level of services need not meet the qualitative standard implied by the full realisation of the relevant right.[319] In circumstances where it is unavoidable to prioritise among groups in providing basic needs due to pressing and demonstrable resource constraints, the needs of marginalised and disadvantaged groups should receive particular consideration and attention.[320]

However, the overarching obligation of the State is to ensure that the rights delineated in the first sub-sections of ss 26 and 27 are realised, albeit, on a progressive basis. This requires developing a substantive understanding of the nature and scope of the relevant rights. The rights listed in these sections, either expressly or by virtue of the very nature of the rights in question,[321] incorporate a qualitative dimension of adequacy, sufficiency and appropriateness. The obligation of progressive realisation should thus primarily be understood to refer to the State's obligation to improve the nature and quality of the services to which people have access so that their underlying purposes are fulfilled.

According to the UN Committee on Economic, Social and Cultural Rights, 'progressive realisation' has a dual character:

> It is on the one hand a necessary flexibility device, reflecting the realities of the real world and the difficulties involved for any country in ensuring full realization of economic, social and cultural rights. On the other hand, the phrase must be read in the light of the overall objective, indeed the *raison d'être*, of the Covenant, which is to establish clear obligations for States parties in respect of the full realization of the rights in question. It thus

---

> as soon as possible. Therefore the burden is on the State to demonstrate that it is making measurable progress toward the full realization of the rights in question.

318 *Grootboom* (note 3 above) para 52.

319 The Court noted in *Grootboom* ibid:

> These are people in desperate need. Their immediate need can be met by relief short of housing which fulfils the requisite standards of durability, habitability and stability encompassed by the definition of housing development in the Act.

In the *Treatment Action Campaign* case, the Court rejected the government's argument that it was not obliged to facilitate access to Nevirapine unless it could provide the 'full package' of care associated with a comprehensive programme for the reduction of mother-to-child transmission of HIV, including the provision of supplements and breast-milk substitutes. See *Treatment Action Campaign* (note 5 above) paras 54–55, 64, 128.

320 The UN Committee on Economic, Social and Cultural Rights has held that State parties 'must give due priority to those social groups living in unfavourable conditions by giving them particular consideration. Policies and legislation should not be designed to benefit already advantaged social groups at the expense of others.' General Comment No 4 (note 221 above).

321 The right to health care services in s 27(1)(*b*) is illustrative of such a right. The delivery of unsafe or negligent health care services cannot be understood to meet the requirements of the right. Thus the UN Committee on Economic, Social and Cultural Rights refers to the 'quality' of the health care services as one of the 'interrelated and essential elements' of the right to health. See General Comment No 14 (note 89 above) para 12(*d*).

> imposes an obligation to move *as expeditiously and effectively* as possible towards that goal.[322] (Emphasis added.)

Thus while the concept of 'progressive realisation' provides the State with a potential justification for failing to ensure reasonable access to socio-economic rights, it can also assist an applicant to establish that the State's acts or omissions are unreasonable. Claimants could rely on the interpretation of 'progressive realisation' by the Court and the UN Committee on Economic, Social and Cultural Rights to argue that the State has not taken timely or effective steps or made sufficient progress in realising the relevant rights.[323]

The Court furthermore cited with approval the views of the UN Committee on Economic, Social and Cultural Rights that 'retrogressive measures ... would require the most careful consideration and would need to be fully justified by reference to the totality of the rights provided for in the Covenant and in the context of the full use of the maximum available resources'. The Court's endorsement of the UN Committee's views that 'retrogressive measures' require particular justification creates the basis for challenging the withdrawal of social programmes or the reduction of benefits under such programmes.[324] Among the 'violations through acts of commission' identified in the Maastricht Guidelines on Economic, Social and Cultural Rights are:

> The calculated obstruction of, or halt to, the progressive realization of a right protected by the Covenant, unless the State is acting within a limitation permitted by the Covenant or it does so due to a lack of available resource or *force majeure*.[325]

The major interpretative difficulty which arises in relation to the concepts of 'progressive realisation' and 'retrogressive measures' is whether they should be assessed in relation to particular individuals or groups, or in respect of the entire population. The former interpretation would imply that the State is placed under a burden of justification if the benefits being received by a particular individual or group are reduced, even if there is an overall improvement in access to the benefits assessed in relation to the entire population. The converse would apply in the case of the latter interpretation – the State is not required to justify the reduction of benefits to any individual or particular group provided there is no overall, statistical decrease in access to benefits.

---

[322] UN Committee on Economic, Social and Cultural Rights, General Comment No 3 (note 85 above) para 9. As noted, the Court expressly endorsed this meaning of the phrase 'progressive realisation' (note 313 above).

[323] Among the 'violations through acts of omission' identified in the *Maastricht Guidelines on Economic, Social and Cultural Rights* (note 100 above) para 15(*g*) is: 'The failure to remove promptly obstacles which it is under a duty to remove to permit the immediate fulfilment of a right guaranteed by the Covenant'.

[324] See the discussion in Scott and Macklem (note 315 above) 80–84.

[325] *The Maastricht Guidelines on Economic, Social and Cultural Rights* (note 100 above) para 14(*f*).

In its judgment in the case of *'Five Pensioners' v Peru*,[326] the Inter-American Court of Human Rights adopted the latter interpretation. The case concerned a series of reductions in the amount of the pension payments which had been legislatively guaranteed to the pensioners at the time of their retirement. The Committee found a violation of the right to property in art 21 and a right of recourse to a competent court or tribunal in art 25 of the American Convention on Human Rights (1969). However, it found no violation of art 26 of the Convention which protects the progressive achievement of economic, social and cultural rights. The Court reasoned as follows:

> Economic, social and cultural rights have both an individual and collective dimension. This Court considers that their progressive development, about which the United Nations Committee on Economic, Social and Cultural Rights has already ruled, should be measured in function of the growing coverage of economic, social and cultural rights in general, and of the right to social security and to a person in particular, of the entire population bearing in mind the imperatives of social equity, and not a function of the circumstances of a very limited group of pensioners, who do not necessarily represent the prevailing situation.[327]

The concern with regard to a presumption against retrogression in favour of individuals or groups is that it can obstruct redistributive measures which reduce or even eliminate the benefits received by more advantaged groups in order to achieve a more equitable distribution of benefits.[328]

On the other hand, the purpose of human rights norms is precisely concerned with the well-being of each individual and group. As the Court observed in *Grootboom*, a statistical advance in the realisation of economic and social rights will not necessarily be judged reasonable if those measures fail to treat everyone with care and concern.[329] The better view would accordingly be to expose all retrogressive measures, including those affecting only particular individuals or groups, to close scrutiny in the light of the overall requirement of reasonable conduct in realising the rights. Retrogressive measures would thus not be absolutely prohibited but may be justifiable where the State can show, for instance, that such measures are necessary to achieve equity in the realisation of the right or a more sustainable basis for the adequate realisation of the rights. However, weighty justifications should be required where the retrogressive measures result in depriving marginalised and vulnerable groups of access to basic social services.

---

[326] Judgment of 28 February 2003, Inter-Am. Ct. H.R. (Ser. C) No 98.

[327] Ibid para 147.

[328] See the discussion by Tara Melish of the 'Five Pensioners' Case: 'The Inter-American Court of Human Rights: Beyond Progressivity' in M Langford (ed) *Social Rights Jurisprudence: Emerging Trends in International and Comparative Law* (2008) 372–408 at 386–387 and 398–400.

[329] *Grootboom* (note 3 above) para 44.

Finally, even when the State is unable to make measurable progress in realising the rights because of resource constraints or other difficulties, it is under an obligation to formulate a transparent and participatory plan or strategy for the realisation of the rights.[330] It is also under a 'process obligation' to monitor the implementation of its programmes and to make appropriate adjustments in the light of changing circumstances. Thus in *Grootboom*, the Court noted that '[c]onditions do not remain static and therefore the program will require continuous review'.[331]

The processes of formulating and implementing such plans have substantial potential to promote the type of deliberative and participatory democracy encouraged by transformative constitutionalism. They also provide an important remedial tool for systemic socio-economic rights violations.[332]

4.4.4 Resource constraints

In contrast to the provisions entrenching civil and political rights or even the general limitations clause (s 36), ss 26 and 27 expressly refer to the availability of the State's resources. However, as previously argued and as the Court itself acknowledged, the enforcement of all rights has resource implications.[333] In contrast to civil and political rights, the distributive and resource implications of socio-economic rights are given much more prominence in the debates concerning their justiciability. The resources required to guarantee civil and political rights are less obvious because in most democratic societies the State has already invested in the infrastructure, such as the court and electoral systems, required to guarantee these rights. In contrast, the distribution of welfare and other socio-economic benefits has largely been relegated to private institutions such as the family and the market.[334] Placing an obligation on the State to ensure that everyone has access to socio-economic rights will therefore require a degree of intervention which has significant implications for pre-existing policy and resource distributions. This is an unavoidable consequence of a constitutional commitment to the fulfilment of socio-economic rights.

---

[330] The UN Committee on Economic, Social and Cultural Rights has held that 'the obligations to monitor the extent of the realization, or more especially of the non-realization, of economic, social and cultural rights, and to devise strategies and programmes for their promotion, are not in any way eliminated as a result of resource constraints'. General Comment No 3 (note 85 above) para 11. The Committee regards the duty to formulate a transparent and participatory strategy and plan of action for the realization of the rights, including indicators and benchmarks, as part of the core obligations of States Parties to the Covenant. See General Comment No 14 (note 89 above) para 43(*f*); General Comment No 15 (note 89 above) para 37(*f*). See also *The Maastricht Guidelines on Economic, Social and Cultural Rights* (note 100 above) para 7.

[331] *Grootboom* (note 3 above) para 43.

[332] See further chapter 8, part 8.6.

[333] See chapter 2, part 2.4.4.

[334] See chapter 2, part 2.4.5.

As noted above, the Court has expressly indicated that the availability of resources will be a factor in the assessment of the reasonableness of the State's conduct.[335] Government is afforded the latitude to demonstrate that the measures it has adopted are reasonable, taking into account its resource and capacity constraints and the overall claims on its resources. The Court has said that although its orders in enforcing socio-economic rights claims may have budgetary implications, they are not 'in themselves directed at rearranging budgets'.[336]

This raises the question as to how the resource-based justifications raised by the State will be assessed. Is a court confined to the existing budgetary allocations of particular government departments or spheres of government, or can it scrutinise budgetary and even macroeconomic policies more broadly to assess the reasonableness of budgetary allocations?[337] The latter gives rise to institutional considerations regarding the appropriateness and capability of the courts to make these determinations.

The second issue raised by a defence of resource constraints is the appropriate standard of scrutiny to be applied by a court. In *Soobramoney*, the Court scrutinised the claim within the context of the budget of the KwaZulu-Natal provincial health department. The broader question of whether the health budget of the provincial department was reasonable in the light of its constitutional obligations appears not to have been raised. However, as observed previously, the Court expressly drew attention to the polycentric implications of ordering an overall increase in renal dialysis facilities.[338]

In *Grootboom*, the State did not pertinently raise resource constraints. Its defence was premised on the argument that its existing housing policy was reasonable and complied with constitutional obligations. In the *Treatment Action Campaign* case, the issue of resource constraints was pertinently raised by the State. In its judgment, the Court undertook a relatively detailed scrutiny of the nature and extent of these constraints. It held that the actual provision of Nevirapine would not impose an undue burden on the State in facilities where the necessary HIV testing and counselling facilities already existed.[339] However, expanding the programme to hospitals and clinics where such facilities had not yet been established would undoubtedly have significant resource implications. The provincial health authorities responsible

---

[335] In *Grootboom* (note 3 above) para 46 the Court held:

> There is a balance between goals and means. The measures must be calculated to attain the goal expeditiously and effectively but the availability of resources is an important factor in determining what is reasonable.

[336] Ibid para 38.

[337] As Moellendorf (note 56 above) 330 observes:

> 'Available resources' is, however, ambiguous as it has both narrow and broad senses. It may mean those resources that a ministry or department has been allotted and has budgeted for the protection of the right. Alternatively, it may mean any resources that the State can marshal to protect the right. These are the two extreme senses of the terms. To be sure, between the narrowest interpretation and the broadest lie other senses.

[338] *Soobramoney* (note 2 above) para 28. See further the discussion in part 4.2.2 above.

[339] See further the discussion of the *Treatment Action Campaign* case in part 4.3.3 above.

for implementing the testing and counselling programme claimed that they faced both financial and capacity constraints in extending the programme. The TAC and the other respondents argued that it was cost-effective to implement a comprehensive policy for the use of Nevirapine, which included testing and counselling. Such a policy would result in 'significant savings' for the State in later years, as it would reduce the number of HIV-positive children who would have to be treated in the public health system.[340]

The Court held that it was not necessary to deal with the cost-effectiveness argument, because there had been a significant change in conditions since the proceedings were implemented. Some provinces – such as Gauteng and KwaZulu-Natal – were in the process of expanding their provision of Nevirapine at public health facilities beyond the test sites.[341] According to the Court, these developments demonstrated that substantial progress could be made 'provided the requisite political will is present'.[342] Moreover, the Court was informed during the hearing of the appeal that the government had made 'substantial additional funds' available for the treatment of HIV, including the reduction of mother-to-child transmission of HIV.[343] The Court drew the unassailable conclusion that budgetary constraints were 'no longer an impediment', and that it should now 'be possible to address any problems of financial incapacity that might previously have existed'.[344] Had the State not made substantial additional funds available for HIV-treatment, the Court may have been compelled to engage with the cost-effectiveness arguments raised by the TAC. This would have drawn the Court into a much more direct evaluation of resource allocation priorities.

Finally, as the above analysis of the *Khosa* case shows, the Court was prepared to undertake a close scrutiny of the State's defence regarding resource constraints.[345] It found the cost implications of extending access to social grants to permanent residents to be minor in the context of the total cost of the social grants programme. The lack of a genuine resource constraints obstacle to the extension contributed to the Court's assessment that the legislation in question was unreasonably restrictive.

The jurisprudence suggests that orders with clear budgetary and resource implications will be made in circumstances where government does not place convincing evidence before the court demonstrating that it lacks available resources or has other competing urgent claims on its resources.[346]

---

[340] *Treatment Action Campaign* (note 5 above) para 116.

[341] Ibid para 118.

[342] Ibid para 119.

[343] Ibid para 120.

[344] Ibid.

[345] See the discussion of *Khosa* in part 4.3.4 above.

[346] For an analysis of the Constitutional Court's approach to resource allocation questions, see generally T Roux 'Legitimating transformation: Political resource allocation in the South African Constitutional Court' (2003) 10 *Democratization* 92–111.

A situation which arises not infrequently in the South African context is one where departments or provincial or local governments do not spend their budgetary allocations, usually due to bureaucratic or capacity constraints.[347] While the latter situation may raise complex questions regarding the appropriate remedy, judicial intervention in these circumstances does not raise significant separation of powers obstacles. The executive and legislature have already allocated the resources for the implementation of the relevant socio-economic programmes. A positive court order in these circumstances does not countermand existing policy, but is rather aimed at securing the more effective implementation of the programme in question.[348]

The cases thus far have all been ones where the resource implications of putting in place or extending a programme were relatively minor or could be accommodated within existing budgetary allocations. The cases which will present particular challenges are those where the resource implications of the claim are extensive and provision has not been made for such expenditure within existing budgetary frameworks. Examples of recent cases are the challenge to the differential age of eligibility applicable to men and women for state grants for the aged,[349] and the application for the extension of the age limit for the child support grant to cover children between the ages of 14 and 18 years.[350] Even more challenging is the large gap in social assistance provisioning in South Africa. The Constitution confers the right on 'everyone' to have access to 'social security, including, if they are unable to support themselves and their dependents, appropriate social assistance'.[351] The current system of social assistance excludes large numbers of poor people who do not fall into one of the

---

[347] The Joint Parliamentary Budget Committee on Expenditure notes in its report in terms of s 32 of the Public Finance Management Act 1 of 1999 for the fourth quarter and year-to-date 2007/08 financial year that '[u]nder-expenditure and virements due to vacancies and goods and services continue to impact negatively on service delivery and budget outcomes in a number of departments'. (16–17). Available at http://www.pmg.org.za/docs/2008/comreports/080623jcbudgetreport.htm (accessed on 15 April 2009).

[348] It will be recalled that the Court identified the reasonable implementation of programmes as one of the criteria for assessing its reasonableness: *Grootboom* (note 3 above) para 42. On the remedial challenges posed by structural inefficiencies and incapacities within government departments, see chapter 8, part 8.6.3.

[349] The sex differential in the age of eligibility for the grant for the aged in the Social Assistance Act 13 of 2004 was challenged in *Roberts v Minister for Social Development* Case No: 32838/05 (North Gauteng High Court). Prior to judgment being handed down the State amended s 10 of the Social Assistance Act to provide for the equalisation of the age of eligibility for the old age pension over a three-year period (s 1 of the Social Assistance Amendment Act 6 of 2008).

[350] *Mahlangu v Minister for Social Development* Case No 025754/05 (North Gauteng High Court). This matter was argued before Mavundla J on 4 and 5 March 2008. At the time of finalising this manuscript judgment had not been handed down, and a political decision to phase-in the extension of the child support grant to children up to the age of 18 years was imminent.

[351] Section 27(1)(*c*) read with (2) of the Constitution.

groups targeted for social grants (primarily the aged, persons living with disabilities and children), but face endemic structural unemployment.[352]

The transformative potential of socio-economic rights will be severely diluted if the courts adopt the view that the availability of resources for their realisation can only be assessed within the parameters of existing budgetary allocations to the relevant departments or spheres of government. As Darrel Moellendorf observes, even if the purpose of the express inclusion of the phrase 'available resources' in ss 26(2) and 27(2) is to signal that 'the protection of these rights are more sensitive to budgetary limitations than is the protection of other rights ... [they] must have some role in guiding policy rather than being merely dependent upon it, if they are to be real rights and not mere priorities'.[353] The question then becomes, how should the courts fulfil their constitutional mandate to enforce these rights without usurping the role of the other branches and spheres of government to distribute resources equitably among various legitimate priorities under South Africa's democratic constitution?

Undoubtedly, claims involving significant budgetary implications warrant a measure of respect by the judiciary for the resource allocation decisions of the other branches of government. The courts may not have the evidence before them to assess the impact of such a decision on other needs and priorities. The legislative and executive branches are institutionally better placed to hear a range of diverse public submissions and to weigh the competing needs and priorities entailed by such a decision. It is also the primary responsibility of these institutions to design and adopt macroeconomic and budgetary policies which enable the equitable and effective realisation of socio-economic rights. However, as previously argued, the legislative and executive branches of government may not comply with their socio-economic rights obligations due to oversight, bureaucratic inertia or capture by powerful interest groups. In adjudicating socio-economic rights claims, courts should not simply take refuge in the theoretical institutional advantages of the other branches of government. Instead they should closely scrutinise the actual conduct and decisions of these branches in relation to the issues at stake in the litigation. The mere fact that the realisation of a socio-economic right will have extensive resource implications does not constitute an automatic ground for judicial non-intervention.[354] The constitutional com-

---

[352] On poverty and inequality in South Africa, see generally chapter 2, part 2.2.2.

[353] Moellendorf (note 56 above) 332. The UN Committee on Economic, Social and Cultural Rights interprets the phrase 'to the maximum of [States Parties'] available resources' in art 2 of the International Covenant on Economic, Social and Cultural Rights to include 'both the resources existing within a State as well as those available from the international community through international cooperation and assistance'. Statement of UN Committee on Economic, Social and Cultural Rights, 'An Evaluation of the Obligation to Take Steps to the "Maximum of Available Resources" under an Optional Protocol to the Covenant' Thirty-eighth sess, UN doc. E/C.12/2007/1, 10 May 2007 para 5.

[354] Karin Lehmann argues (note 195 above) 193–197 that litigants have generally been too timid in urging judicial scrutiny of government's resource allocation priorities.

mitment to socio-economic rights will indeed acquire 'a hollow ring' if the courts refrain from engaging with the resource implications of their fulfilment.[355]

Of particular importance in assessing justifications based on resource constraints is whether there is evidence of serious consideration by the legislature and executive of the implications of their constitutional obligations in relation to socio-economic rights as well as meaningful public participation in informing the relevant policy choices. The UN Committee on Economic, Social and Cultural Rights has stated that in assessing 'whether a State party has taken reasonable steps to the maximum of its available resources to achieve progressively the realization of the provisions of the Covenant, the Committee places great importance on transparent and participative decision-making processes at the national level'.[356] Other considerations that it will take into account in evaluating the justifiability of resource constraints in communications brought in terms of the Optional Protocol to the International Covenant on Economic, Social and Cultural Rights, include:

(*a*) the extent to which the measures taken were deliberate, concrete and targeted towards the fulfillment of economic, social and cultural rights;
(*b*) whether the State party exercised its discretion in a non-discriminatory and non-arbitrary manner;
(*c*) whether the State party's decision (not) to allocate available resources is in accordance with international human rights standards;
(*d*) where several policy options are available, whether the State party adopts the one that least restricts Covenant rights;
(*e*) the time frame in which the steps were taken;
(*f*) whether the steps had taken into account the precarious situation of disadvantaged and marginalized individuals or groups and, whether they were non-discriminatory, and whether they prioritized grave situations or situations of risk.[357]

These considerations, while formulated in the context of an international human rights complaints procedure, can offer useful guidance to the courts in assessing the State's reliance on resource constraints in the context of ss 26. However, in order to engage in a substantive assessment of this justification based on considerations such as those referred to above, it will be necessary for State respondents to place detailed evidence before the court of the considerations and processes which informed their relevant policy choices and budgetary allocations.[358] While demonstrable and jus-

---

355 See Pieterse (note 189 above) 408–409; Bilchitz (note 78 above) 225–234.

356 UN Committee on Economic, Social and Cultural Rights, Statement (note 353 above) para 11.

357 Ibid para 8.

358 See, for example, the observations of Murphy J in *Centre for Child Law v MEC for Education, Gauteng,* 2008 (1) SA 223 at 227E–F concerning the lack of evidence presented by the State concerning its budgets or the existence of any contingency fund to meet its constitutional obligations to children housed in a school of industry. See the discussion of the case in chapter 5, part 5.2.4.

tifiable resource constraints constitute a valid reason for a court to decline relief, O'Regan J reminds us in the *Metrorail* case:

> This last criterion [resource constraints] will require careful consideration when raised. In particular, an organ of State will not be held to have reasonably performed a duty simply on the bald assertion of resource constraints. Details of the precise character of the resource constraints, whether human and financial, in the context of the overall resources of the organ of State will need to be provided.[359]

Organs of state must be required to show that their conduct is reasonable in the light of their constitutional obligation to realise the socio-economic rights in ss 26(1) and 27(1). To succeed they will have to show that relevant resource allocation and policy decisions have been informed by a serious and carefully reasoned consideration of their constitutional obligations. The burden of adducing evidence regarding the availability of resources, distributive decisions, and the overall onus of proof in respect of the defence of resource constraints should rest on the State as this information is squarely within its own sphere of knowledge and expertise.[360]

If existing budgetary allocations are inadequate for the realisation of a particular socio-economic right, the State should be required to provide good reasons justifying this situation. These could include, for example, an overall resource scarcity due to factors beyond its control (such as an economic recession) which compels the State to apportion limited resources among competing constitutionally mandated priorities.

If it is not possible to ensure the full realisation of the right under current circumstances, the State should nevertheless be required to show that it has allocated a reasonable amount of resources for the provision of short-term measures of relief for those whose needs are urgent. As the Court stated in *Grootboom*, the recognition of immediate needs in nationwide government programmes 'requires it to plan, budget and monitor the fulfilment of immediate needs and the management of crises'.[361] It has been argued that in cases where the service or resource in question constitutes a basic social need and its denial has a severe impact on the complaint group, this should trigger a particularly close scrutiny of the State's resource-based justifications.[362] Particularly compelling reasons should be required from the State in these

---

[359] *Rail Commuters Action Group v Transnet Ltd t/a Metrorail* (note 101 above) para 88.

[360] As Grosskopf JA stated in *Eskom v First National Bank of Southern Africa Ltd* 1995 (2) SA 386 (A) 392C–E:

> As a matter of fairness and sound judicial policy it seems reasonable that, where one party has the means of establishing a particular fact and his opponent not, the onus should rather be on the former than on the latter.

[361] *Grootboom* (note 3 above) para 68. The UN Committee on Economic, Social and Cultural Rights has underlined that 'even in times of severe resource constraints whether caused by a process of adjustment, of economic recession, or by other factors the vulnerable members of society can and indeed must be protected by the adoption of relatively low-cost targeted programmes'. General Comment No 3 (note 85 above) para 12.

[362] See the discussion in part 4.4.2(*c*) above.

circumstances.[363] The UN Committee on Economic, Social and Cultural Rights has also emphasised that the State is subject to obligations to monitor and adopt remedial plans and strategies pertaining to the realisation of socio-economic rights – even in times of severe resources constraints.[364]

Finally, even where a judicial decision enforcing socio-economic rights has considerable resource implications, it should be borne in mind that courts enjoy extensive remedial flexibility under the Constitution to accord government a measure of discretion in deciding precisely how it will marshal the resources necessary to give effect to its obligations. This is an important mechanism for enabling the judicial enforcement of socio-economic rights while respecting the democratic mandate and expertise of the other branches of government and civil society participation in relation to the particular policy and distributional choices to be made.[365]

It is difficult to describe a single threshold which should be applied in evaluating the resource constraints justification in the context of socio-economic rights claims. As Langa CJ observed in the context of commenting on the various standards which have been adopted in comparative law to assess whether adequate 'reasonable accommodation' has been made in the context of equality jurisprudence:

> [T]he utility of ... these phrases is limited as ultimately the question will always be a contextual one dependant not its compatibility with a judicially created slogan but with the values and principles underlying the Constitution. Reasonable accommodation is in a sense, an exercise in proportionality that will depend intimately on the facts. [366]

I have sought to illustrate that the 'exercise in proportionality' in the context of socio-economic rights claims must be informed by a proper analysis of the normative commitments of the relevant rights and the impact of the deprivation of the particular resource or service at issue on the claimant group. A rigorous analysis of this kind is essential for socio-economic rights to have substantive meaning to those marginalised by poverty. In addition, requiring the State to demonstrate that it is doing all that it reasonably can to increase its control over resources, and to allocate and spend them efficiently and reasonably in meeting its constitutional obligations, fosters a culture of justification and dialogue encouraged by transformative constitutionalism.[367]

---

[363] *The Maastricht Guidelines on Violations of Economic, Social and Cultural Rights* (note 100 above) para 14(*g*) lists as an example of a 'violation of commission', the 'reduction or diversion of specific public expenditure, when such reduction or diversion results in the non-enjoyment of such rights and is not accompanied by adequate measures to ensure minimum subsistence rights for everyone'.

[364] General Comment No 3 (note 85 above) para 11.

[365] On remedies for socio-economic rights violations, see generally chapter 8.

[366] *MEC for Education: KwaZulu-Natal v Pillay* 2008 (1) SA 474 (CC), 2008 (2) BCLR 99 (CC) para 76 (footnotes omitted).

[367] On a dialogic conception of transformative constitutionalism, see chapter 2, part 2.2.4.

4.4.5 The general limitations clause and burden of proof

As discussed above, alleged breaches of the positive duties imposed by socio-economic rights are evaluated in terms of the criteria in the second sub-sections of ss 26 and 27. The criteria in ss 26(2) and 27(2) play the dual role of both defining the content and scope of the relevant rights,[368] and the basis on which the State can attempt to justify its failure to provide access to these rights. Litigants can thus argue that the State has failed to comply with its positive duties in that it has made insufficient progress towards the realisation of the right in question, or that it has failed to make optimum use of its 'available resources'. On the other hand, the State may argue that its failure to provide the relevant service to the applicants is not unreasonable, given its overall shortage of resources and/or taking into account the latitude of time afforded by the concept of 'progressive realisation'.[369]

Given this dual role which the second sub-sections of ss 26 and 27 play, the Court has acknowledged that '[t]here is a difficulty in applying section 36 of the Constitution to the socio-economic rights entrenched in sections 26 and 27 of the Constitution'.[370] It correctly observes that if a legislative measure fails to pass the requirement of reasonableness for the purposes of ss 26 and 27, 'section 36 can only have relevance if what is "reasonable" for the purposes of that section is different to what is "reasonable" for the purposes of sections 26 and 27'.[371] However, the Court was of the view that it was not necessary to decide the issue in the context of the *Khosa* case. It therefore expressly refrained from deciding whether a different test or threshold of 'reasonableness' applies in terms of ss 26 and 27 to the one applicable to the general limitations analysis in terms of s 36.[372] It is therefore unclear what role, if

---

368 In *Treatment Action Campaign* (note 5 above) para 39 the Court held that: 'Sections 27(1) and 27(2) must be read together as defining *the scope* of the positive rights that everyone has and the corresponding obligations on the State to "respect, protect, promote and fulfil" such rights' (emphasis added). In *Khosa* (note 6 above) para 43, the Court held: 'Section 27(2) exists as an internal limitation on the content of section 27(1) and *the ambit* of the s 27(1) right can therefore not be determined without reference to the reasonableness of the measures adopted to fulfil the obligation towards those entitled to the right in section 27(1)'. See further K Iles 'Limiting socio-economic rights: Beyond the international limitations clauses' (2004) 20 *SAJHR* 448–465 at 453–455; M Pieterse 'Towards a useful role for section 36 of the Constitution in social rights cases? *Residents of Bon Vista Mansions v Southern Metropolitan Local Council*' (2003) 120 *SALJ* 41–48.

369 *Grootboom* (note 3 above) paras 30–39.

370 *Khosa* (note 6 above) para 83.

371 Ibid.

372 Ibid para 84. See also the academic literature referred to by the Court in n 88 of the judgment. Even if there was a different threshold for reasonableness in terms of ss 26(2) and 27(2) and s 36, Mokgoro J held that she was satisfied for the reasons given in the judgment 'that the exclusion of permanent residents from the scheme for social assistance is neither reasonable nor justifiable within the meaning of section 36' (ibid). Compare the minority judgment of Ngcobo J in which the justificatory analysis is conducted entirely in terms of the general limitations clause. He concluded that the limitation of social

any, s 36 has to play in the context of a socio-economic rights claim framed as a violation of the positive duties imposed by these rights.[373]

In practice, under the Court's current jurisprudence relating to the positive duties imposed by socio-economic rights, reasonableness in terms of ss 26(2) and 27(2) carries the main justificatory burden.[374] However, I have sought to illustrate through my critique of reasonableness review that the conflation of the stages of rights definition, the determination of infringements, and the justifiability of limitations has certain practical consequences for the adjudication of the positive duties imposed by socio-economic rights.[375]

The second sub-sections of ss 26 and 27 have the potential to facilitate a relational process of evaluating the justifiability of restricting rights for weighty reasons consistent with a democratic society committed to the values of human dignity, equality

---

grants (excluding the grants payable in respect of children) to South African citizens was reasonable and justifiable in terms of s 36(1) of the Constitution (ibid paras 105–134).

[373] Bilchitz (note 78 above) 175–176 suggests that the internal limitation in ss 26(2) and 27(2) and the general limitations clause in s 36 have the following distinctive role:

> The internal limitation is focused on a particular right, for example, the right to have access to adequate health care services. It is suggested that the enquiry requires us to consider whether, in the context of this particular right, and the competing priorities in relation to this particular right, the measures taken by the State are reasonable. Section 36, on the other hand, involves a more global enquiry. It requires us to situate the right to have access to health-care services and the measures adopted by the state against other rights that people have in the Bill of Rights and the obligations that they impose on the state. It allows for the consideration of legitimate government purposes other than those relating to the particular right that is in focus, and requires a broader consideration of the impact of a measure on the society beyond the particular sphere of a particular right.

For a similar analysis, see Iles (note 368 above) 464–465.

[374] Ignatius Rautenbach argues that 'the requirement of reasonableness in ss 26(2) and 27(2) serves the purpose of a special limitation provision that overlaps to such an extent with the general limitations clause that there is no room for the application of the general limitation clause after a conclusion has been reached that the state's justification of why it failed to provide adequate access is rejected.' I M Rautenbach 'The limitation of rights and "reasonableness" in the right to just administrative action and the rights to access to adequate housing, health services and social security' (2005) 4 *TSAR* 627–654 at 653. He illustrates that the Constitutional Court has incorporated within its reasonableness analysis in terms of ss 26(2) and 27(2) the criteria traditionally forming part of the s 36 analysis: the importance of the purpose of the limitation, the nature and extent of the limitation, and less restrictive means for achieving the State's purposes (647–654). Similarly Woolman and Botha (note 244 above) 41 argue that an analysis of the socio-economic rights jurisprudence to date 'does not suggest that the Court is likely to place constraints on its FC ss 26(2) and 27(2) "reasonableness" analysis in the service of creating a meaningful allocation of analytical responsibilities between FC ss 26(2) and 27(2), and FC s 36. Indeed … the Court is unlikely to jettison the freedom that an open-ended reasonableness standard – under FC ss 26(2) and 27(2) – offers in the name of such an "abstract" good as doctrinal coherence.' (footnotes omitted).

[375] See part 4.4.2 above.

and freedom.[376] In this respect, the analysis is similar to that occurring under the general limitations clause. However, there is no clear first stage of analysis in which the content and scope of the relevant right is interpreted independently from a consideration of criteria such as resource constraints which may justify a limitation of the right. This is in contrast with the general approach of the Court to constitutional analysis in relation to civil and political rights, and the negative duties imposed by socio-economic rights.[377] In these situations the justifiability of resource constraints are evaluated in terms of the general limitations clause. Thus, for example, in *Minister of Home Affairs v National Institute for Crime Prevention and the Re-integration of Offenders (NICRO)*,[378] the Court evaluated resource-based justifications for the limitation of prisoners' right to vote in terms of s 36. It held that the factual basis for such a justification would have to be clearly established, and it would have to be shown by the State that the extension of the right to vote to prisoners would place an 'undue burden' on its resources.[379]

In the absence of a principled consideration of the content and scope of the relevant rights and the impact of their infringement on the claimants, the focus of the analysis tends to weigh disproportionately on the State's justificatory arguments. As argued above, this not only undermines the normative status of socio-economic rights as constitutional rights, but weakens a significant jurisprudential platform for claimants to articulate their own understanding of what the rights entail and the impact on them of socio-economic deprivations. A method explored above for overcoming (or at least mitigating) some of these defects in the reasonableness model of review is to incorporate a more substantive analysis of the relevant rights and a contextual application of the normative requirements to the facts and circumstances of particular cases.[380] This will enable the assessment of the reasonableness of the State's acts or omissions to be conducted in dialogic engagement with the preceding principled and contextual analysis.

A further distinction in a justification analysis in terms of ss 26(2) and 27(2) and s 36 is that a threshold requirement for the application of s 36(1) is that the limitation must be 'in terms of law of generation application'.[381] There is no similar requirement in ss 26(2) and 27(2). Frequently, the absence of adequate legislative or other measures will form the basis of a claim in terms of ss 26 and 27. In these circumstances, reliance on the general limitations clause will be excluded unless the lack of a relevant programme has its origin in a law of general application. However, where the policy or programme in question originates in a law of general application and has

[376] On the role of the limitations clause in fundamental rights analysis under the South African Constitution, see Woolman and Botha (note 244 above).

[377] On the approach to justification adopted in respect of the negative duties imposed by the rights in ss 26 and 27, see part 4.6 below.

[378] 2005 (3) SA 280 (CC), 2004 (5) BCLR 445 (CC).

[379] Ibid paras 47–51.

[380] See part 4.4.2 above.

[381] See generally chapter 3, part 3.2.4.

the characteristics of law, the general limitations clause is not in principle excluded, provided some independent significance can be given to it.[382] The advantage of a law of general application in the form of legislation is that the reasons for the limitation of rights, and the nature and extent of the limitation, are subject to an open and transparent debate by elected representatives.[383] The opportunities for such open deliberation on the justifiability of restrictions to socio-economic rights are more constrained in the case of executive programmes and policies.[384]

The lack of the traditional two-stage approach in relation to positive socio-economic rights claims also means that there is no clear allocation of the burden of persuasion and justification. The general approach is that the applicant bears the burden at the first stage of persuading the court regarding the content and scope of the relevant right and that the respondent's conduct has infringed their right. If this is successful, the burden shifts to the respondent to show that the infringement can be justified in terms of the stringent requirements of the general limitations clause.[385] In cases involving the positive duties imposed by socio-economic rights, it is not clear whether the burden should be on the applicant to show that the measures adopted by the State are unreasonable. An alternative approach would be to require the applicant to show only that they lack access to a socio-economic resource or service corresponding to the rights in ss 26 and 27. The burden would then shift to the State to show that its failure to ensure such access is reasonable in the circumstances.[386]

Given the fact that the policy and resource considerations motivating a failure to extend access to the rights is uniquely within the State's own purview, it is submitted that the State should at least bear an evidentiary burden and a burden of persuasion regarding the reasonableness of its conduct or omissions.[387] In practice applicants, particularly specialist NGOs, will adduce evidence and attempt to persuade the courts that there are no valid policy reasons or genuine resource shortages preventing the State from extending access to the relevant right.[388] The socio-economic

---

382 See also chapter 3, part 3.2.4 at 67–69 and accompanying text.

383 Liebenberg (note 114 above) 28.

384 On the power of the executive branch of government in modern democracies, see further chapter 2, note 210 and accompanying text.

385 See *Minister of Home Affairs v National Institute for Crime Prevention and the Re-integration of Offenders (NICRO)* (note 378 above) paras 34–36; I Currie and J de Waal *The Bill of Rights Handbook* 5th ed (2005) 27–28; Woolman and Botha (note 244 above) 3–6; 42–47.

386 See generally P de Vos 'Pious wishes or directly enforceable human rights? Social and economic rights in South Africa's 1996 Constitution' (1997) 13 *SAJHR* 67 at 92–94.

387 On the distinction between burden of proof properly so called and an evidentiary burden, see P J Schwikkard 'The standard and burden of proof and evidential duties in civil trials' in P J Schwikkard, S E van der Merwe et al *Principles of Evidence* 3 ed chapter (2009) 32.3.

388 For example, in the *Treatment Action Campaign* case (note 5 above), the TAC placed an impressive array of medical, public health and economic evidence placed before the Court in support of its arguments.

jurisprudence to date indicates that the Court does not adopt a rigid approach to allocating the burden of proof and persuasion to either party. It tends to evaluate reasonableness in the light of all the evidence and arguments presented in the case. However, placing the burden to present evidence and arguments in relation to the reasonableness of its measures on the State may well be critical in ensuring that socio-economic rights litigation is practically accessible to disadvantaged groups.[389] At the very least a failure to present such evidence should lead to negative inferences being drawn regarding the reasonableness of the State's conduct.[390]

4.4.6 Direct access to socio-economic services and resources?

Reasonableness review has also been criticised for allegedly creating only an indirect entitlement to the formulation and implementation of a reasonable government programme.[391] On this reading, the jurisprudence does not confer any direct entitlements on individuals and groups to claim concrete resources and services from the State. However, the Court's socio-economic rights jurisprudence does not necessarily preclude direct relief to individuals.

In *Grootboom*, the Court asserted that '[n]either s 26 nor s 28 entitles the respondents to claim shelter or housing immediately upon demand', and therefore the High Court order ought not to have been made.[392] The State's obligation in terms of s 26 was to devise and implement a coherent, co-ordinated program designed to meet its s 26 obligations. The Court went on to grant a declaratory order concerning the State's obligation to devise and implement a reasonable housing programme, incorporating reasonable measures to provide relief for those in urgent housing need, and living in 'intolerable conditions or crisis situations'.[393] The Court's unwillingness to affirm a direct right to emergency accommodation in *Grootboom* appears to have been influenced by two main considerations, one of a more pragmatic and the other of a more principled nature. First, a settlement agreement had been entered into between the *Grootboom* community and the Oostenberg municipality and the Western Cape provincial government concerning the amelioration of the conditions

---

389 On the difficulties which reasonableness review presents to disadvantaged groups and organisations in successfully mounting a challenge to government's programmes, see Liebenberg (note 188 above) 178–179.

390 I am indebted to Geoff Budlender for alerting me to this possibility in email correspondence.

391 This was one of the major critiques raised by the *amici curiae* in their submissions in the *Treatment Action Campaign* (note 5 above). See also Liebenberg (note 188 above) 176, 188. For an argument that the obligation to create a '"reasonable" overall system for protection' of socio-economic rights as opposed to individual entitlements constitutes an appropriate approach to the judicial enforcement of socio-economic rights, see Sunstein (note 233 above) 130.

392 *Grootboom* (note 3 above) para 95.

393 Ibid para 99.

in which the respondents were living.[394] Following an application to the Court in which it was alleged that this settlement agreement had not been complied with, the Court 'crafted an order putting the municipality on terms to provide certain rudimentary services'.[395] In delivering its judgment, the Constitutional Court accordingly did not have to deal with the immediate crisis situation of the applicants, and focused exclusively on the systemic question of the proper interpretation of the obligations imposed by s 26.[396]

Second, the Court expressed concern regarding the equity of an order which gave 'a special dispensation' to the respondent community 'on account of their extraordinary circumstances' when 'it is a painful reality that their circumstances were no worse than those of thousands of other people, including young children, who remained at Wallacedene'.[397] This suggests that the Court's primary concern with granting an order granting direct benefits to applicants is its own institutional limitations in ensuring the equitable allocation of resources to all those similarly placed.[398]

In *Treatment Action Campaign*, the Court responded to the minimum core arguments of the *amici curiae* in the following terms:

> We therefore conclude that section 27(1) of the Constitution does not give rise to a self-standing and independent positive right enforceable irrespective of the considerations mentioned in section 27(2).[399]

However, this statement can simply be read as the Court affirming its position that the positive obligations imposed by s 27(1) are qualified or limited by the criteria in s 27(2). The Court was not called upon to grant individual relief, as the application was brought as a public interest case by the Treatment Action Campaign and others. The Court made mandatory orders against the State which would benefit the entire class of HIV-positive women giving birth in the public hospitals and clinics and their newborn infants.[400] There were indications in the oral argument before the Constitutional Court that a primary concern with individually enforceable positive socio-economic rights was fairness to other groups not represented before the Court. Sachs J posed the following questions to counsel for the *amici curiae*, Adv Wim Trengove during oral argument:

---

394 Ibid para 5. This settlement order and its impact on the *Grootboom* litigation is discussed in chapter 8, part 8.4.2.

395 Ibid.

396 See in this regard A Sachs (note 114 above) 595.

397 The Court in *Grootboom* (note 3 above) para 81 accepted that the community was not engaged in an orchestrated land invasion 'as a deliberate strategy to gain preference in the allocation of housing resources over thousands of other people who remained in intolerable conditions and who were also in urgent need of housing relief'.

398 On institutional competence in socio-economic rights adjudication, see chapter 2, part 2.4.8.

399 *Treatment Action Campaign* (note 5 above) para 39.

400 On mandatory orders in socio-economic rights cases, see chapter 8, part 8.5.3.

> Does it mean that somebody living up in the mountains can come to court and say he wants water from a tap, even if the money spent on meeting his particular claim could be used to furnish water for 10,000 people living lower down on the plains?...[C]ould it be that the Constitution implied that those individuals with the sharpest elbows (and the best lawyers) would get a house, water and electricity? Should the Constitution be read as handing over to each judge in each court the right and duty to decide who should have priority access to social goods in short supply?[401]

However, there may be situations where it is clearly appropriate and not inequitable to other groups to order the provision of tangible benefits to the particular individuals or groups before the court. For example, the claimants may suffer serious and irreparable harm if they are not afforded some concrete relief, even if it is only on a temporary basis, until they can be integrated in other medium- to long-term programmes. As will be seen in the discussion of evictions jurisprudence, the courts have been increasingly willing to order temporary alternative accommodation to persons evicted from their homes in situations where it is just and equitable to do so.[402]

Furthermore, there may be sufficient evidence and information before a court in a particular case which enables it to make a positive order without prejudicing the needs of other disadvantaged groups who are not before the court. An example in this regard is the *Khosa* case where the Court was able to conclude that the extension of social grants to all permanent residents would not unduly strain the social security budget.[403] Such an order would therefore not undermine the social security rights of other beneficiaries of the State's social assistance programme. Accordingly the Court was willing to 'read in' the category of permanent residents in the relevant legislation.[404]

While there will be cases in which the only appropriate remedy is a general order for the State to enact a programme, the possibility of direct positive relief should not be categorically excluded.[405] The circumstances of a particular case may reveal that justice will not be served by simply ordering the formulation and implementation of a reasonable programme. The courts should not ignore the hardship which individual claimants will suffer if there is no response tailored to their particular needs and circumstances.[406] One of the institutional advantages of the courts is that they are

---

[401] Sachs (note 114 above) 598. The author was also present in Court during this interchange.

[402] See the jurisprudence discussed in chapter 6.

[403] See part 4.3.4 above.

[404] *Khosa* (note 6 above) para 98.

[405] Scott and Alston (note 42 above) 254–255 describe the chilling effect that the exclusion of direct relief might have on socio-economic rights cases:

> However, while public interest groups may well wish to seek standing under s 38(*d*) to bring constitutional claims about breach of framework procedural duties, individual claimants will understandably wish to see something geared more to their own situation and are unlikely to wish to bring constitutional cases purely as constitutional triggers for general policy processes.

[406] On the importance of socio-economic rights cases resulting in tangible benefits for disadvantaged groups, see M Pieterse 'Eating socioeconomic rights: The usefulness of rights

well placed, through the hearing of individualised evidence, to detect the impact of general legislative and executive acts and omissions on marginalised individuals and groups.[407]

As with the resource constraints defence, the State should be required to place cogent evidence and arguments before the courts concerning the alleged 'floodgate' implications of granting direct relief.[408] These arguments should be exposed to searching scrutiny before it is decided to deny direct forms of relief to claimants. Sections 26 and 27 appropriately encourage the fulfilment of socio-economic rights through comprehensive, co-ordinated state programmes. However, there is nothing in the formulation of these sections that precludes a remedy awarding direct benefits to defined individuals and groups. When such programmes are lacking, appropriate relief may, depending on the context of the case, consist of both an order that the State adopt such a general programme as well as the granting of interim or permanent forms of relief in favour of the claimants.

Whether individual relief is appropriate in a particular case should not turn on a restrictive interpretation of reasonableness review, but rather on what constitutes the most appropriate and effective remedy in the particular circumstances of the case. This reading allows courts to interpret the socio-economic rights in ss 26 and 27 in a manner which gives the courts maximum flexibility to craft a remedy which most effectively protects the interests and values at stake in the particular case.[409]

4.5 DEVELOPING THE INTERRELATIONSHIP BEWEEN EQUALITY AND SOCIO-ECONOMIC RIGHTS

Under South Africa's transformative Constitution, socio-economic rights have an important role to play in advancing a society based on social justice. Such a society implies dismantling structural inequalities in access to economic resources and social services.[410] Interpreted in the light of the transformative commitments of the Constitution, socio-economic rights are concerned not only with absolute deprivation, but also a more equitable distribution of socio-economic resources and services. Similarly the value and right to equality in the Constitution (s 9) extends not only to civil and political freedoms, but is also concerned with equal access and non-discrimination in relation to socio-economic benefits. Thus equality is defined in the Constitution to include 'the full and equal enjoyment of all rights and freedoms'.[411] It

talk in alleviating social hardship revisited' (2007) 29 *HRQ* 796–822.

[407] See Pieterse (note 189 above) 391–392 and 395–396. Dixon (note 206 above) 402–403 describes the 'blind spots of perspective' affecting legislatures when legislators 'fail to anticipate the impact of laws on rights because they do not appreciate, adequately, the perspective of rights claimants with very different life experiences and viewpoints'.

[408] See further Scott & Alston (note 42 above) 267–268.

[409] See also chapter 8, part 8.5.3(*a*).

[410] See generally chapter 2, part 2.2.3.

[411] Section 9(2). On the interdependence between rights, see generally chapter 2, part 2.4.3.

is significant in this context that the Promotion of Equality and Prevention of Unfair Discrimination Act 4 of 2000[412] incorporates a directive principle which includes socio-economic status[413] as a possible ground of prohibited discrimination given 'overwhelming evidence of the importance, impact on society and link to systemic disadvantage and discrimination'.[414]

There is a mutually reinforcing relationship between socio-economic rights and the right to equality which should find expression in the interpretation of both rights.[415] Pierre de Vos puts it thus:

> To put it more forcefully: it would be difficult to come to grips with the nature of the obligations imposed by social and economic rights without a solid understanding of the way in which the Constitutional Court has developed the concept of substantive equality. At the heart of this approach is an understanding that the right to equality – and the concomitant interlinking value of human dignity – and the social and economic rights are two sides of the same coin. Both sets of rights have been included in the Bill of Rights to ensure the achievement of the same objective, namely the creation of a society in which all people can achieve their full potential as human beings, despite apparent differences created by race, gender, disability and sexual orientation, and despite differences in the social and economic status of such individuals.[416]

Although the Court did not explicitly decide the *Treatment Action Campaign* and *Grootboom* cases in terms of an equality analysis, it has been argued that the failure to make reasonable provision for the socio-economic needs of the disadvantaged groups in these cases can also be understood in terms of an equality rights paradigm.[417] The fact that, in the South African context, poverty intersects with and reinforces other

---

412 This legislation was enacted to give effect to s 9 of the Constitution.

413 'Socio-economic status' is defined in the Act to include 'a social or economic condition or perceived condition of a person who is disadvantaged by poverty, low employment status or lack of or low-level educational qualifications' (s 1(xxvi)).

414 Section 34(1) of the Promotion of Equality and Prevention of Unfair Discrimination Act. Pending a recommendation by the Equality Review Committee as to its express inclusion as a prohibited ground of discrimination, the Act states that nothing prevents a court from making a determination that this ground is included within the definition of prohibited grounds of discrimination in terms of s 1(xxii) of the Act. Complainants may also institute proceedings on this ground (section 34(2)(*b*)).

415 See G Brodsky & S Day 'Beyond the social and economic rights debate: Substantive equality speaks to poverty' (2002) 14 *CJWL* 185–219; M Jackman 'Constitutional contact with the disparities in the world: Poverty as a prohibited ground of discrimination under the Canadian *Charter* and human rights law' (1994) II *RCS* 76–122; L A Williams '*The justiciability of water rights:* Mazibuko v City of Johannesburg' (2009) 36 *Forum Devel Stud* 5–48 at 44–45.

416 P de Vos 'Grootboom, the right of access to housing and substantive equality as contextual fairness' (2001) 17 *SAJHR* 258–276 at 265.

417 See, for example, De Vos ibid; Roux (note 346 above) 97; Liebenberg and Goldblatt (note 216 above).

forms of systemic disadvantage on grounds of race, gender and disability also supports an argument of indirect discrimination.[418]

The interrelationship between equality and socio-economic rights is especially significant in the context of transforming the patterns of gendered disadvantage and inequality which are deeply inscribed on South African society.[419] Women's structurally disadvantaged position arises from the intersection of race, poverty and gendered social roles. Their disadvantaged status is further entrenched where other axes of discrimination – such as living with a disability, being HIV-positive,[420] gay or a non-national – intersect with the aforementioned grounds.[421]

Women (particularly those living in rural areas and informal settlements on urban peripheries) bear a disproportionate burden of reproductive work such as caring for children and ill or elderly relatives, collecting fuel and water for household use, cooking, cleaning and other work associated with keeping households and extended families going. As much as it can be rewarding, this work is time-consuming, and physically and emotionally draining.[422] This burden is exacerbated when the State cuts or fails to provide basic social services such as potable water, health care, good and accessible school facilities and social security. This in turn prevents women from participating as equals in the political, economic and cultural spheres of our society. Writing in the Canadian context, Gwen Brodsky and Shelagh Day observe:

> The fact is that, for women, poverty enlarges every dimension of women's inequality, not just the economic dimension. Poor women get women's inequality writ large. They are sexually commodified and subordinated in their daily interactions, and they accept sexual commodification and subordination in order to survive; they lose reproductive decision-making autonomy about when and whether to bear children as well as sexual autonomy in relationships; they are subject to stereotyping as sexually irresponsible women, as whores, and bad mothers; their vulnerability to assault and rape is magnified; their ability to care for their children is compromised; and they have no political voice or influence. Without access to adequate social assistance and social services, including transitional housing,

---

418 See, for example, B Porter (note 195 above) 61–62; G Brodsky & S Day 'Denial of the means of subsistence as an equality violation' (2005) *AJ* 149–170 at 163–164.

419 See chapter 2, part 2.2.2 at notes 15–17.

420 See in this regard, A Meerkotter 'The impact of the HIV/AIDS epidemic on women's citizenship in South Africa' in A Gouws (ed) *(Un)thinking Citizenship: Feminist Debates in Contemporary South Africa* (2005) 157–174.

421 On the impact of poverty on women with disabilities, see T Emmett 'Disability, poverty, gender and race' in B Watermeyer, L Swartz, T Lorenzo, M Schneider & M Priestley (eds) *Disability and Social Change – A South African Agenda* (2006) 207–233. See further Liebenberg & Goldblatt (note 216 above) 339–341.

422 See in this regard the observations of Goldstone J in *President of the Republic of South Africa v Hugo* 1997 (4) SA 1 (CC), 1997 (6) BCLR 708 (CC) para 37. See further D Budlender 'Women and poverty' (2005) 64 *Agenda* 30–36. For a discussion of the stereotypes and burdens of reproductive work borne by women in the context of the HIV/AIDS epidemic, see Meerkotter (note 420 above) 157–174.

> access to training and education, and effective legal rights, including *Charter* rights, women are much less able to resist or escape their subordination.[423]

Given the critical importance of adequate social provisioning for the transformation of women's gendered realities, it is hardly surprising that women's organisations were prominent and active in the campaign for the inclusion of socio-economic rights in the Constitution.[424]

Without an active State role in providing good quality social services and facilitating equitable access to resources, the attainment of substantive gender equality remains illusory.[425] The realisation of socio-economic rights is thus critical to the attainment of substantive gender equality.[426]

The values of substantive equality should also inform the interpretation of socio-economic rights to encourage a jurisprudence which is sensitive and responsive to the gendered realities and needs of women's lives.[427] For example, the rights of everyone to have access to housing, health care services, and social security will not foster substantive gender equality if they are not interpreted to include shelters and specifically designed health care interventions and social services (such as counselling) for survivors of domestic violence, rape and other forms of violence against women.[428] Interpreting the rights to fair labour practices (s 23), social security (s 27) and the child's right to social services (s 28(1)(*c*)) to include the duty to establish a public network of high quality child care facilities (particularly in informal settlements and rural areas) will facilitate the ability of many women to obtain employment and participate in development programmes. Such services are essential to the 'full and equal'

---

423 Brodsky & Day (note 415 above) 219.

424 On civil society campaigns for the inclusion of socio-economic rights in the Constitution, see generally, chapter 1, parts 1.4–1.5. See, for example, the submission by the Women's National Coalition to Theme Committee 4 (Bill of Rights) of the Constitutional Assembly, 5 July 1995 (copy on file with author).

425 See S Liebenberg 'Social and economic rights: A critical challenge' in S Liebenberg (ed) *The Constitution of South Africa from a Gender Perspective* (1995) 79–96; L Seth 'Social action litigation in India' in S Liebenberg (ed) ibid 97–111.

426 Section 8 of the Promotion of Equality and Prevention of Unfair Discrimination Act 4 of 2000 expressly prohibits unfair discrimination on the grounds of gender in a number of socio-economic spheres: see, particularly, s 8(*e*)(i). In addition, the Act requires the taking of special promotional measures to promote the achievement of equality with regard to race, gender and disability in the public and private sector. See ss 26, 27 and 28.

427 For a critique of the *Grootboom* judgment for its failure to integrate the value of gender equality, see D M Chirwa and S Khoza 'Towards enhanced citizenship and poverty eradication: A critique of *Grootboom* from a gender perspective' in A Gouws (ed) (note 420 above) 137–156 at 148–149.

428 On positive State duties to protect women from violence, see H Combrinck 'Positive state duties to protect women from violence: Recent South African developments' (1998) 20 *HRQ* 666–690. See further UN Committee on Economic, Social and Cultural Rights, General Comment No 16 (Thirty-fourth sess, 2005) *Article 3: The equal right of men and women to the enjoyment of all economic, social and cultural rights,* UN doc E/C.12/2005/3.

enjoyment by women of all the rights in the Bill of Rights.[429] Moreover, the design of social programmes should not reinforce gender stereotypes,[430] but strive to facilitate a more equitable sharing of reproductive and other forms of 'gendered work'.[431]

Developing the interrelationship between equality and socio-economic rights is also significant for other disadvantaged and marginalised groups. The Constitutional Court's decision in the *Khosa* case was expressly based on an interrelationship between the right to equality in s 9 of the Constitution and socio-economic rights.[432] The fact that the exclusion of permanent residents from the social grants scheme constituted unfair discrimination against a vulnerable group was a significant factor in the Court's finding that the programme was not a reasonable measure for realising the right to social assistance in terms of s 27(1)(*c*) of the Constitution.[433] This illustrates how the value of 'equality' has a significant role to play in the courts' assessment of the reasonableness of the State's measures in relation to socio-economic rights.

As the *Khosa* decision illustrates, measures which result in the deepening of patterns of systemic inequality and disadvantage experienced by marginalised groups will be exposed to particularly close scrutiny. In assessing the progressive realisation of socio-economic rights, a court should be alert to forms of unfair discrimination against any group in terms of s 9(3) of the Constitution. Equality as a right and a foundational constitutional value can thus play an important role in the evaluation of the reasonableness of the State's measures in relation to socio-economic rights. It can guide the assessment of whether the State's resource allocation priorities and policy choices in the sphere of socio-economic rights are consistent with the transformative vision of the Constitution.

---

429 Section 9(2). On the duty of the State in relation to the establishment of care facilities for children and dependent family members, see B Goldblatt 'Citizenship and the right to child care' in A Gouws (ed) (note 420 above) 117–136; UN Committee on Economic, Social and Cultural Rights (Thirty-fourth sess, 2005), General Comment No 16 (note 428 above) para 24.

430 See the discussion by Liebenberg and Goldblatt (note 216 above) 350–352. For example, women's receipt of welfare benefits has often exposed them to pernicious stereotypes, based on an intersection of gender, race and poverty. For a discussion of this issue in the context of the US Supreme Court decision in *Wyman v James* 400 U.S. 309 (1971), see T Ross 'The rhetoric of poverty: Their immorality, our helplessness' (1991) 79 *Geo LJ* 1499–1546 at 1522–1525. For a discussion of similar trends in the South African context, see B Goldblatt 'Gender and social assistance in the first decade of democracy: A case study of South Africa's child support grant' (2005) *Politikon* 239.

431 On the obligation of States to eliminate gendered patterns of conduct and roles for men and women, see for example: art 5 of the Convention on the Elimination of All Forms of Discrimination Against Women; art 2(2) of the Protocol to the African Charter on Human and Peoples' Rights on the Rights of Women in Africa; UN Committee on Economic, Social and Cultural Rights (Thirty-fourth sess, 2005), General Comment No 16 (note 428 above) para 7; paras 23–24.

432 See part 4.3.4 above.

433 *Khosa* (note 6 above) paras 49, 82.

There will be circumstances where the State is able to demonstrate that it cannot meet everyone's socio-economic rights under current circumstances given resource constraints and competing claims on resources. In these situations the State is constrained to prioritise among various groups in extending access to the rights. As Mokgoro J observed in *Khosa*:

> It is also important to realise that even where the State may be able to justify not paying benefits to everyone who is entitled to those benefits under section 27 on the grounds that to do so would be unaffordable, the criteria upon which they choose to limit the payment of those benefits (in this case citizenship) must be consistent with the Bill of Rights as a whole. Thus if the means chosen by the Legislature to give effect to the State's positive obligation under section 27 unreasonably limits other constitutional rights, that too must be taken into account.[434]

In the jurisprudence on substantive equality under s 9 of the Constitution, the position of marginalised and disadvantaged groups is accorded special consideration. In assessing the fairness of discrimination in terms of ss 9(3) and (4), one of the factors which the Court takes into account is the 'position of the complainants in society and whether they have been victims of past patterns of discrimination'.[435] As Currie and De Waal observe, '[d]ifferential treatment that burdens people in a disadvantaged position is more likely to be unfair than burdens placed on those who are relatively well off'.[436] This concern should also be reflected in the setting of priorities by the State in the progressive realisation of socio-economic rights. Complex issues arise when the State argues that it is necessary to prioritise in its provision of socio-economic rights among different disadvantaged groups.[437] Such a claim should be treated with a measure of scepticism given the overall resources available to a middle-income country such as South Africa.

It should also be borne in mind that the purpose of socio-economic rights is to ensure that everyone in society is able to enjoy access to these rights. A failure to interrogate the adequacy of the State's allocation of resources to fulfil this purpose will leave intact and legitimate existing distributions of wealth and the pervasive class-based inequalities of our society. It will not facilitate the transformation of our society in a participatory, egalitarian direction. Resource-based justifications for a failure to ensure that disadvantaged groups have access to socio-economic rights

---

434 *Khosa* (note 6 above) para 45.

435 *Harksen* (note 160 above) para 52. See also s 14(3)(*c*) of the Promotion of Equality and Prevention of Unfair Discrimination Act 4 of 2000.

436 Currie and De Waal (note 385 above) 244.

437 In the case of *Roberts v Minister of Social Development* (note 349 above), the State argued that the earlier age (60 years) at which poor women qualified for a grant for the aged compared to poor men (65 years) in terms of the Social Assistance Act 13 of 2004 constituted an affirmative action measure in favour of women. For a description of the arguments of the *amici curiae* in the case, arguing that the distinction between poor women and men in the age of eligibility for the old age grant was not justifiable, see S Heleba 'Towards equalising the age for accessing pensions' (2007) 8 *ESR Review* 14–18.

should thus be carefully scrutinised.[438] The State should be placed under a burden to show that it has explored all reasonable alternatives to avoid distinguishing between different disadvantaged groups in extending access to socio-economic rights.

A substantive approach to equality requires positive measures of support to be extended to disadvantaged groups to enable them to enjoy full and equal access to their constitutional rights.[439] In terms of s 9(2) of the Constitution, 'legislative and other measures designed to protect or advance persons, or categories of persons, disadvantaged by unfair discrimination' may be taken 'to promote the achievement of equality'. Positive measures are required to progressively 'eradicate socially constructed barriers to equality and to root out systematic or institutionalised under-privilege'.[440] The goal of such measures should be to ensure that everyone gains access, as expeditiously as possible, to the resources and services that enable them to live with dignity and participate as equals in society. This well-established dimension of equality rights should also underscore the importance of positive measures in the context of socio-economic rights. It is a fallacy to regard equality rights as entailing only the negative duty to refrain from unfair discrimination in contrast to the positive duties required in the context of socio-economic rights.[441] The effective realisation of both rights requires positive measures and a commitment of resources from the State.

The above discussion illustrates the various interrelated dimensions of equality and socio-economic rights jurisprudence. Taking this interrelationship seriously is more likely to lead to a jurisprudence which is responsive to the complex, multifaceted realities of poverty and inequality in South Africa. Nevertheless, certain types of claims are likely to fit more comfortably within the jurisprudential traditions and paradigms of either equality rights or socio-economic rights.

Thus equality law and jurisprudence is well developed in respect of claims entailing the exclusion of a certain group from an existing social programme or the failure of

---

[438] On the interpretation of the concept of 'available resources' in ss 26(2) and 27(2), see part 4.4.4 above.

[439] As O'Regan J observed in *Brink v Kitshoff NO* 1996 (4) SA 197 (CC), 1996 (6) BCLR 752 (CC), the purpose of the constitutional equality clause is to prohibit patterns of group-based disadvantage and harm, and 'to permit positive steps to redress the effects of such discrimination.' (para 42). On the need for social programmes which are responsive to the particular needs and circumstances of differently placed disadvantaged groups, see Liebenberg and Goldblatt (note 216 above) 351–352.

[440] Per Moseneke J (as he then was) in *Minister of Finance v Van Heerden* 2004 (6) SA 121 (CC), 2004 (11) BCLR 1125 (CC) para 31. In terms of chapter 5 of the Promotion of Equality and Prevention of Unfair Discrimination Act 4 of 2000, organs of State and certain private entities are to adopt positive measures to eradicate all forms of unfair discrimination and to promote the achievement of substantive equality.

[441] Remedying unfair discrimination requires positive measures such as those contemplated in the orders which an equality court is empowered to make in terms of s 21 of the Promotion of Equality and Prevention of Unfair Discrimination Act. These include, for example, 'an order to make specific opportunities and privileges unfairly denied in the circumstances available to the complainant in question' (s 21(2)(*g*)).

an existing programme to reasonably accommodate the needs of a disadvantaged group.[442] It is likely to prove more difficult to persuade a court that the absence of a social programme amounts to a violation of equality rights, particularly where the omission cannot easily be shown to amount to discrimination against a group on one or more of the traditional grounds of prohibited discrimination.[443] This is particularly the case in relation to systemic socio-economic inequalities. Although 'socio-economic status' is recognised as a potential ground of prohibited discrimination in the Promotion of Equality and Prevention of Unfair Discrimination Act, it has a less secure footing as a 'directive principle' than other grounds of prohibited discrimination.[444] Such a case is likely to encounter the orientation of equality jurisprudence towards individualised, status-based recognition claims as opposed to the redress of systemic socio-economic inequalities (redistributive claims).[445]

Where the relief sought is the adoption or enactment of a programme to extend access to social goods and services, the claim may be better framed as an infringement of the positive duties imposed by socio-economic rights. However, where there is evidence showing that the absence of such a programme is due to, or perpetuates, unfair discrimination based on prohibited grounds, both socio-economic rights and equality rights should be raised as causes of action. This is necessary for the emergence of a jurisprudence which develops the interdependent dimensions of the right to equality and socio-economic rights. As argued in chapter 2, a jurisprudence which takes seriously the interrelationships between rights in the Bill of Rights promotes the transformative purposes of the Constitution.[446]

---

[442] One of the factors listed in the Promotion of Equality and Prevention of Unfair Discrimination Act in determining the fairness or unfairness of discrimination is 'whether and to what extent the respondent has take such steps as being reasonable in the circumstances to – (i) address the disadvantage which arises from or is related to one or more of the prohibited grounds; or (ii) accommodate diversity.' (s 14(3)(*i*)). On the interpretation of 'reasonable accommodation' in the context of our constitutional jurisprudence on equality, see *MEC for Education: KwaZulu-Natal v Pillay* (note 366 above) paras 71–79.

[443] 'Discrimination' in terms of the Promotion of Equality and Prevention of Unfair Discrimination Act is defined to mean 'any act or omission, including a policy, law, rule, practice, condition or situation which directly or indirectly (*a*) imposes burdens, obligations or disadvantage on; or (*b*) withholds benefits, opportunities or advantages from, any person on one or more of the prohibited grounds.' (s 1(viii)).

[444] See note 413 above.

[445] See in this regard S Fredman 'Redistribution and recognition: Reconciling inequalities' (2007) 23 *SAJHR* 214–234 at 228–229.

[446] See chapter 2, part 2.4.3.

4.6 NEGATIVE DUTIES

4.6.1 Introduction

In *Grootboom*, the Court held that s 26(1) incorporates 'at the very least, a negative obligation placed upon the State and all other entities and persons to desist from *preventing or impairing* the right of access to adequate housing'.[447] It went on to hold that this negative duty 'is further spelt out in sub-s (3) which prohibits arbitrary evictions'.[448]

The Court does not explain what types of conduct would amount to a prevention or impairment of the right of access to adequate housing. The terminology used is broad enough to incorporate a lack of positive action on the part of the State which has the effect of impairing access to housing. It is furthermore clear that the Court regards this negative duty to be binding not only on organs of State, but also 'all other entities and persons'. In the *Treatment Action Campaign* case, the Court confirmed that this interpretation also extended to s 27(1).[449] It held that this negative obligation was 'relevant to the challenges to the measures adopted by government for the provision of medical services to combat mother-to-child transmission of HIV'.[450] However, the Court did not make any specific finding regarding the nature of the negative violations of s 27(1). Presumably this would include the restrictions which government placed on doctors at public hospitals and clinics other than the research and training sites in prescribing nevirapine to reduce the risk of mother-to-child transmission of HIV.[451] However, the Court's overall finding is that the breach of s 27 consisted of a failure to devise and implement a reasonable and comprehensive programme for the reduction of mother-to-child transmission of HIV.[452]

In an early High Court decision, *Residents of Bon Vista Mansions v Southern Metropolitan Local Council*,[453] Budlender AJ held that the disconnection by a local authority of the water supply to the residents constituted a *prima facie* breach of the applicants' constitutional right to have their existing access to water respected in terms of s 27(1)(*b*). In the absence of justification for this disconnection, the applicants were entitled to have their supply reconnected.

---

[447] *Grootboom* (note 3 above) para 34 (emphasis added). The Court referred in this regard to the *Certification Judgment, Ex parte Chairperson of the Constitutional Assembly: In re Certification of the Constitution of the Republic of South Africa, 1996* 1996 (4) SA 744 (CC), 1996 (10) BCLR 1253 (CC) para 78 in which it held that socio-economic rights could at the very minimum be 'negatively protected from improper invasion'. See further chapter 1, part 1.6.

[448] Ibid.

[449] *Treatment Action Campaign* (note 5 above) para 46.

[450] Ibid.

[451] See the Court's order at ibid para 135, 2(*c*)(i).

[452] Ibid para 135, 2(*a*) and (*b*).

[453] 2002 (6) BCLR 625 (W).

4.6.2 The *Jaftha* case

The case of *Jaftha*[454] is significant in that it is the first decision in which the Constitutional Court elaborates on what it means by 'negative duties' in the context of s 26 (and, by implication, s 27), and adopts a distinctive model of review to these negative violations.

This case involved a challenge to the constitutionality of provisions of the Magistrates' Courts Act 32 of 1944 that permitted the sale in execution of people's homes in order to satisfy (sometimes trifling) debts. The effect of such sales-in-execution would be the eviction of the applicants from their state-subsidised homes. It was also common cause that if the applicants were evicted, they would have no suitable alternative accommodation, and would not be eligible again for a housing subsidy from the State.[455]

The Court characterised the provisions of the Act as authorising a negative violation of s 26(1) in that it permitted 'a person to be deprived of existing access to adequate housing'.[456] This negative duty is not subject to the qualifications in subsection (2) relating to reasonableness, resource constraints and progressive realisation. Deprivation of existing access to housing (and by implication, other socio-economic rights) constitutes a limitation of their rights which can only be justified in terms of the stringent requirements of the general limitations clause (s 36), including the requirement of law of general application.[457] The Court expressly did not elaborate on all the circumstances which would constitute a violation of the negative duties imposed by the Constitution.[458] However, as noted above, the deprivation of people's existing access to housing by the relevant provisions of the Magistrates' Courts Act was held to constitute a limitation of s 26(1). The Court highlighted the severe impact of a deprivation of housing on persons like the applicants in the circumstances of the case:

> In the present matter access to housing already exists. Relative to homelessness, to have a home one calls one's own, even under the most basic circumstances, can be an empowering and dignifying human experience. The impugned provisions have the potential of undermining that experience. The provisions take indigent people who have already benefited from housing subsidies and, worse than placing them at the back of the queue to benefit again from such subsidies in the future, put them in a position where they might never again acquire such assistance, without which they may be rendered homeless and never able to restore the conditions for human dignity. Section 66(1)(*a*) is therefore a severe limitation of an important right.[459]

---

[454] Note 8 above.

[455] Ibid para 12. The disadvantaged and impoverished circumstances of the applicants are described in paras 3–5 of the Court's judgment.

[456] Ibid paras 31–34.

[457] See generally on s 36, chapter 3, part 3.2.4.

[458] Ibid para 34.

[459] Ibid para 39.

In conducting the limitations analysis in terms of s 36, the Court closely scrutinised the purposes that the relevant provisions of the Act were designed to serve, and found them to be overbroad. They permitted execution against the homes of debtors in circumstances 'where execution will be unjustifiable because the advantage that attaches to a creditor who seeks execution will be far outweighed by the immense prejudice and hardship caused to the debtor'.[460] It considered the Minister's argument that the possible over-breadth of the scheme was cured by other provisions of the Act that permit debtors to approach the courts to set aside or stay a warrant of execution that has been issued on good cause shown, or to request that the debt be repaid in instalments.[461] The Court held that these provisions did not offer adequate protection to debtors in that many debtors in similar situations to the appellants were unaware of the relevant provisions. Even with awareness, indigent people were likely to encounter significant obstacles in accessing the courts to claim protection.[462] Thus the fact that the relevant provisions of the Act created the possibility for unjustified sales-in-execution to occur was sufficient to render the legislative scheme overbroad. The Court demonstrated considerable sensitivity to the real life constraints faced by disadvantaged groups in asserting their legislative rights. These circumstances were deemed relevant considerations in assessing the constitutionality of the legislative scheme.

The Court thus concluded that the relevant provisions were not justifiable in terms of the general limitations clause.[463] By way of remedy it 'read in' provisions to the Act requiring judicial oversight of executions against the immovable property of debtors taking into consideration 'all relevant circumstances'.[464] Among the guiding factors set out in its judgment for the exercise of judicial oversight is whether an order authorising the sale-in-execution would be 'grossly disproportionate':

> This would be so if the interests of the judgment creditor in obtaining payment are significantly less than the interests of the judgment debtor in security of tenure in his or her home, particularly if the sale of the home is likely to render the judgment debtor and his or her family completely homeless.[465]

The Court also acknowledged that part of the value of a home to poor people is that it can be used to leverage capital. It thus held that the circumstances in which the debt arose was a relevant consideration, particularly where a judgment debtor willingly puts up his or her house as security for the debt.[466] A further consideration is the finding of 'creative alternatives' allowing for debt recovery but which use the

---

[460] Ibid para 43.
[461] Sections 62 and 73.
[462] *Jaftha* (note 8 above) paras 47–49.
[463] Ibid paras 35–51.
[464] Ibid paras 52–67. On the reading-in remedy applied in this case, see further chapter 8, part 8.3.3 at notes 48–56 and accompanying text.
[465] Ibid para 56.
[466] Ibid para 58.

sale-in-execution of the debtor's home 'only as a last resort'.[467] Thus the fact that a person might be rendered homeless is a weighty consideration in judicial oversight over sales-in-execution.

The close scrutiny which the Court applied to the justificatory arguments and the proportionality assessment in *Jaftha*[468] is similar to the approach adopted by the European Court of Human Rights in the case of *Connors v United Kingdom*.[469] The eviction of a gypsy family from a halting site by a local authority on the grounds of alleged anti-social behaviour was challenged as a violation of art 8 of the European Convention on Human Rights.[470] The Court noted that art 8 'concerns rights of central importance to the individual's identity, self-determination, physical and moral integrity, maintenance of relationships with others and a settled and secure place in the community'.[471] The effect of the eviction was to render the family concerned homeless, 'with the adverse consequences on security and well-being which that entails'.[472] The seriousness of the impact of the eviction accordingly 'required particularly weighty reasons of public interest by way of justification and the margin of appreciation to be afforded to the national authorities must be regarded as correspondingly narrowed'.[473]

The *Jaftha* case illustrates that the interest of poor people in the protection of their homes is an important consideration in a judicial process which was previously solely concerned with protecting the interests of creditors. Prior to this decision, a judgment creditor was entitled to a writ of execution against immovable property

---

[467] Ibid para 59. The relevant factors that a court might consider in determining whether there is good cause to order execution are in summary: 'the circumstances in which the debt was incurred; any attempts made by the debtor to pay off the debt; the financial situation of the parties; the amount of the debt; whether the debtor is employed or has a source of income to pay off the debt and any other factor relevant to the particular facts of the case before the court.' (para 60).

[468] See the analysis by Rautenbach (note 374 above) 647.

[469] *Connors v United Kingdom* (2005) 40 EHRR 189.

[470] Article 8 reads:

(1) Everyone has the right to respect for his private and family life, his home and his correspondence;

(2) There shall be no interference by a public authority with the exercise of this right except such as is accordance with the law and is necessary in a democratic society in the interests of national security, public safety or the economic well-being of the country, for the prevention of disorder or crime, for the protection of health or morals, or for the protection of the rights and freedoms of others.

[471] *Connors v United Kingdom* (note 469 above) para 82.

[472] Ibid para 85.

[473] Ibid para 86. Although the relevant UK legislation entitled the applicants to apply for a judicial review of the decision to evict them, it did not provide an opportunity for an examination of the facts in dispute between the parties. The fact that UK law did not provide for an inquiry by a court into the substantive justification for the evictions of gypsy families on halting sites led the European Court of Human Rights to find a violation of art 8 of the Convention.

once the debtor had insufficient movables to satisfy the debt. The clerk of the court had no discretion to refuse the writ. *Jaftha* affirms that the interests of both creditors and debtors facing the loss of their homes must be considered and a proportional solution found in the light of the particular facts and circumstances of the case. In this respect the decision represents a transformative approach to a legal process in which the values and interests underpinning housing rights were previously considered irrelevant.[474]

4.7 NEGATIVE AND POSITIVE DUTIES: BEYOND THE CONCEPTUAL DIVIDE

The Constitutional Court's decision in *Jaftha* demonstrates that the Court will apply a different model of review to positive conduct or legislation which deprives people of their existing access to socio-economic rights. Such conduct or legislation is regarded as a *prima facie* breach of the rights in ss 26 and 27. The burden is on the State to justify them according to the stringent purpose and proportionality requirements of the general limitations clause. In contrast, the internal limitations of ss 26(2) and 27(2) allow the State a greater margin to rely on resource constraints and the latitude of progressive realisation with regard to an omission to fulfil the positive duties to fulfil socio-economic rights.

The stronger model of review applied to negative as opposed to positive duties suggests that in circumstances where people lack access to socio-economic resources and services, the State will be exposed to less robust forms of constitutional accountability. Evaluating State omissions more leniently is premised on the assumption that the State is not implicated in current distributions of resources and services. This ignores the myriad ways in which the State structures and legitimates current distributions through a plethora of institutions, policies, legislation, and the enforcement of common law rules. These policies and rules both determine access to public benefits and resources, and to private resources distributed through market and family institutions. As Lucy Williams argues:

> [T]he stubborn persistence of poverty, in both developed and developing countries, largely results from political and legal decisions and institutions that generate and sustain a sharply unequal distribution of wealth and resources. Far from being natural or neutral, legal rules, norms and practices play a central part in maintaining poverty by according privilege to and legitimating certain values, interests, and concerns over others. Legal precepts shape social roles by assigning power and responsibility in social relationships, whether within the family or in the workplace.[475]

---

[474] The implications of the *Jaftha* judgment for court processes to declare mortgaged property executable are considered in chapter 7, part 7.3.2.

[475] L A Williams 'Beyond labour law's parochialism: A re-envisioning of the discourse of redistribution' in J Conaghan, R M Fischl & K Klare (eds) *Labour Law in an Era of Globalization: Transformative Practices and Possibilities* (2002) 93–114 at 96. See also the discussion in chapter 2, part 2.4.5.

This is particularly evident in the light of South Africa's apartheid history which produced entrenched patterns of systemic poverty and inequality.

It is difficult and somewhat arbitrary to know whether to classify situations as involving a breach of the negative and positive duties imposed by socio-economic rights. Violations of socio-economic rights often involve a complex matrix of positive conduct and omissions.[476] The intertwinement of negative and positive duties is well illustrated by the eviction cases discussed in the following chapter. The negative duty of the State not to deprive people unjustifiably of access to housing in the context of housing is inextricably linked with the duty of relevant organs of State to take positive measures to provide alternative accommodation to those who face homelessness as a result of an eviction.

Furthermore, Ida Koch points out that, 'the conception of non-interference as less demanding than provision of goods and services is untenable'.[477] Non-interference in existing rights may have considerable budgetary implications. These may exceed the resources required for the provision of a social benefit, depending on the consequences:

> For example, the interest of a State party in obtaining ownership of a certain residential property may be so great that the costs connected with abstaining from expropriation, i.e. showing *respect* for the right to private property exceeds those of *fulfilling* the right to housing by providing accommodation to the person or persons who becomes homeless as a consequence of the expropriation. Non-interference may require highly 'positive measures'.[478]

Finally, a precondition for the effective guarantee of all rights and the various duties they impose is the establishment of appropriate institutional machinery.[479] This includes, for example, the appointment and training of public officials, monitoring mechanisms, and the establishment and maintenance of judicial and quasi-judicial accountability mechanisms. All of these require positive measures and an intensive investment of resources.

It is therefore highly debatable whether the different model of review adopted for the negative and positive duties imposed by socio-economic rights is justified under our transformative Constitution. There seems to be little principled justification for subjecting claims by people who lack access to socio-economic rights to a less stringent review standard than those involving a deprivation of existing access. As noted above, socio-economic rights violations often arise as a result of a complex matrix of omissions, positive conduct by organs of State and private parties, and background rules of statutory, customary or common law which sanction these acts or omissions.

---

[476] This is illustrated by the facts of the *Treatment Action Campaign* case. See also the discussion in 4.3.3 above.

[477] I E Koch 'Dichotomies, trichotomies or waves of duties?' (2005) 5 *HRLR* 81–103 at 102–103.

[478] Ibid 92.

[479] Ibid.

A simple classification of a case as entailing a breach of negative or a positive obligation and the consequential application of a different standard of review is bound to constitute a narrow perspective on the relevant facts and issues at stake. While it may make for neater jurisprudential conceptual analysis, this perspective is unlikely to lead to transformative remedies which are responsive to the complex realities within which socio-economic deprivations are embedded.

It is better therefore to avoid formalistic distinctions between negative and positive duties and to develop an approach to socio-economic rights which is attuned to the substantive values and interests at stake in particular cases. I have argued previously that a transformative approach to the adjudication of socio-economic rights requires transcending the dichotomies between negative and positive rights which pervade classical liberal theory.[480]

4.8 DEFENDING SOCIAL PROGRAMMES

The cases examined thus far have entailed claims against the State based on the socio-economic rights provisions in the Constitution. However, socio-economic rights can also serve to assist the State in defending pro-poor legislation and programmes against attack by powerful private interests in society.

This is illustrated by the *Kyalami Ridge* case[481] in which the Ministry of Public Works relied on its constitutional obligation to assist people in crisis situations to defend its decision to establish a transit camp on the grounds of a prison which it owned in order to temporarily house destitute flood victims. This decision was challenged by a neighbouring residents' association on the grounds that there was no legislation authorising the government to establish the transit camp and that the decision was unlawful in that it contravened the town planning scheme and environmental legislation.

The Constitutional Court held that none of the laws relied on by the association excluded or limited the government's common law power to make its land available to flood victims pursuant to its constitutional duty to provide them with access to housing.[482] Furthermore, procedural fairness did not require government to do more in the circumstances than it had undertaken to do, namely to consult with the Kyalami residents in an endeavour to meet any legitimate concerns they might have as to the manner in which the development will take place. The Court observed in this regard:

> To require more would in effect inhibit the government from taking a decision that had to be taken urgently. It would also impede the government from using its own land for a constitutionally mandated purpose, in circumstances where legislation designed to regulate land use places no such restriction on it.[483]

---

[480] See chapter 2, part 2.4.4.

[481] Note 4 above.

[482] Ibid para 51.

[483] Ibid para 109.

A similar case decided by the Western Cape High Court, Cape Town in *Stock v Minister of Housing*[484] concerned an application for an interim interdict by neighbouring property owners to prevent the further construction and occupation of a Temporary Residential Area (TRA) on adjacent land in Philippi. The purpose of the TRA was to house inhabitants of the Boys Town informal settlement pending their accommodation in formal housing as part of the N2 Gateway Project. The Court found that the applicants had established a clear right to the relief sought. The respondents (national, provincial and local government) had failed to grant them a hearing prior to the decision to establish the TRA,[485] and had not complied with the provisions of the Land Use Planning Ordinance 15 of 1985 (LUPO).[486] This resulted in harm to their proprietary interest as their plans for a proposed industrial development on their land had been disrupted and would be negatively affected by the construction of the TRA.[487]

Nevertheless the Court declined to exercise its discretion to grant interim relief interdicting the further construction of the TRA, as to do so would be 'to the detriment of the implementation of desperately needed housing' and be contrary 'to all the important principles which underlie the Constitution'.[488] The Court was of the view that resolving the housing crisis in the greater Cape Town area was not only 'essential to the sustainability of development of this area' but also 'for the long term democratic stability within this area, not to say the entire country'.[489]

The Court referred to the Constitutional Court's decision in *Port Elizabeth Municipality*[490] in support of an approach that strives for a balance between property rights and the housing rights of the poor whose dignity 'is assailed when homeless people are driven from pillar to post in a desperate quest for a place where they and their families can rest their heads'.[491] This constitutional imperative together with the fact that the applicants had contemplated a settlement agreement tolerating the presence of the TRA on the adjacent land for a period of two years (albeit subject to a series of conditions),[492] motivated the dismissal of the application. However, the respondents were ordered to remove all encroachments on the applicants' land. The

[484] 2007 (2) SA 9 (C).

[485] See s 3(1) of the Promotion of Administrative Justice Act 3 of 2000. Counsel for the applicants had argued that the case was distinguishable from the *Kyalami Ridge* case (note 4 above) in that the provision of temporary housing was not as urgent as it was on the facts of *Kyalami Ridge*. This meant that it was reasonable to consult with the neighbouring property owners and to consider their views before a decision affecting their property rights was taken. The court accepted this argument (19B–G).

[486] *Stock v Minister of Housing* (note 484 above) 14E–16G, 18G.

[487] Ibid 16H–18G.

[488] Ibid 19I.

[489] Ibid 18I–J.

[490] Note 7 above.

[491] Ibid 19E–G (citing *Port Elizabeth Municipality* ibid para 18); 20A–B.

[492] Ibid 19G–I.

Court also emphasised the importance of the obligation on state officials to comply with the rule of law in relation to the regulatory environment governing the construction of such temporary settlements.[493] The failure to comply with the provisions of LUPO in this case was held to be unacceptable and the respondents were penalised in costs.[494]

The above case underscores the fact that legislative and executive conduct aimed at realising socio-economic rights will not be immune from challenge for breaches of other provisions of the Bill of Rights, such as the right to just administrative action. A further example is the constitutional challenge to the regulations promulgated under the Medicines and Related Substances Act 101 of 1965 which sought to establish a pricing system for medicines in order to make them more transparent and affordable for consumers. In his judgment in *Minister of Health v New Clicks SA (Pty) Ltd (Treatment Action Campaign as Amicus Curiae)*,[495] Moseneke J (as he then was), emphasised the importance of legislative and other measures aimed at securing affordable medicines for the realisation of socio-economic rights such as the right to health care.[496] Various aspects of these regulations were set aside by the Constitutional Court, primarily for being inconsistent with the primary legislation.

These decisions illustrate the significance of Karl Klare's understanding of transformative constitutionalism as 'an enterprise of inducing large-scale social change through nonviolent political processes grounded in law'.[497] Ngcobo J similarly alludes to the requirement that all constitutional rights and values be respected in the process of transformation:

> [T]ransformation is a process. There are profound difficulties that will be confronted in giving effect to the constitutional commitment of achieving equality. We must not underestimate them. The measures that bring about transformation will inevitably affect some members of the society adversely, particularly those coming from the previously advantaged communities. It may well be that other considerations may have to yield in favour of achieving the goal we fashioned for ourselves in the Constitution. What is required, though, is that the process of transformation must be carried out in accordance with the Constitution.[498]

---

[493] Ibid 20E–F.

[494] Ibid 20G.

[495] 2006 (2) SA 311 (CC), 2006 (1) BCLR 1 (CC).

[496] Ibid paras 704–707.

[497] K Klare 'Legal culture and transformative constitutionalism' (1998) 14 *SAJHR* 146–188 at 150.

[498] *Bato Star Fishing (Pty) Ltd v Minister of Environmental Affairs and Tourism* 2004 (4) SA 490 (CC), 2004 (7) BCLR 687 (CC) para 76. The Court also emphasised in *Bel Porto School Governing Body v Premier of the Province, Western Cape* (note 103 above) para 7 that '[t]he process of transformation must be carried out in accordance with the provisions of the Constitution and its Bill of Rights'.

4.9 CONCLUSION

This chapter has analysed and evaluated the approach of the courts to the obligations imposed by the rights in ss 26 and 27 in the context of cases brought against organs of State.

The Constitutional Court has developed a different model of review, depending on whether a particular case is characterised as entailing a breach of the positive or negative duties imposed by the relevant socio-economic rights.[499] Where it is alleged that the State has breached its positive duties in terms of ss 26 and 27, the State's measures are assessed in terms of the overarching standard of reasonableness. A number of specific, but non-exhaustive criteria have been developed to assess reasonableness in this context. Thus the State is required to adopt and reasonably implement a comprehensive and coherent programme which is capable of facilitating the progressive realisation of the particular right. A key element is the requirement that the programme which is designed to advance the progressive realisation of the rights cannot omit short-term measures of relief for those in desperate need and living in intolerable conditions. In this respect the Court's jurisprudence represents a challenge to economic theories which have as their exclusive focus the improvement of the aggregate welfare of the population over the medium to long term. The Court has sought to ensure that the value of human dignity is given prominence within the evaluative framework of reasonableness review.

A key strength of reasonableness review is its sensitivity to the contexts of different types of socio-economic rights cases and the range of different values and interests that are at stake in these cases. Reasonableness review is capable of accommodating a broad range of challenges to the design and implementation of the State's socio-economic programmes. It promotes dialogic engagement on the content and purposes of socio-economic rights which accords with the deliberative aspects of South Africa's constitutional democracy. Paradoxically, this strength is also the potential weakness of reasonableness review. Reasonableness review can easily degenerate into a weak, normatively empty standard of review when its relationship to the transformative values and purposes of South Africa's Constitution is not clearly developed.

The minimum core approach has the advantage of infusing the socio-economic rights in ss 26 and 27 with a basic normative content. Its major advantage is that it requires particular judicial vigilance and heightened justification when people are deprived of access to basic needs. However, particularly when tied to a single overarching standard such as survival, it becomes too reductive in its account of the values or interests which should be given priority attention in the realisation of socio-economic rights. It fails to do justice to the complexity of the interests and values at stake in various socio-economic rights cases, and the diverse needs of differently situated groups in society. This determinacy and closure of the survival-based standard

---

[499] See in this regard, *Jaftha* (note 8 above) paras 31–34.

can operate to exclude and marginalise groups whose needs do not fulfil the threshold requirement of biological survival.

However, if the minimum core obligation idea is linked to a broader set of constitutional values, it can be incorporated within the framework of reasonableness review without sacrificing the openness and context-sensitivity of this standard. The concept of minimum core obligations serves the purpose in adjudication of requiring the State to discharge a heavy burden of justification when individuals or groups are lacking access to a basic resource or service with correspondingly severe impacts.

Whether or not the courts explicitly accept the concept of a minimum core obligation, reasonableness review as a whole should be firmly anchored in a more substantive account of the content and values protected by the rights in ss 26(1) and 27(1). In the absence of such an account, the criteria for a reasonable government programme developed in cases such as *Grootboom* and *TAC* bear no necessary relationship to the normative commitments underpinning the relevant rights. This creates precisely the risk of judicial retreat into 'structural good governance standards' warned of by scholars such as Danie Brand.[500] For example, without taking seriously the normative commitments implied by the rights in ss 26(1) and 27(1), it is impossible to conduct a rights-based evaluation of the State's justifications for failing to realise these rights. Justifications such as resource constraints are bound to win the day in socio-economic rights litigation unless courts consistently require the State to demonstrate the values and purposes underpinning these and other constitutional rights have been the lodestar of the relevant policy decisions.

A robust judicial role in developing the content of the socio-economic rights in ss 26 and 27 appears at first blush to detract from the deliberative, participatory forms of democracy which I have argued transformative constitutionalism seeks to foster.[501] However, the courts should be understood as a significant forum for deliberation on the fundamental normative commitments on which our young democracy is founded. They have been given the responsibility to pronounce on the meaning and implications of the rights in the Bill of Rights. Through the approaches adopted in both the substantive and remedial stages of socio-economic rights litigation, courts can enhance deliberative democracy by stimulating dialogic engagement by the other branches of government and the broader public on the meaning and implications of socio-economic rights.

Of particular importance in developing the substantive meaning of socio-economic rights and the obligations that they impose on the State in the particular circumstances of a case is the willingness and ability of a court to detect forms of systemic marginalisation and deprivation. This requires careful and detailed analysis of the historical context in which the particular claim arises, the political, economic, social and cultural situation of the claimant group, and the impact of the denial of the benefit in question on them. As Moseneke DCJ argues in an extra curial lecture:

---

[500] Brand (note 52 above) 51.

[501] See chapter 2, part 2.2.4.

> Much is to be said for the contextual approach to constitutional adjudication. The contextual approach posits that legal enquiry in adjudication should be migrated from 'abstract comparison of similarly situated individuals to an exploration of actual impact of the alleged rights violation within the existing socio-economic circumstances.' This is also another way of stating that transformative jurisprudence needs to contextualise violations within actual, live conditions. Decisions on violation of constitutional rights must be seen in the context of socio-economic conditions of the groups concerned in the light of social patterns, power relations and other systemic forms of deprivation, which may be relevant. Also the historical context of the case must be heard.[502]

The richer the evidence before a court of relevant historical and contextual factors pertaining to the claim, the better placed it will be to develop interpretations of socio-economic rights which are responsive to the needs of groups marginalised by systemic poverty and inequality.

Developing an interpretation of socio-economic rights that is sensitive to multiple, overlapping forms of deprivation and socio-economic marginalisation, also requires attention to the interrelationships between the various rights in the Bill of Rights. This chapter has explored the significance of the interrelationship between equality rights and socio-economic rights, particularly for promoting substantive gender equality in various spheres of socio-economic life. The decision of the Constitutional Court in *Khosa*[503] illustrates how the values and interests protected by equality rights and socio-economic rights can be taken into account to enrich the interpretation of the respective rights. Thus the fact that depriving permanent residents of social grants constituted unfair discrimination against them and implicated other important constitutional rights and values such as life and dignity were significant factors in the Court's finding that the legislation did not comply with the constitutional requirement of reasonable measures to realise the right to social assistance in s 27(1)(*c*) read with (2).

A further issue addressed in this chapter is the implications of the different model of review which the Constitutional Court has developed in respect of the negative and positive duties imposed by socio-economic rights for the development of a transformative jurisprudence. In essence, where people are deprived of existing access to socio-economic rights, justifications must comply with the stringent threshold of the general limitations clause (s 36). Where people lack access to socio-economic rights, compliance by the State with its positive duties in terms of ss 26 and 27 is assessed according to the more open and variable criteria of reasonableness review. The following chapter on evictions jurisprudence highlights the fact that in many socio-economic rights cases, negative and positive duties are intertwined. This makes

[502] D Moseneke 'The Fourth Bram Fischer Memorial Lecture: Transformative adjudication' (2002) 18 *SAJHR* 309–319 at 318–319 (citation to C Albertyn & B Goldblatt 'Facing the challenge of transformation: Difficulties in the development of an indigenous jurisprudence of equality' (1998) 14 *SAJHR* 248–276 at 261).

[503] Note 6 above.

a conceptual distinction in the model of review applicable to negative and positive duties difficult to apply in practice and, as I have previously sought to demonstrate, the distinction rests on a shaky theoretical foundation.[504]

The alternative approach argued for above in interpreting and applying reasonableness review, narrows the gap between the models of review applicable to negative and positive duties. Thus a high standard of justification is applied where the State has omitted to take positive measures to ensure that disadvantaged groups have access to basic social resources and services. This would be similar to the analysis in terms of the general limitations clause and the approach adopted with respect to negative deprivations of socio-economic rights. It would incorporate a proportionality analysis, requiring the State to show that it had exhausted all reasonable alternatives to ensure that disadvantaged groups do not experience a denial of access to basic needs, including the adoption of temporary measures which alleviate the immediate crisis of the group in question. The more serious the impact of a deprivation or lack of access to a particular right, the higher the threshold of justification on the State. If the measures adopted by the State increase the socio-economic vulnerability of disadvantaged groups, this should trigger a stringent review of the State's justifications.[505] As Sachs J observed in *PE Municipality*:

> Our society as a whole is demeaned when State action intensifies rather than mitigates their marginalisation. The integrity of the rights-based vision of the Constitution is punctured when governmental action augments rather than reduces denial of the claims of the desperately poor to the basic elements of a decent existence.[506]

The final theme examined in this chapter is the role of socio-economic rights in enabling the State to defend remedial and redistributive measures against legal challenges brought by more powerful social groups. As the jurisprudence suggests, socio-economic rights can play a potentially significant role in supporting such measures. However, realising the full potential of this dimension requires lawyers for the State to consistently invoke arguments based on socio-economic rights to defend pro-poor legislative measures and social programmes.

The fact that legislation and programmes have the broad goal of realising socio-economic rights does not constitute a justification for their failure to respect other constitutional rights or values. This is an important consequence of a commitment to law-based processes of transformation under a constitutional democracy.[507]

However imperfect and limited, courts provide an important forum for disadvantaged groups to articulate their needs within the powerful discourse of human rights law. When courts vindicate their rights, the result can be a deepening of democracy, particularly when litigation occurs in the context of a broader programme of

---

[504] See chapter 2, part 2.4.4 and part 4.7 above.

[505] See also the discussion of retrogressive measures in part 4.4.3 above.

[506] *Port Elizabeth Municipality* (note 7 above) para 18.

[507] See Klare (note 497 above) and accompanying text.

social mobilisation and advocacy.[508] However, the transformative potential of socio-economic rights will not be realised if the courts are reticent to explore the substantive purposes and values they seek to protect and promote.

This chapter has sought to illustrate that reasonableness review can be reconceived so that it incorporates a substantive interpretation of the socio-economic rights described in ss 26(1) and 27(1). In so doing, the weighing of the reasonableness of the State's justifications can occur within a framework which takes seriously the normative commitments of socio-economic rights. This remains a major challenge in the development of a transformative jurisprudence on socio-economic rights in South Africa.

---

508 On the potential and limitations of social rights litigation, see chapter 2, part 2.3.2.

CHAPTER 5

Children, Education, Persons Deprived of their Liberty

Sections 28(1)(*c*), 29 and 35(2)(*e*)

In this chapter *Page*

5.1 INTRODUCTION

This chapter analyses how the courts have approached cases concerning the socio-economic rights of particular beneficiary groups as well as specific rights which do not follow the same formula as those within the cluster of rights in ss 26 and 27. Specifically, the interpretation of the provisions dealing with the socio-economic rights of children (s 28(1)(*c*)), educational rights (s 29), and the socio-economic rights of persons deprived of their liberty (s 35(2)(*e*)) are examined.

5.2 CHILDREN'S SOCIO-ECONOMIC RIGHTS

5.2.1 The special needs and circumstances of children

There are many features of childhood that render children uniquely vulnerable as a group. This requires that special attention be paid both to the nature of their needs, and the manner in which these needs are fulfilled. Their vulnerability arises from their physical characteristics, special emotional and developmental needs, their dependence on adult care and guidance, lack of legal capacity and inability to access many government services without adult assistance.

Children growing up in poverty are particularly vulnerable, and are disadvantaged in a range of areas.[1] For example, malnutrition in early childhood not only threatens a child's survival, but has profound effects on their future health and physical and mental development.[2] Moreover, a number of children in South Africa are growing up in child-headed households without adult care as a result of the HIV/AIDS epidemic in South Africa. This renders them particularly vulnerable to the devastating consequences of physical, psychological and material deprivation.[3] Other especially vulnerable groups of children include children subject to violence and trauma,[4] children of

---

[1] According to the 2006 General Household Survey, about 68% (12.3 million) children in South Africa lived in households with an income of less than R1 200 per month in that year. *General Household Survey* 2006 Statistics South Africa (Pretoria) analysed by the Children's Institute, UCT at 69. This study further indicates that about 16% of all children in South Africa lived in households experiencing child hunger in 2006 (79). For a further breakdown of children's poverty and access to social services, see P Proudlock, M Dutschke, L Jamieson, J Monson & C Smith (eds) *South African Child Gauge* 2007/2008 (2008). Available at http://www.ci.org.za/depts/ci/pubs/pdf/general/gauge2007/Child-Gauge2007.pdf (accessed on 1 June 2009). See generally J Streak 'Child poverty in South Africa and implications for policy: Using indicators and children's views to gain perspective' in E Coetzee & J Streak (eds) *Monitoring Child Socio-Economic Rights in South Africa: Achievements and Challenges* (2004) 9–49.

[2] The primary international treaty protecting children's rights, the United Nations Convention on the Rights of the Child (1989, ratified by South Africa on 16 June 1995) affirms that every child has 'the inherent right to life'. It imposes a duty on States Parties to ensure 'to the maximum extent possible the survival and development of the child'. (arts 6(1) and (2)). See also art 5 of the African Charter on the Rights and Welfare of the Child (1990, ratified by South Africa on 7 January 2000). On the role of international law in interpreting children's socio-economic rights, see generally S Rosa & M Dutschke 'Child rights at the core: The use of international law in South African cases on children's socio-economic rights' (2006) 22 *SAJHR* 224–260.

[3] See the study by S Giese, H Meintjies, R Croke & R Chamberlain *Health and Social Services to Address the Needs of Orphans and Other Vulnerable Children in the Context of HIV/AIDS in South Africa: Research Report and Recommendations* (2003). Available at http://www.ci.org.za/site/frames.asp?section=publications (accessed on 27 April 2009); B Goldblatt & S Liebenberg 'Giving money to children: The State's constitutional obligations to provide child support grants to child headed households' (2004) 20 *SAJHR* 151–164. See also s 137 of the Children's Amendment Act 41 of 2007 which makes special provision for a 'supervising adult' for child-headed households. At the time of finalising the manuscript, the Act had not been brought into operation.

[4] See generally R Lockhat & A van Niekerk 'South African children: A history of adversity, violence and trauma' (2000) 5 *Ethnicity and Health* 291–302.

refugees and asylum-seekers,[5] unaccompanied foreign children,[6] children subject to sexual exploitation,[7] children with disabilities and chronic illnesses,[8] children awaiting trial or convicted of crimes,[9] and children of families evicted from their homes.[10]

Furthermore, children generally live their lives within the institution of the family. The family can be a source of nurture and protection of a child's rights and well-being. As such it is an important institution in liberal democracies for meeting children's social and economic needs. However, it is also a context within which children can experience abuse and neglect of their needs, and are relatively powerless to obtain redress on their own behalf.[11] Additionally, in the context of poverty, many parents and caregivers struggle to provide children with the basic necessities for their survival and development.

Traditional liberal discourse has tended to shield the institution of the family from State intervention both for the purposes of protecting children and to assist family members to provide for the socio-economic needs of children.[12] As Marius Pieterse has argued, this traditional liberal view of the private sphere combined with neo-liberal discourses which emphasise private and familial responsibility for people's social and economic welfare continues to undermine the effective realisation of children's rights.[13]

---

5 See UN Convention on the Rights of the Child (note 2 above) art 22; African Charter on the Rights and Welfare of the Child (note 2 above) art 23.

6 See, for example, *Centre for Child Law v Minister of Home Affairs* 2005 (6) SA 50 (T).

7 See the UN Convention on the Rights of the Child (note 2 above) art 34; African Charter on the Rights and Welfare of the Child (note 2 above) art 27.

8 See UN Convention on the Rights of the Child (note 2 above) art 23; African Charter on the Rights and Welfare of the Child (note 2 above) art 13; United Nations Convention on the Rights of Persons with Disabilities (2006) art 7.

9 See UN Convention on the Rights of the Child (note 2 above) art 40; African Charter on the Rights and Welfare of the Child (note 2 above) art 17. See also *S v Z and 23 Similar Cases* 2004 (4) BCLR 410 (E), [2004] 1 All SA 438 (E).

10 See A Nolan 'Security of tenure from a children's rights perspective' (2006) 7 *ESR Review* 22–26; UN Committee on Economic, Social and Cultural Rights, General Comment No 7 (Sixteenth sess, 1997) *The right to adequate housing (art 11(1) of the Covenant): Forced evictions* UN doc E/1998/22 para 10.

11 Even older children may face a range of psychological barriers in seeking redress for abuse against powerful family members. See generally G M Spies 'Restorative justice: A way to support the healing process of a child exposed to incest' (2009) 22 *Acta Criminologica* 15–24; L M Richter & A R L Dawes 'Child abuse in South Africa: Rights and wrongs' (2008) 17 *Child Abuse Review* 79–93 at 87.

12 On the public/private divide in classic liberal legal theory, see generally chapter 2, part 2.4.5.

13 M Pieterse 'Reconstructing the private/public dichotomy? The enforcement of children's constitutional rights and care entitlements' (2003) 1 *TSAR* 1–19.

Finally, children do not participate in elections[14] and have traditionally not been given a voice in matters which profoundly affect their lives and welfare. Traditional views which ignore the agency of children and their evolving capacities to make decisions in fundamental matters concerning their welfare are increasingly being challenged. These matters range from consent to surgical operations or medical treatment,[15] decisions relating to the termination of a pregnancy,[16] and a say on access and custody questions in divorce proceedings.[17] These developments recognise the child as a person in their own right, and not simply an extension of their parents

[14] A 'child' in s 28 is defined as 'a person under the age of 18 years'. The right to vote in s 19(3) of the Constitution is confined to 'adult citizens'.

[15] The new Children's Act 38 of 2005 introduces significant changes to the ages at which children may consent to surgical operations or medical treatment on their own behalf or on behalf of their own children. In terms of the Child Care Act 74 of 1983, a child could consent to surgical operations at 18 years, and to medical treatment at 14 years (s 39(4)). Section 129 of the 2005 Act contains more nuanced standards which take into account the level of maturity and understanding of the particular child. Thus a child over the age of 12 years can consent to surgical operations and medical treatment provided the child 'is of sufficient maturity and has the mental capacity to understand the benefits, risks, social and other implications' of the treatment or surgical operation. In the case of surgical operations, the child must be duly assisted by his or her parent or guardian. See also s 130 relating to the age of consent for HIV-testing. At the time of writing this provision was not yet in operation.

[16] Minors are entitled to consent to the termination of a pregnancy in terms of the Act subject only to a duty on a medical practitioner, midwife or nurse to 'advise such minor to consult with her parents, guardian, family members or friends before the pregnancy is terminated'. However, a termination of pregnancy may not be denied to a minor if she chooses not to consult them. See s 5(1)–(3) of the Choice on Termination of Pregnancy Act 92 of 1996.

[17] The right of the child to express him- or herself and to have their views taken into account in accordance with their age and maturity is recognised in art 12 of the UN Convention on the Rights of the Child (note 2 above). See further arts 4 and 7 of the African Charter on the Rights and Welfare of the Child (note 2 above). Section 28(1)(*h*) of the Constitution gives every child the right 'to have a legal practitioner assigned to the child by the State, and at State expense, in civil proceedings affecting the child, if substantial injustice would otherwise result.' In *Soller NO v G* 2003 (5) SA 430 (W) para 27, the court described the role of the legal practitioner in terms of s 28(1)(*g*) as follows:

> The legal practitioner stands squarely in the corner of the child and has the task of presenting and arguing the wishes and desires of that child. This task is not without certain inbuilt limitation. The legal practitioner does not only represent the perspective of the child concerned. The legal practitioner should also provide adult insight into those wishes and desires which have been confided and entrusted to him or her as well as apply legal knowledge and expertise to the child's perspective. The legal practitioner may provide the child with a voice but is not merely a mouthpiece.

or other care-takers.[18] As Sachs J affirmed in *S v M (Centre for Child Law as Amicus Curiae)*:[19]

> Every child has his or her own dignity. If a child is to be constitutionally imagined as an individual with a distinctive personality, and not merely as a miniature adult waiting to reach full size, he or she cannot be treated as a mere extension of his or her parents, umbilically destined to sink or swim with them.[20]

In certain circumstances, recognising the right of children to make decisions and gain access to government services in their own name may be crucial to ensuring that they can access and benefit from socio-economic rights, such as health care and social security.[21]

5.2.2 Interpreting children's 'basic' socio-economic rights

The 'basic' socio-economic rights of children entrenched in s 28(1)(*c*) of the Constitution are not qualified as are the socio-economic rights in ss 26 and 27.[22]

Except for the right to basic 'social services', all the basic rights referred to in s 28(1)(*c*) have their counterpart in the rights protected in ss 26 and 27. There is some disputation as to the scope of a child's right to 'social services' in s 28(1)(*c*).[23] It can be given a narrow interpretation referring to the social welfare services which typically form the other major component of the mandate of the Department of Social

---

[18] See also J Sloth-Nielsen 'Realising children's rights to legal representation and to be heard in judicial proceedings: An update' (2008) 24 *SAJHR* 495–524. For a useful survey of the legal provisions relating to the age thresholds applicable to children in South Africa, see P Mahery & P Proudlock *Legal Guide to Age Thresholds for Children* 4 ed (2008) Children's Institute, University of Cape Town and Centre for Child Law, University of Pretoria.

[19] 2008 (3) SA 232 (CC), 2007 (12) BCLR 1312 (CC).

[20] Ibid para 18. See also the postscript of Sachs J in *Christian Education South Africa v Minister of Education* 2000 (4) SA 757 (CC), 2000 (10) BCLR 1051 (CC) para 53, lamenting the fact that a *curator ad litem* had not been appointed to represent the voice and interests of children in the case, which concerned the constitutionality of corporal punishment in independent schools. According to Sachs J ibid:

> A curator could have made sensitive enquiries so as to enable their [the learners at these schools] voice or voices to be heard. Their actual experiences and opinions would not necessarily have been decisive, but they would have enriched the dialogue, and the factual and experiential foundations for the balancing exercise in this difficult matter would have been more secure.

[21] See, for example, L Gerntholtz 'HIV testing and treatment, informed consent and AIDS orphans' (2003) 4 *ESR Review* 11–14; Goldblatt and Liebenberg (note 3 above).

[22] As Julia Sloth-Nielsen points out, socio-economic entitlements can also be derived from s 28(1)(*d*) of the Constitution which requires children 'to be protected from maltreatment, neglect, abuse or degradation'. See J Sloth-Nielsen 'The child's right to social services, the right to social security, and primary prevention of child abuse: Some conclusions in the aftermath of *Grootboom*' (2001) 17 *SAJHR* 210–231 at 230–231. On the factors which make children living in poverty particularly vulnerable to abuse, see the discussion in Richter and Dawes (note 11 above) 85–87.

[23] See, for example, the discussion of the literature by Julia Sloth-Nielsen ibid 218–220.

Development. These are services delivered usually by social workers and NGOs and include services to child victims of physical or mental abuse or neglect; protection and assistance to children temporarily or permanently separated from their families; special support services provided to children with disabilities; and protection of children from economic exploitation, drug abuse, sexual exploitation and abuse.[24]

A broad interpretation of the phrase would encompass all categories of social services usually provided by the State such as health care, water delivery services, sanitation, child care facilities, social security and education.[25] The delivery of these services would traverse a range of government departments and programmes, and not be restricted to those provided by the Department of Social Development. On this broader reading, 'social services' would encompass all forms of social provisioning by the State necessary to ensure children's survival and physical, mental, emotional and moral development. A broad interpretation of the phrase 'social services' would better promote the achievement of the underlying purposes of children's socio-economic rights. These are, as expressed in the United Nations Convention on the Rights of the Child, the right of every child 'to a standard of living adequate for the child's physical, mental, spiritual, moral and social development'.[26] Such a right would also incorporate the right to social security in s 27(1)(*c*) which is the only right which does not have a direct counterpart in s 28(1)(*c*).[27]

The entitlements in s 28(1)(*c*), with the exception of 'shelter', are qualified by the adjective, 'basic' which suggests that children are to be guaranteed essential levels of health care services, food, and other social services necessary for their survival and proper development. 'Shelter' as a basic form of housing would also be consistent with this interpretation.[28] However, as discussed below, the Constitutional Court in

[24] See, for example, the social welfare programmes described in the Department of Social Development's Annual Report for 2007/08, presented to the Portfolio Committee on Social Development, November 2008 at 12–24 (document on file with author).

[25] *The New Shorter Oxford English Dictionary* (1993) gives as one of the primary meanings of 'social services': 'a service provided esp. by the State for the benefit of the community, esp. education, health and housing'.

[26] Article 27(1). The preamble of the UN Convention on the Rights of the Child (note 2 above) also notes that 'childhood is entitled to special care and assistance'.

[27] The UN Convention on the Rights of the Child (note 2 above) recognises the right of every child to benefit from social security (art 26).

[28] *The New Shorter Oxford English Dictionary* (1993) gives as among the meanings of 'shelter': 'A structure giving protection from rain, wind, or sun; anything serving as a shield or a place of refuge from the weather … **e** A place providing accommodation or refuge for the homeless, the oppressed, etc.' See also the interpretation of the concept of 'shelter' by the Western Cape High Court, Cape Town in *Grootboom v Oostenberg Municipality* 2000 (3) BCLR 277 (C) at 288B–C.

Grootboom[29] disagreed that 'shelter' in the context of s 28(1)(*c*) implied a rudimentary form of housing.[30]

The absence in s 28(1)(*c*) of the equivalent qualifying phrases encountered in ss 26(2) and 27(2) suggests that the State is obliged to ensure that all children enjoy immediate and effective access to a basic level of these social services and resources.[31] According to this interpretation, a failure to ensure the basic socio-economic needs of children due to resource constraints or other reasons is justifiable only in terms of the criteria and proportionality analysis required by the general limitations clause.[32] Requiring weighty reasons and heightened scrutiny of the State's justificatory arguments in terms of s 36 accords with the justification for including a separate provision in the Constitution dealing with children's socio-economic rights – the special needs and vulnerability of children, particularly those living in poverty.[33]

---

29 *Government of the Republic of South Africa v Grootboom* 2001 (1) SA 46 (CC), 2000 (11) BCLR 1169 (CC) *('Grootboom')*.

30 Ibid para 73. See note 45 below and accompanying text.

31 A number of academic commentators have argued in favour of such an interpretation. See P de Vos 'The economic and social rights of children and South Africa's transitional Constitution' (1995) 10 *SAPR/L* 233–259 at 255 (although not identical, s 30(1)(*c*) of the transitional Constitution is similar to s 28(1)(*c*) of the 1996 Constitution); G van Bueren 'Alleviating poverty through the Constitutional Court' (1999) 15 *SAJHR* 52–74 at 57; C Scott & P Alston 'Adjudicating constitutional priorities in a transnational context: A comment on *Soobramoney's* legacy and *Grootboom's* promise' (2000) 16 *SAJHR* 206–268 at 258–262; M Pieterse (note 13 above) 5; L Stewart 'Interpreting and limiting the basic socio-economic rights of children in cases where they overlap with the socio-economic rights of others' (2008) 24 *SAJHR* 472–494 at 493–494. See also *Centre for Child Law v Minister of Home Affairs* (note 6 above) para 17. In *Centre for Child Law v MEC for Education* 2008 (1) SA 223 (T) at 227I–J Murphy J held as follows:

> What is notable about the children's rights in comparison to other socio-economic rights, is that section 28 contains no internal limitation subjecting them to the availability of resources and legislative measures for their progressive realisation. Like all rights, they remain subject to reasonable and proportional limitation, but the absence of any internal limitation entrenches the rights as unqualified and immediate.

32 In this sense, the socio-economic rights of children correspond to an 'obligation of result' identified in the *Maastricht Guidelines on Violations of Socio-Economic Rights*. An 'obligation of conduct' 'requires action reasonably calculated to realize the enjoyment of a particular right' whereas an 'obligation of result' 'requires States to achieve specific targets to satisfy a detailed substantive standard' (para 7). On the Maastricht Guidelines, see chapter 3, note 17.

33 In the constitutional drafting process, the Panel of Constitutional Expert identified 'two underlying reasons' for not subjecting the children's socio-economic rights to the qualifications applicable to the socio-economic rights of 'everyone' in ss 26 and 27:

> The vulnerability, lack of maturity and comparative innocence of children render them deserving of more effective protection. Also, children cannot be expected to participate actively in the human rights discourse, in defining its scope, or articulating its social dimensions and implications, as adults can be expected to do. The difference in formulation means that the state would undertake to make a greater effort in order to secure the rights of children.

5.2.3 The Constitutional Court's jurisprudence

In both the *Grootboom*[34] and *Treatment Action Campaign* cases,[35] the High Court and Constitutional Court were presented with arguments that the facts of these cases also constituted a breach of the rights of children to shelter and basic health care services respectively.[36] The Western Cape High Court in *Grootboom* did not find a breach of s 26,[37] but held that the right of children to shelter in s 28(1)(*c*) of the Constitution had been infringed.[38] It held further that a joint reading of s 28(1)(*b*)[39] and (*c*) and (2)[40] creates a derivative right for parents to shelter with their children. Davis J reasoned as follows:

> As the family must be maintained as a unit parents of the children who are granted shelter should also be entitled to such shelter. The bearer of the right now becomes the family. The justification for such a conclusion is that a failure to recognise the parents would prevent the children and indeed their parents who, to a considerable extent owing to the ravages of apartheid are unable to provide adequate shelter for their own children.[41]

This reasoning recognises the responsibility of the State to assist families to meet their socio-economic needs when they are unable to do so owing to structural historical and social forces. However, the difficulty with the High Court's reasoning in interpreting ss 26 and 28(1)(*c*) is that the short-term provision of shelter for adults is dependent on their being parents or primary caregivers of children. This leaves out of consideration other groups of adults who have urgent shelter needs.

On appeal, the Constitutional Court held that the 'carefully constructed constitutional scheme for the progressive realisation of socio-economic rights would make little sense if it could be trumped in every case by the rights of children to get shelter

---

Memorandum by the Panel of Constitutional Experts to the Chairpersons and Executive Director of the Constitutional Assembly, 5 February 1996, 2 para 3.3 (document on file with author).

34 Note 29 above.

35 *Minister of Health v Treatment Action Campaign (No 2)* 2002 (5) SA 721 (CC), 2002 (10) BCLR 1033 (CC) (*'Treatment Action Campaign'*).

36 On the *Grootboom* and *Treatment Action Campaign* cases, see generally chapter 4, part 4.3.

37 *Grootboom v Oostenberg Municipality* (note 28 above). Davis J held that the respondents had produced 'clear evidence that a rational housing programme has been initiated at all levels of government and that such programme has been designed to solve a pressing problem in the context of scarce financial resources'. (286H–I).

38 The High Court interpreted 'shelter' in terms of s 28(1)(*c*) as a basic form of the more extensive concept of 'adequate housing' in s 26. It thus held that s 28(1)(*c*) 'appears to provide for a right to be protected from the elements in circumstances where there is no need to remove such children from their parents'. (287H–288A).

39 Section 28(1)(*b*) provides that every child has the right 'to family care or parental care, or to appropriate alternative care when removed from the family environment'.

40 Section 28(2) provides that '[a] child's best interests are of paramount importance in every matter concerning the child'.

41 *Grootboom v Oostenberg Municipality* (note 28 above) 289C–D.

from the State on demand'. [42] It held that s 28(1)(*b*) and (*c*) must be read together. While the former provision defines those responsible for giving care, the latter 'lists various aspects of the care entitlement'.[43] According to the Court, the primary duty to fulfil a child's socio-economic rights rests on that child's parents or family where the child is being cared for in the family:

> It follows that section 28(1)(*c*) does not create any primary State obligation to provide shelter on demand to parents and their children if children are being cared for by their parents or families.[44]

The Court also disagreed that 'shelter' in s 28(1)(*c*) represented a rudimentary form of housing, holding that it 'embraces shelter in all its manifestations'.[45]

According to the Court, the State's primary obligation towards children who are being cared for by their families is to 'provide the legal and administrative infrastructure necessary to ensure that children are accorded the protection contemplated by section 28'.[46] This obligation would 'normally be fulfilled by passing laws and creating enforcement mechanisms for the maintenance of children, their protection from maltreatment, abuse, neglect or degradation, and the prevention of the other forms of abuse of children mentioned in section 28'.[47]

The Court furthermore referred to the State's obligation under ss 25, 26 and 27 to provide access to the relevant socio-economic rights protected by these sections 'on a programmatic and co-ordinated basis, subject to available resources'.[48] It held that one of the ways in which the State would meet its s 27 obligations was through the provision of maintenance grants and other material assistance to families in need.[49] As the children who were respondents in the *Grootboom* case were in the care of their parents, and 'not in the care of the State, in any alternative care, or abandoned', the Court held that the State did not incur any obligation in terms of s 28(1)(*c*) to provide them with shelter and, through them, their parents.[50]

The Court's reasoning has rightly been criticised for failing to affirm the right of parents, other caregivers and children to State assistance for the fulfilment of their

---

[42] *Grootboom* (note 29 above) para 71.
[43] Ibid para 76.
[44] Ibid para 77.
[45] Ibid para 73.
[46] Ibid para 78.
[47] Ibid. See also *S v M (Centre for Child Law as Amicus Curiae)* (note 19 above) para 20:

> No constitutional injunction can in and of itself isolate children from the shocks and perils of harsh family and neighbourhood environments. What the law can do is create conditions to protect children from abuse and maximise opportunities for them to lead productive and happy lives. (Footnotes omitted.)

[48] Ibid.
[49] Ibid.
[50] *Grootboom* (note 29 above) para 79.

shelter and other basic socio-economic needs.[51] According to the Convention on the Rights of the Child, 'parent(s) or others responsible for the child have the primary responsibility to secure, within their abilities and financial capabilities, the conditions of living necessary for the child's development'. However, States have a duty 'in accordance with national conditions and within their means' to 'take appropriate measures *to assist* parents and others responsible for the child to implement this right *and shall in the case of need provide material assistance and support programmes*, particularly with regard to nutrition, clothing and housing'.[52] (Emphasis added.)

As Marius Pieterse has pointed out, by characterising the State's primary duty in terms of s 28(1)(*c*) as the enforcement and regulation of parent's common law and statutory duties towards their children, the Court minimises the State's role in ensuring children's socio-economic welfare. This serves to reinforce both the traditional dichotomy between the public and private spheres in classic liberal theory,[53] and neo-liberal economic theories which seek to limit the State's role in securing people's social and economic welfare.[54] He argues that:

> It may therefore be said that *Grootboom* largely insulates public institutions from social accountability towards children, and instead views child welfare almost exclusively as a private responsibility. This is problematic not only in light of the limited financial capacity of many private sphere actors, but also in light of the law's traditional hesitance to disrupt private relationships and the notorious ineffectiveness of private remedies.[55]

The Court is clearly reluctant to recognise direct entitlements to the provision of social and economic goods and services even when this is strongly suggested by the text of the relevant provisions. *Grootboom* is an early indication that its preferred mode of evaluating the State's compliance with its duties in terms of s 28(1)(*c*) is via reasonableness review in terms of ss 26 and 27.[56]

---

[51] See, for example, Julia Sloth-Nielsen (note 22 above) 229–230 who argues that the Court's reasoning may encourage families in dire poverty to abandon their responsibilities 'and leave their children at the doorstep of the state, where at least the state's obligation to provide will then be assured'. She points out that this would 'work against stated welfare policies of family preservation, family reintegration, and support to children within the family or kinship environment' (ibid). It is ironic, given the severe impact that family poverty has on children's wellbeing, that the Court justifies its unwillingness to impose a duty on the State to assist parents to meet the shelter needs of their children on the basis that children 'could become stepping stones to housing for their parents instead of being valued for who they are'. *Grootboom* (note 29 above) para 71.

[52] Article 27(1), (2) and (3). See also art 20(1) and (2) of the African Charter on the Rights and Welfare of the Child (note 2 above).

[53] See also chapter 2, part 2.4.5.

[54] M Pieterse (note 13 above).

[55] Ibid 11–12. See also E Bonthuys 'Realising South African children's basic socio-economic claims against parents and the state: What courts can achieve' (2008) 22 *Int J of Law, Policy and the Family* 333–355.

[56] The Court in *Grootboom* (note 29 above) para 74 held that '[t]he obligation created by s 28(1)(*c*) can properly be ascertained only in the context of the rights and, in particular,

In the *Treatment Action Campaign* case the Court appears to retreat from the clear suggestion of the *Grootboom* case that the State's duty to provide for children's socio-economic needs is triggered only when children are physically separated from their families. Thus the Court held that children are entitled to the protection contemplated by s 28 'when the implementation of the right to parental or family care is lacking'.[57] In *Treatment Action Campaign*, the Court was dealing with children born to mothers who were too poor to afford private medical care and who were, as a result, dependent on State health care facilities.[58] However, the Court did not conclude that these children enjoyed an unqualified, direct claim to the provision of health care services (subject only to justification in terms of the general limitations clause). Instead, the Court relied on the denial of the right of children to basic health care services to support its finding that the government's rigid policy on Nevirapine was unreasonable because the policy excluded and harmed a particularly vulnerable group. Their precarious position was described in the following terms:

> Their needs are 'most urgent' and their inability to have access to Nevirapine profoundly affects their ability to enjoy all rights to which they are entitled. Their rights are 'most in peril' as a result of the policy that has been adopted and are most affected by a rigid and inflexible policy that excludes them from having access to Nevirapine.[59]

The approach of the Court in *Treatment Action Campaign* to the argument based on the right of children to basic health care services illustrates its discomfort with interpreting the socio-economic rights provisions in the Constitution to confer a directly enforceable entitlement to social resources and services. The Court is clearly more comfortable applying a model of reasonableness review to the positive obligations imposed by the socio-economic rights provisions in the Constitution, even in contexts where the formulation of the right clearly suggests a directly enforceable entitlement.

5.2.4 Children lacking family care: Towards direct entitlements?

A body of High Court jurisprudence has developed affirming children's direct entitlements to socio-economic support, particularly in contexts where they lack family care. Thus in *Centre for Child Law v Minister of Home Affairs*,[60] the court dealt with an application brought on behalf of a number of unaccompanied foreign children designated for deportation challenging their conditions of detention in a repatriation camp and the procedures for assessing their personal circumstances. In particular, the application was aimed at preventing the detention of the children with adults at the Lindela repatriation camp, and ensuring that they were brought before a children's court for inquiries to be conducted in terms of the Child Care Act 74 of

---

the obligations created by ss 25(5), 26 and 27 of the Constitution'.

[57] *Treatment Action Campaign* (note 35 above) para 79.

[58] Ibid.

[59] Ibid para 78.

[60] Note 6 above.

1983. Such inquiries are directed at ascertaining whether the child is a child in need of care and whether the child should be removed to a place of safety.

The Court noted that the curator's report revealed 'that insufficient resources, inadequate administrative systems and procedural oversights in the handling of children, as well as the inaccessibility of legal representation in the adjudication process, have further exacerbated the crisis now existing in the treatment of unaccompanied foreign children'.[61] De Vos J referred to the Constitutional Court's holding in *Grootboom* that the primary duty for fulfilling a child's socio-economic rights rests on the child's parents or family. According to De Vos J:

> [T]his suggests that the State is under a direct duty to ensure basic socio-economic provision for children who lack family care, as do unaccompanied foreign children. There is thus an active duty on the State to provide those children with the rights and protection set out in s 28.[62]

The Court granted a range of orders against the State respondents concerning the procedures and treatment applicable in respect of unaccompanied foreign children.[63] These included bringing the children presently in detention to a Children's Court for the purposes of enquiries in terms of the Child Care Act, conducting inquiries into the personal circumstances of each of these children, and providing them with legal representation in terms of s 28(1)(*h*) of the Constitution if it appeared that a substantial injustice would otherwise result.[64] The respondents were also ordered to report back to the Court on their compliance with these directions.[65]

Another case which concerned the socio-economic needs of children in a context outside of family care is *The Centre for Child Law v MEC for Education, Gauteng.*[66] The case concerned a challenge to the poor conditions existing at the JW Luckhoff High School, a school of industry in Gauteng.[67] These conditions included broken windows; a lack of doors to provide privacy in showers and toilets; thin, dirty blankets; an absence of security due to a lack of access control and perimeter fencing around the institution; and a lack of psychological and therapeutic services.[68] In particular, the children were bitterly cold due to the inclement weather, their lack of warm clothing and the disrepair of the building.[69] An immediate solution proposed

---

[61] Ibid para 14.
[62] Ibid para 17.
[63] Ibid para 31.
[64] Ibid.
[65] Ibid.
[66] Note 31 above.
[67] Children who are deemed to be children in need of care are placed at the school by way of an order in terms of s 15(1)(*d*) of the Child Care Act 74 of 1984.
[68] *Centre for Child Law v MEC for Education, Gauteng* (note 31 above) 226G–227D.
[69] Ibid 227D–F.

by the applicants was the immediate provision of sleeping bags to keep the children relatively warm at night.[70]

The respondents argued that the provision of sleeping bags would overstretch their budget and amount to inequality by favouring the children at this school above others at similar institutions.[71] However, given that there was only one other school of industry in Gauteng, Murphy J calculated that at worst the state would have to provide about 150 sleeping bags at an estimate of between R30 000 and R70 000.[72] This was 'possibly less than the amount spent by the respondents in defending this litigation'.[73] The Court held that the 'minimal costs or budgetary-allocation problems in this instance are far outweighed by the urgent need to advance the children's interests in accordance with our constitutional values'.[74] The equality argument was rejected on the following basis:

> It can never be a defence to a violation of constitutional rights to argue without qualification that the remedy should not be granted, lest others, similarly denied their rights, should seek the same remedy, at significant cost to the State. While levelling down may have its place when considering remedies for infringements of rights with pecuniary consequences, in cases such as the present, where the fundamental right to dignity is central, and where costs are foreseeable, manageable and containable, levelling up is the appropriate and desirable remedy.[75]

Murphy J affirmed that the duty 'to provide care and social services to children removed from the family environment rests upon the state', and that 'the government must provide appropriate facilities and meet the children's basic needs'.[76] He held that this duty was not being fulfilled and was being frustrated by 'bureaucratic silence and inertia' as well as by misguided undertakings to seek resources from private institutions.[77]

The court found that the conditions in which the children were accommodated as well as the lack of psychological and therapeutic services at the school of industry[78] violated ss 28(1)(*b*) and (*c*), 28(2), 10, and 12(1)(*c*) and (*e*) of the Constitution. A

---

[70] Ibid 227D.

[71] Ibid 227E–G.

[72] Ibid 227H.

[73] Ibid.

[74] Ibid 228B.

[75] Ibid C–E (referring to the metaphor of 'equality with a vengeance', leading to 'equal graveyards' discussed by Ackermann J in *National Coalition for Gay and Lesbian Equality v Minister of Home Affairs* 2000 (2) SA 1 (CC), 2001 (1) BCLR 39 (CC) para 77).

[76] Ibid 228F–G.

[77] The government had offered to seek to meet its constitutional obligations to the children by seeking to raise funds from the Red Cross and the non-governmental sector. The Court held that this proposal 'is way off the mark and reflects its fundamental misunderstanding of its constitutional duty' (228F–G).

[78] In this regard, the Court pointed out that the purpose of children being sent to schools of industry is care and rehabilitation:

range of orders were made against the respondent which included the provision of sleeping bags to the children, the installation of perimeter and access control at the school, the provision of psychological and therapeutic support services, and the initiation of a developmental quality assurance process. The court retained a supervisory jurisdiction over the implementation of its order given 'the dilatory and lackadaisical approach taken so far'.[79]

This judgment affirms the interdependence betweens socio-economic rights and civil and political rights such as the rights to human dignity and security of the person. It also demonstrates the capacity of courts to make direct, pragmatic orders for the improvement of the material conditions of children's lives. The Court was also clear that the State cannot seek to divest itself of its constitutional obligations to children by making them conditional on support from non-governmental actors.

The State's obligations to provide social grants and other social services to children who lack parental care remain to be clarified in the important area of child-headed households. This phenomenon is fuelled by the HIV/AIDS epidemic ravaging South Africa.[80]

5.2.5 Conclusion

The *Grootboom ratio* reinforces the public/private dichotomy in classic liberal legal theory by placing the obligations imposed by s 28(1)(*c*) on the parents and family members of children living with their families. The Court is careful to emphasise that the State's duty in these circumstances is indirect – namely, to create the necessary 'legal and administrative infrastructure' for the maintenance of children and their protection from maltreatment, abuse, neglect or degradation.[81] The jurisprudence is unsatisfactory for its failure to affirm that the State is under a direct duty to assist families living in poverty to meet the socio-economic needs of the children in their care. As noted previously, this is an obligation binding on South Africa in terms of the UN Convention on the Rights of the Child.[82] However, the Court failed to consider the provisions of this important Convention in interpreting the State's obligations in terms of s 28(1)(*c*).[83]

> Psychological and social support is a critical ingredient of State care, absent parental support. It is common cause that there is no such resource in place at the school. There is no psychologist. There is no social worker. (229C).

[79] Ibid 230E–231F.
[80] See note 3 above and accompanying text.
[81] *Grootboom* (note 29 above) para 78.
[82] Note 2 above and accompanying text.
[83] Compare the detailed consideration of the UN Convention on the Rights of the Child and the African Charter on Human and People's Rights in interpreting s 28(2) of the Constitution in *Director of Public Prosecutions, Transvaal v Minister for Justice and Constitutional Development* 2009 (4) SA 222 (CC), 2009 (7) BCLR 637 (CC) paras 75–79. On the duty of courts in terms of s 39(1)(*b*) to consider international law in interpreting the Bill of Rights, see further chapter 3, part 3.3.2(*b*).

In *Treatment Action Campaign*, the Court was at pains to clarify that the State is obliged to provide basic health care services to children when their parents are impoverished and reliant on the public health care sector. Nevertheless, the Court continued to refrain from giving independent meaning and effect to children's socio-economic rights in s 28, preferring to decide the case in terms of the overall framework of reasonableness review developed in the context of ss 26 and 27.

If claims brought on behalf of children for access to socio-economic rights are to be evaluated in terms of the reasonableness standard, it is apposite, given the special needs and vulnerability of children, that the courts require stringent standards of justification from the State.[84] The fact that children will suffer serious harm to their health and future development should they not receive certain social services should be a compelling ground for finding that a failure to put in place and implement the necessary social programmes is unreasonable. In evaluating arguments based on budgetary constraints, the State should be put to a stringent standard of proof and justification regarding the availability of resources to fulfil children's basic socio-economic needs. In particular, relevant organs of State should be required to show that in formulating their social policies and budgetary allocations, they have prioritised the fulfilment of children's socio-economic needs to ensure their survival and development.

The recognition of direct duties on the State to fulfil the socio-economic rights of children in circumstances when they are removed from or lack family care is a positive development in the jurisprudence of the High Courts. It illustrates that orders requiring the direct provision of social services to defined beneficiaries constitutes 'just and equitable relief' in appropriate circumstances, and can also be practically feasible.

5.3 THE RIGHT TO EDUCATION

5.3.1 Basic education

Section 29(1)(*a*) is also formulated as a direct right of 'everyone to a basic education, including adult basic education'. To date there has not been a major test case in which the Constitutional Court has pronounced on the nature and scope of the right to

[84] Kenneth Creamer has suggested that a 'higher standard of reasonableness' review is appropriate in assessing State programmes which affect children's socio-economic rights. He argues for this higher standard on the basis of a reading of the Constitution which requires children's needs to be prioritised. The higher standard of reasonableness review should include such factors as the rapid implementation of relevant programmes and the requirement that programmes are effectively designed to reach all children in need. See K Creamer 'The impact of South Africa's evolving jurisprudence on children's socio-economic rights in budget analysis' (2002) IDASA Occasional Papers at 17; K Creamer 'The implication of socio-economic rights jurisprudence for government planning and budgeting: The case of children's socio-economic rights' (2004) 8 *LDD* 221–234. See also S Liebenberg 'Taking stock: The jurisprudence on children's socio-economic rights and its implications for government policy' (2004) 5 *ESR Review* 3–6.

basic education. It has said *obiter* in respect of the right to basic education in s 32(*a*) of the interim Constitution, that this provision 'creates a positive right that basic education be provided for every person and not merely a negative right that such a person should not be obstructed in pursuing his or her basic education'.[85]

The legislature has sought to define the parameters of 'basic education' by providing that it is compulsory for a learner to attend school from the age of seven until the age of 15 years or the ninth grade, whichever comes first.[86] Provincial governments are obliged to ensure that there are sufficient places in public schools for all learners living within the province.[87] Whether basic education for the purposes of s 29(1)(*a*) can be equated with the compulsory phase of schooling remains to be tested in the jurisprudence.

In developing the normative content of the right to basic education, helpful guidance can be obtained from the so-called 'Four A' standards identified by the UN Committee on Economic, Social and Cultural Rights in interpreting the right to education in art 13 of the International Covenant on Economic, Social and Cultural Rights.[88] Thus in order to be compatible with the obligations undertaken in terms of art 13, education 'in all its forms and at levels shall exhibit the following interrelated and essential features': availability, accessibility, acceptability and adaptability.[89]

Section 29(1)(*a*) also expressly includes 'adult basic education'. According to the National Department of Education, 'adult basic education subsumes both literacy and post-literacy as it seeks to connect literacy with basic (general) adult education on the

---

[85] *Gauteng Provincial Legislature, Ex parte: In re Dispute Concerning the Constitutionality of Certain Provisions of the Gauteng School Education Bill of 1995* 1996 (3) SA 165 (CC), 1996 (4) BCLR 537 (CC) para 9 (hereafter '*In re School Education Bill of 1995*'). However, the main issue in this case was whether the State was under a positive duty to assist in the establishment of educational institutions based on a common culture, language or religion to give effect to s 32(*c*) of the interim Constitution. The Court held that there was no such positive duty on the State.

[86] Section 3(1) of the South African Schools Act 84 of 1996 ('the Schools Act'). This phase of education is the General Education Certificate (GEC). The White Paper on Education and Training (1995) paras 13–15 defines basic education as 'appropriately designed programmes to the level of the proposed General Education Certificate (GEC), whether offered in school to children, or through other forms of delivery to young people and adults'.

[87] Ibid s 3(6).

[88] UN Committee on Economic, Social and Cultural Rights, General Comment No 13 (Twenty-first sess 1999) *The right to education (art 13 of the Covenant)* UN doc E/2000/22 para 6.

[89] Ibid. See the elaborations provided by the Committee in para 6(*a*)-(*d*). See also the standard of 'fiscal and instructional adequacy' proposed by Woolman and Fleisch. S Woolman & B Fleisch *The Constitution in the Classroom: Law and Education in South Africa 1994–2008* (2009) 135–137.

one hand and with training for income generation on the other hand'.[90] Again this right has been the subject of almost no litigation despite indications that it is poorly funded and implemented.[91]

The lack of internal qualifiers or limitations suggests that the right to basic education in s 29(1)(*a*) requires direct realisation. This right can be violated through non-compliance with positive duties such as ensuring an adequate provision of primary schools in all areas of the country, or of negative duties such as policies, legislation or conduct which have the effect of depriving certain learners of their existing access to schooling.[92] Should the State have cogent reasons for failing to ensure the fulfilment of this right, such as apartheid-inherited structural inequalities in the education system and resource constraints, it must seek to do so in terms of the criteria of the general limitations clause (s 36).[93] As noted in chapter 4, this includes the requirement of a law of general application.[94]

Moreover, as Stu Woolman and Brahm Fleisch point out, the courts have sufficient remedial flexibility to craft remedies which do not impose unrealistic obligations on the State or schools, but nevertheless require concrete measures designed to remedy the violation with all due diligence.[95]

The heightened protection accorded to the right to basic education can be justified on the basis that it is the foundation of all further learning, and is crucial for the development, effective functioning and ability of people to earn a living in contemporary societies.[96] Without a basic education people's life chances are severely

---

[90] The Department of Education's Policy Document on Adult Basic Education and Training (1997) 5. Available at http://www.education.gov.za/Documents/policies/Policy Document/ABET.pdf (accessed on 12 January 2010).

[91] See P Rule '"The time is burning": The right of adults to basic education in South Africa' (2006) 39 *Journal of Education* 113–134. The Adult Basic Education and Training Act 52 of 2000 aims at establishing 'a national co-ordinated adult basic education and training system which promotes co-operative governance and provides for programme-based adult basic education and training'. (Preamble). See also the National Norms and Standards for Funding Adult Learning Centres (NSF–ALC), Government Notice 1769 of 2007, *Government Gazette* 30576, 14 December 2007.

[92] This could include, for example, the exclusion of pregnant learners from school or racial and other forms of discrimination in school policies which have the effect of depriving learners of their right to a basic education.

[93] See F Veriava & F Coomans 'The right to education' in D Brand & C Heyns (eds) *Socio-Economic Rights in South Africa* (2005) 57–83 at 62–63.

[94] See chapter 4, part 4.4.5 at notes 381–384 and accompanying text.

[95] Woolman & Fleisch (note 89 above) 125–126. See also the remedy of participatory structural interdicts discussed in chapter 8, part 8.6.

[96] According to art 13(1) of the International Covenant on Economic, Social and Cultural Rights (1966) education 'shall be directed to the full development of the human personality and the sense of its dignity, and shall strengthen the respect for human rights and fundamental freedoms'. It should further 'enable all persons to participate effectively in a free society, promote understanding, tolerance and friendship among all nations and all

constrained and their ability to participate fully in the political and economic life of a society is compromised.[97]

The post-apartheid South African educational landscape is still characterised by deep disparities in the quality of education and schooling, with historically black schools operating under conditions of severe resource and infrastructure backlogs.[98] As O'Regan J notes in her partially dissenting judgment in *MEC for Education: KwaZulu-Natal v Pillay*,[99] although the position of black children in the post-apartheid period 'ha[s] improved somewhat', the 'pattern of disadvantage engraved onto our education system by apartheid has not been erased'.[100] She goes on to observe that, 'although the law no longer compels racially separate institutions, social realities by and large still do.'[101]

A major question relating to the interpretation of the right to basic education is whether it permits the charging of school fees. Post-apartheid education policy has permitted schools to charge school fees subject to a system of full or partial exemption for poor learners.[102] In contrast, international law generally endorses a right to free and compulsory primary education.[103] Research in the South African context indicates that the charging of schools fees and the secondary costs associated with schooling (uniforms, transport, textbooks, costs associated with extracurricular activities) are a significant barrier for poor learners to access education.[104]

---

racial, ethnic or religious groups, and further the activities of the United Nations for the maintenance of peace'.

97 See the discussion of a purposive approach to the right to basic education by F Veriava & F Coomans 'The right to education' (note 93 above) 61–65.

98 See, for example, *The National Policy on an Equitable Provision of an Enabling School Physical Teaching and Learning Environment and National Norms and Standards for School Infrastructure* (2008). Available online at http://www.education.gov.za/Documents/policies/System-Planning/norms%20and%20standards.pdf (accessed on 12 January 2010).

99 2008 (1) SA 474 (CC), 2008 (2) BCLR 99 (CC).

100 Ibid para 123.

101 Ibid para 124.

102 Section 39 of the Schools Act 84 of 1996 read with the regulations entitled 'The Exemption of Parents from the Payment of School Fees' Government Notice 1293, *Government Gazette* 19347, October 1998.

103 See, for example, International Covenant on Economic, Social and Cultural Rights (1966) arts 13(2)(*a*) and 14; UN Committee on Economic, Social and Cultural Rights, General Comment No 11 (Twentieth sess 1999) *Plans of Action for Primary Education* UN doc E/2000/22 para 7; General Comment No 13 (note 88 above); UN Convention on the Rights of the Child (note 2 above) art 28(1)(*a*); African Charter on the Rights and Welfare of the Child (note 2 above) art 11(3)(*a*).

104 S Wilson 'Out of site, out of mind: Relocation and access to schools in Sol Plaatje' (2003). Available at http://web.wits.ac.za/Academic/Centres/CALS/Education/ResearchReports.htm (accessed on 27 April 2009).

The problems associated with the implementation of the system of exemption from school fees have been extensively documented both in research[105] and in litigation proceedings.[106] It can be argued that fees make schooling economically inaccessible for many poor learners. Faranaaz Veriava and Fons Coomans argue further that the system of charging school fees unfairly discriminates against poor learners on the basis of both race and class:

> Since schools are reliant on school fees to supplement school budgets, those schools in wealthier communities are able to raise funds through school fees that will be able to provide learners with the sufficient facilities necessary for a basic education, while those schools situated in poor communities where parents cannot pay school fees will not be able to provide such facilities. This, it is argued, has resulted in the 're-stratification' of public schools because it creates and reinforces apartheid era class and race inequalities.[107]

The Department of Education has responded to these evident shortcomings in the system of school fees by introducing a new policy framework.[108] The revised policy provides for the concept of 'fee free' schools for the poorest two quintiles.[109] These schools are guaranteed an 'adequate' budgetary allocation from provincial govern-

---

105 See the literature and research discussed by F Veriava & F Coomans 'The right to education' (note 93 above) 68–71; F Veriava 'The amended legal framework for school fees and school funding: A boon or a barrier' (2007) 23 *SAJHR* 180–194 at 183–186; D Roithmayr 'Access, adequacy and equality: The constitutionality of school fee financing in public education' (2003) 19 *SAJHR* 382–429. For an account of the contestation surrounding the interpretation of educational rights in policy-making in South Africa, see S Wilson 'Taming the Constitution: Rights and reform in the South African education system' (2004) 20 *SAJHR* 418–447.

106 See, for example, *Centre for Applied Legal Studies v Hunt Secondary School*, Case No 10091/2006, 15 June 2007 (ZAKZNHC). This case was brought as a class action suit and in the public interest on behalf of poor learners attending the respondent school concerning the inadequate implementation of the exemption system. A comprehensive settlement was reached in this matter just prior to argument, and was made an order of court by consent. Order available at http://web.wits.ac.za/NR/rdonlyres/5D8CF2A2-1D6F-42A6-B88D-EF0514E8DA6E/0/HuntRoad_Consent_Order.doc (accessed 27 April 2009). See further F Veriava 'Enforcing the current laws on school fees' (2003) 4(2) *ESR Review* 6–11.

107 F Veriava & F Coomans 'The right to education' (note 93 above) 70. See further D Roithmayr (note 105 above). For an alternative perspective on the constitutionality of school fees, see B Fleisch & S Woolman 'On the constitutionality of school fees: A qualified defence' (2004) 22 *Perspectives in Education* 111–123; Woolman & Fleisch (note 89 above) chapter 7.

108 The background and policy considerations informing this policy shift can be found in: Department of Education *Plan of Action: Improving Access to Free and Quality Basic Education* (14 June 2003). Available at http://www.info.gov.za/view/DownloadFileAction?id=70189 (accessed on 27 April 2009).

109 The aim is to extend the 'no fee' schools to 60% of schools. See the Minister of Finance, Budget Speech, 2009. Available at http://www.treasury.gov.za/documents/national%20 budget/2009/speech/speech.pdf (accessed on 27 April 2009).

ments to compensate for their inability to charge school fees.[110] For the remaining schools, it is permissible to continue charging fees, but subject to an improved exemption system which includes greater protections against various forms of discrimination in the schooling system experienced by learners whose parents struggle to pay school fees.[111] The constitutionality of this new legislative and policy framework pertaining to school fees remains to be tested.

5.3.2 Further and higher education

In contrast to the right to basic education, everyone's right to 'further education' is internally qualified. Thus the state must, 'through reasonable measures', make this right 'progressively available and accessible'.[112] Given the similar phrasing to that encountered in ss 26(2) and 27(2) it is likely that the courts will apply a similar standard of 'reasonableness' review to evaluate compliance with the obligations imposed by the right to further education.[113] Although the phrase 'within its available resources' does not appear in s 29(1)(*b*), genuine and substantiated resources constraints are implicit in an evaluation of the reasonableness of the State's acts or omissions.[114]

Veriava and Coomans argue that, despite legislative distinctions relating to further and higher education,[115] the right should be interpreted to encompass all education of a higher level than basic education, including higher education.[116] While international standards do not require further education to be provided free, they support 'the progressive introduction of free education', particularly secondary education.[117]

---

[110] These school allocations are based on national per learner funding norms and minimum standards which establish the amount that provinces ought to allocate per learner in each quintile. The national department also sets an 'adequacy benchmark', which it considers the minimally adequate amount for a learner's right to a basic education to be fulfilled.

[111] See s 41(5) of the South African Schools Act 84 of 1996. For a critical evaluation of the new policy framework in respect of school fees, see F Veriava (note 105 above) 187–194.

[112] Section 29(1)(*b*).

[113] On reasonableness review, see chapter 4, part 4.3.3.

[114] On the evaluation of resource constraints in socio-economic rights adjudication, see chapter 4, part 4.4.4.

[115] The Further Education and Training Colleges Act 16 of 2006 defines 'further education and training' as ... 'all learning and training programmes leading to qualifications at levels 2 to 4 of the National Qualifications Framework or such further education and training levels determined by SAQA and contemplated in the South African Qualifications Authority Act, 1995 (Act No. 58 of 1995), which levels are above general education but below higher education' (s 1). The Higher Education Act 101 of 1997 defines 'higher education' as 'all learning programmes leading to qualifications higher than grade 12 or its equivalent in terms of the National Qualifications Framework' (s 1). This would include universities and technikons.

[116] Veriava & Coomans (note 93 above) 74–75.

[117] Ibid. See International Covenant on Economic, Social and Cultural Rights (1966), art 13(2)(*b*) and (*c*); UN Convention on the Rights of the Child (note 2 above) art 28(1)(*b*) and (*c*); and the African Charter on the Rights and Welfare of the Child (note 2 above) art

Moreover, all forms of education should be subject to reasonable and appropriate admission criteria and policies that protect against unfair discrimination on grounds such as race,[118] gender,[119] sexual orientation, religion and culture, [120] disability,[121] and socio-economic status.[122] In this respect the right to equality protected in s 9 of the

11(3)(*b*) and (*c*). Higher education should also be economically accessible to students with academic potential and aptitude: see in this regard, UN Committee on Economic, Social and Cultural Rights, General Comment No 13 (note 88 above) paras 11–14.

[118] *Matukane v Laerskool Potgietersrus* 1996 (3) SA 223 (T), [1996] 1 All SA 468 (T). The school concerned had rejected black learners' application to a parallel medium primary school on the basis that it would detrimentally affect the Afrikaans culture and ethos of the school. The Court found that this policy unlawfully discriminated against pupils on the basis of their race.

[119] This could include, for example, the exclusion of pregnant learners from schooling, although appropriate adaptations may have to be made to accommodate their special situation and needs. The African Charter on the Rights and Welfare of the Child (note 2 above) requires that 'States Parties ... shall take all appropriate measures to ensure that children who become pregnant before completing their education have an opportunity to continue with their education on the basis of their individual ability' (art 11(6)). The Department of Education has adopted a policy entitled *Measures for the Prevention and Management of Learner Pregnancy* (2007). Available at http://www.doh.gov.za/docs/measures-pregnancy-f.html (accessed on 27 April 2009).

[120] See, for example, the Constitutional Court's decision in *MEC for Education: KwaZulu-Natal v Pillay* (note 99 above). In this case, the Court held schools were obliged to adjust their uniform codes and other policies so as to reasonably accommodate sincerely held religious and cultural forms of expression. The case concerned the prohibition imposed by a public school in terms of its Code of Conduct of the wearing of a nose stud by a Hindu pupil. The Court affirmed that a society such as ours which 'values dignity, equality and freedom must therefore require people to act positively to accommodate diversity' (para 75).

[121] This could include, for example, unequal educational access and provisioning for children with special educational needs. On the equal right of children and adults with autism to education, see the decision of the European Committee of Social Rights in terms of the Revised European Social Charter (1996) in *International Association Autism-Europe v France* Complaint No 13/2002 (European Committee on Social Rights). Available at http://www.coe.int/t/dghl/monitoring/socialcharter/Complaints/CC13Merits_en.pdf (accessed on 27 April 2009).

[122] The ground of socio-economic status (possibly in combination with other grounds such as race) could possibly form the basis of a challenge to the implementation of school fees policies and the secondary costs associated with schooling which have a disparate impact on learners from impoverished families. The ground of 'socio-economic status' is included as a directive principle in s 34 of the Promotion of Equality and Prevention of Unfair Discrimination Act 4 of 2000. It is defined to include 'a socio-economic condition or perceived condition of a person who is disadvantaged by poverty, low employment status or lack of or low-level educational qualifications' (s 1(1)(xxvi)). On the interrelationship between equality and socio-economic rights, see chapter 4, part 4.5.

Constitution together with the Promotion of Equality and Prevention of Unfair Discrimination Act 4 of 2000 complements the educational rights protected in s 29.

5.3.3 Education in the language of one's choice

Section 29(3) entrenches the right of everyone to receive education 'in the official languages of their choice in public educational institutions where that right is reasonably practicable'. It goes on to provide:

> In order to ensure the effective access to, and implementation of, this right, the state must consider all reasonable educational alternatives, including single medium institutions, taking into account –
> (*a*) equity;
> (*b*) practicability; and
> (*c*) the need to redress the results of past racially discriminatory laws and practices.

The tortuous nature of this provision is the product of a compromise in the constitutional negotiations between the National Party's efforts to secure constitutional protection for single medium Afrikaans schools and the ANC's determination that single medium schools should not be used to perpetuate racial exclusion in education.[123] A number of judgments have sought to ensure that the maintenance of single medium Afrikaans schools do not become a pretext for racial discrimination in the admissions policy of these schools.[124] In *Laerskool Middelburg v Departementshoof, Mpumalanga Departement van Onderwys*, [125] Bertelsmann J furthermore held as follows:

> Die reg op 'n enkelmedium openbare onderwysinstelling is duidelik ondergeskik aan die reg wat elke Suid-Afrikaner het op onderwys in 'n sodanige instelling en moet wyk wanneer daar 'n duidelike bewese behoefte bestaan om onderwysfasiliteite met ander kultuur gemeenskappe te deel.[126]

The Schools Act 84 of 1996 read together with the *Norms and Standards Regarding Language Policy in Public Schools*[127] (hereafter 'the Norms and Standards') seeks to give effect to the obligations in s 29(3) of the Constitution. In terms of s 6(2) of the Act,

---

[123] See B Fleisch & S Woolman 'On the constitutionality of single-medium public schools' (2007) 23 *SAJHR* 34–67 at 37–38. The authors also provide a useful overview of the historical significance of educational language issues in the South African context.

[124] *Matukane v Laerskool Potgietersrus* (note 118 above); *Laerskool Middelburg v Departementshoof, Mpumalanga Departement van Onderwys* 2003 (4) SA 160 (T), [2002] 4 All SA 745 (T); *Seodin Primary School v MEC Education, Northern Cape* 2006 (4) BCLR 542 (NC), [2006] 1 All SA 154 (NC); *High School Ermelo v The Head of Department* [2008] 1 All SA 139 (T).

[125] Ibid.

[126] Ibid 173F. ('The right to a single-medium public educational institution is clearly subordinate to the right which every South African has to education in a similar institution and has to make way where there is a clearly proven need to share educational facilities with other cultural societies. ')

[127] Government Notice R1701, *Government Gazette* 18546, December 1997. These norms are promulgated in terms of s 6(1) of the Schools Act which provides that the Minister of Education may, subject to the Constitution and the Act, by notice in the *Government*

the governing body of a public school 'may determine the language policy of the school subject to the Constitution, this Act, and any applicable provincial law'.[128] According to the Norms and Standards, it is 'reasonably practicable to provide education in a particular language of learning and teaching if at least 40 in Grades 1 to 6 or 35 in Grades 7 to 12 learners in a particular grade request in a particular school'.[129]

In *Minister of Education, Western Cape v Governing Body of Mikro Primary School* ('*Mikro*'),[130] the Supreme Court of Appeal held that the function of determining the language policy of a public school vested, in terms of s 6(2) of the Schools Act, with the governing body of that school, subject to the Constitution, the Act and any applicable provincial law. Section 6(1) of the Schools Act authorises the Minister of Education to determine norms and standards for language policy in public schools, but it does not authorise the Minister 'him- or herself to determine the language policy of particular schools, nor does it authorise him or her to authorise any other person or body to do so'.[131] The Court held that s 29(2) was a right against the State.[132] The State was obliged to give effect to this right by considering various reasonable educational alternatives, including single medium institutions. According to Streicher JA:

> This is clear indication that, in terms of s 29(2), everyone has a right to be educated in an official language of his or her choice at a public educational institution to be provided by the State if reasonably practicable, but not the right to be so instructed at each and every public educational institution subject only to it being reasonably practicable to do so.[133]

The Court accordingly held that the provincial education authorities did not have the right to instruct the principal of a school to admit certain learners, and to have them taught in English contrary to the single medium Afrikaans policy of the school as determined by its governing body. Such actions were unlawful, and the appeal against the setting aside of these decisions by the court *a quo* was dismissed.[134] The court *a quo's* order that the 21 learners who had been admitted to the Mikro school by the department against the wishes of the principal and governing body were to be placed by the department at another suitable school (or schools) was also upheld.

Gazette, after consultation with the Council of Education Ministers, determine norms and standards for language policy in public schools.

[128] Another of the functions of the governing body of a public school is to determine the admission policy of a public school. See s 5(5) of the Schools Act.

[129] Ibid s D3.

[130] 2006 (1) SA 1 (SCA), 2005 (10) BCLR 973 (SCA).

[131] Ibid para 33. In this regard, the SCA expressly disapproved of Bertelsmann J's interpretation of the Norms and Standards as providing a mechanism for the alteration of the language policy of a public school. See *Laerskool Middelburg v Departementshoof, Mpumulanga Departement van Onderwys* (note 124 above) 170I–171A and 171J–172A.

[132] Ibid para 31.

[133] Ibid.

[134] The Court *a quo*'s judgment is reported as *Governing Body, Mikro Primary School v Minister of Education, Western Cape* 2005 (3) SA 504 (C), 2005 (10) BCLR 973 (C).

The right of the governing bodies of public schools to establish their language policy free from interference by provincial educational authorities was again considered by the Supreme Court of Appeal in *Hoërskool Ermelo v Head of Department of Education, Mpumalanga.*[135] The case concerned attempts by the provincial department of education to require a school with a single medium Afrikaans policy to admit learners to the school to be taught in English. It had become 'evident that there was a need for English tuition in the Ermelo circuit beyond the available capacity'.[136] When the principal and governing body of the school refused to admit English-speaking learners, the department appointed an interim committee to determine the language policy of Hoërskool Ermelo in order to make it possible 'for the 113 learners who cannot be accommodated elsewhere to attend the school'.[137]

A letter was also sent in advising the school that the head of department had decided to withdraw, in terms of s 22 of the Schools Act, the function of the governing body to determine the language policy of the school.[138] The interim committee proceeded to change the language policy of the school to English and Afrikaans ('parallel medium') teaching and learning. Twenty learners were admitted in 2007 in terms of the amended policy and were being taught in English at the school.[139] The validity of the decisions of the department to withdraw the function of the governing body to determine the language policy of the school and to appoint an interim committee to determine the language policy, and the decision of the interim committee to amend the language policy of the school from Afrikaans medium to parallel medium were challenged.

Snyders JA for the Court stated at the outset that the case was not 'as at first blush appears, about language policy at schools, a highly emotive issue in the South African context, but rather about the principle of legality and proper exercise of administrative power'.[140] Her judgment turns on the interpretation of the department's powers in terms of the Schools Act. She held that the department's power to withdraw the functions of a governing body on reasonable grounds applies only to the additional functions which a governing body may apply to the head of department to be allocated in terms of s 21 of the Schools Act. It does not apply to the function of the governing body to determine the language policy of a school. The Court reasoned thus:

> The Act authorises only the governing body to determine the language policy of an existing school and nobody else. As nobody else is empowered to exercise that function, it is inconceivable that s 22 was intended to give the head of department the power

[135] 2009 (3) SA 422 (SCA). This was an appeal against a full bench of the High Court (Ngoepe JP, Seriti J and Ranchod AJ): *High School Ermelo v The Head of Department* (note 124 above).

[136] Ibid para 6.

[137] Ibid para 11.

[138] Ibid. Section 22 permits the Head of Department, on reasonable grounds and subject to a number of procedural requirements, to withdraw a function of a governing body.

[139] Ibid para 13.

[140] *Hoërskool Ermelo v Head of Department of Education, Mpumalanga* (note 135 above) para 3.

> to withdraw that function, albeit on reasonable grounds, and appoint somebody else to perform it, without saying so explicitly.[141]

In this regard, the Supreme Court of Appeal expressly overruled its *obiter dictum* in the *Mikro* case in which it held that the department's remedies if a governing body unreasonably refused to change its language policy lay in the use of ss 22 and 25 of the Schools Act.[142] Snyders JA held that s 25 of the Act could not be relied on by the department as authority for the establishment of an interim committee to perform the function of the governing body and change the language policy of the school. The jurisdictional prerequisite for such a step is if the Head of Department has reasonable grounds for determining that a governing body 'has ceased to perform functions allocated to it in terms of this Act or has failed to perform one or more of such functions'.[143] In the present case the facts did not support a reasonable conclusion that the governing body had ceased to determine the language policy of the school.[144]

The Court rejected an interpretation of the Act that would permit the department to withdraw the function of the governing body to determine the language policy of a school in terms of s 22 and then determine that the governing body has ceased to exercise this function, thereby triggering the right to appoint an interim committee in terms of s 25. According to Snyders JA such an interpretation 'enables a functionary to abuse power and makes possible indirectly that which cannot be attained directly'.[145]

She further held that the decision of the interim committee to change the language policy of the school violated the Promotion of Administrative Justice Act 3 of 2000 ('PAJA'). Their decision had not been taken independently of the department's instruction to 'ensure that the Language policy determined by [them] will enable the learners to be admitted at Hoërskool Ermelo as a matter of urgency'.[146] In terms of the Hoërskool Ermelo judgment, the only remedy for the provincial education authorities if they are dissatisfied with the language policy determined by the governing body of a school is to apply for a review of the language policy if they can make out a case in terms of PAJA.[147] The Court accordingly set aside the various decisions of the educational department and of the interim committee. It did, however, order that the learners who had been enrolled at the school in terms of the parallel medium language policy would be entitled to be taught and write their examinations in English until the completion of their school careers.[148]

---

[141] Ibid para 21.
[142] Ibid paras 23–30. See also the separate concurring judgment of Brand JA.
[143] Section 25(1) of the Schools Act.
[144] *Hoërskool Ermelo v Head of Department of Education, Mpumalanga* (note 135 above) para 27.
[145] Ibid.
[146] Ibid para 31.
[147] Ibid para 32.
[148] Ibid. Order, para 34.

The interpretation of the Schools Act by the Supreme Court of Appeal gives national and provincial educational authorities very narrow grounds for intervening in the language policy determined by the governing body of a public school if they are of the opinion that it does not give proper effect to s 29(2) of the Constitution.

It is important to note that s 29(2) of the Constitution does not confer upon schools the right to maintain single medium institutions. The latter are one of the mechanisms which may be considered to give effect to the right of everyone to receive education in the official language or languages of their choice in public educational institutions. However, the criteria which must guide the choice of a particular mechanism in terms of s 29(2) are equity, practicability, and the need to redress the results of past racially discriminatory laws and practices. In addition, the provisions of s 29 must be read holistically so that the choice of a particular mechanism to give effect to language rights in education in terms of s 29(2) should not undermine the unqualified right of everyone to a basic education, or reasonable access to further education in terms of s 29(1). Thus a determination of language policy by the governing body of a school which fails to take into account all the aforesaid criteria is subject to review in terms of PAJA on the grounds that relevant considerations were not considered,[149] alternatively, that the decision is unconstitutional or unlawful.[150]

A further alternative is the amendment of the provisions of the Schools Act to provide a clearer basis and mechanisms for holding schools accountable for complying with their constitutional obligations in terms of s 29(2). For example, where the maintenance of the single language policy of a school effectively deprived pupils in the area of their rights to education in a language of their choice or perpetuated the racial legacy of apartheid education, educational authorities and learners should be entitled to require that the school make provision for teaching and learning in other languages. Single medium public schools should not constitute a justification for the continuation of racially exclusive public schools. This undermines the criterion of equity in s 29(2) and certainly runs counter to the Constitution's express commitment to fostering diversity.[151] As O'Regan J observes in *MEC for Education: KwaZulu-Natal v Pillay*:

> Many Black learners are educated in township schools where there are generally no White learners at all. Many White learners are educated in schools where there is only a sprinkling of Black learners. The absence of racial integration in our schools remains a problem for us all. It deprives young South Africans of the ability to meet, and to learn and play together.[152]

---

[149] Section 6(2)(*e*)(iii) of PAJA.

[150] Section 6(2)(*i*) of PAJA.

[151] In *MEC for Education: KwaZulu-Natal v Pillay* (note 99 above) para 65, Langa CJ observed that the Constitution's commitment to affirming diversity 'is totally in accord with this nation's decisive break from its history of intolerance and exclusion'. He goes further by stating that our constitutional project 'not only affirms diversity, but promotes and celebrates it' (ibid). See also *Minister of Home Affairs v Fourie; Lesbian and Gay Equality Project v Minister of Home Affairs* 2006 (1) SA 524 (CC), 2006 (3) BCLR 355 (CC) para 60.

[152] Note 99 above, para 124.

A strong case can be made that racially exclusive education undermines the pedagogic goals of education which include preparing learners to function effectively in a diverse, multicultural society and global context.[153] The maintenance of single medium schools should also not have the effect of perpetuating class-based inequalities in education. Thus poor families should not be precluded from choosing public schools for their children which offer a superior quality education (or simply education of an acceptable quality) to that offered by another school in the area which caters for the language preferences of their children. This outcome would similarly be inconsistent with the guiding criteria of equity and the need for redress in determining the language policy of schools.

Public schools should not be permitted to maintain language policies which have the effect of excluding poor, black learners. A full bench of the High Court in the *Hoërskool Ermelo* case suggested that this was the attitude of the school, and underscored its inconsistency with the constitutional values of redress and equal access to public institutions:

> It is clear that the attitude of the applicants is to consign learners wanting to be taught in English to any conditions anywhere, as long as they do not set foot at their school. This is a callous attitude towards the educational interests of learners from other sections of the communities. It is reminiscent of the pre-democratic era, when the educational rights of white learners were better catered for than those of learners of a different colour. Under the present constitution, all learners have equal rights to state facilities irrespective of language or colour.[154]

The underlying purposes of the right to education in the official language of one's choice are to enable children to be schooled in the language that is most conducive to their educational progress and to foster linguistic diversity. However, there are other important objectives of educational rights including equitable access to quality education, and training learners to function effectively and to be respectful of difference in a racially and culturally diverse society. Section 29(2) enjoins public schools and educational authorities to take all these considerations into account in formulating balanced and fair language policies.[155] It does not mandate the perpetuation of homogenous and exclusive educational enclaves under the guise of language rights.

---

153 According to the International Covenant on Economic, Social and Cultural Rights (1966) 'education shall enable all persons to participate effectively in a free society, promote understanding, tolerance and friendship among all nations and all racial, ethnic or religious groups, and further the activities of the United Nations for the maintenance of peace' (art 13(1)). See also UN Convention on the Rights of the Child (note 2 above) art 29(1)(*d*).

154 Note 124 above, para 66.

155 As the Constitutional Court noted in *In re School Education Bill of 1995* (note 85 above) para 52:

> The theme of reducing the discrepancies in the life chances of all South Africans runs right through the Constitution. ... Thus the dominant theme of the Constitution is the achievement of equality, while considerable importance is also given to cultural diversity and language rights,

5.3.4 Independent educational institutions

The final subsection of s 29 gives everyone the right 'to establish and maintain, at their own expense, independent educational institutions' subject to certain conditions.[156] Such institutions (*a*) may not discriminate on the basis of race; (*b*) must be registered with the state; and (*c*) must maintain standards that are not inferior to standards at comparable public educational institutions.[157]

Section 29(3) clarifies that there is no right to State support for private educational institutions although, in terms of s 29(4), the State is not precluded from providing subsidies. In interpreting s 32(*c*) of the interim Constitution, the Constitutional Court held that there was no State obligation to support schools based on a common culture, language or religion.[158] This provision establishes '*a defensive right* to a person who seeks to establish such educational institutions and it protects that right from invasion by the state, without conferring on the state an obligation to establish such educational institutions'.[159] This interpretation has been placed beyond doubt in the drafting of s 29(3) of the 1996 Constitution, and is also in accordance with international law in this field.[160] There is thus no positive obligation on the State to support schools based on a particular language, religious or cultural affiliation.

Although the State is at liberty to provide financial support to such schools in terms of s 29(4), it must ensure that the support does not amount to unfair discrimination against schools based on a prohibited ground of discrimination. Such unfair discrimination could include privileging certain schools of a particular language or religious affiliation in granting financial support.[161] However, providing differential financial support to independent schools based on their socio-economic circumstances and needs would represent a manifestation of substantive equality, and would not amount to unfair discrimination.[162]

---

so the basic problem is to secure equality in a balanced way which shows maximum regard for diversity.

After the finalisation of this manuscript, the Constitutional Court handed down judgment in an appeal by the Department of Education against the Supreme Court of Appeal's judgment. See the postscript, chapter 9 part 9.2.

156 See S Woolman 'Defending discrimination: On the constitutionality of independent schools that promote a particular, if not comprehensive, vision of the good life' (2007) 22 *Stell LR* 31–52.

157 Section 29(3).

158 Section 32(*c*) of the interim Constitution provides that every person shall have the right 'to establish, where practicable, educational institutions based on a common culture, language or religion, provided that there shall be no discrimination on the ground of race.'

159 *In re School Education Bill of 1995 (Gauteng)* (note 85 above) para 7.

160 Ibid paras 45–90. See also the decision of the UN Human Rights Committee, *Waldman v Canada*, Comm No 694/1996, Report of the Human Rights Committee, Vol II, General Assembly Official Records, Fifty-fifth Sess Suppl No 40 (A/55/40) 86–101 para 10.6.

161 See *Waldman* ibid.

162 See also the analysis by Veriava & Coomans (note 93 above) 80–81.

5.3.5 Conclusion

There can be little doubt that post-apartheid society has failed to transform the education system in accordance with the constitutional dictates of social justice. Fifteen years since the end of apartheid, the South African education system still manifests deep, systemic inequalities based largely on class and race. Of particular concern is the fact that millions of impoverished black children still receive an inferior quality education in overcrowded, under-resourced public schools.[163]

In contrast to the sphere of housing and health rights, there have been very few test cases dealing with the right to education in s 29. The majority of cases have dealt with access by English-speaking learners to schools which have sought to rely on s 29(2) of the Constitution to retain their single medium Afrikaans status. While access to existing educational institutions is clearly a critical issue in the transformation of South Africa's education system, the potential of s 29(1) to stimulate an improvement in both the quantity and quality of educational provisioning in South Africa remains to be realised. This includes the building of more schools, the improvement of educational resources available to disadvantaged schools, and the training and employment of more and better qualified educators in these schools.

Finally, good educational outcomes for disadvantaged learners depend on the realisation of a number of other rights such as adequate nutrition, decent housing and a safe and secure learning environment.[164] This underscores the fact that none of the rights can be realised in isolation, given their interdependence.[165]

5.4 PERSONS DEPRIVED OF THEIR LIBERTY

5.4.1 Interpreting section 35(2)(*e*)

Section 35(2)(*e*) of the Constitution guarantees to everyone who is detained, including every sentenced prisoner, the right 'to conditions of detention that are consistent with human dignity, including at least exercise and the provision, at state expense, of adequate accommodation, nutrition, reading material and medical treatment'.[166] The formulation of this provision suggests that it extends to all persons who are detained, including awaiting trial prisoners, prisoners serving a custodial sentence, juveniles in

---

[163] See the analysis and evidence cited by Woolman & Fleisch (note 89 above) on the inadequacies and inequities in the provision of basic education in South Africa: chapter 5 at 137–150.

[164] See, for example, the study by Budlender and Woolard on the positive impact of social assistance grants on children's schooling: D Budlender & I Woolard *The Impact of the South African Child Support and Old Age Grants on Children's Schooling and Work* (2006).

[165] On the interdependence between rights, see chapter 2, part 2.4.3.

[166] Section 35(2)(*f*) also entitles detained persons to communicate with, and be visited by various persons, including that person's chosen medical practitioner.

reform schools or schools of industry, or persons detained in mental health facilities in terms of the provisions of the Mental Health Care Act 17 of 2002.[167]

Like the children's socio-economic rights in s 28(1)(*c*), the rights in s 35(2)(*e*) are not qualified with reference to the criteria contained in ss 26(2) and 27(2). This suggests that prisoners enjoy a direct and immediate entitlement to the goods and services guaranteed by this provision. It further implies that the evaluation of limitations to these rights, for example based on resource constraints, should occur in terms of the stringent requirements of the general limitations clause (s 36).[168] In addition, the section provides a clear standard against which the State's acts and omissions in relation to the socio-economic conditions of prisoners are to be evaluated. These conditions must be 'consistent with human dignity'. They include 'at least' the various services and goods listed in s 35(2)(*e*), but extend beyond this to incorporate whatever goods and services are necessary to ensure conditions of detention that are consistent with human dignity. As observed by Kruger J in *Huang v Head of Grootvlei Prison*:[169]

> The right to humane conditions of detention and the specific duties in section 35(2)(*e*) encompass a minimum set of duties as indicated by the words, 'including at least'.

The purpose of s 35(2)(*e*) is to prescribe a basic minimum standard of provisioning for a particular group who, due to the fact of their detention, are in a particularly vulnerable position. Failure to fulfil this standard is a limitation of the relevant right and requires a compelling justification in terms of s 36. The strong constitutional protection afforded to the socio-economic rights of persons deprived of their liberty is appropriate, given the vulnerabilities of their particular situation. In the first place, prisoners and persons detained in mental health care facilities are totally dependent on the State for the fulfilment of all their basic needs.[170] The fact that they are detained

---

[167] On the rights of persons with mental illnesses or disabilities, see further the *UN Principles for the Protection of Persons with Mental Illness and the Improvement of Mental Illnesses and the Improvement of Mental Health Care* General Assembly Res 46/119, 46 UN General Assembly Official Records Supp (No 49) 189, UN doc A/46/49 (1991); UN Declaration on the Rights of Disabled Persons, General Assembly Res 3447, 1975; UN Committee on Economic Social and Cultural Rights, General Comment No 5 (Eleventh sess, 1994), *Persons with disabilities* UN doc E/1995/22 paras 33–34; United Nations Convention on the Rights of Persons with Disabilities (2006) art 14(2).

[168] See also the views of M Pieterse 'The potential of socio-economic rights litigation for the achievement of social justice: Considering the example of access to medical care in South African prisons' (2006) 50 *Journal of African Law* 118–131 at 121–123; J C Mubangizi 'Public health, the South African Bill of Rights and the socio-economic polemic' (2002) 35 *TSAR* 343–352 at 349.

[169] Case No 992/2003 (ZAFSHC) (unreported judgment of 15 May 2003) para 30. The views of N Steytler in *Constitutional Criminal Procedure* (1998) at 192 are cited with approval in this regard.

[170] As noted by Pillay J in *N v Government of the Republic of South Africa* (No 1) 2006 (6) SA 543 (D), 2007 (1) BCLR 84 (D) at para 7: 'Incarcerated persons are wards of the State' (para 7).

already constitutes a limitation (albeit justified) of their rights to human dignity and freedom of the person. Moreover, in the South African context it is well known that conditions in prisons[171] and mental health facilities[172] are generally poor.

Prisoners are incarcerated in conditions of serious overcrowding which expose them to a lack of privacy and security of the person, and exposure to HIV and other diseases. HIV-positive prisoners are particularly vulnerable as prison conditions increase their risk of being exposed to a range of opportunistic infections.[173] Moreover, the status of being a prisoner or mental health care patient carries significant social stigma. As Pieterse notes, prisoners in particular are widely regarded as undeserving of constitutional protection, particularly when they receive services or treatment to which many in the general populace lack access.[174]

5.4.2 International standards

The UN Standard Minimum Rules for the Treatment of Prisoners contain a detailed set of standards for the nature of medical services to be provided to prisoners, as well as the conditions of their detention, including facilities, food, sanitation, hygiene and exercise.[175] Although the International Covenant on Civil and Political Rights (1966)[176] does not expressly guarantee the socio-economic rights of detained persons,

---

[171] In his annual report for the period 1 April 2007 to 31 March 2008 in terms of s 90(4) of the Correctional Services Act 111 of 1998, the Acting Inspecting Judge of Prisons, Judge Ntlupheko James Yekiso states at 6:

> The JIOP [Judicial Inspectorate of Prisons] holds the views that the extent of overcrowding in our prisons remains the driving force behind many of the problems faced in our correctional system. Although good results have been recorded by government in reducing the number of prisoners from 190 180 in April 2003 to 161 639 in December 2007, most of our prisons remain heavily overcrowded resulting in inhumane conditions of detention.

The report goes on to record that of the 237 operational prisons in South Africa, 90 are occupied at levels of between 100 and 150%, 67 are occupied at levels of between 150 and 200%, and 17 are occupied at levels of more than 200% (chapter 3, 21). The report is available at: http://judicialinsp.dcs.gov.za/Annualreports/Annual%20Report%202007-2008.pdf (accessed on 1 June 2009).

[172] For example, staff/bed ratios in South African mental health services are considerably lower than those in developed countries. See C Lund & A J Flisher 'Staff/bed and staff/patient ratios in South African public sector mental health services' (2002) 92 *SAMJ* 161–164; C Lund & A J Flisher 'Community/hospital indicators in South African public sector mental health services' (2003) 6 *The Journal of Mental Health Policy and Economics* 181–187.

[173] See the observations of Pillay J in *N v Government of the Republic of South Africa* (No 1) (note 170 above) para 29.

[174] M Pieterse (note 168 above) 121–122, 128.

[175] Standard Minimum Rules for the Treatment of Prisoners, adopted by the First United Nations Congress on the Prevention of Crime and the Treatment of Offenders (1955) and approved by the Economic and Social Council, Res 663C, 31 July 1957, and 2076, 13 May 1977, particularly Rules 8–26. See also the Basic Principles for the Treatment of Prisoners adopted and proclaimed by General Assembly Res 45/111 of 14 December 1990.

[176] Ratified by South Africa on 10 December 1998.

the UN Committee on Civil and Political Rights (which supervises States Parties' obligations under the Covenant) has held the conditions of detention and treatment of prisoners may, in certain circumstances, amount to a violation of art 7 of the Covenant which prohibits cruel, inhuman and degrading treatment.[177] This is another illustration of the interdependence between civil and political rights and socio-economic rights. According to the Committee, States Parties are under an obligation, regardless of their level of development, to ensure compliance with certain minimum standards regarding conditions of detention:

> These include, in accordance with rules 10, 12, 17, 19 and 20 of the Standard Minimum Rules for the Treatment of Prisoners, minimum floor space and cubic content of air for each prisoner, adequate sanitary facilities, clothing which shall be in no manner degrading or humiliating, provision of a separate bed and provision of food of nutritional value adequate for health and strength.[178]

These minimum requirements must be observed even under conditions of economic or budgetary constraints.[179]

In *Purohit & Moore v The Gambia*,[180] the African Commission on Human and Peoples' Rights considered a communication concerning outdated mental health legislation and poor conditions of detention of mental health patients detained in a psychiatric facility. The Commission affirmed its previous jurisprudence that exposing persons to 'personal suffering and indignity' violated their right to human dignity.[181] The Commission found that the relevant legislation and conditions of detention violated the right to respect for human dignity and the prohibition of cruel, inhuman or degrading treatment contained in art 5 of the African Charter on Human and Peoples' Rights (1981).[182]

It also considered the applicability of art 16 of the African Charter which confers on every individual 'the right to enjoy the best attainable state of physical and mental health'. States Parties are obligated to 'take the necessary measures to protect the health of their people and to ensure that they receive medical attention when they are sick'.[183] Article 18(4) states that: 'The aged and disabled shall also have the right to special measures of protection in keeping with their physical or moral needs.' The Commission noted the realities in many African countries where resource constraints inhibit the full enjoyment of the right to health. It accordingly read into art 16 an obligation on [the] part of States Parties to the African Charter 'to take concrete and targeted steps, while

177 *Albert Womah Mukong v Cameroon*, Comm No 458/1991, Report of the Human Rights Committee, Vol II, General Assembly Official Records, Forty-ninth Sess Suppl No 40 (A/49/40) para 9.4.

178 Ibid para 9.3.

179 Ibid.

180 (2003) AHRLR 96 (ACHPR 2003).

181 Ibid para 58 (referring to its decision in *John K. Modise v Botswana*, Comm No 97/93 (2000) paras 59–61).

182 Ratified by South Africa on 9 July 1996.

183 Articles 16(1) and (2).

taking full advantage of its available resources, to ensure that the right to health is fully realised in all its aspects without discrimination of any kind'.[184]

The Commission found that the scheme of the 'Lunatics Detention Act' (the principal legislation governing mental health in The Gambia) was 'lacking in terms of therapeutic objectives as well as the provision of matching resources and programmes of treatment of persons with mental disabilities'.[185] Moreover, the steps that the State had taken to improve the nature of care given to mental health patients were insufficient. In addition to arts 5, 16 and 18(4), the Commission found violations of arts 2 (non-discrimination), 3 (equality before the law), 7(1)(*a*) and (*c*) (the right to have one's cause heard), and 13(1) (the right of all citizens to participate freely in the government of their country) of the Charter. It recommended the repeal of the Lunatics Detention Act and its replacement with new human rights compliant legislation, as well as the provision of adequate medical and material care for persons suffering from mental health problems. This decision of the African Commission affirms the rights of persons with mental disabilities to be detained in conditions consistent with human dignity. The right to health in the African Charter on Human and Peoples' Rights is interpreted to place positive obligations on the State to ensure adequate material and therapeutic conditions to mental health patients.

5.4.3 South African common law and legislation

According to the South African common law, prisoners retain all their basic rights and liberties save those expressly abridged by law or necessarily incompatible with the fact of their detention.[186] This is consistent with the UN Basic Principles for the Treatment of Prisoners (1990) which provides:[187]

> Except for those limitations that are demonstrably necessitated by the fact of incarceration, all prisoners shall retain the human rights and fundamental freedoms set out in the Universal Declaration of Human Rights, and, where the State concerned is a party, the International Covenant on Economic, Social and Cultural Rights, and the International Covenant on Civil and Political Rights and the Optional Protocol thereto, as well as such other rights as are set out in other United Nations covenants.

---

[184] *Purohit & Moore v The Gambia* (note 180 above) para 84.

[185] Ibid paras 83 and 85.

[186] *Whittaker v Roos & Bateman*; *Morant v Roos & Bateman* 1912 AD 92 at 122; *Goldberg v Minister of Prisons* 1979 (1) SA 14 (A) at 39C–F; *Minister of Justice v Hofmeyr* 1993 (3) SA 131 (A) at 141G–H. This is also referred to as the 'residuum principle': a prisoner retains all personal rights save those expressly removed or abridged by law. See generally D Van Zyl Smit *South African Prison Law and Practice* (1992).

[187] General Assembly Resolution 45/111 para 5.

As Pieterse observes, the effect of the 1996 Constitution has been to extend the 'residuum principle' of the common law to incorporate the civil, political, economic, social and cultural rights in the Bill of Rights.[188]

The socio-economic rights which the Constitution guarantees to prisoners are given concrete specification in Chapter III of the Correctional Services Act 111 of 1998. It is titled 'custody of all prisoners under conditions of human dignity'.[189] The overall purpose of the Act is to promote 'the social responsibility and human development of all prisoners and persons subject to community corrections'.[190] Chapter III regulates, among others, the conditions for the safe custody of prisoners, their admission to prison, conditions of accommodation, nutrition, hygiene, clothing and bedding, exercise, health care, contact with the community, development and support services, and access to reading material.[191]

The Correctional Services Act makes provision for the Minister of Correctional Services, with the concurrence of the Minister of Finance and the Minister of Public Works, to enter into a contract with any person to construct, finance and operate any prison or part of a prison (so-called 'joint venture prisons').[192] The contractor is obliged to enforce the sentences of the courts in the manner prescribed by the Act, to detain all prisoners 'in safe custody whilst ensuring their human dignity', and to promote 'the social responsibility and the human development of all prisoners'.[193]

The running of a prison by a contractor is subject to further controls and oversight by the Commissioner of Correctional Services.[194] The State is ultimately responsible for ensuring that the constitutional rights of prisoners are respected and fulfilled through exercising appropriate oversight and control over the running of prisons by private contractors. Moreover, in appropriate circumstances, prisoners may have direct recourse against private contractors running joint venture prisons for violations of their constitutional rights.[195]

---

188 Pieterse (note 168 above) 124. See also the observations by the Court in *August v Electoral Commission* 1999 (3) SA 1 (CC), 1999 (4) BCLR 363 (CC) paras 18–19; *S v Makwanyane* 1995 (3) SA 391 (CC), 1995 (6) BCLR 665 (CC) paras 143–144; and *Ehrlich v Minister of Correctional Services* 2009 (2) SA 373 (E) paras 7–9.

189 One of the objects of the Act in its long title is to provide for 'the custody of all prisoners under conditions of human dignity'. See also s 2(*c*) of the Act. See generally D van Zyl Smit (note 186 above).

190 Section 2(*c*).

191 See also s 41 of the Act concerning development and support services to sentenced prisoners.

192 Section 103.

193 Section 104(1).

194 See ss 104–112 of the Act.

195 Section 8(2) provides for the possibility of horizontal application of a provision in the Bill of Rights 'if, and to the extent that, it is applicable taking into account the nature of the right and the nature of any duty imposed by the right'. Where prisons are run by private contractors under a joint venture agreement, s 35(2)(*e*) of the Constitution could ground a cause of action against the relevant private contractor, either separately or jointly with the

The Mental Health Care Act 17 of 2002 also regulates the conditions of admission, treatment and care to be provided to mental health care users, and specifies that their person, human dignity and privacy must be respected.[196]

5.4.4 Relevant jurisprudence

There have been a number of High Court decisions enforcing the socio-economic rights of prisoners protected in s 35(2)(*e*) of the Constitution. In *Van Biljon v Minister of Correctional Services*,[197] the Western Cape High Court, Cape Town, directed the respondents to supply two HIV-positive applicants with antiretroviral medication which had been prescribed for them in fulfilment of their right to be provided with adequate medical treatment at State expense.

The Court held that HIV-positive prisoners were more vulnerable than those living with HIV outside the prison context because of their heightened exposure to opportunistic infections due to overcrowding and the prevalence of tuberculosis and pneumonia in prison.[198] This justified providing them with treatment 'which is better able to improve their immune systems than that which the State provides for HIV patients outside.'[199] Thus the standard of adequate medical treatment for HIV-positive prisoners could not per se be determined by what the State provides for HIV patients in the general population.[200]

The Court was somewhat equivocal on the role that budgetary factors should play in interpreting the guarantee of 'adequate medical treatment' in s 35(2)(*e*). On the one hand, it held that resource constraints could not justify treatment that did not meet the standard of 'adequacy'.[201] On the other hand, the Court held that resource availability was nonetheless relevant in determining what constituted 'adequate' medical treatment:

> What is 'adequate medical treatment' cannot be determined in vacuo. In determining what is 'adequate', regard must be had to, *inter alia*, what the State can afford. If the prison authorities should, therefore, make out a case that as a result of budgetary constraints they cannot afford a particular form of medical treatment or that the provision of such medical treatment would place an unwarranted burden on the State, the Court may very well decide that the less effective medical treatment which is affordable to the State must in the circumstances be accepted as 'sufficient' or 'adequate medical treatment'.[202]

State. Moreover, in terms of s 39(2) of the Constitution, the development of common law delictual remedies in this context should be informed by the 'spirit, purport and objects' of s 35(2)(*e*). On the application of socio-economic to private actors, see chapter 7.

196 See ss 6(1), 8(1), (2) and (3) and 9–18 of the Act.

197 1997 (4) SA 441 (C), 1997 (6) BCLR 789 (C).

198 Ibid para 54.

199 Ibid.

200 Ibid para 55.

201 Ibid para 49.

202 Ibid.

Nevertheless, the Court found that anti-retroviral therapy was the internationally recognised medical treatment for HIV-positive patients, and that without this treatment the immune system of the patient would inexorably deteriorate, leading to opportunistic infections and ultimate death.[203] Moreover, the Minister had failed to make out a case that they could not afford the relevant treatment.[204] The respondents had furthermore failed to consider evidence relating to the cost-effectiveness of the provision of prophylactic antiretroviral treatment to HIV-positive persons.[205] Accordingly, the Court concluded that anti-retroviral therapy constituted the 'adequate medical treatment' to which the applicants were entitled in terms of s 35(2)(*e*) of the Constitution. The Court directed the respondents to supply the antiretroviral medication which had been prescribed to two of the applicants to them as long as such medication continued to be prescribed on medical grounds. The order was expressly limited to the anti-retroviral therapy which had been medically prescribed. The Court declined to make a general declaratory order to the effect that all HIV-positive prisoners were entitled to anti-retroviral therapy when they reached the symptomatic stage of the HIV virus or when their CD4 counts were less than 500/ml.[206]

A better reading of s 35(2)(*e*) is that the adequacy of the medical treatment should be determined in the light of the value of human dignity expressly referred to in s 35(2)(*e*), and considering relevant international and comparative law standards. Justifications, including those based on resource constraints, for failing to meet the threshold of adequacy should be evaluated in terms of s 36.[207]

The leading case thus far on the medical treatment due to prisoners under the Constitution is *N v Government of Republic of South Africa* ('*N*').[208] An application was brought by 15 HIV-positive prisoners serving sentences at the Westville Correction Centre and the Treatment Action Campaign. They sought an order that the relevant government departments immediately remove the restrictions that prevent the applicants, and all other similarly situated prisoners at Westville Correctional Centre who

---

[203] Ibid para 59.

[204] Ibid paras 56, 60.

[205] Ibid para 57.

[206] According to Brand J this would amount to dictating to medical practitioners when they must prescribe anti-retroviral therapy (ibid paras 32–34). He could also not exclude the possibility that a medical practitioner may prescribe a form of antiretroviral treatment which the respondents could show was 'unaffordable to the State and/or that there [was] less expensive but equally – or almost equally – effective anti-viral treatment available' (ibid paras 61–62). For a criticism of this aspect of the Court's order, see C Ngwena & R Cook 'Rights concerning health' in D Brand & C Heyns (eds) *Socio-Economic Rights in South Africa* (2005) 107–151 at 134. The general entitlement of HIV-positive prisoners to anti-retroviral therapy was addressed in the case of *N v Government of Republic of South Africa* (No 1) (note 170 above).

[207] See note 168 above and accompanying text. See further F ka Mdumbe 'Socio-economic rights: *Van Biljon* versus *Soobramoney*' (1998) 13 *SAPR/L* 460–470 at 469.

[208] Note 170 above.

meet the criteria as set out in the National Department of Health's *Operational Plan for Comprehensive HIV and AIDS Care, Management and Treatment for South Africa*, from accessing antiretroviral treatments at an accredited public health facility. They furthermore sought a positive order for the respondents to immediately provide such treatment in accordance with the Operational Plan. The applicants relied on both s 27 and s 35(2)(*e*) of the Constitution.[209] Resource constraints had not been raised by the respondents, their attitude being that they were complying with their obligations.[210]

Following a detailed evaluation of the evidence, the Court found that the respondents were guilty of 'dilatoriness and lack of commitment'[211] in ensuring that the applicants could access antiretroviral treatment in terms of the Operational Plan, particularly 'in circumstances where life and death mattered'.[212] The Court concluded that the respondent's implementation of the relevant laws and policies pertaining to treatment for HIV-positive persons as it pertained to prisoners was unreasonable on the following three grounds: its inflexibility; the unjustified and unexplained delays which characterised the process; and the irrational manner in which appointments were scheduled for the applicants at King Edward Hospital, a hospital accredited by the Department of Health for providing anti-retroviral therapy.[213] The Court referred to s 237 of the Constitution which requires constitutional obligations to be performed 'diligently and without delay'.[214] It also endorsed O'Regan J's dicta in *Rail Commuters Action Group v Transnet Ltd t/a Metrorail* that a proportionately greater response is required from the State 'the graver the threat to fundamental rights'.[215] The court granted an order in similar terms to that sought by the applicants, including a structural interdict.[216]

In contrast to the court in *Van Biljon v Minister of Correctional Services*, the court in the *N* case did not analyse the concept of 'adequate' medical treatment in s 35(2)(*e*), and the obligations it imposed on the State. It preferred to conduct its entire analysis in terms of the reasonableness criteria developed in the *Grootboom* and *Treatment Action Campaign* cases.[217] It is unclear whether the Court was reading implied reasonableness criteria into s 35(2)(*e*), or applying s 27(1)(*a*) read with (2) of the Constitution. The Court engaged in a serious and substantive analysis and evaluation of the evidence

---

209 Ibid para 17.
210 Ibid para 25.
211 Ibid para 24.
212 Ibid para 23.
213 Ibid para 30.
214 Ibid para 31.
215 Ibid. *Rail Commuters Action Group v Transnet Ltd t/a Metrorail* 2005 (2) SA 359 (CC), 2005 (4) BCLR 301 (CC) para 88.
216 On structural relief in socio-economic rights litigation, see generally chapter 8, part 8.6.
217 The Court initially held that the case was both about s 27 of the Constitution and s 35(2)(*e*). It observed that these provisions dealt with the obligations 'directly applicable to the class of persons such as [the] applicants'. *N v Government of the Republic of South Africa* (note 170 above) para 17. On the application of the reasonableness criteria developed in the *Grootboom* and *Treatment Action Campaign* cases to the facts of the case, see paras 25–31.

presented and carefully considered what remedy would be most appropriate and effective. However, it is unfortunate that the Court missed the opportunity to engage in a normative interpretation of s 35(2)(*e*) and its interrelationship with s 27 in relation to detained persons.

There have been a number of High Court cases in which the lawfulness of other aspects of the conditions of detention of prisoners has been considered. In *Strydom v Minister of Correctional Services,*[218] the High Court ruled that the applicant and the other occupants of the Maximum Security Section of Johannesburg Prison have the right to have access to electricity in their cells. Schwartzman J ruled that access to electricity was not a mere comfort or diversion, but could make the difference between mental stability and derangement given the circumstances in which high security prisoners are held. Noting that they spend 18 hours of each day of what remains of their lives, or a substantial portion thereof, in what is in effect solitary confinement, he held:

> To deprive them entirely and in perpetuity of this prospect could also result in their being 'treated and punished in a cruel or degrading manner' (section 12(1)(*c*) of the Constitution or their being detained in conditions that are inconsistent with human dignity (section 35(2) of the Constitution).[219]

The case of *Huang v Head of Grootvlei Prison,*[220] concerned the intersection between the right to adequate nutrition in s 35(2)(*e*) and the cultural rights of prisoners. Kruger J affirmed the right of Taiwanese prisoners to receive raw food and prepare it in accordance with their Eastern tradition. It also granted leave to the applicants to approach the Court on supplemented papers for an order that their special food be provided at State expense.[221] The Court referred to s 8(3) of the Correctional Services Act 111 of 1998 which provides that, where 'reasonably practicable, dietary regulations must take into account religious requirements and cultural preferences'. The case is a good illustration of the fact that socio-economic rights are not commodities intended solely to meet people's physical needs, but in many circumstances, also protect the expressive, cultural and religious dimensions of human identity.

In *Ehrlich v Minister of Correctional Services,*[222] Plasket J reviewed and set aside in terms of PAJA the decision of the Head of Mdantsane Prison to deny the applicant access to a gymnasium in the prison at which he had been running a karate development programme for the previous two years. He held that this decision deprived the applicant of his right to participate in a development programme as envisaged in s 41(5) of the Correctional Services Act, 1998, and was unlawful, procedurally unfair and unreasonable in terms of s 6 of PAJA. The reasonableness of the decision to terminate the karate programme was evaluated in the light of the constitutional right and value of human

---

[218] 1993 (3) BCLR 342 (W).
[219] Ibid para 15.
[220] Note 169 above.
[221] Ibid para 35.
[222] Note 188 above.

dignity and the constitutionally inspired objectives of the Correctional Services Act.[223] Thus Plasket J held:

> [The decision] infringed the statutory right of every participant and affected them in their dignity in the sense that they were denied access to an undertaking that not only had the potential to break the boredom and monotony of incarceration but also to contribute to their personal development and rehabilitation. In this sense the decision undermined important purposes of the Correctional Services Act.[224]

It was declared that the applicant was entitled 'as of right and forthwith' to take part in the karate development programme and, for this purpose, to be granted supervised access to the gymnasium in the A-section of the prison.[225] In addition, and in order to ensure effective compliance with the order, the Head of Mdantsane Prison was ordered to file an affidavit, confirming that medium category prisoners at the Mdantsane Prison, including the applicant, had been granted supervised access to the relevant gymnasium in order to take part in the karate development programme.[226] The *Ehrlich* case illustrates how the interpretation of the Correctional Services Act and the evaluation of the reasonableness of administrative action taken in terms of the Act should be informed by the constitutional rights of prisoners.[227]

The appalling conditions in South African prisons and the seeming inability of the State to guarantee conditions of detention consistent with human dignity has given rise to cases in which the courts have released prisoners on bail when they have not been accorded the treatment necessitated by their medical condition,[228] overturned decisions of the Parole Board to refuse medical parole to seriously ill prisoners,[229] or converted custodial sentences to correctional supervision on appeal.[230] As Pieterse notes:[231]

> Where the state is unable to satisfy a prisoner's health-related needs, it is clear from judgments such as *Vanqa, Stanfield and Du Plooy* that section 35(2)(*e*) can successfully be relied upon to challenge the validity of the continued detention of the prisoner … . Individual

[223] Ibid paras 8–10.
[224] Ibid para 43. The Court also held that the decision was unreasonable in that it had an unequal impact on the applicant: 'its unreasonableness lies in its defiance of the constitutional value and fundamental right of equality.' (para 44).
[225] Ibid para 45. Order (*b*).
[226] Ibid para 45. Order (*d*).
[227] See also *Ehrlich v Minister of Correctional Services* (note 188 above). In this case the respondents were directed to comply with various provisions of the Correctional Services Act pertaining to the provisioning of library services, and the implementation of sentencing plans, as well as sport, recreation, arts and culture, and training and development programmes for offenders at Mdantsane Prison.
[228] *S v Vanqa* 2000 (2) SACR 37 (Tk).
[229] *Stanfield v Minister of Correctional Services* 2004 (4) SA 43 (C), 2003 (12) BCLR 1384 (C) (see particularly the court's observations at para 125); *Du Plooy v Minister of Correctional Services* [2004] 3 All SA 613 (T).
[230] *S v Cloete* 1995 (1) SACR 367 (W).
[231] Pieterse (note 168 above) 129.

prisoners thus stand to derive significant individual benefit from successful reliance on section 35(2)(*e*).

The interpretation of s 35(2)(*e*) remains somewhat confused and underdeveloped in our constitutional jurisprudence. This is regrettable given the vulnerability of the affected group, and their general exposure to degrading and life-threatening conditions of detention. It remains to be tested to what extent s 35(2)(*e*) can be relied upon to challenge the systemic conditions of overcrowding and undignified living conditions which characterise South African prisons. Apart from systemic relief in the form of mandatory orders to improve conditions in particular prisons, delictual remedies for damages suffered by prisoners as a result of a failure by prison officials to ensure constitutionally compliant conditions of detention could be pursued.[232]

5.5 CONCLUSION

The Constitution has made express provision for the socio-economic rights of particular groups who are in vulnerable, dependent situations. These rights are generally formulated in a way which suggests a basic level of provisioning, and are not subject to the internal limitations or qualifications encountered in ss 26(2) and 27(2). Despite the more direct formulation of the socio-economic rights of children (s 28(1)(*c*)) and of persons deprived of their liberty (s 35 (2)(*e*)), the courts have, with some exceptions, tended to apply the reasonableness model of review developed in the *Grootboom* and *Treatment Action Campaign* cases to claims based on these rights.[233]

The availability of the general limitations clause provides the State with an opportunity to seek to justify its failure to ensure the immediate fulfilment of these rights. There is accordingly little justification for the courts to avoid recognising what the Constitution clearly intended: the imposition of a heightened duty on the State to ensure a basic level of socio-economic provisioning to certain particularly vulnerable groups. The consideration of possible legitimate reasons for failing to secure the basic needs of these groups is not excluded, but must be evaluated in terms of the stringent requirements of the general limitations clause.

The ambiguity inherent in the approach of the courts to these specific socio-economic guarantees in the Constitution suggests a lingering discomfort with the positive duties and distributional implications of these rights. Enforcing these duties clearly requires a delicate and skilful interaction with the other branches. But it should not result in a denial of their distributional implications, nor an abdication on the part of courts of their duty to craft innovative and effective remedies when breaches are identified. Until this nettle is firmly grasped, the transformative potential of socio-economic rights will be curtailed.

---

[232] See, for example, *Mxolisi v Minister of Correctional Services* [2008] ZAGPHC 107. As held by Salduker J: 'Prisoners are at the mercy of their gaolers. It is to them that prisoners look for protection and safe custody. Their gaolers have a duty to maintain their safe custody until they leave the prison.' (para 59).

[233] On the reasonableness model of review, see generally chapter 4, parts 4.3 and 4.4.

CHAPTER 6

A New Paradigm for Evictions Law

Section 26(3)

In this chapter *Page*

6.1 INTRODUCTION

The interests and values protected by housing as a human right are particularly threatened when people face evictions from their homes. As the African Commission on Human and Peoples' Rights has observed:

> Wherever and whenever they occur, forced evictions are extremely traumatic. They cause physical, psychological and emotional distress; they entail losses of the means of economic sustenance and increase impoverishment. They can also cause physical injury and in some cases sporadic deaths. Evictions break up families and increase existing levels of homelessness.[1]

In the apartheid era forced removals and evictions in terms of influx control policies and their associated legislation were used to achieve the purposes of racial segregation and subordination.[2] Residence by black persons in urban areas was strictly controlled

---

[1] *The Social and Economic Rights Action Centre and the Centre for Economic and Social Rights v Nigeria*, Comm No 155/96 (2001) AHRLR 60 (ACHPR 2001) para 63. See also UN Committee on Economic, Social and Cultural Rights, General Comment No 7 (Sixteenth sess, 1997) *The right to adequate housing (art 11 (1) of the Covenant): Forced evictions*, UN doc E/1998/22.

[2] In terms of the Black Land Act 27 of 1913 (repealed by the Abolition of Racially Based Land Measures Act 108 of 1991) and the Development Trust and Land Act 18 of 1936 (repealed by the Additional Appropriation Act 28 of 1992), the African population was restricted to 13 % of South Africa's Land. They were precluded from owning or occupying land outside of the reserved areas. The implementation of this legislation and the administrative control of Africans were achieved through the Black Administration Act 38 of 1927 (repealed by the Repeal of the Black Administration Act and Amendment of Certain Laws

through requiring their presence to be functional to the labour needs of white business.[3] In areas such as the Western Cape, which followed a coloured labour preference policy, systemic homelessness for Africans was further entrenched.[4] Forced evictions and removals were effected through a range of legislation such as the pernicious Group Areas Act 36 of 1966 and Prevention of Illegal Squatting Act 52 of 1951.[5]

Black occupiers were in a powerless position as they enjoyed few legislative or common-law rights, and their interest in preserving their homes received scant legal recognition in the context of evictions from public or private land. In contrast, the property rights of the landowner were extensively protected in the common law and in legislation.[6] Between 1963 and the late 1980s, approximately 3,5 million people were removed from their land and homes.[7] Citing Prof Colin Bundy, Moseneke DCJ describes the impact of these forced evictions and relocation as follows:

> Bundy makes the point that 'trauma, frustration, grief, dull dragging apathy and [the] surrender of the will to live' are indeed some of the effects of forcible evictions on the human condition. And, the consequences span over multiple areas of social life: frequently it is the case that families are left homeless, their social support structures severed and their welfare services, jobs and educational institutions, rendered inaccessible.[8]

Act 28 of 2005). This legislation paved the way for the 'Bantustan policy' enacted through the Representation between the Republic of South Africa and Self-governing Territories Act 46 of 1959 and the National States Citizenship Act 26 of 1970. The latter two pieces of legislation were repealed by sched 7 of the Constitution of the Republic of South Africa 200 of 1993.

[3] Key influx control legislation was the Black (Urban Areas) Act 21 of 1923 and the Black (Urban Areas) Consolidation Act 25 of 1945. Both pieces of legislation were repealed by the Abolition of Racially Based Land Measures Act 108 of 1991.

[4] See in this regard the judgment of Ngcobo J in *Residents of Joe Slovo Community, Western Cape v Thubelisha Homes, Minister for Housing and Minister of Local Government and Housing, Western Cape (Centre on Housing Rights and Evictions and Community Law Centre, University of the Western Cape as amici curiae)* [2009] ZACC 16, 2009 (9) BCLR 847 (CC) ('*Joe Slovo*') paras 192–197.

[5] See C O'Regan 'No more forced removals: An historical analysis of The Prevention of Illegal Squatting Act' (1989) 5 *SAJHR* 361–394.

[6] For example, s 3B of the Prevention of Illegal Squatting Act 52 of 1951 permitted landowners to demolish, without prior notice to any person and without obtaining a court order, structures erected on their land without consent. This provision was declared in conflict with s 26(3) of the Constitution in *Despatch Municipality v Sunridge Estate and Development Corporation (Pty) Ltd* 1997 (4) SA 596 (SE), 1997 (8) BCLR 1023 (SE) at 1037B. For an overview of the legal landscape regulating evictions of persons from their homes during the apartheid era, see A J van der Walt *Constitutional Property Law* (2005) 410–416.

[7] C Bundy 'Land, law and power: Forced removals in the historical context' in C Murray & C O'Regan (eds) *No Place to Rest: Forced Removals and the Law in South Africa* (1990) 3–13, 8.

[8] *Joe Slovo* (note 4 above) para 98 (citing Bundy ibid 10–11).

The recognition of the housing rights in s 26 of the Constitution has created a powerful constitutional foundation for transforming evictions law in South Africa. One of the fundamental purposes of the human right to housing is to protect people against the misery and the multitude of negative effects on people's well-being and livelihoods created by homelessness. The trauma and consequences of homelessness are particularly severe in circumstances where people are forcibly evicted from their homes. Section 26(3) of the Constitution was designed to protect people's interests in their homes when faced with eviction or demolition. It reads:

> No one may be evicted from their home, or have their home demolished, without an order of court made after considering all the relevant circumstances. No legislation may permit arbitrary evictions.

The Court in *Government of the Republic of South Africa v Grootboom*[9] ('*Grootboom*') observed that s 26(3) is a special manifestation of the obligation in s 26(1) on the State and private parties to refrain from preventing or impairing people's access to housing.[10]

The first part of this chapter focuses on the leading jurisprudence in which the obligations of organs of State in relation to the eviction of unlawful occupiers from their homes have been developed. Much of the jurisprudence has evolved in the context of the interpretation of key pieces of legislation enacted to give effect to s 26(3), particularly the Prevention of Illegal Eviction from and Unlawful Occupation of Land Act 19 of 1998 ('PIE').[11] It commences with an analysis of the leading case interpreting PIE in the light of s 26 of the Constitution, *Port Elizabeth Municipality v Various Occupiers*[12] ('*Port Elizabeth Municipality*'), and the subsequent jurisprudence it has influenced. This jurisprudence illustrates how the courts have explicitly sought to interpret legislation regulating evictions so as to promote the interests and values protected by s 26 of the Constitution.

---

[9] 2001 (1) SA 46 (CC), 2000 (11) BCLR 1169 (CC).

[10] On the Constitutional Court's approach to the review of negative duties, see chapter 4, part 4.6.

[11] PIE repealed the old Prevention of Illegal Squatting Act 52 of 1951 referred to above. Another key piece of legislation regulating evictions is the Extension of Security of Tenure Act 62 of 1997 (ESTA). The scope of ESTA is quite restrictive. It applies chiefly in rural and peri-urban areas (s 2), and extends only to an occupier who resides on land belonging to another person and who has (or on 4 February 1997 or thereafter had) consent or another right in law to do so (s 1(*x*)). It expressly excludes labour tenants in terms of the Land Reform (Labour Tenants) Act 3 of 1996. Most evictions of people from their homes fall under either PIE or ESTA, or are governed by other legislation protecting security of tenure, for example, the Informal Protection of Land Rights Act 31 of 1996. For a discussion of the jurisprudence in terms of ESTA and other land reform legislation, see P J Badenhorst, J M Pienaar & H Mostert *Silberberg and Schoeman's The Law of Property* 5 ed (2006) chapter 22; A J van der Walt *Constitutional Property Law* (2005) chapters 6 and 7.3.

[12] 2005 (1) SA 217 (CC), 2004 (12) BCLR 1268 (CC).

The second part of the chapter examines the jurisprudence pertaining to the obligations of organs of State in eviction applications brought by private parties against unlawful occupiers.[13] The judgments of the Supreme Court of Appeal and the Constitutional Court in *President of the Republic of South Africa v Modderklip Boerdery (Pty) Ltd (Agri SA, Amici Curiae)*[14] ('*Modderklip*') provide a powerful theoretical underpinning for the constitutional duties imposed on public organs in the context of eviction applications brought by private parties. A number of significant High Court judgments pertaining to the joinder of local authorities in eviction applications by private parties have further elaborated on the housing rights dimensions of all applications to evict people from their homes.

The impact of s 26 on eviction applications brought in terms of health and safety legislation is considered in the following part through an analysis of the leading Constitutional Court decision in *Occupiers of 51 Olivia Road, Berea Township and 197 Main Street, Johannesburg v City of Johannesburg* ('*Occupiers of 51 Olivia Road*').[15] The final part analyses and considers the implications of the recent decision of the Constitutional Court in *Residents of Joe Slovo Community, Western Cape v Thubelisha Homes* ('*Joe Slovo*').[16] This decision has significant implications for organs of State seeking to evict and relocate a community for the purposes of upgrading an informal settlement.

The chapter concludes with an analysis of the influence of the housing rights in s 26 of the Constitution on the emergence of a new paradigm for evictions law in South Africa.

6.2 INTERPRETING PIE IN THE LIGHT OF SECTION 26

6.2.1 Introducing PIE

PIE was enacted with the clear purpose of protecting both constitutional housing and property rights in an evictions context.[17] PIE applies to the eviction of unlawful occupiers in respect of all land in South Africa.[18] An 'unlawful occupier' is defined in s 1 of PIE as 'a person who occupies land without the express or tacit consent of

---

[13] The jurisprudence pertaining to the impact of housing rights on the private common-law rules pertaining to evictions and property is considered in chapter 7, part 7.3.1.

[14] 2005 (5) SA 3 (CC), 2005 (8) BCLR 786 (CC) ('*Modderklip (CC)*'). The Supreme Court of Appeal judgment is reported as *Modderfontein Squatters, Greater Benoni City Council v Modderklip Boerdery (Pty) Ltd (Agri SA and Legal Resources Centre, Amici Curiae); President of the Republic of South Africa v Modderklip Boerdery (Pty) Ltd (Agri SA and Legal Resources Centre, Amici Curiae)* 2004 (6) SA 40 (SCA), 2004 (8) BCLR 821 (SCA) ('*Modderklip (SCA)*').

[15] 2008 (3) SA 208 (CC), 2008 (5) BCLR 475 (CC).

[16] Note 4 above.

[17] The preamble of PIE refers to the content of both ss 25(1) and 26(3) of the Constitution.

[18] Section 2 of PIE read with ss 5, 6 and 7.

the owner or person[19] in charge, or without any other right in law to occupy such land'.[20] It excludes –

(*a*) a person who is an occupier in terms of ESTA, 1997; and

(*b*) a person whose informal right to land is protected in terms of the Interim Protection of Informal Land Rights Act, 31 of 1996.[21]

Section 4 of PIE regulates proceedings for the eviction of an unlawful occupier by an owner or person in charge of land. It applies '[n]otwithstanding anything to the contrary contained in any law or the common law'.[22] In addition to procedural protections such as adequate notice of pending eviction proceedings,[23] PIE requires that, before granting an eviction order, a court must be of the opinion 'that it is just and equitable to do so, after considering all the relevant circumstances, including the rights and needs of the elderly, children, disabled persons and households headed by women'.[24] Where the occupier has occupied the land in question for more than six months, the Act specifies additionally that the court must consider 'whether land has been available or can reasonably be made available by a municipality or other organ of state or other land owner for the relocation of the unlawful occupier'.[25] Provision is also made for the owner or person in charge of land to institute urgent proceedings for the eviction of an unlawful occupier.[26]

Separate provision is made in s 6 of PIE for evictions at the instance of an organ of state. It permits an organ of state to institute proceedings for the eviction of an

[19] The *Joe Slovo* case (note 4 above) is the leading decision in which the question of the consent required in terms of s 1 of PIE is considered in the five judgments delivered in this case. See further part 6.5 below.

[20] In *Ndlovu v Ngcobo; Bekker v Jika* 2003 (1) SA 113 (SCA), [2002] 4 All SA 384 (SCA) ('*Ndlovu*'), the Supreme Court of Appeal interpreted 'unlawful occupiers' to include not only those who unlawfully took possession of land (so-called 'squatters'), but also persons who once had lawful possession, but whose possession subsequently became unlawful (referred to as cases of 'holding over'). PIE thus applies to situations where occupiers refused to vacate property after the lawful termination of a lease agreement or the sale in execution of property pursuant to the calling up of a mortgage bond. On the impact of s 26(3) on common-law ejectment applications, see further chapter 7, part 7.3.1(*b*).

[21] PIE s 1(xi).

[22] Ibid s 4(1).

[23] Ibid s 4(2)–(5). On the nature of the procedural protections conferred by PIE, see, for example, *Cape Killarney Property Investments (Pty) Ltd v Mahamba* 2001 (4) SA 1222 (SCA), [2001] 4 All SA 479 (A). See also UN Committee on Economic, Social and Cultural Rights, General Comment No 7 (Sixteenth Sess, 1997) *The right to adequate housing (art 11(1) of the Covenant): Forced evictions*, UN doc E/1998/22 paras 14 and 16; *Basic Principles and Guidelines on Development-Based Evictions and Displacement*, UN Special Rapporteur on Adequate Housing as a Component of the Right to an Adequate Standard of Living UN doc A/HRC/4/18, 5 February 2007, paras 37–42; 45–46. See also note 248 below.

[24] Ibid s 4(6).

[25] Ibid s 4(7).

[26] Ibid s 5.

unlawful occupier from land that falls within its jurisdiction if the consent of the organ of State for the erection of a building or structure is required and has not been obtained, or it is in the public interest to grant such an order.[27] The 'public interest' in this context is defined to include 'the interest of the health and safety of those occupying the land and the public in general'.[28] The discretion of a court to grant such evictions is also subject to the overriding considerations of justice and equity, which include substantive considerations pertaining to the circumstances of the occupation, the period of residence on the land, and the availability to the unlawful occupier of suitable alternative accommodation or land.[29] The procedural protections applicable in s 4 also apply to eviction at the instance of an organ of state.[30] Finally, PIE provides for the mediation of any dispute in terms of the Act.[31]

6.2.2 *Port Elizabeth Municipality*

Port Elizabeth Municipality is the leading Constitutional Court judgment on the interpretation of PIE.[32] The judgment illuminates how PIE must be interpreted to promote the purposes and values underpinning s 26(3). The case concerned an eviction application brought in terms of s 6 of PIE by the Port Elizabeth Municipality against about 68 people who were occupying informal dwellings erected on privately owned land within the jurisdiction of the Municipality. Most of them had settled on the undeveloped land after being evicted from other land in the vicinity. The Municipality was responding to a neighbourhood petition in launching the application.[33]

The Court commenced its judgment with a detailed historical and contextual analysis of the nature and role of forced evictions during the apartheid era, and the transformative purposes that s 26(3) of the Constitution and PIE were intended to promote.[34] It held that PIE had to be interpreted and applied within a 'defined and carefully calibrated constitutional matrix'.[35] This matrix explains how courts should

---

[27] Ibid s 6(1)(*a*) and (*b*). This provision does not apply 'where the unlawful occupier is a mortgagor and the land in question is sold in a sale of execution pursuant to a mortgage'. According to Yacoob J in the *Joe Slovo* case (note 4 above) paras 94–101, the requirements of s 6(1)(*a*) and (*b*) are disjunctive in the sense that existence of either of these two jurisdictional requirements would entitle the State to bring an eviction application in terms of s 6. Langa CJ and Van der Westhuizen J concurred in the judgment of Yacoob J. See also *Baartman v Port Elizabeth Municipality* 2004 (1) SA 560 (SCA) para 9.

[28] Ibid s 6(2).

[29] Ibid s 6(3). In *Joe Slovo* (note 4 above) para 101, Yacoob J held in addition that 'an eviction cannot ordinarily be just and equitable unless the public interest requires it'.

[30] Ibid s 6(6).

[31] Ibid s 7.

[32] *Port Elizabeth Municipality* (note 12 above).

[33] See the background provided by the Court in *Port Elizabeth Municipality* ibid paras 1–3.

[34] Ibid paras 8–23.

[35] Ibid para 14.

approach the conflict between property and housing rights which arises when applications for the eviction of unlawful occupiers from their homes are brought.[36] In the first place, property rights are not absolute, but incorporate the important social dimension of promoting the public interest, particularly given South Africa's history of colonial and racist dispossession.[37]

Moreover, under the Constitution, 'the normal ownership rights of possession, use and occupation' are counterposed to 'a new and equally relevant right not arbitrarily to be deprived of a home'.[38] In other words, PIE should not merely be seen as an expression of 'judicial philanthropy in favour of the poor',[39] but must be interpreted in the light of the fact that even unlawful occupiers are now the bearers of constitutionally enshrined housing rights. The judgment elaborates on the substantive interests people have in their homes and which are threatened in an eviction context in the following terms:

> Section 26(3) evinces special constitutional regard for a person's place of abode. It acknowledges that a home is more than just a shelter from the elements. It is a zone of personal intimacy and family security. Often it will be the only relatively secure space of privacy and tranquillity in what (for poor people in particular) is a turbulent and hostile world. Forced removal is a shock for any family, the more so for one that has established itself on a site that has become its familiar habitat.[40]

---

[36] The Supreme Court of Appeal has emphasised that the application of PIE and the guarantees in s 26(3) are restricted to eviction from a person's 'home'. It held that, although a person 'can conceivably have more than one home, the term does … . require an element of regular occupation coupled with some degree of permanence.' *Barnett v Minister of Land Affairs* 2007 (6) SA 313 (SCA), 2007 (11) BCLR 1214 (SCA) para 38. Accordingly, PIE did not apply 'to holiday cottages erected for holiday purposes and visited occasionally over weekends and during vacations, albeit on a regular basis, by persons who have their habitual dwellings elsewhere'. Ibid para 40. See also *Ndlovu* (note 20 above) para 20 (PIE does not extend to buildings occupied purely for commercial purposes).

[37] Ibid para 16 (citing Ackermann J's judgment in *First National Bank of SA Limited t/a Westbank v Commissioner for the South African Revenue Services; First National Bank of SA Limited t/a Westbank v Minister of Finance* 2002 (4) SA 768 (CC), 2002 (7) BCLR 702 (CC) paras 50–52.

[38] Ibid para 23.

[39] Ibid para 14.

[40] Ibid para 17. Sachs J refers also to a report of UN-Habitat which explains that adequate housing is recognised as a fundamental human right because of its integral connections with other dimensions of human well-being such as personal security, privacy, health, protection from the elements 'and many other attributes of a shared humanity'. United Nations Housing Rights Programme, Report No 1, 'Housing Rights Legislation: Review of International and National Legal Instruments' (2002) 1. On housing as a right in the South African Bill of Rights, see the analysis by Kirsty McLean: 'Housing' in Woolman et al (eds) *Constitutional Law of South Africa* 2nd ed, original service (2006) chapter 55.

The fact that people have housing rights which may conflict with property rights in an eviction application fundamentally changes the traditional approach of courts in eviction applications. This new role is described in the following terms by Sachs J:

> The judicial function in these circumstances is not to establish a hierarchical arrangement between the different interests involved, privileging in an abstract and mechanical way the rights of ownership over the right not to be dispossessed of a home, or vice versa. Rather, it is to balance out and reconcile the opposed claims in as just a manner as possible taking account of all the interests involved and the specific factors relevant in each particular case.[41]

In performing this balancing and reconciling function, the Court must take into account the social function of property and land rights in terms of s 25 of the Constitution, as well as the fact that the Constitution does not 'sanction arbitrary seizure of land, whether by the State or by landless people'.[42] However, the Court cautioned that the term 'land invasion' must be used with caution, as it is applied to a range of situations from the relatively long-term occupation of land by desperate people with nowhere else to go, to the deliberate, premeditated occupation of a large tract of land.[43]

The rights in s 26(3) are described as 'defensive rather than affirmative' in character:

> The landowner cannot simply say: this is my land, I can do with it what I want, and then send in the bulldozers or sledgehammers.[44]

A further feature of the cluster of constitutional provisions is that they acknowledge, through s 26(3), 'that eviction of people in informal settlements may take place, even if it results in loss of a home'.[45] In elaborating on the availability to the unlawful occupier of suitable alternative accommodation as a factor in determining whether it is just and equitable to grant an order for eviction in terms of s 6(3) of PIE, the Court notes again that there is 'no unqualified constitutional duty on local authorities to ensure that in no circumstances should a home be destroyed unless alternative accommodation or land is made available'.[46] However, the Court immediately thereafter stipulates that a court 'should be reluctant to grant an eviction against relatively settled occupiers unless it is satisfied that a reasonable alternative is available, even if only as an interim measure pending ultimate access to housing in the formal housing

---

[41] Ibid para 23.

[42] Ibid para 20.

[43] Ibid n 22. The Court refers in this context to *Grootboom* (note 9 above) para 92 and the judgment in *Port Elizabeth Municipality v People's Dialogue on Land and Shelter* 2000 (2) SA 1074 (SE). See also *City of Cape Town v Unlawful Occupiers, Erf 1800, Capricorn (Vrygrond Development)* 2003 (6) SA 140 (C), 2003 (8) BCLR 878 (C).

[44] Ibid para 20.

[45] Ibid para 21.

[46] Ibid para 28.

programme'.[47] This suggests that, in the absence of exceptional circumstances such as an orchestrated land invasion, eviction orders should generally require organs of State to take reasonable measures to ensure alternative accommodation for occupiers who will be left homeless, even if it is only on a temporary basis pending their integration in a long-term housing programme.[48]

This obligation to consider alternative accommodation is expressly linked to the Court's reasoning in *Grootboom* that statistical progress in advancing access to housing does not constitute sufficient compliance with the constitutional obligations imposed by s 26. A flexible approach is required which treats everyone 'with care and concern'.[49] The existence of a programme 'designed to house the maximum number of homeless people over the shortest period of time in the most cost effective manner', while going 'a long way towards establishing a context that would ensure that a proposed eviction would be just and equitable', is not determinative 'of whether and under what conditions an actual eviction order should be made in a particular case'.[50] This constitutes a crucial affirmation that the obligation of the State to make serious and sustained efforts to ensure alternative accommodation to those facing homelessness pursuant to an eviction is not satisfied by a generalised programme that 'works in theory'.[51] What is required is an individualised assessment by organs of State of the actual needs and situation of the occupiers in the particular case.[52] This individualised consideration of people's needs is vital if socio-economic rights are to fulfil their role as a meaningful human rights guarantee. As expressed by Sachs J:

> In a society founded on human dignity, equality and freedom, it cannot be presupposed that the greatest good for the many can be achieved at the cost of intolerable hardship for the few, particularly if, by a reasonable application of judicial and administrative statecraft, such human distress could be avoided.[53]

A further factor to be taken into account in determining the justice and equity of an eviction is whether 'proper discussions, and where appropriate, mediation' have been attempted.[54] This reinforces the right of people who face the loss of their home to be heard and have their views taken into account. In seeking to resolve the conflict between property and housing rights in eviction cases, 'the procedural and substantive aspects of justice and equity cannot always be separated'.[55] People facing eviction have constitutionally protected housing rights which entitle them to participate

---

[47] Ibid para 28.

[48] See the observations of Sachs J in relation to the possible role of places of temporary settlement in serving 'to cushion removals and place the persons concerned in a position to re-establish themselves pending access to secure housing'. Ibid n 28.

[49] Ibid para 29; *Grootboom* (note 9 above) para 44.

[50] Ibid para 29.

[51] Ibid.

[52] Ibid.

[53] Ibid.

[54] Ibid para 43. See further paras 39–47.

[55] Ibid para 39.

in the process of finding a just solution to the conflict between their rights and the landowner's property rights. In the words of Sachs J:

> Thus, those seeking eviction should be encouraged not to rely on concepts of faceless and anonymous squatters automatically to be expelled as obnoxious social nuisances. Such a stereotypical approach has no place in the society envisaged by the Constitution; justice and equity require that everyone is to be treated as an individual bearer of rights entitled to respect for his or her dignity.[56]

The significance of the *Port Elizabeth Municipality* decision lies in its insistence that unlawful occupiers, who enjoyed minimal rights under the previous legislative and common-law regime, are now the bearers of constitutional rights, specifically the housing rights in s 26. This confers on them interrelated procedural and substantive protections in the context of legal steps to evict them from their homes.

In this context, the courts have an exacting and particular constitutional responsibility. In the clash between property rights and 'the genuine despair of people in dire need of accommodation', they should not automatically privilege property rights.[57] Their role is to strive for a just and equitable solution which attempts to reconcile the interests of landowners and unlawful occupiers. In doing so, they must take into account the purposes and values protected by property and housing rights, the broader historical and social context, as well as the specific circumstances relevant in each particular case.[58]

Justice and equity are the prerequisites for granting an eviction order in terms of PIE. The Act gives effect to the requirement in s 26(3) of the Constitution that a court must consider 'all the relevant circumstances' before granting an order evicting people from their homes. It is evident from the *Port Elizabeth Municipality* judgment that the Court does not confine the circumstances which are considered relevant in eviction applications to the legal grounds justifying an eviction of an unlawful occupier in terms of the common law.[59] As the Court stated in relation to the interpretation of PIE:

> The court is not resolving a civil dispute as to who has rights under land law; the existence of unlawfulness is the foundation for the enquiry, not its subject matter. What the court is called upon to do is to decide whether, bearing in mind the values of the Constitution, in upholding and enforcing land results it is appropriate to issue an order which has the effect of depriving people of their homes. Of equal concern, it is determining the

---

[56] Ibid para 41.

[57] Ibid para 23.

[58] Ibid.

[59] See in this regard the interpretation of the concept of 'relevant circumstances' in s 26(3) by the Supreme Court of Appeal in *Brisley v Drotsky* 2002 (4) SA 1 (SCA), 2002 (12) BCLR 1229 (SCA) paras 38 and 42 ('*Brisley*'), and its judgment in *City of Johannesburg v Rand Properties (Pty) Ltd* 2007 (6) SA 417 (SCA), 2007 (6) BCLR 643 (SCA) paras 40–41. See the analysis of *Brisley* in chapter 7, part 7.4.1.

conditions under which, if it is just and equitable to grant such an order, the eviction should take place.[60]

Even when unlawfulness is established, 'the eviction process is not automatic', and the 'courts are called upon to exercise a broad judicial discretion on a case by case basis'.[61] In exercising this discretion, a court would be entitled to go beyond the facts established on the papers before it, and play a more inquisitorial role in procuring 'ways of establishing the true state of affairs, so as to enable it properly to "have regard" to relevant circumstances'.[62]

The nature of the discretion which vests in the courts to decide whether an eviction would be 'just and equitable' and, if so, what conditions should attach to the eviction order is broad and expansive.[63] Significant factors in determining whether an eviction will be just and equitable in the particular circumstances of a case include: compliance with the procedural requirements stipulated in PIE; the circumstances and length of time of the occupation;[64] the 'rights and needs' of vulnerable groups such as the elderly, children, disabled persons and households headed by women;[65] reasonable conduct by the relevant organ of State in making suitable alternative accommodation available; and whether efforts have been made to resolve the dispute through mediation or other forms of face-to-face engagement with 'equality of voice' for all concerned.[66]

The *Port Elizabeth Municipality* judgment suggests a fluid, dialogic relationship between property rights and housing rights as opposed to an implacable confrontation between two static, fixed rights.[67] This relationship is mediated by the search for

---

[60] *Port Elizabeth Municipality* (note 12 above) para 32.

[61] Ibid para 31.

[62] Ibid para 32. For an illustration of this more inquisitorial role played by courts in the wake of the *Port Elizabeth Municipality* judgment, see the judgment by Bertelsmann J in *Ritama Investments v Unlawful Occupiers of Erf 62 Wynberg* Case No 30782/05 ZAGPHC (unreported judgment of 27 January 2006).

[63] *Port Elizabeth Municipality* (note 12 above) paras 30–31.

[64] Ibid paras 26–27.

[65] These groups are specifically referred to in s 4(6) of PIE. In *ABSA Bank v Murray* 2004 (2) SA 15 (C), 2004 (1) BCLR 10 (C) ('*Murray*'), Binns-Ward AJ held that the rights of occupiers that would generally be relevant in an eviction application in terms of PIE include 'the right to human dignity, the right not to be treated in a cruel, inhumane and degrading way, the constitutional rights of children and the availability of alternative accommodation within the context of the State's obligation to provide access to it'. He went on to hold that: 'The "needs" would be the considerations which would have to be satisfied to give substance to the rights' (para 28). The effect of an eviction on a person's 'basic rights, including that person's constitutional socio-economic rights' would be an influential consideration (para 29).

[66] *Port Elizabeth Municipality* (note 12 above) para 30.

[67] See also the observations by Binns-Ward AJ in *Murray* (note 65 above) paras 32 and 35–36 (referring to 'the misdirected extremes in the dichotomous conceptual approaches to the proper construction' of PIE).

contingent solutions which seek to achieve 'micro-justice'[68] in the concrete circumstances of particular cases. This quest must occur within the normative framework of constitutional rights and values. This relational, context-sensitive adjudication of conflicts between rights is one of the features of a transformative approach to the adjudication of constitutional rights.[69]

6.2.3 Evictions at the instance of organs of State

A critical element of the protection provided by housing rights is the provision of alternative accommodation to those who face homelessness following an eviction from their homes.[70] Both prior and subsequent to the *Port Elizabeth Municipality* judgment, the courts have underscored the duty of organs of State in relation to the provision of alternative accommodation for people facing eviction from their homes. These developments have occurred primarily in the context of the considerable delay by the State in enacting the emergency housing programme envisaged in *Grootboom*. Entitled *Housing Assistance in Emergency Housing Circumstances*, this programme was finally adopted by the National Department of Housing in April 2004, and constitutes chapter 12 of the National Housing Code. However, the programme has been plagued by considerable delays and problems in its implementation, particularly by local authorities who have generally failed to anticipate and plan proactively for emergency housing situations. The latter includes situations where people are evicted or face imminent eviction.[71]

City of Cape Town v Rudolph[72] ('*Rudolph*') was a significant case heard prior to the adoption of the emergency housing programme and the Constitutional Court's judgment in *Port Elizabeth Municipality*. The City had brought an application in the Western Cape High Court for the eviction of a community occupying a structure in a park owned by the City in Valhalla Park. As in the *Grootboom* case, this community's housing situation was desperate, given their impoverished circumstances and the huge backlog in the supply of housing. Many members had been on housing waiting lists for more than a decade.[73] The application for eviction was based in the first instance on the common law, alternatively, on the provisions governing urgent eviction proceedings under PIE.[74] The City also sought an alternative order declaring

---

[68] On the onerous duty of the courts to strive for justice at the micro-level in the context of large-scale inherited structural inequities, see *Port Elizabeth Municipality* (note 12 above) para 38.

[69] See also chapter 3, part 3.2.4 at notes 72–74 and accompanying text.

[70] See also G Budlender 'The right to alternative accommodation in forced evictions' in J Squires, M Langford & B Thiele (eds) *The Road to a Remedy: Current Issues in the Litigation of Economic, Social and Cultural Rights* (2005) 127–138.

[71] On the implementation and impact of the *Grootboom* order, including the adoption of the emergency housing programme, see chapter 8, part 8.4.2.

[72] 2004 (5) SA 39 (C), 2003 (11) BCLR 1236 (C).

[73] *Rudolph* ibid 1240G–1241A.

[74] Section 5 of PIE.

PIE unconstitutional in that it infringed 'the fundamental rights of property owners'.[75] The community filed a counter-application for an order declaring that the Council's housing programme did not comply with its obligations as laid down in *Grootboom* to make short-term provision for people in Valhalla Park who are in crises or desperate situations.

Selikowitz J held that the provisions of PIE were applicable to the eviction, and dismissed the challenge to that Act's constitutional validity. He held that PIE did not amount to an arbitrary deprivation of property rights,[76] and was enacted pursuant to the constitutional duty to protect the rights of occupiers.[77] In addition, the circumstances did not warrant the granting of an urgent interim eviction order in terms of s 5 of PIE. The Court thus dismissed the City's application for the eviction of the community.

Turning to the counter-application, the Court found that the local authority had failed to implement the requisite programme to provide for people in urgent need.[78] The Court referred to 'a direct causal link' between 'the deliberate and sustained failure by the Council to make any provision for people in the applicants' situation, and their occupation of the park'.[79] The Court's order included a supervisory component, requiring the Council to report back to it on the steps it was taking to comply with its constitutional obligations to make short-term provision for people in Valhalla Park who were in a crisis or a desperate situation. This included giving 'adequate priority and resources' to the needs of people in the area 'who have no access to a place where they may lawfully live'.[80]

Although the eviction application was dismissed on the grounds that the City had not established an entitlement to urgent relief in terms of s 5 of PIE, the *Rudolph* case illustrates how an eviction application can trigger an order compelling an organ of State to take positive measures to provide urgent housing relief in terms of s 26(2) of the Constitution. *Rudolph* is a good illustration of the interdependence of the three subsections of s 26, and of the negative and positive duties they impose.

In *Transnet t/a Spoornet v Informal Settlers of Good Hope*,[81] the High Court postponed *sine die* an eviction application in terms of s 4(7) of PIE brought by Transnet

---

[75] *Rudolph* (note 72 above) 1242F–G.

[76] See also *Ndlovu* (note 20 above) para 17.

[77] The Court in *Rudolph* (note 72 above) 1252H–I also dismissed the applicant's attempt to rely on common-law remedies for the ejectment of the respondents. It held:

> To hold that the common-law remedies available in our law for the eviction of unlawful occupiers exist alongside the remedies provided for in PIE, at the option of the applicant, or at all, would fundamentally undermine the overall purpose of PIE and particularly the purpose of the protections provided for therein.

[78] *Rudolph* (note 72 above) 1274–1275.

[79] Ibid 1276E.

[80] Ibid 1280J (Order para 2.1.3). On the structural interdict granted in this case, see chapter 8, part 8.6.2 at notes 335–347 and accompanying text.

[81] [2001] 4 All SA 516 (WLD) ('*Transnet*').

against a community occupying land designated as part of the rail reserve. It held that the third respondent, the local authority within whose area of jurisdiction the land fell, had failed to appreciate its constitutional and statutory obligations relating to the provision of accommodation to persons in urgent housing need.[82] It furthermore ordered Transnet 'to conduct a survey to enable it (and the court when the matter is reinstated) to assess the needs and rights of the persons presently illegally occupying the Rail Reserve and the prospect, if any, of relocating the communities to a safer and healthier site'.[83] It justified this order on the basis that the applicant was better placed to allege and prove the circumstances which were relevant when it sought to evict a large group of homeless people. Browde AJ reasoned thus:

> The applicant is an organ of State as defined in section 1 (viii) of the Act read with section 239 of the Constitution. It is a company created by statute and controls immovable and movable assets countrywide on a large scale. Consequently I believe that it is the public duty of the applicant to place before the court as much information as it can to enable the court to deal equitably with the two communities which the applicant seeks to evict.

The Court thus affirmed the duty of public organs to assist the courts in ascertaining as much of the relevant circumstances as possible. This reasoning reinforces the public responsibilities created by eviction applications, particularly those involving a large group of disadvantaged persons. These persons lack the resources to collate and present to the courts a comprehensive account of the circumstances of the community, and the rights and needs of the especially vulnerable groups referred to in PIE such as the elderly, children, disabled persons and households headed by women.

Judgments such as *Port Elizabeth Municipality*, *Rudolph* and *Transnet* underscore the need for a court to have before it as rich and detailed a factual matrix as possible to enable a substantive assessment of the justice and equity of an eviction application.

6.3 EVICTIONS FROM PRIVATE LAND: *MODDERKLIP* AND RELATED JURISPRUDENCE

The cases considered in the previous part concerned applications for eviction at the instance of an organ of State. This part considers the obligations of organs of State, particularly local authorities, when applications are brought for the eviction of impoverished occupiers from private land. The impact of s 26 on common-law principles and doctrines pertaining to evictions is considered in chapter 7.[84]

The *Modderklip* case dealt with the State's duties in the context of a private landowner's unsuccessful efforts to execute an eviction order granted in terms of s 4 of PIE against a community occupying his land.[85] At the time of the landowner's

[82] Ibid 520A–521H.

[83] Ibid 524D.

[84] See chapter 7, part 7.3.1.

[85] The judgment in the original eviction application is reported as *Modderklip Boerdery (Pty) Ltd v Modder East Squatters* 2001 (4) SA 385 (W).

attempted execution of order the community numbered approximately 40 000, of whom roughly a third were allegedly illegal immigrants. The owner was confronted by a demand from the sheriff of the High Court for a deposit of R1,8 million to secure the costs of the eviction, an amount far exceeding the value of the part of the property which was being occupied. After attempts to get various organs of State to assist in enforcing the eviction order failed, the owner applied to the High Court for a declaratory order obliging the State to assist in vindicating his property rights in terms of the Constitution. The owner and Agri SA (intervening as *amicus curiae*) also requested a mandamus requiring the State to adopt a comprehensive plan to solve the needs of the occupiers for secure accommodation. Such an order was regarded as essential to avoid the reoccupation of the land by the community.

The High Court granted an order in terms of which the State was obliged to submit a comprehensive plan to the court and the parties indicating in what manner it would fulfil its obligations to assist the landowner in enforcing the eviction order. The State was also required to report on the adoption of a scheme for the provision of accommodation, alternatively, access to land to qualifying occupiers in the community.[86] The Court's reasoning was based on the duty of the State to protect the owner's constitutional property rights in terms of s 25(1). In order to do so effectively, it was imperative that alternative land be made available for the settlement of the occupiers once they had been removed from the Modder East farm. The Court relied on ss 25(5) and 26 of the Constitution in support of this proposition.

The State appealed against the enforcement order to the Supreme Court of Appeal which also considered a late application by the Modderklip community for leave to appeal against the original eviction order.[87] The Supreme Court of Appeal denied the community leave to appeal against the eviction order. In relation to the enforcement order, the Court reasoned that the failure to provide land for occupation by the community in terms of s 26(1) effectively made it impossible for the landowner to execute the eviction order. The State had no plan for the 'immediate amelioration of the circumstances of those in crisis'.[88] This resulted in a breach of the owner's property rights in terms of s 25(1) of the Constitution.[89] Effectively, the State had breached its duties in terms of s 7(2) of the Constitution to 'protect' the owner's property rights by failing to fulfil its responsibilities to a community in desperate need of accommodation.[90] The Supreme Court of Appeal also held that the rights to equality and non-discrimination in terms of s 9(1) and (2) had been breached by the

[86] *Modderklip Boerdery (Edms) Bpk v President van die Republiek van Suid-Afrika* 2003 (6) BCLR 638 (T), [2003] 1 All SA 465 (T) 693A–694H.

[87] *Modderklip (SCA)* (note 14 above).

[88] Ibid para 22 citing *Grootboom* (note 9 above) para 64.

[89] Ibid para 28.

[90] Ibid paras 26–28.

fact that the State permitted the public burden of accommodating a homeless community to be borne by a single, private person.[91]

In his judgment for the Court, Harms JA (as he then was) underscored the fact that the occupiers were the beneficiaries of a right of access to housing in terms of s 26(1) of the Constitution and that the State had failed in its duty to have a plan in place for those in desperate housing need.[92] In response to the argument made on behalf of the municipality and the province that any order for the provision of accommodation to the community would amount to 'queue-jumping' and disrupt existing priorities and orderly planning in the provision of housing, Harms JA pointed out that there was no evidence that the occupation took place with any intent to gain an advantage in the housing allocation process, and that the land was occupied under the mistaken impression that it belonged to the municipality.[93] Moreover, in terms of the *Grootboom* judgment the State was under an obligation 'to ensure, at the very least, that evictions are executed humanely'.[94] According to the Court, it was 'abundantly clear by now, the order cannot be executed – humanely or otherwise – unless the State provides some land'.[95] This was a factor that 'must be taken into account without granting the Gabon residents priority'.[96]

By way of remedy, the Court declared that the owner was entitled to the payment of damages by the Department of Agriculture and Land Affairs in respect of the land occupied by the community.[97] It furthermore declared that the residents were entitled to occupy the land until alternative land was made available to them by the State.[98]

The State appealed against this decision to the Constitutional Court. The Court did not consider it necessary to resolve the case on the basis of the landowner's property rights (s 25) or the housing rights of the occupiers (s 26).[99] Instead it found a violation of the principle of the rule of law in s 1(*c*) as well as the right of access to courts or other independent forums protected in s 34 of the Constitution. It held that the first obligation, arising from the principle of the rule of law, is that the State is obliged to provide the necessary mechanisms for citizens to resolve the disputes

---

91 Ibid para 31.

92 Ibid para 22.

93 Ibid para 25.

94 Ibid para 26 citing *Grootboom* (note 9 above) para 88.

95 Ibid.

96 Ibid.

97 The damages were to be calculated in terms of s 12(1) of the Expropriation Act 63 of 1975 which provides that in respect of the expropriation of property or the taking of a right to use property, compensation must not exceed the amount which the property would have realised if sold in the open market by a willing seller to a willing buyer; and an amount to make good any actual financial loss caused by the expropriation or the taking of the right.

98 Ibid paras 51–52. On the 'constitutional damages' remedy granted in the *Modderklip* case, see further chapter 8, part 8.7.2.

99 *Modderklip (CC)* (note 14 above) para 26.

that arise between them.[100] The corollary of this obligation is the entitlement of every citizen to have access to courts or other independent forums provided by the State for the settlement of such disputes.[101] The effective execution of orders was also integral to the rule of law and the right to have access to courts or other independent forums. In this case, it required the active participation of the State.[102] The obligation to ensure that court orders are effectively executed goes beyond providing the institutions and mechanisms for resolving disputes. It also requires the State 'to take reasonable steps, where possible, to ensure that large-scale social disruptions in the social fabric do not occur in the wake of the execution of court orders, thus undermining the rule of law'.[103]

The Court held that the State's failure to take steps to assist the landowner to vindicate his property and, at the same time, avoid the large-scale social disruption caused by the eviction of a large community with nowhere to go was unreasonable. The State's rationale for failing to assist the landowner and occupiers was ostensibly to discourage 'queue-jumping' with respect to housing, but this was not supported on the facts of the case.[104] The Court affirmed that the progressive realisation of the right of access to housing or land for the homeless requires 'careful planning', 'fair procedures' and 'orderly and predictable processes'.[105] Land invasions should always be discouraged.[106] At the same time, these measures should not be 'unduly hamstrung so as to exclude all possible adaptation to evolving circumstances'.[107] The importance of finding flexible, pragmatic and humane solutions to extraordinary cases[108] was emphasised. In the words of Langa ACJ (as he then was) for the Court:

> If social reality fails to conform to the best laid plans, reasonable and appropriate responses may be necessary. Such responses should advance the interests at stake and not be unduly disruptive towards other persons. Indeed, any planning which leaves no scope whatsoever for relatively marginal adjustments in the light of evolving reality, may often not be reasonable.[109]

In the final analysis it was unreasonable for the State 'to stand by and do nothing in circumstances where it was impossible for Modderklip to evict the occupiers because of the sheer magnitude of the invasion and the particular circumstances of the occupiers'.[110]

---

[100] Ibid para 39.
[101] Ibid paras 39–40.
[102] Ibid para 42.
[103] Ibid para 43.
[104] Ibid para 50.
[105] Ibid para 49.
[106] Ibid.
[107] Ibid.
[108] Ibid para 47.
[109] Ibid para 49.
[110] Ibid para 48.

The remedy granted by the Supreme Court of Appeal was substantially upheld by the Constitutional Court.[111] The State was required to compensate the landowner for the occupation of its property, such compensation to be calculated on the basis of s 12(1) of the Expropriation Act 63 of 1975.[112] Similarly, the order expressly declares 'that the residents are entitled to occupy the land until alternative land has been made available to them by the state or the provincial or local authority'.[113]

All three judgments in the *Modderklip* case confirm that the State may not abdicate its responsibilities in a dispute between private parties where important constitutional rights are threatened and State intervention is required for their protection.[114] It is unfortunate that the Constitutional Court, in contrast to the Supreme Court of Appeal, chose to avoid identifying the interests pertaining to the property and housing rights so clearly at stake in the circumstances of the case. While the principle of the rule of law and the right of access to courts are also implicated by the facts of the *Modderklip* case, the State's abdication of its responsibility towards both the landowner and the community directly affected their respective property and housing rights.[115] Nevertheless the relational interaction between the various constitutional rights and duties affirmed in the *Port Elizabeth Municipality* judgment also pervades the Constitutional Court's judgment in *Modderklip*. Pragmatic and humane solutions must be sought to eviction-related conflicts which are consonant with the rights and values protected in the Constitution. Such solutions cannot be achieved without active State involvement.

Both the Supreme Court of Appeal and the Constitutional Court affirmed the principle that where an eviction will place persons in a situation of desperate housing need they should generally have access to some form of accommodation (albeit on a temporary basis) pending their integration in long-term development programmes.[116] This represents a specific manifestation of the principle laid down in *Grootboom* that the State should put in place and implement a reasonable programme which provides immediate relief 'for people who have no access to land, no roof over their heads, and

---

[111] Ibid para 68.

[112] Ibid. Order para 3(*d*).

[113] Ibid. Order para 3(*c*).

[114] The Supreme Court of Appeal highlighted the State's duty in terms of s 7(2) of the Constitution to protect citizens against violations of their rights perpetrated by private parties: see (note 14 above) para 27. For a commentary on this protective duty of the State in the context of the *Modderklip* case, see A J van der Walt 'The State's duty to protect property owners v the State's duty to provide housing: Thoughts on the *Modderklip* case' (2005) 21 *SAJHR* 144–161 at 159–161. See also the discussion of the State's duty to protect socio-economic rights in chapter 3, part 3, 3.2.2.

[115] See Van der Walt ibid 156–157 and 159.

[116] As noted previously, there may be exceptions where, for example, a community deliberately invades land or housing in order to secure preference in housing provision. See the discussion by Geoff Budlender (note 70 above) at 130–131.

who are living in intolerable conditions or crisis situations'.[117] As Browde AJ observed in *Transnet v Informal Settlers of Good Hope*:

> No longer can there be tolerated an attitude by government – at any level – that people may have no home of any kind nor even any basic shelter from the elements as was the position for so much of the twentieth century.[118]

In subsequent jurisprudence, the courts have emphasised that relevant organs of State such as municipalities cannot disavow their responsibilities in an eviction application brought by a private landowner against an unlawful occupier. There have been a series of High Court cases decided in terms of PIE in which municipalities have been joined as parties to the proceedings. The purpose of such joinder is to place information before the court on the availability of suitable alternative accommodation and to facilitate mediation of the dispute between the parties.[119]

The case of *Lingwood v The Unlawful Occupiers of R/E of Erf 9 Highlands*[120] ('*Lingwood*') concerned an eviction application in terms of PIE by owners who had recently purchased residential property which was occupied by 19 adults and eight children. Prior to the sale of the property the impoverished occupiers had been paying rental in respect of the property to a person whose identity and relationship to the property was unclear.[121] The respondents sought the joinder of the City of Johannesburg Metropolitan Municipality on the basis of the City's constitutional and statutory obligations to make provision for temporary emergency shelter for persons such as the respondents who, upon eviction, would have no suitable alternative accommodation available to them.[122] However, the joinder application was not properly served on the City of Johannesburg, and the respondents elected not to proceed with the application. The City was accordingly not a party to the proceedings,[123] but in response to applicants' eviction papers being served on it pursuant to s 4(2) of PIE, it filed a notice stating that it did 'not have any land and/or alternative suitable accommodation available to accommodate the respondents'.[124] Mogagabe AJ held that this 'terse and unsubstantiated statement' was insufficient to ascertain whether

---

[117] *Grootboom* (note 9 above) para 99.
[118] Note 81 above at 520B.
[119] In terms of s 4(2) of PIE, written and effective notice of proceedings for the eviction of unlawful occupiers by the owner or person in charge of land must be served both on the unlawful occupier at least 14 days before the hearing of the proceeding as well as the 'municipality having jurisdiction'. In *Cashbuild (South Africa) (Pty) Ltd v Scott* 2007 (1) SA 332 (T), the Court held that upon receipt of a s 4(2) notice the City was obligated to apply its mind to mediation, its legal interest arising from its obligation under s 7(1) of PIE to facilitate meetings and mediation between the interested parties to the dispute.
[120] 2008 (3) BCLR 325 (W).
[121] Ibid paras 3–5.
[122] Ibid para 12.
[123] Ibid para 17.
[124] Ibid para 15.

the City was complying with its constitutional and statutory obligations in terms of the Housing Act 107 of 1997.[125]

According to the Court, the non-availability of suitable alternative accommodation to unlawful occupiers did not *per se* render an eviction order unjust or inequitable.[126] Nevertheless, the availability of suitable alternative accommodation or land was 'one of the factors, if not the most important factor, for a Court to have regard to in determining whether it is just and equitable to issue an eviction order'.[127] The importance of mediation in attempting to arrive at equitable and pragmatic solutions to the clash between property and housing rights in eviction situations was also emphasised.[128]

Given the purposes and underlying philosophy of PIE, read in the light of s 26 of the Constitution, the judge held that the joinder of the City to the proceedings was essential.[129] Such joinder was for the purpose of furnishing the envisaged comprehensive programme for the realisation of the right of access to adequate housing and the provision of temporary emergency housing as an interim measure,[130] and to facilitate mediation between the parties with a view to achieving a mutually acceptable solution.[131] It accordingly ordered the application to be postponed *sine die*, and ordered the respondents to join the City to the proceedings. It further directed the parties 'to engage in mediation in an endeavour to exploring all reasonable possibilities of securing suitable alternative accommodation or land and/or of achieving solutions mutually acceptable to the parties'.[132]

In the subsequent decision of *Sailing Queen Investments v The Occupants La Colleen Court*[133] ('*Sailing Queen Investments*'), Jajbhay J also stayed an application for eviction brought in terms of s 4 of PIE, and directed that the City of Johannesburg Metropolitan Municipality be joined to the proceedings. He expressly disagreed with the unreported decision of Boruchowitz J in *Xantium Trading 387 (Pty) Ltd v Molefe*[134] refusing the application for joinder of the local authority in a PIE eviction applica-

---

[125] Ibid.

[126] Ibid para 27.

[127] Ibid para 18. See also the observation of Bertelsmann J in *Ritama* (note 62 above) at 13:
'Normally the information regarding available housing for the homeless will be critical to determine on what terms and conditions justice and equity would best be served if an eviction order has to be made.'

[128] Ibid para 37 citing *Port Elizabeth Municipality* (note 12 above) paras 36 and 37, and *Modderklip (CC)* (note 14 above) para 55.

[129] The City was 'a necessary and interested party' by virtue of its constitutional and statutory obligations. Ibid para 37.

[130] Ibid para 32. The court held that PIE did not impose an obligation on a private landowner to provide alternative accommodation to unlawful occupiers facing eviction. This obligation rested on the State and/or its responsible organs: paras 19–25.

[131] Ibid para 37.

[132] Ibid para 38 (Order).

[133] 2008 (6) BCLR 666 (W).

[134] Case No 23758/ 05 ZAGPHCJ (unreported judgment of 2 April 2007).

tion. He held that the obligation of the municipality to ensure that the 'desperately poor' have access to alternative accommodation if evicted as well as their role in acting as mediator in eviction applications made it vital that they be joined as a party in private evictions.[135] The joinder of the local authority in cases concerning the eviction of socio-economically marginalised groups from private property was deemed 'necessarily incidental to the vindication of the respondents' constitutional rights of access to adequate housing, protection from arbitrary evictions, and dignity'.[136]

A number of other judgments have confirmed the importance of local authorities placing substantive information before a court to enable them to exercise a proper discretion in eviction applications brought by private landowners in terms of PIE.

In *ABSA Bank v Murray*,[137] the court referred to the obligation of municipalities to report to the court 'in respect of any of the factors affecting land and accommodation availability and the basic health and amenities consequences of an eviction, especially on the most vulnerable such as children, the disabled and the elderly'.[138] It held that the failure to provide such a report not only rendered the service of a s 4(2) notice in terms of PIE superfluous and costly for applications, but frustrated important objectives of PIE. Such reports 'should be the norm and not the exception'.[139] In *Ritama Investments v The Unlawful Occupiers of Erf 62, Wynberg*,[140] the Court again affirmed that meaningful information regarding available housing for the homeless is critical in order to determine whether an eviction order should be made at all and, if so, on what terms and conditions justice and equity would be served.[141]

A detailed and sophisticated elaboration of the duty of municipalities to provide meaningful information to courts in eviction applications from private land is provided by Masipa J in *Blue Moonlight Properties 39 (Pty) Limited v The Occupiers of Saratoga Avenue*[142] ('*Blue Moonlight Properties*'). Judge Masipa emphatically rejected the inference in the City's papers that it is not under an obligation to assist persons facing homelessness pursuant to their eviction from private land.[143] She held that such a stance was inconsistent with s 26 of the Constitution as interpreted in the *Grootboom* judgment,[144] the Housing Act 107 of 1997, and the *Programme for Housing Assistance*

---

[135] Ibid para 14. See further paras 15–16.

[136] Ibid para 17. This position has been confirmed in the recent unreported judgment of the Supreme Court of Appeal in *The Occupiers of Shorts Retreat, Pietermaritzburg v Daisy Dear Investments (Pty) Ltd* [2009] ZASCA 80 (3 July 2009).

[137] Note 65 above.

[138] Ibid para 41.

[139] Ibid para 42.

[140] Note 62 above.

[141] Ibid 9–10.

[142] 2009 (1) SA 470 (W), 2009 (3) BCLR 329 (W).

[143] Ibid para 37.

[144] Note 9 above.

in Emergency Circumstances adopted in terms of the Housing Act.[145] In performing their special judicial role as described in the *Port Elizabeth Municipality* judgment of reaching just and equitable decisions in eviction applications, courts require municipalities to provide them with comprehensive, meaningful and specific information. It is insufficient simply to file a generic report dealing generally with the housing programmes adopted by the relevant municipality.[146] This lack of specificity is aggravated when the municipality adopts the position that its plans expressly exclude persons in the position of the occupiers in the relevant eviction application.[147] The municipal report must be appropriately tailored to the circumstances of the particular case and deal with the personal circumstances of the particular occupants facing eviction, particularly when they are impoverished and face homelessness. As expressed by the Court:

> Such cases require extra vigilance and compassion on the part of the courts. Hence the need to get specific information from the City regarding a specific case. A one-fits-all solution in eviction cases is, therefore, not only unworkable but also unacceptable.[148]

In order to submit a proper report which gives the court 'a full picture' of whether land has been made available, or can reasonably be made available, to a specific group of unlawful occupiers it is necessary for the municipality to 'investigate the circumstances of a case as well as consult with the stakeholders, where necessary'.[149] The Court found that the inadequate report provided by the City in the instant case was in breach of its constitutional and statutory obligations.[150] It postponed the eviction application *sine die* and ordered the City to provide a report to the Court on 'what steps it has taken and in future can take to provide emergency shelter or other housing for the first respondents in the event of their eviction as prayed'.[151] It also provided the applicants with an opportunity to comment on the aforesaid report.[152]

The *Blue Moonlight Properties* judgment draws a clear link between the obligations of organs of State in terms of the *Grootboom* judgment and the exercise by the courts of their discretion to make just and equitable orders in eviction cases in terms of PIE. This illustrates the interrelatedness of all three subsections of s 26. Important guidance is also provided on the obligations of local authorities in relation to the eviction of unlawful occupiers from private land. The judgment stresses that an individualised assessment of the circumstances of the occupiers in question is necessary, and that

---

145 Ibid paras 25–36. See notes 70–71 above and accompanying text. See also chapter 8, part 8.4.2.
146 Ibid paras 57–58.
147 Ibid para 58–62.
148 Ibid para 64.
149 Ibid para 66.
150 Ibid para 73.
151 Ibid para 78.
152 Ibid.

relevant officials must make special efforts to secure alternative accommodation for those who will be rendered homeless as a result of an eviction.

Instead of the private law paradigm through which the eviction of persons from private property was traditionally viewed, the judgments discussed above exemplify the new approach envisaged for a court by when it evaluates the justice and equity of an eviction order in terms of PIE. As expressed by Sachs J:

> [A court] is called upon to balance competing interests in a principled way and promote the constitutional vision of a caring society based on good neighbourliness and shared concern. The Constitution and PIE confirm that we are not islands unto ourselves. The spirit of *ubuntu*, part of the deep cultural heritage of the majority of the population suffuses the whole constitutional order. It combines individual rights with a communitarian philosophy. It is a unifying motif of the Bill of Rights, which is nothing if not a structured, institutionalised and operational declaration in our evolving new society of the need for human interdependence, respect and concern.[153]

A caring society founded on mutual interdependence and respect cannot be promoted without proactive and meaningful State involvement whenever persons face homelessness due to their eviction from public or private land. It is only when organs of State are able to assist in resolving eviction disputes through discussions, mediation and the provision of suitable alternative accommodation that solutions can be reached which respect both the landowner's property rights and the occupier's housing rights. Judgments such as the *Lingwood,*[154] *Sailing Queen Investments*[155] and *Blue Moonlight Properties*[156] epitomise this transformative approach to the socially disruptive clash between property and housing rights in eviction applications.

There is a further line of cases in which eviction orders are granted (usually subject to a delayed date for the execution thereof) accompanied by a positive order against the relevant organs of State to provide temporary alternative accommodation to those facing homelessness as a result of the eviction. In *Property Lodging Investments (Pty) Ltd v The Unlawful Occupiers of Erf 705, Halfway Gardens,*[157] the City of Johannesburg had been cited as a party in the eviction application. The South Gauteng High Court ordered the unlawful occupiers to vacate the private property which they were occupying. It also made an order directing the City to provide short-term alternative accommodation for the respondents 'who are in a crisis or a desperate situation', in compliance with its constitutional and statutory obligations, by no later than the date stipulated for their eviction.

In *Grobler v Msimanga,*[158] the South Gauteng High Court held that the Randfontein Local Municipality had failed to provide any detailed information on the provision

---

[153] *Port Elizabeth Municipality* (note 12 above) para 37 (footnotes omitted).
[154] *Lingwood* (note 120 above).
[155] *Sailing Queen Investments* (note 133 above).
[156] *Blue Moonlight Properties* (note 142 above).
[157] Case No: 6292/06 ZAGPHC (unreported judgment 30 November 2006).
[158] [2008] 3 All SA 549 (W).

of alternative accommodation to the occupiers facing eviction from the private land in question.[159] The Municipality had adopted the approach that no land was available to accommodate the community and had failed to appreciate its constitutional and statutory duties to provide emergency accommodation in the case of an eviction order.[160] The eviction application was granted,[161] but the carrying out of the order postponed for a ten-month period. In addition, the Municipality was ordered:

> to offer and provide to those respondents who are evicted and are, at that time, desperately in need of housing, assistance with relocation to a temporary settlement area as described in Chapter 12 of the National Housing Code, within its municipal area, which temporary accommodation is to consist of a place where they may live secure against eviction, in a structure that is waterproof, and with access to basic sanitation, water and refuse services.[162]

To this end, the Municipality was also required to take all steps necessary to obtain land for the purposes of the relocation of the respondents and all other unlawful occupiers of the property.[163]

A recent judgment of the Supreme Court of Appeal dealt with the limits of orders which can be made against municipalities in relation to the purchasing of specific land for alternative accommodation. In *Dada NO v Unlawful Occupiers of Portion 41 of the farm Rooikop*,[164] the South Gauteng High Court found that the Ekurhuleni Metropolitan Municipality had failed to put in place any plan to provide emergency relief in terms of alternative accommodation and basic services in respect of a group of 76 households facing eviction from private land.[165] The owners of the land in question had offered the land for sale to the municipality for a purchase price of R250 000. The court directed the municipality to purchase the property from the applicants for this sum, and to forthwith make provision of essential services to the occupiers of the property.[166]

This order to purchase specific property was overturned by the Supreme Court of Appeal in *Ekurhuleni Metropolitan Municipality v Dada NO* ('*Dada*')[167]. The Supreme Court of Appeal held that the judge in the court *a quo* was impelled to make such an order by 'a preconceived notion' that 'it was time to get things moving'.[168] In doing so,

[159] Ibid paras 216–217.
[160] Ibid para 235.
[161] For a critique of the Court's approach in this case to its discretion to grant eviction orders in terms of PIE, see chapter 7, part 7.3.1(*c*) at notes 177–184 and accompanying text.
[162] Ibid para 254. Order 6.
[163] Ibid order 7.
[164] 2009 (2) SA 492 (W).
[165] Ibid paras 45–48. This judgment was delivered in respect of a counterclaim against the Municipality by the occupiers. The Municipality had been joined as a respondent by the landowner (a Trust) in their application to evict the occupiers in terms of s 4 of PIE.
[166] Ibid para 50.
[167] 2009 (4) SA 463 (SCA)
[168] Ibid para 13.

he overlooked the principle of 'progressive realisation' in relation to housing rights, as well as crafting an order not specifically sought by the parties.[169] The Supreme Court of Appeal held that the court *a quo* 'was perhaps right in coming to the conclusion that the municipality had not dealt with the problems of the informal settlement on the property with the measure of alacrity which could reasonably be expected of them'.[170] However, this did not justify an approach which disregarded relevant statutory provisions and precepts of appropriate relief in the circumstances.[171] The order against the municipality to purchase the land was set aside, but an order relating to the provision of essential services to the community was upheld. The main application relating to the eviction of the occupiers was to be set down for hearing and dealt with by the court of first instance.

The Supreme Court of Appeal's judgment in the *Dada* case should be understood in the light of the specific circumstances of the relief sought, and the need to permit organs of State a reasonable margin of discretion in deciding precisely how their constitutional duties to occupiers should be fulfilled.[172] The principles established both by the Supreme Court of Appeal and the Constitutional Court in cases such as *Modderklip* concerning the State's constitutional obligations to vulnerable occupiers facing eviction from private land have not been negated by this judgment.

Cases such as *Modderklip* and the other cases discussed in this part dealing with eviction from private land destabilise the notion of a strict dichotomy between public and private law. They illustrate how the housing rights in s 26 of the Constitution have transformed cases which were previously regarded as involving purely private and procedural law into ones with significant public dimensions.[173] In commenting on the attitude adopted by the State in *Modderklip*[174] that the case was an exclusively civil law matter, with the State's responsibility restricted to providing the institutions and mechanisms for the enforcement of court orders, André van der Walt observes:[175]

> The attitude that the eviction is possible under civil law and that its execution in the present case is a 'simple' and 'mundane' matter of private law is inspired by the now outdated extreme minimal-state privatism of nineteenth century *laissez-faire* politics. In order to adopt this attitude, the state had to bracket out a number of factors that are in fact inextricably linked up with the social, political and legal context of the case. Neither the SCA

---

[169] Ibid.

[170] Ibid para 14.

[171] Ibid.

[172] Cassim AJ (note 164 above) para 37 conceded that the approach he adopted 'may well be viewed not only as ordering the State to fulfil its obligations, but also telling it how to do so and this would be a breach of the rule on separation of powers' (references omitted).

[173] See also *Port Elizabeth Municipality* (note 12 above) paras 16–17. On the public/private dichotomy in classic liberal theory, see chapter 2, part 2.4.5.

[174] See *Modderklip (CC)* (note 14 above) para 24.

[175] Van der Walt (note 114 above) 148.

nor the Constitutional Court was willing to accept this bracketing-out or the attitude underlying it.

6.4 EVICTIONS FOR HEALTH AND SAFETY REASONS: *OCCUPIERS OF 51 OLIVIA ROAD*

Occupiers of 51 Olivia Road is a significant case which provided the courts with an opportunity to consider the implications of s 26, particularly s 26(3), in a context outside of the land reform legislation adopted post 1994. The case arose out of the Johannesburg City Council's applications to evict a substantial number of poor residents of alleged unsafe buildings in the Johannesburg inner city in terms of the National Building Regulations and Building Standards Act 103 of 1977 ('the NBRSA').[176] The spate of evictions in terms of this legislation throughout Johannesburg formed part of the Johannesburg City Council's Inner City Regeneration Strategy.[177]

Section 12(4)(*b*) of the NBRSA provides that if a local authority 'deems it necessary for the safety of any person, it may by notice in writing, served by post or delivered ... order any person occupying or working or being for any other purpose in any building, to vacate such building immediately or within a period specified in such notice'. Failure to comply with such a notice is a criminal offence in terms of s 12(6) of the Act. The NBRSA does not expressly provide for a court order in respect of the issuing of a s 12(4)(*b*) notice. However, it was the practice of the City to apply for a court order authorising the eviction of residents who failed to comply with the notices issued in terms of s 12(4)(*b*) of the Act. Moreover, there is no express provision in the NBRSA requiring a court to consider 'all the relevant circumstances' before ordering the eviction of applicants.

The High Court held that the NBRSA and other relevant municipal by-laws must be interpreted in the light of the constitutional right of access to adequate housing in s 26 of the Constitution, specifically s 26(3).[178] It held that the issuing by a municipality of a notice to vacate unsafe buildings in terms of s 12(4)(*b*) of the NBRSA does not automatically require a court to make an eviction order, but merely triggers the court's discretion.[179] Factors the court will consider in exercising its discretion are the degree of emergency and desperation of the people living in these buildings, the

---

[176] Reliance was also placed on s 20 of the Health Act 63 of 1977 which placed a duty on local authorities to 'take all lawful, necessary and reasonably practicable measures' to ensure safe and hygienic conditions within their district. However, the case turned primarily on the interpretation of the relevant provisions of the NBRSA.

[177] For a detailed historical and social analysis of the background of this case, see Centre for Housing Rights and Evictions (COHRE) 'Any room for the poor? Forced evictions in Johannesburg, South Africa' (8 March 2005). Available at http://www.cohre.org/store/attachments/Any_Room_for_the_Poor_8Mar05.pdf (accessed on 30 June 2009).

[178] *City of Johannesburg v Rand Properties (Pty) Ltd* 2007 (1) SA 78 (W), 2006 (6) BCLR 728 (W) para 36.

[179] Ibid para 29.

period that they have been occupying the buildings, and the requirements of non-arbitrariness and due process in s 26(3) of the Constitution.[180]

The Court found that the City had no programme in place as required by the *Grootboom* judgment to provide temporary accommodation for persons such as the respondents. They would face homelessness if evicted as they were too poor to secure alternative accommodation.[181] If evicted, the applicants would be far worse off than in their current accommodation.[182] The suggestion by the applicants that the occupiers relocate to one of the informal settlements far away from the city centre was rejected by the Court as being inconsistent with the African philosophical concept of *ubuntu*. *Ubuntu* pervades the Constitution and emphasises the interconnectedness of individual and communal welfare, and 'the responsibility to each that flows from our connection'.[183] The eviction of the applicants would deprive them of their livelihood as many of them eke out a living through informal economic activities (such as waste recycling and domestic work) in the inner city of Johannesburg. Jajbhay J referred in this context to 'the right to work' (which is not expressly included in the text of the South African Constitution) as 'one of the most precious liberties that an individual possesses':

> An individual has as much right to work as the individual has to live, to be free and to own property. To work means to eat and consequently to live. This constitutes an encompassing view of humanity.[184]

The applicant was directed 'to devise and implement within its available resources a comprehensive and co-ordinated programme to progressively realise the right to adequate housing of people in the inner city of Johannesburg who are in a crisis situation or otherwise in desperate need of accommodation'.[185] The City was furthermore interdicted from evicting or seeking to evict the occupiers pending the implementation of the aforementioned programme; alternatively, until such time as suitable alternative accommodation was provided to them.[186]

The case was appealed by the City to the Supreme Court of Appeal.[187] The Supreme Court of Appeal overruled the High Court on the question of whether the courts had any discretion to refuse an eviction order if the requirements of the NBRSA were satisfied. It confirmed its interpretation of s 26(3) articulated in *Brisley v Drotsky*[188] that the only 'relevant circumstances' which s 26(3) requires a court to take into account are those which are relevant in terms of existing common or statutory

---

[180] Ibid para 29 read with para 36.
[181] Ibid paras 22, 47.
[182] Ibid para 57.
[183] Ibid para 63.
[184] Ibid para 64.
[185] Ibid 749H (Order, para 3 of the Court's order).
[186] Ibid 749I (Order, para 4).
[187] *City of Johannesburg v Rand Properties* (note 59 above).
[188] Note 59 above.

law.[189] The Court held that the only legally relevant criterion in this case was whether a municipality deemed it 'necessary for the safety of any person' to order a notice to vacate in terms of s 12(4)(*b*) of the NBRSA.[190]

However, the Court went on to hold that it could not ignore 'the consequences that might follow upon eviction', observing that '[i]t seems probable that, once evicted, at least some of the respondents will be left without any shelter at all, and will have no resources with which to secure any'.[191] The eviction would place people in a situation of crisis and desperate need, thereby triggering the *Grootboom* obligation to ensure that there is a programme in place to cater for their emergency shelter needs.[192] The Court went on to hold that it was 'not satisfied that the City has pursued with any vigour the application under Chapter 12 [of the Housing Code]'.[193]

The Supreme Court of Appeal was not prepared to follow the High Court in making the eviction order conditional on the provision of alternative accommodation. It held that the City was entitled to evict the occupiers in terms of s 12(4)(*b*) of the NBRSA 'even if the effect of complying with the order will be that they are left without access to adequate housing'.[194] It accordingly upheld the appeal against the High Court's refusal of the eviction order.[195] However, the eviction order was coupled with an order in terms of which the City was ordered to provide temporary accommodation to those evicted from the building and who were desperately in need of housing assistance. This temporary accommodation was to consist of 'at least the following elements: a place where they may live secure against eviction; a structure that is waterproof and secure against the elements; and with access to basic sanitation, water and refuse services'.[196] The location of this alternative accommodation had to be determined by the City 'after consultation' with respondents.[197] It granted a limited supervisory order in the form of requiring the City of Johannesburg to serve on the respondents' attorneys of record and the *amici curiae*, as well as filing with the registrar, a compliance affidavit within four months of the order.[198]

---

[189] In *Brisley* the Supreme Court of Appeal held that the courts had no broad, general equitable discretion in terms of s 26(3) to take into account factors such as the personal circumstances of an unlawful occupier or the availability of suitable alternative accommodation. Ibid paras 41–44. The legally relevant circumstances in this case were the common-law entitlements of an owner to recover possession of his or her property when a former tenant is in unlawful occupation thereof (para 45). See further the discussion of the *Brisley* decision in chapter 7, part 7.3.1(*b*).

[190] *City of Johannesburg v Rand Properties* (note 59 above) paras 40–41, 49.

[191] Ibid para 76.

[192] Ibid paras 5, 47, 77.

[193] Ibid para 77.

[194] Ibid para 68.

[195] Ibid para 78.

[196] Ibid. Order para 2.1.

[197] Ibid. Order para 2.3.

[198] Ibid. Order para 2.4.

The occupiers appealed against the judgment and order of the Supreme Court of Appeal to the Constitutional Court.[199] Two days after the application for leave to appeal and argument was heard in the matter, the Constitutional Court issued an interim order, requiring the City and occupiers to 'engage with each other meaningfully ... in an effort to resolve the differences and difficulties aired in this application in the light of the values of the Constitution, the constitutional and statutory duties of the municipality and the rights and duties of the citizens concerned'.[200] The engagement order was also directed at alleviating the plight of the applicants by making the two buildings concerned 'as safe and as conducive to health as is reasonably practicable'.[201] The parties were ordered to report back to the Court on the results of the engagement.[202] The Court indicated further that account would be taken of the contents of the report in the preparation of the judgment or in issuing further directions should this become necessary.[203]

The outcome of this 'meaningful engagement' order was a comprehensive settlement agreement between the parties. This agreement included steps for rendering the buildings safer and more habitable, as well detailed provisions relating to the relocation of the occupiers to alternative accommodation in the inner city. The latter included the identification of the relevant buildings, the nature and standard of the accommodation to be provided, and the calculation of the rental to be paid. The agreement further stipulated that this alternative accommodation was being provided 'pending the provision of suitable permanent housing solutions' being developed by the City 'in consultation' with the occupiers concerned.[204] This settlement agreement was endorsed by the Court on 5 November 1997.[205]

The judgment of the Constitutional Court dealt with three major issues. The first concerned its reasons for making the engagement order, and the purposes and nature of such engagement. It affirmed the basic principle that in situations where people face homelessness due to an eviction, public authorities should generally engage seriously and in good faith with the affected occupiers with a view to finding humane and pragmatic solutions to their dilemma. The Court chose not to decide the arguments raised by the occupiers, and elaborated on by the *amici curiae*[206] in their

[199] *Occupiers of 51 Olivia Road* (note 15 above).

[200] Ibid para 5. Interim order para 1.

[201] Ibid. Interim order para 2.

[202] Ibid. Interim order para 3.

[203] Ibid. Interim order para 4.

[204] Settlement agreement between City of Johannesburg and the Occupiers of 51 Olivia Road, Berea Township and 197 Main Street, Johannesburg dated 29 October 2007 (copy on file with author). The terms of the engagement order are summarised by the Court at paras 24–26.

[205] Ibid para 27.

[206] The Community Law Centre (UWC) and Centre on Housing Rights and Evictions (COHRE) were joint *amici curiae* in both the Supreme Court of Appeal and the Constitutional Court. A copy of the *amici curiae* submissions is available at http://www.consti-

submissions, that the issuing of the s 12(4)(*b*) notices by the City constituted administrative action and was therefore subject to the hearing or public inquiry procedures in terms of s 3, alternatively, s 4 of the Promotion of Administrative Justice Act 3 of 2000 ('PAJA').[207] Similarly, the Court declined to decide whether the eviction was subject to s 6 of PIE.[208] Instead the Court derived the legal basis for the requirement of 'meaningful engagement' directly from a range of constitutional provisions.

The duty is primarily derived from the various subsections of s 26 of the Constitution. Every level of government is obliged to act consistently with the constitutional obligation on the State to take reasonable measures to extend access to adequate housing. This includes the obligation to respect the inherent dignity of every person and to treat human beings as human beings.[209] Whether there has been meaningful engagement is furthermore one of the 'relevant circumstances' to be taking into account in terms of s 26(3) of the Constitution.[210] The failure of a municipality to engage meaningfully, or an unreasonable response in the engagement process, 'would ordinarily be a weighty consideration against the grant of an ejectment order'.[211] The judgment furthermore refers to the obligation on local authorities to 'provide services to communities in a sustainable manner, promote social and economic development, and encourage the involvement of communities and com-

---

tutionalcourt.org.za/uhtbin/cgisirsi/joJDP6Ac5p/MAIN/175670035/523/8183 (accessed 30 June 2009).

207 *Occupiers of 51 Olivia Road* (note 15 above) paras 7, 9, 39. It is unfortunate that the Court did not avail itself of this opportunity to clarify the applicability of the public inquiry and other procedures provided for in s 4 of PAJA when an eviction is a result of an administrative action which 'materially and adversely affects the rights of the public'. See in this regard G Quinot 'An administrative law perspective on "bad building" evictions in the Johannesburg inner city: *City of Johannesburg v Rand Properties (Pty) Ltd* 2007 ZASCA 25 (RSA)' (2007) 1 *ESR Review* 25–28.

208 Ibid para 38. It will be recalled that a court may grant an order for the eviction of unlawful occupiers in terms of PIE at the instance of organs of State if it is in the public interest to do so (s 6(1)(*b*)). The public interest is defined as including 'the interest of the health and safety of those occupying the land and the public in general' (s 6(2)). Again, the Court's failure to decide on the applicability of PIE and its relationship with the NBRSA in the context of evictions for health and safety reasons leaves the legal framework governing such evictions unclear.

209 Ibid para 10. In support hereof, the Court cites its judgment in *Grootboom* (note 9 above) paras 82–83 and 87. The latter paragraph sets out the Court's expectation that the local municipality would have taken steps 'to resolve the difficulty on a case-by-case basis' after investigation of the circumstances of the settlement on the New Rust land from which the *Grootboom* community had been evicted before occupying the sportsfield in Wallacedene. It also cites *Port Elizabeth Municipality* (note 12 above) para 39 on the importance of engaging in a proactive and respectful manner in order to find 'sustainable reconciliations' of the different interests involved in eviction applications.

210 Ibid paras 18, 22.

211 Ibid para 21.

munity organisation in matters of local government'.[212] Reference is also made to the State's obligation to fulfil the objectives in the preamble of the Constitution to '[i]mprove the quality of life of all citizens and free the potential of each person' as well as its obligation to 'respect, protect, promote and fulfil the rights in the Bill of Rights'.[213] According to the Court, the most important rights in this present context are human dignity and the right to life.[214] It concludes with the observation that 'a municipality that ejects people from their homes without first meaningfully engaging with them acts in a manner that is broadly at odds with the spirit and purpose of the constitutional obligations ... taken together'.[215]

The objectives of such engagement are to ascertain what the consequences of an eviction might be, whether the city could help in alleviating those dire consequences, whether it is possible to render the buildings concerned relatively safe and conducive to health for an interim period, whether the City had any obligations to the occupiers in the prevailing circumstances, and when and how the City could or would fulfil these obligations.[216] The Court explicitly links the objectives of meaningful engagement with the duty of municipalities to act reasonably in relation to people's housing needs in terms of s 26(2) as elaborated upon in the *Grootboom* judgment.[217] Thus the Court states:

> Every homeless person is in need of housing and this means that every step taken in relation to a potentially homeless person must also be reasonable if it is to comply with section 26(2).[218]

A number of the key features of 'meaningful engagement' in the context of an eviction can be distilled from the judgment. Meaningful engagement requires reasonable responses that are consistent with the right of access to adequate housing protected in s 26(2). This includes serious consideration of the alternative accommodation needs and circumstances of the particular occupiers. In this regard Yacoob J observes:

> It may in some circumstances be reasonable to make permanent housing available and, in others, to provide no housing at all. The possibilities between these extremes are almost endless. It must not be forgotten that the City cannot be expected to make provision for housing beyond the extent to which available resources allow. As long as the response of the municipality is reasonable, that response complies with section 26(2).[219]

The nature and extent of the engagement must depend on the context. Thus 'the larger the number of people potentially to be affected by eviction, the greater the need for structured, consistent and careful engagement' involving 'competent sensi-

---

[212] Ibid para 16 referring to s 152(*b*), (*c*) and (*e*) of the Constitution.
[213] Ibid, referring to s 7(2) of the Constitution.
[214] Ibid, referring to ss 10 and 11 of the Constitution.
[215] Ibid.
[216] Ibid para 14.
[217] Ibid para 17.
[218] Ibid.
[219] Ibid para 18.

tive council workers skilled in engagement'.[220] In a small municipality where the numbers of people affected by evictions are much smaller, ad hoc engagement may be appropriate.[221] Meaningful engagement requires that the parties engage with each other reasonably and in good faith. Intransigent attitudes or the 'making of non-negotiable, unreasonable demands' undermines the deliberative process.[222] Proactive solutions must be pursued and civil society organisations should facilitate the engagement process in every possible way.[223] Finally, the engagement process must be characterised by transparency as 'secrecy is counter-productive to the process of engagement'.[224] In eviction proceedings at the instance of a municipality, 'a complete and accurate account of the process of engagement including at least the reasonable efforts of the municipality within that process' must be provided to the court.[225]

The Court concluded that the Supreme Court of Appeal should not have granted the eviction order in the circumstances of the case in the absence of meaningful engagement between the parties.[226] According to *Occupiers of 51 Olivia Road*, 'meaningful engagement' is an obligation on public authorities derived directly from the various constitutional provisions referred to above. It would accordingly apply whenever public authorities seek to evict people from their homes in circumstances that expose them to potential homelessness, regardless of the common law or legislative source of the power to evict.

The second major issue dealt with in the Constitutional Court's judgment concerned the proper interpretation of s 12(4)(*b*) of the NBRSA in the light of s 26 of the Constitution.[227] The Court held that, although the Supreme Court of Appeal was correct in concluding that a local authority's right to issue a notice to vacate to occupiers in terms of the aforesaid section was not necessarily conditional on their having access to adequate housing, it did not follow that the availability of suitable alternative accommodation or land was not a relevant consideration when making a decision to issue a notice to vacate in terms of s 12(4)(*b*).[228] The fact that people would be rendered homeless consequent upon a decision to evict was a highly relevant consideration which a municipality should take into account in exercising its discretion

---

[220] Ibid para 19.
[221] Ibid.
[222] Ibid para 20.
[223] Ibid.
[224] Ibid para 21. This gives expression to transparency as a relevant criterion in the assessment of reasonable action by the State in realising socio-economic rights. See *Minister of Health v Treatment Action Campaign (No 2)* 2002 (5) SA 721 (CC), 2002 (10) BCLR 1033 (CC) para 123, and chapter 4, part 4.3.3 at note 111 and accompanying text.
[225] Ibid.
[226] Ibid para 23. On the outcome and implications of the 'meaningful engagement' order, see further chapter 8, part 8.5.3(*b*) at notes 268–284 and accompanying text.
[227] Interpreting legislation so as to 'promote the spirit, purport and objects of the Bill of Rights' is an injunction imposed upon courts by s 39(2) of the Constitution.
[228] Ibid para 43.

to issue a notice to vacate. It seems self-evident that the legitimate public purpose of ensuring safe accommodation is undermined when people are literally thrown out on the streets of a city without recourse to alternative accommodation. This exposes them to a range of threats to their safety and well-being.

The Court emphasised that local authorities are under an obligation to function in a systematic, integrated manner in realising their constitutional obligation to progressively realise the right of access to adequate housing. This requires different departments not to function in isolation from each other with 'one department making a decision on whether someone should be evicted and some other department in the bureaucratic maze determining whether housing should be provided'.[229] By failing to affirm the relevance of the availability of alternative accommodation in the decision by the city to issue notices to vacate, the Supreme Court of Appeal had not fully appreciated 'the interrelationship between section 12(4)(*b*) of the Act and section 26(2) of the Constitution'.[230]

The third aspect which is considered in the judgment is the constitutionality of s 12(6) of the NBRSA which imposes criminal liability for a failure to comply with a notice to vacate without provision for judicial oversight of the eviction. The Constitutional Court held that this provision falls foul of s 26(3) which prohibits the eviction of people from their home in the absence of a court order made after considering all the relevant circumstances. This provision, according to the Court, 'deserves a generous construction'.[231] Yacoob J observes:

> The provisions of section 26(3) would be virtually nugatory and would amount to little protection if people who were in occupation of their homes could be constitutionally compelled to leave by the exertion of the pressure of a criminal sanction without a court order.[232]

By way of remedy the Court read appropriate wording into the section to provide for judicial oversight of evictions in terms of s 12(4)(*b*) of the NBRSA.[233]

The Court expressly declined to deal with the systemic issue of whether the City had put in place a reasonable plan for the permanent housing of the occupiers and the many other poor people resident in the inner city.[234] It held that this issue was adequately dealt with by the undertaking of the City in the settlement agreement to pursue 'permanent housing solutions' in consultation with the occupiers. It saw no reason to doubt that negotiations on this issue with the occupiers would continue in

---

229 Ibid para 44.

230 Ibid.

231 Ibid para 49.

232 Ibid. The question of the constitutionality of the use of criminal law to compel the evictions of the poor was expressly left open, save that the Court noted that imprisonment was not involved in this matter. See the remarks at footnote 42 of the judgment (ibid).

233 Ibid para 54. Order para 6. On 'reading in' remedies in the context of socio-economic rights litigation, see chapter 8, part 8.3.3.

234 Ibid paras 32–36.

good faith,[235] and that the City would proceed in a similar manner in relation to other occupiers in the same position as the appellants.[236] In addition, the Court expressed its reservations about acting as the 'court of first and last instance' in an abstract and generalised evaluation of whether the City's housing plan was reasonable in relation to the entire class of similarly-placed occupiers.[237] If necessary, particular occupiers could bring a case to the High Court making specific allegations concerning the compliance of the City with its housing obligations in relation to them.[238]

In many respects, the Constitutional Court judgment is a welcome affirmation of the principle of participatory, deliberative democracy in resolving conflicts involving constitutional rights such as housing. The Court derived a general obligation on public authorities to consult meaningfully with persons whom they seek to evict from their homes directly from various constitutional provisions, particularly s 26. A failure to engage meaningfully is to be treated by courts as a weighty consideration against the grant of an eviction order.

The engagement between state officials and local communities must fulfil certain criteria to be considered 'meaningful'. These criteria bear many of the hallmarks of a deliberative conception of democracy.[239] Participants must approach the process with openness and respect for the humanity of the other party as well as the constitutional rights and values at stake. They should be open to reason and persuasion and not cling implacably to fixed positions. All relevant information should be placed on the table to enable the taking of informed decisions. The process should not be seen as a winner-take-all bargaining process. It should be designed to enable and empower disadvantaged and marginalised communities to participate meaningfully in the process. This requires local authorities to put in place mechanisms that can facilitate the 'structured, consistent and careful' engagement process conducted by 'competent sensitive council workers skilled in engagement'.[240] As noted above, civil society organisations are encouraged to be involved and support marginalised groups in the engagement process.

If meaningful engagement is to constitute a significant mechanism in the adjudication of socio-economic rights claims, it is important that the outcome of such engagement is consistent with constitutional rights and values. In *Occupiers of 51 Olivia Road* the Court scrutinised and endorsed the agreement reached pursuant to its engagement order. It did so because 'meaningful engagement' on various matters had been specifically ordered by it upon the conclusion of the parties' argument before it on the application for leave to appeal.[241] However, it emphasised that 'the process of

[235] Ibid para 34.
[236] Ibid para 35.
[237] Ibid paras 34–35.
[238] Ibid para 35.
[239] On the relationship between deliberative democracy and transformative constitutionalism, see chapter 2, part 2.2.4.
[240] *Occupiers of 51 Olivia Road* (note 15 above) para 19.
[241] Ibid paras 27–30.

engagement should take place before litigation commences unless it is not possible or reasonable to do so because of urgency or some other compelling reason'.[242]

In this context, courts and the participants in engagement processes should be aware that there is no guarantee that the process or outcome of such engagement will respect and vindicate the relevant constitutional rights. This is a particular concern given the power imbalance which exists between deeply disadvantaged groups facing homelessness in an eviction situation, and local authorities or private landowners. Communities who lack the support of NGOs or public interest lawyers are particularly vulnerable in this context, and may not be in a position to secure the effective protection of their housing and other rights in an engagement process. As noted, not all engagement orders will be subjected to judicial scrutiny and approval.

There is a need for regulatory measures and the allocation of appropriate resources to help ensure that engagement processes in these contexts are fair and empowering to the communities concerned. However, just as important for ensuring the protection of the rights of marginalised communities is the need for a substantively reasoned interpretation of the obligations imposed by s 26.[243] Judgments which elaborate on the nature and implications of housing rights in an eviction context provide the constitutional normative framework within which the search for particular solutions through meaningful engagement between the parties must take place. In this regard, important guidance on the normative framework can be obtained from the aspects of the *Olivia Road* judgment which engage with the substantive implications of s 26(3).

First, no eviction of persons from their home may take place without judicial control. The right to insist that a court authorise any attempt to evict them from their homes is an important safeguard for communities when they believe their rights are not being respected by public authorities in the engagement process.

Second, the Court affirmed that when exercising its discretion to grant an eviction order, relevant legislation must be read in the light of s 26 of the Constitution. In terms of s 26(2), organs of State must take reasonable measures to realise progressively the right of access to adequate housing. In the *Grootboom* judgment the duty to take reasonable measures includes making short-term provision for those 'who have no access to land, no roof over their heads, and who are living in intolerable conditions or crisis situations'.[244] In the context where people face homelessness as a result of an eviction, the availability of suitable alternative accommodation or land is a highly relevant factor in terms of s 26(3) of the Constitution. As the Constitutional Court said in the *Port Elizabeth Municipality* judgment, 'a court should be reluctant to grant an eviction against relatively settled occupiers unless it is satisfied that a reasonable

---

242 Ibid para 30.

243 On the significance of substantive reasoning in the interpretation of human rights guarantees, see chapter 2, part 2.4.2.

244 *Grootboom* (note 9 above) paras 52, 99, Order para 2(*b*). See also chapter 4, part 4.3.

alternative is available, even if only as an interim measure pending ultimate access to housing in the formal housing programme'.[245]

With regard to legislation dealing with evictions for reasons of health and safety, the context of particular cases should guide the formulation of an appropriate order. In the *Occupiers of 51 Olivia Road* case, the settlement order endorsed by the Court provided for interim measures to render the buildings more safe and habitable pending the relocation of the occupiers. If the safety concerns are more urgent, it may be appropriate to grant an immediate eviction order, but coupled with an order that the State provide temporary provision of suitable alternative accommodation where the eviction order will render the occupiers homeless. In such situations not only are the occupiers deprived of access to housing, but they are exposed to violations of a range of other constitutional rights such as the right to human dignity (s 10), security of the person (s 12), privacy (s 14), and the right of children to shelter (s 28(1)(*c*)). In these circumstances, courts should also consider making an order requiring the parties to engage meaningfully with each other concerning long-term housing solutions for the affected group.

Finally, perhaps the most significant implication of the *Olivia Road* judgment is the Constitutional Court's confirmation that the phrase, 'relevant circumstances' in s 26(3) of the Constitution is not simply a redundant injunction for courts to take into account the circumstances which are relevant in terms of the existing common law or the applicable legislation governing evictions.[246] Section 26(3) is intended to transform the existing legal framework pertaining to evictions by requiring courts to take into account a range of considerations which are relevant to the purposes and values underlying the right of access to housing in s 26 of the Constitution. This includes the personal circumstances of the occupiers, whether meaningful engagement has taken place, and the provision of alternative accommodation to those facing homelessness.

6.5 EVICTIONS FOR THE PURPOSE OF UPGRADING INFORMAL SETTLEMENTS: *JOE SLOVO*

The recent judgment of the Constitutional Court in *Joe Slovo*[247] considers the implications of s 26 of the Constitution in circumstances where the State seeks to evict and relocate a large, settled community from their homes in order to facilitate a major housing development.[248]

---

245 *Port Elizabeth Municipality* (note 12 above) para 28.

246 As noted above, this has been the approach followed by the Supreme Court of Appeal in its judgment in *Brisley* (note 59 above) and its judgment in the *Occupiers of 51 Olivia Road* case (note 15 above).

247 Note 4 above.

248 Of particular relevance in this context are the *UN Basic Principles and Guidelines on Development-Based Evictions and Displacement* developed under the auspices of the UN Special Rapporteur on Adequate Housing as a Component of the Right to an Adequate Standard

The case concerned an eviction application brought by various organs of State against 4 386 households comprising about 20 000 people from the Joe Slovo informal settlement on the outskirts of Cape Town. The land on which they were settled is owned by the City of Cape Town, but it did not participate in the eviction proceedings.[249] According to government[250] and Thubelisha Homes,[251] the eviction and relocation of the community to 'temporary resettlement units' ('TRUs') located in Delft, some 15 km away from their present homes, was required to enable the upgrading and building of formal housing in terms of the N2 Gateway Project. The N2 Gateway Project is a key pilot project of the *Breaking New Ground Policy* (BNG).[252] In terms of this policy, the Department of Human Settlements seeks to eradicate informal settlements through structured *in situ* upgrading and, where this is not possible, through relocation of the relevant communities.

A decision was taken that *in situ* upgrading of the Joe Slovo site was not feasible and the community should accordingly be relocated to Delft. An initial commitment that 70% of those relocated would be able to return to low-income housing in the upgraded development did not materialise in Phase 1 of the Project.[253] The trust between communities and organs of State was further eroded by the fact that rentals in the development were substantially higher than initially envisaged and greater emphasis was placed on bonded housing. This rendered the housing opportunities inaccessible to the vast majority of the families in the Joe Slovo community.[254] In addition, many residents feared that the relocation to Delft would destroy their already fragile livelihood and communal networks, and that they would lack access to the schools, transport and other facilities on which they depended in the Joe Slovo settlement. Following resistance by the residents to their eviction and relocation, the housing authorities applied for and obtained an eviction order from the Western

---

of Living. See UN doc A/HRC/4/18, 5 February 2007 (Annex 1). These Principles and Guidelines contain international normative standards for evictions which are planned in order to serve the public good, such as urban renewal programmes, slum upgrades, housing renovation and city beautification (para 8).

[249] Ibid para 11.

[250] The organs of State primarily involved in seeking the eviction of the Joe Slovo residents were the national Minister for Housing, and the MEC for Local Government and Housing, Western Cape.

[251] Thubelisha Homes was a company established by the State to undertake various housing functions.

[252] The full title is the *Comprehensive Plan for the Development of Sustainable Human Settlements* which was adopted by Cabinet in September 2004. Available at http://www.fslgh.gov.za/BREAKING%20NEW%20GROUND.pdf (accessed on 13 July 2009) para 13.4. See also the judgment of Ngcobo J in the *Joe Slovo* judgment (note 4 above) paras 203–208.

[253] The other 30% was to be reserved for residents of backyard dwellings in kwa-Langa.

[254] See *Joe Slovo* (note 4 above): paras 31–34 (per Yacoob J); para 307 (per O'Regan J); paras 371–376 (per Sachs J). The income of the majority of the families in the Joe Slovo settlement was below R3 500 per month.

Cape High Court in terms of PIE.[255] The residents of Joe Slovo appealed to the Constitutional Court and judgment was handed down on 10 June 2009.

The appeal succeeded in part and was dismissed in part. The Court agreed on the outcome and a common order.[256] However, five different judgments were delivered by Yacoob J, Moseneke DCJ,[257] Ngcobo J,[258] O'Regan J, and Sachs J.[259] The judgments differ on the reasoning in support of the order.

There are five essential features of the order handed down by the Court.[260] First, the Court agreed with the High Court judgment of Hlophe JP that an eviction order was just and equitable in the circumstances. A schedule for the eviction of the community over a ten-month period, commencing on 17 August 2009 and ending on 21 June 2010, is annexed to the Court's order.[261] Second, the order to vacate 'is conditional upon and subject to' the applicants being relocated to temporary residential units situated in Delft 'or another appropriate location'.[262] Third, the order contains a detailed specification of the nature and quality of the alternative accommodation which must be provided.[263] Fourth, it imposes an obligation on the respondents to ensure that 70% of the new homes to be built on the site of the Joe Slovo informal settlement are allocated to those people who are currently resident there or who were resident there but voluntarily relocated to the TRUs in Delft after the N2 Gateway Housing Project had been launched.[264] In this regard, the Court records that the respondents have indicated that the total number of low-income BNG houses (low-cost government housing available at low rentals) to be built at the site of Joe Slovo will not number fewer than 1500. They are directed to inform the Court and the parties within 14 days of the order 'if this number has changed or is likely to change whereupon the Court may issue further directions in this regard'.[265] Finally, the order requires an ongoing process of meaningful engagement between the residents and

---

[255] *Thubelisha Homes v Various Occupiers* Case No 13189/07 ZAWCHC (unreported judgment of 10 March 2008). The application was initially brought as an urgent proceeding for eviction in terms of s 5 of PIE. After a number of developments in the litigation, the High Court treated the application as a s 6 application ('Eviction at instance of organ of state'). This approach was endorsed by the Constitutional Court. See the reasoning of Yacoob J in *Joe Slovo* (note 4 above) paras 86–93.

[256] See the short judgment for the Court which summarises the grounds on which all the justices agreed that the order should be made: *Joe Slovo* (note 4 above) paras 1–10.

[257] Sachs J concurred in the judgment by Moseneke DCJ.

[258] Langa CJ and Van der Westhuizen J concurred in the judgment of Yacoob J.

[259] Moseneke DCJ and Mokgoro J concurred in the judgment of Sachs J.

[260] The Order is set out in para 7 of the judgment.

[261] See Annexure 'A' to the Order of Court dated 10 June 2009.

[262] *Joe Slovo* (note 4 above) para 7. Order para 4.

[263] Ibid. Order paras 9–10.

[264] Ibid. Order para 17.

[265] Ibid. Order para 18.

respondents concerning various aspects of the eviction and relocation process.[266] The parties are directed to report to Court on the implementation of the order and the allocation of permanent housing opportunities to those affected by the order.[267]

Three major themes emerge from the reasons for the order in the five separate judgment in this case.

The first theme concerns the residents' defence that they were not 'unlawful occupiers' in terms of PIE and thus a fundamental jurisdictional requirement for an eviction application in terms of this legislation was not fulfilled. They argued that the City of Cape Town, both through its positive conduct as well as omissions over the 15-year period the community had occupied the land, had given express or tacit consent to their occupation.[268] Furthermore, no notice of termination of this consent had been given prior to the launching of the eviction application in terms of PIE.

Yacoob J (with the concurrence of Langa CJ and Van der Westhuizen J) found that the residents had neither express nor tacit consent to occupy the land.[269] In their separate judgments Moseneke DCJ, O'Regan J, and Sachs J held that the conduct of the City gave rise to an inference that the occupiers had tacit or express consent to be on the land.[270] However, they found that the consent had been withdrawn and the residents were on notice that they would be required to vacate the land for the purposes of upgrading the site for the N2 Gateway development.[271] Ngcobo J similarly found that the residents were not unlawful occupiers. However, his reasoning was that landless people are shielded by the Constitution from eviction until alternative accommodation is found, and accordingly cannot be regarded as unlawful occupiers.[272] Despite having 'grave doubts whether the provisions of section 6(1) are the appropriate vehicle for dealing with the situation of the residents in this particular case',[273] he nevertheless proceeds to adjudicate the dispute in terms of PIE as '[e]ffect must ... be given to the statute that the government has resorted to in order to secure the eviction and relocation of the residents'.[274] This approach effectively disregards, without a substantive justification, a vital jurisdictional requirement for triggering eviction applications in terms of PIE.

---

[266] Ibid. Order paras 5 and 11. The parties were required to report to the Court if the phase of the engagement to be completed by 30 June 2009 resulted in an agreement between the parties. The Court would then consider whether it was appropriate to issue an order giving effect to the agreement. Order paras 6–7.

[267] The reporting to the Court on the broader implementation of the order was required to take place not later than 1 December 2009. See ibid para 16. See also chapter 8, part 8.6.2 at notes 331-334 and accompanying text.

[268] See judgment of Yacoob J, ibid para 43.

[269] Ibid paras 40–83.

[270] See ibid paras 154–156, 271–278, 341–358 respectively.

[271] See ibid paras 157–160, 281–291, 359–362 respectively.

[272] Ibid paras 214–216.

[273] Ibid para 218.

[274] Ibid para 219.

Of particular relevance to a transformative conception of the influence of constitutional housing rights on evictions law is the private law paradigm applied by Yacoob J to the interpretation of the concepts of 'express or tacit consent' in s 1 of PIE.[275] Moseneke DCJ voiced the following criticism of this approach:

> We are … required to understand the provisions [of PIE], to the extent that it is feasible, in a way that is protective of people who are homeless or otherwise vulnerable to arbitrary evictions. I am accordingly unable to support an understanding of the notion of consent that seeks to make a distinction between ostensible and actual consent; that equates consent that is required in the statute to a requirement of 'voluntary agreement'; and that seeks to rely on concepts of estoppel and ostensible consent in the law of contract in order to narrow down the proper reach and protection afforded by the word 'consent' in the sphere of public law. Section 39(2) of the Constitution requires a court to craft a just outcome that is in harmony with the guarantees of the Constitution rather than a mechanistic application of legal rules of private law in a terrain which is clearly intended to give fulsome protection derived from the Bill of Rights.[276]

The second major theme traversed in the judgments is whether the respondents acted reasonably in seeking the eviction of the occupiers. The two important aspects of reasonableness identified by O'Regan J in her judgment are, first 'whether the N2 Gateway Housing Project is reasonable within the meaning of section 26', and second, 'whether the processes to implement the plan have been reasonable'.[277] The latter aspect of reasonableness 'overlaps with the requirement stipulated in PIE that an eviction may not be ordered unless it is "just and equitable to do so"'.[278] The Court was unanimous that there were no grounds for reviewing the reasonableness of the N2 Gateway Project, the decision that an *in situ* upgrade of the land on which the Joe Slovo community was situated was not possible, and the consequent need to relocate the community to a temporary resettlement area. It was deemed appropriate to afford State authorities a generous margin of discretion in relation to the relevant policy choices.[279]

In her judgment, O'Regan J emphasises the importance of fair procedures in terms of PAJA and 'meaningful engagement' in the reasonable implementation of

---

[275] These concepts are central to the definition of an 'unlawful occupier' in terms of PIE. See notes 18–20 above and accompanying text.

[276] *Joe Slovo* (note 4 above) para 146. See also the judgment of Sachs J at para 343.

[277] Ibid para 294. Sachs J emphasises that the obligation of reasonable implementation extended to 'every step' in the process leading up to the eviction:

> It begins with the initial tolerance of the settlement on the land, proceeds to the devising of the Project, follows with the programme of actual implementation, and only concludes with the ultimate decision to institute eviction proceedings. The question to be asked in relation to each of these steps is: does the conduct of the Council measure up to the test of reasonableness as required by the Constitution? (para 353).

[278] Ibid para 294.

[279] See, for example, paras 115–116 (Yacoob J); para 174 (per Moseneke DCJ); paras 228–229 (per Ngcobo J); para 295 (per O'Regan J); and paras 364–368 (per Sachs J).

government plans to realise socio-economic rights.[280] This is a welcome affirmation of the need for participatory, dialogic decision-making in realising socio-economic rights.[281] However, its transformative implications are undermined by the readiness of the Court to find that the acknowledged inadequacies in the engagement process did not vitiate the ultimate decisions taken concerning the Joe Slovo community. The flawed nature of the engagement between the officials and community is described as follows by Sachs J in his judgment:

> There can be no doubt that there were major failures of communication on the part of the authorities. The evidence suggests the frequent employment of a top-down approach where the purpose of reporting back to the community was seen as being to pass on information about decisions already taken rather than to involve the residents as partners in the process of decision-making itself.[282] (Footnotes omitted.)

This top-down form of engagement represents the antithesis of 'the need for structured, consistent and careful engagement' by 'competent sensitive council workers skilled in engagement' which was endorsed by the Court in *Occupiers of 51 Olivia Road*.[283] Nevertheless the Court was prepared to conclude for a variety of reasons that the greater good which the N2 Gateway project sought to achieve – the need

---

[280] This aspect was elaborated upon in some detail in the submissions of the *amici curiae*: see note 206 above. See O'Regan J's engagement with these arguments at paras 296–301.

[281] The *UN Basic Principles and Guidelines on Development-Based Evictions and Displacement* (note 248 above) para 38 state that:

> All potentially affected groups and persons, including women, indigenous peoples and persons with disabilities, as well as others working on behalf of the affected, have the right to relevant information, full consultation and participation through the entire process, and to propose alternatives that the authorities should duly consider.

See also the detailed standards of procedural fairness stipulated in these *Guidelines* at para 37. These include:

> [The] holding of public hearing(s) that provide(s) affected persons and their advocates with opportunities to challenge the eviction decision and/or to present alternative proposals and to articulate their demands and development priorities.

In the *Joe Slovo* case, O'Regan J was not persuaded that the authorities could be compelled to hold a public inquiry in terms of s 4 of PAJA nor 'that the failure to hold a public inquiry could be said to be unreasonable within the meaning of section 26(2)' (para 300).

[282] Ibid para 378 (footnotes omitted). See also para 113 (per Yacoob J); paras 166–167 (per Moseneke DCJ); para 301 (per O'Regan J).

[283] *Occupiers of 51 Olivia Road* (note 15 above) para 19. The Court further held at para 21:

> In any eviction proceedings at the instance of a municipality therefore, the provision of a complete and accurate account of the process of engagement including at least the reasonable efforts of the municipality within that process would ordinarily be essential. The absence of any engagement or the unreasonable response of a municipality in the engagement process would ordinarily be a weighty consideration against the grant of an ejectment order.

See also in this connection *Joe Slovo* ibid para 166 (per Moseneke DCJ) and para 247 (per Ngcobo J).

for the project and the need for 'realism and practicality'[284] – outweighed the defects in the engagement process.

This fails to take seriously the Court's own insight that procedure and substance are inextricably connected. Meaningful participation is not only an expression of the dignity of citizens, but is indispensable to ensuring that both the design and implementation of programmes to realise socio-economic rights are effective and sustainable. According to O'Regan J, a consideration that weighed heavily in the balance in finding that 'the failure to have a coherent and meaningful strategy of engagement' did not render the plan 'unreasonable to the extent that the respondents have failed to establish a right to evict the occupiers' was the fact that '[t]housands of other households have already co-operated with the respondents in the hope that their co-operation will hasten the building of the housing project and result in their receiving permanent housing'.[285] However, the fact that some desperate members of impoverished communities elect to 'co-operate' with State authorities without insisting on their constitutional and statutory rights to meaningful engagement and due process, should not disqualify others from insisting on their rights.

The Court sought to remedy some elements of the defects in the engagement process through requiring meaningful engagement on various aspects of the eviction and relocation process, including the very significant issue of '[t]he prospect in due course of the allocation of permanent housing to those relocated to temporary residential accommodation units, including information regarding their current position on the housing waiting list, and the provision of assistance to those relocated with the completion of application forms for housing subsidies'.[286] However, the Court did not find that the manifest defects in the engagement process rendered the eviction and relocation of the residents unjust.[287]

In the *Joe Slovo* case there were serious prior questions which should have been explored through meaningful engagement, for example, the feasibility of an *in situ* upgrade, which would have been far less disruptive and arguably more effective than the massive relocation of a fragile community. If the courts are willing to condone

---

[284] See ibid para 117 (per Yacoob J). In a similar vein, O'Regan J writes that fair process 'should not result in unnecessary and prolix requirements that may strangle government action'. (para 296).

[285] Ibid paras 302–303.

[286] See ibid para 7. Order para 11.7.

[287] Although the engagement order made by the Court makes provision for 'any other relevant matter upon which [the parties] agree to engage' (ibid order para 5.3), it is unlikely that the community will be in a position to exert a meaningful influence on the substantive merits of the development decisions. The balance of power will be skewed in favour of the State authorities by the default situation in the order. This is acknowledged by Sachs J when he observes at para 405:

> It is important to note that the order of this Court requires meaningful engagement in relation to the stage the process has now reached. This does not envisage re-opening the basic modalities of the upgrading and relocation scheme. But it does bring the community directly into helping to achieve maximum fairness in relation to potentially divisive features of the implementation.

manifestly inadequate consultation and engagement processes, our socio-economic rights jurisprudence will fail to foster the values of participatory democracy which lie at the heart of transformative developmental processes.

The third theme dealt with in *Joe Slovo* was the evaluation of whether the eviction of the community was 'just and equitable', as required by s 6(1) of PIE. Major considerations in upholding the eviction order were the squalid and dangerous conditions currently prevailing in the Joe Slovo settlement[288] and the State's objective of constructing improved housing through the N2 Gateway Project.[289] However, the Court was not prepared to uphold an eviction order without substantive guarantees concerning the nature and quality of the alternative accommodation to be provided in Delft, and a firm guarantee that 70% of BNG houses at the site of Joe Slovo would be allocated to those forced to relocate as a result of the upgrading programme.[290] It also required engagement on the prospects of permanent housing opportunities for those relocated to the temporary resettlement units.[291] The Court's reasoning in this regard is best expressed by Moseneke DCJ:

> No matter how commendable the government's intentions are regarding the intended use of the land from which the community has been removed without the solid promise of alternative housing, evictions may turn out to be a method of brutal state control and a far cry from the progressive realisation of the socio-economic rights our Constitution guarantees. Courts must remain vigilant to ensure that when the government seeks to evict a community in pursuit of commendable housing plans, the plans must include the guarantee that those who are evicted and relocated have a reasonable opportunity of accessing adequate housing within a reasonable time in relation to the housing projects concerned.[292]

Many of the judgments underscore that suitable alternative accommodation is a fundamental prerequisite for the justice and equity of an eviction by State authorities of a large, settled community.[293] In his judgment Moseneke DCJ is particularly sensitive to the need for 'special concern where settled communities face the threat of being uprooted to other neighbourhoods distant from employment, schooling and other social amenities'.[294] The eviction was made 'conditional upon and subject to' the provision of alternative accommodation.[295] Moreover, detailed standards were

---

[288] Both Moseneke DCJ and Ngcobo J make a conscious effort to locate the conditions existing within informal settlements within their historical context of the forced removals, influx control policies and the 'coloured labour preference policy' in the Western Cape during the apartheid era. See ibid paras 147, 150 and 163; and paras 191–198 respectively.

[289] See, for example, ibid paras 387–388 (per Sachs J).

[290] See, for example, the sentiments expressed by Moseneke DCJ at para 138.

[291] Ibid para 7. Order para 11.7.

[292] Ibid para 172. See also para 170.

[293] See, for example, ibid: paras 105(*c*)–107 (per Yacoob J); para 214 (per Ngcobo J); paras 313–315 (O'Regan J).

[294] Ibid para 165.

[295] Ibid para 7. Order para 4.

specified for the temporary residential units to be provided in Delft.[296] In addition, the respondents were required to engage with the communities about aspects that are of special concern when impoverished communities are relocated far from their established social networks and livelihood opportunities.[297] Of particular importance in this context is the requirement of engagement on '[t]he provision of transport facilities to the affected residents from the temporary residential accommodation units to amenities, including schools, health facilities and places of work'.[298] However, as meaningful engagement does not necessarily require the parties to agree on every issue,[299] there is no guarantee that the community will receive the assistance required to access these facilities at Delft. Making concrete provision for these facilities would have given effect to the Court's own insight that housing rights 'entail more than bricks and mortar'.[300]

In conclusion, the *Joe Slovo* judgment is the strongest affirmation to date of suitable alternative accommodation as a critical factor in evaluating the justice and equity of evicting a large settled community. However, it raises serious concerns regarding the ease with which organs of State may be able to justify not complying with the principles of procedural fairness in PAJA and the constitutional tenets of meaningful engagement established in *Occupiers of 51 Olivia Road*.

6.6 TOWARDS A NEW PARADIGM

The evictions jurisprudence discussed in this chapter exhibits many of the features of a transformative approach to the adjudication of socio-economic rights.

The previous precarious position of unlawful occupiers in South African common law and statutory law has been transformed by the fact that they are now the bearers of constitutionally protected housing rights. The Constitutional Court and other courts in South Africa have interpreted s 26(3) to confer not only procedural guarantees, but also a number of substantive guarantees for those facing eviction from their home.

In its judgment in *Port Elizabeth Municipality v Various Occupiers*, the Constitutional Court elaborated on the substantive purposes which s 26(3) seeks to advance in an eviction context, and the connection between housing rights and a number of other values and interests protected by internationally recognised human rights. This analysis of the relevant rights is situated within a rich historical account of the role of forced evictions and dispossession in achieving the purposes of the apartheid regime, and the new legal and social context within which s 26(3) and relevant legislation must be interpreted. In this respect, the *Port Elizabeth Municipality* judgment exemplifies

---

[296] Ibid. Order para 10.

[297] This aspect is highlighted in the submissions of the *amici curiae* (note 206 above) paras 91–129 above.

[298] Ibid. Order para 11.6.

[299] See para 244 (per Ngcobo J).

[300] *Grootboom* (note 9 above) para 35.

the type of substantive and contextual legal reasoning which epitomises a transformative approach to the adjudication of human rights.[301]

The Court also provided guidance in *Port Elizabeth Municipality* on the approach to be adopted by courts in evaluating conflicting property and housing rights in an eviction context. It rejected as inappropriate judicial approaches which categorically or presumptively favour one right over the other. Instead an attempt must be made 'to balance out and reconcile the opposed claims in as just a manner as possible taking account of all the interests involved and the specific factors relevant in each particular case'.[302] This relational balancing between different constitutional rights in striving to achieve solutions which provide the maximum possible protection to the interests and values protected by both rights is consonant with the deliberative ethos of the Constitution.

The recognition of the substantive nature of the housing rights guaranteed in s 26 of the Constitution has fundamentally changed the legal framework governing evictions law in South Africa. Evictions of people from their homes are no longer exclusively questions of private law or policy choices to be made by the legislature or executive. Both public and private actors are now bound by the negative and positive duties imposed by s 26. This has eroded the public/private dichotomy in cases involving the eviction of people from their homes.[303]

The previously dominant paradigm that the eviction of unlawful occupiers from land and housing constituted a private dispute to be resolved in accordance with the rules and procedures of civil law is illustrated by the attitude adopted by various State respondents in response to the request by Modderklip Boerdery (Pty) Ltd to enforce the eviction order.[304] The Director-General in the Department of Agriculture and Land Affairs described the issue in the case as the execution of the eviction order 'which is a mundane matter regulated by the private law and civil proceedings'.[305] Modderklip Boerdery (Pty) Ltd, according to the deponent, could 'vindicate its property through the simple expedient of having the eviction order executed'.[306] The provision of alternative accommodation for the occupiers of the land was, according to the deponent, a matter 'constitutionally reserved for the Executive'.[307] In rejecting this approach as 'plainly wrong'[308] the Supreme Court of Appeal underscored the critical role of public officials in protecting both property and housing rights in situations of conflicts between private landowners and homeless occupiers. The Constitutional Court reached a similar conclusion, although its analysis centred on the implications

---

301 See also chapter 2, parts 2.4.2 and 2.4.3.
302 Ibid para 23.
303 On the significance of transcending the public/private dichotomy for transformative constitutionalism, see chapter 2, part 2.4.5.
304 See *Modderklip (SCA)* (note 14 above) paras 15–17.
305 Ibid para 15.
306 Ibid.
307 Ibid.
308 Ibid para 17.

of the case for the rule of law and s 34 of the Constitution.[309] However, it too stressed that State involvement was critical in resolving the impasse and social pressures created when the protection of property rights would lead to large-scale homelessness. As the Court observed, the eviction of a large community with nowhere to go 'would cause unimaginable social chaos and misery and untold disruption'.[310] In response to this social reality the State was obliged to make reasonable adjustments in its 'orderly and predictable' plans and procedures designed to ensure progressive access to housing or land for the homeless.[311]

The public dimensions of evictions are underscored by the constitutional role of the State as the ultimate guarantor of everyone's right of access to adequate housing in terms of s 26.[312] By virtue of its constitutional obligations, the State has a fundamental interest in all eviction applications which result in homelessness, regardless of whether the eviction is instituted by an organ of state or private entity. It has affirmative duties to protect the constitutional rights at stake in eviction applications and to facilitate dialogic, mediated solutions that strive to reconcile these rights to the maximum extent possible in the concrete circumstances of particular cases.

The public dimensions of eviction applications have been developed further in cases such as *Lingwood* [313] and *Sailing Queen Investments*[314] in which courts have ordered the joinder of the State as a party to eviction proceedings brought by private landowners. The purpose of such joinder is to permit an order to be made against the relevant local authorities to facilitate mediation between the parties and to provide information to the court relating to alternative accommodation for those facing eviction. In *Port Elizabeth Municipality*, the Constitutional Court sanctioned a more proactive role for courts in ensuring that relevant organs of State provide them with detailed and specific information regarding the surrounding circumstances and impact of an eviction. The nature and specificity of the information to be provided is elaborated upon in the judgment of Masipa J in the *Blue Moonlight Properties* case.[315] The reporting order requires the City of Johannesburg to detail the steps it will take to provide emergency accommodation to the occupiers in the event of an eviction order. It also makes provision for a response from the occupiers to this report. This illustrates the proactive role which courts are required to play in fulfilling their con-

[309] *Modderklip (CC)* (note 14 above) paras 39–51.
[310] Ibid para 47.
[311] Ibid para 49.
[312] The State is under a general duty in terms of s 7(2) 'to respect, protect, promote and fulfil the rights in the Bill of Rights'. See further chapter 3, part 3.2.2. Section 26(2) is a specific manifestation in the context of housing rights of the positive duties inherent in s 7(2). It requires the State to take reasonable measures to achieve the progressive realisation of access by everyone to housing rights. See also *Murray* (note 65 above) para 40.
[313] *Lingwood* (note 120 above).
[314] *Sailing Queen Investments* (note 133 above).
[315] *Blue Moonlight Properties* (note 142 above).

stitutional and legislative responsibilities to ensure that an eviction complies with the requirements of justice and equity.[316]

A further significant feature of the evictions jurisprudence under the constitutional order is its emphasis on participatory, dialogic solutions to the conflicting rights and public policy imperatives which often lie at the heart of eviction applications. In striving for the optimal reconciliation of these rights and policy objectives, the message of cases such as *Port Elizabeth Municipality* and *Modderklip* is that there is no universal blueprint which can be applied to all eviction cases. Neither is it possible to simply resort to general plans, processes and mechanisms if these do not generate an adequate solution to the circumstances and needs of the particular case. As Sachs J observed in *Port Elizabeth Municipality*:

> Every situation has its own history, its own dynamics, its own intractable elements that have to be lived with (at least for the time being), and its own creative possibilities that have to be explored as far as reasonably possible.[317]

In its decision in *Occupiers of 51 Olivia Road*,[318] the Constitutional Court derived an obligation of meaningful engagement in the context of proposed evictions from a range of constitutional provisions, particularly s 26. The nature of the engagement process required is elaborated upon in some detail in the judgment. It requires organs of State to plan proactively, to anticipate situations where evictions may lead to urgent housing need, and to ensure that it puts in place the structures and personnel required to engage meaningfully with disadvantaged communities.

Cases such as *Port Elizabeth Municipality* and *Occupiers of 51 Olivia Road* have emphasised the importance of procedural fairness and the need for parties to seek dialogic solutions to eviction conflicts through mediation or meaningful engagement. However, the willingness of the Constitutional Court in *Joe Slovo* to effectively condone the lack of procedural fairness and manifestly inadequate engagement process raises concerns about the extent of the Court's commitment to these principles. If engagement is to be meaningful and entrenched as part of the new paradigm in eviction disputes, consequences must attach to the State's failure to adhere to the deliberative requirements so carefully elaborated in *Occupiers of 51 Olivia Road*.

The processes and outcomes of meaningful engagement must furthermore be consistent with the rights and obligations of all parties involved. This is vital as disadvantaged communities may lack the support, experience and resources to ensure the protection of their housing and other rights in the engagement process. Meaningful engagement facilitates participatory democracy in resolving eviction disputes. However, it should constitute a mechanism for protecting and realising rights, and not a vehicle for pressuring marginalised groups to negotiate away their rights.

It is therefore crucial that the courts ensure that clear guiding principles are provided on the nature of the obligations imposed by s 26 in an eviction context.

---

316 *Port Elizabeth Municipality* (note 12 above) para 32.

317 Ibid para 31.

318 *Occupiers of 51 Olivia Road* (note 15 above).

Meaningful engagement between public officials and communities must respect and promote these principles in order to produce results consistent with constitutional obligations. A number of guiding principles can be distilled from the jurisprudence.

In the first instance, s 26(3) cannot be interpreted in isolation but forms an integral part of the entire scheme of s 26 in which all three subsections are interrelated. Section 26(3) rests on the fundamental safeguard that no-one may be evicted from their home without an order of court 'made after considering all the relevant circumstances'. Moreover, legislation may not permit 'arbitrary' evictions. In *Occupiers of 51 Olivia Road,* the Constitutional Court affirmed the fundamental importance of judicial oversight in respect of all evictions of people from their homes.[319] Legislation such as PIE was enacted to give concrete effect to s 26(3). It sets out detailed procedural safeguards which apply in eviction applications. It also contains a number of substantive considerations which provide guidance on the type of 'relevant circumstances' which must be considered by a court in eviction applications. Circumstances which are particularly relevant are contextual factors relating to the housing circumstances and needs of vulnerable occupiers.

In addition, the availability of suitable alternative accommodation will usually be a critical issue when marginalised and disadvantaged groups are evicted from their homes. It is in this context that the Constitutional Court's affirmation of the interdependence of the three subsections of s 26 is especially significant. Thus the negative obligation not to deprive people unjustifiably of their access to housing is integrally linked to a positive duty on relevant organs of State to take reasonable measures to ensure that those facing homelessness have access to suitable alternative accommodation. This is a manifestation of the principle established in the *Grootboom* case that short-term measures of relief must be adopted to assist those in urgent housing need or living in intolerable conditions.

The courts have approached the issue of alternative accommodation in eviction applications in one of two ways. They have regarded alternative accommodation as a weighty factor in determining whether an eviction is justifiable in the circumstances.[320] This may result in a stay of the eviction order pending the provision of information to the court on suitable measures to ensure alternative accommodation to the affected groups.[321] Alternatively, they have held that the eviction of impoverished groups into a situation of homelessness triggers a positive duty to provide some form of temporary accommodation in a *Grootboom*-type programme designed for these situations.[322]

---

319 *Occupiers of 51 Olivia Road* (note 15 above) paras 47–51.

320 See *Port Elizabeth Municipality* (note 12 above) para 28 and *Occupiers of 51 Olivia Road* (note 15 above) paras 42–46.

321 See, for example, the order granted in *Blue Moonlight Properties* (note 142 above) para 78.

322 *Grobler v Msimanga* (note 158 above). See also the judgment of the Supreme Court of Appeal in the *Occupiers of 51 Olivia Road* case: *City of Johannesburg v Rand Properties* (note 59 above) para 77.

The obligations of organs of State in relation to alternative accommodation for those facing homelessness is not satisfied by referring to its general housing plans and policies. Reasonable steps must be taken by relevant organs of State that are tailored to the particular needs and circumstances of the affected community. If challenged in court, details of the specific measures being taken or planned to secure emergency shelter or housing for those applicants who will be homeless as a result of the eviction will have to be provided.[323] The strongest affirmation to date of alternative accommodation as a critical factor in evaluating the justice and equity of eviction applications is the Constitutional Court's judgment in *Joe Slovo*. This is complemented by the detailed substantive standards prescribed by the Court concerning the 'adequacy' of the alternative accommodation to be provided. This confirms that s 26 does not simply amount to a generalised entitlement to a reasonable housing programme, but gives rise to concrete entitlements in an eviction context.[324]

As the above analysis illustrates, the courts have developed a number of principles relating to the interpretation of s 26(3) in the context of s 26 as a whole. These principles must guide efforts to explore participatory, dialogic solutions to eviction conflicts. While these principles have developed primarily in the context of litigation in terms of PIE and the NBRSA, they should infuse the interpretation of all legislation regulating evictions, including ESTA.[325] The Constitutional Court has made it clear in the *Occupiers of 51 Olivia Road* decision[326] that all statutes regulating the eviction of people from their homes must be interpreted in the light of s 26 of the Constitution.[327] This is required by the general injunction contained in s 39(2) of the Constitution that when interpreting legislation courts must 'promote the spirit, purport and objects of the Bill of Rights'. Where it is not reasonably possible to interpret legislation to give effect to these principles, the relevant provisions should be declared unconstitutional.[328] A consistent application of these principles will result in the new paradigm for adjudicating eviction disputes under the influence of constitutional housing rights gradually displacing the traditional paradigm premised on the hierarchical system of private law property rights.

---

[323] *Port Elizabeth Municipality* (note 12 above) para 29; Blue *Moonlight Properties* (note 142 above).

[324] See in this regard, chapter 4, part 4.4.6.

[325] For a critical appraisal of the performance of the Land Claims Court established in 1996 under the Restitution of Land Rights Act 22 of 1994, see T Roux 'Pro-poor court, anti-poor outcomes: Explaining the performance of the South African Land Claims Court' (2004) 20 *SAJHR* 511–543.

[326] *Occupiers of 51 Olivia Road* (note 15 above).

[327] Ibid para 43.

[328] Legislation can only be interpreted in conformity with constitutional obligations insofar as it is reasonably capable of such a construction. See *Govender v Minister of Safety and Security* 2001 (4) SA 273 (SCA); *Investigating Directorate: Serious Economic Offences v Hyundai Motor Distributors (Pty) Ltd: In re Hyundai Motor Distributors (Pty) Ltd v Smit NO* 2001 (1) SA 545 (CC) para 24.

CHAPTER 7

Socio-Economic Rights in Private Law

7.1 INTRODUCTION

Classic legal liberalism is premised on a firm conceptual divide between public and private law. The common law, particularly private law, has historically been regarded as a self-contained system of 'natural' rights and liberties shielded from regulatory intervention based on public law norms and values, particularly those associated with the human rights law.[1] The role of the State in constructing and enforcing common-law

[1] See generally chapter 2, part 2.4.5. See also J Nedelsky 'Reconceiving autonomy: Sources, thoughts and possibilities' (1989) 1 *Yale J of Law and Feminism* 7–36 at 15–17.

doctrines and rules is rendered invisible in classic liberal ideology.[2] There is a general failure to acknowledge how common-law rules and institutions structure access to socio-economic resources in diverse areas of contract law, property law, delict (tort law), family law and succession.[3] For example, the non-recognition of gay marriages, Muslim and African customary law marriages, and heterosexual, cohabiting life partnerships has profound implications for the socio-economic security of the more vulnerable partners in these relationships.[4] As Frank Michelman points out in relation to the rules of contract and property:

> Suppose everyone has a constitutionally super-valued interest in having 'access to sufficient food and water'.[5] Food-sellers exercising powers under the law of contract to set highly profitable prices for their wares, and landowners exercising rights and privileges under the law of property to convert land from food production to game parks, may threaten those interests as gravely as any state official ever would be likely to do.[6]

The traditional resistance to applying constitutional rights to private law is partially motivated by a fear of undermining the individual autonomy which common-law rules and institutions are perceived to safeguard.[7] This understanding privileges a version of 'negative' freedom and rights premised on the notion that public law regu-

---

[2] On the influence of liberalism in South African legal culture and doctrine, See generally S Woolman & D Davis 'The last laugh: *Du Plessis v De Klerk*, classical liberalism, creole liberalism and the application of rights under the interim and final constitutions' (1996) 12 *SAJHR* 361–404.

[3] As Jennifer Nedelsky (note 1 above) at 19 observes:

> The common law has been informed and shaped by particular conceptions of fairness, freedom and progress. The 'neutral rules of the game' correspond to a particular vision of the good society which gives advantages to some players over others in systemic, if not perfectly predictable ways.

[4] In *Volks NO v Robinson* 2005 (5) BCLR 446 (CC) the Constitutional Court held that the failure of the Maintenance of Surviving Spouses Act 27 of 1990 to make provision for the surviving partner of a permanent heterosexual life partnership to claim maintenance from the estates of their deceased partners did not constitute unfair discrimination. Compare *Daniels v Campbell NO* 2004 (5) SA 331 (CC), 2004 (7) BCLR 735 (CC) in which the words 'spouse' and 'survivor' in this Act and the Intestate Succession Act 81 of 1987 were held to include spouses in Muslim marriages. See C de Villiers '*Daniels v Campbell NO:* The long battle of a woman married according to Muslim personal rights to acquire ownership of her home' (2003) 4 *ESR Review* 8–10. In *Bhe v Magistrate, Khayelitsha (Commission for Gender Equality as Amicus Curiae); Shibi v Sithole; South African Human Rights Commission v President of the Republic of South Africa* 2005 (1) SA 580 (CC), 2005 (1) BCLR 1 (CC) relevant provisions of the Black Administration Act 38 of 1927 and associated regulations as well as the customary law rule of male primogeniture were declared unconstitutional. On the impact of the rule of primogeniture on access to property by women, female children and extra-marital children, see paras 91–94 of the judgment.

[5] Referring to s 27(1)(*b*) of the Constitution.

[6] F I Michelman 'The Bill of Rights, the common law, and the freedom-friendly state' (2003–2004) 58 *Miami L Rev* 401–448 at 414.

[7] See Woolman & Davis (note 2 above) 385.

lation of the 'private sphere' undermines individual autonomy.[8] In contrast, a more substantive understanding of autonomy recognises that the fostering of autonomy requires both restraint and positive social intervention in order to facilitate the ability of all people to make choices and pursue their life plans.[9] Elevating negative liberty to a privileged value entrenches existing distributions of power and resources, and reinforces the marginalised position of those excluded from participation in the social and economic institutions of society. In the South African context, this conception operates to entrench the socio-economic legacy of South Africa's colonial and apartheid history.[10]

The Constitution, particularly through its commitment to socio-economic rights and substantive equality, is explicitly committed to the redress and transformation of these patterns of socio-economic disadvantage and marginalisation. This commitment is reinforced by the express constitutional provisions governing the application of the rights and values in the Bill of Rights to private relations, and requiring their normative content to direct the development of the common law and customary law.

Section 8(1) states that the Bill of Rights 'applies to all law, and binds the legislature, the executive, the judiciary and all organs of state'. Section 8(2) specifies that a provision in the Bill of Rights 'binds a natural and juristic person if, and to the extent that, it is applicable, taking into account the nature of the right and the nature of any duty imposed by the right'. In order to give effect to the horizontal application of a right in the Bill of Rights, a court 'must apply, or if necessary develop, the common law to the extent that legislation does not give effect to that right'.[11] The court may also develop 'rules of the common law to limit the right provided that the limitation is in accordance with section 36(1)'.[12] In terms of s 39(2), every court, tribunal or forum is obliged when interpreting legislation or when developing the common law or customary law to 'promote the spirit, purport and objects of the Bill of Rights'.

Sections 8 and 39(2) are crucial mechanisms for holding private entities and law accountable for infringements of the rights in the Bill of Rights. No exercise of public or private power is immune from critical scrutiny and re-evaluation in the light of the rights and values of the Constitution. There are only better or worse

---

[8] On the concept of 'negative' liberty and rights, see chapter 2, part 2.4.4.

[9] Nedelsky (note 1 above) demonstrates how the experience of autonomy is fostered or undermined in the choices we make about how we organise our society and economy, in the benefits, resources and opportunities that are extended or denied. See also S Liebenberg 'The value of freedom in interpreting socio-economic rights' (2009) *AJ* 149–176.

[10] See Kriegler J's observations on the 'pervading misconception[s]' and 'egregious' caricature[s]' of the impact of direct horizontality on South African society in his separate judgment in *Du Plessis v De Klerk* 1996 (3) SA 850 (CC), 1996 (5) BCLR 658 (CC) para 120.

[11] Section 8(3)(*a*).

[12] Section 8(3)(*b*).

constitutional justifications for leaving intact, invalidating or changing the particular legal rule (whatever its source) which is subject to challenge. Shielding common-law rules from judicial review in terms of constitutional rights and values, particularly in the sphere of socio-economic rights, will have the effect of perpetuating the power and privileged position of those who already enjoy access to socio-economic resources.

The Constitutional Court has held that it is erroneous to conceive of South Africa's post-apartheid constitutional legal order in terms of a fragmented set of self-contained bodies of law. Thus in *Pharmaceutical Manufacturers Association of SA: In Re Ex Parte President Republic of South Africa*[13] ('*Pharmaceutical Manufacturers*'), Chaskalson P (as he then was) stated:

> I cannot accept this contention, which treats the common law as a body of law separate and distinct from the Constitution. There are not two systems of law, each dealing with the same subject-matter, each having similar requirements, each operating in its own field with its own highest Court. There is only one system of law. It is shaped by the Constitution which is the supreme law, and all law, including the common law, derives it force from the Constitution and is subject to constitutional control.[14]

This conception of the post-apartheid legal system is not premised on rigid divisions between public and private law. There is 'one system of law' in which all legal rules – whether sourced in legislation, common law or customary law – are subject to critical re-evaluation in the light of constitutional norms and values.[15]

The first part of this chapter analyses ss 8 and 39(2) as the constitutional vehicles for applying constitutional rights in private law. It proceeds to consider their specific application in the sphere of socio-economic rights. Attention is paid to both existing jurisprudence and conceptual issues such as when it is appropriate to develop existing common-law remedies or to craft new remedies to give effect to constitutional rights. The second part of the chapter examines the influence of socio-economic rights in selected areas of property law and contract.[16] It concludes by exploring the methodological and ideological obstacles which constrain the potentially transformative impact of socio-economic rights in private law.

---

[13] 2000 (2) SA 674 (CC), 2000 (3) BCLR 241 (CC).

[14] Ibid para 44.

[15] See J C Froneman 'The horizontal application of human rights norms' (2007) 21 *Speculum Juris* 13–24 at 24.

[16] For an initial exploration of the application of socio-economic rights in selected areas of private law, see S Liebenberg 'The application of socio-economic rights to private law' (2008) 3 *TSAR* 464–480.

7.2 APPLYING SOCIO-ECONOMIC RIGHTS IN PRIVATE LAW: SECTIONS 8 AND 39(2)

7.2.1 Introduction

As noted above, ss 8 and 39(2) are the two main constitutional provisions mandating and providing a methodology for the horizontal application of rights in the Bill of Rights. The interpretation of the two provisions and their interrelationship is subject to ongoing academic controversy and debate.[17]

The courts have not been consistent, nor has a clear methodology emerged to guide the application of the rights in the Bill of Rights to private law in terms of s 8, s 39(2), or a combination of these provisions. In *Khumalo v Holomisa*[18] (*Khumalo*), the Constitutional Court relied on s 8 to apply freedom of expression (s 16) directly to the common-law rules of defamation. However, subsequently it has preferred to rely on s 39(2) to give affect to the Bill of Rights in legal relations between private parties,[19] or in developing the common law in cases involving organs of state.[20]

This chapter focuses on the significance of both ss 8 and 39(2) for applying socio-economic rights in legal relations between private parties. However, attempts to accord distinctive roles to ss 8 and 39(2) remain fraught with theoretical and conceptual difficulties.[21] In this debate the oft-drawn distinction between direct and indirect

---

[17] For a comprehensive discussion of this issue, see S Woolman 'Application' in S Woolman *et al* (eds) *Constitutional Law of South Africa* 2 ed (Original Service 2005) chapter 31.

[18] 2002 (5) SA 401 (CC), 2002 (8) BCLR 771 (CC).

[19] See, for example, *Barkhuizen v Napier* 2007 (5) SA 323 (CC), 2007 (7) BCLR 691 (CC) ('*Barkhuizen*') in which the Court held that constitutional challenges to contractual terms should ordinarily occur through the development of the notion of public policy consistent with 'the values that underlie our constitutional democracy as given expression by the provisions of the Bill of Rights' (paras 29–30). Compare the views of Langa CJ in his separate judgment disagreeing with the judgment of Ngcobo J (for the majority) to the extent that it holds that the only acceptable approach to challenging the constitutionality of contractual terms is indirect application under s 39(2). The Chief Justice preferred to keep open the possibility of a direct application in terms of s 8 of certain rights in the Bill of Rights to contractual terms or the common law that underlies them. However, he was of the view that 'the distinction between direct and indirect application will seldom be outcome determinative' (para 186).

[20] *Carmichele v Minister of Safety and Security* 2001 (4) SA 938 (CC), 2001 (10) BCLR 995 (CC), *S v Thebus* 2003 (6) SA 505 (CC), 2003 (10) BCLR 1100 (CC), *Masiya v Director of Public Prosecutions Pretoria (Centre for Applied Legal Studies and Another, Amici Curiae)* 2007 (5) SA 30 (CC), 2007 (8) BCLR 827 (CC), *Murray v The Minister of Defence* 2009 (3) SA 130 (SCA), 2008 (11) BCLR 1175 (SCA) para 5. For a critique of the 'over-reliance' on s 39(2) by the Constitutional Court, see S Woolman 'The amazing, vanishing Bill of Rights' (2007) 124 *SALJ* 762–794 at 763.

[21] For a recent discussion of these difficulties, see P J Sutherland 'Ensuring contractual fairness in consumer contracts after *Barkhuizen v Napier* 2007 5 SA 323 (CC) – part 1' (2008) 19 *Stell LR* 390–413 at 397–406.

application obfuscates more than it clarifies.[22] Although an exhaustive survey of the academic debate on this issue will not be undertaken, it is apposite at the outset to provide a brief overview of my preferred reading of the respective roles of s 8 and s 39(2) as mechanisms for giving effect to the Bill of Rights in relationships between private parties. Thereafter the specific jurisprudence on these sections and their implications for the application for socio-economic rights to private law is analysed.

7.2.2 The respective roles of sections 8 and 39(2): A preferred reading

As the heading of s 8 of the Constitution indicates, it is the primary provision governing the application of the Bill of Rights. Section 8(1) states that the Bill of Rights 'applies to *all law*, and binds the legislature, the executive, the judiciary and all organs of state'. (Emphasis added.) Section 8(2) specifies that, a provision of the Bill of Rights is binding on a natural or a juristic person 'if, and to the extent that, it is applicable, taking into account the nature of the right and the nature of any duty imposed by the right'. The point of departure is that the Bill of Rights applies to all law – whether public or private, or sourced in statute, the common law or customary law. Section 8(2) qualifies s 8(1) by providing a specific description of the circumstances in which the Bill of Rights binds a private party.

In determining whether, and to what extent, a provision in the Bill of Rights should bind a private party regard must be had to 'the nature of the right and the nature of any duty imposed by the right'. As Currie and de Waal observe, the question whether a particular provision in the Bill of Rights is horizontally applicable 'cannot be determined *a priori* and in the abstract'.[23] The application of a provision of the Bill of Rights in private relationships 'also depends on the nature of the private conduct in question and the circumstances of a particular case'.[24] In other words, the application of a provision in the Bill of Rights to a private party must be a context-sensitive determination taking into account the appropriateness of imposing the particular duty on the particular private party concerned. Currie and de Waal also correctly caution that 'a resort to context or circumstances of a particular case should not be used to frustrate the clear intention of the drafters of the 1996 Constitution – to extend the direct operation of the provisions of the Bill of Rights to private conduct'.[25]

Section 8(3) describes the methodology for applying a right to private parties. Thus, in the absence of legislation giving effect to the particular right, the courts 'must apply, or if necessary develop, the common law'.[26] It may at the same time 'develop

[22] For an argument that the distinction between direct and indirect application remains salient, see I Currie & J de Waal *The Bill of Rights Handbook* 5 ed (2005) 72–78.

[23] Ibid 53. See further the five considerations identified by the authors as relevant in making a determination in terms of s 8(2): 52–55.

[24] Ibid.

[25] Ibid.

[26] Section 8(3)(*a*).

rules of the common law to limit the right, provided that the limitation is in accordance with section 36(1)'.[27] Thus legislation and the common law are the primary vehicles for giving effect to the horizontal application of the Bill of Rights, including, where necessary, the development of new remedies not previously recognised in the common law. As discussed below, difficult questions will arise as to the appropriateness of applying or extending the scope of application of an existing common-law remedy to give effect to a constitutional right,[28] or developing a new remedy to give proper effect to a constitutional right in private relationships.[29] This includes situations where the existing private common law fails to give effect to a positive duty imposed by any right in the Bill of Rights.[30] However, whether an existing common-law remedy is extended or a new remedy is developed to give effect to a constitutional right, both are part of South Africa's 'one system of law' which is shaped and controlled by the Constitution.[31]

The focus in s 8 should be, as Stu Woolman argues, on 'the prescriptive content of the substantive rights found in sections 9–35 of the Constitution'.[32] As has been previously argued, the development of the substantive content of the rights in the Bill of Rights should be informed by the founding values of the Constitution in general, and the Bill of Rights in particular.[33] However, these values ultimately ground con-

---

[27] Section 8(3)(*b*).

[28] In *K v Minister of Safety and Security* 2005 (6) SA 419 (CC), 2005 (9) BCLR 835 (CC) para 16, O'Regan J characterised these situations as 'deciding cases within the framework of an existing rule'. In this context, she identifies two possibilities:

> [F]irstly, a court may merely have to apply the rule to a set of facts which it is clear fall within the terms of the rule or existing authority. The rule is then not developed but merely applied to facts bound by the rule. Secondly, however, a court may have to determine whether a new set of facts falls within or beyond the scope of an existing rule. The precise ambit of each rule is therefore clarified in relation to each new set of facts. A court faced with a new set of facts, not on all fours with any set of facts previously adjudicated, must decide whether a common-law rule applies to this new factual situation or not. If it holds that the new set of facts falls within the rule, the ambit of the rule is extended. If it holds that it does not, the ambit of the rule is restricted, not extended. (ibid)

[29] This constitutes the introduction of a 'new rule'. See *K v Minister of Safety and Security* ibid. See further part 7.2.5 below.

[30] As Johan van der Walt '*Progressive* indirect application of the Bill of Rights: Towards a co-operative relation between common law and constitutional jurisprudence' (2001) 17 *SAJHR* 341–363 at n 44, 355 argues, with reference to Wesley Hohfeld's analysis of rights, liberties, duties and non-rights:

> The relation between liberties and non-rights remains a legal relationship, irrespective of the law's apparent refusal to intervene in the relationship. A legal system that allows for the existence of liberties and non-rights (the absence of a right that would terminate the liberty and change it into a duty) that are inconsistent with constitutional principles would not be able to claim that it is not itself involved in the unconstitutional behaviour.

[31] See *Pharmaceutical Manufacturers* (note 13 above) para 44.

[32] Woolman (note 20 above) 776.

[33] See chapter 2, part 2.4.2, and chapter 3, part 3.3.1. See also *Dawood v Minister of Home Affairs; Shalabi v Minister of Home Affairs; Thomas v Minister of Home Affairs* 2000 (3) SA 936

crete substantive rights which must give rise to 'appropriate relief'[34] when these rights are infringed or threatened by public bodies, as well as private parties when the right in question is found to be applicable to the natural or juristic person concerned in terms of s 8(2).

What is the role then of s 39(2), which requires courts and other bodies '[w]hen interpreting any legislation, and when developing the common law or customary law ... to promote the spirit, purport and objects of the Bill of Rights'? I read this provision as an interpretive injunction which applies whenever courts are interpreting legislation or developing the common law or customary law.[35] It requires legislation to be interpreted so that, whenever reasonably possible, it is consistent with the Bill of Rights. When a specific provision in the Bill of Rights is found to be horizontally applicable in terms of s 8(2), the courts must apply or develop the common law to give effect to the right insofar as legislation does not do so. In this context the function of the interpretive injunction in s 39(2) is to require the courts to ensure that the development of the common law not only gives effect to the specific provision of the Bill of Rights at issue, but is also consonant with the overall 'objective normative value system' established by the Bill of Rights.[36] It plays the further role of ensuring that even when a court finds that no specific substantive right is applicable in terms of s 8(2) to a dispute between private parties, it should nonetheless ensure that the common law is developed to be in line with the overall 'spirit, purport and objects' of the Bill of Rights. As Stu Woolman argues:

> [I]ndirect application [in terms of section 39(2)] was not meant to 'avoid' actual constitutional analysis in terms of the specific substantive provisions of the Bill of Rights. It enables a court to go beyond the limited substantive provisions of the Bill of Rights. Section 39(2) promises an expansive understanding of judicial review under the Bill of Rights, not a cramped understanding.[37]

In other words, s 39(2) requires courts to go beyond an exclusive focus on particular substantive rights and to consider how the general ethos and purposes of the Bill of Rights can be actively promoted in the interpretation of legislation and the development of the common law or customary law.[38] The Constitutional Court has endorsed an expansive understanding of s 39(2). Thus in *K v Minister of Safety and Security*, O'Regan J writes:

> The overall purpose of section 39(2) is to ensure that our common law is infused with the values of the Constitution. It is not only in cases where existing rules are clearly

(CC), 2000 (8) BCLR 837 (CC) at para 35 (human dignity as a value informs the interpretation of possibly all the fundamental rights in the Bill of Rights).

[34] See s 38 of the Constitution.

[35] The heading of s 39 is 'Interpretation of Bill of Rights'.

[36] See *Carmichele* (note 20 above) para 56. On the application of s 39(2) to social legislation such as PIE, see further part 7.3.1(*c*) below.

[37] Woolman (note 20 above) 777.

[38] See *Thebus* (note 20 above) para 28. See further part 7.2.4 below.

> inconsistent with the Constitution that such an infusion is required. The normative influence of the Constitution must be felt throughout the common law. Courts making decisions which involve the incremental development of the rules of the common law in cases where the values of the Constitution are relevant are therefore also bound by the terms of section 39(2). The obligation imposed upon courts by section 39(2) of the Constitution is thus extensive, requiring courts to be alert to the normative framework of the Constitution not only when some startling new development of the common law is in issue, but in all cases where the incremental development of the rule is in issue.[39]

The Court has been criticised for retreating from its initial methodology of testing private common-law rules for consistency with the substantive rights in the Bill of Rights in terms of ss 8(2) and (3)[40] in favour of a loose resort to vaguely defined values in terms of s 39(2).[41] It could be argued that, provided s 39(2) is applied in a sufficiently robust and substantive manner, not much is lost through routing horizontal application cases through this provision as opposed to ss 8(2) and (3). Johan van der Walt argues, for example, that the distinction between direct and indirect horizontal application may in the end amount to 'a choice between two vocabularies, one which does not shy away from directly invoking constitutional principles within the context of the common law, and one that prefers to let the common law principles themselves perform the required mediation between existing law and constitutional challenges to such law'.[42] Neither s 8 nor s 39(2) requires that the impact of the Bill of Rights on the body of private law should be mitigated or softened. On the contrary, both provisions mandate and enable the application of the rights in the Bill of Rights to private law.

However, the danger exists that an over-reliance on s 39(2) will result in a failure by the courts to engage systematically with the normative implications of substantive constitutional rights in private law disputes. The result will be that the testing of private law rules against constitutional rights will be both less rigorous and robust than the constitution-makers intended. As Woolman argues:

> By continually relying on s 39(2) of the Constitution to decide challenges both to rules of common law and to provisions of statutes, the court obviates the need to give the specific substantive rights in Chapter 2 the content necessary to determine the actual validity of

---

[39] *K v Minister of Safety and Security* (note 28 above) para 17. See also *Thebus* ibid para 28. As Davis J stated in *Advtech Resourcing (Pty) Ltd t/a Communicate Personnel Group v Kuhn* 2008 (2) SA 375 (C), [2007] 4 All SA 1368 (C):

> [Section] 39(2) of the Constitution mandates courts to engage in a normative enquiry as to the foundational framework from which will radiate the principles upon which each rule of law should be grounded. ... This obligation is not limited to situations when the Bill of Rights applies to natural or juristic persons in terms of s 8 of the Constitution, but is *an interpretative obligation* that is imposed on all courts, *even in the absence of a direct conflict between the common law and [a] specific provision of the Bill of Rights*; that is where the rule of common law falls short of the spirit, purport or objectives of the Constitution. (para 24; emphasis added, references omitted.)

[40] This initial approach was adopted in *Khumalo* (note 18 above). See further 7.2.3(*b*) below.

[41] This is the thrust of Woolman's critique (note 20 above).

[42] Van der Walt (note 30 above) 355.

> the rule being challenged in the instant matter and of similar rules challenged in subsequent matters. This strategy also enables the court to skirt the nuanced process of justification that s 36 of the Constitution or some other express limitations clause in a specific substantive right might require. The persistent refusal to give rights identifiable content, by avoiding direct application, results in a Bill of Rights increasingly denuded of meaning.[43]

Developing the substantive content of the rights in the Bill of Rights has been identified as a key feature of transformative adjudication under the South African Constitution.[44] A methodology for horizontal application which avoids engagement with the substantive content of the various rights in the Bill of Rights runs the risk of undermining the transformative goals of the Constitution. This danger exists particularly in the case of socio-economic rights given their lack of historical recognition in the common law. If socio-economic rights are to play a vital role in the fundamental transformation of traditional common-law paradigms it becomes imperative that the courts engage seriously with their normative content and underlying purposes.

I turn now to examine the specific jurisprudence on ss 8 and 39(2), and explore its implications for the application of socio-economic rights in private law.

7.2.3 Section 8

(*a*) Section 8(1)

The statement in s 8(1) that the Bill of Rights applies to 'all law' and binds 'the judiciary' suggests that the Bill of Rights is intended to apply directly to the common law in disputes between private parties. However, in *Khumalo* O'Regan J held this interpretation of the inclusion of 'the judiciary' in s 8(1) would render s 8(2) and (3) redundant.[45] Thus the direct application of a right in the Bill of Rights to the common law in disputes between private parties is primarily governed by ss 8(2) and 8(3). In *K v Minister of Safety and Security*[46] O'Regan J indicated that the inclusion of the judiciary in s 8(1) read in conjunction with s 39(2) 'creates an expressly normative legal system founded on the norms articulated in our Constitution'.[47]

The application of the Bill of Rights to 'all law' in s 8(1) establishes that the Bill of Rights applies to all forms of law in South Africa – whether statutorily derived, the common law or customary law. However, as noted above, the extent and methodology of applying rights in the Bill of Rights to legal disputes between private parties (where an organ of State or legislation is not involved) will be determined by ss 8(2) and (3).

---

[43] Woolman (note 20 above) 763.

[44] See chapter 2, part 2.4.2.

[45] *Khumalo* (note 18 above) paras 30–31.

[46] Note 28 above.

[47] Ibid paras 15 and 19. This case concerned a delictual claim based on vicarious liability against an organ of state.

(*b*) Section 8(2)

Section 8(2) provides broad criteria for determining when a provision in the Bill of Rights will bind a private party. Its formulation suggests that there are no definitive categories of rights or duties which can be excluded from horizontal application in any *a priori* fashion. Thus s 8(2) provides that:

> A provision of the Bill of Rights binds a natural or a juristic person if, and to the extent that, it is applicable, taking into account the nature of the right and the nature of any duty imposed by the right.

In *Khumalo* the Constitutional Court gave an indication of the considerations relevant to determining whether a right in the Bill of Rights has direct horizontal application. The case concerned the question whether the right of freedom of expression in s 16 altered the applicable common law rules pertaining to an action for defamation against a media defendant. The Court held that the right of freedom of expression 'is integral to a democratic society' and is 'constitutive of the dignity and autonomy of human beings'.[48] The media play a central role in upholding democracy and the right to freedom of expression enables them to fulfil this role.[49] It went on to hold that:

> Given the intensity of the constitutional right in question, coupled with the potential invasion of that right which could be occasioned by persons other than the State or organs of State, it is clear that the right to freedom of expression is of direct horizontal application in this case as contemplated by section 8(2) of the Constitution.[50]

A court must accordingly decide in the context of a particular dispute between private parties whether the nature of the right at issue in the case, and the nature of any duty imposed by that right render it capable of application in the dispute. The degree to which a particular right will be binding on a private party thus depends on a contextual evaluation of the nature of the right and duties which are in question in particular cases, as well as the nature of the private entity concerned.[51] This inevitably involves a policy judgment as to whether a duty imposed by the right should be imposed on a private party in the particular context of the case. As Currie and De Waal argue,[52] and *Khumalo* clearly implies, it is not necessary for the power exercised by a private entity to approximate that of the State. It is enough that the exercise of private law rights and liberties has the potential to limit the enjoyment of constitutional rights by others. The commitment of the Constitution to transform existing inequitable

---

[48] Ibid para 22.
[49] Ibid para 24.
[50] Ibid para 33.
[51] As Alfred Cockrell 'Private law and the Bill of Rights: A threshold issue of "horizontality"' in *Butterworths Bill of Rights Compendium* (Issue 14 May 2004) notes, s 8(2) 'proceeds on the assumption that constitutional rights might be agent-relative and context-sensitive, inasmuch as their direct application against private agencies will depend on the circumstances of the case and the characteristics of the particular person.' Ch 3A8 at 13.
[52] Note 22 above at 53.

power relations and patterns of poverty supports an expansive interpretation of the provisions in the Constitution governing horizontal application.[53]

Early academic contributions suggested that socio-economic rights were unsuited for horizontal application in that it would be too burdensome to impose the positive duties to provide socio-economic rights on private parties.[54] However, as early as the *Government of the Republic of South Africa v Grootboom* ('*Grootboom*') decision,[55] the Court indicated that at least some of the duties imposed by socio-economic rights were binding on private parties. Thus the Court held that s 26(1) of the Constitution imposes 'at the very least, a negative obligation upon the State *and all other entities and persons* to desist from preventing or impairing the right of access to adequate housing'.[56] (Emphasis added.) The Court subsequently confirmed in *Minister of Health v Treatment Action Campaign (No 2)*[57] ('*Treatment Action Campaign*') that this negative duty was sourced in the first subsection of ss 26 and 27.[58] In the *Grootboom* and *Treatment Action Campaign* judgments, the Court did not elaborate on its understanding of the 'negative duty' imposed by socio-economic rights.

However, in its subsequent decision in *Jaftha v Schoeman; Van Rooyen v Stoltz*[59] ('*Jaftha*') it held that 'any measure which permits a person to be deprived of existing access to adequate housing, limits the rights protected in section 26(1).'[60] Such measures can only be justified in terms of the general limitation clause (s 36). This suggests that private law rules which permit people to be deprived of the existing access which they enjoy to socio-economic rights are inconsistent with ss 26(1) and 27(1) of the Constitution, and are subject to justification in terms of s 36.

The situation in relation to the positive duties imposed by socio-economic rights is more complex.[61] Does the fact that ss 26(2) and 27(2) expressly place this positive duty on the State imply that the positive duties imposed by socio-economic rights cannot bind private parties in appropriate circumstances? Such a reading would confine the horizontal application of ss 26 and 27 to the negative duties imposed by ss 26(1) and 27(1). There is some suggestion to support this reading in the following statement made by the Court in the *Treatment Action Campaign* case:

> We therefore conclude that section 27(1) of the Constitution does not give rise to a self-standing and independent positive right enforceable irrespective of the considerations mentioned in s 27(2). Sections 27(1) and 27(2) must be read together as defining the scope

---

[53] See chapter 2, part 2.4.5.

[54] For an early view expressed in this regard, see H Cheadle and D Davis 'The application of the 1996 Constitution in the private sphere' (1997) 13 *SAJHR* 44–66 at 59–60.

[55] 2001 (1) SA 46 (CC), 2000 (11) BCLR 1169 (CC).

[56] Ibid para 34.

[57] 2002 (5) SA 721 (CC), 2002 (10) BCLR 1033 (CC).

[58] Ibid para 46.

[59] 2005 (2) SA 140 (CC), 2005 (1) BCLR 78 (CC).

[60] Ibid para 34.

[61] On the positive duties imposed by ss 26 and 27, see chapter 4. The positive duties imposed by ss 28(1)(*c*), 29 and 35(2)(*e*) are discussed in chapter 5.

> of the positive rights that everyone has and the corresponding obligations *on the State* to 'respect, protect, promote and fulfil' such rights. The rights conferred by ss 26(1) and 27(1) are to have 'access' to the services *that the State is obliged to provide* in terms of ss 26(2) and 27(2).[62] (Emphasis added.)

However, this statement can also be read simply to indicate that the positive duties which rest on the State to take legislative and other measures to progressively achieve the full realisation of the socio-economic rights generated by s 27(1) are not unqualified and must take account of resource constraints.

An approach which does not rely on an abstract distinction between negative and positive duties for the purpose of determining the extent of horizontal application of ss 26 and 27 is more theoretically coherent and consonant with the transformative purposes of socio-economic rights.[63] One of the fundamental purposes of ss 26 and 27 is to protect and advance people's access to socio-economic rights. As Stephen Ellman observes, 'Section 27(2) states part of what the state must do to implement these rights; it does not tell us that only the state need do anything.'[64] Both public and private actors and institutions can unjustifiably deprive people of their access to socio-economic rights and, in appropriate contexts, both sets of actors and institutions should bear positive duties to facilitate access to these rights. Section 8(2) of the Constitution provides a nuanced and contextual framework for determining whether in a particular case it is reasonable to impose negative or positive duties on a non-State actor. This will inevitably be a value judgment which must be made in the light of the transformative commitments of the Constitution which include the redress of socio-economic deprivations and systemic inequalities.

---

[62] *Treatment Action Campaign* (note 57 above) para 39.

[63] For a critique of the conceptual divide between negative and positive duties in relation to socio-economic rights, see chapter 2, part 2.4.4.

[64] S Ellman 'A constitutional confluence: American "state action" law and the application of South Africa's socio-economic rights guarantees to private actors' in P Andrews & S Ellman (eds) *The Post-Apartheid Constitutions: Perspectives on South Africa's Basic Law* (2001) 444–480 at 461. Jonathan Klaaren argues that the requirement of 'reasonable legislative and other measures' in ss 26(2) and 27(2) read in conjunction with ss 26(1) and 27(1) can be interpreted to include judicial measures thereby requiring the courts to develop the private common law so as to facilitate access to socio-economic rights. See J Klaaren 'A remedial interpretation of the *Treatment Action Campaign* decision' (2003) 19 *SAJHR* 455–468 at 461; J Klaaren 'An institutional interpretation of socio-economic rights and judicial remedies after *TAC*' in H Botha, A J van der Walt, J van der Walt (eds) *Rights and Democracy in a Transformative Constitution* (2003) 105–115. Marius Pieterse 'Indirect horizontal application of the right to have access to health care services' (2007) 23 *SAJHR* 157–179 at 163 argues that positive duties can be derived from ss 26(1) and 27(1) which are capable of binding private parties:

> Subject to the (express and implied) limitations on horizontal application derived from s 8 of the Constitution, all obligations inherent in s 27(1)(*a*) *except* for that set out in s 27(2) should in principle be viewed as capable of attaching to private entities.

There are many examples which illustrate the potential application of both negative and positive obligations in the context of socio-economic rights claims to private actors. Thus in the context of the right of access to adequate housing, private law rules of property which permit people to be unjustifiably deprived of their access to adequate housing may be regarded as inconsistent with s 26 of the Constitution. Similarly, the contractual arrangements between medical aid schemes and their members may unreasonably and unjustifiably allow for the termination of membership or the coverage of particular medical treatments previously funded.[65]

There are certain contexts in which it is particularly appropriate to impose positive duties on private actors to protect or facilitate people's access to socio-economic rights. Such situations may arise where there is a special relationship between the parties, or where the private entity has significant power to control access to a particular social resource or service. Thus, for example, the Constitutional Court has held that the duty to secure the socio-economic rights of children in s 28(1)(*c*) rests primarily on their parents and families, and only in default of such parental or family care, on the State.[66] Furthermore, it may be appropriate to impose a legal duty on large corporations to make provision for the housing needs of their workers in contexts where the company relies primarily on migrant labour. The health rights in ss 27, 28(1)(*c*) and 35(2)(*e*) can be interpreted to place duties on large pharmaceutical companies to ensure that their patent rights do not prevent the economic accessibility of crucial drugs and medical treatments.[67] Such cases may not necessarily give rise to a direct claim against the corporation concerned. However, recognising the obligation of powerful pharmaceutical manufacturers to ensure the accessibility and

---

[65] While the relationship between medical aid schemes and their members is regulated by the Medical Schemes Act 131 of 1998, the Act nonetheless permits a broad latitude for medical schemes and their members to regulate their contractual arrangements. The provision of medical aid is particularly susceptible to forms of indirect discrimination based on the prohibited grounds in terms of s 9(4) of the Constitution. For example, scheme rules may exclude or provide significantly reduced cover for certain types of medical treatment which have an exclusive or disproportionate significance for particular groups such as women, persons living with HIV/AIDS, or with mental health conditions. Some forms of redress are provided through legislation such as ss 24(2)(*e*) and (*f*) of the Act and various provisions of Promotion of Equality and Prevention of Unfair Discrimination Act 4 of 2000 (PEPUDA). However, to the extent that legislative remedies are inadequate to vindicate the intersecting constitutional rights to equality and health care in this context, judicial remedies must be found in the existing common law or developed.

[66] See the discussion of the Constitutional Court's jurisprudence in relation to children's socio-economic rights in chapter 5, part 5.2.

[67] See the analysis of a possible application of s 27 in this scenario by S Ellman (note 64 above) 459–469.

affordability of medicines should influence the interpretation of relevant international agreements,[68] and legislation regulating patents and pharmaceutical pricing.[69]

Section 8(2) thus requires courts to do sustained interpretative work in coming to grips with the nature of the particular socio-economic right and the duties which should be imposed in a legal dispute between private parties. The Constitutional Court's judgment in *Khumalo* suggests that the application of any right in the Bill of Rights to a private party should depend on the power of the private party concerned to undermine the interests and values protected by the particular right. Given the significant power of a network of private institutions and rules to influence access to socio-economic rights, courts should be slow to conclude that a particular socio-economic right is not applicable in a dispute between private parties, particularly when the social and economic context reveals significant disparities of power between the parties.

(c) Section 8(3)

Having established that a right binds the private entity in a particular case, s 8(3) prescribes the mechanism through which this 'horizontal' application is to take effect. In the first place a court must consider whether there is legislation which gives adequate effect to the right. If not, the court must consider whether an existing common-law rule gives effect to the right. If the existing common law is deficient, the court is obliged to develop the common law to give effect to the right and may at the same time develop rules of the common law to limit the right in accordance with s 36(1).[70]

---

[68] Of particular significance in this context is the World Trade Organisation's treaty on the Trade Related Aspects of Intellectual Property Rights (TRIPS) and the Doha Declaration on the TRIPS Agreement and Public Health WT/MIN(01)/Dec/2, 14 November 2001.

[69] Such legislation in the South African context, includes the Patents Act 57 of 1978, the Medicines and Related Substances Act 101 of 1965, and the Competition Act 89 of 1998. In his separate judgment in *Minister of Health v New Clicks South Africa (Pty) Ltd (Treatment Action Campaign and Another as Amici Curiae)* 2006 (2) SA 311 (CC), 2006 (1) BCLR 1 (CC) Moseneke J (as he then was) recognised the critical role of regulatory measures to ensure access to affordable medicines as a component of the right of access to health care (paras 704–707). On the significance of health care rights to the intellectual property entitlements of pharmaceutical companies, see W P Nagan 'International intellectual property, access to health care, and human rights: South Africa v United States' (2001–2002) 14 *Florida J of Int Law* 155–191; C Onyemelukwe 'Access to anti-retroviral drugs as a component of the right to health in international law: Examining the application of the right in Nigerian jurisprudence' (2007) 7 *AHRLJ* 446–474; D M Chirwa 'The right to health in international law: Its implications for the obligations of state and non-state actors in ensuring access to essential medicine' (2003) 19 *SAJHR* 541–566.

[70] Thus in *Khumalo* (note 18 above), the Constitutional Court affirmed that the development of the common law of defamation to recognise the defence of 'reasonable publication' by the Supreme Court of Appeal in *National Media Ltd v Bogoshi* 1998 (4) SA 1196 (SCA), 1999 (1) BCLR 1 (SCA) struck an appropriate balance between the protection of freedom

In giving effect to the horizontal application of constitutional rights, the courts are thus enjoined in the first instance to apply appropriate legislation which gives effect to the relevant rights. This is understandable given the democratic legitimacy of legislation which, in terms of the Constitution, should also be adopted, following broad and inclusive public deliberation and participation.[71] Such processes should enable legislatures to craft balanced and comprehensive schemes which take into account and attempt to reconcile diverging rights and interests.[72] The Constitutional Court has held that a key criterion of reasonableness in assessing compliance with the State's positive duties in terms of ss 26 and 27 is the adoption of a comprehensive, co-ordinated programme to give effect to the relevant socio-economic rights. The Court has further indicated that such a programme may require putting in place national framework legislation.[73]

Moreover, an important nexus exists in this context between the duties imposed by socio-economic rights on private parties and the duty of the State 'to protect' the socio-economic rights of more vulnerable members of society against powerful private actors.[74] This duty to protect places an obligation on the State to enact and enforce the necessary legislation to regulate and enable private actors to fulfil their duties in socio-economic spheres.[75] This duty is particularly important in the context of the privatisation of many social services which are recognised as socio-economic rights in the Constitution and international law.[76]

It is therefore incumbent on the State to protect and give effect to socio-economic rights in relation to both public authorities and private parties through the enactment

---

of expression on the one hand, and the value of human dignity on the other (paras 28; 39–42).

[71] See ss 59 and 72 of the Constitution.

[72] The significance of public participation in legislative processes was highlighted in *Doctors for Life International v Speaker of the National Assembly* 2006 (6) SA 416 (CC), 2006 (12) BCLR 1399 (CC).

[73] *Grootboom* (note 55 above) para 40.

[74] On the 'duty to protect' in the context of socio-economic rights, see generally chapter 3, part 3.2.2. On the State's 'duty to protect' discourse in the context of constitutional property law jurisprudence, see A J van der Walt 'Transformative constitutionalism and the development of South African property law (part I)' (2005) 4 *TSAR* 655–690; A J van der Walt 'Transformative constitutionalism and the development of South African property law (part 2)' (2006) 1 *TSAR* 1–31.

[75] The Court in *Grootboom* (note 55 above) para 35 stated:

> A right of access to adequate housing also suggests that it is not only the State who is responsible for the provision of houses, but that other agents within our society, including individuals themselves, must be enabled by legislative and other measures to provide housing.

[76] See, for example, the State's duty to regulate the provision of water services operated or controlled by third parties in terms of arts 11 and 12 of the International Covenant on Economic, Social and Cultural Rights (1966). See Committee on Economic, Social and Cultural Rights, General Comment No 15 (Twenty-ninth sess, 2002) 'The right to water' UN doc E/C.12/2002/11 paras 23–24, 44(*b*).

of legislation. Where adequate and effective regulatory legislation exists, litigants will be required to rely on such legislation to protect their socio-economic rights against infringements by private parties.[77] Where litigants allege that legislation which is intended to give effect to a particular right in the Bill of Rights unconstitutionally excludes them and similarly situated groups from the rights and benefits it provides, they will be obliged to challenge the constitutionality of the legislation concerned.[78]

The courts are enjoined in terms of s 39(2) of the Constitution to interpret legislation so as to 'promote the spirit, purport and objects of the Bill of Rights'. This requires courts to interpret legislation, insofar as is reasonably possible, to protect and give effect to the rights and foundational constitutional values.[79] The purpose of socio-economic rights is to ensure that everyone has access to the socio-economic

---

[77] On the duty of litigants to base their cases on any legislation enacted to regulate constitutional rights, see *Bato Star Fishing (Pty) Ltd v Minister of Environmental Affairs* 2004 (4) SA 490 (CC), 2004 (7) BCLR 687 (CC) para 25; *South African National Defence Union v Minister of Defence* 2007 (5) SA 400 (CC), 2007 (8) BCLR 863 (CC) para 52 ('*SANDU*'); *Fuel Retailers Association of Southern Africa v Director-General: Environmental Management, Department of Agriculture, Conservation and Environment, Mpumalanga Province* 2007 (6) SA 4 (CC), 2007 (10) BCLR 1059 (CC) paras 36–39; paras 59–62; *MEC for Education: KwaZulu-Natal v Pillay* 2008 (1) SA 474 (CC), 2008 (2) BCLR 99 (CC) para 40. The situation is more complex where there is a dispute as to whether particular legislation is intended to give effect to a constitutional right. Thus the Supreme Court of Appeal has referred with apparent approval to the argument that the rule precluding direct reliance on constitutional rights 'operates only if and when, on a proper interpretation of the legislation read with the constitutional right to which it gives effect, the legislation is intended to be exhaustive of the right, that is, if parliament intended to *cover the field*'. (Emphasis added.) See *New Clicks* (note 69 above) and *City of Johannesburg v Mazibuko* 2009 (3) SA 592 (SCA) paras 11; 12–13. Complex questions of application and jurisdiction also arise when there is overlapping legislation of relevance to the protection of a particular constitutional right. An example of the latter situation is the applicability of the Labour Relations Act 66 of 1995 and the Promotion of Administrative Justice Act 3 of 2000 in the context of the right of public sector employees to fair labour practices in terms of s 23(1) of the Constitution. On the jurisdictional and normative complexities in this context, see *Fredericks v MEC for Education and Training, Eastern* Cape 2002 (2) SA 693 (CC), 2002 (2) BCLR 113 (CC), *Chirwa v Transnet Limited* 2008 (4) SA 367 (CC), 2008 (3) BCLR 251 (CC); *Nakin v MEC, Department of Education, Eastern Cape* 2008 (6) SA 320 (Ck), 2008 (6) BCLR 643 (Ck).

[78] This constitutes legislation which, in the parlance of the *New Clicks* (note 69 above), is intended to 'cover the field'. See *SANDU* ibid para 51:

> [W]here legislation is enacted to give effect to a constitutional right, a litigant may not bypass that legislation and rely directly on the Constitution without challenging that legislation as falling short of the constitutional standard.

[79] See *Govender v Minister of Safety and Security* 2001 (4) SA 273 (SCA), 2001 (11) BCLR 1197 (SCA) para 11; *Investigating Directorate: Serious Economic Offences v Hyundai Motor Distributors (Pty) Ltd; In re Hyundai Motor Distributors (Pty) Ltd v Smit NO* 2001 (1) SA 545 (CC), 2000 (10) BCLR 1079 (CC) para 22. An interpretation of legislation which is consistent with the Constitution should be preferred insofar as reasonably possible without unduly straining the legislative text and scheme. See *Hyundai* ibid para 24.

services and resources referred to in the relevant provisions. These must be adequate in quality and quantity to facilitate the development of people to their full potential and their participation as equals in all spheres of our society.[80] Legislation which regulates or determines access to socio-economic rights must thus be interpreted purposively to give full effect to these rights.[81]

However, in determining whether to require reliance on legislative measures for giving effect to the horizontal application of socio-economic rights, courts must be cognisant of the very real limitations and constraints of legislatures in ensuring the effective protection of constitutional rights. The South African Parliament and provincial legislatures, like most other modern legislatures, are subject to the constraints of time and resource pressures, they are at a relative disadvantage to the executive in relation to technical expertise and resources, and subject to capture by powerful business and interest groups in society.[82] This situation results in imperfect legislation which may disregard or neglect the rights of particular groups, frequently those who are politically, economically and socially marginalised.[83] In these situations, there are manifest legal difficulties in the way of obtaining a remedy to compel the enactment of such legislation. Litigants must look to the courts in terms of s 8(3) to find a remedy in terms of the existing common law or, where necessary, to develop a new common-law remedy to give effect to the relevant constitutional rights.

This responsibility cannot be avoided in the name of deference to legislative choices. As Justice Johan Froneman has argued, the conventional wisdom of deferring to legislative choices to avoid considering whether long-standing private law rules require significant reform prevents courts doing 'their bit in eradicating distorting patterns of interpersonal, social and economic domination'.[84] He argues that this type of judicial minimalism in the face of entrenched patterns of socio-economic deprivation and inequality in areas regulated by private law will 'tend to assist only a transfer of power between elites, not the substantive transformation of the character of our society that the best reading of the Constitution requires'.[85]

Section 8(3)(*a*) and (*b*) gives the courts the tools to develop rules which seek to synthesise and achieve the best reconciliation possible between the competing rights

---

[80] See also the discussion in chapter 2, part 2.4.2.

[81] For an example of the interpretation of legislation (albeit in the context of litigation against a public authority) to promote the objectives and values underlying the right of access to adequate housing in s 26, see *Occupiers of 51 Olivia Road, Berea Township and 197 Main Street, Johannesburg v City of Johannesburg* 2008 (3) SA 208 (CC), 2008 (5) BCLR 475 (CC) paras 42–46.

[82] See the discussion in chapter 2, part 2.4.7.

[83] For a discussion of the 'blind spots' and 'burdens of inertia' in legislative processes, see R Dixon 'Creating dialogue about socio-economic rights: Strong-form versus weak-form judicial review revisited' (2007) 5(3) *I Con* 391–418 at 402–406. See *SANDU* (note 77 above).

[84] J C Froneman (note 15 above) 16–17.

[85] Ibid 21–22.

and values which may be at stake in a particular case.[86] Thus in developing common-law remedies to give effect to the horizontal application of a socio-economic right, rules may also be developed which limit the scope of its application, provided that the limitation is 'reasonable and justifiable in an open and democratic society based on human dignity, equality and freedom' (s 36(1)).

Section 8(3) clearly indicates that constitutional rights, which are not adequately protected in legislation or the existing common law, must be vindicated through the protection of new constitutionally inspired remedies. In developing such remedies, courts should resist any inclination to confine the remedial possibilities within existing common-law paradigms. Socio-economic rights were not part of the previous private law tradition in South Africa, and the constitutional recognition of socio-economic rights requires a fundamental transformation of this body of law to give proper effect to these rights. This will require the development of new and innovative remedies. The horizontal application of socio-economic rights requires a radical break with conventional patterns of thought about the way in which the law should regulate relationships between non-State actors. A full appreciation of the nature and direction of this change will require serious and systematic engagement with the substantive content of socio-economic rights and their application to the various fields of private law.

7.2.4 Section 39(2)

Section 39(2) of the Constitution imposes a general duty on every court, tribunal or forum when interpreting any legislation, and when developing the common law or customary law to 'promote the spirit, purport and objects of the Bill of Rights'. In *Carmichele v Minister of Safety and Security*[87] ('*Carmichele*') the Constitutional Court held that this provision places a general duty on the courts to develop the common law and customary law so that they are consonant with the 'objective normative value system' established by the Constitution.[88] This provision suggests that the development of the common law or customary law should not occur on the basis of a narrow, formalistic construction of the relevant rights in the Bill of Rights. Instead, courts should seek 'to promote' the overall purposes, values and spirit of the Bill of Rights when developing the law. This suggests an active effort to bring common-

[86] See, for example, the reconciliation of the competing values of human dignity and freedom of expression in the context of defamation claims in the cases of *National Media Ltd v Bogoshi* (note 70 above) and *Khumalo* (note 18 above).

[87] Note 20 above, para 54 (the development of the common law under the influence of constitutional values in terms of s 39(2) is generally referred to in the literature as the 'indirect' horizontal application of the Bill of Rights).

[88] *Carmichele* ibid para 56; *S v Thebus* (note 20 above) paras 27–28.

and customary law rules and doctrines into alignment with a broad construction of the spirit, purposes and values of the Bill of Rights.[89]

Section 39(2) requires the courts when adjudicating run-of-the-mill commercial, contractual, family and property law cases to consider whether applicable common- and customary law principles require development to give effect to the underlying purposes and values of the Bill of Rights, including the socio-economic rights. The purpose of socio-economic rights is not only to ensure that people have access to basic social services and economic resources, but also to facilitate greater equity and social justice in socio-economic relations in South Africa. This understanding emerges particularly from a purposive approach to the interpretation of the Bill of Rights which takes the interrelationship between rights seriously.[90] A key area of interdependence exists between socio-economic rights and equality as a founding constitutional value[91] and a substantive right in s 9 of the Constitution.[92] Thus, for example, s 9(2) of the Constitution defines equality to include 'the full and equal enjoyment of all rights and freedoms'. The duty in terms of s 39(2) to promote more equitable social and economic relationships through appropriate development of the various spheres of private law regulating these relationships emerges particularly from this interrelationship between equality and socio-economic rights.

7.2.5 Development of the common law or a new constitutional remedy?

Whether the path taken to the horizontal application of constitutional rights is s 8(2) read with (3), or s 39(2), the question arises when it is appropriate to develop existing common-law remedies and doctrines to give effect to constitutional rights and values, or to develop an entirely new remedy sourced in the Constitution.[93] The case law dealing with the relationship between common-law and constitutional remedies to vindicate constitutional rights illustrates the complexity of this issue. Although the cases discussed all involve organs of State as parties to the proceedings, similar questions arise in respect of the application of the Bill of Rights to private common-law rules.

In *Tswelopele Non-Profit Organisation v City of Tshwane Metropolitan Municipality*[94] ('*Tswelopele*'), the Supreme Court of Appeal was reluctant to develop the common-law remedy of the mandament van spolie to provide the relief of reconstruction

---

[89] See in this regard *K v Minister of Safety and Security* (note 28 above) para 17 (cited in the text accompanying note 39 above). See also *Thebus* (note 20 above) para 28. See also part 7.2.2 above.

[90] On the implications of an interpretive approach which seeks to develop the interrelationship between the rights in the Bill of Rights, see chapter 2, part 2.4.3.

[91] Sections 1 and 7(1) of the Constitution. See further chapter 3, part 3.3.1.

[92] On the implications of an interdependent interpretation of equality and socio-economic rights, see chapter 4, parts 4.3.4 and 4.5.

[93] See in this regard notes 28–31 above and accompanying text.

[94] 2007 (6) SA 511 (SCA).

of dwellings unlawfully destroyed by municipal officials. Instead it chose to craft a remedy 'special to the Constitution'[95] to provide this relief. The constitutional right primarily at stake was s 26(3) read in conjunction with the foundational constitutional value of the rule of law.[96] The Court, per Cameron JA (as he then was), stated:

> The Constitution preserves the common law, but requires the courts to synchronise it with the Bill of Rights. This entails that common-law provisions at odds with the Constitution must either be developed or put at nought; but it does not mean that every common-law mechanism, institution or doctrine needs constitutional overhaul; nor does it mean that where a remedy for a constitutional infraction is required, a common law figure with an analogous operation must necessarily be seized upon for its development. On the contrary: it may sometimes be best to leave a common-law institution untouched, and to craft a new constitutional remedy entirely.[97]

The effect of the Court's reluctance to apply or develop the existing common-law remedy of the mandament van spolie is that the latter remedy remains confined to 'the interim restoration and physical control and enjoyment of physical property – not its reconstituted equivalent'.

The facts of *Tswelopele* arguably represented precisely the kind of situation in which it would have been appropriate to develop an existing common-law remedy to provide relief.[98] There exist previous precedents of the application of the mandament to require the reconstruction of informal dwellings under apartheid.[99] The policy reasons for failing to make an established common-law remedy available in these situations are not clearly explained in the judgment. Furthermore, the sharp distinction drawn between common-law and constitutional remedies, and the caution that common-law institutions must sometimes be left 'untouched' does not sit comfortably with the notion of a single system of law deriving its force from the Constitution.[100] Even if there were good reasons for the creation of a new constitutional remedy in

---

[95] Ibid para 27.

[96] Ibid paras 2 and 25–26.

[97] Ibid para 20 (footnotes omitted).

[98] Ibid para 24. For an argument that a restrictive interpretation of the mandament in the specific context of an informal dwelling 'that can quickly, easily and cheaply be replaced using fungible and even used materials' is unnecessary and out of step with the values and interests protected by s 26, see A J van der Walt 'Developing the law on unlawful squatting and spoliation' (2008) 125 *SALJ* 24–36. As Van der Walt points out, the requirements for this new constitutional remedy and its scope of application are unclear (36).

[99] See *Fredericks v Stellenbosch Divisional Council* 1977 (3) SA 113 (C); *Rikhotso v Northcliff Ceramics (Pty) Ltd* 1997 (1) SA 526 (W). See further D G Kleyn 'Die mandament van spolie as besitsremedie' (1986) *DJ* 1–16; A J van der Walt 'Squatting, spoliation and the new constitutional order' (1997) 60 *THRHR* 522–529 and M Blumberg '*Mandament van spolie* – restoration of the *status quo ante* revisited' (1997) 60 *THRHR* 529–533.

[100] See *Pharmaceutical Manufacturers* (note 13 above) and accompanying text. See also Roederer's argument that common law and constitutional remedies should be viewed as part of a single seamless matrix: C Roederer 'Post-matrix legal reasoning: Horizontality and the rule of values in South African law' (2003) 19 *SAJHR* 57–81.

these circumstances, the judgment does not provide general guidance on the types of considerations which should inform a judicial decision to give effect to a constitutional right through the development of existing common-law remedies, or the crafting of an entirely new constitutional cause of action.

There are clearly situations in which it is appropriate to provide a direct constitutional remedy as opposed to requiring litigants to rely on existing common-law remedies. In these cases the most effective, expeditious form of relief for the violations of constitutional rights at issue is a remedy derived directly from the Constitution.

In *MEC, Department of Welfare, Eastern Cape v Kate*[101] ('*Kate*'), the Supreme Court of Appeal confirmed an award of damages in the form of back pay and interest for an unlawful delay in the payment of a social grant in terms of the Social Assistance Act 59 of 1992.[102] The Supreme Court of Appeal held that the denial of the substantive right of access to social assistance in s 27(1)(*c*) of the Constitution lay at the heart of Mrs Kate's claim.[103] In responding to the provincial government's argument that relief should be pursued through an ordinary delictual claim and not through a claim for constitutional damages, Nugent JA held that the relief permitted by s 38 for infringements of constitutional rights was 'not a remedy of last resort, to be looked to only when there is no alternative – and indirect – means of asserting and vindicating constitutional rights'.[104] Given the 'direct breach of a substantive constitutional right (as opposed to merely a deviation from a constitutionally normative standard)' and the 'endemic breach' of the rights in issue, the court held that a constitutional remedy of damages was appropriate.[105] In this case, a direct constitutional remedy as opposed to an indirect common-law remedy ensured the more effective and flexible relief required to vindicate the egregious breaches of the right to social assistance and administrative justice at issue in the case.

In *President of Republic of South Africa v Modderklip Boerdery (Pty) Ltd*[106] both the Supreme Court of Appeal and the Constitutional Court granted relief to a private

---

101 2006 (4) SA 478 (SCA), [2006] 2 All SA 455 (SCA).

102 See also the judgment of Froneman J in the court *a quo* in *Kate v MEC for the Department of Welfare, Eastern Cape* 2005 (1) SA 141 (SE), [2005] All SA 745 (SE), particularly at paras 20 and 31.

103 *Kate* (note 101 above) para 22.

104 Ibid para 27. In *Fose v Minister of Safety and Security* 1997 (3) SA 786 (CC), 1997 (7) BCLR 851 (CC) the Constitutional Court held that constitutional damages was not an appropriate remedy in the circumstances of the particular case as the rights in question could be adequately vindicated through normal delictual damages.

105 Ibid.

106 *Modderfontein Squatters, Greater Benoni City Council v Modderklip Boerdery (Pty) Ltd (Agri SA and Legal Resources Centre, Amici Curiae); President of the Republic of South Africa v Modderklip Boerdery (Pty) Ltd (Agri SA and Legal Resources Centre, Amici Curiae)* 2004 (6) SA 40 (SCA), 2004 (8) BCLR 821 (SCA) ('*Modderklip (SCA)*') paras 41–44; 51–52; *President of the Republic of South Africa v Modderklip Boerdery (Pty) Ltd (Agri SA and Others, Amici Curiae)* 2005 (5) SA 3 (CC), 2005 (8) BCLR 786 (CC) ('*Modderklip (CC)*') paras 53–68. See the analysis of the *Modderklip* judgments in chapter 6, part 6.3.

landowner in the form of an award of constitutional damages against the State for failing to assist the owner to execute an eviction order obtained in terms of the Prevention of Illegal Evictions from and Unlawful Occupation of Land Act 19 of 1998 (PIE) against a large community occupying the land in question. The Supreme Court of Appeal found that the owner's constitutional property rights had been infringed, and also found that relevant organs of State had failed to adequately protect the occupiers' housing rights in terms of the Constitution.[107] The Constitutional Court, on the other hand, found a violation of the right of access to court in s 34 and the rule of law enshrined in s 1(*c*) of the Constitution.[108] However, it upheld, in all essential aspects, the remedy of damages granted by the Supreme Court of Appeal to vindicate the infringement of constitutional rights.[109] Section 26 rights were taken into account in the determination of appropriate relief, as the Court held that it was also important to have regard to 'the general tone and purpose of legislation enacted to govern evictions, read with the relevant constitutional provisions'.[110] The Court accordingly declared that the residents were entitled to occupy the land 'until alternative land has been made available to them by the State or the provincial or local authority'.[111]

The decision to develop the existing common law or to fashion new remedies based on constitutional provisions should be made after a careful scrutiny of the existing common law within its historical and social context. In the context of socio-economic rights, courts should consider whether existing legal rules facilitate or impede access to socio-economic rights. This historical and contextual analysis will enable the courts to gain a better appreciation of the desirability of transforming or leaving intact existing common-law rules and doctrines in a particular field. André van der Walt points out, for example, that given the central role of property law in serving the colonial and apartheid project in South Africa, it is appropriate to reconsider 'the underlying structure of the property regime and its effect on the entrenchment of privilege and power embodied in property holdings' whenever the courts have to consider the appropriateness of common-law remedies in a particular case.[112]

7.2.6 Transformation of the common law and legal culture

A significant constraining factor on the transformation of common-law doctrines and rules under the influence of the normative value system of the Constitution

---

[107] *Modderklip (SCA)* ibid paras 16–17, 21–28.
[108] *Modderklip (CC)* (note 106 above) paras 39–51.
[109] Ibid paras 53–66. On the remedial aspects of *Modderklip* chapter 8, part 8.7.2.
[110] Ibid paras 55–56.
[111] *Modderklip (SCA)* (note 106 above) para 52; *Modderklip (CC)* (note 106 above) para 68 (Order 3(*c*)).
[112] Van der Walt (note 98 above) 32.

is the nature of legal culture[113] in South Africa and traditional understandings of the 'internal logic' and processes through which common-law development takes place.[114]

According to received wisdom, the evolution or development of the common law takes place incrementally on a case-by-case basis to fill gaps in the law in accordance with its own conceptual structures and doctrines.[115] The legislature is seen as the appropriate institution, given its democratic legitimacy, to bring about any far-reaching changes in the doctrinal structure and normative content of the common law.[116] But even then the presumption is applied that a statute does not alter the common law more than necessary.[117] The influence of this understanding of the common law is strongly evident in South African legal culture and tradition, and continues to exert a powerful grip on our collective legal imagination in the constitutional era.[118] It runs beneath the surface of the controversy regarding the nature and extent to which the Bill of Rights should influence developments in various spheres of the common law, and the respective roles of the judiciary and legislature in realising constitutional rights. It is also manifest in arguments that the values which the Constitution proclaims as foundational to the democratic order are already 'inherent' in the common law thus obviating the need for any dramatic changes.[119]

---

[113] On the disjuncture between South Africa's legal culture and the transformative commitments of the Constitution, See generally Karl Klare 'Legal culture and transformative constitutionalism' (1998) 14 *SAJHR* 146–188; A J van der Walt 'Legal history, legal culture and transformation in a constitutional democracy' (2006) 12 *Fundamina* 1–47.

[114] Van der Walt ibid 7–8.

[115] See Van der Walt's discussion of the preference in South African legal culture for giving effect to constitutional rights and values through 'incremental, "interstitial changes" that fill up small gaps in existing common-law doctrine, while they oppose larger changes that would affect the logic or direction of doctrine substantively' (footnotes omitted). Ibid 8.

[116] Van der Walt ibid 8–9. See *Masiya v Director of Public* Prosecutions (note 20 above), paras 30–31. See also O'Regan J's dissenting judgment on the question of remedy in *Minister of Home Affairs v Fourie (Doctors for Life International and Others, Amici Curiae); Lesbian and Gay Equality Project v Minister of Home Affairs* 2006 (1) SA 524 (CC), 2006 (3) BCLR 355 (CC).

[117] See the discussion of *Grobler v Msimanga* [2008] 3 All SA 549 (W) in part 7.3.1(*c*) below.

[118] See, for example, the cautious approach to reforming the common law suggested by the Constitutional Court in *Carmichele* (note 20 above) para 55:

> This requires not only a proper appreciation of the Constitution and its objective, normative value system, but also a proper understanding of the common law. We have previously cautioned against overzealous judicial reform. … Not only must the common law be developed in a way which meets the s 39(2) objectives, but it must be done in a way most appropriate for the development of the common law within its own paradigm.

See also *Masiya v Director of Public Prosecutions* (note 20 above) para 31.

[119] For an insightful analysis of the disjuncture encountered in the jurisprudence between a transformative interpretation of the foundational constitutional values of human dignity, freedom and equality and a preservative, classic liberal interpretation, see D Bhana and

There is an evident tension between the notion that the development of the common law requires gradual, cautious changes and the transformative character of the Constitution which envisages a substantial and substantive change in both public and private patterns of socio-economic disadvantage and marginalisation. It is particularly manifest in the sphere of the horizontal application of socio-economic rights given the absence of a conceptual foundation in our existing common law for recognising entitlements to socio-economic resources and services. This tension will be examined further in the context of the specific jurisprudence discussed in parts 7.3 and 7.4 below.

A further factor which constrains fundamental changes in common-law doctrine to give effect to the purposes and values of socio-economic rights is the privileging of negative rights and liberties in our legal culture.[120] Our private law provides strong protection to vested private property rights[121] and the negative freedom to contract freely without undue judicial intervention (expressed in the doctrine *pacta sunt servanda*). In the post-constitutional era a measure of reinforcement has been found for these common-law rights and doctrines in constitutional rights and values such as aspects of the property clause (s 25), and freedom and dignity as foundational constitutional values.[122]

However, these rights and doctrines must be considered and weighed within an integrated normative framework which includes the Constitution's commitment to socio-economic rights and substantive equality. If the rights and values associated with socio-economic rights are marginalised in the adjudication of legal disputes between private parties, the law will be skewed in favour of those already able to wield the power that access to property and economic resources provides. The ultimate consequence will be to undermine the Constitution's commitment to eradicating entrenched patterns of socio-economic disadvantage. The privileging of negative rights and liberty in constitutional adjudication is not merely a question of the methodology of applying the constitution to the private law, but a substantive ideological choice.[123] This choice can only be made by disregarding the values and purposes which the socio-economic rights in our Constitution were intended to promote.

The second part of this chapter considers the extent of influence of socio-economic rights in selected areas of private property and contract law.

M Pieterse 'Towards a reconciliation of contract law and constitutional values: *Brisley* and *Afrox* revisited' (2005) 122 *SALJ* 865–895 at 876–884.

120 See chapter 2, part 2.4.4.

121 See in this regard A J van der Walt *Constitutional Property Law* (2005) 404–416.

122 See, for example, the analysis of the jurisprudence in part 7.3.1(*c*) below. See also the discussion of Cameron JA's concurring judgment in *Brisley v Drotsky* 2002 (4) SA 1 (SCA), 2002 (12) BCLR 1229 (SCA) in part 7.4.1 below at notes 243–250 and accompanying text.

123 I am grateful to my colleague Prof Geo Quinot for this observation in the course of commenting on the chapter.

7.3 SOCIO-ECONOMIC RIGHTS IN SELECTED AREAS OF PROPERTY LAW

7.3.1 The eviction of people from their homes

(*a*) Introduction

The focus in this part is on the impact of s 26 (the right of access to housing) on private law rules and procedures regulating the eviction of persons from their homes.[124] The eviction of unlawful occupiers from their homes is the locus of tension between the traditional hegemony of private property rights in common law and the vital human interests which people have in secure tenure of their homes. The common-law right of an owner to evict unlawful occupiers from their property forms part of what André van der Walt describes as:

> a complex web of rules and practices premised on a deep-level commitment to the supremacy of private individual ownership in a free market, resulting in seemingly natural and neutral outcomes that systematically favour the exclusivity of private ownership over alternative or reformist rules and practices premised on notions of access to land and the protection of vulnerable and marginalised groups and individuals against arbitrary, unwarranted or unfair eviction.[125]

Rights in relation to deprivation and expropriation of property are constitutionally protected through ss 25(1)–(3). Security of tenure, equitable access to land and housing rights are also constitutionally protected through ss 25(4)–(9) and 26. Cumulatively the latter provisions pose a fundamental challenge to the deeply entrenched idea that ownership of immovable property is the dominant or exclusive right to be considered in applications for the eviction of people from their homes.

The impact of housing rights on the law pertaining to evictions is examined in two primary contexts. The first is the approach of the courts to developing the common law applicable to evictions in the constitutional era prior to the coming into force of PIE or in cases in which the courts have held that PIE is inapplicable. This legislation was enacted with the express purpose of creating a constitutionally compliant regulatory framework governing the eviction of unlawful occupiers from their homes. Second, the general approach of the courts to the interpretation of PIE in the context of eviction applications where the land occupied is privately owned is considered.[126] Both these contexts assist in illuminating the extent to which the constitutional recognition of housing rights has influenced courts to apply a transformed legal paradigm in eviction cases. It is necessary at the outset to briefly sketch the pre-

[124] Chapter 6 focuses primarily on the obligations which have been imposed on organs of state in respect of the eviction of persons from their homes.

[125] A J van der Walt 'Exclusivity of ownership, security of tenure and eviction orders: A critical evaluation of recent case law' (2002) 18 *SAJHR* 372–420 at 410.

[126] For a detailed consideration of PIE and the jurisprudence applicable to the obligations of organs of state in terms of this legislation, see chapter 6, part 6.2.

constitutional common-law rules governing an action for the ejectment of occupiers of immovable property by a landowner.

This power of property rights in the case of the pre-constitutional common law is reflected in the remedy of *rei vindicatio* which takes the form of an action for ejection in the case of the occupation of immovable property. To succeed, the owner is merely required to allege and prove ownership of the property, and the fact that the defendant is in possession of the property. If these allegations are not contested, the only defence available to the occupier is to allege and prove a valid right to occupy the property in terms of legislation or arising, for example, from a lease agreement. In the event of the owner acknowledging a right of occupation by the occupier such as a lease agreement, he or she must prove that the right is no longer enforceable in law because it has expired or been terminated.[127] When an occupier has no valid right of occupation, the owner's property rights trump any other considerations pertaining to the eviction, such as the hardship or homelessness which the occupier might experience upon eviction.[128]

The recognition of constitutional housing rights in the 1996 Constitution signalled the need for a seismic change in the legal landscape applicable to evictions. Section 26 of the Constitution read as a whole aims at advancing and protecting access to housing. Section 26(3) creates specific procedural and substantive safeguards for people facing eviction from their home, or the demolition of their home.[129] It reads as follows:

> No one may be evicted from their home, or have their home demolished, without an order of court made after considering all the relevant circumstances. No legislation may permit arbitrary evictions.

In *Grootboom*, the Constitutional Court considered the eviction of persons from their homes to be a specific manifestation of the negative duty in s 26(1) which is 'further spelt out' in s 26(3).[130] As noted above, the Court held that this negative duty is

---

127 For the classic exposition of these rules, see *Graham v Ridley* 1931 TPD 476 at 479; *Chetty v Naidoo* 1974 (3) SA 13 (A) at 20A–E. The power of ownership as a common-law institution is captured by the following statement of Jansen JA in *Chetty v Naidoo* ibid:

> [I]t may be difficult to define *dominium* comprehensively ... but there can be little doubt ... that one of its incidents is the right of exclusive possession of the *res*, with the necessary corollary that the owner may claim his property wherever found, from whomsoever holding it. It is inherent in the nature of ownership that possession of the *res* should normally be with the owner.

128 The metaphor of private property rights as a 'trump card' is derived from the work of André van der Walt. See, for example, *Constitutional Property Law* (2005) 417. Van der Walt argues that 'both the common law regarding property in land and existing property holdings were fundamentally shaped and affected by the deeply politicized intervention of apartheid laws and policies'. (416).

129 See further chapter 6, part 6.1.

130 *Grootboom* (note 55 above) para 34.

horizontally applicable as it is binding both upon the State and 'all other entities and persons'.[131]

(*b*) Impact of section 26(3) on common-law ejectment actions

Section 26 has given rise to legislation which has fundamentally changed the common law described above governing the eviction of people from their homes. Of particular significance in this context is the enactment of PIE which applies to unlawful occupiers in respect of all land throughout South Africa.[132] However, prior to the coming into force of PIE, there were a number of cases which grappled with the implications of s 26(3) in the common-law application for ejectment. It is also instructive to examine the approach of the courts to the nature and implications of s 26(3) of the Constitution in eviction applications brought in terms of the common law and in which PIE has been held to be inapplicable.

In *Ross v South Peninsula Municipality*[133] ('*Ross*'), the Western Cape High Court held that s 26(3) of the Constitution altered the common law by vesting in the court an equitable discretion to determine the incidence of onus in an ejectment application.[134] This meant that the Clerk of the Magistrate's Court or the Registrar of the High Court could not issue eviction orders in applications for default judgment as this would effectively deprive the courts of an opportunity to consider 'all the relevant circumstances' as required by s 26(3).[135] Section 26(3) also altered the traditional rules of onus by requiring the plaintiff to allege and prove the circumstances known to it which were relevant to the granting of an eviction order.[136] Some guidance as to these circumstances could be found in ss 4(6) and (7) of PIE referring to 'the rights and needs of the elderly, children, disabled persons and households headed by women'.[137]

In contrast to this serious attempt to consider the implications of s 26(3) for common-law actions for ejectment, Flemming DJP (as he then was) adopted a highly restrictive approach to the impact of s 26(3) on existing law in the subsequent case of *Betta Eiendomme (Pty) Ltd v Ekple-Epoh*[138] ('*Betta Eiendomme*'). In the first instance he held that s 26(3) was of vertical application only,[139] thus preventing it from having any impact on the existing private law applicable to evictions. Second, he held that the court in *Ross* was incorrect to refer to PIE in seeking guidance on the meaning of 'relevant circumstances' for the purposes of s 26(3).[140] Rather, regard must be had in

[131] Ibid.
[132] See s 1 (xi) read with s 2 of PIE.
[133] 2000 (1) SA 589 (C).
[134] Ibid 595G.
[135] Ibid 595H.
[136] Ibid 595J–596I.
[137] Ibid 595I–599C. PIE had not yet commenced at the time of this case.
[138] 2000 (4) SA 468 (W).
[139] Ibid para 7.3.
[140] Ibid para 8.2.

interpreting 'relevant circumstances' to factors such as 'the unfairness of causing loss to the owner so that the impertinence of land grabbing can stand', the owner's liability for 'land taxes and ... for water and electricity left unpaid by the unlawful occupier', and 'the factual question of how the exercise of the court's decision in a particular way will fit into society, its law and its sense of fairness'.[141] These are circumstances of which the court may take judicial notice, once the fact of the plaintiff's ownership of the land and the defendant's unlawful occupation have been established.[142] Given that the Court held that s 26(3) was of vertical application only, the above views on the meaning of 'relevant circumstances' are *obiter*. Nevertheless they are illustrative of the reflexive privileging of property interests, and the absence of any acknowledgment of the human interests which occupiers have in not being evicted from their homes.[143]

In the subsequent decision of *Ellis v Viljoen*[144] ('*Ellis*'), a full bench of the Western Cape High Court held that PIE was not applicable to an eviction application against an occupier who initially took up occupation of the land with consent.[145] In considering the direct application of s 26(3) of the Constitution to the common-law action for ejectment the court held that *Ross* had been wrongly decided 'insofar as it was there held that "a plaintiff seeking to evict a person from his or her home is now required to allege relevant circumstances which entitled the court to issue such an order"'.[146] It reasoned that s 25(1) of the Constitution, which provides that '[n]o one may be deprived of property except in terms of law of general application, and that no law may permit arbitrary deprivation of property', reinforced the landowner's common-law right to reclaim ownership of her land upon proof of ownership and the defendant's possession of the property. In other words, s 26(3) brought about no change in the onus or burden of proof in legal proceedings for ejectment. The Court found that such an approach was 'eminently consonant' with the constitutional protection of property rights in s 25(1).[147]

The Court fails to develop a balanced normative framework in which the purposes and values underlying both property and housing rights are recognised. Instead, the common-law position in which property rights are accorded overriding significance is simply reaffirmed. This effectively denudes s 26(3) of much of its potential to transform the common law pertaining to the eviction of people from homes.

---

[141] Ibid para 12.1–12.3.

[142] Ibid para 15.4.1.

[143] See the critique of T Roux 'Continuity and change in a transforming legal order: The impact of section 26(3) of the Constitution on South African law' (2004) 121 *SALJ* 466–492 at 482.

[144] 2001 (4) SA 795 (C), (2001) 5 BCLR 487 (C).

[145] Ibid at 799G–802A. This restrictive approach to the application of PIE to 'holding over' situations was subsequently overruled by the Supreme Court of Appeal in *Ndlovu v Ngcobo; Bekker v Jika* 2003 (1) SA 113 (SCA), [2002] 4 All SA 384 (SCA). See notes 165–169 above and accompanying text.

[146] Ibid 804 I-J (citing *Ross* (note 133 above) 596H-I).

[147] Ibid 805E-F.

The Supreme Court of Appeal had occasion to consider the implications of s 26(3) for the common law of ejectment in *Brisley v Drotsky* ('*Brisley*').[148] The case concerned an action for ejectment in circumstances where a lessee remained in occupation of the premises following the cancellation of a lease agreement by the owner. The first major point of contention in the case concerned the validity under the new constitutional dispensation of the common-law principle that clauses in contracts in which parties agree that any variation to the contract should be reduced to writing (so-called 'non-variation clauses') should be strictly enforced. The Court found that the *Shifren* principle[149] remains applicable. It then considered the lessee's argument that the mere fact that the lessor was the owner and the lessee was in unlawful occupation of the property did not, without more, entitle the owner to an eviction order.[150]

She contended that the circumstances under which the lease agreement had been cancelled as well as the socio-economic circumstances of herself, her mother and her child were relevant circumstances which the court *a quo* should have taken into account.[151] In this regard, she relied on the decision in *Ross*. Harms JA (as he then was) held that the court in *Ross* had erred in referring to the type of circumstances which would be relevant in terms of ss 4(6) and (7) of PIE as a guide to s 26(3).[152] The circumstances which were relevant in terms of PIE could not be regarded as indicative of the kinds of circumstances which would be relevant in terms of s 26(3) before it had been determined whether s 26(3) conferred a discretion on the court and what the nature of such discretion is.[153]

However, the Supreme Court of Appeal held that the court in *Betta Eiendomme* had erred in finding that s 26 had only vertical application, and did not apply to natural and juristic persons. Referring to s 8(2) of the Constitution, the Court held that there is no reason why s 26(3) could not (or should not) be applied to natural and juristic persons.[154] The Court further affirmed that, prior to ordering an eviction of a person from his or her home, a court was obliged in terms of s 26(3) to consider 'all the relevant circumstances'. However, it disagreed with the following academic commentary on the nature of the circumstances that were relevant in terms of s 26(3):

> The relevant circumstances which the court must consider before it makes such an order should include at least the personal circumstances of those being deprived of accommodation, and the availability of alternative accommodation. These were among the factors

[148] Note 122 above.

[149] According to this principle laid down in *SA Sentrale Ko-op Graanmaatskappy Bpk v Shifren* 1964 (4) SA 760 (A), the effect of a non-variation clause in a written agreement is that parties are not permitted to alter the contract by a subsequent oral agreement. See further the discussion of this aspect of the *Brisley* decision ibid in part 7.4.1 below.

[150] *Brisley* (note 122 above) para 35.

[151] Ibid.

[152] Ibid para 38.

[153] Ibid.

[154] Ibid para 40.

> which were considered relevant to the exercise of a court's discretion in issuing an ejectment order in terms of s 46(2) of the repealed Group Areas Act 36 of 1966 (*S v Govender* 1986 (3) SA 969 (T) at 971H-J). These factors should be weighed against the reasons for the party seeking the order (for example, an illegal occupation, a default on bond or rent payments, the resettlement of a community in another area).[155]

According to the Court, while s 26(3) required that all the relevant circumstances be considered, it did not say that any circumstances will be relevant.[156] The only circumstances that could be relevant in this context were those that were *legally* relevant. Section 26(3) vests no equitable discretion in the courts to refuse an eviction order in circumstances where the owner would otherwise be entitled in law to such an order.[157] The situation was different where legislation such as PIE or the Extension of Security of Tenure Act 62 of 1997 ('ESTA') expressly limited the common-law rights of an owner through conferring a discretion on the courts to grant an eviction order subject to considerations of justice and equity.[158] The wide construction of 'relevant circumstances' by Goldstone J in *S v Govender*[159] should similarly be read in the context of the discretion expressly conferred upon the courts to order an eviction where a person had been convicted of offences in terms of the Group Areas Act.[160]

As the tenant had no common-law right (the lease agreement having been validly cancelled) or statutory right to remain in occupation of the property, the Court accordingly had no discretion to refuse an eviction order.[161] The personal circumstances raised by the tenant were accordingly not relevant circumstances which could be taken into account in terms of s 26(3).[162] The appeal was accordingly dismissed with the added sting of an award of costs on an attorney-and-client scale.

The 'relevant circumstances' which must be considered by a court in terms of s 26(3) are thus confined to those that are relevant in terms of the existing common law pertaining to ejectment or any applicable statutory provisions. The *status quo* in which the equities of the situation, the occupier's interests in retaining occupation of her home, and the personal circumstances of the parties are irrelevant in an ejectment action at common law was confirmed. Although judicial oversight of evictions is a vital safeguard, the Supreme Court of Appeal's interpretation of 'relevant circumstances' in s 26(3) strips this phrase of independent, substantive content.[163] The injunction in s 26(3) requiring the courts to consider 'all the relevant circumstances'

---

155 Ibid para 41–42. S Liebenberg 'Housing' in D Davis, H Cheadle and N Haysom (eds) *Fundamental Rights in the Constitution: Commentary and Cases* (1997) 349–350.
156 Ibid para 42.
157 Ibid.
158 Ibid para 43.
159 Cited in quotation accompanying note 155 above.
160 Ibid para 44.
161 Ibid para 45.
162 Ibid.
163 For criticisms of the interpretation in the *Brisley case*, see Van der Walt (note 121 above) 422–424; Roux (note 143 above) 484–491.

before making an order for the eviction of people from their homes or the demolition of homes is rendered superfluous by the Supreme Court of Appeal's interpretation.[164] The effect of this interpretation is to minimise the potential transformative impact of housing rights on the common law.

The impact of the Supreme Court of Appeal's restrictive interpretation of s 26(3) in *Brisley* has been limited, as shortly thereafter the Supreme Court of Appeal held in *Ndlovu v Ngcobo; Bekker v Jika*[165] (*'Ndlovu'*) that PIE applied to a tenant holding over subsequent to the lawful termination of a lease agreement.[166] The Court emphasised that PIE had to be interpreted so as to promote 'the spirit, purport and objects' of s 26(3).[167] Given the historical and social context of South Africa, the Court held that there was no reason to assume that the legislature intended to deprive the vulnerable class of occupiers holding over after the termination of their right of occupation of the protections in PIE.[168] The Court refers to the fact that the legislature in giving effect to social rights may legitimately 'impinge or impact upon common-law rights, sometimes dramatically'.[169]

It is significant that this generous approach to the 'spirit, purport and objects' of s 26(3) in interpreting legislation is not followed when the development of the common law is required. While this is explicable to some extent given the democratic mandate of the legislator, the Supreme Court of Appeal's minimalist interpretation of s 26(3) suggests a reluctance in coming to terms with the constitutional mandate of the courts to develop existing common-law doctrine in line with the transformative ethos of the Constitution. At the very least the Supreme Court of Appeal in *Brisley* should have located s 26(3) within the broader context of ss 26(1) and (2) and the overall purport of the section to promote and protect people's access to housing. The shadow cast by *Brisley* still lingers over evictions applications not governed by PIE

---

164 In his separate judgment in *Brisley,* Olivier JA held that s 26(3) has the effect of vesting in the courts an equitable discretion to stay the execution of an eviction order (paras 82–87). This at least accords some independent significance to the phrase, 'all relevant circumstances' although not, I would argue, one which embraces the full transformative implications of s 26(3).

165 Note 145 above.

166 Ibid. In *Transnet (Pty) Limited v Zaaiman* (326/07) [2008] ZAECHC 17 (11 March 2008) para34, Erasmus J held that a court will generally 'be less sympathetic to recalcitrant ex-lessees and ex-owners than it is to squatters; not by virtue of legal principle, but because usually such persons are less deserving of protection in the circumstances surrounding their occupancy'.

167 Ibid para 16.

168 Ibid.

169 Ibid.

or similar legislation,[170] as well as the interpretation of other legislation authorising evictions.[171]

(c) Property rights and the interpretation of PIE

The leading case on the interpretation of PIE is *Port Elizabeth Municipality v Various Occupiers* (*'Port Elizabeth Municipality'*).[172] The judgment and its implications have been analysed in chapter 6.[173] This part focuses on the implications of the common-law paradigm of property rights for the interpretation of PIE.

In *Port Elizabeth Municipality*, the Constitutional Court held that PIE had to be interpreted through the lens of s 26(3) of the Constitution. This represents a transformation of the common-law paradigm governing the ejectment of people from their homes. Instead of 'privileging in an abstract and mechanical way the rights of ownership over the right not to be dispossessed of a home, or vice versa', courts must strive for a just solution which balances and reconciles the competing interests in the context of the specific case.[174] The Court in *Port Elizabeth Municipality* was at pains to emphasise the broad, open-ended and context-sensitive nature of the discretion given to the courts by PIE in considering all relevant circumstances pertaining to an eviction. As described by Sachs J:

> The combination of circumstances may be extremely intricate, requiring a nuanced appreciation of the specific situation in each case. Thus, though there might be a sad uniformity in the conditions of homelessness and desperation which lead to unlawful occupations, on the one hand, and the frustration of landowners at being blocked by intruders from enjoyment of their property, on the other, the actual details of the relationships involved are capable of infinite variation. It is not easy to classify the multitude of places and relationships involved. This is precisely why, even though unlawfulness is established, *the eviction process is not automatic* and why the courts are called upon to exercise *a broad judicial discretion on a case by case basis*.[175] (Emphasis added.)

---

[170] The correctness of the approach in *Brisley* to the impact of s 26(3) on the common law acquires particular significance in the light of the proposed amendments to PIE that will undo the ruling in the *Ndlovu* case by excluding its application to tenants holding over. See s 2 of the Prevention of Illegal Eviction from and Unlawful Occupation of Land Amendment Bill [B8–2008].

[171] See, for example, the constrained interpretation of the impact of s 26 of the Constitution on s 12(4)(*b*) of the National Building Regulations and Building Standards Act 103 of 1977 by the Supreme Court of Appeal in *City of Johannesburg v Rand Properties (Pty) Ltd* 2007 (6) SA 417 (SCA), 2007 (6) BCLR 643 (SCA). On appeal, the Constitutional Court held that the Supreme Court of Appeal 'did not wholly embrace the interrelationship between s 12(4)(*b*) of the Act and s 26(2) of the Constitution'. See *Occupiers of 51 Olivia Road* (note 81 above) paras 45–46, and the discussion in chapter 6, part 6.4.

[172] 2005 (1) SA 217 (CC), 2004 (12) BCLR 1268 (CC).

[173] Chapter 6, part 6.2.2.

[174] See *Port Elizabeth Municipality* (note 172 above) paras 17–23; 30–38.

[175] Ibid para 31 (footnotes omitted).

Thus a narrow and formalistic approach in cases is eschewed in circumstances where the housing rights of homeless people clash with the property rights of landowners. Instead courts are required to 'infuse elements of grace and compassion into the formal structures of the law' and 'to balance competing interests in a principled way'.[176]

The Court does not attempt to arrive at easy or superficial resolutions of the tension between property and housing rights by walking the well-worn path of privileging property rights, and failing to recognise the human rights interest which people have in maintaining occupation of their homes. Instead a conscious attempt is made to give full effect to the normative significance of housing as a constitutional right through a generous interpretation of the procedural and substantive protections PIE confers on unlawful occupiers.

The Constitutional Court's approach in *Port Elizabeth Municipality* can be contrasted with the more conservative approach to the interpretation of PIE adopted in the *Grobler* case.[177] Du Plessis AJ held that 'it could never have been the intention of the legislature to provide a discretion to a court to refuse an eviction order if a property owner is entitled to such an order, and therefore ... the intention of the legislature was never to vary the common law in this regard'.[178] Such an interpretation of PIE would amount to an expropriation or constructive expropriation of the owner's property, rendering the State liable for compensation.[179] The Court construed ss 4(7)–(12) of PIE as being confined to the 'principles and procedures according to which the courts should grant eviction orders, and in particular, to emphasize circumstances and facts which should be taken into account by the courts in formulating eviction orders'.[180]

However, once an eviction order is made it triggers the State's duties to provide emergency accommodation in terms of ss 26(1) and (2).[181] The Court accordingly ordered the Randfontein Local Municipality (the third respondent in the case) to offer and to provide temporary accommodation within its municipal area in terms of chapter 12 of the National Housing Code 'to those respondents who are evicted and are, at that time, desperately in need of housing'.[182]

The Court's restrictive interpretation of the nature of the judicial discretion to order an eviction in terms of PIE is illustrative of the tendency to interpret social legislation in ways which are maximally preservative of the privileged status accorded

---

[176] Ibid para 37.

[177] Note 117 above.

[178] Ibid para 180. See the express reliance by the Court on the presumption that 'an Act does not alter the common law more than is necessary' (para 136).

[179] Ibid para 177.

[180] Ibid para 180.

[181] Ibid para 209. See the discussion in the *Grobler* judgment of the implications of *Grootboom* (note 55 above) and subsequent jurisprudence at ibid paras 184–244. See also chapter 8, part 8.4.2.

[182] Ibid para 254. Order para 6.

to property rights in traditional common-law doctrine. Thus the court insists that in a situation of unlawful occupation of land there should be no balancing under PIE of the interests protected by s 26 rights and the affected landowner's property rights.[183] Housing rights only come into play once an eviction is ordered by the court, thereby triggering an obligation on the relevant local authority to provide emergency accommodation. The latter obligation is derived from the requirement in *Grootboom* that reasonable short-term measures must be taken to provide relief for people facing homelessness.[184]

Once the housing rights of the occupiers are no longer in direct conflict with the owner's private property rights, a generous interpretation is given to the public dimensions of the obligations imposed by s 26. This is inconsistent with the approach to PIE endorsed by the Constitutional Court in the *Port Elizabeth Municipality* case in which courts are required to strive for a reconciliation of the property and housing interests at stake in eviction applications from private land, and are vested with a broad discretion regarding all aspects of eviction applications.

Grobler, which was handed down over four years after the judgment in *Port Elizabeth Municipality*, is indicative of the extent to which traditional conceptions of property rights continue to inhibit the potential of legislation such as PIE to transform eviction law by requiring equal consideration for housing rights.

7.3.2 Execution against mortgaged residential property

Another area in which the courts have had to consider the impact of s 26 on property rights is in proceedings to obtain default or summary judgments against those defaulting on their home loans and to declare the mortgaged property executable. The implications of the decision of the Constitutional Court in *Jaftha*[185] have been of particular relevance in this context. *Jaftha* concerned a challenge to the execution procedures in the Magistrates' Courts Act 32 of 1944 which permitted execution against the state-subsidised housing of low-income residents for debts unrelated to the property.[186] The Constitutional Court held that 'any measure which permits a person to be deprived of existing access to adequate housing, limits the rights in section 26(1)'. The justifiability of such a measure must be evaluated in terms of the stringent requirements of s 36 of the Constitution (the general limitations clause).[187] Having found that s 66(1)(*a*) of the Act constituted an unjustifiable limitation of s 26(1) of the Constitution, the Court read in provisions requiring judicial over-

183 Ibid para 206.

184 See further in this regard, chapter 4 at notes 127–131 and accompanying text.

185 Note 59 above.

186 See the analysis of *Jaftha* in chapter 4, part 4.6.2. The cash loans concerned were minor amounts for the purpose of purchasing basic groceries.

187 Ibid para 34.

sight of executions against immovable property after a consideration 'of all relevant circumstances'.[188]

The implications of the *Jaftha* decision for the law and procedures pertaining to the execution by banks against residential property secured by a mortgage bond were considered by the Western Cape High Court, Cape Town in *Standard Bank of SA Ltd v Snyders and Eight Similar Cases*.[189] The question was whether banks were entitled to orders that the homes in question be declared executable as part of their applications for default or summary judgments on the main debt. A related question concerned whether the Registrar was permitted in terms of Rule 31(5)(*a*) of the Uniform Rules of Court ('the Rules') as part of an application for default judgment to grant an order declaring the immovable property to be executable.[190] Blignaut J observed that, prior to the advent of the Constitution, the effect of orders declaring particular immovable property executable, 'was simply of a procedural nature'.[191] It allowed 'a judgment creditor to execute against the immovable property of the debtor without first having to execute against his movable property'.[192] The effect of *Jaftha* was that 'the remedy in question has now acquired a very different significance' in that it is 'no longer simply a question of procedural law'.[193] Defaulting debtors now had important rights in that 's 26(3) of the Constitution has introduced a pre-requisite for the granting of such an order, namely that the court must consider all relevant circumstances'.[194] Blignaut J held that the effect of the reasoning in *Jaftha* was that the Registrar did not have the power to issue an order declaring immovable property to be executable.[195]

---

188 Ibid para 67. On the remedial aspects of *Jaftha*, see chapter 8, part 8.3.3 at notes 48–56 and accompanying text. In *Menqa v Markom* 2008 (2) SA 120 (SCA), [2008] 2 All SA 235 (SCA), the Supreme Court of Appeal held that the requirement of judicial oversight in *Jaftha* applied to sales in execution which occurred prior to the *Jaftha* judgment. The sale in execution and all subsequent sales of the property were declared null and void, and could not be saved by s 70 of the Magistrates' Courts Act which provided that a sale in execution after registration of transfer of immovable property was not liable to be impeached as against a purchaser in good faith and without notice of any defect. Van Heerden JA held that if the effect of s 70 was to render sales in execution which had occurred without judicial oversight unimpeachable, this would 'indeed defeat the whole purpose of the Constitutional Court ruling in the *Jaftha* case' (at para 21).

189 2005 (5) SA 610 (C).

190 Ibid para 3. Rule 31(5)(*a*) permits a plaintiff, whenever a defendant is in default of delivery of a notice of intention to defend or a plea, and where 'each of the claims is for a debt or liquidated demand,' to 'file with the Registrar a written application for judgment against such defendant'. The Registrar had adopted the position in the present case that, in the light of the *Jaftha* decision, she did not have the power to grant an order declaring the immovable property to be executable.

191 Ibid para 20.

192 Ibid.

193 Ibid para 22.

194 Ibid.

195 Ibid para 7.

The Court held further that the bank's summons in each case was defective in that it 'should contain a suitable allegation to the effect that the facts alleged by it (which should be identified) are sufficient to justify an order in terms of section 26(3) of the Constitution'.[196] In this way the defendant would be alerted as to her constitutional rights. The Court granted default or summary judgment for the applicable monetary claims in each case, but dismissed an order declaring the properties executable. However, it granted leave to the plaintiff to apply again on amplified papers, and after notice to the respective defendants, for an order permitting execution against the immovable property of the defendants.[197]

Standard Bank appealed against this judgment to the Supreme Court of Appeal. In its judgment in *Standard Bank of South Africa Ltd v Saunderson*[198] ('*Saunderson*'), the Supreme Court of Appeal distinguished the facts of the current case from that of *Jaftha*. The latter case was concerned with provisions of the Magistrates' Courts Act authorising the clerk of the court to issue a warrant of execution against the home of a debtor for unrelated debts, when there was insufficient movable property to satisfy the judgment debt.[199] *Saunderson* had its origins in an agreement by a borrower to register a mortgage bond against the title of her property. The essential character of the mortgage bond is that, upon default, the lender is entitled to sell the property to satisfy the outstanding debt. The mortgage bond, as described by the Court, 'thus curtails the right of property at its root, and penetrates the rights of ownership, for the bond-holder's rights are fused into the title itself'.[200] The effect of having a debt secured by a mortgage bond is that a creditor can apply immediately to have the property declared executable without having to take execution against movable property first.

The Supreme Court of Appeal held that the High Court had misunderstood *Jaftha* in that s 26(1) was at issue in that case, not s 26(3). Furthermore, the Constitutional Court had not decided that s 26(1) is compromised in all cases where execution is levied against residential property. It was only when a writ of execution would deprive a person of 'adequate' housing that s 26(1) rights would be implicated, thus requiring justification in terms of s 36(1). Executing against a luxury or holiday

---

196 Ibid para 24.

197 Ibid paras 30–31. See also the different interpretation of the implications of s 26 and the *Jaftha* decision for legal proceedings to declare mortgaged property executable by the South Gauteng High Court, Johannesburg in *Nedbank Ltd v Mortinson* 2005 (6) SA 462 (W). For a summary of the differences in the decisions of the Western Cape High Court, Cape Town and the South Gauteng High Court, Johannesburg in this regard, see *Campus Law Clinic, University of KwaZulu-Natal v Standard Bank of South Africa Ltd* 2006 (6) SA 103 (CC), 2006 (6) BCLR 669 (CC) para 14. See also *Absa Bank Ltd v Xonti* 2006 (5) SA 289 (C).

198 2006 (2) SA 264 (SCA).

199 Section 66(1)(*a*) of the Magistrates' Courts Act 32 of 1944.

200 *Saunderson* (note 198 above) para 2.

home would not 'implicate the right of access to adequate housing at all'.[201] In the *Jaftha* case, the sale in execution deprived the debtors of title to the home purchased through a state subsidy with the result that they were disqualified from obtaining other State-aided housing.[202] The Court held that the present case did not require it to decide whether s 26(1) may be compromised where the property in question did in fact constitute 'adequate housing'.[203] It was of the view that cases where execution against mortgaged property conflicted with s 26(1) were 'likely to be rare'.[204] The Court was, however, prepared to contemplate the possibility of a court delaying execution 'where there is a real prospect that the debt might yet be paid'. However this did not change the approach to pleadings in such a case.[205]

The onus was on the defendants to show that the orders for execution would infringe their s 26(1) right, and such infringement would not necessarily occur because the property in question was residential.[206] A burden of justification would only rest upon the bank once the defendant had shown that the execution would breach his or her s 26 rights. The practical implications hereof are that the bondholder's summons 'need not attempt to justify in advance a possible constitutional infringement'.[207]

The Supreme Court of Appeal further overruled the High Court and held that the Registrar was entitled, in terms of Rule 31(5) of the Uniform Rules of Court, in granting default judgments to declare immovable properties executable.[208] It held that there could be no objection to the Registrar entering judgment in accordance with Rule 31(5) in cases in which the constitutional validity of an order of execution was not disputed. The Registrar in such circumstances was not exercising a judicial function nor did it entail 'the mechanical grant of an order in circumstances where

---

[201] Ibid para 17.

[202] *Jaftha* (note 59 above) para 12.

[203] *Saunderson* (note 198 above) para 19.

[204] It referred in this regard to *Jaftha* (note 59 above) para 58 in which Mokgoro J held that the circumstances in which the debt arose was '[a]nother factor of great importance' in determining the justifiability of an execution order. Thus:

> If the judgment debtor willingly put his or her house up in some or other manner as security for the debt, a sale in execution should ordinarily be permitted where there has not been an abuse of court procedure. The need to ensure that homes may be used by people to raise capital is an important aspect of the value of a home which courts must be careful to acknowledge.

See also the argument advanced in this regard by L Steyn 'Safe as houses? Balancing a mortgagee's security interest with a homeowner's security of tenure' (2007) 11 *LDD* 101–119.

[205] *Saunderson* (note 198 above) para 20.

[206] Ibid.

[207] Ibid para 25.

[208] Ibid para 23. The Court specifically declined to rule on the constitutionality of High Court Rule 45(1) which permits a writ of execution to be issued against immovable property only where a return of service indicates that there is insufficient movable property to satisfy the writ, as the validity of this rule was not before the Court (para 22).

that would be constitutionally impermissible'.[209] Nevertheless, Registrars 'ought in any event to be cautioned to refer matters for hearing in open court even where a defendant raises a constitutional objection informally by approaching the Registrar and objecting to the order'.[210]

Moreover, given the fact that most defaulting debtors were unlikely to obtain legal advice, it was desirable that they be informed that s 26(1) may affect the bond-holder's claim to execution. The Court reasoned thus:

> Should it be held that the negative obligation of s 26(1) binds even the bond-holder, the debtor would have the right to invoke circumstances that may persuade a court to grant extenuation in the execution of the order (albeit that the bond-holder's summons need not attempt to justify in advance a possible constitutional infringement).[211]

The appeal against the High Court's order was upheld, and the High Court's order was supplemented declaring the mortgaged property to be specially executable.[212] The Supreme Court of Appeal's order included a practice direction which affects all summonses initiating action in which the relief sought includes an order declaring immovable property executable. Such a summons must henceforth draw the defendant's attention to s 26(1) of the Constitution, and inform her that should she claim that the order for execution will infringe this right, it is incumbent on her to place information supporting that claim before the court.[213]

The sequel to this case was an attempt by the Campus Law Clinic at the University of KwaZulu-Natal to appeal this judgment to the Constitutional Court on a public interest basis, alternatively, to have the matter determined on the basis of a direct access application.[214] It had not been a party to the proceedings in the Supreme Court of Appeal, nor had it intervened as *amicus curiae*. The Constitutional Court refused the applications for leave to appeal and direct access. It held that many of the arguments which the Campus Law Clinic wished to make went to the question of the constitutionality of s 27A of the Supreme Court Act 59 of 1959 and Rules 31(5) and 45(1) of the Uniform Rules of Court. These provisions are all concerned with the circumstances in which a creditor might execute against immovable property and the procedure which must be followed before such execution is permitted.[215] The question of the constitutionality of these provisions had not been before the Supreme Court of Appeal or the Western Cape High Court.[216] While the issues raised by the

---

[209] Ibid para 24.

[210] Ibid.

[211] Ibid.

[212] Ibid para 27.

[213] Ibid.

[214] *Campus Law Clinic, University of KwaZulu-Natal v Standard Bank of South Africa Ltd* (note 197 above). In terms of s 167(6)(*a*) of the Constitution read together with Constitutional Court Rule 18, a case may be brought directly to the Constitutional Court when it is in the interests of justice and with leave of the Constitutional Court.

[215] Ibid para 5.

[216] Ibid para 16.

Law Clinic raised important questions of public interest, the Court held that it was not in the interests of justice for it to consider the matter *de novo* as a court of first and last instance. It held that the interests of justice require that the issues 'be dealt with in a comprehensive manner on the basis of a fully prepared record to which all interested parties have had the opportunity to contribute'.[217]

A subsequent decision of the North Gauteng High Court, Pretoria in *ABSA Bank Ltd v Ntsane*[218] ('*Ntsane*') rejected an application for default judgment against the defendants on the full amount owing in terms of a mortgage bond (R62 042.43) and an order declaring the immovable property of the defendants executable.[219] The defendants, a husband and wife married in community of property, had obtained ownership of their home through various land reform statutes, facilitating the upgrading of leasehold rights to full ownership.[220] They did not receive any State assistance to purchase their home, hence the registration of the mortgage bond over the property.[221] At the time of the application for default judgment, the defendants were in arrears with their agreed periodic payments on the bond in an amount of R18.46.[222] It was also clear that if the defendants lost their home they would not qualify for a housing subsidy which was only payable to first-time property owners.[223]

The Court held that the bank's right to commercial activity and to rely on the agreements underlying the registration of mortgage bonds had to be balanced against 'the right to adequate housing that the defendants indubitably enjoy'.[224] The potential infringement of s 26 arose from the calling up of a bond in circumstances where the unpaid amount on the bond was as minimal as in the present case. As Bertelsmann J held:

> To allow such a result in a country where housing is at a premium and poverty and the legacy of a previous dispensation deny millions the fundamental right to a roof over their heads infringes the fundamental right to adequate housing and may also … be in conflict with the right to dignity.[225]

The Court held that, even if it erred in finding that attempts to enforce the repayment of the full outstanding amount of the bond in the circumstances of this case constituted an infringement of the defendants' constitutional right to adequate

---

217 Ibid para 27.

218 2007 (3) SA 554 (T).

219 In this regard, the decision in *Nedbank v Mortinson* (note 197 above) was followed, obliging the Registrar to refer all cases in which mortgaged property is sought to be declared executable heard in open motion court.

220 *Ntsane* (note 218 above) paras 55–59.

221 Ibid para 60.

222 Ibid paras 14–20.

223 Ibid para 62.

224 Ibid para 71.

225 Ibid para 83. See also para 86 in which the Court referred to the fact that the debt in question was 'so small that it should readily be capable of execution against movable assets'.

housing, default judgment should still not be granted. The insistence of ABSA Bank in these circumstances of executing against the only home the defendants have in circumstances where there were alternative ways of obtaining payment of the arrears constituted a *prima facie* abuse of the system and the processes of this Court.[226] In these circumstances, a Court should refuse to grant such an application 'unless and until the plaintiff has persuaded the Court by acceptable evidence that no other reasonable alternative exists to enforce its right'.[227]

Given the difficulties which courts have in conducting the necessary inquiries for determining whether an order declaring immovable property executable should be granted despite the seemingly small arrears, the Court held that the application for default judgment should be accompanied by an affidavit setting out 'sufficient facts to persuade the Court to grant the prayer that the property be declared executable'.[228]

The judgment ends with a recommendation for the banking and financial services sector to give serious consideration to the creation of a speedy and inexpensive remedy such as an arbitration tribunal for facilitating proportional resolutions of disputes between debtors and creditors in cases where execution against people's homes for relatively small amount of arrears are sought.[229]

The Supreme Court of Appeal's judgment in *Saunderson* indicates that s 26(1) and the *Jaftha* decision have had an influence on the normal rules of pleadings in cases in which plaintiffs seek to declare mortgaged residential property executable. Defaulting home owners now have the right to be notified that their s 26(1) rights may be affected by such an order, and that they are entitled to place supporting information before a court to support such a claim. If the homeowner is able to make out a case that her s 26 rights will be infringed by such an order, the courts must consider whether an order permitting the sale in execution will be reasonable and justifiable in the circumstances.

However, as the Constitutional Court observed in *Jaftha*, indigent people (even if they are notified in a summons of their s 26 rights) face considerable difficulties in approaching a court to claim protection.[230] Given this fact, it is unfortunate that the Supreme Court of Appeal held that a Registrar was authorised to grant orders declaring properties specially executable in granting default judgment.

In contrast, the judgment in *Ntsane* underscores the important role of judicial oversight in ensuring that all the affected interests in applications declaring mortgaged property executable are considered and evaluated within a balanced normative framework. Such a framework must include the values and interests protected by the housing rights in s 26. The aspect of judicial oversight of execution against mortgaged property could be addressed through possible future constitutional challenges to

[226] Ibid paras 85 and 91.
[227] Ibid para 88.
[228] Ibid para 96.
[229] Ibid paras 97–98.
[230] *Jaftha* (note 59 above) para 47.

s 27A of the Supreme Court Act 59 of 1959, and Rules 31 and 45(1) of the Uniform Rules of Court. Given the fact that execution against people's mortgaged homes raises complex questions concerning the balance to be struck between contractual, property and housing rights, it is appropriate that these matters are determined by the courts.[231] The Constitutional Court has consistently held that procedures which result in people being deprived of access to their homes must be subject to judicial oversight and control.[232]

7.4 SOCIO-ECONOMIC RIGHTS IN SELECTED AREAS OF CONTRACT LAW

This part examines the jurisprudence in cases in which the relevant contracts have implicated the socio-economic rights which form the focus of this work.[233] It incorporates a discussion of the Constitutional Court decision in *Barkhuizen v Napier*[234] ('*Barkhuizen*') in view of its significance in establishing the general approach to be followed in testing the constitutional validity of particular contracts.

The analysis suggests that thus far socio-economic rights have failed to have a meaningful impact on the law of contract. It is not contended that constitutionally entrenched socio-economic rights will produce incontrovertible resolutions to contractual disputes. There are clearly competing rights, values and policy considerations at stake in contractual disputes, and courts have the exacting task of balancing and attempting to achieve an optimal reconciliation of these values and rights. My argument is rather that the transformative purposes of the Constitution will be frustrated if socio-economic rights and their underlying values are marginalised in the process of identifying and weighing the rights and values at stake in contractual disputes.

7.4.1 *Brisley v Drotsky*

In *Brisley v Drotsky*[235] ('*Brisley*') the appellant's attempt to rely on an oral variation of the written contract of lease regarding the due date for rent payments was defeated on the basis of a non-variation clause contained in the written agreement. She argued that the non-variation clause was contrary to the principles of *bona fides* (good

---

[231] The context-specific balancing of competing rights and interests was emphasised in *Jaftha*. In this case the competing interests were those of judgment creditors seeking execution against the immovable property of debtors, on the one hand, and that of judgment debtors who face the loss of their homes. See particularly *Jaftha* (note 59 above) para 59.

[232] See *Jaftha* ibid; *Occupiers of 51 Olivia Road* (note 81 above) paras 49–50.

[233] On the relevance of socio-economic rights to the law of contract, see generally Pearmain 'Contracting for socio-economic rights: A contradiction in terms? (1)' (2006) 69 *THRHR* 287–301; Pearmain 'Contracting for socio-economic rights: A contradiction in terms? (2)' (2006) 69 *THRHR* 466–478.

[234] *Barkhuizen* (note 19 above).

[235] Note 122 above. See further the discussion on *Brisley* at part 7.3.1(*b*) above.

faith).[236] This argument was rejected on the grounds that, although the principle of good faith is a foundational principle underlying contract law and finds expression in its particular rules and principles, it does not constitute an independent or 'free-floating' basis for the setting aside or non-enforcement of contractual provisions.[237] The Supreme Court of Appeal, in the words of Gerhard Lubbe, 'therefore rejected a vision that would accord good faith any direct or overt relevance in the judicial determination of whether a contract has been concluded, or is defeasible or otherwise enforceable'.[238] In the alternative, it was argued, relying on *Sasfin v Beukes*,[239] that although non-variation clauses were not generally in conflict with the principles of good faith, the enforcement of the clause in the present case was so unfair that it would be contrary to the public interest for a court to enforce it. The Court held that the *Sasfin* principle was not directly applicable, as the non-variation clause was not in itself invalid.[240] It further held that a high threshold of 'exceptional unfairness'[241] would have to be applied if the *Sasfin* principle were to be extended to prevent the enforcement of contractual terms that were not *per se* in conflict with the public interest. The unfairness would have to be of such a degree that it was 'inimical to the interests of the community'.[242]

In his separate concurring judgment in *Brisley*, Cameron JA clearly affirms that all law, including the common law of contract, derives its force from the Constitution and is 'subject to constitutional control'.[243] Public policy as a ground for nullifying or declining to enforce contractual terms 'is now rooted in our Constitution and the fundamental values it enshrines'. These values include 'human dignity, the achievement of equality and the advancement of human rights and freedoms, non-racialism and non-sexism'.[244] However, the Constitution and its value system does not give

---

[236] *Brisley* (note 122 above) para 11. The principle of the general binding effect of non-variation clauses was established in *SA Sentrale Ko-op Graanmaatskappy Bpk v Shifren* (note 149 above).

[237] Ibid. The court referred in this regard to D B Hutchison 'Non-variation clauses in contract: Any escape from the *Shifren* straitjacket?' (2001) 118 *SALJ* 720–746. In *Bank of Lisbon & SA Ltd v De Ornelas* 1988 (3) SA 580 (A), the *exceptio doli generalis* as a general equitable remedy in our contract law was rejected. For a critical evaluation of the majority decision in *Bank of Lisbon*, and an endorsement of the substantive reasoning in Jansen JA's dissenting judgment in the case, see Froneman (note 15 above) 18–19.

[238] G Lubbe 'Taking fundamental rights seriously: The Bill of Rights and its implications for the development of contract law' (2004) 121 *SALR* 395–423 at 397.

[239] *Sasfin v Beukes* 1989 (1) SA 1 (A). See also *Magna Alloys and Research (SA) (Pty) Ltd v Ellis* 1984 (4) SA 874 (A).

[240] *Brisley* (note 122 above) para 31.

[241] Ibid para 32.

[242] Ibid para 31. For a criticism of the Court's restrictive interpretation of the *Sasfin* principle, and suggestions for a basis for distinguishing subsequent cases, see Lubbe (note 238 above) 417–419.

[243] Ibid para 88.

[244] Ibid para 91 citing s 1(*a*) and (*b*) of the Constitution.

courts 'a general jurisdiction to invalidate contracts on the basis of judicially perceived notions of unjustness or to determine their enforceability on the basis of imprecise notions of good faith'.[245] Contractual freedom, 'shorn of its obscene excesses', informs the constitutional value of dignity.[246] In this context, Cameron JA cites H L A Hart's depiction of rules conferring private powers as making a citizen, 'a private legislator'.[247] He concludes that the constitutional values of dignity, equality and freedom 'require that the courts approach their task of striking down contracts or declining to enforce them with perceptive restraint'.[248]

Cameron JA's judgment is a welcome affirmation that the content of public policy in contract law must be rooted in the Constitution and the 'objective value system'[249] it embodies. More problematic, however, is the suggestion that contract autonomy, 'shorn of its obscene excesses', represents an expression of the constitutional values of freedom and dignity. The bargains which the majority of people make are seldom an expression of private freedom in a context of systemic, intertwined class, race and gendered power disparities. The judgment does not consider the implications of constitutional values for the weaker party in a contractual relationship, particularly where their economic survival and basic needs are at stake. Support for the strict enforcement of contracts as the basic point of departure in private law adjudication is found in constitutional values. The courts are cautioned to exercise restraint in interfering with private contracts on the basis of 'vague' notions of good faith and public policy.

The realities referred to above would suggest rather that concepts such as good faith and public policy be given a more robust content and role in mandating judicial control of contractual relationships. In developing the content and role of these doctrines in the constitutional era, a much more rigorous engagement with constitutional values such as social justice and the other values underpinning socio-economic rights is required than occurred in the *Brisley* judgment.

The *Brisley* decision illustrates the Supreme Court of Appeal's insistence on the strict enforcement of contracts and the limited role envisaged for infusing open-ended normative values and standards such as good faith and public policy with constitutional rights and values in the evaluation of contractual disputes. In considering whether the enforcement of the non-variation clause would, in the circumstances of the case, be contrary to public policy, the Court failed to consider the implications of the housing rights in s 26 of the Constitution. The relevance of s 26(3) was confined to the question of its possible impact on the granting of an eviction order against a former tenant following the lawful cancellation of the lease agreement.[250] A con-

[245] Ibid para 93.
[246] Ibid para 94.
[247] H L A Hart *The Concept of Law* (1961) 40–41 cited at ibid para 94.
[248] Ibid.
[249] *Carmichele* (note 20 above) para 56.
[250] *Brisley* (note 122 above) para 35. The Court's evaluation of the relevance of s 26(3) to the eviction of the tenant is discussed in part 7.3.1(*b*) above.

sideration of s 26 rights would not necessarily have altered the court's conclusion regarding the validity of the non-variation clause and the cancellation of the contract. Nonetheless, it would have brought to the surface the full range of rights and values implicated by the particular contract and the strict enforcement of the non-variation clause in the original contract. This would have paved the way for a serious attempt to come to grips with the content and implications of socio-economic rights for contract law in South Africa.

7.4.2 *Afrox Health Care Bpk v Strydom*

In the same year, the Supreme Court of Appeal had occasion to consider arguments in which the impact of socio-economic rights on contract law were directly raised. *Afrox Healthcare Bpk v Strydom* ('*Afrox*')[251] concerned a challenge to a clause in a contract between a patient and a private hospital exempting the hospital from liability for the negligence of its staff. The respondent had instituted an action for damages against the hospital for breach of contract based on alleged negligent post-operative treatment by a nurse employed by the hospital.

The respondent relied on three alternative grounds. First, that the exemption clause, which formed part of the documentation signed by him during the admission procedures of the hospital, was contrary to the public interest. He argued that the public interest had to be interpreted, as required by s 39(2) of the Constitution, to promote the spirit, purport and objects of the Bill of Rights, particularly the right of access to health care services in s 27(1)(*a*) of the Constitution.[252] Second, he argued that the clause was unenforceable as it was unreasonable, unfair and in conflict with the principle of *bona fides*. Finally, the respondent argued that he was not bound by the exemption clause because he was unaware of its terms at the time of signing the admission documents. Because such a clause was unexpected in the context of a contract by a patient for medical treatment with a hospital, the admissions clerk was under duty to bring the contents of the clause to his attention.

The Court endorsed a high threshold for determining whether a contractual term was unenforceable on the grounds of conflicting with the public interest. It held that a contractual term is only contrary to the public interest when it, either due to extreme unfairness or other policy considerations, conflicts with the interests of the community.[253] The words of warning of Smalberger JA in *Sasfin (Pty) Ltd v Beukes*[254] are quoted with approval:

> The power to declare contracts contrary to public policy should, however, be exercised sparingly and only in the clearest of cases, lest uncertainty as to the validity of contracts result from an arbitrary and indiscriminate use of the power. ... In grappling with this often difficult problem it must be borne in mind that public policy generally favours

---

[251] 2002 (6) SA 21 (SCA).

[252] *Afrox* (note 251 above) paras 15–16.

[253] Ibid para 10.

[254] *Sasfin v Beukes* (note 239 above) 9B-F.

> the utmost freedom of contract, and requires that commercial transactions should not be unduly trammelled by restrictions on that freedom.[255]

The Court acknowledged that the notions of public policy and public interest in contract law had now to be interpreted in the light of the rights and values enshrined in the Constitution.[256] The respondent's contention that the enforcement of the exemption clause was contrary to the public interest because of the unequal bargaining power present at the time of the conclusion of the contract was dismissed on the grounds that the respondent had adduced no evidence that he was in fact in a weaker bargaining position than the private hospital concerned.[257]

The Court proceeded to consider the argument that an exemption clause such as the one in question in a contract for medical services was contrary to public policy in that it directly or indirectly breached the right of access to health care services in s 27(1)(*a*) of the Constitution.[258] The contract was concluded before the coming into force of the 1996 Constitution, and accordingly it was held that there was no question of a direct breach of s 27(1)(*a*) of the Constitution as its operation was not retrospective.[259] Nevertheless, the Court was prepared to assume in favour of the respondent that s 27(1)(*a*) of the Constitution had to be taken into account in determining whether the clause was contrary to the 'spirit, purport and objects' of the Constitution in terms of s 39(2).[260]

According to the Court, the respondent correctly conceded that the exemption clause was not directly in conflict with s 27(1)(*a*) in that it did not prevent access to health care services, and did not prohibit hospitals from insisting on legally acceptable conditions for the rendering of medical services.[261] The respondent's argument was that the clause was contrary to the public interest in that it undermined a core value protected by s 27(1)(*a*), namely the rendering of medical services in a professional, non-negligent manner.[262] The Court rejected this interpretation on the basis that the hospital nursing staff's professional conduct was secured by relevant professional codes and the sanction of damage to the hospital's reputation and competitiveness should its staff render services in a negligent manner.[263] Furthermore, it held that

---

255 *Afrox* (note 251 above) para 8 (portions of the quote omitted).

256 Ibid para 18. The Court cited with approval Cameron JA's dictum in *Brisley* (note 122 above) that '[i]n its modern guise "public policy" is now rooted in our Constitution and the fundamental values it enshrines' (para 91). See also *Mort NO v Henry Shields-Chiat* 2001 (1) SA 464 (C) at 474J–475E; *Barkhuizen* (note 19 above) paras 28–29.

257 Ibid para 12.

258 Ibid para 14.

259 Ibid paras 16–17.

260 Ibid.

261 Ibid para 19.

262 Ibid para 20.

263 Ibid para 21.

contractual autonomy, which finds expression in the doctrine of *pacta sunt servanda*, was a competing value also supported by constitutional values.[264]

The Court disposed of the respondent's second argument that the exemption clause conflicted with the principle of good faith by endorsing the restrictive interpretation of the role of this principle in contract law upheld in *Brisley*.[265] Abstract principles such as 'good faith' could justify and explain existing rules of contract and lead to the formation and changing of such rules, but did not vest in the courts a discretion based on equity in relation to the enforcement of contractual provisions. In this regard, Brand JA held that a court had to act, not on the basis of abstract ideas, but on the basis of crystallised and established legal rules.[266]

The Court also dismissed the argument that a clause exempting a health services provider from negligence in the context of a contract for the rendering of medical treatment was unexpected, thereby placing a duty on the hospital to alert a prospective patient to such a clause. It held that, objectively speaking, such a clause was not unexpected and that exemption clauses were the rule rather than the exception in standard contracts. The Court saw no reason in principle to distinguish private hospitals from other service providers.[267]

The Court's reasoning rests on a particularly formalistic and impoverished interpretation of s 27(1)(*a*) and the values and interests it protects.[268] Section 39(2) specifically mandates the courts to transcend a literal interpretation of the relevant provisions and to look to their 'spirit, purport and objects'.[269] The Court held that the exemption clause did not impede access to health care services, nor did s 27(1)(*a*) prohibit the imposition of legally enforceable conditions for the rendering of such services. But

---

[264] *Afrox* (note 251 above) paras 22–23. The Court cited Cameron JA's concurring judgment in *Brisley* (note 122 above) para 94 that the constitutional values of human dignity, equality and freedom 'require that the Courts approach their task of striking down contracts or declining to enforce them with perceptive restraint'. For a critique of the reliance on Cameron JA's statement in *Afrox* and a nuanced analysis of the interplay of the constitutional values of human dignity, equality and freedom in a contractual context, see Lubbe (note 238 above) 420–421.

[265] *Brisley* (note 122 above) para 22.

[266] *Afrox* (note 251 above) paras 31–32.

[267] Ibid paras 35–36.

[268] Contrast in this regard the substantive, contextual reasoning in the court *a quo*, *Strydom v Afrox Healthcare Ltd* [2001] 4 All SA 618 (T). Mavundla AJ (as then was) held that s 27 of the Constitution protects not only access to health care services, but also the 'legitimate expectation' which a prospective patient has when he 'goes to seek medical care in an institution, be it private or public ... that the services will be accorded to him by professional and trained people, who will perform their duty with skill and care' (627). He held that the defendant was accordingly under a duty to bring the exemption clause to the attention of the plaintiff, and to explain its import to him. The clause in question was held to be *contra bonis mores* and unenforceable in law.

[269] See notes 35–39 above and accompanying text.

this begs the question as to whether a clause exempting a health services provider from medical negligence is lawful in terms of s 27(1)(*a*) of the Constitution.

The spirit, purport and objects of the health rights in s 27(1)(*a*) go beyond a claim simply for minimal access to health care services through public institutions. The right to health in international human rights law incorporates a qualitative dimension and requires the rendering of services to appropriate professional and scientific standards.[270] The negligent rendering of health care services – whether by public or private institutions – undermines the very interests and purposes which a right of access to health care services is intended to protect. These include the protection of one's life, bodily integrity and health. A fundamental safeguard in our legal system against the threats to health posed by the negligent rendering of medical services is undermined by the denial of a judicial remedy.[271]

Moreover, the Court provides no substantive reasoning as to why the doctrine of *pacta sunt servanda* should be preferred in the specific circumstances of the case over the value of ensuring a remedy to those who suffer damages as a result of negligent medical care. The latter value has its origin in the constitutionally enshrined right of access to health care services, one of the socio-economic rights which the Constitutional Court has held are fundamental to the transformative objectives of the Constitution.[272] Sanctity of contract, on the other hand, as Pearmain points out, 'is not a right in the Bill of Rights. It is a principle of the common law that is not inconsistent with the Constitution in certain, but not all, circumstances.'[273] The Court in *Afrox* treated the contract in question as simply another commercial transaction instead of evaluating the public policy considerations relating to the enforcement of the exemption clause in the light of the special nature of a contract between a patient and a hospital for the provision of health care services.[274] This was a contract for the provision of a constitutionally enshrined right and the 'spirit, purport and objects'

---

[270] See the interpretation by the UN Committee on Economic, Social and Cultural Rights of the right to health in art 12 of the International Covenant on Economic, Social and Cultural Rights: General Comment No 14 (Twenty-second sess, 2000), UN doc E/C.12/2000/4, para 12(*d*). See further Pieterse (note 64 above) 166–167.

[271] See also *Pearmain* (1) (note 233 above) 300–301.

[272] *Soobramoney v Minister of Health, KwaZulu-Natal* 1998 (1) SA 765 (CC), 1997 (12) BCLR 1696 (CC) paras 8–9; *Grootboom* (note 55 above) para 23.

[273] Pearmain (1) (note 233 above) 299. For further critiques of the *Afrox* decision, see T Naudé & G Lubbe 'Exemption clauses – A rethink occasioned by *Afrox Health Care Bpk v Strydom*' (2005) 122 *SALJ* 441–463; Bhana and Pieterse (note 119 above); D Tladi 'One step forward, two steps back for constitutionalising the common law: *Afrox Health Care v Strydom*' (2002) 17 *SAPR/PL* 473–478; D Brand 'Disclaimers in hospital admission contracts and constitutional health rights' (2002) 3(2) *ESR Review* 17–18.

[274] See further Naudé & Lubbe ibid 459–462. In the subsequent case of *Johannesburg Country Club v Stott* 2004 (5) SA 511 (SCA) the Supreme Court of Appeal left open the question whether an exemption clause which excluded liability for damages for the negligent causing of the death of another was against public policy. The court held that it was 'arguable that to permit such exclusion would be against public policy because it runs

of this right should have played a far greater role in the court's evaluation of the enforceability of the exemption clause. Similarly, the Court should have taken judicial notice and accorded greater weight to the inequalities in bargaining power inherent in relationships between health service providers and patients.[275]

7.4.3 *Mpange v Sithole*

The approach of the Supreme Court of Appeal in *Afrox* can be contrasted to the more substantive analysis in *Mpange v Sithole* [276] ('*Mpange*') of the implications of the housing rights in s 26 of the Constitution on the availability of the common-law remedies of specific performance and reduction of rental.

In cases concerning a landlord's failure to maintain the premises let in a reasonably fit condition, the courts have tended to refuse an order against the lessor to effect the necessary repairs.[277] The underlying assumption is that the lessee will be in a position to afford the repairs, and recover the costs from the lessor either in the form of a set-off against rental or a claim against the lessor for the amount of the repairs.[278] However, as Satchwell J observed, this option is not easily available to poor tenants (such as the ones before the court) who lack the resources and skills to undertake the renovations required to render the premises habitable.[279] She also recognised that it would not be a feasible option for tenants in this situation to decline to rent the premises and seek alternative accommodation, alternatively, to report the respondent to the municipal authorities and have the building declared a health hazard and unfit for human habitation. Such approaches ignore the relevant social realities: that there is a shortage of accommodation for poor people in Gauteng and that poor people are at the mercy of slum landlords if they wish to avoid homelessness.[280]

The Court held that where 'a court's exercise of discretion implicates constitutional rights, it must be interpreted and applied with appropriate regard to the spirit, purport and objects of the Bill of Rights and with due consideration given to international law'.[281] In circumstances where tenants are too poor to cover the costs of repairing the building themselves, courts should exercise their discretion in favour of an order of specific performance.[282] This approach is mandated by the right of access to adequate housing in s 26(1) as well as the rights to dignity and privacy in

---

counter to the high value the common law and, now, the Constitution place on the sanctity of life.' (para 12, footnotes omitted). See also Pearmain (1) (note 233 above) 301.

[275] As Naudé & Lubbe (note 273 above) 461 observe, '[t]he court's dismissal of the allegation that patients are in a weak bargaining position was all too quick'.

[276] 2007 (6) SA 578 (W).

[277] See the cases cited in n 19 of *Mpange* ibid.

[278] See *Mpange* ibid para 37 and cases cited at note 20.

[279] Ibid.

[280] Ibid para 47.

[281] Ibid para 49 (footnotes omitted).

[282] Ibid paras 36–58.

ss 10 and 14.[283] In support of her interpretation of the scope of s 26(1), Satchwell J referred to the qualitative dimensions of the right to adequate housing as well as the need for effective remedies against landlords who fail to maintain dwellings let in an adequate and healthy condition.[284] Both these aspects have been endorsed by the UN Committee on Economic, Social and Cultural Rights.[285]

However, in the light of the fact that the registered owner of the property had not been joined in the application, the remedy of specific performance could not be awarded. Instead the court granted a remedy in the form of an interdict against the landlord from charging in excess of a specified reduced rental.[286] Although such an order would not cure the disrepair of the premises which implicates the applicants' rights, 'it nevertheless provides an incentive to the respondent to effect such repairs in order to regain the full amount of the rental'.[287] It would also provide the applicants with spare cash in the form of saved rental moneys to make some improvements to their living conditions.[288] In this regard the court also declined to follow a line of case law holding that where lessees remain in occupation of the premises let, they remain liable for the full rental even though they do not have full use and enjoyment of the premises.[289]

The court did not develop a new rule of the common law, as the authoritative position is that the courts retain a discretion regarding an award of specific performance.[290] It nevertheless affirmed that the exercise of this discretion should be informed by constitutional rights, including the right of access to adequate housing, and that specific performance should generally be awarded where tenants are too poor to effect the repairs themselves. In so doing, the court departed from previous authority which refused to exercise the discretion to grant specific performance in favour of tenants where landlords failed to maintain the premises let.

7.4.4 *Barkhuizen v Napier*

The leading case in which the Constitutional Court has considered the impact of constitutional rights on contractual terms is *Barkhuizen*.[291] The case is therefore indicative of the methodological and substantive approach followed by the Constitutional Court in this context.

---

[283] Ibid paras 50–58.
[284] Ibid paras 51–52.
[285] General Comment No 4 (Sixth sess, 1991) *The right to adequate housing* (art 11(1) of the Covenant), UN doc E/1992/23 paras 8 and 17.
[286] *Mpange* (note 276 above) paras 64–74; 83–89.
[287] Ibid para 74.
[288] Ibid.
[289] See the cases cited in *Mpange* (note 276 above) para 66 and n 35.
[290] See *Benson v SA Mutual Life Assurance Society* 1986 (1) SA 776 (A) at 781–783. See further GF Lubbe 'Contractual derogation and the discretion to refuse an order for specific performance' in G Glover (ed) *Essays in Honour of A J Kerr* (2006) 77–99.
[291] Note 19 above.

At issue was the effect of the constitutional right of access to court (s 34)[292] on the validity of a 90-day time limitation clause for issuing summons in a short-term motor vehicle insurance contract. The High Court had held that the time-bar clause in the contract was unenforceable as it constituted an unjustifiable limitation of the right of access to court in s 34 of the Constitution. On appeal, the Supreme Court of Appeal affirmed that the common law of contract was subject to the Constitution which meant 'that courts are obliged to take fundamental constitutional values into account while performing their duty to develop the law of contract in accordance with the Constitution.'[293] While this did not give courts the general power to refrain from enforcing contractual terms on the basis of their own perceptions of justice or 'imprecise notions of good faith',[294] they were obliged to invalidate contractual terms that were offensive to public policy. The content of public policy is to be determined having regard to the 'founding constitutional values of human dignity, the achievement of equality and the advancement of human rights and freedoms, non-racialism and non-sexism'.[295] Cameron JA reiterated the views expressed in his concurring judgment in *Brisley* that 'the liberty to regulate one's life by freely engaged contractual arrangements' gave expression, in appropriate circumstances, to the constitutional values of autonomy and dignity.[296] This required courts to be generally cautious in 'intruding on apparently voluntarily concluded arrangements'.[297] An important factor in determining whether the constitutional values of dignity and equality required the Court to develop the common law of contract so as to invalidate the term was the relative bargaining position of the parties.[298] However, in the present case the court held that the evidence was so scant regarding the plaintiff's bargaining position vis-à-vis the insurer that the broader constitutional challenge could not get off the ground.[299]

---

[292] Section 34 reads as follows:

> Everyone has the right to have any dispute that can be resolved by the application of law decided in a fair public hearing before a court or, where appropriate, another independent and impartial tribunal or forum.

[293] *Napier v Barkhuizen* 2006 (4) SA 1 (SCA), 2006 (9) BCLR 1011 (SCA).

[294] Ibid para 7 (referring to its judgment in *Brisley* (note 122 above) para 93.

[295] Ibid.

[296] Ibid para 13 (referring to *Brisley* (note 122 above) para 94).

[297] Ibid (referring to *Brisley* (note 122 above) para 95).

[298] Ibid. The Court referred in this regard to its judgments in *Brisley* (note 122 above), *Afrox* (note 251 above) and *Johannesburg Country Club v Stott* (note 274 above).

[299] The time-bar clause had been raised by way of a special plea by the insurance company to a summons issued by the plaintiff some two years after the claim he lodged with the insurance company for damages to the insured motor vehicle had been repudiated. It was agreed between the parties that the special plea would be adjudicated on the basis of an agreed brief statement of facts concerning the insurance contract, the accident, the notification of the claim, the repudiation of the claim, and the institution of legal action. No further facts were included in the statement of case. See in this regard *Barkhuizen* (note 19 above) paras 2–7.

The specific challenge to the time-bar clause based on s 34 of the Constitution was also rejected by the Supreme Court of Appeal. Cameron JA distinguished the Constitutional Court decisions dealing with curtailed statutory prescription periods on the basis that these cases dealt with pre-existing rights to legal redress in the form of compensation for personal injuries in respect of which the legislator had superimposed an unreasonable time-bar for instituting legal proceeding.[300] The present case dealt with a contractually negotiated time-limit in a context in which the plaintiff had no 'pre-existing entitlement' against the insurer.[301] In other words, the time-bar restriction 'arose from the very agreement that defined the ambit of the right in creating it'.[302] According to the Court, s 34 of the Constitution did not prohibit contractual arrangements which created rights subject to a stipulation that, in order to be enforceable, a claim had to be instituted within a limited time-period.[303]

On appeal, Ngcobo J writing for the Constitutional Court commenced his judgment by setting out the 'proper approach to constitutional challenges to contractual terms'.[304] He held that the High Court had erred in directly applying s 34 of the Constitution to the time-bar clause in the insurance contract in terms of s 8(2) and (3) of the Constitution.[305] This gave rise to difficulties in identifying a law of general application for the purposes of applying the general limitations clause in s 36,[306] as well as conceptual difficulties in the application of s 172(1)(*a*).[307] According to the Court, constitutional challenges to contractual clauses would usually give rise to the question whether the clause was contrary to public policy.[308] Public policy was 'now deeply rooted in our Constitution and the values which underlie it'.[309] This implied that in determining whether a contractual term is contrary to public policy and accordingly unenforceable, courts must refer 'to the values that underlie our constitutional democracy as given expression by the provisions of the Bill of Rights'.[310] In other words, the Court preferred to use s 39(2) as the conduit for interpreting (and

---

300 *Mohlomi v Minister of Defence* 1997 (1) SA 124 (CC), 1996 (12) BCLR 1559 (CC) (invalidating the six months time bar for instituting action in terms of the Defence Act 44 of 1957); *Moise v Greater Germiston Transitional Local Council: Minister of Justice and Constitutional Development Intervening (Women's Legal Centre as Amicus Curiae)* 2001 (4) SA 491 (CC), 2001 (8) BCLR 765 (CC) (striking down the 90-day notice requirement for instituting legal proceedings against a local authority in terms of the Limitation of Legal Proceedings (Provincial and Local Authorities) Act 94 of 1970).

301 *Napier v Barkhuizen* (note 293 above) paras 20–21.

302 Ibid para 22.

303 Ibid paras 26–27.

304 *Barkhuizen* (note 19 above) paras 23–30.

305 Ibid para 23.

306 Ibid para 24.

307 Ibid paras 25–26. This provision requires a court to invalidate, to the extent of its inconsistency, 'any law or conduct' that is inconsistent with the Constitution.

308 Ibid para 28.

309 Ibid (footnote omitted).

310 Ibid paras 29–30.

where necessary developing) common-law doctrines such as public policy so as to be consonant with the rights and values of the Constitution.[311]

Turning to the question whether public policy tolerated time limitation clauses in contracts between private parties, the Court held that there was no reason in logic or principle why such clauses were not acceptable, subject to considerations of reasonableness and fairness.[312] Time limits for instituting litigation were important safeguards against unreasonable delays in bringing and finalising litigation. As indicated by the Court in *Mohlomi v Minister of Defence*,[313] such delays had various detrimental consequences for the administration of justice.[314] The applicable standard for determining whether a time-bar clause for instituting litigation complied with s 34 was 'the availability of an initial opportunity to exercise the right that amounts, in all the circumstances ... to a real and fair one'.[315] The Court confirmed that this standard was not confined to statutorily imposed prescription periods, but also applied to time-limitation clauses in contracts. It held that the distinction drawn by the Supreme Court of Appeal between statutory and contractual time-bar provisions was 'somewhat narrow and formalistic'.[316] Although there was a conceptual difference in the two situations, the common law[317] and constitutional purpose of ensuring that disputes were resolved by courts and independent tribunals was applicable to both.[318]

According to the Court, there were two factors relevant to determining the fairness of the time-bar clause in the present case. The first question to be determined was whether the clause itself was unreasonable. If the clause was found to be reasonable, the second question concerned whether the courts should nevertheless refrain from enforcing it in the light of the circumstances and reasons for non-compliance with the relevant time limits.[319] In this respect, the onus was on the party seeking to avoid the enforcement of the clause to show why its enforcement would be unfair or unreasonable in the given circumstances.[320]

---

[311] See notes 19–20 and accompanying text. Langa CJ in his separate judgment doubted whether s 39(2) represents 'the only acceptable approach to challenging the constitutionality of contractual terms'. He preferred to leave open the possibility 'that certain rights may apply directly to contractual terms or the common law that underlies them' (para 186).

[312] Ibid para 48.

[313] Note 300 above.

[314] These consequences are summarised by the Court in *Mohlomi* (note 300 above) para 11 (quoted in *Napier v Barkhuizen* (note 293 above) para 47).

[315] Ibid para 50 (citing *Mohlomi* (note 300 above) para 12).

[316] Ibid para 54.

[317] In this regard the Court referred to the principle recognised since *Nino Bonino v De Lange* 1906 TS 120 that contracting parties may not prevent one another from having disputes arising from the contract resolved by a court of law. Ibid para 54.

[318] Ibid para 55.

[319] Ibid para 56.

[320] Ibid paras 58 and 69.

On the first issue, the Court found that the 90-day time limit for issuing summons was not so 'manifestly unreasonable' that it offended public policy. Reasonableness in this context had to be assessed 'by reference to the circumstances of the parties',[321] and a disparity of bargaining power between the contracting parties was a relevant factor in this context.[322] However, the Court held that in the present case there was no evidence 'to suggest that the contract was not freely concluded between parties with equal bargaining power or that the applicant was not aware of the clause'.[323] Furthermore, the applicant had not provided reasons for his non-compliance with the time clause, and thus the Court was unable to evaluate whether the enforcement of the clause against him would be unfair or unjust to the applicant and thus contrary to public policy.[324]

Finally, the Court observed that the current law as interpreted in *Brisley* envisages a limited role for good faith 'not as a self-standing rule, but as an underlying value that is given expression through existing rules of law'.[325] It expressly refrained from deciding whether this limited role for good faith was appropriate under the Constitution as it was of the view that the facts of the case did not require this question to be answered.[326]

In his dissenting judgment, Sachs J held that the surrounding context of the case, particularly the nature of documentary evidence was sufficient to enable the Court to make a finding regarding the substantive fairness of the time-limitation clause. The time-bar clause formed part of the 'fine print' in an addendum to a standard form contract. There were a number of factors in the available evidence which established that, from an objective perspective, the 'tendency' of the clause in the context of the contract as a whole was to 'vitiate standards of reasonable and fair dealing that the legal convictions of the community would regard as intrinsic to appropriate business firm/consumer relationships in contemporary society'.[327] The judgment seeks guidance on evolving standards of public policy in this context from a historical survey of notions of consensus and public policy in contract law, contemporary international practice, statutory reform in South African consumer protection law, and norms contained in various statutes regulating prescription periods.[328] Of particular importance was the fact that the clause had 'the effect of significantly limiting a right to have a dispute settled by a court, a right long recognised by the common law and now

[321] Ibid para 64.
[322] Ibid para 65.
[323] Ibid para 66.
[324] Ibid para 84.
[325] Ibid para 82. See the discussion of *Brisley* (note 122 above) in para 7.4.1 above.
[326] Ibid. In her separate concurring judgment, O'Regan J expressed the view that this aspect of the majority judgment was unnecessary to the decision in the case, and expressly declined to consider it until raised in an appropriate matter (para 120).
[327] See particularly *Barkhuizen* (note 19 above) para 146 and the factors summarised in para 183.
[328] Ibid paras 151–176.

guaranteed as a fundamental right by the Constitution.'[329] Sachs J concluded that the clause offended public policy as understood in the light of the rights and values of the constitutional dispensation.[330]

Moseneke DCJ concurred in the outcome proposed by Sachs J. In his separate judgment he held that the majority erred by assessing the consistency of the impugned clause with public policy by reference to the circumstances and conduct of the parties to the contract.[331] Instead, the proper approach 'would be to look at the time bar stipulation itself within the context of the entire agreement with a view to assessing whether it evinces a tendency or reasonable likelihood to deprive the claimant of the right to approach the court for redress'.[332] He found that the clause was unreasonably short and denied the insured a reasonable opportunity to have the dispute decided by an independent tribunal on several grounds. These included the practical difficulties of issuing summons within 90 days of repudiation of the claim, the lack of proportionality in the burdens imposed on the insured and the benefits reaped by the insurance company, the lack of reciprocity, and the statutory trend towards providing a standard three-year prescription period for delictual debts.[333]

Although the contract in *Barkhuizen* was not specifically concerned with a socio-economic right, as Sachs J points out, car insurance is a virtual necessity and a matter of considerable public concern in modern societies.[334] Restrictive time-bar clauses in standard form insurance contracts clearly weigh disproportionately in favour of the interests of the major commercial insurance companies, regardless of whether the particular client belongs to the middle classes.[335] The effect of allowing such unilaterally imposed and clearly one-sided clauses[336] to prevail is, in the words of Moseneke DCJ, 'to extol the *laissez faire* notions of freedom of contract at the expense of public notions of reasonableness and fairness'.[337] This is of heightened concern in contexts where basic constitutional rights such as access to court are at stake. This right serves as the guarantee of all rights in our legal system, including the socio-economic rights guaranteed in the Bill of Rights.

The majority judgment set a high threshold of 'manifest unreasonableness' for vitiating a time-bar clause in a contract. This suggests an approach which regards the

329 *Barkhuizen* (note 19 above) para 183.
330 See also the separate judgment of Moseneke DCJ concurring in the judgment of Sachs J.
331 Ibid paras 94–95.
332 Ibid para 96.
333 Ibid paras 112–117.
334 Ibid para 144.
335 The plaintiff was a software developer and the vehicle in question was a BMW. See *Napier v Barkhuizen* (note 293 above) para 15; *Barkhuizen* (note 19 above) para 2.
336 See Sachs J's observations in *Barkhuizen* (note 19 above) at para 147.
337 Ibid para 104.

principle of *pacta sunt servanda* as having presumptive force as a normative standard.[338] The majority finds constitutional reinforcement for the maxim of *pacta sunt servanda* in the founding constitutional values. Thus Ngcobo J states:

> [P]*acta sunt servanda*] ... as the Supreme Court of Appeal has repeatedly noted, gives effect to the central constitutional values of freedom and dignity. Self-autonomy, or the ability to regulate one's own affairs, even to one's own detriment, is the very essence of freedom and a vital part of dignity.[339]

Although the Court considers the purpose of s 34 in the context of the jurisprudence on statutory prescription periods, there is very little attempt to engage with the distinctive purposes which s 34 serves in the context of contracts between private parties, particularly in the context of contracts between consumers and major insurance companies. While the prevention of self-help is undoubtedly an important purpose of s 34, the right to access to courts also provides an important safeguard against abuse of power and oppressive conduct in contractual disputes between private parties.

Judicial control of disputes in public and private law is not only a fundamentally important principle in a constitutional democracy, but is a substantive right enshrined in the Bill of Rights. There is a very steep discrepancy between the 90-day contractual time-bar clause in *Barkhuizen* and the general norm of a three-year prescription period in the Prescription Act 68 of 1969 and the Institution of Legal Proceedings against certain Organs of State Act 40 of 2002. These considerations strongly suggest that the clause in question should have been regarded as contrary to public policy for unreasonably curtailing the right of access to court. At the very least, the burden should have been placed on the insurance company to justify that such a clause was reasonable and justifiable in terms of the purpose and proportionality requirements of s 36.[340]

7.4.5 Evaluation

Cases such as *Brisley*, *Afrox* and *Barkhuizen* illustrate that, even under a transformative Constitution, South African contract law is still strongly influenced by classic liberal notions of individual autonomy and freedom of contract. This manifests the privileging of form over substance in the judicial scrutiny of contractual arrangements,

---

[338] D Bhana 'The role of judicial method in the relinquishing of constitutional rights through contract' (2008) 24 *SAJHR* 300–317.

[339] *Barkhuizen* (note 19 above) para 57.

[340] As previously noted, the majority found that there was a fundamental difficulty in identifying a 'law of general application' for the purposes of applying s 36. Compare, however, the approach outlined in *Khumalo* (note 18 above) para 31. The route followed in the latter case was direct application of the Bill of Rights to the common law in terms of ss 8(2) read with (3). See part 7.2.3(*b*) above. As discussed, the majority held in *Barkhuizen* that the constitutionality of contractual terms fell to be evaluated in terms of s 39 of the Constitution. Nevertheless, even if this route is followed, there seems to be little justification for excluding the 'spirit, purport and objects' of a limitations analysis in terms of s 36 in evaluating the constitutionality of contractual terms.

and a preference for relying on 'crystallised rules' of contract law over open-ended standards such as fairness and good faith.[341] It is further reflected in the restricted impact of constitutional rights such as socio-economic rights and the right of access to court on existing rules and doctrines in this sphere.

In the sphere of contract law, the Supreme Court of Appeal has tended to minimise the impact of socio-economic rights on the various doctrines, principles and rules of contract law, particularly by applying a narrow and formalistic interpretation of the relevant rights. In order to do justice to the injunction in s 39(2) of the Constitution to harmonise common-law rules and principles with the spirit, purport and object of the Bill of Rights, courts are required to engage with the broader purposes and values which all the rights, including socio-economic rights, seek to promote.

A J Barnard-Naudé points out that, '[t]he South African law of contract is not *fundamentally* individualistic and formal'.[342] However, its values such as good faith, fairness and reasonableness have been marginalised in favour of a formalistic, rule-bound approach which favours the interests of the commercially powerful at the expense of those in a weaker bargaining position.[343] The open-ended standards of good faith and reasonableness enable a careful and critical evaluation of the impact of constitutional rights and their underlying purposes and values on particular contracts. It allows the courts to identify all the rights, values and policy considerations which are implicated in the specific circumstances and set of relationships involved in the contractual dispute before them.[344]

The concern that this will promote subjectivity and judicial law-making is misplaced. The Constitution itself endorses a form of value-based reasoning in which policy choices are rendered transparent and particular decisions justified in the light of constitutional rights and values.[345] This process is impeded when concepts such as good faith, equity and reasonableness in contractual dealings are accorded a dimin-

---

[341] See also *South African Forestry Company Limited v York Timbers Limited* 2003 (1) SA 331 (SCA), and *Hartley v Pyramid Freight (Pty) Ltd t/a Sun Couriers* 2007 (2) SA 599 (SCA). For a critique of this approach see A J Barnard 'To wonderland through the looking-glass: Conceiving a critical legal argument for contractual justice in the South African law of contract' (2006) 17 *Law and Critique* 153–170; A J Barnard-Naudé 'The decision in *Hartley v Pyramid Freight (Pty) Ltd:* Justice miscarried?' (2007) 18 *Stell LR* 497–507.

[342] Barnard ibid at 161.

[343] Ibid.

[344] As Deeksha Bhana and Marius Pieterse (note 119 above) 894 argue:

> This dogmatic adherence to legal rules (at the expense of open-ended standards such as good faith and equity) for the sake of certainty strips the common law of its inherent potential and accordingly frustrates legal and social transformation.

[345] On the nature of judicial discretion in the context of the open-ended legal standards of contract law, see Lubbe (note 238 above) 417–418.

ished role.[346] It is also impeded when negative liberty manifested in non-interference with sanctity of contract enjoys a privileged normative status.[347]

In the context of contracts which regulate access to constitutionally protected socio-economic rights courts should be particularly alert to terms which may undermine the purposes of these rights. In this area public policy considerations, and the reasonableness and good faith of the relevant contractual terms, should be exposed to a form of heightened scrutiny. As Gerhard Lubbe argues:

> It might also be necessary to differentiate contracts concluded between commercial parties from contracts concluded by individuals in respect of the basic needs of human existence (which involve what in Germany is referred to as 'Daseinsvorsorge'), eg in relation to housing, education and health. This becomes particularly problematic in so far as these needs are served by contracts concluded with commercially orientated entities, under which intrinsically human needs become commercial commodities, as is exemplified by the facts at issue in *Afrox*.[348]

The continued diminished role of open-ended evaluative standards in contract law in the post-constitutional era does not bode well for allowing socio-economic rights and the interests and values they protect to have a meaningful influence on our contract law. As noted previously, this does not imply that one set of rights or values will automatically be determinative. Rather it requires that the validity and enforcement of contracts be considered within the balanced normative framework supplied by the Bill of Rights.

Given the reticence of the courts to undertake a more robust evaluation of the fairness of contractual provisions in the light of constitutional rights and values, legislative intervention has become critical. The Consumer Protection Act 68 of 2008 should provide the impetus towards developing contract law in South Africa so as to be consonant with the constitutional purpose of promoting social justice in South Africa.[349]

7.5 CONCLUSION

This chapter has examined the application of constitutional rights and values to private law through the mechanisms of ss 8 and 39(2) of the Constitution. The application of these provisions in the specific context of socio-economic rights has been critically evaluated.

---

346 On the role of the doctrine of good faith in enabling a consideration of constitutional rights and values, see *Mort NO v Henry Shields-Chiat* (note 256 above) 474J–475E.

347 On the conceptual power of negative liberty in South African law, and the need to develop a concept of positive liberty which is more consonant with the constitutional goals of social justice and participatory democracy, see S Liebenberg (note 9 above).

348 Lubbe (note 238 above) 422–423. See also Pearmain (1) (note 233 above) 296–299.

349 The Consumer Protection Act 68 of 2008. On the need for this legislation, see T Naudé 'Unfair contract terms legislation: The implications of why we need it for its formulation and application' (2006) 17 *Stell LR* 361–385.

The second part of the chapter has focused on the application of socio-economic rights in selected areas of property law and contract law. This analysis shows that the housing rights in s 26 of the Constitution has had a substantial impact on the procedural and substantive law relating to the eviction of people from their homes. However, despite the clearly transformative import of s 26(3) and the substantive interpretation of PIE in the *Port Elizabeth Municipality* case,[350] the influence of the pre-constitutional common-law paradigm pertaining to evictions continues to be felt in evictions jurisprudence, particularly when applying s 26(3) to the applicable common law.

In the sphere of contract law, the influence of a classic liberal paradigm is still pervasive. This paradigm tends to minimise the impact of human rights standards in areas of law regulating 'autonomous' private relationships. This is particularly evident in the jurisprudence which has directly or indirectly considered the impact of socio-economic rights on contractual relationships. Traditional notions of sanctity of contract and judicial restraint have generally prevailed over any transformation of existing doctrines inspired by socio-economic rights and their underlying purposes and values. Moreover, the potential of socio-economic rights to invite a critical re-evaluation of traditional approaches has been restricted by the reduced role accorded to open-ended standards such as good faith and reasonableness in contract law. These standards could serve as conduits for the application of the normative value system underpinning socio-economic rights in contract law. Even when the application of socio-economic rights in the sphere of contract law is acknowledged, their impact is diminished by the particularly narrow and formalistic interpretation given to these rights in cases such as *Brisley*[351] and *Afrox*.[352]

In the end both methodological and ideological considerations constrain the potentially transformative influence of socio-economic rights on private law rules and doctrines. The methodological obstacles relate to a reluctance to alter fundamentally the existing doctrinal logic, institutions and rules of private law under the influence of constitutional rights and values, particularly in relation to socio-economic rights. The ideological obstacles relate to the privileging of negative liberties and vested rights over the positive obligations and the ideals of substantive social and economic justice.

These trends will continue unless the powerful hold which the classic liberal ideology of minimising state and judicial interference in private relationships has in our legal culture is loosened. The foundational constitutional value of freedom is concerned with the political, social and economic relationships that foster the dignity and capabilities of people. This requires the judiciary to play an active role in aligning the rules and institutions of private law with this new normative value system. As Froneman J stated in the *Kate* decision:

---

[350] *Port Elizabeth Municipality* (note 172 above).
[351] *Brisley* (note 122 above).
[352] *Afrox* (note 251 above).

> [T]he Judge who fails to examine the existing law with a view to ensuring the effective realisation of constitutional rights and values that were not recognised before is not, as is so often presumed by proponents of this course, merely neutrally and objectively applying the law. That will only ever be true if the existing common law proceeds from a fair and equal baseline, an assumption that will not often be open to the present judiciary in South Africa … given our unequal past. More often than not such a supine approach will effectively result in a choice for the retention of an unequal and unjust *status quo*.[353]

[353] *Kate v MEC for the Department of Welfare, Eastern Cape* (note 102 above) para 16.

CHAPTER 8

Responsive Remedies

In this chapter *Page*

8.1 INTRODUCTION

Classic liberal legalism is premised on a model of negative rights accompanied by strict boundaries between the roles and functions of the three branches of government. This is a product of the insistence on a clear divide between law and politics and a concomitant anxiety to restrain the incursion of the judiciary into the 'political' terrain in the process of adjudication.[1] This background ideology can have a powerful restraining effect on the boldness and imagination with which courts approach the remedial dimensions of socio-economic rights litigation.

Moreover, to the extent that the courts' remedial approach to constitutional rights violations is premised on an unarticulated private law model of adjudication, this will also limit the willingness of courts to innovate and experiment in designing effective remedies. Traditional private law litigation is premised on an adversarial contest between individuals or clearly defined groups of individual or legal persons. As the Constitutional Court pointed out in the *Metrorail* case, private law remedies 'tend to be retrospective in effect, seeking to remedy loss caused rather than to prevent loss in the future'.[2] In their analysis of constitutional remedies Iain Currie and Johan de Waal, point out that the harm caused by the violation of constitutional rights is not merely to the individual applicants, 'but a harm to society as a whole: the violation impedes the realisation of the constitutional project of creating a just and democratic society'.[3] Thus the purpose of constitutional remedies is not only to provide effective relief to those who have experienced the violation, but also to deter future violations of the rights.[4]

Sabel and Simon caution against overstating the differences between common-law and public interest litigation. They observe that many common-law remedies share public law's regulatory and institutional restructuring purposes and effects. This is described by the authors as the 'destabilization aspect of common law regulation'.[5] Nevertheless, there is an important difference between the objectives of private law

---

1 See generally chapter 2, parts 2.4.4; 2.4.6–2.4.7.

2 *Rail Commuters' Action Group v Transnet Ltd t/a Metrorail* 2005 (2) SA 359 (CC), 2005 (4) BCLR 301 (CC) para 80 ('*Metrorail*').

3 I Currie & J de Waal *The Bill of Rights Handbook* 5 ed (2005) 196. On the tension between the corrective and distributive dimensions of remedial justice, see C Mbazira '"Appropriate, just and equitable relief" in socio-economic rights litigation: The tension between corrective and distributive forms of justice' (2008) 125 *SALJ* 71–94.

4 See *Fose v Minister of Safety and Security* 1997 (3) SA 786 (CC), 1997 (7) BCLR 851 (CC) para 96; *Saunderson v Attorney-General, Eastern* Cape 1998 (2) SA 38 (CC), 1997 (12) BCLR 1675 (CC) para 38.

5 C F Sabel & W H Simon 'Destabilization rights: How public law litigation succeeds' (2004) 117 *Harv LR* 1016–1101 at 1059. The development of the duty of care to strangers and the immunity for competitive injury are given as examples of the regulatory function

remedies and constitutional law remedies in human rights litigation. Common-law regulation of market and family institutions both constitutes and enables economic and social relations in these spheres. It assumes the normality of the current paradigm and changes in the regulatory framework tend to be 'incremental', rather than fundamental.[6] The focus of human rights litigation is on ensuring that public and private institutions respect and give effect to the obligations imposed upon them by human rights norms. A transformative conception of socio-economic rights should resonate with broader strategies to redress the underlying causes of systemic poverty, including those which arise from the distribution of power and wealth in a market economy. It should seek to identify and challenge those rules of public and private law which perpetuate entrenched patterns of socio-economic disadvantage and marginalisation.

Crafting effective remedial responses to violations of socio-economic rights requires courts to come to grips with the fact that these violations are the product of systemic injustices perpetrated against classes of people over generations. In this context, a lack of access, or inadequate access, to socio-economic rights can often not be remedied by a once-and-for-all court order sounding in money.[7] Innovative responses are required which incorporate, but also transcend, the traditional repertoire of private law remedies.

The Constitutional Court has emphasised the broader significance of developing effective and, if need be, innovative remedies to vindicate constitutional rights:

> Particularly in a country where so few have the means to enforce their rights through the courts, it is essential that on those occasions when the legal process does establish that an infringement of an entrenched right has occurred, it be effectively vindicated. The courts have a particular responsibility in this regard and are obliged to 'forge new tools' and shape innovative remedies, if needs be, to achieve this goal.[8]

This is particularly relevant in socio-economic rights cases, where impoverished communities often lack access to legal services, and cannot afford to engage in ongoing litigation to secure an effective remedy.[9]

This chapter analyses the wide range of remedial options which are available to the South African courts under the Constitution to respond to socio-economic rights violations. It commences with an overview of the courts' remedial powers in constitutional litigation and the applicable principles which have developed through the jurisprudence. The remainder of the chapter examines the jurisprudence on the

---

of the common law. Antitrust and insolvency law entail remedies for the restructuring of business institutions (1059–1062).

6 See further chapter 2, part 2.4.5; chapter 7, part 7.2.6.

7 For a discussion of these features of socio-economic rights litigation, see W Trengove 'Judicial remedies for violations of socio-economic rights' (1999) 1 *ESR Review* 8–11.

8 *Fose* (note 4 above) para 69 (footnotes omitted); M Swart 'Left out in the cold? Crafting constitutional remedies for the poorest of the poor' (2005) 21 *SAJHR* 215–240.

9 See the observations of Cameron JA (as he then was) in *Permanent Secretary, Department of Welfare, Eastern Cape Provincial Government v Ngxuza* 2001 (4) SA 1184 (SCA), 2001 (10) BCLR 1039 (SCA) paras 11–12.

different kinds of constitutional remedies and explores their potential to promote transformative responses to various kinds of socio-economic rights violations. The impact of the remedies granted in some of the leading socio-economic rights judgments such as *Government of the Republic of South Africa v Grootboom*[10] ('*Grootboom*') and *Occupiers of 51 Olivia Road, Berea Township and 197 Main Street, Johannesburg v City of Johannesburg*[11] ('*Occupiers of 51 Olivia Road*'), for example, are also considered.[12]

8.2 CONSTITUTIONAL REMEDIES

The courts have wide remedial powers to grant effective remedies in litigation under the Bill of Rights. Section 38 of the Constitution provides that anyone with standing[13] in terms of this section 'has the right to approach a competent court, alleging that a right in the Bill of Rights has been infringed or threatened, and the court may grant appropriate relief, including a declaration of rights'. This provision has to be read in conjunction with s 172 of the Constitution which provides that a court deciding a constitutional matter within its power 'must declare that any law or conduct that is inconsistent with the Constitution is invalid to the extent of its inconsistency'.[14] In addition, the court may make any order that is 'just and equitable', including an order 'limiting the retrospective effect of the declaration of invalidity', and making an order 'suspending the declaration of invalidity for any period and on any conditions, to allow the competent authority to correct the defect'.[15]

In *Fose v Minister of Safety and Security*[16] *('Fose')* the Court held that the appropriateness of the remedy was determined by its efficacy, 'for without effective remedies for breach, the values underlying and the rights entrenched in the Constitution cannot properly be upheld or enhanced'.[17] This requires careful attention to the nature of the constitutional infringement in the particular case and the 'probable impact' of a specific remedy. The objective of the remedy is twofold – to provide suitable relief to the victims of a violation of constitutionally protected rights and to deter future violations of these rights.[18]

Kriegler J describes the role of courts in crafting remedies for constitutional violations as an 'attempt to synchronise the real world with the ideal construct of a constitutional world created in the image of [the supremacy clause]'.[19] However, courts

[10] 2001 (1) SA 46 (CC), 2000 (11) BCLR 1169 (CC).
[11] 2008 (3) SA 208 (CC), 2008 (5) BCLR 475 (CC).
[12] See parts 8.4.2 and 8.5.3(*b*) respectively below.
[13] On the standing provisions in the Bill of Rights, see chapter 3, part 3.2.3.
[14] Section 172 (1)(*a*).
[15] Section 172(1)(*b*)(i) and (ii).
[16] Note 4 above.
[17] *Fose* (note 4 above) para 69. See also *National Coalition for Gay and Lesbian Equality v Minister of Home Affairs* 2000 (2) SA 1 (CC), 2000 (1) BCLR 39 (CC) paras 65, 81–82.
[18] See the observations by Kriegler J in *Fose* (note 4 above) paras 96 and 97.
[19] *Fose* (note 4 above) para 94.

may be confronted with a number of interrelated challenges in achieving this synchronisation.[20] These may include designing a remedy in circumstances when the violation of a constitutional right requires extensive positive measures and has substantial resource implications. In these situations there are usually a range of possible policy solutions to remedy the violation, and the court may not know in advance what would be the optimal solution. Second, they may face the challenge of ensuring speedy and effective relief in circumstances where a violation of rights may have serious and irreparable consequences for the applicant group. Third, courts must consider the implications of the relief they give not only to the successful litigant, but also to other groups that may be similarly situated to the applicants or who may be adversely affected by the order.[21] Finally, the courts must consider whether another branch of government may be best suited to remedy the particular constitutional violation. The latter entails separation of powers considerations. However, the inquiry, particularly at the remedial phase, should not be premised on a rigid functional separation between the various branches, but rather proceed on the basis of which branch of government – separately or in collaboration – is best placed to ensure effective and equitable relief for the constitutional violation.[22] This is consonant with the co-operative, dialogic model of the separation of powers doctrine which I have argued a transformative reading of the 1996 Constitution supports.[23]

The extent to which these themes recur is evident from the examination which follows of the diverse remedies available to the courts in socio-economic rights litigation. Particular attention is paid to how the courts have responded to the challenges they pose. Finally, the potential of the various remedial possibilities to foster transformative responses to socio-economic rights violations is explored.

8.3 DECLARATIONS OF INVALIDITY AND ASSOCIATED REMEDIES

8.3.1 Introduction

In terms of s 172(1), a court is obliged to declare any law or conduct which is found to be inconsistent with the Constitution invalid to the extent of its inconsistency.[24]

---

[20] See the observations of Ngcobo J in *Hoffmann v South African Airways* 2001 (1) SA 1 (CC), 2000 (11) BCLR 1211 (CC) para 45.

[21] See Currie & De Waal (note 3 above) 197. Thus the Constitutional Court has stated in *NCGLE v Minister of Home Affairs* (note 17 above), that constitutional litigation has 'a wider public dimension. The bell tolls for everyone' (para 82).

[22] See discussion on structural interdicts in 8.6 below.

[23] See chapter 2, part 2.4.7.

[24] See, for example, *Dawood v Minister of Home Affairs; Shalabi v Minister of Home Affairs; Thomas v Minister of Home Affairs* 2000 (3) SA 936 (CC), 2000 (8) BCLR 837 (CC) paras 17 and 59. Insofar as reasonably possible, legislation must be interpreted to be consistent with the Constitution in order to 'promote the spirit, purport and objects of the Bill of Rights' (s 39(2)). See in this regard *Investigating Directorate: Serious Economic Offences v Hyundai Motor Distributors (Pty) Ltd; In re Hyundai Motor Distributors (Pty) Ltd v Smit NO*

When a law or conduct is declared invalid, the courts have wide powers to control the consequences of the declaration of invalidity through granting 'just and equitable' remedies. These may include limiting the retrospective effect of a declaration of invalidity, suspending the declaration for a period subject to any conditions,[25] severing constitutionally defective provisions of legislation, and reading particular provisions into the legislation.

The ability of the courts to control the consequences of a declaration of invalidity through these mechanisms is particularly important in the context of legislation and programmes which give effect to various socio-economic rights. If these laws and programmes were simply declared invalid (for example, on the basis of an unconstitutional exclusion of a certain group) the consequence would be that large numbers of current beneficiaries would be deprived of access to much needed social benefits. Such a result would be incompatible with the underlying purpose and values of the Constitution.[26] Furthermore, seeking to remedy constitutional defects without invalidating legislation which enacts important social programmes, respects the institutional responsibilities and competencies of the legislative and executive branches of government. These branches of government have the primary mandate under the Constitution to give effect to socio-economic rights through comprehensive social legislation and programmes.[27]

2001 (1) SA 545 (CC), 2000 (10) BCLR 1079 (CC) para 24 ('*Hyundai Motor Distributors*'); *Daniels v Campbell NO* 2004 (5) SA 331 (CC), 2004 (7) BCLR 735 (CC). However, such interpretation must not be 'unduly strained'. See *Hyundai Motor Distributors* ibid, para 24; *Director of Public Prosecutions, Transvaal v Minister for Justice and Constitutional Development* 2009 (4) SA 222 (CC), 2009 (7) BCLR 637 (CC) paras 82–84; 158.

[25] As noted above, these two options are specifically referred to in s 172(1)(*b*)(i) and (ii) of the Constitution.

[26] See, for example, the Canadian case of *Schachter v Canada* [1992] 2 SCR 679 which concerned an equality challenge under s 15 of the Canadian Charter of Rights and Freedoms to the exclusion of natural parents from the benefits available to adoptive parents under the Unemployment Insurance Act, 1971. The Canadian Supreme Court described the striking down of the relevant legislative provision providing for unemployment benefits to remedy a breach of equality rights as 'equality with a vengeance' which would create 'equal graveyards' (15G). This description was referred to with approval by Ackermann J in *NCGLE v Minister of Home Affairs* (note 17 above) paras 77–78.

[27] See *Grootboom* (note 10 above) paras 39–40. In its recent judgment in *Head of Department: Mpumalanga Department of Education v Hoërskool Ermelo (Federation of Governing Bodies for South African Schools as Amicus Curiae)* [2009] ZACC 32 (judgment unreported at the date of writing), the Constitutional Court emphasised that the broad remedial powers in s 172(1)(*b*) are not limited to circumstances where a court makes an order of constitutional invalidity in respect of law or conduct under section 172(1)(*a*). A court is thus at large to forge a 'just and equitable' remedy aimed at resolving 'the actual underlying dispute between the parties' even where a declaration of invalidity has not been made (para 97).

8.3.2 Severance

Severance entails the excision of unconstitutional words or sections from legislation. The basic criteria for determining when severance will be an appropriate remedy were laid down by Kriegler J in *Coetzee v Government of the Republic of South Africa; Matiso v Commanding Officer, Port Elizabeth Prison*:[28]

> [I]f the good is not dependent on the bad and can be separated from it, one gives effect to the good that remains after the separation if it still gives effect to the main objective of the statute. The test has two parts: first, is it possible to sever the invalid provisions and second, if so, is what remains giving effect to the purpose of the legislative scheme?[29]

However, as Currie and De Waal point out, this 'apparently simple two-part test of Kriegler J may be extremely difficult to apply in practice'.[30] It is not always a straightforward matter to determine how severance of the constitutionally objectionable portions of a statute will affect the remainder, and what the overall impact of the excision will be on the purpose of the legislative scheme in question.

The Court has also extended the remedy of severance to include 'notional severance'. This device is employed when it is not possible to achieve a precise excision of certain words or provisions from legislation. In these circumstances, the Court subjects the statute's provisions to a particular condition or interpretation.[31] However, the Court has held that it will only employ notional severance when it is the actual presence of words or provisions which are constitutionally offensive, not when the defect arises from an unconstitutional omission of provisions of a statute.[32] In these cases, the Court has held that other remedial options must be used such as 'the reading in' remedy or a suspended declaration of invalidity.[33]

8.3.3 'Reading in' remedies

When a legislative omission gives rise to the infringement of a constitutional right, a possible remedy is the 'reading in' of particular words in a statute. This situation usually arises when a statute is under-inclusive in the sense that it unconstitutionally excludes certain groups from the ambit of the protection it provides or the benefits it confers. However, the remedy is not confined to under-inclusive statutes, and can, to a limited extent, be used to recraft legislative provisions to render them constitutionally consistent.[34]

---

[28] 1995 (4) SA 631 (CC), 1995 (10) BCLR 1382 (CC).

[29] Ibid para 16 (footnote omitted).

[30] Currie & De Waal (note 3 above) 203.

[31] See, for example, the order formulated by Ackermann J in *Ferreira v Levin NO; Vryenhoek v Powell NO* 1996 (1) SA 984 (CC), 1996 (1) BCLR 1 (CC) ('*Ferreira*') para 114. See also *First National Bank of SA Ltd t/a Wesbank v Commissioner for the South African Revenue Services ; First National Bank of SA Limited t/a Wesbank v Minister of Finance* 2002 (4) SA 768 (CC), 2002 (7) BCLR 702 (CC) para 114.

[32] *NCGLE v Minister of Home* Affairs (note 17 above) paras 63–64.

[33] Ibid.

[34] See *S v Manamela (Director-General of Justice Intervening)* 2000 (3) SA 1 (CC), 2000 (5) BCLR 491 (CC) para 56. In this case the court 'severed' a reverse onus presumption and

In *National Coalition for Gay and Lesbian Equality v Minister of Home Affairs*,[35] ('*NCGLE v Minister of Home Affairs*') the Constitutional Court formulated guidelines for determining when a 'reading in' remedy would be appropriate. In summary:

(1) A court should be able to define with 'sufficient precision' how a statute should be altered to render it constitutionally compliant.[36]
(2) The court should strive to be 'as faithful as possible to the legislative scheme within the constraints of the Constitution'.
(3) A 'reading in' remedy should not result in an 'unsupportable budgetary intrusion'. In determining the budgetary implications of reading in a particular group, the court should 'consider the relative size of the group which the reading in would add compared to the group already enjoying the benefits'.
(4) Where 'reading in would, by expanding the group of persons protected, sustain a policy of long standing or one that is constitutionally encouraged, it should be preferred to one removing the protection completely'.[37]

These guidelines seek to achieve a balance between ensuring immediate access to the statutory benefits for the excluded group, and avoiding excessive judicial intrusion in the legislature's duty to enact legislation giving effect to constitutional rights. Courts must be particularly cautious not to impose their own conceptions of appropriate policy in circumstances where there is not one correct policy choice, but rather a range of reasonable policy options that would adequately vindicate the constitutional right in question.[38] In these circumstances a suspended declaration of invalidity with appropriate interim relief to affected parties, may constitute the more appropriate remedy.[39]

The Constitutional Court has used the 'reading in' remedy in three major socio-economic rights cases to date. In *Khosa v Minister of Social Development; Mahlaule v Minister of Social Development*[40] ('*Khosa*'), the Court read the excluded group of 'permanent residents' into relevant provisions of the Social Assistance Act 59 of 1992 and the Welfare Laws Amendment Act 106 of 1997. It held that their exclusion from the social grants scheme established by this legislation violated both the right against

read in an evidential presumption in its place. See also *S v Singo* 2002 (4) SA 858 (CC), 2002 (8) BCLR 793 (CC).

[35] Note 17 above.

[36] This is exemplified by the cases extending the benefits accorded to heterosexual married couples to same sex life partners: See, for example, *Du Toit v Minister for Welfare and Population Development (Lesbian and Gay Equality Project as Amicus Curiae)* 2003 (2) SA 198 (CC), 2002 (10) BCLR 1006 (CC); *Satchwell v President of the Republic of South Africa* 2002 (6) SA 1 (CC), 2002 (9) BCLR 986 (CC).

[37] *NCGLE v Minister of Home Affairs* (note 17 above) para 75.

[38] See in this regard the warning sounded by Ngcobo J in *Director of Public Prosecutions, Transvaal v Minister for Justice and Constitutional Development* (note 24 above) against courts unnecessarily dictating the content of policies to the executive (para 184).

[39] See the observations of O' Regan J in *Dawood v Minister of Home Affairs* (note 24 above) paras 62–64. On suspended declarations of invalidity, see part 8.3.5 below.

[40] 2004 (6) SA 505 (CC), 2004 (6) BCLR 569 (CC).

unfair discrimination (s 9(3)) and the right of access to social security, including social assistance (s 27(1)(*c*) read with (2)).[41] The Court confirmed that in considering the 'reading in' remedy, remedial precision was an important consideration related 'directly to respect for the role of the Legislature'.[42] 'Reading in' was considered a more appropriate remedy than granting an immediate or suspended declaration of invalidity. Declaring the provisions which limited the payment of social grants to South African citizens invalid was deemed inappropriate as it would extend the net of eligibility too wide. All categories of residents (including non-national visitors within South Africa) who satisfied the other conditions of eligibility would be entitled to apply for social grants.[43] The judgment was expressly confined to the exclusion of permanent residents as a category of non-citizens from the legislation. The Court indicated that it 'may be reasonable to exclude from the legislative scheme workers who are citizens of other countries, visitors and illegal residents, who have only a tenuous link with this country'.[44]

A suspended declaration of invalidity was not considered a 'just and equitable' order as there were compelling reasons not to delay payment of social grants any further to the applicants and those similarly situated.[45] In her judgment, Mokgoro J highlighted the grave consequences of the denial of the right of access to social security for permanent residents:

> They are relegated to the margins of society and are deprived of what may be essential to enable them to enjoy other rights vested in them under the Constitution. Denying them their right under section 27(1) therefore affects them in a most fundamental way. In my view this denial is unfair.[46]

Even if interim relief were given to the applicants during the period of suspension, other permanent residents would be barred from applying for the relevant social grants during the period of suspension. A significant background consideration in granting the 'reading in' remedy was undoubtedly the relatively negligible financial implications of the inclusion of permanent residents in the social grants scheme.[47]

The second socio-economic rights case in which the Constitutional Court granted the 'reading in' remedy was *Jaftha v Schoeman; Van Rooyen v Stoltz*[48] ('*Jaftha*'). The Court held that s 66(1)(*a*) of the Magistrates' Courts Act 32 of 1944 was unconstitutional to the extent that it allowed for sales-in-execution against immovable pro-

---

[41] See the discussion of the judgment in chapter 4, part 4.3.4.
[42] *Khosa* (note 40 above) para 88.
[43] Ibid para 88.
[44] Ibid para 59.
[45] Ibid.
[46] Ibid para 77. See also para 80.
[47] See *Khosa* (note 40 above) para 62 ('an increase of less than 2% on the present cost of social grants').
[48] 2005 (2) SA 140 (CC), 2005 (1) BCLR 78 (CC).

perty without appropriate judicial oversight.[49] The remedy for the 'over-breadth' of the scheme was to read in a provision requiring that such sales-in-execution against immovable property could only be authorised by a court 'after consideration of all relevant circumstances'.[50]

The Court rejected the argument of the Minister of Justice and Constitutional Development that the most appropriate remedy would be to strike down the impugned section and to suspend the declaration of invalidity for a period in order to allow the Legislature to correct the defect on the grounds that it would 'not be in the interests of justice and good governance'.[51] A central consideration in favour of a remedy reading words into s 66 of the Magistrates' Courts Act was the limited range of legislative options for curing the constitutional defect.[52] This was not a case where a range of reasonable policy options for remedying the defect existed, or where the interests of other groups not before the Court would potentially be prejudiced by a reading in order.

The Court held that it was not appropriate to specify a comprehensive list of factors that would be relevant to the exercise of the judicial discretion in these circumstances, given the range of different circumstances in which execution against the homes of debtors could be sought to satisfy a debt.[53] However, it held that some guidelines should nonetheless be provided to ensure proper consideration of the constitutionally protected housing rights of debtors.[54] In this respect the Court endorsed a proportionality inquiry in which the creditor's interests in obtaining payment of a debt were weighed against 'the interests of the judgment debtor in security of tenure in his or her home, particularly if the sale of the home is likely to render the judgment debtor and his or her family completely homeless'.[55] A central element in the proportionality inquiry is whether there are alternative mechanisms for the creditor to secure payment of the debt without resorting to the drastic step of execution against a person's home.[56]

The third case in which the 'reading in' remedy was granted is *Occupiers of 51 Olivia Road.*[57] Section 12(6) of the National Building Regulations and Building Standards Act 103 of 1977 ('NBRSA') was found to be inconsistent with s 26(3) of the Constitution in that it compelled people to leave their homes 'on pain of a criminal sanction in the absence of a court order'.[58] However, the Court held that it was not just and equitable to set the provisions of s 12(6) aside as it was 'appropriate to

---

49 See the discussion of the judgment in chapter 4, part 4.6.2.
50 Ibid. See the order of the Court at para 67.
51 Ibid para 63.
52 Ibid. See the order of the Court at para 67.
53 Ibid. See the limitations analysis, particularly paras 40–43, para 53.
54 Ibid para 56.
55 Ibid.
56 Ibid para 59.
57 Note 11 above.
58 Ibid para 49. See the discussion of the judgment in chapter 6, part 6.4.

encourage people to leave unsafe or unhealthy buildings in compliance with a court order for their eviction'.[59] A criminal sanction had this effect and reduced the need for a forced eviction at the instance of the State.[60] Accordingly the most effective means of remedying the constitutional defect was to read in the following proviso after the end of s 12(6):

> This subsection applies only to people who, after service upon them of an order of court for their eviction, continue to occupy the property concerned.[61]

The 'reading in' remedy was deemed appropriate as there was not a wide scope for legislative choice in remedying the unconstitutionality of the relevant provision.[62]

The Court also underscored that, before making an order for eviction in terms of the NBRSA, a court is obliged to 'take into account all relevant circumstances' as well as affording the occupier a reasonable time within which to vacate the property.[63] In other words, s 12 of the NBRSA had to be read so as to be consonant with s 26 of the Constitution.[64] Without striking down the legislative provisions giving local authorities the power to seek the eviction of people from unsafe buildings, the Court sought to bring them into conformity with housing rights and their underlying values. It did so through employing a combination of a 'reading in' remedy and reminding courts to read statutory provisions in conformity with constitutional rights. Of particular importance in this context, was the reminder to courts that the availability of alternative accommodation for those facing homelessness pursuant to an eviction was a relevant consideration in the exercise of their discretion.[65]

In conclusion, there is little principled distinction between the remedies of severance and 'reading in'.[66] Both are aimed at remedying a constitutional violation while preserving the legislative scheme as far as possible. Both may have budgetary implications and may, depending on the circumstances, interfere with the legislature's purpose to a greater or lesser extent. For example, where access to a benefit such as a social grant is subject to an unconstitutional condition, such as consent to excessively intrusive surveillance requirements, the constitutional defect may be remedied by the excision of the relevant condition. This may have the effect of increasing the number of grant

---

[59] Ibid para 50.

[60] The Court noted that the constitutionality of the use of criminal law to compel evictions of the poor was not raised, and expressly declined to express any opinion on it, save to note that s 12(6) of the NBRSA did not provide for imprisonment. Ibid para 50, n 42.

[61] Ibid para 51 and Order (6) para 54.

[62] Ibid para 51.

[63] Ibid para 50.

[64] Earlier in its judgment, the Court observed that the Supreme Court of Appeal had failed to appreciate that the statutory provisions providing for eviction in these circumstances had to be read consistently with the constitutionally guaranteed housing rights in s 27. See ibid paras 42–46.

[65] Ibid.

[66] This point was accepted by the Constitutional Court in *NCGLE v Minister of Home Affairs* (note 17 above) paras 67–68.

beneficiaries. Persons who were previously deterred owing to the invasion of privacy mandated by the offensive provision may now be willing to apply for the grant.[67]

Ultimately a court must weigh up whether the degree of intrusion in the legislative provisions through the remedies of severance or 'reading in' is warranted by the clear and immediate relief provided by a moderate degree of judicial re-drafting of a legislative provision in order to render it constitutionally compliant. As Ackermann J pointed out in *NCGLE v Minister of Home Affairs*:

> The only relevant enquiry is what the consequences of such an order are and whether they constitute an unconstitutional intrusion into the domain of the legislature. Any other conclusion would lead to the absurdity that the granting of a remedy would depend on the fortuitous circumstance of the form in which the legislature chose to enact the provision in question.[68]

Ultimately, whatever remedy is provided by the court, the legislature retains a discretion to amend the remedy through drafting an entirely new legislative scheme provided such a scheme is consistent with the Constitution.[69]

Severance and 'reading in' will generally not constitute appropriate relief in circumstances where there are a number of reasonable policy options available for remedying the defect.[70] The ultimate policy choice is likely to be more sustainable, effective and equitable if it is adopted by the relevant legislature after a broad and deep process of public debate and participation. Considerations of both institutional competence and democratic legitimacy are particularly acute in this context. Finally, the remedies of severance and 'reading in' will also be inappropriate when the constitutional defect can only be remedied through organs of state undertaking a series of positive steps and structural reforms over a period of time.[71]

8.3.4 Limiting the retrospective effect of declarations of invalidity

According to the doctrine of objective constitutional invalidity accepted by the court, unconstitutional conduct or legislation is deemed to be unconstitutional from the date of the conduct, or the coming into effect of the relevant legislation. If the legislation came into effect prior to the Constitution, then the invalidity dates from the date of the coming into force of the Constitution.[72]

---

[67] See, for example, the United States Supreme Court decision in *Wyman v James* 400 US 309 (1971) upholding intrusive conditions for accessing social benefits in the context of the United States. For a critique of the judgment, see T Ross 'The rhetoric of poverty: Their immorality, our helplessness' (1991) 79 *Geo LJ* 1499–1547 at 1522–1525.

[68] Note 17 above, para 68.

[69] See *Zondi v Member of the Executive Council for Traditional and Local Government Affairs* 2005 (3) SA 589 (CC), 2005 (4) BCLR 347 (CC) paras 121–123.

[70] Ibid para 123.

[71] See part 8.6 below.

[72] *Ferreira* (note 31 above) paras 27–28.

However, the courts have a discretion based on justice and equity in terms of s 172(1)(*b*)(ii) of the Constitution to limit the retrospective effect of the declaration of invalidity. In *S v Bhulwana; S v Gwadiso*[73] ('*Bhulwana*') the Court described the considerations relevant to the discretion to limit the retrospective effect of an order of invalidity in the following terms:

> Central to a consideration of the interests of justice in a particular case is that successful litigants should obtain the relief they seek. It is only when the interests of good government outweigh the interests of the individual litigants that the Court will not grant relief to successful litigants. In principle too, the litigants before the Court should not be singled out for the grant of relief, but relief should be afforded to all people who are in the same situation as the litigants.[74]

Thus a court must weigh the consideration of giving effective relief not only to the applicants, but other similarly situated groups against the potentially disruptive effects on the administration of justice of a retrospective order of invalidity.[75]

In *Occupiers of 51 Olivia Road*,[76] the Court held that it was not just and equitable for the 'reading in' of the provision for judicial oversight in s 12(6) of the NBRSA to operate retrospectively. The 'reading in' proviso was thus held not to apply to 'cases in which people have already been convicted of a contravention of s 12(6) of the Act and the period for lodging of an application for leave to appeal has expired with no notice of appeal having been lodged'.[77]

It is not clear why the Court did not give a similar order to that given in *National Coalition*[78] permitting the courts to condone a late noting of an appeal against any conviction in terms of s 12(6). The conviction of persons for failing to comply with an order to vacate their homes without judicial oversight amounts to a form of summary eviction which the Constitution expressly prohibits in terms of s 26(3). In these circumstances, it is questionable whether it is in accordance with justice and equity to allow such convictions to stand in the constitutional era.

8.3.5 Suspended declarations of invalidity

In terms of s 172(1)(*b*)(ii), a court may suspend a declaration of invalidity 'for any period and on any conditions, to allow the competent authority to correct the defect'. As Kent Roach and Geoff Budlender note, the suspended declaration of invalidity 'recognizes the need for positive government action to enforce rights'.[79] The effect of such an order is that an unconstitutional state of affairs is allowed to continue

---

[73] 1996 (1) SA 388 (CC), 1995 (12) BCLR 1579 (CC).
[74] Ibid para 32.
[75] See further in this regard Currie & De Waal (note 3 above) 208–209.
[76] Note 11 above.
[77] *Occupiers of 51 Olivia Road* (note 11 above) paras 52 and 54 (Order (7)).
[78] *NCGLE v Minister of Home Affairs* (note 17 above) paras 97 and 106 (Order para 2.2).
[79] K Roach & G Budlender 'Mandatory relief and supervisory jurisdiction: When is it appropriate, just and equitable' (2005) 122 *SALJ* 325–351 at 339.

for a temporary period, pending correction by the legislature or another competent authority. If the constitutional defect is cured before the expiry of the prescribed period, the declaration of invalidity is of no further consequence and the new law or conduct takes effect. If the competent authority fails to correct the constitutional defect before the expiry of the prescribed period, the declaration of invalidity in respect of the relevant law or conduct takes effect on the relevant date.[80]

The point of departure is the principle articulated in *Bhulwana*[81] that a successful litigant in constitutional litigation should ordinarily obtain the relief that they seek.[82] However, there are circumstances which warrant a departure from this principle in the form of a suspended declaration of invalidity.[83] As a declaration of invalidity ordinarily has immediate effect, the burden is on the party seeking the suspension order to provide information and arguments to the court in support of such an order.[84]

A suspension order will usually be an appropriate remedy in two primary circumstances. First, it comes into consideration when the immediate striking down of a statutory scheme would result in an unacceptable legal position. In these situations, as stated by Iain Currie and Johan De Waal, the courts 'must determine whether a declaration of invalidity with immediate effect will result in a situation that is more inconsistent with the Constitution than the existing situation'.[85] Typically this occurs when the immediate striking down of a legislative scheme results in a lacuna in the regulatory framework governing a particular sphere.[86]

Second, the context of a particular case may indicate that it is preferable to afford the appropriate authority an opportunity to design a comprehensive and balanced scheme to cure the constitutional defect, rather than the court attempting to cure the defect itself. This situation usually arises when there are a range of reasonable policy options to cure the defect and the particular choices are better made through democratic institutions and broad consultative processes. The deliberative ideals of transformative constitutionalism are better served in these circumstances by requiring an inclusive and transparent dialogue between institutions of government and civil

---

[80] See in this regard, *Executive Council, Western Cape Legislature v President of the Republic of South Africa* 1995 (4) SA 877 (CC), 1995 (10) BCLR 1289 (CC) para 106.

[81] Note 73 above.

[82] Ibid para 32.

[83] In *Minister of Home Affairs v Fourie (Doctors for Life International and Others, Amici Curiae); Lesbian and Gay Equality Project v Minister of Home Affairs* 2006 (1) SA 524 (CC), 2006 (3) BCLR 355 (CC), O'Regan J provides a succinct summary of the circumstances in which a departure from this principle is warranted (para 170).

[84] See *Mistry v Interim National Medical and Dental Council of South Africa* 1998 (4) SA 1127 (CC), 1998 (7) BCLR 880 (CC) para 37.

[85] Currie & De Waal (note 3 above) 212. See *S v Ntuli* 1996 (1) SA 1207 (CC), 1996 (1) BCLR 141 (CC) paras 24–28.

[86] See also *Moseneke v Master of the High Court* 2001 (2) SA 18 (CC), 2001 (2) BCLR 103 (CC).

society regarding the most effective and equitable manner of giving effect to the relevant constitutional right.[87]

However, it would be inappropriate to suspend an invalidity order when the effect thereof would be to allow a 'manifestly indefensible' violation of a constitutional right to continue.[88] The effect of a suspended declaration of invalidity may be to deprive a successful plaintiff of much needed relief or protection during the period of suspension. This undermines the ordinary principle that 'a successful litigant should receive at least some practical relief'.[89] However, as noted above, the Court has held that this is not 'an absolute rule'.[90]

A *via media* sanctioned by the Court has been the grant of interim relief to the applicants and others similarly situated. It has also issued guidelines to State officials on how they should deal with similar situations during the period of suspension. In this way, the courts have been placed in a position to mitigate the effects of an unconstitutional state of affairs during the period when an invalidity order is suspended. In *Zondi v Member of the Executive Council for Traditional and Local Government Affairs*[91] (*'Zondi'*) the Court declared certain provisions of the Pound Ordinance (KwaZulu-Natal) Act 32 of 1947, to be unconstitutional and invalid on the basis that they infringed the constitutional rights of access to courts and equality. The Court suspended the declaration of invalidity to permit the legislature to re-craft the leg-

87 See, for example, *Fraser v Childen's Court, Pretoria North* 1997 (2) SA 261 (CC), 1997 (2) BCLR 153 (CC); *Dawood* (note 24 above) para 63; and *Zondi* (note 69 above) para 128. As noted by Roach and Budlender (note 79 above), 'the delayed declaration of invalidity is often seen as a means to provide governments with space and time to select the precise means by which to comply with the Constitution' (340).

88 See, for example, *Coetzee* (note 28 above) para 18; *De Lange v Smuts NO* 1998 (3) SA 785 (CC), 1998 (7) BCLR 779 (CC) para 106. In *Bhe v Magistrate Khayelitsha (Commission for Gender Equality as Amicus Curiae); Shibi v Sithole; South African Human Rights Commission v President of the Republic of South Africa* 2005 (1) SA 580 (CC), 2005 (1) BCLR 1 (CC), the Court held that the importance of the rights in question and the vulnerability of the affected groups, meant that the Court could not 'afford to suspend the declaration of invalidity to a future date and leave the current legal regime in place pending rectification by the Legislature' (para 108). An immediate declaration of invalidity was accordingly given in respect of the customary law of primogeniture as regulated by the Black Administration Act 38 of 1927. Pending what it hoped would be expeditious legislative reform of the customary law of intestate succession, it put in place a 'substitute regime' based on s 1 of the Intestate Succession Act 81 of 1987 (with appropriate adaptations to cater for polygynous unions). See the Reform of Customary Law of Succession and Related Matters Bill B10 – 2008 which was opened for public comment. Available at http://www.pmg.org.za/bill/20080310-reform-customary-law-succession-and-regulation-related-matters-bill-b1 (accessed 21 July 2009).

89 *Fourie* (note 83 above) para 133.

90 Ibid.

91 Note 69 above.

islative provisions pertaining to the impounding of livestock.[92] However, it held that the infringement of constitutional rights during the period of the suspension of the invalidity order could 'not be allowed to continue in the interim'.[93] Pending the revision of the pound legislation the Court made a range of orders relating to notice of trespass to stockowners and judicial supervision of the process of sales in execution of impounded livestock.[94]

The difficulty in determining when it is appropriate to grant immediate judicial relief to litigants and other similarly situated groups as opposed to suspending a declaration of invalidity in order to allow the legislature to cure the defects is illustrated in *Fourie.*[95] The Court found the common-law definition of marriage and s 30(1) of the Marriage Act 25 of 1961 to be inconsistent with the Constitution to the extent that it did not permit same-sex couples to enjoy the status, entitlements, benefits and responsibilities it accords to heterosexual couples.[96] However, the Court declined to grant an immediate remedy reading the words 'or spouse' into s 30(1) of the Act to enable the applicants and other persons in same sex relationships to solemnise a valid marriage. The effect of such a remedy would have been to grant immediate relief to the applicants 'while at the same time leaving Parliament free, if it chose, to amend the law so as to provide an alternative statutory mechanism to enable same-sex couples to enjoy their constitutional rights as outlined in this judgment'.[97]

This form of relief was deemed inappropriate because the case involved status which required a secure remedy in the form of an 'enduring and stable' legislative framework as opposed to an ad hoc, temporary solution.[98] Referring to the 'deep public and private sensibilities' that the case evoked, the Court adopted the view that Parliament was the most appropriate institution to find 'the best ways of ensuring that same-sex couples are brought in from the legal cold'.[99] A further factor in the decision to grant a suspended declaration of invalidity in respect of the statutory and common-law regime pertaining to marriage was the different legislative options for enabling same-sex couples to enjoy the status, benefits and responsibilities accorded to heterosexual married couples.[100] At the same time the Court deemed it necessary to include 'certain guiding principles of special constitutional relevance' to avoid unnecessary litigation and disputes regarding what would constitute appropriate

---

92 It held that any attempt to excise or read words into the Ordinance would render the legislation 'unworkable' and amount to excessive judicial involvement with the details of law-making. *Zondi* (note 69 above) paras 126–127.

93 *Zondi* (note 69 above) para 129.

94 Ibid para 134 and the order at para 135.

95 Note 83 above.

96 Ibid paras 109 and 114.

97 Ibid para 135.

98 Ibid para 136.

99 Ibid para 138.

100 Ibid paras 139–147.

legislative recognition for gay couples.[101] The Court also declined to provide any interim remedy to enable the particular applicants and others in their position to solemnise a same-sex marriage during the period of suspension, as such a 'stop-gap' mechanism would not accord with the stability normally associated with a marriage commitment, nor enhance the dignity of same-sex relationships.[102]

In dissenting from the decision of the majority to suspend its declaration of invalidity in respect of the statutory and common law definition of marriage, O'Regan J reasoned as followed:

> There can be no doubt that it is necessary that unconstitutional laws be removed from our statute book by Parliament. It is equally necessary that provisions of the common law which conflict with the Constitution are developed in a manner that renders them in conformity with it. It would have been desirable if the unconstitutional situation identified in this matter had been resolved by Parliament without litigation. The corollary of this proposition, however, is not that this Court should not come to the relief of successful litigants, simply because an Act of Parliament conferring the right to marry on gays and lesbians might be thought to carry greater democratic legitimacy than an order of this Court. The power and duty to protect constitutional rights is conferred upon the courts and courts should not shrink from that duty. The legitimacy of an order made by the Court does not flow from the status of the institution itself, but from the fact that it gives effect to the provisions of our Constitution. Time and time again, there will be those in our broader community who do not wish to see constitutional rights protected, but that can never be a reason for a court not to protect those rights.[103]

This illustrates that it is often a difficult call whether immediate relief or a suspended declaration of invalidity should be granted. The view of the majority in *Fourie* was clearly motivated by a sense that an inclusive legislative process would produce a more widely accepted and sustainable legal regime for gay marriages. However, it was not prepared to leave Parliament entirely to its own devices and laid down the normative parameters within which the legislative deliberations should occur.[104]

In its decision in *Nyathi v MEC for the Department of Health, Gauteng*[105] ('*Nyathi*') the Constitutional Court held that it was appropriate to suspend its declaration of invalidity in respect of s 3 of the State Liability Act 20 of 1957 for a period of 12 months as the legislature was best placed to formulate appropriate procedures and accounting mechanisms to enable judgment creditors to execute against the assets of the State.[106] However, pending new legislation and in order to ensure that unsatisfied court orders were speedily settled, the Court assumed a supervisory jurisdiction over the State's compliance with these orders.[107]

---

[101] Ibid paras 148–153.
[102] Ibid para 154.
[103] Ibid para 171.
[104] See also notes 91-94 above and accompanying text.
[105] 2008 (5) SA 94 (CC), 2008 (9) BCLR 865 (CC).
[106] Ibid para 88.
[107] See further the discussion of *Nyathi* in part 8.9.3 below.

The question of whether a suspended declaration of invalidity could be extended after its expiration arose following the Constitutional Court's decision in *Mashavha v President of the Republic of South Africa*[108] ('*Mashavha*'). In this case the Court confirmed the High Court's declaration of invalidity of a presidential proclamation ceding the administration of the Social Assistance Act 59 of 1992 to the provincial governments on the grounds of its conflict with s 235(6) and (8), read with s 126 and sched 6 of the interim Constitution.[109] The order of invalidity was suspended for a period of 18 months, given the need for a holistic solution to problems plaguing the administration of social grants and the 'Herculean task' of establishing a new institutional framework for which the national government required sufficient time.[110] Specifically there were two Bills before Parliament at the time which aimed to deal comprehensively with the delivery of social assistance, namely the Social Security Agency Bill[111] and the new Social Assistance Bill.[112]

The sequel to the suspended declaration of invalidity in the *Mashavha* case was an urgent application by the Minister for Social Development together with provincial Executive Councils for direct access to the Constitutional Court seeking a further suspension of the invalidity order initially granted by the Court.[113] However, as the application was brought on the day following the expiry of the 18-month period, the Court held that it had no power to 'retrospectively extend' the suspension period and resuscitate legislation which had been declared invalid.[114] It would have been a different matter if the State had approached the Court for an extension of the suspension period prior to its expiry. The Court had previously held in *Zondi II*[115] that its remedial jurisdiction in terms of s 172(1) of the Constitution extended to varying the period of suspension and the conditions attached to suspension, if necessary, 'to reflect the justice and equity required by the facts of the case'.[116] However, this power only subsists during the period of the suspension order and terminates once the invalidity order comes into effect upon the lapsing of the period. If the purpose of suspended declarations of invalidity is to be served, it is thus essential that the State takes timeous positive action to ensure that a replacement legislative framework is put

[108] 2005 (2) SA 476 (CC), 2004 (12) BCLR 1243 (CC).

[109] The Court held that social assistance 'is a matter which cannot be regulated effectively by provincial legislation and that requires to be regulated or co-ordinated by uniform norms and standards that apply generally throughout the Republic, for effective performance'. Ibid para 57.

[110] *Mashavha* (note 108 above) para 69.

[111] This Bill was subsequently enacted as the South African Social Security Agency Act 9 of 2004.

[112] This Bill was subsequently enacted as the Social Assistance Act 13 of 2004.

[113] *Ex Parte: Minister of Social Development* 2006 (4) SA 309 (CC), 2006 (5) BCLR 604 (CC).

[114] Ibid paras 39–40. See also *Minister of Justice v Ntuli* (note 85 above).

[115] *Zondi v MEC, Traditional and Local Government Affairs* 2006 (3) SA 1 (CC), 2006 (3) BCLR 423 (CC) ('*Zondi II*').

[116] Ibid para 39.

in place prior to the expiry of the suspension period. If there are legitimate reasons for seeking an extension of the suspension order,[117] this application must be launched prior to the expiry of the relevant period.

A thorough substantive analysis of the rights implicated in a particular case is essential in determining whether a suspended declaration of invalidity constitutes an appropriate remedy as well as the terms of the suspension order. This is illustrated by the Supreme Court of Appeal's judgment in *City of Johannesburg v Mazibuko* ('*Mazibuko (SCA)*').[118] The Court found that the installation of prepayment water meters (PPMs) in Phiri, Soweto, was unlawful.[119] However, it held that an order obliging the City to remove the prepayment meters was not an appropriate remedy because the residents of Phiri were 'better off with meters and preferred to have them'.[120] The Court also accepted the following submissions of the City: there was no other mechanism which allowed a guaranteed monthly delivery of free water; the City had incurred a 'massive capital expenditure' through the installation of the meters; and the campaign to encourage residents to pay for water services (Operation Gcin'manzi') had been effective, 'enabling the City to plan for the extension of basic water infrastructure to the estimated 105 000 households that do not have access to basic water'.[121] The declaration of unlawfulness in respect of the PPMs was thus suspended for a two-year period to enable the City to amend its by-laws so as 'to legalise the use of prepayment meters in so far as it may be possible to do so'.[122] In this regard, the Supreme Court of Appeal was of the view that the City, by amending its bylaws, may 'to at least some extent ... alleviate the problems caused by the unauthorized installation of the prepayment meters'.[123] This would enable the City to retain the PPMs 'at least in respect of consumers who prefer to have them and possibly also in respect of those who cannot pay a deposit or who do not pay their accounts'.[124]

The Supreme Court of Appeal failed to engage substantively with the residents' arguments that the automatic disconnection of water through the PPMs breached their rights to procedurally fair administrative action in terms of the Promotion of Administrative Justice Act 3 of 2000 ('PAJA') and s 4(3) of the Water Services Act 108 of 1997. The latter provision requires fair and equitable procedures for the

---

117 See the separate concurring judgment of Ngcobo J in *Ex Parte: Minister of Social Development* (note 113 above) for an indication of the factors that the Court may consider relevant in an application for an extension of the suspension period (particularly at para 50).

118 2009 (3) SA 592 (SCA); 2009 (8) BCLR 791 (SCA) ('*Mazibuko (SCA)*').

119 See also the discussion of the mandatory order granted in this case in respect of the challenge pertaining to the sufficiency of the free water supply provided by the City at 8.5.3(*a*) below.

120 *Mazibuko* (note 118 above) para 59.

121 Ibid.

122 Ibid para 62. Order paras 5 and 6.

123 Ibid para 60.

124 Ibid.

discontinuation of people's water supply.[125] Similarly the Supreme Court of Appeal did not deal with the argument that the imposition of PPMs in impoverished black communities compared to the credit supply option offered to communities in historically white areas constituted unfair discrimination. Such discriminatory treatment arguably implicates various grounds of review in terms of PAJA.[126] As a result, the terms of the suspended order neglects these further dimensions of the alleged unlawfulness of the PPMs, and the impact thereof on impoverished communities such as the residents of Phiri.[127]

This analysis of the cases indicates that there are various considerations which should guide the exercise of a court's remedial discretion to suspend a declaration of invalidity. These include the importance of immediate relief to the litigants and others in a similar position; the need for equity and an opportunity for other social groups not represented in the litigation to be heard; and the particular institutional competencies of the various branches of government in relation to remedying the violation.[128] Giving proper weight to these considerations in the exercise of a court's remedial discretion depends on an in-depth analysis and appreciation of the social and political context in which a particular breach of constitutional rights occurs and the mechanisms which are likely to be the most effective and equitable in remedying the particular violation.

The Constitutional Court has attempted to balance and reconcile these considerations by crafting nuanced orders. Such orders have provided the legislature with an opportunity to cure the constitutional defect through appropriate legislation while ordering interim relief. The objective of these interim measures during the period of suspension is to minimise the impact of the temporary continuation of an unconstitutional state of affairs on litigants and similarly situated groups.

These types of orders illustrate a flexible, dialogic approach to the interaction between the judiciary, the other branches of government, and civil society

---

125 Compare in this regard, the judgment of Tsoka J in *Mazibuko v The City of Johannesburg (Centre on Housing Rights and Evictions as amicus curiae)* [2008] 4 All SA 471 (W) ('*Mazibuko (HC)*') paras 83–93. The High Court ordered the City to provide each applicant and other similarly placed residents of Phiri Township with 'the option of a metered water supply installed at the cost of the City of Johannesburg' (para 183.5).

126 Compare in this regard, the High Court judgment ibid paras 151–156.

127 See further the critique by J Dugard & S Liebenberg 'Muddying the waters: The Supreme Court of Appeal's judgment in the *Mazibuko* case' (2009) 10(2) *ESR Review* 11. The Constitutional Court judgment in *Mazibuko v City of Johannesburg (Centre on Housing Rights and Evictions as amicus curiae)* 2009 ZACC 28 was handed down on 8 October 2009. It is discussed in the postscript, chapter 9, part 9.4.

128 Thus, for example, in dissenting from the decision of the majority to suspend the declaration of invalidity in respect of the common-law definition of marriage in *Fourie* (note 83 above), O'Regan J noted that the courts bear a special responsibility for ensuring that the common law 'is in conformity with the Constitution' (para 167, citing *Carmichele v Minister of Safety and Security (Centre for Applied Legal Studies Intervening)* 2001 (4) SA 938 (CC), 2001 (10) BCLR 995 (CC) para 33 ('*Carmichele*')).

organisations in constitutional rights litigation. They also illustrate a concern to achieve a pragmatic, but substantively just resolution of the dispute in the context of the particular circumstances of the case. However, as the discussion of the suspended declaration of unlawfulness granted by the Supreme Court of Appeal in the *Mazibuko* cases suggests, the efficacy of the remedy depends on a substantive analysis of the full range of constitutional rights implicated in the particular case.

8.4 DECLARATIONS OF RIGHTS

8.4.1 General features

Section 38 of the Constitution specifically provides that a declaration of rights is one of the forms of 'appropriate relief' that a court may consider when it is approached by anyone alleging that their rights in the Bill of Rights are infringed or threatened. The Constitutional Court has distinguished its constitutional obligation in terms of s 172(1)(*a*) of the Constitution to declare law or conduct that is inconsistent with the Constitution invalid to the extent of its inconsistency from its power to make declaratory orders. Thus it has the power to make declaratory orders even where it has not found conduct to be in conflict with the Constitution.[129] A declaration of rights is an optional remedy which may constitute appropriate relief in the circumstances of a particular case.

In considering when declaratory orders should be made, the Court has held that the principles developed at common law and under s 19(1)(*a*)(iii) of the Supreme Court Act 59 of 1959[130] 'will provide helpful guidance'.[131] However, the particular context of constitutional matters may introduce different or additional considerations.[132]

Declaratory orders in which no consequential relief for any party is claimed, are not enforceable through, for example, contempt of court proceedings. However, as a

---

[129] *Metrorail* (note 2 above) para 106. Where law or conduct is found to be inconsistent with the Constitution, an invalidity order in terms of s 172(1)(*a*) of the Constitution is obligatory (ibid).

[130] Section 19(1)(*a*)(iii) provides that a High Court has the power in respect of persons or cases falling within its jurisdiction, 'in its discretion, and at the instance of any interested person, to enquire into and determine any existing, future or contingent right or obligation, notwithstanding that such person cannot claim any relief consequential upon the determination'. On declarations of rights, see generally A C Cilliers, C Loots & H C Nel *Herbstein and Van Winsen The Civil Practice of the High Courts and the Supreme Court of Appeal of South Africa* 5 ed (2009) chapter 43. A declaratory order is defined as 'an order by which a dispute over the existence of some legal right or obligation is resolved. The right or obligation can be existing, prospective or contingent and no specific consequential relief need by claimed' (1428 referring to *Naptosa v Minister of Education, Western Cape* 2001 (2) SA 112 (C) at 125).

[131] *Metrorail* (note 2 above) para 106.

[132] Ibid. See also *Islamic Unity Convention v Independent Broadcasting Authority* 2002 (4) SA 294 (CC), 2002 (5) BCLR 433 (CC).

declarator stipulates what parties' obligations are in terms of the law and Constitution, it is expected that they will adopt the necessary measures to comply therewith. In rejecting the argument made on behalf of the State in *Minister of Health v Treatment Action Campaign (No 2)*[133] ('*Treatment Action Campaign*') that a distinction should be drawn between declaratory and mandatory orders against Government, the Court held:

> Even simple declaratory orders against government or organs of State can affect their policy and may well have budgetary implications. Government is constitutionally bound to give effect to such orders whether or not they affect its policy and has to find the resources to do so.[134]

The Court has also confirmed that, while declaratory orders can be accompanied by mandatory and prohibitory orders, they can also stand on their own.[135] In *Rail Commuters Action Group v Transnet Ltd t/a Metrorail* ('*Metrorail*')[136] the Constitutional Court observed that a declaratory order 'is a flexible remedy which can assist in clarifying legal and constitutional obligations in a manner which promotes the protection and enforcement of our Constitution and its values'.[137]

A pure declaratory order in constitutional cases will usually describe the relevant breach of constitutional rights, but leave it to the executive and legislative branches of government to decide on the precise means or policy measures which should be adopted to remedy the breach.[138] The grant of exclusively declaratory relief is sometimes accompanied by a statement of confidence that the parties will take the necessary steps to comply with the order.[139]

Another circumstance in which declaratory relief may be appropriate is where a particular matter may be a moot issue between the parties, but the court nevertheless

---

[133] 2002 (5) SA 721 (CC), 2002 (10) BCLR 1033 (CC) para 12.

[134] Ibid para 99.

[135] Note 2 above, para 107.

[136] Ibid.

[137] Ibid.

[138] Ibid para 108. In the Canadian case of *Eldridge v British Columbia (Attorney General)* [1997] 3 SCR 624, the Canadian Supreme Court confined itself to a declaratory order to the effect that the government of British Columbia had breached s 15 (right to equality) of the Canadian Charter of Rights and Freedoms by failing to provide sign language interpretation for deaf patients in the health system. A declaration, as opposed to some form of injunctive relief, was considered an appropriate order as there were a 'myriad options available to the government that may rectify the unconstitutionality of the current system', and it was not 'the court's role to dictate how this is to be accomplished' (paras 95–96).

[139] Thus in *Metrorail* (note 2 above) the Court declared that respondents 'have an obligation to ensure that reasonable measures are taken to provide for the security of rail commuters whilst they are making use of rail transport services' provided by the respondents (para 111). The Court held that it was not persuaded that the declaratory order should be accompanied by some form of mandatory relief as '[t]here is nothing to suggest on the papers that Metrorail and the Commuter Corporation will not take steps to comply with the terms of the order' (para 109).

considers it appropriate to confirm that a constitutional violation has occurred.[140] Among the factors which will guide a Court in determining whether it is in the interests of justice that it should hear a matter even if it is moot is 'the nature and extent of the practical effect that any possible order might have' as well as 'the importance of the issue'.[141] A declaratory order in circumstances where there is no live controversy between the parties serves the purpose of providing a public, authoritative confirmation that the applicant's constitutional rights have been violated. It may also assist in deterring future violations of constitutional rights by clarifying the constitutional duties which apply in particular circumstances. However, declaratory orders will not be appropriate when they do not provide effective relief for a particular constitutional breach and in deterring future violations.

The following section examines the repercussions of the purely declaratory orders made in the *Grootboom* judgment[142] as a case study illustrating the shortcomings, but also the potential far-reaching effects of such orders in socio-economic rights litigation.

8.4.2 The declaratory orders made in *Grootboom* and their impact

After allowing the appeal in part,[143] the Court in *Grootboom* made three declaratory orders, specifying the nature of the State's obligations in terms of s 26 of the Constitution in relation to its housing programme in the area of the Cape Metropolitan Council.

First, it declared that s 26(2) of the Constitution 'requires the State to devise and implement within its available resources a comprehensive and co-ordinated program progressively to realise the right of access to adequate housing'.[144] Second, it held that this programme 'must include reasonable measures such as, but not necessarily limited to, those contemplated in the Accelerated Managed Land Settlement Program,[145] to provide relief for people who have no access to land, no roof over their heads, and who are living in intolerable conditions or crisis situations'.[146] Finally, it held that at the date of the launch of the application, the State housing programme in the area of

---

[140] See, for example, *MEC for Education: KwaZulu-Natal v Pillay* 2008 (1) SA 474 (CC), 2008 (2) BCLR 99 (CC).

[141] Ibid para 32. See also *Independent Electoral Commission v Langeberg Municipality* 2001 (3) SA 925 (CC), 2001 (9) BCLR 883 (CC) para 11.

[142] Note 10 above.

[143] The judgment of the Constitutional Court in *Grootboom* is discussed in chapter 4, part 4.3.

[144] *Grootboom* (note 10 above) para 99 (Order para 2(*a*)).

[145] This programme had been designed by the Cape Metropolitan Council to assist in meeting urgent short-term housing needs while the medium- and long-term objectives of the nationwide housing programme were being fulfilled. However, at the time when litigation in the *Grootboom* case commenced, the programme had not been implemented. See *Grootboom* (note 10 above) paras 60–65.

[146] *Grootboom* (note 10 above) para 99 (Order para 2(*b*)).

the Cape Metropolitan Council fell short of compliance with these requirements 'in that it failed to make reasonable provision within its available resources for people in the Cape Metropolitan area with no access to land, no roof over their heads, and who were living in intolerable conditions or crisis situations'.[147]

In its judgment the Court elaborated on the key flaw in the State's housing programme. Despite major achievements in the progressive realisation of access to housing, there was 'no express provision to facilitate access to temporary relief for people who have no access to land, no roof over their heads, for people who are living in intolerable conditions and for people who are in crisis because of natural disasters such as floods or fires, or because their homes are under threat of demolition'.[148] These immediate needs could be met 'by relief short of housing which fulfils the requisite standards of durability, habitability and stability encompassed by the definition of housing development in the [Housing] Act [107 of 1997]'.[149]

It has been argued that the Grootboom community did not receive adequate relief due to the fact that the Court confined itself to making purely declaratory orders.[150] However, a widely misunderstood feature of the case is the fact that at the hearing of the case before the Constitutional Court, the 'immediate crisis situation' of the applicants was the subject of a settlement agreement between the community and the relevant organs of state.

Some four months after argument in the case (but before judgment was handed down), an urgent application was made to Court on behalf of the Grootboom community in which it was revealed that the government had failed to comply with the agreement. Consequently, the Court, 'after communication with the parties, crafted an order putting the municipality on terms to provide certain rudimentary services'.[151] In terms of this order the respondents were ordered to provide basic sanitation services, water and R200 000 for the purposes of waterproofing the applicant's existing accommodation.[152] The order specifies the nature and number of toilets and taps to be made available to the Grootboom community, as well as the requirement that their shelters be adequately waterproofed. The order also made provision for the provincial and local government to report back to the court on the implementation of the order by 6 November 2000 and for a response thereto by the Grootboom community.

The main difficulty with the settlement agreement, which was made an order of Court, is that it failed to make any express or appropriate provision for the

---

147 Ibid. (Order para 2(*c*)).

148 *Grootboom* (note 10 above) para 52.

149 Ibid.

150 Swart (note 8 above) 221.

151 *Grootboom* (note 10 above) para 5.

152 Order dated 21 September 2000 on file with the author. For a detailed account of the *Grootboom* litigation and the implementation of the various orders made, see K Pillay 'Implementation of *Grootboom*: Implications for the enforcement of socio-economic rights' (2002) 6 *LDD* 255–277.

accommodation of the Grootboom community in the medium to long term. It appears to have been tacitly accepted between the parties that the community could continue to reside on the Wallacedene sports field on a temporary basis until housing became available to them under one of the State's housing programmes for the broader Wallacedene area. As Kameshni Pillay points out in her study of the implementation of the various *Grootboom* orders, the main difficulty with the settlement order is that it represented an ad hoc arrangement and did not make any provision for security of tenure for the community. She observes that the lack of permanent resolution to their housing problems was a source of great insecurity for the community.[153] Their accommodation on the sports field was intended to be temporary, and over the period of the nine years since the judgment was handed down, the Grootboom community has been gradually relocated to permanent accommodation provided in the broader Wallacedene housing development programme.[154]

Given the negotiated settlement which was made an order of court, the Constitutional Court was relieved of the burden of having to decide on direct relief for the Grootboom community in its judgment.[155] The Court thus confined itself to considering whether the State's housing programme in the area of the Cape Metropolitan Council was consistent with s 26 of the Constitution. It is in this context that the declaratory orders set out above were made.[156]

There was a considerable delay in adopting the programme for urgent housing needs envisaged in the Court's declaratory orders. Only in August 2003 did the national and provincial ministers of housing approve a new programme entitled '*Housing Assistance in Emergency Housing Situations*'. This programme was incorporated in the National Housing Code published in terms of s 4 of the Housing Act 107 of 1997. It came into operation in April 2004.[157]

---

[153] Pillay ibid 265.

[154] The schedule of relocation to permanent accommodation has depended on whether various members of the community selected contractor-built housing or if they elected to participate in the provision of housing through the Peoples' Housing Process (PHP). Telephonic interview with Steve Kahanovitz of the Legal Resources Centre on 28 July 2009. The Legal Resources Centre represented parts of the Wallacedene community subsequent to the handing down of the *Grootboom* judgment by the Constitutional Court.

[155] The court *a quo* in *Grootboom* declared that the State was obliged to provide shelter to the applicant children and their parents until such time as the parents were able to shelter their own children. See *Grootboom v Oostenberg Municipality* 2000 (3) BCLR 277 (C) at 293H-J. Although the court was not prescriptive as to the nature of the shelter to be provided, it provisionally indicated 'that tents, portable latrines and a regular supply of water (albeit transported) would constitute the bare minimum' (292I-J–293A-C). It also ordered the respondents to present a compliance report to the court on its implementation of the order (294A-C).

[156] See notes 144 to 147 above and accompanying text.

[157] National Housing Code, chapter 12, *Housing Assistance in Emergency Housing Situations* ('*Emergency Housing Programme*'). The Housing Code which contains the details of national

The South African Human Rights Commission, which had intervened as a joint *amici curiae* in the case, indicated that it would 'monitor and, if necessary, report' in terms of its constitutional powers and functions on the efforts made by the State to comply with its s 26 obligations in accordance with the judgment.[158] However, the Court's order does not expressly mention any involvement by the Human Rights Commission in the monitoring of the implementation of the order. Subsequent to the judgment, the Commission was involved in relatively extensive efforts to monitor the plans to provide permanent accommodation for the Grootboom community within the Cape Metropolitan Council's long-term Development Plan for Wallacedene.[159]

The Commission appeared to be under the impression that it was bound to report to the Constitutional Court on its monitoring of the respondents' implementation of the judgment. In a letter to the Constitutional Court dated 14 November 2001, the Commission reported in relative detail on the difficulties which the relevant organs of state were experiencing in implementing the order.[160] These included a dispute between the City of Cape Town (the local authority) and the Western Cape Provincial Government as to which organ bore responsibility for the implementation of the order. There also appeared to be a lack of clarity regarding the meaning and implications of the declaratory order handed down by the Constitutional Court. The Human Rights Commission itself appeared uncertain as to whether the steps taken by the local and provincial government in relation to the Grootboom community constituted adequate compliance with the court order.[161] Given the declaratory nature of the order, the Court was no longer seized of the *Grootboom* case. Chaskalson P (as he then was) advised that the Commission's reports should be directed to the legislature

housing policy is binding on the provincial and local spheres of government in terms of s 4(6) of the Housing Act.

[158] The powers of the South African Human Rights Commission are set out in s 184 of the Constitution. They include the power 'to investigate and to report on the observance of human rights'; and 'to take steps to secure appropriate redress where human rights have been violated' (s 184(2)(*a*) and (*b*)). In addition, the Commission is obliged annually to require relevant organs of state to provide it with information on the measures they have taken towards the realisation of the various constitutionally entrenched socio-economic rights (s 184(3)). For an account of the Commission's role in terms of s 184(3), see D G Newman 'Institutional monitoring of social and economic rights: A South African case study and a new research agenda' (2003) 19 *SAJHR* 189–216. The powers and functions of the Human Rights Commission are further regulated by the Human Rights Commission Act 54 of 1994.

[159] Pillay (note 152 above) 271–274.

[160] Letter addressed by the Chairperson of the South African Human Rights Commission, Dr Barney Pityana to the Justices of the Constitutional Court in the matter of *Government of South Africa v Grootboom and Others*, CCT 11/00 dated 14 November 2001 (copy on file with author).

[161] Ibid 6.

and possibly the public, based on its investigations as well as the information provided to the Commission by organs of state in terms of s 184(3) of the Constitution.[162]

As Kameshni Pillay points out, both the provincial and local government appear to have interpreted their obligations in terms of the *Grootboom* judgment to encompass the formulation and implementation of a plan for permanent housing for all people within the broader Wallacedene area.[163] Moreover, the Commission's monitoring efforts were concentrated on the housing plans of the local and provincial government for people living in the Wallacedene area of the Western Cape. There does not appear to have been a sustained effort to monitor the general obligation of the State in terms of s 26 of the Constitution to devise and implement a programme to cater for all those in urgent housing need.[164]

It remains to be tested whether the Emergency Housing Programme in Chapter 12 of the National Housing Code fulfils the constitutional obligations in terms of s 26 as elaborated in the *Grootboom* judgment. The main objective of the programme is 'to provide temporary assistance in the form of secure access to land and/or basic municipal engineering services and/or shelter in a wide range of situations of exceptional urgent housing need through the allocation of grants to municipalities'.[165] An 'emergency housing situation' is deemed to exist when the Emergency Housing Steering Committee on application by a municipality and/or the province deems that people, 'owing to situations beyond their control', face homelessness in a range of situations.[166]

The programme is intended to benefit all groups who are unable to address their emergency housing needs from their own resources and may be extended to a number of groups not catered for in the standard qualification criteria pertaining to other housing programmes in the Code such as those earning more than the minimum prescribed amount, unlawful residents, minors heading households, persons

---

162 Transcript of letter to the Chairperson of the South African Human Rights Commission dated 10 December 2001 (on file with author).

163 Pillay (note 152 above) 271–274.

164 Pillay reports that according to interviews with staff of the South African Human Rights Commission, 'numerous letters were addressed to the [National] Department [of Housing] but no response was received'. Ibid 272.

165 *Emergency Housing Programme* (note 157 above) 12.2.1.

166 These include homelessness as a result of natural or man-made disasters such as industrial accidents; residence in dangerous conditions such as on land which is prone to dangerous flooding or dolomitic undermining; living in the way of engineering or other services or proposed services; eviction or threatened imminent eviction from land or from unsafe buildings in situations where proactive steps ought to be taken to forestall such consequences; the demolition or threatened imminent demolition of their homes; displacement as a result of a state of civil conflict or unrest; living in conditions that pose immediate threats to life, health and safety and require emergency assistance; or are otherwise in a situation of exceptional housing need that can reasonably be addressed only by resettlement or other appropriate assistance in terms of the programme. Ibid 12.3.1(*a*) and (*b*).

without dependants, and persons who have previously received housing assistance.[167] A dedicated fund is established for the programme within the budget of the National Department of Housing under the control of the Director-General. Applications for assistance in the form of grants must be submitted by municipalities via the Housing Department of their provincial government.[168] The grant must be used by municipalities to provide land and the infrastructure for services and shelter.[169]

The programme in its current form raises two major concerns from the perspective of providing relief for those in urgent housing need or living in intolerable conditions.

The first concern is the design of the programme and whether it fulfils the criteria of providing urgent assistance for those in housing crises. In her evaluation of the emergency housing programme, Jeannie van Wyk points out that it is a relatively time-consuming process to access land, apply the relevant standards and allocate grants under the programme.[170] It requires proactive planning and the anticipation of evictions or other causes of homelessness so that one of the measures envisaged in Chapter 12 of the Code may already be in place to deal with the housing crisis when it occurs. The programme cannot be accessed 'in a matter of hours' and is thus unsuited to dealing with a housing crisis that has already occurred for which there has been no prior planning.[171]

The need for a proper assessment of potential housing crises and the preparation of a plan for submission to the relevant provincial authorities was also underscored by the Supreme Court of Appeal in *City of Johannesburg v Rand Properties (Pty) Ltd*.[172] It held that it was not satisfied that the City had pursued with 'any vigour' an application under Chapter 12 to deal with the crisis of homelessness that would be triggered by the eviction of persons from accommodation deemed unsafe by the City in terms of the provisions of the NBRSA.[173] The Court put it thus: 'Writing a letter or two is not enough. Plans are one thing, execution is another.'[174]

The second concern relates to the ambit of the emergency housing programme. The definition of 'emergency housing situations' is on its face fairly broad and would

---

[167] Ibid 12.3.2.

[168] Ibid 12.3.3. Applications for assistance are considered by the Emergency Housing Steering Committee (EHSC). For a summary of the procedures to be followed by local authorities to access emergency housing assistance, see J van Wyk 'The complexities of providing emergency housing assistance in South Africa' (2007) 1 *TSAR* 35–55 at 43–44.

[169] Ibid 12.3.4.

[170] Ibid 44.

[171] Ibid.

[172] 2007 (6) SA 417 (SCA), 2007 (6) BCLR 643 (SCA) para 26. The judgment is discussed in chapter 6, part 6.4.

[173] Ibid para 77.

[174] Ibid.

seem to extend to the situations contemplated in the declaratory orders made in the *Grootboom* case.[175]

However, in a judgment of the South Gauteng High Court, Epstein AJ rejected a claim by the Harry Gwala Informal Settlement for temporary sanitation facilities and high mast lighting in key areas to enhance community safety and access by emergency vehicles.[176] It was argued on behalf of the community that the conditions in which they were living posed an immediate threat to their lives, health and safety and they were accordingly entitled to emergency assistance in terms of Chapter 12 of the Housing Code.[177] Acting Justice Epstein held that it was apparent from the affidavits and photographs taken of the settlement that the applicants live in 'squalid and putrid conditions'.[178] Nevertheless, he held that their situation did not fall within the ambit of an emergency housing situation in terms of Chapter 12 as they had access at least to a basic level of services consisting of water, refuse removal and pit latrines.[179] Moreover, their situation was not 'for reasons beyond their control' in that they had an option to relocate to another area (Chief Albert Luthuli Extension 4) where they would have access to permanent services.[180] Finally, they were not in a situation where their existing shelter has been destroyed or damaged.[181] The applicants' reliance on Chapter 13 of the Housing Code dealing with the provisions of grants to municipalities for the purposes of the *in situ* upgrading of informal settlements was also rejected by the Court.[182]

This judgment raises the question whether Chapter 12 can be invoked in situations where communities are living in conditions of chronic squalor and insecurity due to a lack of basic services. Epstein AJ was of the view that such situations which comprised part of the 'normal' reality of communities living in informal settlements such as Harry Gwala settlement did not fall within the remit of Chapter 12.[183] However,

---

[175] See notes 144 to 147 above and accompanying text.

[176] *Nokotyana v The Ekurhuleni Metropolitan Municipality* Case No: 08/17815 ZAGPJHC 14 (unreported judgment of 24 March 2009). An order by consent was granted pertaining to the provision by the respondent municipality of communal water taps and refuse removal (para 7).

[177] Ibid paras 14 and 18.

[178] Ibid para 19.

[179] Ibid.

[180] Ibid. The applicants disputed that they would have access to schools and electricity in Extension 4, and their refusal to relocate was not without reason (para 4).

[181] Ibid.

[182] Ibid paras 21–30.

[183] The judgment notes that the community have been living on the land in question since the 1980s. Ibid para 18. An appeal against this judgment was argued in the Constitutional Court on 11 August 2009. The judgment in *Nokotyana v The Ekurhuleni Metropolitan Municipality* [2009] ZACC 33 was handed down on 19 November 2009. It is briefly discussed in the postscript, chapter 9, part 9.3.

the *Grootboom* judgment contemplates urgent relief not only for those who are literally homeless or landless, but also for those 'living in intolerable conditions'.[184]

There can be little doubt that a lack of access to hygienic toilets and the absence of street lighting pose a threat to people's health and safety. For example, women are particularly vulnerable to violence in unlit public spaces, and access to emergency health and other services is seriously compromised when emergency vehicles cannot find their way in informal settlements. As the Court noted in *Grootboom*, housing 'entails more than bricks and mortar'.[185] It includes essential social services such as water and sanitation.[186] Squalid and unsanitary conditions due to a lack of decent services should not be 'normalised' by refusing to recognise the very real threats to health and safety which they pose. Such conditions require an urgent response via the mechanism of Chapter 12 of the National Housing Code or other appropriate programmes. The absence of programmes catering for people's urgent needs in these circumstances renders all spheres of government, but particularly national government,[187] vulnerable to a constitutional challenge for failing to take reasonable measures to realise the socio-economic rights in ss 26 and 27.

The State was tardy in adopting the programme envisaged in the declaratory orders in the *Grootboom* case, and the constitutionality of the emergency housing programme eventually adopted has yet to be tested. Nevertheless, the *Grootboom* order has had a significant impact on the jurisprudence pertaining to the eviction of people from their homes. As discussed in chapter 6, various courts have found that the relevant local authority failed to comply with its obligations in terms of *Grootboom* to develop and implement a housing programme for those in desperate need. This finding has significantly influenced the types of orders handed down in eviction applications. These have included the dismissal or postponement of the main eviction application, mandatory orders against the local authority concerned to ensure the provision of emergency accommodation to those evicted who were in urgent housing need, and orders requiring officials to 'engage meaningfully' with those facing eviction with a view to finding humane solutions to their housing plight.[188]

A further trend has been for the courts to grant a temporary stay of eviction applications brought by private landowners in terms of the Prevention of Illegal Eviction from and Unlawful Occupation of Land Act 19 of 1998 ('PIE'), pending the joinder of the relevant local authority. The purpose of such joinder is to enable the local

---

[184] See notes 146–147 and accompanying text.

[185] *Grootboom* (note 10 above) para 35.

[186] Ibid.

[187] In *Grootboom* (note 10 above) para 40, the Court held that all spheres of government were responsible for implementing part of the comprehensive, co-ordinated programme required to realise socio-economic rights, but that 'the national sphere of government must assume responsibility for ensuring that laws, policies, programs and strategies are adequate to meet the State's s 26 obligations.'

[188] See particularly the jurisprudence discussed in chapter 6, parts 6.2–6.5. See also part 8.5.3(*b*) below.

authority to be involved in tripartite mediation[189] and to place information before the court on its plans and programmes for the provision of temporary emergency accommodation to those in desperate housing need.[190]

8.4.3 Declaration of rights as appropriate relief in socio-economic rights cases

It has been suggested that the Court in *Grootboom* should have been more proactive in compelling, and possibly even supervising, the implementation of an emergency housing programme.[191] However, the order was clearly intended by the Court to prod Government into developing an appropriate programme for responding to urgent housing needs. The declaratory order was an expression of faith in Government's willingness and capacity to do so. This is consistent with the general remedial approach of the Court to allow Government to exercise the first choice when there is a range of complex policy choices for giving effect to a particular right. A dialogic conception of the relationship between the different branches of government and civil society would also favour remedies which serve as a catalyst for Government to adopt appropriate programmes and legislation to give effect to constitutional rights through transparent and participatory processes.[192]

As previously noted, the *Grootboom* judgment has had a far-reaching impact on the jurisprudence pertaining to the eviction of people from their homes. Although the courts have not affirmed an unqualified right to alternative accommodation for persons evicted from their homes, the availability of alternative accommodation for those who face homelessness as a result of an eviction is a central consideration in determining whether an eviction order should be made. In a number of cases, eviction orders have either been refused due to the lack of temporary alternative accommodation, or the grant of an eviction order has been accompanied by mandatory orders against local authorities to ensure the provision of some form of alternative accommodation.[193] These types of orders are usually made when an unlawful occupation results from a crisis of homelessness and poverty (as in the *Grootboom* case), as opposed to an orchestrated attempt to invade land to gain some advantage in the

---

[189] On the role of municipalities in facilitating mediation in relation to the eviction of unlawful occupiers, see s 7 of PIE and *Port Elizabeth Municipality v Various Occupiers* 2005 (1) SA 217 (CC), 2004 (12) BCLR 1268 (CC) ('*Port Elizabeth Municipality*') paras 39–47. The developments are discussed in chapter 6, part 6.2.2.

[190] See the jurisprudence discussed in chapter 6, part 6.3.

[191] See, for example, the following academic criticisms of the purely declaratory nature of the order in *Grootboom*: Pillay (note 152 above) 274–276; D Bilchitz 'Giving socio-economic rights teeth: The minimum core and its importance' (2002) 119 *SALJ* 484–501 at 500–501.

[192] On the potential of social rights litigation to stimulate democratic processes of transformation, see generally chapter 2, part 2.3.2. See also part 8.6 below.

[193] See note 188 above.

allocation of housing.[194] Moreover, as described above, public authorities have been required to 'engage meaningfully' with communities facing evictions in a number of cases.[195] These trends illustrate how general declaratory orders describing the obligations of the State to devise and implement a reasonable programme to give effect to socio-economic rights can give rise to the grant of tangible relief to particular litigants in subsequent litigation.

However, the benefits of this dialogic and evolutionary approach must be weighed against the consequences for the applicants and similarly situated groups of being denied immediate relief. The delays in implementing the programme specified in the *Grootboom* orders undoubtedly had serious repercussions for those in urgent housing need. This has been mitigated to some extent by the reluctance of the courts to grant eviction orders without being satisfied that the authorities have made provision for some form of alternative accommodation.

Although the emergency housing programme has now been enacted, there are evident problems with its implementation. This may be due to defects in the design of the programme by the national housing department, or to a failure by provincial and local spheres of government to plan proactively in order to access funds under the programme for the purposes of dealing effectively with housing crises within their jurisdiction. Until the constitutionality of the programme itself is challenged or a new programme developed, the responsibility rests with the courts to ensure that disadvantaged groups facing eviction are not left without a roof over their heads.

In the light of the *Grootboom* experience, it is submitted that three primary considerations should guide a court in determining whether a purely declaratory order constitutes appropriate relief for infringements of constitutional rights. In the first place, a court must consider the consequences of a lack of immediate and effective relief for those whose socio-economic rights have been violated. If delayed relief will have a serious impact on the claimants and others in similar circumstances, a purely declaratory order will not constitute appropriate relief. The deliberative nature of our constitutional democracy will be subverted if immediate and concrete forms of material relief are not given to those who are facing severe forms of socio-economic deprivation. Their voices will be effectively silenced if the courts do not ensure expeditious interventions to meet their basic needs.[196]

Second, a purely declaratory order is only appropriate when a court has good grounds for believing that the State understands its obligations, and that it will take effective and expeditious steps to fulfil the obligations described in the order.

---

194 *Grootboom* (note 10 above) para 92; *Port Elizabeth Municipality* (note 189 above) para 55; *President of the Republic of South Africa v Modderklip Boerdery (Pty) Ltd* 2005 (5) SA 3 (CC), 2005 (8) BCLR 786 (CC) para 49 ('*Modderklip (CC)*'). See also G Budlender 'The right to alternative accommodation in forced evictions' in J Squires, M Langford & B Thiele (eds) *The Road to a Remedy: Current Issues in the Litigation of Economic, Social and Cultural Rights* (2005) 127–138.

195 See notes 188–190 above and accompanying text.

196 See also the discussion in part 8.5.3(a) below.

A final consideration is whether the applicants and groups in similar circumstances will have an opportunity to engage meaningfully with the relevant organs of state on the measures to be adopted to give effect to the order. Courts should be particularly alert to facts indicating that the avenues for litigants and broader civil society organisations to influence the decisions pertaining to the adoption of a particular programme are effectively blocked. The deliberative ideals of the Constitution will be undermined by an order which leaves the method of compliance entirely in the hands of organs of the state.

The Court's confidence that the State would take steps to comply with its declaratory order in *Grootboom* may have been warranted in the light of the fact that it was the first major test case in which the Court elaborated on the nature of the obligations imposed by s 26 of the Constitution. However, in the light of the evident failure of all three spheres of government to fulfil their duties expeditiously in terms of the judgment, a more robust remedial approach is called for in subsequent cases in which it is shown that the State has failed to comply with its positive obligations in terms of s 26.

8.5 PROHIBITORY AND MANDATORY INTERDICTS AND ORDERS

8.5.1 Introduction

The purpose of interdicts is to prevent or to compel certain conduct. As Currie and De Waal point out, they are essentially aimed at future events.[197] Section 38 of the Constitution enables a litigant not only to seek 'appropriate relief' for infringements of rights that have already occurred, but also to prevent 'threatened' infringements. The common-law requirements for a permanent interdict are 'a clear right, injury actually committed or reasonably apprehended, and the absence of similar protection by any other ordinary remedy'.[198]

The common-law requirements for the granting of an interim interdict are a *prima facie* right, a well-grounded apprehension of irreparable harm, the absence of an alternative satisfactory remedy, and the balance of convenience favouring the granting of interim relief. However, these traditional requirements are subject to development in terms of s 39(2) of the Constitution to provide effective and appropriate relief for violations of constitutional rights.[199]

8.5.2 Prohibitory orders

In the context of socio-economic rights cases, a prohibitory interdict may be considered in situations where there is a threatened interference with people's existing

[197] Currie & De Waal (note 3 above) 216.

[198] *Setlogelo v Setlogelo* 1914 AD 221 at 227.

[199] See, for example, the discussion by Currie and De Waal (note 3 above) 216 at n 142 of the development of the standard of 'a serious question to be tried' in relation to interim interdicts in various constitutional matters, particularly by the Land Claims Court.

access to socio-economic rights. This could include, for example, the expulsion of a child from school, the termination of social security benefits, or the discontinuation of water services.

In *Residents of Bon Vista Mansions v Southern Metropolitan Local Council*,[200] Budlender AJ held that the disconnection by a local authority of the existing water supply to the applicants constituted a *prima facie* breach of its constitutional duty to respect the right of (existing) access to water, which required constitutional justification.[201] The applicants had shown that they had a *prima facie* right to a continuing supply of water which was being infringed by the disconnection.[202] They had no other satisfactory remedy and the balance of convenience 'weighed heavily in their favour'.[203] Accordingly an interim interdict was granted in terms of which the Council was ordered to restore the water supply to Bon Vista Mansions, where the applicants lived.[204]

8.5.3 Mandatory orders

Where the violation of a socio-economic right consists of a failure to take particular steps or adopt measures in order to give effect to a positive duty, a mandatory order may constitute appropriate relief. Such an order requires the respondent to act in the manner specified in the particular order.[205] As is the case in relation to prohibitory orders, a failure to comply with such an order exposes the respondent to the risk of being held in contempt of court and committed to prison.[206] The common law has, however, precluded committal for contempt in relation to orders for the payment of a sum of money (orders *ad pecuniam solvendam*). The latter issue is discussed further in part 8.9 below in the context of the enforcement of judgments sounding in money against organs of state.

This part focuses on two types of mandatory orders which are typically encountered in socio-economic rights litigation: orders for the provision of benefits and services, and orders of 'meaningful engagement' and mediation.

---

[200] 2002 (6) BCLR 625 (W).

[201] Ibid para 27.1.

[202] Ibid para 34.

[203] Ibid.

[204] Ibid para 35.

[205] On the power of the courts to make mandatory orders against an organ of state, see generally *Saunderson* (note 4 above) para 39; *New National Party of South Africa v Government of the Republic of South Africa* 1999 (3) SA 191 (CC), 1999 (5) BCLR 489 (CC) para 46.

[206] Contempt proceedings are usually initiated through the issuing of a rule nisi, requiring the respondent to show cause as to why they should not be held in contempt before a committal order is granted. See *Eveleth v Minister of Home Affairs* 2004 (3) All SA 322 (T), 2004 (11) BCLR 1223 (T). On the procedures and standard of proof required for committal to prison for contempt of court, see *Fakie NO v CCII Systems (Pty) Ltd* 2006 (4) SA 326 (SCA) ('*Fakie NO*').

(*a*) Orders for the provision of benefits and services

The *Treatment Action Campaign* judgment placed it beyond doubt that the courts are not confined to making general declaratory orders relating to the State's non-compliance with the constitutional duties imposed by socio-economic rights. Neither are the courts limited to issuing general mandatory orders requiring the State to adopt a 'reasonable programme' to give effect to particular socio-economic rights.[207] In appropriate circumstances, a mandatory order may be issued requiring the State to provide or extend the provision of socio-economic goods and services to defined groups or classes of persons.

The primary underlying concern with orders requiring concrete benefits to be provided to particular groups relates to the institutional capacity and legitimacy of the courts to make decisions which have direct policy and distributional implications.[208] A court may not be in a position to ascertain whether its order will have inequitable consequences for other disadvantaged groups who are not represented before the court. In *Grootboom*, the Court expressed its disquiet regarding the equity of an order which gave 'a special dispensation' to the respondent community 'on account of their extraordinary circumstances' when 'it is a painful reality that their circumstances were no worse than those of thousands of other people, including young children, who remained at Wallacedene'.[209] Albie Sachs describes this dilemma as follows:

> [C]ould it be that the Constitution implied that those individuals with the sharpest elbows (and the best lawyers) would get a house, water and electricity? Should the Constitution be read as handing over to each judge in each court the right and duty to decide who should have priority access to social goods in short supply?[210]

However, this concern should not be overstated as an obstacle to providing direct benefits to litigants. Both principled considerations relating to the interpretation of socio-economic rights and the evidence in a particular case may establish that ordering the State to provide tangible benefits to a defined class of persons will not be inequitable. Thus, for example, the claimants may suffer serious and irreparable

---

[207] C Scott & P Alston 'Adjudicating constitutional priorities in a transnational context: A comment on *Soobramoney's* legacy and *Grootboom's* promise' (2000) 16 *SAJHR* 206–268 at 254–255 highlight the chilling effect that the exclusion of orders providing direct forms of relief may have on socio-economic rights litigation:

> [W]hile public interest groups may well wish to seek standing under s 38(*d*) to bring constitutional claims about breach of framework procedural duties, individual claimants will understandably wish to see something geared more to their own situation and are unlikely to wish to bring constitutional cases purely as constitutional triggers for general policy processes.

[208] See the discussion in chapter 2, parts 2.4.6–2.4.8.

[209] *Grootboom* (note 10 above) para 81. The Court accepted, however, that the community had not engaged in an orchestrated land invasion 'as a deliberate strategy to gain preference in the allocation of housing resources over thousands of other people who remained in intolerable conditions and who were also in urgent need of housing relief' (ibid).

[210] A Sachs 'The judicial enforcement of socio-economic rights: The *Grootboom* case' (2003) *Current Legal Problems* 579–601 at 598.

harm if they are not afforded some concrete relief, even if it is only temporarily until they can be integrated in other medium- to long-term programmes. As discussed above, the courts have been increasingly willing to order temporary alternative accommodation to persons evicted from their homes in situations where it is just and equitable to do so.[211] Such orders can be derived from the *ratio* of the *Grootboom* judgment, namely, that the State fails to act reasonably when it fails to provide relief for those in urgent need and living in intolerable conditions.[212] In these circumstances the relief claimed is of such a nature that it should be provided to all groups similarly situated, and it is inappropriate to distinguish between different disadvantaged groups in the absence of a compelling justification such as a severe shortage of resources.

Furthermore, the State may fail to make out a cogent case that a positive order for the provision of benefits or services to the applicants would prejudice the needs of other disadvantaged groups who are not before the court. The evidence in such a case may indicate that justice will not be served by simply ordering the formulation and implementation of a reasonable programme. The courts should not ignore the hardship which the claimants will suffer if the remedy is not tailored to their particular needs and circumstances. After all, one of the institutional advantages of the courts is that they are well placed to detect the impact of general legislative and executive acts and omissions on particular individuals and groups.[213] A substantive approach to the adjudication of socio-economic rights claims would require the State to place cogent evidence and arguments before the courts concerning the alleged 'floodgate' implications of granting direct relief.[214] These arguments should be exposed to searching scrutiny before it is decided to deny direct forms of relief to the claimants.

In *Treatment Action Campaign*,[215] the State argued that the only competent order that the Court could make was to issue a declaration of rights. Such an order would give the Government the latitude 'to pay heed to the declaration made and to adapt its policies insofar as this may be necessary to bring them into conformity with the court's judgment'.[216] This argument is premised on a bounded notion of the separation of powers doctrine which views policy questions to be the sole preroga-

---

[211] See part 8.4.2–3 above.

[212] See notes 146–147 and accompanying text above.

[213] M Pieterse 'Coming to terms with judicial enforcement of socio-economic rights' (2004) 20 *SAJHR* 383–417 at 391–392 and 395–396; R Dixon 'Creating dialogue about socio-economic rights: Strong-form versus weak-form judicial review revisited' (2007) 5 *I Con* 391–418 at 402–403 defends a judicial role in the enforcement of socio-economic rights by highlighting a number of 'blind spots' and 'burdens of inertia' to which legislative processes and their implementation are subject. These include 'blind spots of perspective' when 'legislators may fail to anticipate the impact of laws on rights because they do not appreciate, adequately, the perspective of rights claimants with very different life experiences and viewpoints'.

[214] See the discussion in this regard by Scott & Alston (note 207 above) 267–268.

[215] *Treatment Action Campaign* (note 133 above).

[216] Ibid para 96.

tive of the executive branch of government, and precludes the courts from making orders 'that have the effect of requiring the Executive to pursue a particular policy'.[217] In response, the Court observed that it has not endorsed an interpretation of the separation of powers doctrine based on 'bright line' boundaries between the three spheres of government.[218] Nevertheless, it held 'there are certain matters that are pre-eminently within the domain of one or other of the arms of government and not the others.'[219] Although all arms of government are required to be 'sensitive to and respect this separation', this did not imply 'that Courts cannot or should not make orders that have an impact on policy.'[220]

The Constitution imposes a duty on the State to 'respect, protect, promote and fulfil the rights in the Bill of Rights.'[221] The doctrine of constitutional supremacy and the duty of courts to apply the Constitution and the law 'impartially and without fear, favour or prejudice',[222] means that a court is obliged to consider whether the State has complied with its constitutional obligations:

> If it should hold in any given case that the State has failed to do so, it is obliged by the Constitution to say so. Insofar as that constitutes an intrusion into the domain of the Executive, that is an intrusion mandated by the Constitution itself.[223]

The Court confirmed its wide remedial powers, including the granting of mandatory relief with or without the exercise of some form of supervisory jurisdiction.[224] After briefly surveying a number of comparative jurisdictions, it concluded that there was no suggestion in any of these jurisdictions that 'the granting of injunctive relief breaches the separation of powers'.[225] It went on to hold that such remedies are particularly appropriate when 'the State's obligations are not performed diligently and without delay'.[226] A court should be guided by '[t]he nature of the right infringed and the nature of the infringement' in determining what would constitute appropriate relief in a particular case.[227] The Court reiterated that the central guiding criterion is what would constitute an effective remedy in the circumstances of the case.[228]

Although the Court in *Treatment Action Campaign* made both declaratory and mandatory orders against the State, it declined to exercise a supervisory jurisdiction as it

---

[217] Ibid para 97.
[218] Ibid para 98. On a reconceptualised doctrine of the separation of powers appropriate to a transformative constitution, see chapter 2, part 2.4.7.
[219] Ibid para 98.
[220] Ibid.
[221] Ibid para 99.
[222] Section 165(2) of the Constitution.
[223] *Treatment Action Campaign* (note 133 above) para 99.
[224] Ibid paras 101–106.
[225] Ibid para 112.
[226] Ibid. See s 237 of the Constitution.
[227] *Treatment Action Campaign* (note 133 above) para 106.
[228] Ibid para 102 (citing Ackermann J in *Fose* (note 4 above) para 69).

was invited to do by the applicants.[229] It held that there were no grounds for believing that the Government would not respect and execute the orders of the Court.[230] The *Treatment Action Campaign* orders required government to act 'without delay' to: '[r] emove the restrictions' to the provision of Nevirapine in public hospital and clinics; 'permit and facilitate' its use when medically indicated; 'make provision' for counsellors based at public hospitals and clinics to be trained for the counselling necessary for the use of Nevirapine to reduce the risk of mother-to-child transmission of HIV; and '[t]ake reasonable measures to extend the testing and counselling facilities' at all public hospitals and clinics 'to facilitate and expedite the use of Nevirapine for the purpose of reducing the risk of mother-to-child transmission of HIV'.[231]

An important factor in formulating remedies for the provision of benefits and services is the need to accommodate reasonable changes in policy necessitated by evolving scientific and social evidence. The Court in the *Treatment Action Campaign* case held that the remedy should accommodate the need of the Executive to change and adapt its policies subject to consistency with the Constitution.[232] This aspect was built into the *Treatment Action Campaign* orders by the stipulation that the abovementioned orders 'do not preclude government from adapting its policy in a manner consistent with the Constitution if equally appropriate or better methods become available to it for the prevention of mother-to-child transmission of HIV'.[233]

The above discussion suggests that there are three primary circumstances in which it will be appropriate for a court to make an order requiring the State to provide concrete benefits and services to the applicants or a class of similarly situated people. First, such an order is appropriate where the facts of the case indicate that the State does not have a large measure of policy choice in giving effect to a duty imposed by the particular right. Second, such a mandatory order will usually be appropriate when the provision of direct, speedy and concrete forms of relief to the applicants is required to remedy the violation effectively. In this respect the impact of the denial of the right on the applicants and similarly situated groups is a critical consideration. Third, a mandatory order to provide benefits and services is appropriate when the evidence shows that the State is able to comply with the order through adopting relatively straightforward and expeditious measures.[234] If effectively remedying the breach requires the taking of a complex series of structural reforms over a period

---

229 On the exercise of a supervisory jurisdiction by the courts through reporting orders and structural interdicts, see part 8.6 below.

230 *Treatment Action Campaign* (note 133 above) para 129.

231 Ibid para 135. Orders 3(*a*)-(*d*).

232 Ibid para 114.

233 Ibid para 135. Order 4.

234 In *Hoffmann* (note 20 above), the remedy of 'instatement' was deemed an appropriate remedy for the discriminatory refusal of employment of an HIV-positive flight attendant. Among other considerations, the Court held that there was no suggestion that it would be unfair or unjust for the South African Airways to be ordered to employ the appellant. There were also no major practical impediments to his employment (see para 54).

of time, a structural remedy of the nature described in the following section would probably constitute a more appropriate remedy.[235]

The *Treatment Action Campaign* case is a good illustration of the presence of many of these circumstances. The medical evidence indicated that only appropriate anti-retroviral medication could significantly reduce the risk of mother-to-child transmission of HIV.[236] Nevirapine was government's own drug of choice in the research and training sites,[237] and was recommended without qualification by the World Health Organisation (WHO) for the prevention of *intra-partum* transmission of HIV.[238] Second, the denial of this treatment in hospitals and clinics throughout the public health sector had severe consequences for infants who contracted HIV from their mothers during childbirth. They faced an almost certain death along with grave suffering. In these circumstances there was little scope for further deliberative engagement, and any further delay in the roll-out of anti-retroviral treatment would have severe and irrevocable consequences for the infants and their families. As the Court observed:

> One is dealing here with a deadly disease. Once a drug that has the potential to reduce mother-to-child transmission is available, it is desirable that it be made available without delay to those who urgently need it.[239]

The evidence showed, moreover, that it was within the resources and capacity of the State to extend the provision of Nevirapine throughout the public health sector without excessive complications or delays.[240] In the context of reviewing the relevant policy and resource developments in the case, the Court observed:

> These developments clearly demonstrate that, provided the requisite political will is present, the supply of Nevirapine at public health institutions can be rapidly expanded to reach many more than the 10% of the population intended to be catered for in terms of the test site policy.[241]

Finally, this case was brought as public interest action by the TAC and selected other persons acting in a representative capacity. This enabled the Court to make orders which benefited the entire class of women giving birth in the public health sector in South Africa, and their newborn babies. Thus the Court was in a position to assess the evidence and the State's justifications in relation to the entire group of people potentially affected. This clearly made it easier for the Court to have insight into the scope and consequences of the mandatory orders it issued.[242]

---

[235] See part 8.6 below.
[236] *Treatment Action Campaign* (note 133 above) para 57.
[237] Ibid para 62.
[238] Ibid para 60.
[239] Ibid para 130.
[240] Ibid paras 115–120.
[241] Ibid para 119.
[242] For a discussion of the significance of a court having information relating to the impact of its order on other groups and interests not represented before it, and strategies to

The eviction cases in which organs of State have been ordered to ensure the provision of alternative accommodation to those facing eviction from their homes is a further illustration of the inclination of the courts to make mandatory orders for the provision of material benefits when the impact of the deprivation of the right is severe and there can be little debate about what is needed to provide effective relief.[243] This is illustrated by the Constitutional Court's recent judgment in *Residents of Joe Slovo Community, Western Cape v Thubelisha Homes* ('*Joe Slovo*').[244] The Court upheld the order of the Western Cape High Court requiring the residents to vacate the Joe Slovo informal settlement in order to facilitate the development and upgrading of the settlement as part of the N2 Gateway Project. However, it affirmed their right to adequate alternative accommodation during the upgrading process and set detailed substantive standards for the provision of the temporary residential accommodation at Delft, including the provision of services and facilities.[245] The respondents were furthermore directed to allocate 70% of the low-cost housing to be built at the site of Joe Slovo to the residents thereof.[246] The parties were directed to 'engage meaningfully' with each other concerning certain aspects of the order.[247]

Mandatory relief was given by both the High Court and Supreme Court of Appeal in the *Mazibuko* case.[248] The South Gauteng High Court ordered the City to provide each applicant and other similarly placed residents of the Phiri township with a free basic water supply of 50 litres per person per day. It also ordered that they be given the option of a metered supply installed at the cost of the City of Johannesburg. In its judgment the court highlighted the severe impact on the Phiri resident's life, health and human dignity of the prepayment meter system and the restriction of their water supply to 25 litres per person per day (or 6 kilolitres per household per month[249]).[250]

---

address this problem in adversarial adjudication, see C Mbazira 'Confronting the problem of polycentricity in enforcing socio-economic rights in the South African Constitution' (2008) 23 *SAPR/PL* 30–49.

243 See the jurisprudence discussed in chapter 6.

244 [2009] ZACC 16, 2009 (9) BCLR 847 (CC). The judgment is discussed in chapter 6, part 6.5.

245 Ibid para 7. See particularly the Order para 10.

246 Ibid. Order para 17.

247 See further in this regard part 8.5.3(*b*).

248 Notes 118 and 125 above.

249 The monthly allocation per household is based on a household of eight (8) persons. However, according to the judgment, it was common cause that the average household consists of a minimum of sixteen (16) persons, particularly when account was taken of the backyard residents. See *Mazibuko (HC)* note 125 above) para 168–169.

250 See, for example, *Mazibuko (HC)* (note 125 above) paras 84, 169–179. Thus the court states:

> To expect the applicants to restrict their water usage to compromise their health by limiting the number of toilet flushes in order to save water, is to deny them the right to health and to live a dignified lifestyle (para 179).

It found on the evidence that the City was able to provide 50 litres per person per day without straining its capacity in respect of water and financial resources.[251]

On appeal, the Supreme Court of Appeal found that 42 litres of water per person per day would constitute 'sufficient' water in terms of s 27(1) of the Constitution.[252] However, the Court held that this did not imply that everyone had a claim for the immediate fulfilment of the right.[253] The City's obligation was 'only to act reasonably and to progressively fulfil its obligation to ensure that everyone has access to sufficient water'.[254] Nevertheless the City's free water policy was materially influenced by an error of law in that it was formulated on the assumption that the minimum standard of free water supply in terms of the Water Services Act 108 of 1997 (25 litres per person per day or 6 kl per household per month) superseded its constitutional duties in terms of s 27, and that the City had no obligation to provide free water for those who could not afford to pay.[255]

The Supreme Court of Appeal accordingly reviewed and set aside the City's free water policy. It was not, however, prepared to endorse the High Court's order that the City directly provide the respondents and other similarly placed residents with an increased quantum of free basic water. It held that such an order would be inappropriate as 'the circumstances of the respondents are so dissimilar that it would be impossible to give effect to the order'.[256] In addition, the Court held that it did not have the knowledge or expertise to foresee the costs and logistical implications of such an order. It would therefore 'be irresponsible of a court to usurp the function of the City and to itself revise the City's free water policy'.[257] The matter was referred back to the City for them to 'reconsider and reformulate' a revised free water policy in the light of the Court's finding that 'it was constitutionally obliged to grant each Phiri resident who cannot afford to pay for water access to 42 litres of water per day free in so far as it can reasonably be done having regard to its available resources and other relevant considerations'.[258]

However, the Court also made an interim order intended to respond to the immediate needs of those residents of Phiri who, pending the formulation of the revised policy, would be continuing to 'live in squalor'.[259] In terms of this order the City was obliged to provide each account holder in Phiri who is registered by the City as

---

[251] Ibid para 181.
[252] *Mazibuko (SCA)* (note 118 above).
[253] Ibid paras 26.
[254] Ibid para 27.
[255] Ibid para 38.
[256] Ibid para 39.
[257] Ibid para 42.
[258] Ibid paras 43 and 62 (Order paras 2–3).
[259] Ibid para 44. The Supreme Court of Appeal referred in this context to Ackermann J's underscoring of the need for effective remedies, particularly in a context 'where so few have the means to enforce their rights through the courts'. *Fose* (note 4 above) para 69.

indigent with 42 litres of free water per day per member of his or her household.[260] The order was also intended to place some pressure on the City to adopt a free water policy as soon as possible.[261] The purpose of limiting the interim order to those residents appearing on the City's Register of Indigents was to distinguish between those residents who were able to afford to pay for the water and those who were not.[262]

These remedies in response to the free water claim of the Phiri residents[263] are an illustration of the possibilities of combining both systemic and individual relief. The mandatory order requiring the revision of government policy in line with constitutional requirements ensures that the benefits won in the case are extended to all persons in a similar situation to the Phiri applicants. It also provides the government with latitude to reformulate a new policy in line with the normative guidelines provided by the Court. However, the latitude provided by the Supreme Court of Appeal in this context is unduly broad, given that the City's obligation to formulate a new water policy based on 42 litres per resident who cannot afford to pay is subject to 'its available resources and other relevant considerations'. The breadth of this condition has the potential to undermine the normative standard set by the Court regarding the quantum of water services needed to secure the life, health and dignity of the residents.

The interim order was intended to cater for the immediate needs of the applicants before the court and ensure that they did not go away empty handed pending the systemic revisions of the policy. As the Court stated in *August v Electoral Commission*,[264] '[w]e cannot deny strong actual claims timeously asserted by determinate people, because of the possible existence of hypothetical claims that might conceivably have been brought by indeterminate groups'.[265] This is particularly apposite when the substance of the claims relates to the basic necessities of life such as water.

(*b*) Orders of 'meaningful engagement' and mediation

In the context of eviction applications, the courts have frequently made mandatory orders requiring the parties to engage with each other with a view to exploring mutually acceptable solutions to the dispute, including the possibility of securing suitable alternative accommodation for the occupiers.[266] Such orders may or may not

---

[260] Ibid paras 45 and 62 (Order para 4).

[261] Ibid para 46.

[262] For a critique of the Court's reliance on the Register of Indigents as a basis for determining which residents are entitled to interim relief, see Dugard and Liebenberg (note 127 above) 16.

[263] The second leg of the claim concerned the legality of the prepayment meters installed in Phiri. See in this regard part 8.3.5 above. The Constitutional Court judgment in *Mazibuko v City of Johannesburg (Centre on Housing Rights and Evictions as amicus curiae)* [2009] ZACC 28 handed down on 8 October 2009 is discussed in the postscript, chapter 9, part 9.4.

[264] 1999 (3) SA 1 (CC), 1999 (4) BCLR 363 (CC).

[265] Ibid para 30.

[266] See also chapter 6, parts 6.4–6.5.

be accompanied by a reporting order or structural interdict through which judicial supervision over the engagement process is maintained.[267] They are an example of an innovative type of mandatory order which may be given by a court in socio-economic rights litigation.

The leading case in which an order was made for the parties to 'engage meaningfully' with each other was *Occupiers 51 Olivia Road*.[268] The case concerned an eviction application brought by the City of Johannesburg against residents of alleged 'bad buildings' in the inner City of Johannesburg on health and safety grounds in terms of the provisions of the NBRSA.[269] After argument was heard in the case, the Constitutional Court issued an interim order requiring the City of Johannesburg and the applicants 'to engage with each other meaningfully' in an effort to resolve the disputes between them 'in the light of the values of the Constitution, the constitutional and statutory duties of the municipality and the rights and duties of the citizens concerned'.[270] The parties were required to file affidavits before the Court within two months which reported on the results of this engagement between them.

In giving reasons for the interim 'engagement order' the Court cited its judgment in *Port Elizabeth Municipality*[271] in which it said:

> [T]he procedural and substantive aspects of justice and equity cannot always be separated. The managerial role of the courts may need to find expression in innovative ways. Thus, one potentially dignified and effective mode of achieving sustainable reconciliations of the different interests involved is to encourage and require the parties to engage with each other in a proactive and honest endeavour to find mutually acceptable solutions. Wherever possible, respectful face-to-face engagement or mediation through a third party should replace arm's-length combat by intransigent opponents.[272]

The Court emphasised that engagement is 'a two-way process in which the City and those about to become homeless talk to each other meaningfully in order to achieve certain objectives'.[273] The outcome of this engagement order was a comprehensive agreement between the parties[274] which made provision for the resolution of various aspects of the dispute between them. This agreement contained 'meticulous provision' for rendering the relevant buildings safer and more habitable on an interim basis.[275] It provided for the occupiers to relocate by a specified date to alternative accommodation to be provided in certain identified buildings. The agreement also contained detailed provisions regarding the nature and standard of the accommodation to be provided as well as how the rent in respect of this accommodation was

---

[267] See 8.6 below.
[268] Note 11 above.
[269] For an analysis of the *Occupiers of 51 Olivia Road* case, see chapter 6, part 6.4.
[270] The interim order of 30 August 2007 is reproduced in the judgment at para 5.
[271] Note 189 above.
[272] Ibid para 39 cited in *Occupiers of 51 Olivia Road* (note 11 above) para 12.
[273] Ibid para 14.
[274] Agreement of 29 October 2007 (copy on file with author).
[275] *Occupiers of 51 Olivia Road* (note 11 above) para 25.

to be calculated.[276] It was stipulated that this alternative accommodation was being provided 'pending the provision of permanent housing solutions' being developed by the City 'in consultation' with the occupiers concerned.[277]

This agreement was endorsed by the Court on 5 November 2007. As the Court pointed out, this was the first time that the Constitutional Court had endorsed an agreement between parties 'in circumstances where the parties required approval before important aspects of it came into operation'.[278] Although it would not always be appropriate for a court to approve all agreements entered into consequent upon engagement, the Court held that the deciding factor in the present case was the fact that 'engagement was ordered by this Court, and the parties had been asked to report back on the process while proceedings were pending before it'.[279]

The engagement order by the Constitutional Court clearly fulfilled its objective by facilitating an equitable resolution of the dispute between the parties. It illustrates how a mandatory order by a court for the parties to engage meaningfully with each other can stimulate a dialogic process of engagement leading to the provision of concrete benefits to a particular group.[280] The terms of the detailed agreement struck between the City and the occupiers arguably went further than an order which even a sympathetic court would have granted. For example, a key issue for the occupiers was that any alternative accommodation should be within the inner city in proximity to their existing employment and livelihood opportunities. The Supreme Court of Appeal had resisted any entitlement on the part of the occupiers to alternative accommodation within the inner city.[281] The agreement reached between the parties provides for relocation to buildings being renovated within the inner city.

---

[276] Ibid para 26. The newly renovated buildings provided by the City in terms of this agreement are located within the inner city. Both buildings have provision for privacy for families and for single persons. The agreement also makes provision for access to water, electricity, sanitation and heating facilities. Residents will furthermore not be made to pay more than 25% of their household monthly income and will be guaranteed security against eviction. See affidavit of Moray Hathorn filed with the Court on behalf of the applicants dated 24 October 2007, containing the details of the agreement reached between the parties. The residents relocated to the buildings between 23 and 26 August 2008. See press release of 27 August 2008 issued by Webber Wentzel: 'Inner city residents move into new homes'. Available at http://www.webberwentzel.com/wwb/view/wwb/en/page21361?oid=19399&sn=detai (accessed on 20 July 2009).

[277] Ibid.

[278] Ibid para 29.

[279] Ibid para 30.

[280] For a historically and theoretically significant insider's account of the litigation and the engagement process see S Wilson 'Litigating housing rights in Johannesburg's inner city' in C Jenkins, M du Plessis & K Govender (eds) *Law, Nation-Building and Transformation* (forthcoming Intersite, 2010). Stuart Wilson was a leading member of the legal team in the *Occupiers of 51 Olivia Road*.

[281] See *Rand Properties* (note 172 above) paras 75. Nevertheless the Supreme Court of Appeal held that it would be 'remiss' not to consider the consequences that might follow upon

The judgment establishes that the eviction of residents by local authorities in circumstances where they may become homeless cannot ordinarily take place without a reasonable and good faith effort to engage meaningfully with the affected residents on the range of issues referred to by the Constitutional Court.[282] This is one of the 'relevant circumstances' to be considered by a court in terms of s 26(3) of the Constitution. Where an eviction application is brought without evidence of meaningful engagement between the parties, a court may issue a mandatory order for the parties to engage with each other. The terms of the interim order handed down by the Constitutional Court also suggests that the report of the result of the engagement between the parties may be relevant to further directions issued by a court in an eviction case.[283]

In an article on the case and its aftermath, Kate Tissington, a participant in the engagement process, makes the following observations:

> The process of negotiation and consultation between the two sides has not always been easy. However there is the sense, reinforced by the Constitutional Court judgment, that this is an important 'pilot project' in the inner city and that much rests on getting the process right. The question remains as to how this intensive process can be replicated on a large-scale in the inner city, as well as elsewhere in South Africa, taking into consideration that the reason this case has come so far is because of a dedicated and capacitated pro bono legal team and a progressive judgment from the Constitutional Court.[284]

---

eviction in circumstances where 'it seems probable that, once evicted, at least some of the respondents will be left without any shelter at all, and will have no resources with which to secure any' (para 76). Accordingly the City was ordered to offer and provide 'to those respondents who are evicted and are desperately in need of housing assistance relocation to a temporary settlement area as described in chapter 12 of the National Housing Code (April 2004) within its municipal area'. It specified that this temporary accommodation was to consist of at least the following elements: 'a place where they may live secure against eviction; a structure that is waterproof and secure against the elements; and with access to basic sanitation, water and refuse services' (para 78. Order (*c*) 2.1). Although the Court did not endorse any right to be relocated within the inner city, it did indicate that the City should determine the location of the alternative accommodation 'after consultation (if requested by any respondent)'.

282 *Occupiers of 51 Olivia Road* (note 11 above) para 22.

283 See para 4 of the interim order, 30 August 2007, *Occupiers of 51 Olivia Road* (note 11 above) para 5. As discussed in chapter 6, part 6.4, the Court did not consider it necessary to deal with the systemic issue of whether the City had a reasonable plan in place for the housing of the class of similarly placed occupiers in the inner City of Johannesburg. See part 6.4 at notes 234–238 and accompanying text.

284 K Tissington 'Challenging inner city evictions before the Constitutional Court of South Africa: The *Occupiers of 51 Olivia Road* case in Johannesburg, South Africa' (2008) 5(2) *Housing and ESC Rights Law Quarterly* 1, 3–6. Kate Tissington is employed as a researcher by two of the NGOs involved in supporting this litigation – the Centre for Applied Legal Studies (University of the Witwatersrand) and the Centre on Housing Rights and Evictions (COHRE).

Tissington highlights the systemic problem of ensuring that the benefits won through engagement orders are extended to other groups similarly placed. Engagement orders issued in the absence of a substantive analysis of the constitutional rights and duties of the parties may also result in vulnerable groups being pressurised into settlement agreements which do not adequately protect their constitutional rights.

Shortly after its judgment in the *Occupiers of 51 Olivia Road* matter the Constitutional Court issued an engagement order in an application brought on behalf of refugees and asylum seekers in *Mamba v Minister of Social Development*[285] ('*Mamba*') to oppose the closure of refugee camps by various organs of state. The camps had been established as a safe refuge during the xenophobic violence which exploded in South Africa in the middle of 2008. The closure of the camps was opposed due to the lack of a comprehensive and transparent plan of action for the provision of alternative safe accommodation and appropriate reintegration services. The applicants applied for leave to appeal directly to the Constitutional Court against the dismissal of their application by the South Gauteng High Court.[286] After hearing argument in the matter and pending the final determination of the application for leave to appeal, the Constitutional Court issued an order directing the parties:

> to engage with each other meaningfully and with all other stakeholders ... in order to resolve the differences and difficulties aired in this application in the light of the values of the Constitution, the constitutional and statutory obligations of the respondents and the rights and duties of the residents of the shelters.[287]

However, the scope of the engagement was specifically circumscribed by the requirement that its objective was 'to secure the closure of the camps by no later than 30 September'. Meaningful engagement in this context had to occur in a normative vacuum without substantive guidance from the Court on the implications of the constitutional rights and principles at stake. This raises serious questions about whether the engagement order in this case was capable of effectively vindicating the constitutional rights of the refugees.

Finally, in the *Joe Slovo* case[288] the Court also directed the parties to engage meaningfully with each other in relation to various aspects of the eviction and relocation order. These included an alternative commencement date and timetable for the relocation other than the one contemplated by the Court;[289] the practical aspects of

---

[285] Case No CCT 65/08.

[286] See *Mamba v Minister of Social Development* Case No 36573/08 (T) (unreported judgment of 12 August 2008).

[287] Ibid. Order dated 21 August 2008, para 1. Available at http://www.constitutionalcourt.org.za/uhtbin/cgisirsi/mHd7lE84aN/MAIN/0/57/518/0/O-CCT65-08 (accessed 21 July 2009). A range of other orders were given pertaining to the engagement between the parties and their actions during the process of engagement. The matter was postponed to 16 September 2008 in order to enable the parties to comply with the engagement order.

[288] Note 244 above.

[289] Ibid para 7. Order paras 5–6.

the relocation such as the provision of transport facilities to the affected residents from the temporary accommodation in Delft to schools, places of work and health facilities;[290] and the prospects of being allocated permanent housing in due course.[291] The scope of the meaningful engagement order was thus confined to the practical details of the eviction and relocation order.[292]

8.5.4 Conclusion

Mandatory orders play a crucial role in providing effective remedial relief for violations of socio-economic rights. Orders to provide benefits or services to the applicants or a defined class of people are appropriate in circumstances where urgent and concrete forms of relief are urgently needed, and the nature of the benefits to be provided can be defined clearly and provided relatively expeditiously. The nature and extent of this relief will depend on the context, but must reflect the conviction expressed in *Grootboom* that a society 'must seek to ensure that the basic necessities of life are provided to all if it is to be a society based on human dignity, freedom and equality'.[293]

Mandatory orders requiring the parties to engage meaningfully with a view to reaching a mutually satisfactory and specific resolution to the issues in dispute can also constitute an effective remedy in socio-economic rights litigation. These types of orders can facilitate the participatory and deliberative values of the Constitution in the realisation of socio-economic rights.[294]

However, a challenge presented by these context-specific negotiated orders is to ensure that they benefit other similarly placed persons and institutions who are not parties to the particular litigation. This is an important concern, particularly as other groups may not have the benefit of being supported by NGOs or other civil society organisations in negotiations with the relevant authorities. Thus, for example, in *Khosa*[295] the Court declined to ratify a proposed out-of-court settlement between the parties if it would resolve only the dispute between the parties, but not the broader legal questions which the confirmation proceedings raised.[296]

One way of responding, at least partially, to this challenge is through judgments which illuminate the relevant legal principles and their application to similar cases.[297] Such judgments require a substantive interpretation of the relevant rights and their

---

290 Ibid. Order para 11.

291 Ibid. Order para 11.7.

292 On the approach by the Court to 'meaningful engagement' in the *Joe Slovo* case, see further chapter 6, part 6.5.

293 *Grootboom* (note 10 above) para 44.

294 See generally chapter 2, part 2.2.4.

295 Note 40 above.

296 Ibid para 35. See also the discussion by Mbazira (note 3 above) 90.

297 For a critique of the Constitutional Court judgment for not dealing with certain legal issues of general application in relation to the exercise by local authorities of their powers in terms of s 12(4)(*b*) of the NBRSA in *Occupiers of 51 Olivia Road* (note 11 above), see L

implications. Public authorities and the general public should be placed in a position to know what the rights mean in similar situations so that they can act accordingly. This will also assist in obviating the need for further litigation to clarify the obligations of the parties, a process which is particularly burdensome for disadvantaged groups.

Finally, engagement orders, like other remedies must constitute appropriate and effective relief for violations of constitutional rights. In the absence of a substantive evaluation of the rights at stake, meaningful engagement takes place in a normative vacuum. In this situation, disadvantaged groups are particularly vulnerable to being pressured by more powerful counterparts to negotiate away their constitutional rights.

8.6 REPORTING ORDERS AND STRUCTURAL INTERDICTS

8.6.1 Introduction

In addition to granting mandatory relief, a court may require the respondent to report back to it and the other parties to the litigation on the implementation of the order (a 'reporting order').

Alternatively, it may require the parties to negotiate a plan which will give effect to the relevant rights and report back to the court on a regular basis. At each stage the court issues a set of directions regulating further engagement between the parties and the implementation of the plan. This process is continued until the court is satisfied that the constitutional infringement has been satisfactorily remedied. At both the stages of the approval and implementation of the plan, the applicants (and possibly other independent institutions and experts)[298] are given an opportunity to comment through filing affidavits on the reports filed. This type of order involving ongoing supervision and the issuing of periodic directions by the Court regarding the processes of remedying a violation of constitutional rights will be referred to as a 'structural interdict or order'.[299]

Chenwi & S Liebenberg 'The constitutional protection of those facing eviction from "bad buildings"' (2008) 9 *ESR Review* 12–17.

298 These could include, for example, a court-appointed expert or committee of experts or institutions such as the South African Human Rights Commission or the Commission for Gender Equality. For a proposal on how to involve the Commission in structural orders, see M Ebadolahi 'Using structural interdicts and the South African Human Rights Commission to achieve judicial enforcement of economic and social rights in South Africa' (2008) 83 *NYULR* 1565–1606.

299 Judicial supervision of court orders through the issuing of a 'continuing mandamus' are common in Indian public interest litigation. See the analysis and jurisprudence referred to in S Muralidhar 'India: The expectations and challenges of judicial enforcement of social rights' in M Langford (ed) *Social Rights Jurisprudence: Emerging Trends in International and Comparative Law* (2008) 102–124 at 108–110. The Indian Supreme Court has also involved advocates, expert committees and institutions in assisting it to assess expert evidence and

Both reporting orders and structural interdicts entail a court exercising some form of supervisory jurisdiction in respect of the orders issued in its initial judgment. The purpose of a reporting order is to ensure that there is compliance with the terms of the order. A structural order also enables a court to monitor compliance, but its broader purpose is to facilitate a process of engagement between the parties regarding the specific, detailed measures required to give effect to the normative standards set in the judgment.

8.6.2 Supervisory orders in the jurisprudence of the courts

As early as 1998, the Constitutional Court affirmed its remedial power to make mandatory orders combined with an obligation on respondents to report to the court and the applicants on the manner of their implementation.[300]

The earliest socio-economic rights decision in which a reporting order was given is the High Court decision in the *Grootboom* case.[301] The Court found a violation of s 28(1)(*c*) of the Constitution. In the first part of its order, the Court declared in broad terms that the appropriate organ or department of State was obliged to provide the applicant children and their parents with shelter until such time as the parents were able to shelter their own children. The second part of the order directed the respondents to present reports to the Court on the implementation of the order within a period of three months from the date of the order. The applicants were given an opportunity to deliver their commentary on these reports.[302]

In *Treatment Action Campaign v Minister of Health*,[303] the High Court issued declaratory and mandatory orders requiring the respondent to roll out a comprehensive national programme to prevent mother-to-child transmission of HIV, including the provision of Nevirapine (or other appropriate medication). These orders were accompanied by a reporting order.[304] The High Court did not elaborate on its reasons for issuing a reporting order. However, the order was clearly motivated by the severe consequences of the denial of this life-saving medical intervention, and the Minister of Health's unjustifiable equivocation in extending the programme throughout the public health sector.[305]

Although the Constitutional Court made both declaratory and mandatory orders against the State in the *Treatment Action Campaign* case, it declined to exercise a super-

---

in monitoring the implementation of its orders. See, for example, *Sheela Barse v Union of India* (1993) 4 SCC 204; *Sheela Barse v Union of India* (2002) 5 SCALE 8.

300 See, for example, *Pretoria City Council v Walker* 1998 (2) SA 363 (CC), 1998 (3) BCLR 257 (CC) para 96.

301 Note 155 at 293H-J–294A-C. Davis J referred in this context to Wim Trengove's article (note 7 above) dealing with supervisory orders in the context of socio-economic rights litigation as 'most helpful' (292G-H).

302 Ibid 293H-J–294A-C.

303 *Treatment Action Campaign v Minister of Health* 2002 (4) BCLR 356 (T).

304 Ibid 386I-J–387A-H.

305 Ibid 385–386.

visory jurisdiction as requested by the TAC. However, it expressly confirmed that the power to grant mandatory relief included the power of courts, where appropriate, to exercise a supervisory jurisdiction over the implementation of the order.[306] The Court held:

> In appropriate cases they should exercise such a power if it is necessary to secure compliance with a court order. That may be because of a failure to heed declaratory orders or other relief granted by a Court in a particular case. We do not consider, however, that orders should be made in those terms unless this is necessary. The government has always respected and executed orders of this Court. There is no reason to believe that it will not do so in the present case.[307]

This suggests a rather limited conception of supervisory orders as 'last resort' mechanisms to secure compliance with a court order.

In the immediate aftermath of the judgment, there was a lack of urgency in implementing the Court's rulings at both the national level and in some of the provinces. The TAC was compelled to undertake a range of actions in an effort to ensure the proper implementation of the orders. These included correspondence, meetings, and a complaint to the South African Human Rights Commission. During December 2002 contempt of court proceedings were launched against the national Minister of Health and the Member of the Executive Committee (MEC) for Health of the Mpumalanga province.[308] These proceedings were later withdrawn after guarantees of compliance with the Court's order were obtained.

Although not perfect, a national programme for the prevention of mother-to-child transmission of HIV was subsequently adopted by the Government in response to the *Treatment Action Campaign* judgment. There can be little doubt that lives have been saved as a result of the litigation and surrounding mobilisation. This is largely due to the organising capabilities and dedication of the Treatment Action Campaign. In addition, the *Treatment Action Campaign* judgment and its aftermath had a significant impact in the ultimate adoption of a national anti-retroviral treatment plan for all those living with HIV/AIDS.[309]

However, it is important to bear in mind that other litigants may not be in as strong an organisational position as the TAC to monitor and to take political and further legal action to secure compliance with the mandatory orders in its favour. Kent Roach and Geoff Budlender argue that supervisory remedies should not be

---

[306] *Treatment Action Campaign* (note 133 above) para 104. For a detailed discussion of the *Treatment Action Campaign* judgment, see chapter 4, part 4.3.

[307] Ibid para 129.

[308] *Treatment Action Campaign v MEC for Health, Mpumalanga and Minister of Health* TPD Case No: 35272/02; M Heywood 'Contempt or compliance? The *TAC* case after the Constitutional Court judgment' (2003) 4 *ESR Review* 7–10; M Swart (note 8 above) 223–224.

[309] For an analysis of the use by the Treatment Action Campaign of a combination of legal and mobilisation strategies, see M Heywood 'Shaping, making and breaking the law in the campaign for a national HIV/Treatment Plan' in P Jones & K Stokke (eds) *Democratising Development: The Politics of Socio-Economic Rights in South Africa* (2005) 181–212.

restricted to circumstances when a court is concerned that government will intentionally fail to give effect to its order. A supervisory order should also be seriously considered 'where the consequences of even a good-faith failure to comply with a court order are so serious that the court should be at pains to ensure effective compliance'.[310] Roach and Budlender argue that *Treatment Action Campaign* was illustrative of a case in which '[t]he consequences of non-compliance are irremediable, and so serious that it is necessary to go beyond the mandatory order and do whatever is reasonably possible to ensure effective compliance'.[311]

An examination of the circumstances in which the courts have granted reporting and structural orders suggests that the importance of effective relief being provided to the applicants and other similarly situated groups is at least as important a consideration as concerns about government non-compliance with the orders.

In *August* [312] and the subsequent, related decision of *Minister of Home Affairs v National Institute for Crime Prevention (NICRO)* [313] ('*NICRO*'), the Constitutional Court required the Independent Electoral Commission to make all necessary and reasonable arrangements for prisoners to exercise their right to vote. It also required the Independent Electoral Commission to serve an affidavit on the Minister of Correctional Services and the applicants setting out the manner that they would comply with the order.[314] An important element of publicity was built into these orders by enabling any interested person to inspect the reporting affidavit at the Registrar's Office once it has been lodged.[315] In the *NICRO* judgment, the Court emphasised the importance of effective and expeditious relief to enable prisoners to register and cast their votes in the forthcoming elections.[316] Without the timeous registration of prisoners and the necessary facilities to enable them to cast their votes, they would effectively be denied their right to vote in terms of s 19 of the Constitution. This made it imperative for the Court to supervise the implementation of its order.

A further example of the Constitutional Court issuing a mandamus and exercising supervisory jurisdiction over the process of execution of its order is the case of *Sibiya v Director of Public Prosecutions: Johannesburg* ('*Sibiya (1)*').[317] The Court was concerned about the slow pace at which the substitution of death sentences with alternative sentences was taking place in accordance with relevant legislation in the

---

[310] Roach & Budlender (note 79 above) 333.

[311] Ibid 334. The authors go on to observe:

> It is not over-dramatic to suggest that as a result of the failure by the province to comply effectively with the order of the Constitutional Court a significant number of babies may have been infected with HIV where this was avoidable, with probable fatal consequences (ibid).

[312] Note 264 above, para 10.

[313] 2005 (3) SA 280 (CC), 2004 (5) BCLR 445 (CC) para 80.

[314] Ibid para 80. Order para 5.

[315] Ibid. Order para 6.

[316] *NICRO* (note 313 above) paras 78–79.

[317] 2005 (5) SA 315 (CC), 2005 (8) BCLR 812 (CC) ('*Sibiya (1)*')

aftermath of its landmark decision in *S v Makwanyane*.[318] It accordingly undertook a supervisory jurisdiction in respect of this process. The respondent failed to file the necessary reports and affidavits by the due date, but an extension was granted by the Court.[319] In evaluating the respondents' report and affidavit, the Court held that despite the reasonable detail contained therein, difficulties remained in relation to the information provided.[320] It accordingly held that it was appropriate to continue to supervise the execution of its own order until the process of substitution of the death sentences was complete.[321] The 'hands-on' process of supervision in this case was clearly motivated by the slow pace of the substitution process, and its serious impact on the affected group. Prisoners who had been sentenced to death were exposed to delays and uncertainties concerning the period of their incarceration pending the completion of the substitution process. The Court's decision to assume a supervisory jurisdiction was clearly motivated by the importance of the liberty values at stake in relation to the former death row prisoners who were in limbo in the absence of a proper substitution of their sentence.

In *Nyathi*,[322] the Constitutional Court undertook judicial supervision over the State's compliance with outstanding judgment debts. Judicial oversight was deemed appropriate in this case owing to the serious constitutional consequences of the State's non-compliance with court orders. Madala J underscored the fundamental importance of compliance with court orders to our constitutional democracy:

> Certain values in the Constitution have been designated as foundational to our democracy. This in turn means that as pillar-stones of this democracy, they must be observed scrupulously. If these values are not observed and their precepts not carried out conscientiously, we have a recipe for a constitutional crisis of great magnitude. In a state predicated on a desire to maintain the rule of law, it is imperative that one and all should be driven by a moral obligation to ensure the continued survival of our democracy. That, in my view, means at the very least that there should be strict compliance with court orders.[323]

A similar concern informed the Court's decision to assume a supervisory jurisdiction in *Director of Public Prosecutions, Transvaal v Minister of Justice and Constitutional Development*.[324] The Court held that court orders permitting child complainants in sexual offence cases to testify through intermediaries in terms of s 170A(1) of the Criminal Procedure Act 51 of 1977 as well the creation of child-friendly courts in terms of s 170A(3) were being undermined by the inadequate provision of resources,

---

[318] 1995 (3) SA 391 (CC), 1995 (6) BCLR 665 (CC).

[319] In *Sibiya v Director of Public Prosecutions, Johannesburg High Court* [2006] ZACC 22, 2006 (2) BCLR 293 (CC) paras 6–15 ('*Sibiya (2)*'), the Court provided the reasons for this extension, and described the general approach to be followed with regard to applications for extensions of time in relation to complying with court orders.

[320] Ibid paras 19–20.

[321] Ibid para 21.

[322] Note 105 above. See also part 8.9.3 below.

[323] Ibid para 80 (footnotes omitted).

[324] Note 24 above.

facilities and training.[325] Ngcobo J (as he then was) held that there was 'a disturbing inconsistency between the promises that the laws make and the implementation of the laws'.[326] This negated the constitutional and legislative rights of child complainants of sexual offences who are 'some of the most vulnerable members of society'.[327] The Court held that '[i]n these exceptional circumstances', it was appropriate to call for information as a first step in the supervisory process.[328] The Court accordingly ordered the Director-General for the Department of Justice and Constitutional Development to provide detailed information on the facilities available to give effect to the legislative provisions concerning child complainants and witnesses.[329] The National Director of Public Prosecutions and each of the *amici curiae* in the case were given an opportunity to comment on the report, and the Court indicated that further directions concerning the supervision of its orders may be issued.[330]

In the *Joe Slovo* case, the Constitutional Court directed the parties to report back to the Court in six months' time on the implementation of the Court's order and the allocation of permanent housing opportunities to those affected by the order.[331] As Moseneke DCJ acknowledged, the eviction and relocation of the 20 000 members of an impoverished community exposed them to potentially devastating consequences.[332] Not only do they face a substantial risk of their fragile livelihood strategies being disrupted, but the removal of such a large community is evocative, on a symbolic level, of the evictions and forced removals of black communities during the apartheid era.[333] The Court thus deemed it essential to ensure that 'the deleterious effect of relocation on the applicants would be properly mitigated' both by safeguards concerning the nature and quality of the temporary alternative accommodation to be provided for them in Delft as well as by 'the reasonable prospect of access to adequate housing after the temporary stay in Delft'.[334] It is within this context that the reporting order issued by the Court must be understood.

The High Courts have granted supervisory orders in a number of cases. In *City of Cape Town v Rudolph*,[335] ('*Rudolph*') the Western Cape High Court found that the

---

325 Ibid paras 195–198

326 Ibid para 201.

327 Ibid 200.

328 Ibid para 205.

329 Ibid paras 206, 208 and 209. Order para (*e*).

330 Ibid para 209. Order paras (*f*) and (*g*).

331 Note 244 above, para 7 (Order para 16).

332 Ibid para 170.

333 Ibid para 169.

334 Ibid para 171–173. These concerns are expressed in each of the five judgments written in the Joe Slovo matter. See also the reporting orders issued by the Constitutional Court in its recent judgment in *Head of Department: Mpumalanga Department of Education v Hoërskool Ermelo* (note 27 above) paras 101–106.

335 2004 (5) SA 39 (C), 2003 (11) BCLR 1236 (C). See also the discussion of *Rudolph* in chapter 6 at notes 72–80 and accompanying text.

City of Cape Town had not complied with its obligation in terms of the *Grootboom* judgment to develop and implement a housing programme for those in desperate need.[336] In particular, the City had not put any measures in place providing short-term relief for people in Valhalla Park who were in a crisis or a desperate situation.[337] The Court handed down a structural interdict ordering the City of Cape Town to report back to the Court within four months of the date of the order on the steps it was taking to comply with its constitutional and statutory obligations. The residents were also given an opportunity to comment on the City's reports.[338] A structural interdict was deemed appropriate relief in this case as the City had not been induced by the declaratory order in the *Grootboom* case to comply with its constitutional obligations. The City had also persisted in its 'attitude of denial' by failing to recognise the plight of the residents.[339] As the Court stated, '[s]omething more is therefore necessary'.[340]

The City delivered four reports in response to this structural interdict, and the Court delivered a final judgment in December 2005.[341] It found that, although progress in the right direction had been made, there was still unsatisfactory compliance with the City's constitutional and statutory obligations in terms of the *Grootboom* judgment as well as the court's initial judgment.[342] Nevertheless, it held that a further structural interdict (as requested by the residents) was no longer necessary, as the reports indicated that the City now showed an appreciation and acknowledgment of its obligations. Progress was being made in the provision of emergency housing within the constraints of a limited budget and the policy decisions of provincial and national government.[343] The City had not been shown 'to have failed by reason of incompetence, inattentiveness or intransigence'.[344] The Court accordingly held that it was inappropriate to continue supervising compliance with its orders, and confined itself to a declarator that the City had not complied with its constitutional and statutory duties as stipulated in its original order of 7 July 2003.[345] It held that the applicants could 'always approach the Court in the future to assert their rights if they are dissatisfied with the City's compliance and can show an unjustifiable disregard

---

336 A similar finding was made by the South Gauteng High Court in respect of the City of Johannesburg in *City of Johannesburg v Rand Properties (Pty) Ltd* 2007 (1) SA 78 (W), 2006 (6) BCLR 728 (W).

337 *Rudolph* (note 335 above) 1280 I (Order para 2).

338 Ibid 1281C-E (Order paras 3–7).

339 Ibid 1279D.

340 Ibid 1279C.

341 *City of Cape Town v Rudolph*, Case No 8970/01 (unreported judgment of December 2005).

342 In the words of the Court, '[t]here is no evidence that a programme to deal with short term housing needs is in the process of being adopted or will be implemented'. Ibid 35.

343 Ibid 41.

344 Ibid 40.

345 Ibid 42.

for those rights'.[346] The discharge of the structural interdict, despite unsatisfactory compliance with the original order, was based on the Court's assessment that the immediate threat to the residents' security of tenure had been satisfactorily resolved. Selikowitz J observed in this regard:

> The City no longer seeks to evict the applicants. Having visited the site where the applicants are presently housed, I am satisfied that their immediate crisis situation has been temporarily resolved and that, for the time being, they are not in a desperate situation.[347]

In *N v Government of Republic of South Africa (No 1)*,[348] ('*N*') the KwaZulu-Natal High Court, Durban issued mandatory orders requiring the respondents to remove with immediate effect the obstacles that prevented prisoners at the Westville Correctional Centre from accessing anti-retroviral treatment at an accredited public health facility, and to provide such treatment to the applicants and all other similarly situated prisoners.[349] It also required the respondents to report to the court setting out the manner in which they would comply with these orders, and gave the applicants an opportunity to comment on the report. It ruled that the matter could thereafter be enrolled for hearing.[350] The Court held that, although the respondents 'had shown some sense of commitment' in addressing the plight of HIV-positive prisoners at the Westville Correctional Centre, the measures they had adopted were 'unworkable and characterised by delays, obstacles and restrictions'.[351] This seriously compromised the health of the applicants and similarly situated prisoners.[352] A structural interdict was warranted as the respondents had not produced a comprehensive and workable plan for ensuring timeous anti-retroviral treatment for qualifying HIV-positive prisoners. Moreover, the absence of such a plan resulted in unnecessary suffering and threatened the lives of these prisoners.

The respondents obtained leave to appeal against this judgment.[353] Pending the outcome of the appeal, Pillay J granted an application for interim execution or implementation of the order granted in the main judgment.[354] The respondents failed to comply with this order and instead appealed against the interim execution order while the applicants sought a further order from the court to confirm the implemen-

---

[346] Ibid 41.

[347] Ibid 40.

[348] 2006 (6) SA 543 (D), 2007 (1) BCLR 84 (D). See also the discussion of the *N* judgment in chapter 5, part 5.4.4 at notes 208–217 and accompanying text.

[349] Ibid para 35. Orders 1 and 2.

[350] Ibid para 35. Orders 3–6.

[351] Ibid para 32.

[352] Ibid.

[353] They also obtained leave to appeal against the dismissal by Pillay J of an application for his recusal on the basis that his daughter had acted as the applicants' correspondent attorney in Durban. See *Government of the Republic of South Africa v N* 2006 (6) SA 566.

[354] *N v Government of Republic of South Africa (No 2)* 2006 (6) SA 568 (D).

tation order. The appeal against the implementation order pending the respondents' appeal on the main judgment was heard by Nicholson J.[355]

The Court dismissed the leave to appeal against the interim implementation order as the respondents had not shown that the implementation of the order would cause them irreparable harm. In contrast, the consequence for prisoners living with AIDS of not obtaining timeous anti-retroviral treatment was certain death. It held that the respondents were in contempt of court as they had not filed the affidavit required by the structural interdict issued by Pillay J. In particular, they had failed to report on how they had complied with the order in respect of all similarly situated prisoners at the Westville Correctional Centre.[356] However, Nicholson J interpreted the decision in *Jayiya v Member of Executive Council for Welfare, Eastern Cape*[357] ('*Jayiya*') as precluding any 'legal mechanism such as incarceration to enforce court decrees'.[358] The respondents were given a further chance to comply with the deadline set by Pillay J.[359] The application for leave to appeal by the respondents against the interim execution order of Pillay J was dismissed.[360] The respondents were ordered to comply with the terms of the structural interdict issued by Pillay J in the main judgment and the interim execution order unless and until these orders were set aside on appeal. The date on which the compliance affidavit was to be filed was extended.[361]

According to the attorney acting for the applicants in the *N* case, Dr Adila Hassim,[362] the State complied with this further deadline, and filed the requisite affidavit. The applicants filed a commentary on this affidavit identifying a number of areas of concern to which the State replied.

An intensive process of negotiations followed which, despite a number of serious setbacks, resulted in the Department of Correctional Services adopting a national framework policy for the treatment of HIV-positive prisoners. The supervisory order ultimately passed its 'sell by' date, and the matter has not been set down again for a hearing. Neither has the State prosecuted the appeals that it noted. According to lawyers at the AIDS Law Project who represented the Westville prisoners, the

---

355 *N v Government of Republic of South Africa (No 3)* 2006 (6) SA 575 (D).

356 Ibid, para 28.

357 2004 (2) SA 611 (SCA).

358 Note 355 above paras 29–33. See further the discussion of the *Jayiya* case in part 8.9.2 below.

359 Ibid paras 34 and 40.

360 Ibid para 45.

361 Ibid para 46.

362 Head: Litigation and Legal Services of the AIDS Law Project (ALP) based in Johannesburg. Telephonic interview conducted on 9 September 2008. Helpful information was also obtained from listening to a presentation by another member of the legal team for the applicants, Mr Jonathan Berger, Senior Researcher, AIDS Law Project: J Berger 'Prisoners and the right to health: Learning from the ALP experience at the Westville Correctional Centre', presentation at seminar hosted by the Socio-Economic Rights Project Project, Community Law Centre (UWC), Cape Town, 26 May 2009.

structural interdict forced the Department of Correctional Services to enter into serious negotiations with them regarding a national plan for the provision of antiretroviral treatment to all prisoners.[363] The parties have been able to engage with each other on the detailed elements of a reasonable plan for treating HIV-positive prisoners. Civil society organisations with extensive experience in the rights of persons living with HIV/AIDS have been able to influence the development and content of the new policy adopted by the Department of Correctional Services. There have been notable improvements in the provision of antiretroviral therapy for prisoners at the Westville Correctional Centre.[364]

Other High Court cases in which reporting orders or structural interdicts were granted in cases are *Strydom v Minister of Correctional Services*,[365] *Magidimisi NO v Premier of the Eastern Cape*,[366] *Kiliko v Minister of Home Affairs*,[367] *Centre for Child*

[363] Information obtained from Dr Adila Hassan and Jonathan Berger (ibid).

[364] Ibid. The Treatment Action Campaign subsequently applied successfully for a court order in terms of the Promotion of Access to Information Act 2 of 2000, compelling the Minister of Correctional Services to release a copy of a report by the Judicial Inspectorate of Prisoners into the death of one the Westville prisoners (who had been party to the *N* case). See *Treatment Action Campaign v Minister of Correctional Services* Case no 18379/2008, [2009] ZAGPHC 10 (unreported judgment of 30 January 2009).

[365] 1993 (3) BCLR 342 (W). The Ministry of Correctional Services was ordered to report back to court on a timetable within which the electrical upgrading of the maximum security section of Johannesburg Prison would be commenced and completed. See also chapter 5, notes 218–219 and accompanying text.

[366] [2006] ZAECHC 20 (25 April 2006). The Court ordered the Eastern Cape Government to 'take all the administrative and other steps necessary' to ensure that it complied with prior court orders handed down against it in respect of outstanding amounts owing in terms of social grant payments. The government was further ordered to report back to the court and the applicant's attorneys on 'the manner and extent' of their compliance with this order. Froneman J observed that, in his personal experience, 'these orders have contributed to a better understanding on the part of public authorities of their constitutional legal obligations in particular areas, whilst it has also assisted the judiciary in gaining valuable insight in the difficulties that these authorities encounter in their efforts to comply with their duties' (para 32).

[367] 2006 (4) SA 114 (C), 2007 (4) BCLR 416 (C). The order in this case requires the respondents to report on a detailed list of issues and questions pertaining to the policies and practices of processing asylum seekers at the Cape Town refugee reception office (see para 35). A structural interdict was deemed to be an appropriate order in this case 'as the manner in which the Department discharges its duties and obligations to refugees not only deleteriously affects the freedom and dignity of a substantial number of disadvantaged human beings but also fails to adhere to the values embodied in the constitution' (para 32).

Law v MEC for Education, Gauteng,[368] and *Cele v The South African Social Security Agency*.[369]

This survey of the jurisprudence indicates that reporting orders are usually considered when a court is concerned that there will not be effective compliance with its order, and the consequences of the rights violation in the absence of effective and targeted measures of compliance will be serious. Structural interdicts are also appropriate when the violation of constitutional rights cannot be remedied by a 'once and for all' order, but requires the adoption of a number of interdependent, proactive measures over a period of time.[370] A structural interdict facilitates engagement between the parties on the detailed measures required to vindicate the constitutional rights concerned. As the case of the Westville prisoners illustrates, the negotiations between the parties can result in the adoption of a general policy or programme which benefits all groups in a similar situation to the applicants. In this way, the benefits of the litigation are extended to a broader constituency. The transformative implications of these kinds of structural remedies are explored further in the following part.

8.6.3 The transformative potential of structural remedies

Structural remedies are usually granted when a court deems it appropriate to make an order in general terms, leaving a margin of discretion to the government and the applicants to devise a concrete plan to give effect to the constitutional obligations broadly described in the initial order. The court then satisfies itself at regular intervals

---

368 2008 (1) SA 223 (T). The order requires the first respondent to take various detailed measures to improve the material and therapeutic conditions in which children are cared for in a school of industry, including making arrangements for a developmental quality-assurance process by a multidisciplinary team with expertise in child and youth care and children's rights (230–231). The major factors motivating this order were 'the dilatory and lackadaisical approach' displayed by the authorities in improving conditions at the school and the serious consequences for the enjoyment of the range of rights guaranteed to children under the Constitution (229). Reporting orders and structural interdicts have also been given in the following cases involving children's rights: *Centre for Child Law v Minister of Home Affairs* 2005 (6) SA 50 (T) and *S v Z and 23 Similar Cases* 2004 (4) BCLR 410 (E), [2004] 1 All SA 438 (E). See the discussion of these cases in chapter 5, part 5.2.4.

369 2009 (5) SA 105 (D), 2008 (7) BCLR 734 (D). In this case, the State Attorney was ordered to report to the Deputy Judge President at intervals of not less than three months on the workings of a practice directive which the Court had formulated to regulate the processes for instituting High Court applications seeking relief in respect of social grants payable in terms of the Social Assistance Act (para 37). The practice directive was designed to curb 'the congestion of the court's rolls, the unnecessary commencement of legal proceedings and the incurring of wasteful and unnecessary costs' which current practices in respect of these applications were occasioning (para 28). The adoption of such a directive was held to be part of the inherent power of the High Court in terms of s 173 of the Constitution to protect and regulate its own process, taking into account the interests of justice (para 28).

370 See in this regard, Trengove (note 7 above) 9.

whether the evolving plan and its implementation constitute adequate compliance with the order. As Roach and Budlender observe, general orders of this nature

> may be made either because of the nature of the duty involved (for example, a duty to act reasonably), or because the court is anxious to leave the government with as much latitude as possible to decide precisely how it will comply with its constitutional obligations.[371]

This type of structural interdict is capable of facilitating the 'experimentalist' remedial approach described by Charles Sabel and William Simon in their classic study on new directions in public interest litigation in the United States.[372] These innovative structural remedies represent a departure from the normal finality, and 'command-and-control' features of judicial remedies. Initially a court gives an order which defines the broad goals to be achieved to cure the constitutional violation. The order further requires the respondents, through a process of deliberative engagement and negotiation with the applicants, to devise a plan detailing the concrete measures and steps to be taken in order to meet those goals. The approval of the plan and its implementation are subject to ongoing judicial supervision. However, the court leaves as much latitude as possible for the formulation, implementation and monitoring of the plan to be resolved through deliberative negotiation between the claimants, relevant organs of State and, possibly, other stakeholders.[373] According to Sabel and Simon, a *prima facie* case for this type of structural interdict has two main elements – the failure to meet relevant constitutional and/or legislative standards and a political blockage which makes the relevant public institution unresponsive to reforms through normal political channels and processes.[374]

A prevalent concern regarding structural interdicts is that they infringe the separation of powers doctrine in that the supervising courts are drawn into usurping the functions of executive and administrative authorities through intrusive orders and excessive monitoring of administrative authorities.[375] However, as Sabel and Simon

---

371 Roach & Budlender (note 79 above) 334.

372 Sabel & Simon (note 5 above).

373 The authors observe in relation to these forms of 'experimentalist intervention' that 'whatever the technical legal status of the plans, their function is not so much to coerce obedience as to induce internal deliberation and external transparency' (ibid 1071).

374 Ibid 1062. For a description of the three patterns of political blockage identified by Sabel & Simon, see 1064–1065.

375 See, for example, the reservations expressed by the Supreme Court of Appeal in relation to structural interdicts in *Modderfontein Squatters, Greater Benoni City Council v Modderklip Boerdery (Pty) Ltd (Agri SA and Legal Resources Centre, Amici Curiae); President of the Republic of South Africa v Modderklip Boerdery (Pty) Ltd (Agri SA and Legal Resources Centre, Amici Curiae)* 2004 (6) SA 40 (SCA), 2004 (8) BCLR 821 (SCA) ('*Modderklip (SCA)*'):

> Structural interdicts ... have a tendency to blur the distinction between the executive and the judiciary and impact on the separation of powers. They tend to deal with policy matters and not with the enforcement of particular rights. (para 39)

In *Director of Public Prosecutions, Transvaal v Minister of Justice and Constitutional Development* (note 24 above), Ngcobo J held:

point out these kinds of remedies can in fact be more responsive to separation of powers concerns than the traditional final and specific judicial decrees which can be both 'inefficiently rigid and unnecessarily intrusive on executive authority'.[376] Orders which define the broad goals to be achieved for a programme or institution to be constitutionally compliant, but leave it to the organs of State to define the precise measures to achieve these goals through a participatory process afford a greater margin of policy discretion than final, detailed court orders.

These orders also reinforce the foundational constitutional values of accountability, responsiveness and openness.[377] Executive officials 'must make explicit policies and subject themselves to mechanisms of measurement and monitoring that make their performance more readily assessable'.[378] In response to the critique that orders of this nature are inappropriate because courts are not institutionally capable of compelling resource expenditures, Sabel and Simon observe that in all the cases studied, 'legislatures, agencies or nongovernmental organizations volunteered resources once the courts acted'.[379]

Structural interdicts of this nature also provide a methodology for dealing with the problem of polycentricity in the context of socio-economic rights litigation.[380] The processes through which the implications of the court's intervention for other institutions and groups are examined and incorporated in further negotiated orders are described by Sabel and Simon as 'the web effect'. They argue that:

> The web effect makes it possible to address sequentially – in a sequence determined in the course of problem-solving itself – reforms too complex to be addressed whole. The effect is polycentricity viewed as an aid, not an obstacle, to problem solving.[381]

These types of structural orders enable complex problems involving multiple actors, institutions and processes to be addressed through an incremental process of mutual dialogue and experimental learning. They catalyse a structured process of dialogic engagement between the parties and other stakeholders on the precise standards and measures needed to remedy the particular violation as well as the indicators for measuring compliance with the steps specified in the agreed plan. There is also substantial scope within the framework of structural interdicts for the courts to appoint

> Under our constitutional democracy, courts have no power to supervise or interfere with the exercise by the executive or its functions unless the circumstances amount to a clear disregard by the executive of the powers and duties conferred upon it by the Constitution. (para 183)

On separation of powers concerns in the context of socio-economic rights, see generally chapter 2, part 2.4.7.

376 Sabel & Simon (note 5 above) 1085.

377 Section 1(*d*) of the Constitution.

378 Sabel & Simon (note 5 above) 1093.

379 Ibid 1082.

380 See generally the discussion of 'polycentricity' in chapter 2, part 2.4.8 at notes 230–244 and accompanying text.

381 Sabel & Simon (note 5 above) 1080.

independent experts or preferably interdisciplinary teams of experts to assist them in the process of supervising the plans and reform process.[382]

Sabel and Simon draw the following conclusions from their study of the nature and efficacy of these kinds of 'experimentalist' orders:

> In stigmatizing the status quo, the court's intervention opens the defendant institution up to participation of previously marginalized stakeholders and clears the way for the redefinition of relations among more established ones. Counterintuitively, destabilization through new public law creates opportunities for collaborative learning and democratic accountability that the more certain world of pluralist bargaining under the aegis of courts or legislatures often precludes.[383]

Given these features, structural orders have an important role to play in promoting the participatory and deliberative ethos of the Constitution.[384] They have already been presaged in cases such as *Rudolph*[385] and *N* (the Westville prisoners' case),[386] as well as the eviction cases where orders of meaningful engagement have been given.[387]

Finally, such orders are likely to be more effective in remedying systemic violations which arise from complex institutional processes and a series of decisions taken by diverse actors over a period of time. In these circumstances, there are no obvious, 'quick fix' solutions. Effective and sustainable solutions are more likely to evolve through an iterative process of deliberative negotiations which are subject to periodic judicial control and adjustment for their consistency with the relevant constitutional rights.

---

[382] Ibid 1088–1089.

[383] Ibid 1100–1101.

[384] Sabel and Simon distinguish the kind of deliberative engagement mandated by these experimentalist orders from processes of pluralist bargaining in which participants pursue their own self-interest (1098–1099). The key features of deliberative engagement are described in the following terms:

> In contrast to bargaining, deliberation is centrally committed to reason-giving and openness to persuasion. It insists that the parties remain open to the possibility that they may not fully understand their self-interest and that they be at least hopeful of finding solutions that vindicate common values. It aspires to be a process of learning and solidarity-building rather than simply dispute settlement. (1099)

[385] See notes 335–347 above and accompanying text.

[386] See notes 348–364 above and accompanying text.

[387] See the cases discussed in 8.5.3(*b*) above. In *Occupiers of 51 Olivia Road* (note 11 above), the Court required the outcome of the engagement order to be endorsed by it. It held that a deciding factor in requiring the agreement to be approved by the Court was the fact that meaningful engagement had been ordered by the Court, and the parties had been required to report back on the process while proceedings were pending before it. See ibid paras 27–30. However, it did not assume a supervisory jurisdiction over the implementation of the agreement reached pursuant to the process of engagement. In *Joe Slovo* (note 244 above), the Court issued a reporting order in respect of the implementation of its order, which included directions that the parties 'engage meaningfully' with each other on various aspects of the removal, resettlement and permanent housing of the Joe Slovo community.

In conclusion, the transformative potential of socio-economic rights litigation in South Africa will remain unrealised if the courts do not devise remedies to deal with deeply entrenched patterns of socio-economic deprivation and marginalisation. These are precisely the kinds of cases in which the courts are reluctant to intervene because of their complexity and substantial resource and policy implications. The 'experimentalist' structural interdicts, with their emphasis on collaborative dialogue and learning in pursuing fundamental reforms in a particular sector, offer a significant remedial model for these kinds of cases.[388] These orders have the potential to facilitate the long-term structural reforms required to realise socio-economic rights without the shortcomings of the traditional 'command-and-control' judicial remedies. Structural orders should not be thought of as exceptional, 'last resort' remedies, but as an important remedial tool to deal with systemic socio-economic rights violations.

8.7 CONSTITUTIONAL DAMAGES

8.7.1 Introduction

Fose[389] was the earliest case in which the Constitutional Court considered a claim for 'constitutional damages'.[390] The claim was an adjunct to a claim for delictual damages arising out of alleged assault and torture of the plaintiff by members of the Vanderbijlpark police station. The claim for constitutional damages was based on infringements of the plaintiff's constitutional rights to dignity and not to be unlawfully tortured. It included a claim for punitive damages to deter and prevent future infringements of these rights, and to punish the organs of State responsible for the egregious violations of the plaintiff's rights.[391] In this regard, he alleged that his assault and torture were part of a widespread pattern of abuses at the particular police station.[392]

---

388 The potential of remedies to stimulate dialogic engagement between the institutions of government and affected beneficiaries has been highlighted by the Canadian Supreme Court in *Corbiere v Canada (Minister of Indian and Native Affairs)* [1999] 2 SCR 203:

> The remedies granted under the *Charter* should, in appropriate cases, encourage and facilitate the inclusion in that dialogue of groups particularly affected by legislation. In determining the appropriate remedy, a court should consider the effect of its order on the democratic process, understood in a broad way, and encourage that process. (para 116)

In *Reference re Secession of Quebec* [1998] 2 SCR 217, the Supreme Court held that:

> [A] functioning democracy requires a continuous process of discussion. ... Inevitably, there will be dissenting voices. A democratic system of government is committed to considering those dissenting voices, and seeking to acknowledge and address those voices in the laws by which all in the community must live. (para 68)

389 Note 4 above.

390 See the analysis by Currie & De Waal (note 3 above) 220–222.

391 *Fose* (note 4 above) para 14.

392 Ibid para 12.

The Court held that delictual damages constituted an adequate vindication of the plaintiff's rights, and refused the additional claim for 'constitutional damages'.[393] It gave a number of policy reasons why punitive constitutional damages would not be appropriate in the circumstances of the case. It was not persuaded that such awards would constitute an effective deterrent against police misconduct.[394] Second, in a country of scarce resources, it was inappropriate to pay punitive damages to plaintiffs who were already compensated for their injuries by delictual damages.[395] The Court held that the funds were better spent in addressing the structural and systemic causes of the infringements.[396] However, despite the Court's generally cautious attitude to awards of constitutional damages,[397] it did affirm that 'there is no reason in principle why "appropriate relief" should not include an award of damages, where such an award is necessary to protect and enforce chapter 3 rights'.[398]

In subsequent judgments, the sphere of delictual law has been substantially developed to recognise claims based on constitutional values and rights.[399] In the context of socio-economic rights, damages claims derived directly from the Constitution have been recognised in two primary areas.

8.7.2 Reconciling the protection of property and housing rights: *Modderklip*

The *Modderklip* case dealt with the question of the State's constitutional duty to assist a private landowner to execute an eviction order against unlawful occupiers on his property as well its obligations towards the occupiers.[400] The High Court in the case had granted a structural interdict requiring the State to devise a comprehensive plan, setting out the measures to be adopted to assist the landowner to execute the eviction order, as well as the provision of alternative accommodation for the occupiers.[401]

On appeal, the Supreme Court of Appeal expressed separation of powers reservations regarding structural interdicts.[402] It held that the remedy had to take into

[393] Ibid para 67.
[394] Ibid para 71. See also Kriegler J paras 102–3, and Didcott J paras 84–87.
[395] Ibid para 72.
[396] Ibid.
[397] Ibid. See particularly paras 65–68.
[398] Ibid para 60.
[399] See, for example, *Carmichele* (note 128 above); *Minister of Safety and Security v Van Duivenboden* 2002 (6) SA 431 (SCA), 2004 (2) BCLR 133 (SCA); *Van Eeden v Minister of Safety and Security* 2003 (1) SA 389 (SCA), [2002] 4 All SA 346 (SCA); *Zealand v Minister for Justice and Constitutional Development* 2008 (4) SA 458 (CC), 2008 (6) BCLR 601 (CC) paras 48–52.
[400] *Modderklip (SCA)* (note 375 above); *Modderklip (CC)* (note 194 above). The *Modderklip* judgments are discussed in chapter 6, part 6.3.
[401] *Modderklip Boerdery (Edms) Bpk v President van die Republiek van Suid-Afrika* 2003 (6) BCLR 638 (T), [2003] 1 All SA 465 (T) at 693A–694H.
[402] See note 375 above.

account 'comity between the different arms of the State' as well ensuring that the remedy could be sensibly enforced:

> [T]he State must be able to comply with the order within the limits of its capabilities, financial or otherwise. Policies also change, as do requirements, and all this impacts on enforcement.[403]

The Supreme Court of Appeal held that the structural interdict handed down by the High Court suffered from some of these defects in that it did not specify with sufficient precision what was expected of the State, and it encroached on policy matters by effectively permitting the occupiers preference in the housing queue.[404]

The Court held that the only appropriate relief in the circumstances of the case was a declaratory order that the State was obliged to pay '"constitutional" damages, that is, damages due to the breach of a constitutionally entrenched right'.[405] The advantage of ordering the State to pay damages to Modderklip was, in the words of the Court, that 'the Gabon occupiers can remain where they are while Modderklip will be recompensed for that which it has lost and the State has gained by not having to provide alternative land'.[406] The Court explained why a declaratory order in these terms was just in the circumstances of the case:

> Modderklip will not receive more than what it has lost, the State has already received value for what it has to pay and the immediate social problem is solved while the medium and long-term problems can be solved as and when the State can afford it.[407]

Compensation was to be calculated in terms of s 12(1) of the Expropriation Act 63 of 1975.[408] Significantly, the order expressly declared 'that the residents are entitled to occupy the land until alternative land has been made available to them by the state or the provincial or local authority'.[409]

The Constitutional Court upheld the essential features of this order. The State argued that a pure declaratory order clarifying the parties' rights would have been sufficient to vindicate Modderklip's rights. Modderklip could also bring a separate delictual action against the State.[410] However, the Court held that in the light of the

---

403 *Modderklip (SCA)* (note 375 above) para 39 (footnotes omitted).

404 Ibid para 40.

405 Ibid para 43. For a discussion of the considerations pertaining to the grant of a direct constitutional remedy as opposed to the development of a common-law remedy to remedy a constitutional infringement, see chapter 7, part 7.2.5.

406 Ibid.

407 Ibid.

408 On the measure of damages to be applied, see ibid para 44. Section 12(1) of the Expropriation Act 63 of 1975 provides that in respect of the expropriation of property or the taking of a right to use property, compensation must not exceed the amount which the property would have realised if sold in the open market by a willing seller to a willing buyer; and an amount to make good any actual financial loss caused by the expropriation or the taking of the right.

409 Ibid para 52, Order (*b*)(iii).

410 *Modderklip (CC)* (note 194 above) para 60.

long history of Modderklip's efforts to reclaim its property, it required 'something more effective than the suggested clarification of its rights'.[411] In all the circumstances of the case, a declaration that the respondent was entitled to compensation was deemed the most appropriate remedy.[412] The Constitutional Court also confirmed the Supreme Court of Appeal's order entitling the residents to occupy the land until alternative land was made available to them by the State or the provincial or local authority.[413]

In the *Modderklip* case, both the Supreme Court of Appeal and the Constitutional Court recognised that compensation would constitute appropriate relief for the infringement of the relevant constitutional rights.[414] The remedy of constitutional damages constituted the most effective and expeditious way of vindicating the rights of both the landowner and the occupiers in the circumstances of the case. The landowner was compensated by the State for having to bear the ongoing burden of the unlawful occupation of his property. The order entitling the residents to remain on the land until alternative land was made available to them ensured that their housing rights were protected.

The obvious solution to the dilemma was for the State to expropriate the land in question, and to formalise what was already an established community.[415] In fact, as the Court pointed out, an involuntary acquisition of the property would not be necessary as 'the owner has indicated willingness, indeed eagerness, to sell the land to the State'.[416] The Court expressly declined to decide whether courts had the competence to order the State to expropriate specific property.[417] It noted that it had no information about possible alternative land available to the State to enable its obligations to Modderklip to be fulfilled. If so, 'it would not be just and equitable to order the State to acquire specific land on Modderklip's farm'.[418] In other words, it was reasonable in

---

[411] Ibid.

[412] Ibid para 65. According to the Court it followed that, 'should the State decide to expropriate the land on Modderklip's farm, the sum to be awarded as compensation will be set off against compensation to be given for the expropriation'. Ibid.

[413] Ibid. Order 3(*c*).

[414] The Supreme Court of Appeal identified the relevant infringements of constitutional rights to be those entrenched in ss 7(2), (9)(1) and (2) and 25(1) in respect of Modderklip Boerdery (Pty) Ltd, and s 26(1) in respect of the residents. The Constitutional Court identified the infringements to be the right of the owner entrenched in s 34 read with s 1(*c*) of the Constitution, and the right of the occupiers in terms of s 26 to reasonable responses from the State to their housing predicament.

[415] As the Constitutional Court observed, the settlement comprising approximately 40 000 residents has fenced and numbered erven, streets, basic access to water services, shops and 'modest commercial ventures', and a voluntary civic structure. *Modderklip (CC)* (note 194 above) para 8.

[416] Ibid para 62.

[417] Ibid paras 63–64.

[418] Ibid.

the circumstances to leave the State with a choice of means regarding the particular land on which to settle the community.[419]

The remedy in *Modderklip* was clearly intended by the Supreme Court of Appeal and the Constitutional Court to provide a catalyst for tripartite negotiations between the State, landowner and residents on a satisfactory solution that would respect the constitutional rights of both the landowners and residents. This order can thus also be understood to encourage dialogic engagement between the parties in furtherance of the deliberative ideals of transformative constitutionalism.[420]

8.7.3 Compensation for maladministration of social grants

The second main context in which the courts have considered damages or compensation to be an appropriate remedy for infringements of constitutional rights arises from the systemic failure in the administration of social grants payable in terms of the Social Assistance Act in certain provinces. As Froneman J observed in *Kate v MEC for the Department of Welfare, Eastern Cape* ('*Kate*'):[421]

> The failure in proper administration has led to the situation where the courts have become the primary mechanisms for ensuring accountability in the public administration of social grants.[422]

Most of these cases have been decided in terms of the right to administrative justice,[423] making this a crucially important right for the protection of the social security rights in s 27(1)(*c*) of the Constitution.[424] One of the remedies for long delays in the processing of social grant applications has been to order the respondent to backdate the payment to a date deemed to be a reasonable period for processing a social grant application (usually three months after submitting the application absent special circumstances), and awarding interest on this amount.[425] This remedy has been held to constitute 'appropriate relief' in terms of s 38 of the Constitution.[426]

---

[419] See also *Dada NO v Unlawful Occupiers of Portion 41 of the farm Rooikop* 2009 (2) SA 492 (W) and *Ekurhuleni Metropolitan Municipality v Dada NO* 2009 (4) SA 463 (SCA). See the discussion of these cases in chapter 6, part 6.3 at notes 164–172 and accompanying text.

[420] See D Brand 'The "politics of need interpretation" and the adjudication of socio-economic rights claims in South Africa' in A J van der Walt (ed) *Theories of Social and Economic Justice* (2005) 17–36 at 34–35.

[421] 2005 (1) SA 141 (SE), [2005] 1 All SA 745 (SE).

[422] Ibid para 5.

[423] Section 33 of the Constitution and the PAJA which has been enacted to give effect to this right.

[424] See N de Villiers 'Social grants and the Promotion of Administrative Justice Act' (2002) 18 *SAJHR* 320–349; C Plasket 'Administrative justice and social assistance' (2003) 120 *SALJ* 494–524.

[425] *Mahambehlala v MEC for Welfare, Eastern Cape* 2002 (1) SA 342 (SE), 2001 (9) BCLR 890 (SE) and *Mbanga v MEC for Welfare, Eastern Cape* 2002 (1) SA 359 (SE).

[426] See *Mahambehlala* ibid 356C-D. PAJA was not applied as it had not commenced when the relevant facts arose.

It has been questioned whether compensation in the form of awards of back pay and interest constitute appropriate relief in terms of either s 38 of the Constitution or s 33 read with PAJA for unreasonable administrative delays in the processing of social grants or the unlawful termination of grants.[427] In *Jayiya*,[428] the Supreme Court of Appeal indicated that where a statutory remedy had been enacted to give effect to a constitutional right, it was inappropriate to rely directly on s 38 of the Constitution to claim 'constitutional damages'. Remedies for the delay in processing the applicant's disability grant application had accordingly to be sought in terms of PAJA which only 'exceptionally' permitted a court to direct an administrator to pay compensation.[429]

In the subsequent High Court decision of *Kate*,[430] Froneman J held that Conradie JA's remarks on constitutional damages in the form of back pay and interest were essentially *obiter*, but 'obviously merit serious consideration by a lower court'.[431] In response to Conradie JA's views that 'constitutional damages' may only be awarded where no statutory or common-law remedies exist and that back pay and interest cannot be claimed under PAJA, Froneman J reasoned as follows:

> On the face of it the wording of PAJA does not preclude judicial review under the general rule of law principle of legality, nor does it preclude appropriate constitutional relief under such a claim. The remedies available under PAJA too are couched in wide, open-ended and permissive terms. The fact that disregard of public statutory responsibilities may have become commonplace in this province does not necessarily mean that it can no longer constitute exceptional circumstances for the purposes of s 8(1)(*c*)(ii)(*bb*) of PAJA.[432]

The Court went on to hold that while it was true that the setting aside of unlawful administrative action normally associated with the judicial review of administrative action was inappropriate in this case, this did not 'deprive the courts of the competence to find that conduct unlawful, and, in consequence of that finding, to order

---

427 See, for example, *Ntame v MEC for Social Development, Eastern Cape, and Two Similar Cases* 2005 (6) SA 248 (E).

428 Note 357 above.

429 Ibid paras 8–9. He indicated that these were brief 'tentative comments' since this particular issue was not argued before the Court (para 8). Section 8(1)(*c*)(ii)(*bb*) of PAJA provides that in judicial review proceedings, a court or tribunal may grant 'any order that is just and equitable, including orders ... in exceptional cases directing the administrator or any party to the proceedings to pay compensation'.

430 Note 421 above. The case concerned a three-year delay in the processing of the applicant's disability grant. After approval of her grant, she received regular monthly payments as well as a lump sum in respect of 'back pay'. However, such back pay was significantly less than she was entitled to in respect of the unreasonable delay in the approval of her grant. She applied to court seeking, inter alia, payment of the outstanding amount together with interest on the arrear payments.

431 Ibid para 20. The *obiter* status of these remarks of Conradie JA were confirmed by the Supreme Court of Appeal in *MEC, Department of Welfare, Eastern Cape v Kate* 2006 (4) SA 478 (SCA), [2006] 2 All SA 455 (SCA) para 21 ('*Kate (SCA)*').

432 Ibid (footnotes omitted).

some form of remedial relief'.[433] To hold otherwise would be 'to conflate the *process* of what has become known as review, with the *remedies* that may follow upon judicial scrutiny of a decision which turns out to be unlawful'.[434] The applicant had still not received the monetary equivalent of what she would have received had her application been dealt with properly. According to the Court, the applicant 'was constitutionally entitled to a proper redress of the continuing wrong done to her'.[435] It was of little consequence that 'at various stages over this period the interim Constitution, the final Constitution alone, and now the Constitution and PAJA together, regulated the legal position'.[436] The provincial government was accordingly ordered to pay the applicant the outstanding amount of the social grant that had accrued to her together with interest on the monthly amounts that should have been paid.[437]

On appeal, the Supreme Court of Appeal held that the central right at issue in the case was the substantive right to social assistance in s 27(1)(*c*) of the Constitution. The right to administrative fairness was a means to protecting this right.[438] The Court held that it would narrowly determine whether in this particular case an award of monetary damages arising from a breach of a substantive constitutional right was appropriate.[439]

The MEC, Department of Welfare argued that it would be more appropriate for Mrs Kate to pursue delictual remedies for her loss rather than an award of constitutional damages.[440] The Court confirmed that delictual remedies did play a role in protecting constitutional rights, albeit indirectly,[441] and delictual principles were 'capable of being extended to encompass state liability for the breach of constitutional obligations'.[442] However, it held that the indirect route of vindicating constitutional rights was not invariably to be preferred over granting a direct constitutional remedy in terms of s 38. Nugent JA gave the following two reasons for preferring a direct constitutional remedy in the circumstances of the case:

> First, I see no reason why a direct breach of a substantive constitutional right (as opposed to merely a deviation from a constitutionally normative standard) should be remedied

---

[433] Ibid paras 30–31. As the Court pointed out, the normal paradigm of 'setting aside' decisions could not be applied in cases of systemic past failures to take proper decisions.

[434] Ibid para 30.

[435] Ibid para 31.

[436] Ibid.

[437] Ibid paras 34–35.

[438] *Kate (SCA)* (note 431 above) para 22.

[439] Ibid para 25.

[440] Ibid para 26.

[441] In this context, the Court cited the decisions of the Supreme Court of Appeal in *Van Duivenboden* (note 399 above) and *Minister of Safety and Security v Carmichele* 2004 (3) SA 305 (SCA), [2003] 4 All SA 565 (SCA) para 27 n 41.

[442] *Kate (SCA)* (note 431 above) para 27.

> indirectly. Secondly, the endemic breach of the rights that are now in issue justifies – indeed, it calls out for – the clear assertion of their independent existence.[443]

Purely declaratory relief as proposed by the MEC was deemed inappropriate due to the systemic failure of the government to comply with its constitutional obligations.[444] The appropriateness of a mandamus compelling the relevant public functionaries in the provincial department of welfare to fulfil their constitutional and statutory obligations was also considered. The Court held that generally a mandamus, without an additional remedy of damages, had the capacity to be effective in cases where there was a breach or threatened breach by a public official of a constitutional or statutory duty. However, it held that there were two considerations which 'militate against confining Kate to that preventative remedy'.[445] The first relates to the fact that the primary beneficiaries of the rights at issue in the case were the 'very poorest in society' who lacked the knowledge of their rights and the resources to secure them. As a result it was unlikely that Mrs Kate 'had the capacity or the means that were required to act swiftly once the delay set in and it would be quite unrealistic to expect the remedy to have been effective in her hands'.[446] The second consideration relates to 'broader considerations'.[447] In this regard, the Court raised the concern that mandatory relief would tend to encourage spiralling litigation 'with each applicant attempting to leap-frog over others in order to secure their benefits'.[448] The solution lay in the administration 'getting its house in order' as opposed to encouraging yet more litigation.[449]

In the circumstances, the Court held that the only appropriate remedy was an award of constitutional damages in Mrs Kate's favour. The Court acknowledged that it was 'indeed troubling' that the provincial administration would be spending scarce public resources on settling damages claims arising out of its administrative failures. However, this consideration did not justify withholding a damages remedy. The Court expressed the hope that a resolution to the systemic maladministration in social grants payments would lie in accountability to the legislature if the department was forced to seek additional funds to meet claims for damages in addition to those appropriated for social assistance payments.[450] Regarding the measure of damages, the Court described the nature of the losses experienced by Mrs Kate in the following terms:

> To be held in poverty is a cursed condition. Quite apart from the physical discomfort of deprivation it reduces a human in his or her dignity. The inevitable result of being

[443] Ibid. See also the discussion of *Kate* in chapter 7, part 7.2.5.
[444] Ibid paras 28–29.
[445] Ibid para 31.
[446] Ibid para 31.
[447] Ibid.
[448] Ibid.
[449] Ibid.
[450] Ibid para 32.

> unlawfully deprived of a grant that is required for daily sustenance is the unnecessary further endurance of that condition for so long as the unlawfulness continues.[451]

The damages were calculated on the basis of an amount equivalent to the interest that is recognised in law to be payable when money is unlawfully withheld.[452] The order of the High Court was substantially upheld.[453]

An order of constitutional damages was clearly considered to constitute appropriate relief in this case as it was the most expeditious and effective way of remedying the breach of a substantive constitutional right. The case entailed a breach of two interrelated constitutional rights – the right to just administrative action (s 33)[454] and the right of access to social assistance (s 27(1)(*c*) read with (2)). To have expected a litigant in Mrs Kate's position to pursue delictual remedies would have resulted in further delays and costs. The claim would have been viewed and assessed through the common-law requirements for delictual relief which does not provide an appropriate paradigm for cases of this nature.

In assessing the appropriateness of damages derived directly from an infringement of constitutional rights in this case, Nugent JA conducted a context-sensitive analysis of the nature of the infringement, the position of the applicant and others similarly placed, as well as the most effective means of securing Government's compliance with its constitutional obligations. It is submitted that this approach is the correct one to follow when a court assesses whether an award of direct constitutional damages is appropriate.

In *Njongi v MEC, Department of Welfare, Eastern Cape*,[455] ('*Njongi*') the Constitutional Court upheld an order of the High Court awarding the appellant back pay and interest on the arrear amounts following the unlawful termination of her disability grant. The Court confirmed that all persons affected by the unlawful termination of their grants 'ought to have been placed in the position in which they would have been, absent the unlawful administrative decision'.[456]

8.7.4 Conclusion

Wim Trengove has suggested innovative approaches to damages remedies in the context of socio-economic rights cases.[457] He argues that certain types of socio-economic rights violations are better remedied through awards of preventative damages in favour of an independent state institution such as the South African Human Rights Commission or a human rights non-governmental organisation. These institutions

---

451 Ibid para 33.
452 Ibid.
453 See the Order at para 35.
454 On the possibility of claiming back pay and interest in a case such as this one via s 8(2)(*c*) of PAJA, see C Hoexter *Administrative Law in South Africa* (2007) 507–508.
455 2008 (4) SA 237 (CC), 2008 (6) BCLR 571 (CC).
456 Ibid paras 16, 22. See also the discussion of *Njongi* in part 8.10 below.
457 Trengove (note 7 above) 8–9.

are required to apply the award in programmes aimed at preventing and protecting vulnerable groups against violations of their socio-economic rights.[458]

Similarly, he argues that 'reparations in kind' may be a more appropriate remedy than damages sounding in money because of the difficulty in quantifying the harm done to individual plaintiffs arising from a long-term structural deprivation of services such as education, water and health care.[459] The State may thus be ordered to provide appropriate remedial services for the benefit of the beneficiary class as a whole with ongoing judicial supervision of their implementation.[460]

It is submitted that both traditional and the innovative damages remedies are important remedial options for the courts in the context of socio-economic rights cases. The nature of the analysis conducted by Nugent JA in the *Kate (SCA)* case discussed above should guide the courts' discretion in determining whether an award of damages is appropriate and, if so, the precise form this award should take in the light of the particular facts and circumstances of the case.

8.8 ADMINISTRATIVE REMEDIES

Frequently people's access to socio-economic rights is determined by administrative action taken in terms of social legislation enacted to give effect to socio-economic rights.[461] As noted above, s 33 of the Constitution and PAJA constitute crucial mechanisms for ensuring lawful, reasonable and procedurally fair administrative action in the context of decision-making which affects people's access to legislated social benefits and services.[462]

If a successful application for the review of an administrative decision is brought in terms of PAJA, the usual remedy is the setting aside of the decision, and the remittal of the matter for decision by the administrator, 'with or without directions'.[463] In 'exceptional cases' a court on review may substitute or vary the administrative action or correct a defect resulting from an administrative action.[464]

---

[458] Ibid 8.

[459] Ibid 9.

[460] Ibid.

[461] Sections 26(2) and 27(2) specifically envisage legislative measures 'to achieve the progressive realisation' of the relevant rights.

[462] See N de Villiers (note 424 above); C Plasket (note 424 above).

[463] Section 8(1)(*c*)(i) of PAJA.

[464] Section 8(1)(*c*)(ii)(*aa*) of PAJA. On substitution, See generally *Erf One Six Seven Orchards CC v Greater Johannesburg Metropolitan Council (Johannesburg Administration)* 1999 (1) SA 104 (SCA); *Premier, Mpumalanga, v Executive Committee, Association of State-Aided Schools, Eastern Transvaal* 1999 (2) SA 91 (CC), 1999 (2) BCLR 151 (CC) (endorsing in para 50 the leading common-law judgment on this issue, viz. *Johannesburg City Council v Administrator, Transvaal,* 1969 (2) SA 72 (T)); *Commissioner, Competition Commission v General Council of the Bar of South Africa* 2002 (6) SA 606 (SCA); *Gauteng Gambling Board v Silverstar Development Ltd* 2005 (4) SA 67 (SCA) (see particularly para 28 where the PAJA requirement

In *Minister of Home Affairs v Watchenuka*,[465] the Supreme Court of Appeal held that a blanket prohibition placed by The Standing Committee for Refugee Affairs on asylum seekers seeking employment and studying constituted an infringement of their rights to human dignity and education. The Court confirmed the order of the High Court setting aside the relevant regulation promulgated in terms of the Refugees Act 130 of 1998.[466] However, it held that this did not entitle the applicant to an order directing the Minister to permit her and her son to be employed and to study respectively. Nugent JA held that the discretion to permit particular asylum seekers to work or study had to be exercised in a way that took their constitutional rights and particular circumstances into account.[467] A relevant factor would be whether employment is the only reasonable means for the support of the asylum seeker and his or her family. In these circumstances, what is then in issue 'is not merely a restriction upon the person's capacity for self-fulfilment, but a restriction upon his or her ability to live without positive humiliation and degradation'.[468] In other words, the right to human dignity of asylum seekers were implicated.

The Court accordingly directed The Standing Committee for Refugee Affairs 'to consider and determine whether the first applicant and her son respectively should be permitted to undertake employment and to study pending the outcome of the first respondent's application for asylum, and to cause the appropriate condition to be endorsed upon the permit issued to her in terms of s 22 of the Refugees Act'.[469]

Apart from reviewing and setting aside a decision, the other remedies in s 8 of PAJA are also available.[470] Thus, for example, in cases where the breach consists of a failure to take a decision within a reasonable time,[471] the courts have a broad discretion to grant 'any order that is just and equitable' including directing the taking of the decision, declaring the rights of the parties in relation to the taking of the decision, and directing the parties to do or refrain from doing any act which the courts considers necessary to do justice between the parties, or as to costs.[472]

---

of 'exceptional circumstances' was equated with the common-law approach to substitution).

465 2004 (4) SA 326 (SCA), 2004 (2) BCLR 120 (SCA).

466 Ibid para 20.

467 The Court held that this discretion could either be exercised 'on a case by case basis or by formulating guidelines to be applied by Refugee Reception Officers when issuing permits in particular cases' (ibid para 34).

468 Ibid para 32. See also the considerations relevant to the right of the children of asylum seekers to study in para 36.

469 Ibid para 39.

470 See generally Hoexter (note 454 above) 461–530; I Currie *The Promotion of Administrative Justice Act: A Commentary* 2 ed (2007) 189–195.

471 See ss 6(2)(*g*), 6(3) read with 8(2) of PAJA.

472 See s 8(2)(*a*)–(*d*) of PAJA.

In *Vumazonke v MEC for Social Development, Eastern Cape, and Three Similar Cases*[473] the respondent was ordered to consider and take the relevant decisions required of her in terms of the Social Assistance Act 59 of 1992 and its Regulations within 30 calendar days of the date of the court's order. The taking of decisions on various applications for social grant applications had been long delayed and was another manifestation of the systemic problems in the administration of social grants referred to above.[474] Plasket J observed that the courts in these cases faced the problem of 'the limits of the institutional competence of the courts to engineer administrative efficiency'.[475] In a further effort to redress the dysfunctional operation of the Department of Social Development, the Registrar was directed to serve a copy of his judgment on the chairperson of the Human Rights Commission. The purpose of such service was to enable the chairperson of the Commission to consider 'whether to institute an investigation into the conduct of the respondent's department with a view to proposing concrete steps to ensure that it begins to comply with its constitutional and legal obligations and ceases to infringe constitutional rights on the present grant scale'.[476] The Registrar was further directed to serve a copy of the judgment on the chairperson of the Public Service Commission so that he too could consider instituting an investigation into the respondent's department.[477]

The Constitutional Court has declared unconstitutional legislation which vests wide and unlimited discretionary powers in administrative officials. Such a broad conferral of discretion enables decisions to be taken which breach constitutional rights.[478] It has also provided directions or guidelines on how administrative officials should exercise their discretion to ensure consistency with constitutional rights.

The latter approach is illustrated by the case of *Union of Refugee Women v Director: Private Security Industry Regulatory Authority*.[479] The case concerned an application for the review of decisions of the Private Security Industry Regulatory Authority and its Appeal Committee. It was brought by a group representing refugees in South Africa who had either had their registrations as security service providers withdrawn or had been refused registration. In the alternative they sought an order declaring s 23(1)(*a*) of the Private Security Industry Regulation Act 56 of 2001 to be inconsistent with the Constitution and invalid. Section 23(1)(*a*) of the Act makes South African citizenship or permanent residence a requirement for registration. Section 23(6) provides that, '[d]espite the provisions of subsections (1) ... the Authority may on good cause shown and on grounds which are not in conflict with the purpose of this Act

---

[473] 2005 (6) SA 229 (E).
[474] See the observations of Froneman J in *Kate* at notes 421–422 and accompanying text.
[475] Ibid para 9. See also para 10.
[476] Ibid para 18.
[477] The Public Service Commission is established in terms of s 196 of the Constitution, and its powers and functions are regulated by the Constitution and the Public Service Commission Act 46 of 1997.
[478] See *Dawood* (note 24 above).
[479] 2007 (4) SA 395 (CC), 2007 (4) BCLR 339 (CC).

and the objects of the Authority, register any applicant as a security service provider'. The applicants argued that s 23 discriminated unfairly against persons who were not citizens or permanent residents of South Africa and who were seeking work in the private security industry.

The majority of the Court held that the discrimination was not unfair in that it did not place a blanket ban on refugees seeking employment, it was narrowly tailored for the purpose of screening entrants to the security industry, and was flexible by including the exemption in s 23(6) from the strict requirements of citizenship 'on good cause shown'.[480] The Court accordingly dismissed the challenge to the constitutionality of s 23(1)(*a*) of the Act.

However, it directed that the applicants be given an opportunity to apply for exemption in terms of s 23(6) of the Act. Guidelines were provided in the judgment on the factors which the regulatory authorities ought to consider in determining whether 'good cause' had been established for granting an exemption.[481] The regulatory authorities were directed to make both the current and potential applicants aware of the nature of the information that must be furnished in their applications for exemption, and to consider all such applications in the light of the guidelines provided in the judgment.[482]

8.9 ENFORCEMENT OF COURT ORDERS AGAINST THE STATE

8.9.1 Introduction

In this part, the mechanisms available to the courts to ensure that the State complies with their orders are examined. If court orders in socio-economic rights cases can be ignored with impunity, the entire enterprise of seeking relief for violations of these rights through the courts is undermined.

A major challenge that the courts have had to face has been the emergence of a trend of non-compliance with money judgments against the State.[483] Section 3 of the State Liability Act 20 of 1957 precluded execution or attachment against the assets or property of the state. With this avenue of obtaining satisfaction of the judgment debt closed off, the courts resorted to various strategies in attempts to secure compliance with these orders, including a mandamus combined with a structural interdict,[484] and contempt of court proceedings.[485] This part will focus on the use of contempt of

---

480 Ibid para 67. See, however, the dissenting judgments of Mokgoro J and O'Regan J.

481 Ibid paras 85–87.

482 Ibid. See the Order of the Court para 90.

483 In terms of s 165(5) of the Constitution, '[a]n order or decision issued by a court binds all persons to whom and organs of state to which it applies'.

484 See *Magidimisi NO v Premier of the Eastern Cape* (note 366 above).

485 See part 8.9.3 below.

court remedies and the Constitutional Court's decision in *Nyathi*[486] declaring s 3 of the State Liability Act unconstitutional.

8.9.2 Contempt of court

In terms of the existing common law, a distinction is drawn between orders *ad pecuniam solvendam* (for the payment of a sum of money) and orders *ad factum praestandum* (mandatory orders compelling someone to do or to refrain from doing something). The latter orders can be enforced by applying for an order declaring the defaulting party to be in contempt of court and committing them to prison. A rule *nisi* is usually issued calling upon the person or official to show cause why they should not be held in contempt before that person is committed to prison.

In *Fakie NO*,[487] the Supreme Court of Appeal dealt with the impact of constitutional rights and values on the civil process for committal for contempt of court. In elaborating on the public interest dimension inherent in contempt committal, Cameron JA referred with approval[488] to the following observations of Plasket J in *Victoria Park Ratepayers Association v Greyvenouw CC*:[489]

> It is clear that contempt of court is not merely a mechanism for the enforcement of court orders. The jurisdiction of the Superior Courts to commit recalcitrant litigants for contempt of court when they fail or refuse to obey court orders has at its heart the very effectiveness and legitimacy of the judicial system .... That, in turn, means that the Court called upon to commit such a litigant for his or her contempt is not only dealing with the individual interest of the frustrated successful litigant but also, as importantly, acting as guardian of the public interest.[490]

The Court went on to clarify the requirements and burden of proof applicable to contempt of court proceedings where committal is sought. Thus the burden is on the applicant to prove 'the requisites of contempt (the order; service or notice; non-compliance and *mala fides*) beyond reasonable doubt'.[491] But, once the applicant has proved the order, service or notice, and non-compliance, 'the respondent bears an evidential burden in relation to wilfulness and *mala fides*'.[492] Should the respondent fail to advance evidence that establishes a reasonable doubt as to whether non-compliance was wilful and *mala fide*, contempt will have been established beyond reasonable doubt.[493] The Court expressly confirmed that even where the requirements of civil

---

486 Note 105 above.
487 Note 206 above.
488 Ibid para 38.
489 [2004] 3 All SA 623 (SE).
490 Ibid para 5.
491 *Fakie NO* (note 206 above) para 42.
492 Ibid.
493 Ibid.

contempt are not established, a *declarator* and other appropriate remedies remain available to a civil applicant on proof on a balance of probabilities.[494]

Orders to pay sums of money are usually enforceable through execution against the property of the debtor.[495] However, as noted above, this route was precluded in respect of money judgments obtained against the State by the provisions of s 3 of the State Liability Act. Prior to the Constitutional Court's decision in *Nyathi*,[496] litigants pursued the avenue of declarations of contempt of court against the heads of provincial government departments and the relevant public functionaries in an attempt to get the State to comply with money judgments.[497]

However, in *Jayiya*,[498] the Supreme Court of Appeal cast considerable doubt on whether money judgments against the State were enforceable through contempt proceedings.[499] According to Conradie JA, the common law could not evolve 'in conflict with statute law or basic principles of law' of which legality was one of the fundamental tenets.[500] He held that the decisions of the Eastern Cape High Court had created a situation which endorsed the retrospective creation of a new crime of contempt or the extension of the limits of the existing one. This was prohibited both by the general principles of the common law and by s 35(3)(*l*) of the Constitution.[501] The preclusion of contempt proceedings to enforce money judgments against the State effectively left social grant recipients without an effective remedy to vindicate their constitutional and statutory rights.

In the subsequent High Court decision of *Kate*,[502] Froneman J observed:

> It is one thing to realise the possibility *as a matter of fact* that the Government might refuse to comply with court orders. It is something completely different to hold *as a matter of law* that courts are powerless to devise ways to ensure compliance with court orders in a constitutional state such as ours .... For the courts to do the latter would be to aid and

[494] Ibid para 65. See the declaratory and directory orders upheld by the Court in this case following on the finding that CCII had failed to prove that the default in issue in the case was wilful and *mala fide*: paras 64–65.

[495] For a decision dealing with the impact of s 26 of the Constitution on civil proceedings for the enforcement of judgment debts in the Magistrates' Courts Act 32 of 1944, see *Jaftha* (note 48 above). See the discussion of *Jaftha* in chapter 4, part 4.6.2.

[496] Note 105 above.

[497] *Mjeni v Minister of Health and Welfare, Eastern Cape* 2000 (4) SA 446 (Tk); *East London Transitional Local Council v MEC for Health, Eastern Cape,* [2000] 4 All SA 443 (Ck). In *Mjeni* the Court held that the common-law distinction between orders sounding in money and orders to act should not apply when the State was the judgment debtor as the effect of the provisions of the common law and the State Liability Act was that 'those who sue the State run the risk of obtaining hollow and unenforceable judgments. The State could just ignore such judgments with complete impunity' (453I–454B).

[498] Note 357 above.

[499] Ibid paras 15–18.

[500] Ibid para 18.

[501] Ibid.

[502] Note 421 above.

> abet unconstitutional government, the very antithesis of the courts' duty in terms of the Constitution.[503]

Froneman J construed the *Jayiya* judgment narrowly, holding that the only binding decision was that the wrong orders had been sought against the wrong respondents, and that state functionaries could not be found guilty of the *crime* of contempt of court for non-compliance with a money judgment.[504] The courts could accordingly still make a declaratory order that a State functionary is in contempt of a court order. They could also call upon State functionaries to explain why they had not complied with court orders and require them to explain how they intend complying with those orders. The common-law rule of civil contempt could be developed in this manner without attaching criminal sanctions.[505]

On appeal in the *Kate* case, the Supreme Court of Appeal confirmed that *Jayiya* had 'decided only that a money judgment given against a provincial government ... is not enforceable by incarcerating for contempt a defendant who has been cited nominally for the government if the government fails to comply with the order'.[506]

8.9.3 *Nyathi* and the constitutionality of the State Liability Act

The Constitutional Court's judgment in *Nyathi*[507] handed down on 2 June 2008 represents a major breakthrough in enforcing money judgments against the State. In this case, the Court confirmed an order of constitutional invalidity in respect of s 3 of the State Liability Act 20 of 1957 'to the extent that it does not allow for execution or attachment against the state and that it does not provide for an express procedure for the satisfaction of judgment debts'.[508] The declaration of invalidity was suspended for a period of 12 months to allow Parliament to pass legislation providing for the effective enforcement of court orders.[509]

The Court held that the prohibition on execution against the property of the State in the Act unjustifiably limited the right to equality before the law and equal protection of the law (s 9(1)), the right to dignity (s 10), and the right of access to courts (s 34).[510] The Court interpreted the right to dignity substantively. It held that the State effectively ignored the applicant's desperate need for rehabilitative treatment by failing to comply with the terms of an order for an interim payment of the damages due to him as a result of medical negligence suffered at two State hospitals.[511] Without

---

[503] Ibid para 25.
[504] Ibid para 23.
[505] Ibid para 21.
[506] *Kate (SCA)* (note 431 above) para 19 (footnotes and parentheses omitted).
[507] Note 105 above.
[508] Ibid para 92. Order (1).
[509] Ibid para 92. Order (2).
[510] Ibid paras 36–47.
[511] Ibid para 45.

this treatment, the applicant 'stood a very slim chance of survival'.[512] The applicant was precluded from attaching assets of the State as a mechanism for enforcing the court order in his favour. Madala J highlighted the positive duties imposed on the State by the rights to human dignity and to life in these circumstances:

> It certainly cannot be said ... that the applicant was treated in a manner that showed recognition for his worth and importance as a human being. The State is under a duty to ensure than an individual's right to life is not infringed and is also under a duty to ensure that this right is protected. The State knew how vital the treatment was to the applicant yet did not act to ensure that he received it.[513]

The State Liability Act served the valid purpose of protecting the State's interests by disallowing attachment of its assets, which had 'the potential to disrupt service delivery and interfere with the state's accounting procedures'.[514] However, there were other less restrictive measures by which the State's essential assets and accounting procedures could be protected without completely prohibiting execution or attachment against the State. In addition, the Court was of the opinion that s 3 of the State Liability Act read in conjunction with other legislation and regulations for the enforcement of money claims against the State[515] did not provide an effective procedure for the enforcement of judgment debts. According to the Court:

> The procedures referred to [in the abovementioned legislation] are inaccessible to the majority of creditors and are far too complex to constitute a reasonable fulfilment of the state's obligations in terms of the Constitution. The section does not deal at all with how court orders are to be satisfied.[516]

The majority of the Court held that s 3 of the State Liability Act (read in conjunction with the other legislation referred to above) was not reasonably capable of providing an effective remedy for the enforcement of judgment debts against the State. There was 'a desperate need' for new legislation to be enacted that would provide for a more efficient and effective procedure for the settlement of judgment debts against the State.[517]

The Court furthermore took cognisance of the fact that there were approximately 200 cases against the State for payment of outstanding judgment debts.[518] In order to obtain finality in these cases, the Court assumed a supervisory jurisdiction over the settlement of these orders. The Minister of Justice and Constitutional Development was ordered to compile and provide on affidavit 'a list of all unsatisfied court orders against national and provincial state departments' and to provide the Court with 'a

[512] Ibid.
[513] Ibid (footnotes omitted).
[514] Ibid para 51.
[515] The Public Finance Management Act 1 of 1999; Treasury Regulations, GN R225, GG 27388, 15 March 2005.
[516] *Nyathi* (note 105 above) para 58.
[517] Ibid para 74.
[518] Ibid para 86

plan of the steps it would take to ensure speedy settlement of unsatisfied court orders' by no later than 31 July 2008. The Chief Justice would then issue further directions, as necessary.[519] The Court held that judicial oversight was essential in the circumstances of the case as there was no other effective remedy for ensuring that the State complied with court orders.[520] Relying on the State's sense of moral duty to comply with court orders had proven to be insufficient. Effective compliance with these orders required both new legislation and judicial oversight of compliance.[521]

In the course of its judgment, the Court also pointed out why contempt proceedings did not constitute a satisfactory remedial option for a judgment creditor. It placed a heavy and tedious burden on a successful litigant of taking further legal steps such as the obtaining of a mandamus against the relevant state official followed by contempt proceedings upon non-compliance.[522] Contempt proceedings would tend to be impractical in a context of no mechanisms to enforce judgment debts against State assets coupled with an 'inefficient and ineffective' state administration.[523] As Madala J observed:

> The committal of public officials would only result in the 'naming and shaming' of such officials and would produce no real remedy for the aggrieved litigant who is primarily concerned with the payment of the judgment debt. The potential disruption of already overburdened state departments is also a result which should be avoided.[524]

The minority of the Court disagreed that the constitutional defect lay in the legislative provisions for the enforcement of judgment debts against the State.[525] They were of the view that the source of the problem lay in the unlawful conduct of state officials and 'administrative bungling'. In these circumstances, other remedies were available to obtain payment of the judgment debt such as a mandamus against the relevant state officials responsible for ensuring that the debt was paid.[526]

However, it is submitted that the approach of the majority is more attuned to the circumstances and constraints faced by impoverished litigants in pursuing further litigation to enforce court orders. The majority correctly placed the burden on the State

---

[519] Ibid para 92. Order paras 3 and 4.

[520] Ibid paras 83–85.

[521] Ibid.

[522] Ibid para 75. On the burden of proof resting on applicants in contempt proceedings, see note 491 above and accompanying text.

[523] Ibid paras 77–78.

[524] Ibid para 76.

[525] Per Nkabinde J, Langa CJ and Mpati AJ.

[526] Ibid paras 146–148. The minority referred to Froneman J's remedy of a mandamus combined with a structural interdict in *Magidimisi v The Premier, Eastern Cape* (note 366 above) as a method of obtaining relief in circumstances where the State fails to satisfy a judgment debt (paras 145–149.) However, the majority were of the view that the availability of this remedy did not cure the constitutional defect in the Act as it imposed the expensive and time-consuming burden of litigation on a judgment creditor to obtain payment of the debt owed to it by the State (para 33).

to create an effective legislative and administrative mechanism to enable litigants to enforce court orders.

Subsequent to this judgment, applications for the extension of the suspended declaration of invalidity in respect of the State Liability Act were made by the Minister for Justice and Constitutional Development. The Court extended the period of suspension until 31 August 2011. However, it devised an interim procedure to operate during the period of suspension.[527] This procedure permits execution against the movable property of the State subject to service on the relevant state treasuries of a final court order for the payment of a sum of money which is not satisfied within 30 days of the date of judgment. Should the relevant treasury fail to satisfy the judgment debt within 14 days of service of the order, the judgment creditor may apply for a writ of execution against the movable property owned by the State and used by the relevant department. Provision is also made for parties with a direct and material interest to apply to court for a stay of execution of the attached assets on grounds that it is in the interests of justice for the execution to be stayed.[528] In this context, the Court endorsed the submissions of the *amici curiae* relating to the necessity of an interim order 'that is carefully crafted to balance the interests of the state against those of judgment creditors, particularly people who lack access to legal resources'.[529]

8.10 COSTS ORDERS

Another method which the courts have used to express their displeasure in respect of organs of State that are in dereliction of their constitutional and statutory duties has been to grant a costs order against them. Punitive costs orders such as awards of costs on the scale as between attorney and client and awards *de bonis propriis* (from personal funds) may be resorted to when constitutional rights are undermined by serious and persistent maladministration, or when there has been an abuse of the litigation process.[530]

In *Machi v MEC for Province of KwaZulu-Natal Responsible for Social Welfare and Population Development*[531] the KwaZulu-Natal High Court made a costs order *de bonis propriis* against the MEC under whose responsibility the administration of social grants in terms of the Social Assistance Act fell. From submissions of the State attorney and the Black Sash, Combrink J drew the '[t]he inescapable conclusion' that the Department was guilty of gross maladministration in respect of its functions

---

[527] See orders made on 1 June 2009 and 31 August 2009. The reasons for these orders and the supplementary orders are set out in the judgment of Mokgoro J in *Minister of Justice and Constitutional Development v Nyathi* [2009] ZACC 29 (judgment of 9 October 2009 unreported at the date of writing).

[528] Ibid para 57.

[529] Ibid paras 33–34.

[530] See in this regard C Plasket 'Protecting the public purse: Appropriate relief and costs orders against public officials' (2000) 117 *SALJ* 151–158 at 158.

[531] Case No 4392/04 ZAKZNHC (unreported judgment of 8 March 2005).

under the Social Assistance Act.[532] The court held that a costs order *de bonis propriis* was appropriate when it was found that a respondent had acted unreasonably or negligently, or when his actions were clouded by *mala fides*.[533] *Mala fides* was not confined to cases of immediate and direct bad will, but included cases where a functionary did not pay sufficient attention to what he was required to do under the relevant legislation, or if he misunderstood the scope of his authority.[534]

The order was suspended for a four-month period until 29 July 2005. On this date the respondent and all interested parties were required to place information before the court showing that the backlog in the applications, as well as the appeals, had been either totally addressed or substantially addressed. The Court further ordered that a failure to fulfil this condition would result in immediate implementation of the order together with the issuing of guidelines as to how it should be recovered from the respondent in order to avoid the taxpayer having to foot the relevant bill.[535]

An appeal against the order to the Supreme Court of Appeal was dismissed as 'premature and ill-conceived', as Combrink J's order did not meet the requirements of a final judgment or order. Leave to appeal ought accordingly not to have been granted.[536] Interestingly, the Court observed that the special costs order appeared to have had some effect. It had triggered a substantial effort on the Department to deal with social grants backlogs and the expeditious processing of grants through the appointment of additional staff and the appointment of an ad hoc Appeal Board.[537]

The Constitutional Court decision in *Njongi*[538] concerned the decision of the MEC to raise prescription as a defence to claims by the applicant for 'back-pay'[539] and interest on unpaid disability grant payments following the unlawful stoppage of her grant in November 1997. The cancellation of her grant was part of a mass cut-off of social grants in a 're-registration' drive affecting thousands of Eastern Cape beneficiaries between 1996 and 1998.[540] The Department contended that the prescription period of three years had expired, as prescription had started to run against the applicant prior to 2 June 2005, the date when the administrative decision cancelling her disability grant was reviewed and set aside by the High Court. This argument was

---

532 Ibid para 15.
533 Ibid para 17.
534 Ibid para 18.
535 Ibid para 23.
536 *MEC: Welfare (KZN) v Machi* [2006] ZASCA 78 (31 May 2006).
537 Ibid para 11.
538 Note 455 above.
539 The back pay due to Mrs Njongi was only partially paid by the respondent: see ibid paras 22–23; 28.
540 See the social and legal context described by the Court, ibid paras 8–27.

rejected by the Eastern Cape High Court,[541] but reversed on appeal to a full bench of the Eastern Cape High Court.[542]

The Constitutional Court raised doubts as to whether prescription could legitimately be raised in a social grants claim, the payment of which constituted a constitutional obligation.[543] However, the Court 'reluctantly' concluded that it would not decide the issue in the present case, mainly because it had not been argued and canvassed by the lower courts.[544] It accordingly assumed in favour of the Provincial Government that the obligation to pay the social grant to Mrs Njongi constituted a debt for the purposes of the Prescription Act 68 of 1969.[545] The Court held that in circumstances where the Provincial Government had failed to admit that the administrative decision in question was wrong and to expressly disavow that decision, the debt fell due for the purposes of the Prescription Act on the date that the High Court reviewed and set aside the cancellation of the grant.[546] Accordingly, the claim had not prescribed. However, had the Government disavowed reliance on the administrative action concerned, the debt would have become immediately enforceable. Prescription (assuming it was applicable) would have started to run on the date of disavowal.[547]

After conclusion of argument, the Chief Justice issued directions calling upon the respondents to show cause why 'he should not be ordered to pay the applicant's costs in the application on the scale as between Attorney and Client *de bonis propriis*'.[548] In the end, the Court 'reluctantly' decided not to make a costs order *de bonis propriis* in the circumstance of the case. The Court was highly critical of the manner in which the litigation had been conducted and the advice provided and decisions taken by the MEC, the senior legal advisor of the Department of Welfare and the State Attorney. Yacoob J outlined the approach to be followed by organs of state in deciding whether to invoke prescription in litigation aimed at enforcing constitutional rights such as social security:

> A decision by the State whether or not to invoke prescription in a particular case must be informed by the values of our Constitution. It follows that the Provincial Government too, must take a decision whether to plead prescription to defeat a claim for arrear disability

---

[541] *Njongi v MEC for Social Development, Eastern Cape Province* [2005] ZAECHC 23 (2 June 2005).

[542] *MEC for Welfare v Njongi* [2006] ZAECHC 69 (6 December 2006).

[543] See *Njongi* (note 455 above) paras 41–42.

[544] Ibid para 42.

[545] Ibid para 43.

[546] Ibid para 56.

[547] As the Court observed:

> Indeed, Government at every level must be encouraged to re-evaluate administrative decisions that are subject to challenge and, if found to be wrong, to admit this without qualification and to disavow reliance on them. There are literally thousands of administrative decisions of this kind made every day and it would be quite untenable for each decision to be set aside by a court before the underlying obligation can be enforced. (Ibid para 56)

[548] Ibid para 61.

> grant payments. This is not a decision for the State Attorney to make. It is an important decision and must not be made lightly. It must be made after appropriate processes have been followed and by a sufficiently responsible person in the Provincial Government who must take into account all the relevant circumstances. It is the duty of the State to facilitate rather than obstruct access to social security. This will be a fundamental consideration in making the assessment.[549]

Key facts which should have been taken into consideration by the Provincial Government before invoking prescription were the following: the applicant was poor and vulnerable; she lived with a 100% permanent disability; the disability grant payable to her constituted a constitutional obligation; the arrears accrued as a result of unlawful administrative action by the Provincial Government; and there existed a substantial body of jurisprudence of the Eastern Cape High Courts as well as the Supreme Court of Appeal supporting the reinstatement of social grants in similar circumstances.[550] Ultimately, the appeal succeeded and the appellant was awarded the back pay still owing to her as well as interest on the unpaid grant for the relevant periods.[551] Costs were awarded on the scale as between attorney and client to express the Court's disapproval of the Provincial Government's conduct of the litigation.[552]

In *Biowatch Trust v Registrar, Genetic Resources*,[553] (*'Biowatch'*) the Constitutional Court upheld an appeal by Biowatch against a decision of the North Gauteng High Court, refusing an order of costs against the relevant governmental bodies in Biowatch's favour.[554] Biowatch had been substantially successful in the High Court in its litigation aimed at enforcing their right to information in terms of PAIA pertaining to research on genetically modified organisms. However, to mark its disapproval at the lack of precision in the framing of the request for information to the Registrar, the High Court declined to order the government respondents to pay Biowatch costs. Moreover, it ordered Biowatch Trust to pay the costs of Monsanto SA (Pty) Ltd, which had intervened in the litigation in a (largely unsuccessful) effort

---

[549] Ibid para 79.

[550] Ibid para 80.

[551] Ibid para 92. Order paras 1–8.

[552] Ibid paras 91 and 92. Order para 9. See also *Treatment Action Campaign v Minister of Correctional Services* (note 364 above), in which Southwood J ordered the Minister to pay the costs of his spurious opposition to the applicant's request for information in terms of PAIA on an attorney and client scale. The TAC had requested access to a report of the Judicial Inspectorate of Prisons pursuant to an investigation into the death of a prisoner at the Westville Correctional Centre who was an applicant in the case of *N* (note 348 above). The Court held that the papers in the case 'demonstrate a complete disregard by the Minister and his department of the provisions of the Constitution and PAIA which require that records be made available' (para 36). Similarly, in *Bovungana v RAF* 2009 (4) SA 123 (E) Froneman J awarded costs against the Road Accident Fund on an attorney and client scale for the 'reckless and prejudicial' manner in which the litigation had been conducted.

[553] 2009 (6) SA 232 (CC), 2009 (10) BCLR 1014 (CC).

[554] *Trustees, Biowatch Trust v Registrar: Genetic Resources* 2005 (4) SA 111 (T).

to prevent the disclosure of information by the Registrar.[555] This costs order was also overturned by the Constitutional Court.

The Court held that the defects in the requests for information had not been of such a serious nature that it justified departing from the general rule that in litigation aimed at vindicating constitutional rights[556] the government should usually be required to pay the costs of successful litigation by applicants.[557] It observed that, '[t]he root cause of the dispute was the obduracy of the state officials' refusal to supply information they were duty-bound to give'.[558] In addition, Monsanto SA (Pty) Ltd's intervention in the litigation was necessitated by the failure of the relevant government's agencies 'to grasp the nettle and draw an appropriate line between information to be disclosed and information to be withheld'.[559] In other words, government bodies had failed to exercise the regulatory responsibilities vested in them by the Constitution and PAIA. In these circumstances, the Court held that a costs award requiring the State to bear the costs of both Biowatch Trust and Monsanto SA (Pty) Ltd might have been justified.[560] However, as the issue had not been raised by Monsanto SA (Pty) Ltd, the Court confined itself to setting aside the order against Biowatch Trust to pay Monsanto's costs.[561]

These cases illustrate that costs orders may provide an indirect mechanism for pressurising government officials to give effect to their constitutional obligations. Punitive costs orders have also been granted as an expression of the courts' disapproval of the manner in which the State has conducted litigation against poor and marginalised litigants in socio-economic rights cases. Costs awards do not neces-

---

[555] This company was the South African subsidiary of a multinational biotechnology company involved in the research, development and sale of Genetically Modified Organisms (GMOs). It succeeded in the High Court only to the extent of blocking the disclosure of confidential information.

[556] The two constitutional rights which the Court found were implicated in this litigation were the right of access to information in s 32 of the Constitution, and the environmental rights in s 24. *Biowatch* (note 553 above) para 45.

[557] Ibid para 46. In *Affordable Medicines Trust v Minister of Health* 2006 (3) SA 247 (CC), 2005 (6) BCLR 529 (CC), the Constitutional Court confirmed the general principle that an unsuccessful litigant in constitutional litigation against the State ought not to be ordered to pay costs as this would have 'chilling effect on the litigants who might wish to vindicate their constitutional rights' (ibid para 138). See the further rationales provided for this rule by the Constitutional Court in *Biowatch* (note 553 above) para 23.

[558] Ibid para 49. The Court was critical of Government's 'obstinate refusal' to provide information that it was duty-bound to supply. Thereafter, 'instead of welcoming a judicial decision on questions of considerable public importance, the governmental bodies sought to frustrate the proceedings on purely technical grounds'. Ibid para 47. The State also failed to abandon the costs order made by the High Court in its favour. It was accordingly also ordered to pay the costs of Biowatch's appeal to the Constitutional Court (para 52).

[559] Ibid para 53.

[560] Ibid para 54.

[561] Ibid.

sarily guarantee that government departments which are plagued by administrative inefficiency and incapacity will get their houses in order. However, costs awards, particularly of a punitive nature, may give rise to greater scrutiny and accountability of public servants by the political heads of the relevant departments. If such costs orders are regularly granted against them, public officials may also be held accountable through the mechanisms of the Public Finance Management Act 1 of 1999,[562] and the oversight role of the relevant legislatures.

8.11 CONCLUSION

As the above analysis shows, the courts have a wide repertoire of remedies available to them under the Constitution to respond to violations of socio-economic rights. Apart from the constitutional remedies associated with declarations of invalidity, the courts may grant any order that is 'just and equitable' in the circumstances of the case. The dual aim of constitutional remedies is to ensure that the particular remedy is effective and fair to all parties, including those groups who are not represented before the court. All constitutional remedies have an essential public dimension as they protect and promote the public's interest in ensuring proper compliance with constitutional rights and values. As the Court held in the *Biowatch* case:

> [C]onstitutional litigation, whatever the outcome, might ordinarily bear not only on the interests of the particular litigants involved, but on the right of all those in similar situations. Indeed, each constitutional case that is heard enriches the general body of constitutional jurisprudence and adds texture to what it means to be living in a constitutional democracy.[563]

As with all litigation, the remedy must be tailored to the circumstances of the particular case. Not all socio-economic rights cases require long-range structural relief or innovative damages remedies. In certain cases, appropriate relief will be an immediate remedy such as an interdict restraining a public or private organ from depriving a group of their existing access to a particular social benefit, for example, the threatened cut-off of their water supply.[564] Alternatively, it may be appropriate for a court to read into a legislative scheme regulating access to a socio-economic right, a particular group that has been unconstitutionally excluded (a 'reading-in' remedy).[565] The legislature or an organ of State may be required to adopt a particular process to ensure that the applicants are heard, and that the authority concerned takes proper account of the relevant right and its underlying values.[566] Short-term relief may also

---

[562] See, for example, the comments of the Constitutional Court in *Njongi* (note 455 above) para 90.

[563] *Biowatch* (note 553 above) para 23.

[564] See part 8.5.2 above.

[565] See part 8.3.3 above.

[566] See part 8.8 above.

be granted in the form of a mandatory remedy requiring the respondent to provide a particular service or resource to the applicants.[567]

However, there can be little dispute that there are major structural obstacles that impede access to quality education, health care services, housing, food, water and social security for large proportions of the South African population. Moreover, South Africa is a young democracy facing, in many areas, a lack of institutional capacity and experience to redress large-scale violations of socio-economic rights. In these circumstances, compliance with constitutional rights will not be achieved through a once-off, final judicial decree, but will require an ongoing process of engagement between relevant organs of State, affected communities, civil society organisations and persons with expertise in a particular sphere. Substantive guidance and regular supervision by the courts are required to ensure that these processes of engagement are guided by the normative purposes and values of the relevant socio-economic rights. The model of structural interdicts discussed in this chapter is well suited to facilitating the progressive realisation of socio-economic rights. These remedies have the potential to promote deliberative, participatory resolutions to complex, multi-faceted socio-economic deprivations.[568]

There are encouraging signs that the High Courts are beginning to embrace these types of orders, although the Constitutional Court remains hesitant to endorse the more active judicial role which these forms of structural orders require. The orders of 'meaningful engagement' made by the Court in cases such as *Occupiers of Olivia Road*, and to a lesser degree, in the *Joe Slovo* case suggest that the Constitutional Court may be becoming more bold in experimenting with innovative remedies of this nature.[569]

Structural interdicts require a continuous interaction between the judiciary, the other branches of government and civil society in an iterative effort 'to synchronise the real world with the ideal construct of a constitutional world'.[570] They represent a rupture with the classic liberal model of negative constitutionalism and strictly demarcated boundaries between the roles and functions of the three branches of government. The responsiveness of South Africa's remedial jurisprudence to entrenched patterns of socio-economic marginalisation and inequity depends on an acceptance by the courts of the implications of this rupture.

[567] See part 8.5.3(*a*) above.
[568] See part 8.6 above.
[569] See part 8.5.3(*b*) above.
[570] *Fose* (note 4 above) para 94 (per Kriegler J).

CHAPTER 9

Postscript

In this chapter *Page*

9.1 INTRODUCTION

The three Constitutional Court judgments below were handed down after the cut-off date of 31 August 2009 for the consideration of new case law. Nevertheless I consider it appropriate to include a discussion of these judgments, as the relevant court *a quo* judgments are considered in this book. The judgment of the Constitutional Court in *Mazibuko* is analysed in some detail as it represents the antithesis of the substantive, contextually sensitive approach to the adjudication of socio-economic rights argued for in this book.

9.2 *HEAD OF DEPARTMENT: MPUMALANGA DEPARTMENT OF EDUCATION V HOËRSKOOL ERMELO*

On 14 October 2009 the Constitutional Court handed down its judgment in the appeal against the Supreme Court of Appeal's judgment in the case.[1]

The Court firmly rejected the contention that this case was exclusively about 'the principle of legality and the proper exercise of administrative power'.[2] Moseneke DCJ observed that while these issues did call for resolution, 'the substantive and underlying dispute between the parties was not merely procedural'.[3] The case was also fundamentally 'about the appropriateness of the governing body's inflexible stance on an exclusive medium of instruction'.[4]

A unanimous Court proceeded to overrule the Supreme Court of Appeal's interpretation of s 22 of the South African Schools Act 84 of 1996. Thus it held that

[1] *Head of Department: Mpumalanga Department of Education v Hoërskool Ermelo* [2009] ZACC 32. The judgment of the Supreme Court of Appeal is discussed in chapter 5, part 5.3.3 at notes 135–155 and accompanying text.

[2] Ibid para 38.

[3] Ibid para 39.

[4] Ibid.

the head of a provincial education department is entitled, on reasonable grounds, to withdraw the function of a governing body of a school to determine the language policy of the school. The reasonableness of the relevant grounds must be determined on a case-by-case basis, taking into account the impact of such a withdrawal on the well-being of the school, as well as the broad contextual framework of the Constitution, particularly the rights of access to education and the considerations pertaining to equity and historical redress in s 29.[5]

In exercising his or her power to revoke a function of a school's governing body, the head of department is also obliged to 'observe meticulously the standard of procedural fairness required by section 22(2) and, in the case of urgency, by section 22(3)'.[6] Once the power is legitimately revoked, the head of department must exercise the withdrawn function 'only for as long as, and in a manner necessary to achieve the remedial purpose'.[7]

In exercising its fiduciary duties, including the power to determine a school's language policy, a governing body should refrain from adopting an insular approach, focusing only on its existing learners and parents. In addition to promoting the best interests of its immediate constituencies, it should recognise 'that it is entrusted with a public resource which must be managed ... in the interests of the broader community in which the school is located and in the light of the values of our Constitution'.[8]

However, the Court agreed with the Supreme Court of Appeal that the head of department was not entitled to appoint an interim committee to decide on the language policy of a school in terms of s 25 of the Schools Act. Such a power was only to be exercised when the head of department reasonably determined that a governing body had ceased or failed to perform any of its functions in terms of the Act. It did not apply when the head of department disagreed with the language policy adopted by the governing body.[9] The Court accordingly declared the language policy decided on by the interim committee in the case void and of no legal effect.[10]

However, with a view to resolving the underlying dispute between the parties in a manner consistent with constitutional requirements, it ordered the school governing body of Hoërskool Ermelo to review and determine a language policy in terms of s 6(2) of the Schools Act and in the light of the constitutional matrix outlined in the judgment. The governing body was further ordered to lodge a report on the process followed to determine such a language policy and a copy of the relevant policy with the Court by no later than 16 November 2009. In addition, the head of the Mpumalanga Department of Education was also required to lodge a report by the aforementioned date 'setting out the likely demand for grade 8 English places

[5] Ibid paras 62–74.
[6] Ibid para 73.
[7] Ibid para 88.
[8] Ibid para 80.
[9] Ibid paras 84–89.
[10] Ibid para 94.

at the start of the school year in 2010 and setting out the steps that the Department has taken to satisfy this likely demand for an English or parallel medium high school in the circuit of Ermelo'.[11] The latter order was made in view of evidence of overcrowding and excessively large learner-to-class ratios in the Ermelo circuit other than at Hoërskool Ermelo.[12] The redress of this situation required 'proactive and timely steps by the Department' in order to comply with its constitutional and statutory obligations to provide enough school places for every child in the Ermelo circuit.[13]

The approach adopted by the Constitutional Court is a welcome affirmation of the principle that the Schools Act must be interpreted so as to promote the purposes and values of s 29 of the Constitution. In particular, the responsibility of school governing bodies to determine the language policies of a school incorporates a broader social responsibility to ensure that the relevant policy promotes equitable access to education and ensures the redress of the results of past racially discriminatory laws and practices. As Moseneke DCJ observes:

> Apartheid has left us with many scars. The worst of these must be the vast discrepancy in access to public and private resources. The cardinal fault line of our past oppression ran along race, class and gender. It authorised a hierarchy of privilege and disadvantage. Unequal access to opportunity prevailed in every domain. Access to private or public education was no exception. While much remedial work has been done since the advent of constitutional democracy, sadly deep social disparities and resultant social inequity are still with us.[14]

9.3 *NOKOTYANA V EKURHULENI METROPOLITAN MUNICIPALITY*

On 19 November 2009, the Constitutional Court dismissed the appeal against the *Nokotyana* judgment of Epstein AJ.[15]

The Court held that Chapters 12 and 13 of the National Housing Code were promulgated to give effect to s 26 of the Constitution.[16] In the absence of a challenge to these chapters of the Code, the applicants could not rely directly on s 26 of the Constitution.[17] The Court dismissed the argument that the applicants were entitled to rely on Chapter 12 of the Code on the basis that it is only applicable where the

---

[11] Ibid para 105. Order, para 5.
[12] Ibid paras 11 and 103.
[13] Ibid para 103.
[14] Ibid para 45.
[15] The High Court judgment is discussed in chapter 8, part 8.4.2 at notes 176–187 and accompanying text. The neutral citation of the Constitutional Court's judgment is *Nokotyana v Ekurhuleni Metropolitan Municipality* [2009] ZACC 33 (hereafter '*Nokotyana CC*').
[16] Ibid para 48.
[17] Ibid paras 49–51.

MEC has determined that an emergency exists.[18] This had not occurred in the case, nor had the applicants applied for a declaration to that effect.[19]

The applicants' reliance on Chapter 13 was also dismissed on the grounds that, although the Municipality had applied for assistance to the MEC for Local Government and Housing, Gauteng under this chapter, a decision to upgrade the settlement had not yet been made by the MEC. Services could only be provided in terms of Chapter 13 once a decision to embark on an *in situ* upgrade of an informal settlement had been made by the MEC.[20]

However, the Court found that the delay of more than three years on the part of the MEC to make a decision on the Municipality's application to upgrade the Harry Gwala Informal Settlement to a township was inconsistent with s 237 of the Constitution and with 'the requirement of reasonableness imposed on the government by s 26(2) of the Constitution with regard to access to adequate housing'.[21] In this regard, the Court observed:

> The delay by the Province is the most immediate reason for the dilemma and desperate plight of the residents. As long as the status of the Settlement is in limbo, little can be done to improve their situation regarding sanitation, sufficient lighting to enhance community safety and access by emergency vehicles, as well as a range of other services.[22]

The MEC was accordingly ordered to make a decision on the Chapter 13 application within 14 months of the date of the Court's order.[23]

9.4 *MAZIBUKO V CITY OF JOHANNESBURG*

On 8 October 2009, the Constitutional Court handed down judgment in *Mazibuko v City of Johannesburg*[24] (hereafter '*Mazibuko (CC)*').[25]

In a judgment written for a unanimous Court, O'Regan J dismissed the arguments of the Phiri residents that the free basic water supply of 6 kilolitres per household per month (or 25 litres per person per day) was insufficient to meet their basic needs and thus inconsistent with s 27 of the Constitution.

---

[18] See National Housing Code, chapter 12.3.1.

[19] *Nokotyana CC* (note 15 above) para 40.

[20] Ibid paras 44–45.

[21] Ibid para 56.

[22] Ibid para 58.

[23] Ibid para 63. Order, para 4.

[24] *Mazibuko v City of Johannesburg (Centre on Housing Rights and Evictions as amicus curiae)* [2009] ZACC 28 (hereafter '*Mazibuko (CC)*').

[25] The High Court (*Mazibuko v City of Johannesburg and Others (Centre on Housing Rights and Evictions as amicus curiae)* [2008] 4 All SA 471 (W), hereafter '*Mazibuko (HC)*') and SCA judgments in *Mazibuko* (*City of Johannesburg v Mazibuko* 2009 (3) SA 592 (SCA), 2009 (8) BCLR 791 (SCA), hereafter '*Mazibuko (SCA)*') are discussed in chapter 4, part 4.4.2(*b*) at notes 275–291 and accompanying text; and chapter 8, parts 8.3.5 and 8.5.3(*a*) at notes 248–265 and accompanying text.

The Court's dismissal of the challenge to the sufficiency of the free basic water supply illustrates the shortcomings of reasonableness review unmoored from a substantive analysis of the normative purposes and values underpinning the relevant socio-economic rights. The Court fails to give any independent significance to the right of access to sufficient water in s 27(1)(*b*).[26] Instead the right is subsumed within the overarching qualification of reasonableness in s 27(2).[27] The arguments of the applicants are misconstrued as being equivalent to the concept of a minimum core obligation, and are rejected following the precedent of the previous jurisprudence declining to adopt a minimum core approach.[28] However, the applicants in fact argued that the Court should assess the reasonableness of the measures adopted in respect of the Phiri community in the light of the normative standards and values imposed by s 27(1)(*b*) of the Constitution. Their claim was thus framed within the paradigm of reasonableness review developed by the Court for assessing positive socio-economic rights claims.

Their arguments in this regard are reinforced by the express statutory normative standard set by s 1 of the Water Services Act 108 of 1997 which defines a 'basic water supply' as

> the prescribed minimum standard of water supply services necessary for the reliable supply of *a sufficient quantity* and quality of water of households, including informal households, *to support life and personal hygiene*. (Emphasis added.)

This provision can thus be read as defining the normative criteria which are relevant for determining the sufficiency of the right of access to 'sufficient' water in s 27(1)(*b*) of the Constitution.

Regulation 3 of the regulations relating to compulsory national standards and measures to conserve water[29] defines the minimum standard for 'basic water supply' services to be '... a minimum quantity of potable water of 25 litres per person per day or 6 kilolitres per household per month'[30] subject to certain additional conditions.[31]

The key question in *Mazibuko* was whether the City of Johannesburg acted reasonably by restricting the free basic water supply to all residents to the minimum standard of 25 litres per person per day or 6 kilolitres per household per month. Given that regulation 3 prescribes a minimum standard, the applicants' argument was that the City should have provided more free basic water, taking into account its constitutional obligations to act reasonably in ensuring that an impoverished community had access to sufficient water.

---

[26] This critique of reasonableness review is developed in chapter 4, part 4.4.2.

[27] See the discussion in *Mazibuko (CC)* (note 24 above) paras 46–50.

[28] Ibid paras 52–56.

[29] *Government Gazette*, Gazette No 22355, Notice R509 of 2001 (8 June 2001) published in terms of the Water Services Act 108 of 1997.

[30] Regulation 3(*b*)

[31] Regulation 3(*b*)(i)–(iii).

Relevant considerations which the City should have taken into account in exercising its discretion to provide more than the prescribed minimum of water include the basic water needs of the affected households, the impact on their life, health and dignity of restricting their free basic water supply to 25 litres per person per day, and the available resources of the City. As noted, these are the primary considerations which are relevant to the City's constitutional obligations in terms of s 27(1)(*b*) and (2) of the Constitution read with the definition of a basic water supply in s 1 of the Water Services Act.

The applicants emphasised the relevance of human dignity in determining what constituted a 'sufficient' water supply.[32] They presented detailed first-hand and expert evidence pertaining to the quantity of water required to meet their basic needs of drinking, cooking, sanitation, bathing, house cleaning and laundry. They also presented evidence of the insufficiency of the free water supply to meet these basic needs. An important consideration in determining the sufficiency of their water supply was the fact that the sanitation needs of the Phiri residents were supplied through waterborne sanitation. Additional water was therefore required for toilet flushing. Both the High Court and the Supreme Court of Appeal engaged with the relevant evidence and concluded that substantially more water was required than the 25 litres per day standard to meet the sufficiency criterion in s 27(1)(*b*). The High Court upheld the applicants' argument that 50 litres per person per day was necessary to fulfil this criterion.[33]

The Supreme Court of Appeal undertook a serious analysis of the discrepancies between the evidence of the respective experts for the residents and the City regarding what would constitute a sufficient supply of water for households in the position of the Phiri residents.[34] It concluded that the only real difference between the evidence of the experts was the amount of water required for waterborne sanitation. The expert for the City was of the opinion that 15 litres of water would suffice for this purpose whereas the expert for the residents was of the opinion that 20 litres was required. There were also minor differences in respect of the amounts required for personal washing, cooking and household cleaning. On the basis of this analysis the Supreme Court of Appeal concluded that 42 litres of water per person per day constitutes sufficient water in terms of s 27(1) of the Constitution.[35]

In contrast, the Constitutional Court failed to engage with the substantive evidence regarding the water needs of the Phiri community, taking refuge in the lack

---

[32] Applicants' submissions, *Mazibuko v City of Johannesburg*, 23 July 2009. Available at http://www.constitutionalcourt.org.za/Archimages/13710.PDF, paras 323–326 (hereafter 'Applicants' submissions) (accessed on 25 November 2009). They referred in this regard to the Court's 'repeated emphasis of the close connection and interaction between the socio-economic rights in ss 26 and 27 of the Constitution and the right and value of human dignity' (para 325).

[33] See *Mazibuko (HC)* (note 25 above) paras 167–181.

[34] See *Mazibuko (SCA)* (note 25 above) paras 21–23.

[35] Ibid para 24.

of institutional competence and legitimacy of courts in this context. Thus O'Regan J held:

> It is institutionally inappropriate for a court to determine what the achievement of any particular social and economic right entails and what steps government should take to ensure the progressive realisation of the right. This is a matter, in the first place, for the legislature and executive, the institutions of government best placed to investigate social conditions in the light of available budgets and to determine what targets are achievable in relation to social and economic rights. Indeed, it is desirable as a matter of democratic accountability that they should do so for it is their programmes and promises that are subjected to democratic popular choice.[36]

This represents an avoidance of the special responsibility of the courts, particularly the Constitutional Court, to interpret the normative standards underpinning socio-economic rights in the light of the considerations referred to in s 39(1) of the Constitution, and to scrutinise closely whether the State's conduct or omissions are reasonable as required by ss 26 and 27(2). As has been argued in this book, the reasonableness of the State's acts and omissions can only be assessed in the light of the purposes and values which the entrenchment of particular socio-economic rights seeks to promote.[37] In determining whether the State has acted reasonably in realising these standards, a burden of justification must be placed on it to show that its policy choices and prioritisation of resources is consistent with its constitutional commitments in respect of the realisation of socio-economic rights.[38]

Instead the Constitutional Court adopts a highly deferential approach to the policy choices of the City, and gives a particularly narrow reading of its own application of the reasonableness standard in the cases of *Grootboom*[39] and *Treatment Action Campaign*.[40] Thus the Court states that all it did in *Treatment Action Campaign* 'was to render the existing government policy available to all'.[41] In fact government had only established pilot sites in which it provided nevirapine for the purposes of reducing the rate of mother-to-child transmission of HIV. These pilot sites catered for only 10% of women giving birth in the public health sector.[42] The State was not prepared to give any commitment to the roll-out of the provision of nevirapine throughout the public health sector. It argued on a range of grounds that a roll-out of nevirapine would not constitute an appropriate government policy.[43]

---

36 *Mazibuko (CC)* (note 24 above).

37 See in general chapter 4, part 4.4.2.

38 See further chapter 4, parts 4.4.2(*c*) and 4.4.4.

39 *Government of the Republic of South Africa v Grootboom* 2001 (1) SA 46 (CC), 2000 (11) BCLR 1169 (CC).

40 *Minister of Health v Treatment Action Campaign* 2002 (5) SA 721 (CC), 2002 (10) BCLR 1033 (CC).

41 *Mazibuko (CC)* (note 24 above) para 64.

42 *Treatment Action Campaign* (note 40 above) para 62.

43 See further the discussion of the *Treatment Action Campaign* judgment in chapter 4, part 4.3.1–4.3.3.

In *Mazibuko* the Court affords government a wide latitude in determining the legislative and other measures to be adopted as 'the primary instrument for the achievement of socio-economic rights'.[44] Such measures may be reviewed by a court on the basis that '[i]f government takes no steps to realise the rights, the courts will require government to take steps'.[45] Second, the measures adopted must be consistent with the reasonableness standard adopted by the Court, including making provision for those most desperately in need, and avoiding unreasonable limitations or exclusions in the design or implementation of social programmes.[46] Government should set transparent standards[47] for the realisation of socio-economic rights and can be held politically and legally accountable if the standards set are unreasonable.[48]

While these are valuable tools for holding government accountable for the realisation of socio-economic rights, the Court in *Mazibuko* is at pains to minimise its role in reviewing the substantive reasonableness of the State's programmes and policy choices against the normative standard of ensuring that everyone has access to the relevant socio-economic rights. This suggests a retreat from the more robust criteria for reasonableness review established in the *Grootboom* decision in which the Court held that a reasonable programme 'must be capable of facilitating the realisation of the right'.[49] In other words, reasonableness review does not merely establish abstract standards of reasonable governance, but requires that State conduct be assessed in the light of the rights entrenched in the first subsections of ss 26 and 27.

The Court in *Mazibuko* reduces the analytical work performed by ss 26(1) and 27(1) to almost negligible proportions. Sections 26 and 27 are interpreted as though they were drafted simply to require the State to take reasonable measures in the sphere of socio-economic policy. Moreover, the fact that reasonableness review is a context-sensitive standard does not imply that it is inappropriate to make a substantive assessment of what the right demands of the State in the particular circumstances of a case.

This retreat from a substantive reasonableness standard is further illustrated by the Court's approach to the concept of 'progressive realisation'. Instead of imposing an obligation to progressively improve the quality of access which people enjoy to socio-economic rights, it acquires a process-orientated meaning in the *Mazibuko* judgment. Thus 'progressive realisation' stands for the obligation of government to continuously review its policies, and to be flexible and adaptable to changing circumstances and advocacy on behalf of affected beneficiaries.[50] Again, while these are useful tools of accountability, they avoid the substantive dimension of progressive realisation. Under

---

[44] *Mazibuko (CC)* (note 24 above) para 66.
[45] Ibid para 67.
[46] Ibid.
[47] Ibid para 71.
[48] Ibid para 72.
[49] *Grootboom* (note 39 above) para 41. See the discussion of the criteria of reasonableness review in chapter 4, part 4.3.3.
[50] Ibid paras 40 and 67.

international law, the concept of 'progressive realisation' places a substantive, positive obligation on the State 'to move as expeditiously and effectively as possible' towards achieving the full realisation of socio-economic rights for everyone.[51]

Developing the normative content of socio-economic rights need not imply setting fixed, quantitative standards 'in a rigid and counter-productive manner'.[52] The Court's responsibility is to elaborate on the purposes and values which the rights seek to promote, and to assess the State's provision of social services such as water in the light hereof. If it is found that the relevant policy choices are inconsistent with these normative standards, the relevant organ of state should be required to adapt its programmes so that they are more capable of advancing these goals. As discussed in chapter 8, participatory structural interdicts have a rich potential to facilitate an iterative process of developing social policy in the light of broad normative guidelines established by the courts.

Against the background of a primarily process-orientated approach to reasonableness review, the Court proceeded to dismiss the various grounds on which the residents challenged the reasonableness of the City's free basic water policy. It rejected the Supreme Court of Appeal's finding that the policy was based on a misconception by the City of its constitutional obligations because it considered that it was not obliged to provide a specified amount of free basic water. The Constitutional Court held that the City was not in fact 'under a constitutional obligation to provide any *particular* amount of free water to citizens per month'.[53] It also dismissed the argument that the free basic water allocation of 6 kilolitres per household per month was insufficient for larger households such as Mrs Mazibuko's which comprised three separate households with a total of 20 residents. In this regard, the Court held that it would be administratively too difficult for the City to establish a universal per person allowance.[54]

A consideration which weighed particularly heavily in the Court's finding that the free basic water allocation was reasonable is that persons registered in terms of the City's Indigent Persons Policy were provided with an increased free basic water allocation of 10 kilolitres per household per month.[55] The Court held that this policy introduced a crucial measure of flexibility into the system, enabling poor households (who were often larger than average) to benefit by an additional 4 kilolitres per month. In the absence of this additional allocation, the Court held that it 'may well have been concluded that the policy was inflexible and therefore unreasonable'.[56]

---

[51] See UN Committee on Economic, Social and Cultural Rights, General Comment No 3 (Fifth sess, 1990) 'The nature of States parties obligations (art 2(1) of the Covenant)' UN doc. E/1991/23, para 9.

[52] See the discussion by the Court in *Mazibuko (CC)* (note 24 above) para 60.

[53] Ibid para 85.

[54] Ibid para 89.

[55] Ibid para 93.

[56] Ibid para 95.

The applicants' complaint that the indigent register was under-inclusive[57] and demeaning was dismissed. The Court held that requiring citizens to come forward and identify themselves as indigent was an inevitable requirement of means-tested social benefits. To hold means-testing 'to be constitutionally impermissible would deprive government of a key methodology for ensuring that government services target those most in need'.[58]

A second background consideration which informed the Court's assessment of the reasonableness of the applicants' claim for an increased supply of free basic water was the fact that a fifth of the households in Johannesburg have no access to basic sanitary services, and a tenth of all households have no access to a tap providing clean water within 200 metres of their home.[59] Although the Court did not explicitly reject the applicant's claim on the basis that they were not the most disadvantaged group in respect of water services, this fact clearly had some influence in the assessment of the reasonableness of the City's policy priorities.

An organ of state may be able to justify a reduced allocation of resources to the litigants before the Court on the basis that it must attend to the more urgent needs of other groups who are not before the Court. However, the fact that other groups may be in a more disadvantaged position does not preclude a finding that the State's conduct is unreasonable in relation to the litigants before the Court. Reasonableness must be assessed in context, and the fact that the Phiri residents' sanitation needs were provided through waterborne sewerage increased their basic water needs.

In addition, an organ of state should be placed under a burden of proof that its only option is to redistribute resources from a disadvantaged group to a group suffering a relatively greater disadvantage. In this regard, very little was required from the City in terms of showing that it could not ensure a sufficient basic water supply to all disadvantaged groups. The City was not required to justify why it could not redistribute more resources through, for example, increased cross-subsidisation from commercial and wealthier consumers to meet the basic needs of the poor.[60]

The judgment also dismissed the various grounds on which the residents challenged the legality of the pre-paid water meters installed in the Phiri community. In its judgment, the Supreme Court of Appeal upheld the argument that the installation of the water meters had not been authorised by any law. It held that the City's Water Services by-laws, properly interpreted, only allowed for the installation of pre-paid meters on yard standpipes (service level 2) as a penalty for breaching the prescribed conditions applicable to the provision of water through a yard standpipe. The rel-

[57] Only approximately one-fifth of eligible households had registered in terms of this policy. See ibid para 98.

[58] Ibid para 101.

[59] Ibid paras 7 and 14.

[60] On the significance of redistributive equality in advancing the concept of 'developmental reasonableness' in socio-economic rights jurisprudence, see L A Williams 'The justiciability of water rights: *Mazibuko v City of Johannesburg*' (2009) 36 *Forum for Development Studies* 5–48.

evant by-laws did not permit the use of pre-paid water meters for residents receiving a metered full pressure water connection to their stands (service level 3).[61] Having found that the use of pre-paid meters for service level 3 consumers was unlawful, the Supreme Court of Appeal held that the choice given to the Phiri residents between accepting the installation of a pre-paid water meter or being confined to the delivery of water through a yard standpipe was also unlawful.[62]

In contrast, the Constitutional Court interpreted the by-laws to permit the installation of pre-paid meters in respect of service level 3 consumers.[63] It held that this conclusion was fortified by the Local Government: Municipal Systems Act 32 of 2000 which requires local government to provide accessible pay points and other mechanisms for 'settling accounts or for making pre-payments for services'[64] and which gives local governments the right 'to do anything reasonably necessary for, or incidental to, the effective performance of its functions and the exercise of its powers'.[65] The Court held that the installation of pre-paid meters was reasonably incidental to the provision of services by local government to citizens in a sustainable manner that permits cost recovery.[66] The City accordingly had the power to install such meters, as they were reasonably incidental to the effective performance of its functions.[67]

A second ground of attack on the pre-paid meters was that they resulted in a limitation or discontinuation of the residents' water supply without compliance with the procedural fairness requirements in s 4(3) of the Water Services Act 108 of 1997 read together with the relevant by-laws adopted by the City.[68] The Constitutional Court adopted a particularly restrictive and formalistic interpretation of the Water Services Act and relevant by-laws. It held that they provided for the 'permanent' discontinuation or limitation of the water supply to customers with credit meters. The legislative requirements of notice and an opportunity to make representations prior to the termination of a person's water supply did not apply to situations where the water supply is suspended 'when a customer needs to purchase more credit to maintain the water supply through a pre-paid meter'.[69] These procedural safeguards would therefore only be applicable to persons who have credit meters installed.

The implication of this interpretation is that the fundamental guarantees of procedural fairness provided for in the Water Services Act depend on the technical

---

61 *Mazibuko (SCA)* (note 25 above) paras 50-58. The lowest level of service was service level 1, which provides a tap within 200 meters of each dwelling. Approximately 100 000 households in the City do not have access to even this level of water provision (ibid para 14).

62 Ibid para 58.

63 *Mazibuko (CC)* (note 24 above) paras 106–109.

64 Section 95(*i*).

65 Section 8(2).

66 *Mazibuko (CC)* (note 24 above) para 111.

67 Ibid.

68 Ibid paras 115–122.

69 Ibid para 116.

mechanisms through which a person's water supply is measured. Procedural fairness is exclusively an entitlement of those with credit meters. This interpretation undermines the purpose of s 4(3) of the Water Services Act which was clearly designed to provide 'fair and equitable' procedures for the limitation or discontinuation of water services. It also expressly provides for circumstances in which there can be departures from the requirements of notice and an opportunity to make representations.[70] One would expect exclusions from the procedural safeguards in s 4(3) to be in express terms had this been the legislature's intention.

The leading international human rights law standard on the right to water, General Comment No 15 of the UN Committee on Economic, Social and Cultural Rights, provides that before any action that interferes with an individual's right to water is carried out by a State party, or by any other third party, relevant authorities must ensure that such actions provide for an opportunity for genuine consultation with those affected and timely and full disclosure of information and notice on the proposed measures.[71] Section 233 of the Constitution requires that when interpreting legislation a court 'must prefer any reasonable interpretation of the legislation that is consistent with international law over any alternative interpretation that is inconsistent with international law'. This provides further support for the interpretation that the safeguards in s 4(3) of the Water Services Act were intended to apply to any interference in people's access to water.

O'Regan J held that giving notice and providing an opportunity to be heard in circumstances where people's water supply was limited due to insufficient funds to purchase further credits for the pre-paid meter would give rise to absurd results.[72] However, this begs the question whether pre-paid meters constitute a lawful device for limiting or discontinuing a person's water supply if they are practically incompatible with legislative guarantees of procedural fairness.

The residents also argued that the pre-paid meters were unlawful in that the City did not hold a public enquiry or a notice and comment procedure as required by s 4 of the Promotion of Administrative Justice Act 3 of 2000 ('PAJA') prior to the decision to implement such meters. The Court dismissed this argument on the basis that when 'the Johannesburg City Council adopted the Business Plan of Johannesburg Water which includes Operation Gcin'amanzi, it was exercising executive powers to determine how services should be implemented in the City'.[73] The pre-paid meters were a component of Operation Gcin'amanzi, which was designed to save water through upgrading infrastructure and improving the rate of payment for water services in Soweto.[74]

---

[70] Section 4(3)(*b*)(i)–(iii).

[71] UN Committee on Economic, Social and Cultural Rights, General Comment No 15 (2002) 'The right to water (arts 11 and 12 of the International Covenant on Economic, Social and Cultural Rights), UN doc E/C.12/2002/11, 26 November 2002, para 56.

[72] *Mazibuko (CC)* (note 24 above) para 122.

[73] Ibid para 131.

[74] See generally ibid paras 13–18.

The delivery of water services is comprehensively regulated by the Water Services Act, including the conditions under which water services may be limited or discontinued. In this context, decisions pertaining to the installation of pre-paid meters in the delivery of water services to the Phiri residents would seem rather to constitute 'policy formulation in a narrow rather than a broad sense'.[75] If this is so, the decision of the Johannesburg City Council pertaining to the installation of pre-paid meters would constitute an exercise of administrative rather than executive powers. This broad construction of the executive powers of a municipal council results in the exclusion of the public consultation procedures applicable to administrative action affecting the public. The effect is to reduce the scope for public participation in decisions which affect the enjoyment of constitutionally guaranteed socio-economic rights such as the right of access to sufficient water.

The Constitutional Court decision in *Mazibuko* is also the first case in which the Court has considered whether a measure violated ss 26 or 27 on the ground that it constituted a 'retrogressive measure'. It will be recalled that the Constitutional Court in *Grootboom* expressly endorsed the views of the UN Committee on Economic, Social and Cultural Rights that retrogressive measures require particular justification in the light of the obligation undertaken by States Parties to progressively realise the economic, social and cultural rights in the International Covenant on Economic, Social and Cultural Rights.[76]

The applicants argued that the replacement of the deemed consumption and flat rate system of charging for water in Phiri with the new water provision policy incorporating pre-paid meters and a free allocation of 6 kilolitres per month constituted a retrogressive measure. The deemed consumption of consumers under the previous system was 20 kilolitres of water per household per month, and for this a flat rate of R68.40 was levied. The Court, however, concluded that the residents were now better off, as those consumers with pre-paid meters paid 25% less for 20 kilolitres of water than those still charged on the deemed consumption tariff.[77] Those consumers who registered on the City's Indigent Register were charged even less. The Court observed that the tariff for pre-paid meters at low levels of usage was well below the costs of providing the water services. These costs were cross-subsidised by the tariffs charged to heavier water users.[78]

However, the Court misconstrues the applicants' arguments in relation to retrogressive measures. The introduction of pre-paid water meters was in effect a punitive measure which, given the income levels of the Phiri community, was likely to result

---

[75] See O'Regan J's exposition of the proper approach to be adopted by courts in distinguishing between executive and administrative powers in *Permanent Secretary, Department of Welfare, Eastern Cape v Ed-U College (PE) (Section 21) Inc* 2001 (2) SA 1 (CC), 2001 (2) BCLR 118 (CC) para 21.

[76] See further chapter 4, part 4.3.3.

[77] *Mazibuko (CC)* (note 24 above) para 140.

[78] Ibid para 141.

in many households being left on a regular basis without access to any water beyond the free basic minimum of 6 kilolitres per household per month. They were in substance in a worse position than under the deemed consumption, flat rate system under which they had enjoyed access to an unlimited, un-metered water supply for decades.

While retrogressive measures are not absolutely prohibited, they require that the State be placed under a burden of justification when people's access to a socio-economic right is qualitatively or quantitatively reduced. In *Mazibuko*, the City's justification was that the imposition of pre-paid water meters would result in savings which could be redirected to improving the position of those with more urgent water needs (for example, those on service level two or those with no access to water services). However, as the applicants point out in their submissions, the City did not explain why it was necessary to achieve the constitutional objective of improving the position of those with reduced or no access to water by worsening the position of the Phiri residents who also constitute an impoverished community.[79]

The final ground on which the pre-paid meters were challenged is that they breached the equality and non-discrimination guarantees in s 9 of the Constitution. It was argued that singling out only Soweto for the imposition of pre-paid meters while leaving in place the other three deemed consumption areas in Johannesburg – Alexandra, Ivory Park and Orange Farm – constituted a differentiation which was not rationally connected to a legitimate government purpose. The Court dismissed the s 9(1) challenge on the basis that the targeting of Soweto was not irrational as the problem of unaccounted for water was at its most acute in this area.[80]

The applicants further argued that the system of pre-paid meters breached s 9(3) of the Constitution as it discriminated unfairly between poor black South Africans and wealthy white South Africans. The residents of Phiri were offered only the option of a water supply delivered to their homes (service level 3) on condition that they accepted a pre-paid water meter. If they did not accept a pre-paid meter, they were relegated to the delivery of water services through a yard standpipe (service level 3). They were not offered the option of a credit meter routinely offered in the wealthy, formerly white group areas. Those receiving water through a credit meter have the advantage of a period of grace to pay for water already used as well as the procedural safeguards of a fair hearing and an opportunity to make representations prior to the cut-off of their water.[81]

It was argued further that the measures constituted a form of paternalism which perpetuated racial and class stereotypes. It conveyed a message that poor black consumers were not as capable as white consumers in deciding how best to regulate their affairs.[82] The decision to implement pre-paid water meters only in low-income

[79] Applicants' submissions (note 32 above) paras 286–287.
[80] *Mazibuko (CC)* (note 24 above) para 146.
[81] Applicants' submissions (note 32 above) paras 304–305.
[82] Ibid para 308.4.

deemed consumption areas thus had a serious adverse impact on poor black consumers. This constituted indirect discrimination on the grounds of race and social origin (class).[83] As these are listed grounds, they are presumptively unfair. The absence of any justification from the City rendered the policy unconstitutional.

The Court held that even if the pre-paid water meter system was discriminatory in its impact, it would not be unconstitutional 'if it can be shown that the purpose for which the policy was introduced was not unfair for the purposes of s 9(3)'.[84] It found that, although the affected group had been disadvantaged by severe unfair discrimination in the past, the purpose of the measures was to eradicate severe water losses in Soweto which was 'a laudable, indeed necessary, government objective, clearly tailored to its purpose'.[85] A major criterion for evaluating the fairness of a discriminatory measure is whether it impairs the human dignity of the complainants or has a serious adverse impact on their interests.[86] According to the Court, '[i]t is not clear that the new water policy is harmful at all, in the sense that it is disadvantageous to those consumers who use it'.[87]

It reached this conclusion by comparing tariffs charged to credit meter consumers and those applicable to consumers with pre-paid meters. Credit-meter consumers were charged R131.25 per month for 20 kilolitres of water while pre-paid consumers pay R95.80 per month for the same quantity of water.[88] In addition, the Court observed that credit meter consumers are subject to a range of severe consequences should they fail to pay their water accounts. These included the charging of interest on arrear amounts and possibly being listed with a credit bureau as a defaulter.[89] Indigent consumers on the pre-payment systems can avoid these 'worrying measures'.[90]

The fact that the residents were not offered the option of a credit meter system was dismissed by the Court on the basis that credit meter consumers are also not afforded a choice to switch to the pre-payment system with its reduced tariffs unless certain strict conditions are met. Restricting consumer choice in altering the water delivery system was held to be justifiable in the light of the substantial cost of the installation of either system.[91] The Court concluded that the pre-paid meter system did not amount to unfair discrimination in the sense that it was disadvantageous to the residents of Phiri.[92]

---

[83] The integral connection between geographical areas and race in the South African context for the purposes of establishing indirect racial discrimination was recognised in *Pretoria City Council v Walker* 1998 (2) SA 363 (CC), 1998 (3) BCLR 257 (CC) paras 32–35.

[84] Ibid para 150.

[85] Ibid paras 150 and 154.

[86] See *Harksen v Lane NO* 1998 (1) SA 300 (CC), 1997 (11) BCLR 1489 (CC) para 54.

[87] *Mazibuko (CC)* (note 24 above) para 152.

[88] Ibid para 152.

[89] Ibid para 153 (referring to s 9C(3)(*a*) and (*d*) of the City's Water Service by-laws).

[90] Ibid.

[91] Ibid para 155.

[92] Ibid paras 154 and 157.

The Court's deferential approach to the assessment of the reasonableness of the free basic water policy is echoed in its assessment of the fairness of the pre-paid meter system. Given that there had not been serious contestation that the pre-paid meter system had a discriminatory impact on grounds listed in s 9(3),[93] the presumption of unfairness in s 9(5) should have been applied. Thus the burden should have been on the City to rebut this presumption. Instead, the Court concludes that 'the applicants have not established that the pre-paid meter system is unfairly discriminatory'.[94] The Court again emphasises that government enjoys a broad discretion in the provision of essential services, 'as long as the mechanism it selects is lawful, reasonable and not unfairly discriminatory'.[95]

The Court adopts a particularly narrow frame of reference in its approach to detecting the disadvantages imposed by the pre-paid water meter system on indigent communities. While tariffs are more favourable, an impoverished household is in effect often restricted to the free basic provision of 6 kilolitres per household per month. This has severe consequences for the life, health and dignity of such a household.[96] These consequences are aggravated in the context of a poor urban environment such as Phiri where the HIV-infection rate is likely to be above average.[97] The absence of procedural safeguards prior to the discontinuation of a household's water supply due to an inability to purchase additional water credits places them at a further disadvantage.

The Court's analysis is characterised by an a-contextual and formalist concept of equality. It fails to analyse the differential impacts of a pre-paid- system versus a credit metered water supply in the context of the socio-economic background and realities of the respective communities.

The disadvantage of the credit meter system is that the tariffs are 37% higher than those charged to consumers with pre-paid meters. Furthermore, credit meter consumers face certain financial penalties if they default on their payments. However, the middle- and high-income communities living in the formerly white suburbs of Johannesburg do not suffer severe adverse effects as a result of the higher tariffs and

---

93 Following the analysis in *Walker* (note 83 above).

94 Ibid para 157.

95 *Mazibuko (CC)* (note 24 above) para 156.

96 For a detailed account of the impact of the pre-paid water meter system on the Phiri community, see P Bond and J Dugard 'The case of Johannesburg water: What really happened at the pre-paid "Parish pump"?' (2008) 12 *LDD* 1–28.

97 The serious consequences of a restricted water supply for an impoverished household with members living with AIDS is described in the evidence presented by the President of the Southern African HIV Clinicians Society. This evidence is summarised in the High Court judgment in *Mazibuko (HC)* (note 25 above) at paras 172–173. The fifth applicant, Mr Paki, describes the horrific incident in which two children of a tenant burnt to death in a shack fire. The residents struggled to extinguish the blaze with the inadequate water pressure and supply provided through the pre-paid meter system. See the Constitutional Court judgment in *Mazibuko (CC)* (note 24 above) para 144.

credit control mechanisms. Those households who are experiencing difficulties in meeting their water payments are afforded the ample procedural safeguards of notice, an opportunity to make representations and to conclude an agreement with the water services authority for the payment of arrear charges.[98] In contrast, the impoverished households of Phiri struggle to purchase the additional water credits required to meet their basic needs. The pre-paid water meter system is a technical device which results in the automatic discontinuation of their water services when they do not purchase additional credits over and above the 6 kilolitres of free basic water provided per month. They are denied the opportunities afforded to credit meter consumers of receiving notice and some latitude if they experience difficulties in making their water payments.

The benefits afforded by the statutory procedural safeguards are not merely formal. In the context of a basic need and a fundamental constitutional right, they allow for an individualised consideration of the actual circumstances of the consumer. This is a critical safeguard against the impersonal disconnection of water services, particularly in circumstances that pose a threat to peoples' lives, health and human dignity. The values of human dignity and equality are implicated when an impoverished community is denied the opportunity afforded to affluent communities of making representations on their particular circumstances prior to the disconnection of their water supply.

O'Regan J concludes her judgment for the Court by outlining the value of socio-economic rights litigation in a case such as *Mazibuko* despite its unsuccessful outcome. She highlights the important role of public interest legal organisations in holding organs of State accountable through exacting 'a detailed accounting from government' which can 'impact beneficially on the policy-making process'.[99] In the context of the *Mazibuko* litigation, she observes:

> Having to explain why the Free Basic Water policy was reasonable shone a bright, cold light on the policy that undoubtedly revealed flaws. The continual revision of the policy in the ensuing years has improved the policy in a manner entirely consistent with an obligation of progressive realisation.[100]

While these are certainly valuable features of public interest litigation, the Court downplays the difficulties of holding the State accountable in the absence of judicial guidelines on the values and purposes which the various socio-economic rights seek to promote. Providing minimal guidelines on the goals to be achieved in realising socio-economic rights also renders it more difficult for an organ of state to design appropriate social policies and programmes. Furthermore, litigation is an expensive, time-consuming and draining process, particularly for disadvantaged communities and groups. The resources and energy that are expended on litigation can frequently

---

[98] See ss 4(2)(*c*)(iv) and 21(1)(*f*) of the Water Services Act 108 of 1997 read with ss 9C and 11 of the City of Johannesburg's Water Services by-laws.

[99] *Mazibuko (CC)* (note 24 above) para 163.

[100] Ibid.

produce more sustainable benefits when invested in building strong community organisations and development projects. Developing a concept of reasonableness which is integrally linked to a substantive conception of socio-economic rights can help avoid unnecessary litigation.

The deferential and normatively thin concept of reasonableness review applied in the *Mazibuko* case weakens the capacity of socio-economic rights jurisprudence to contribute meaningfully to transformative social change. The responsiveness of the Court's jurisprudence to conditions of poverty and social deprivation is further undermined by the formalism pervading its analysis of the equality and procedural fairness rights raised by the *Mazibuko* applicants.

The Court's early jurisprudence on socio-economic rights has the potential to evolve into a rich, substantive set of normative criteria for guiding fundamental social and economic reforms in South Africa. It is regrettable that in *Mazibuko* the Court chose to place the narrowest possible construction on these criteria and to engage in a superficial analysis of the impact of the City's water policies on the Phiri community.

Revisiting and developing the early potential of the Court's approach to socio-economic rights is a major challenge for the constitutional adjudication of claims to decent social and economic services and benefits over the next decade.

CHAPTER 10

Conclusion

> The Constitution, like any law, can be interpreted formally and thus allow judges to avoid engagement with substance and evade the search for justice.
>
> Former Chief Justice Pius Langa[1]

There are certain kinds of human suffering and forms of disadvantage which liberal legal systems are generally not attuned to recognise and vindicate through effective legal redress. These arise from the social and economic class divisions in society which create systemically marginalised groups or classes of people. These groups experience threats to their lives and health, as well as various forms of indignity. They are also severely constrained in attempting to fulfil their personal potential, and are vulnerable to exploitation and subordination in a range of relationships.

Economic disadvantage and marginalisation overlap with other forms of systemic discrimination on grounds such as race, gender, disability, HIV-positive status and sexual orientation. Economic injustice and these other forms of social injustice mutually reinforce each other to create what Nancy Fraser describes as 'a vicious cycle of cultural and economic subordination'.[2]

This is particularly evident in the South African context, where race, class and gender divisions assumed a distinctive form and were deeply embedded in the fabric of South African society through the colonial and apartheid systems. The result is that large parts of our society are deprived of the ability to participate as equals in all areas of life – the home, the workplace, community structures, the economy, and the formal and informal institutions through which political and social power are exercised.

Economic and social deprivation and discrimination implicate the central values of human rights law – human dignity, equality and freedom. However, legal systems tend to reproduce and reinforce these social and economic divisions, particularly those that are strongly influenced by classic liberal legal conceptions regarding law and society. In these legal cultures, constitutional rights tend to be formal instead of focusing on the substantive social purposes and outcomes which the particular rights seek to protect and facilitate.

Classic liberal legal culture also privileges civil and political freedoms over economic and social rights, and fails to acknowledge that all dimensions of human welfare are interrelated. The effective protection of human welfare requires a holistic matrix

---

[1] 'Transformative constitutionalism' (2006) 17 *Stell LR* 351–360 at 357.

[2] N Fraser 'From redistribution to recognition? Dilemmas of justice in a "postsocialist age"' in K Olson (ed) *Adding Insult to Injury: Nancy Fraser Debates her Critics* (2008) 9–41 at 16.

of rights as well as an interpretative approach which considers the normative and institutional implications of the interdependence between various rights and values.

Furthermore, classic liberal legal culture is premised on various dichotomous conceptions such as the divide between law/politics, rights/democracy, and negative/positive rights. It also upholds a rigid, bounded conception of the separation of powers between the legislature, executive and judiciary. Participants in legal systems which are based on this conceptual framework are considerably constrained in their capacity to recognise and respond to unjust socio-economic power relations in society. Instead they tend to develop legal doctrines which reflect and reinforce these power relations.[3]

It has been argued in this book that the South African legal culture has historically been strongly influenced by the traditions sketched above. Their influence continues to be felt in the era of constitutional democracy despite a Constitution which is manifestly committed to facilitating fundamental political, social and economic transformation.

One of the clearest signals that the Constitution seeks to break with these traditions and introduce fundamental changes in how we think about rights and the relationship between law and society is the inclusion of an expansive set of justiciable social and economic rights in the Bill of Rights.

In addition, the transformative purposes of the Constitution are conveyed by other provisions and features of the Bill of Rights. Thus the Constitution endorses a rich conception of democracy, extending beyond representative democracy to embrace deliberative and participatory forms of democracy. Instead of the Bill of Rights being viewed as a limit or check on democracy, this book has argued that it is a vehicle for enabling broad social engagement and participation on the meaning and implications of constitutional rights for transformative social change in South Africa.[4] This deliberation and engagement occurs in a number of formal and informal institutional sites and forums, which include the courts. The courts have a particular role and responsibility given their constitutional authority to develop authoritative interpretations of rights which, until revised or developed, will determine the nature and scope of legal and social relationships.

There are a number of features of the Constitution which suggest that the adjudication of constitutional rights is intended to be a site of broad social participation and deliberation in developing the meaning of rights. These include the expansive provisions on legal standing,[5] the express injunction in s 39 that rights must be interpreted so as to 'promote' open-textured constitutional rights and values,[6] as well as the structure of rights adjudication under the Constitution. Thus the two-stage

---

[3] These features of classic liberal legal culture and their implications for the adjudication of socio-economic rights are discussed in chapter 2.

[4] See chapter 2, parts 2.2 and 2.3.

[5] See chapter 3, part 3.2.3.

[6] See chapter 3, part 3.3.1.

approach to constitutional interpretation and the general limitations clause (s 36) facilitates a contextual, relational dialogue on the substantive purposes and values underlying rights, and the justifiability of limitations to rights in terms of the broad criteria of s 36.[7] The Constitution furthermore expressly indicates that rights deliberation in courts and other forums in South Africa should be open to developments in international law and foreign law.[8] No right under the constitution has a firm, immutable meaning which can be derived deductively from formal legal doctrine or philosophical premises. There is considerable scope for contestation and deliberation on the meaning which constitutional rights should assume in their particular social and historical context.

Moreover, the classic liberal dichotomy between negative and positive rights and the privileging of negative constitutionalism cannot be sustained given the text and context of the Constitution. Section 7, the opening provision of the Bill of Rights, requires that the State not only 'respect' rights, but also 'protect, promote and fulfil' them.[9] Various provisions in the Bill of Rights require the State to adopt positive legislative and other measures to give effect to rights, including the various provisions dealing with socio-economic rights. The far-reaching remedial powers and open discretion of the courts to grant 'just and equitable' remedies are also indicative of the extent to which the Constitution strives to ensure that constitutional rights translate into real and effective forms of redress for those whose constitutional rights are violated.[10]

Finally, the Constitution provides that the rights in the Bill of Rights are capable of binding private parties and must influence the development of all areas of law – legislation, customary law and the common law. This is a fundamental departure from the notion that there are firm boundaries between public and private law, and that the primary function of human rights law is the control and limitation of public institutions.[11]

The normative and institutional framework created by the South African Constitution is conducive to creating a legal system which is responsive to social and economic disadvantage and marginalisation. However, the potential of adjudication to support fundamental social and legal reforms based on constitutional rights and values is constrained by the lingering influence of many of the features of classic liberal legal culture described above.[12]

---

[7] See chapter 3, part 3.2.4.

[8] See chapter 3, parts 3.3.2 and 3.3.3.

[9] See further chapter 3, part 3.2.2.

[10] See chapter 2, part 2.4.9 and chapter 8.

[11] See chapter 2, part 2.4.5 and chapter 7.

[12] In this respect I have drawn largely on the work of Karl Klare 'Legal culture and transformative constitutionalism' (1998) 14 *SAJHR* 146–188 and the theoretical scholarship on transformative constitutionalism which it has inspired.

This book has sought to explore alternative approaches to the constitutional interpretation of socio-economic rights which can unlock their potential to promote fundamental changes in South African law.

For example, building on the work of various constitutional scholars, I have argued for a reconceptualised separation of powers doctrine based on a model of dialogic interaction between the three branches of government, affected communities and organisations. In addition, a functional model should displace the territorial, bounded conception of the separation of powers doctrine which continues to surface from time to time in South African constitutional jurisprudence. Instead of policing fixed boundaries, the focus of the courts should be on the institutions (or combination of institutions) which can be most effective in advancing access to socio-economic rights in the particular context of a case. The third feature of a transformed doctrine of separation of powers is the broadening and extension of 'the constitutional dialogue' on socio-economic rights. Even within the constraints of adjudication, there exist interpretative and remedial methods which are capable of stimulating meaningful civic participation in the institutional reforms and social programmes required to realise socio-economic rights.

These theoretical approaches have constituted the prism for analysing and evaluating the socio-economic rights jurisprudence which has developed in the 13 years since the coming into force of the Constitution.

Many aspects of this jurisprudence have the potential to advance the transformative purposes of the Constitution. The reasonableness model of review developed by the Constitutional Court for assessing compliance with the positive duties imposed by socio-economic rights allows substantial space for a consideration of the social and economic context in which rights violations occur.[13] The broadly formulated criteria of reasonableness review – comprehensiveness, transparency, provision for those in urgent need, together with efforts by the Court to develop the interrelationship between socio-economic rights and equality rights[14] – permit a diversity of challenges to socio-economic deprivations and inequities. In this respect, reasonableness review avoids the kind of normative closure that can be induced by overly rigid accounts of the concept of minimum core obligations. Such accounts unduly limit socio-economic rights claims, and lead to the exclusion of various forms of socio-economic disadvantage that do not fit the definition of core obligations.[15] The very

[13] The model and criteria of reasonableness review were developed in the important trilogy of cases, *Soobramoney v Minister of Health (KwaZulu-Natal)* 1998 (1) SA 765 (CC), 1997 (12) BCLR 1696 (CC); *Government of the Republic of South Africa v Grootboom* 2001 (1) SA 46 (CC), 2000 (11) BCLR 1169 (CC); and *Minister of Health v Treatment Action Campaign (No 2)* 2002 (5) SA 721 (CC), 2002 (10) BCLR 1075 (CC). See the discussion in chapter 4, parts 4.2. and 4.3.

[14] See particularly *Khosa v Minister of Social Development; Mahlaule v Minister of Social Development* 2004 (6) SA 505 (CC), 2004 (6) BCLR 569 (CC) discussed in chapter 4, part 4.3.4. See further part -4.5.

[15] See in this regard chapter 4, part 4.4.1.

openness and flexibility of reasonableness review create space for a diversity of voices and perspectives to participate in shaping the meaning of these rights.

However, a fundamental weakness in the model of reasonableness review developed by the Constitutional Court for adjudicating the positive duties imposed by socio-economic rights has been a failure to develop the substantive purposes and values which these rights seek to advance. The consequence hereof is that both organs of State and civil society lack normative guidance on the kinds of processes and outcomes which are consistent with these rights.

The analysis of the jurisprudence demonstrates that the courts have generally failed to engage substantively with these questions. Instead the focus has fallen disproportionately on the criteria for evaluating the State's policy and resource-based justifications in legal challenges based on socio-economic rights.[16] This is illustrated most clearly by the decision of the Constitutional Court in *Mazibuko v City of Johannesburg*[17] (hereafter '*Mazibuko*'). The Court's assessment of the reasonableness of the City's water policies takes place in the absence of a serious, systematic attempt to explore the normative commitments which the entrenchment of the right of access to sufficient water in s 27(1)(*b*) of the Constitution seeks to advance.[18]

This approach has also been extended to those socio-economic rights which are formulated as direct basic entitlements without the internal qualifications encountered in ss 26 and 27. Thus the basic paradigm and principles of reasonableness review have also been applied to the socio-economic rights of children and of persons deprived of their liberty.[19]

In this book I have sought to demonstrate that it is possible to engage with the substantive purposes of socio-economic rights within a reconceived model of reasonableness review. A number of suggestions have been made as to how this might be achieved, drawing on various concepts which have gained traction in international and comparative jurisprudence on socio-economic rights.[20]

Recent socio-economic rights judgments of the Constitutional Court have sought to encourage and enforce deliberative engagement between the parties in finding mutually satisfactory solutions to their disputes. This has occurred in the context of cases dealing with the implications of s 26 of the Constitution for various aspects of the law pertaining to the eviction of people from their homes.[21] This is a

---

[16] See the critique of reasonableness review in chapter 4, part 4.4.2.

[17] *Mazibuko v City of Johannesburg (Centre on Housing Rights and Eviction as amicus curiae)* [2009] ZACC 28.

[18] See chapter 9 (Postscript), part 9.4.

[19] See in this regard, chapter 5.

[20] See particularly chapter 4, part 4.4.

[21] See the discussion in chapter 6 of *Port Elizabeth Municipality v Various Occupiers* 2005 (1) SA 217 (CC), 2004 (12) BCLR 1268 (CC), *Occupiers of 51 Olivia Road, Berea Township and 197 Main Street, Johannesburg v City of Johannesburg* 2008 (3) SA 208 (CC), 2008 (5) BCLR 475 (CC) and *Residents of Joe Slovo Community, Western Cape v Thubelisha Homes, Minister for Housing and Minister of Local Government and Housing, Western Cape (Centre on Housing*

potentially significant development for encouraging participatory, context-specific solutions to rights conflicts. However, in the absence of substantive guidance on the nature and purposes of socio-economic rights, such engagement occurs in a normative vacuum. The absence of such guidance renders disadvantaged communities vulnerable to negotiating away their constitutional entitlements, particularly where such communities are not well-organised and lack the support of public interest lawyers and organisations. It can also lead to ad hoc, localised resolutions of disputes concerning constitutional rights rather than addressing the systemic conditions which lead to rights violations.

Orders of meaningful engagement can allow affected groups and communities to participate actively in defining the detailed measures required to implement their rights. They can be particularly useful in the context of the structural, participatory remedies referred to below. However, they cannot substitute for the constitutional responsibility of the courts to develop the normative implications of constitutional rights.

Developing the substantive content of socio-economic rights should not imply a comprehensive, fixed narrative as to their meaning. On the contrary, in interpreting these (and indeed all constitutional) rights, courts should transparently explore a range of traditions in philosophical, social and political theory that can assist in developing a substantive account of the normative commitments promoted by the relevant rights. At the same time, they should be attentive to a diversity of voices, with particular attention to those whose voices are suppressed in the broader political and social context. Judges should be conscious of the fluid social and political contexts in which rights claims are made, and their potential to entrench and create new patterns of social disadvantage.

A process of dialectical engagement between theoretical discourses and social context offers the best chance of developing interpretations of socio-economic rights

Rights and Evictions and Community Law Centre, University of the Western Cape as amicus curiae) [2009] ZACC 16, 2009 (9) BCLR 847 (CC). See also the judgment of the Constitutional Court in *Abahlali Basemjondolo Movement SA v Premier of the Province of KwaZulu-Natal* [2009] ZACC 31 (judgment of 14 October 2009) in which s 16 of the KwaZulu-Natal Elimination and Prevention of Re-emergence of Slums Act 6 of 2007 was declared inconsistent with s 26(2) of the Constitution. Section 16 compelled owners or municipalities to institute eviction proceedings against unlawful occupiers within a period determined by the responsible Member of the Executive Council by notice in the *Gazette*. The majority of the Court held that section 16 introduced 'the coercive institution of eviction proceedings' which undermined the procedural and substantive protections which are integral to the 'dignified framework that has been developed for the eviction of unlawful occupiers' (ibid para 122). These protections include 'proper engagement' which 'would include taking into proper consideration the wishes of the people who are to be evicted; whether the areas where they live may be upgraded *in situ*; and whether there will be alternative accommodation. The engagement would also include the manner of eviction and the timeframes for the eviction' (ibid para 114). See also the minority judgment of Yacoob J at para 69.

which can support broader initiatives to address the underlying structural causes of impoverishment in South Africa. While the interpretation of constitutional rights should always be provisional and continuously evolving, the responsibility of the courts to interpret rights, and the consequences thereof, cannot be avoided. Judges have considerable power in the interpretative choices they make to influence the kind of legal system we develop in South Africa. This legal system can in turn help shape a political culture which is more responsive to the claims of those who experience systemic social and economic disadvantage.

Naturally, this represents in many respects an ideal conception of the processes of constitutional interpretation which the realities of limited time, resources and evidence in litigation frequently do not allow. Nevertheless it indicates the type of interpretative approach which is most likely to promote a constitutional jurisprudence which is attuned to the myriad ways in which conditions of poverty and social marginalisation affect people's human dignity, freedom and equality – the foundational values of the Constitution. The implications of social deprivation for constitutional values is well illustrated in the following observations of Mokgoro J in *Khosa v Minister of Social Development; Mahlaule v Minister of Social Development*:[22]

> The denial of welfare benefits therefore impacts not only on permanent residents without other means of support, but also on the families, friends and communities with whom they have contact. Apart from the undue burden that this places on those who take on this responsibility, it is likely to have a serious impact on the dignity of the permanent residents concerned who are cast in the role of supplicants.[23]

The interpretative approach I have outlined also points to the importance of lawyers, civil society organisations and others involved in socio-economic rights litigation to place before the court a rich tapestry of historical and social evidence pertaining to the claim. This is indispensable if we are to take seriously the Constitutional Court's own affirmation that rights 'need to be interpreted and understood in their social and historical context'.[24]

A second major area of weakness identified in the constitutional jurisprudence on socio-economic rights is the limited impact which these rights have had on various areas of private law. The high-water mark has occurred in the context of jurisprudence which has considered the impact on s 26 (housing rights) of the Constitution on the law pertaining to the eviction of people from their homes. Legislation such as the Prevention of Illegal Eviction from and Unlawful Occupation of Land Act 19 of 1998 ('PIE'), enacted to give effect to s 26(3) of the Constitution, has fundamentally changed the legal paradigm pertaining to such evictions.

The courts have recognised that applications to evict people from their homes raise fundamental questions of human rights law which cannot be resolved through the previous private law-orientated doctrinal frameworks and rules. Unlawful occupiers

---

[22] Note 14 above.

[23] Ibid para 76.

[24] *Grootboom* (note 13 above) para 25.

are entitled to a detailed set of procedural and substantive protections when faced with eviction from their homes.[25] These protections are derived from the various interests and values which the recognition of housing as a human right is designed to protect.

However, the protections are less robust in areas of property law not governed by reform statutes such as PIE, which are explicitly committed to the protection of the housing rights in s 26 of the Constitution. This is illustrated by an examination of the jurisprudence in the post-constitutional era pertaining to common-law ejectment applications and to execution against mortgaged residential property.[26] Moreover, despite the contextual, nuanced interpretation of PIE by the Constitutional Court in *Port Elizabeth Municipality v Various Occupiers*,[27] the power of the private property law paradigm still has considerable potential to constrain a transformative interpretation of land reform legislation such as PIE.[28]

The area of traditional private law in which socio-economic rights have had the least impact is that of contract law. Even under a transformative Constitution, South African contract law is still strongly influenced by classic liberal notions of individual autonomy and freedom of contract. This is manifest in the privileging of form over substance in the judicial scrutiny of contractual arrangements, as well as the limited impact of constitutional rights on existing rules and doctrines in this sphere.

In cases such as *Brisley v Drotsky*[29] and *Afrox Health Care Bpk v Strydom*,[30] the Supreme Court of Appeal has adopted a particularly narrow and formalistic interpretation of the rights to housing and health care respectively.[31] This approach fails to do justice to a substantive interpretation of these rights, relevant international law standards and the injunction in s 39(1)(*a*) of the Constitution requiring courts to 'promote the spirit, purport and objects of the Bill of Rights' when developing the common law. A contrasting illustration of the potential of socio-economic rights to influence the development of common-law rules of contract is the High Court judgment of *Mpange v Sithole*.[32] Through applying substantively interpreted housing rights to the common-law rules of lease, the law in this sphere was developed to be more responsive to the needs and circumstances of impoverished groups.

Even a fundamental civil right – the right of access to courts enshrined in s 34 of the Constitution – has not had a substantive influence on the law of contract. The decision of the Constitutional Court in *Barkhuizen v Napier*[33] underscored the presumptive force of the classic doctrine of *pacta sunt servanda*. This judgment repre-

[25] See the jurisprudence discussed in chapter 6, parts 6.2 and 6.3.
[26] See chapter 7, part 7.3.
[27] Note 21 above.
[28] See chapter 7, part 7.3.1(*c*).
[29] 2002 (4) SA 1 (SCA), 2002 (12) BCLR 1229 (SCA).
[30] 2002 (6) SA 21 (SCA), [2002] 4 All SA 125 (SCA).
[31] See chapter 7, parts 7.4.1 and 7.4.2.
[32] 2007 (6) SA 578 (W).
[33] 2007 (5) SA 323 (CC), 2007 (7) BCLR 691 (CC).

sents an important missed opportunity to allow constitutional rights such as access to court to provide an important safeguard against the power of private corporations to impose unjust and one-sided contractual terms.[34]

The final substantive area of law which has been examined in this book is the remedial power of the courts in socio-economic rights cases. I have sought to demonstrate the range and diversity of remedies which are at the disposal of the courts to fashion effective responses to different types of socio-economic rights violations. In many respects, the courts have demonstrated a flexible and nuanced approach to designing appropriate remedies. Their efforts to 'synchronise the real world with the ideal construct of the constitutional world'[35] is evident from much of the jurisprudence examined in chapter 8.

However, the transformative potential of this remedial jurisprudence will be constrained while the Constitutional Court remains hesitant to endorse structural mandatory relief in the context of socio-economic rights cases. The types of structural orders described in the final chapter are the most effective remedial option for redressing violations of socio-economic rights which require a series of structural reforms to be adopted over a period of time.[36] In this context a court order will define the broad goals to be achieved for the State or even a private entity to be constitutionally compliant. The parties are then ordered to enter into a process of engagement regarding the optimal methods of achieving these goals and the set of concrete measures to be adopted. The court maintains periodic supervision over the process and may issue further directions to ensure that the process and outcomes are in alignment with the normative goals it has defined in its initial judgment.

These remedies have substantial potential to promote the kind of deliberative and participatory engagement which resonates with the transformative ethos of the Constitution.[37] Structural remedies will not constitute appropriate or effective relief in all socio-economic rights cases. Sometimes an infringement can be more effectively and speedily remedied, for example, by direct mandatory orders, 'reading in' remedies,[38] or orders for the payment of constitutional damages.[39] However, structural relief constitutes a valuable remedy for particular types of socio-economic rights violations and their use should not be discouraged on the basis of restrictive conceptions of the separation of powers doctrine and judicial competence. A promising sign that the Constitutional Court may in future be more receptive to structural orders in

---

[34] See chapter 7, part 7.4.4. Compare the minority judgments of Moseneke DCJ (concurred in by Mokgoro J) and of Sachs J.

[35] I borrow in this regard Kriegler J's evocative phrase from his judgment in *Fose v Minister of Safety and Security* 1997 (3) SA 786 (CC), 1997 (7) BCLR 851 (CC) para 94.

[36] See chapter 8, part 8.6.

[37] See chapter 2, part 2.2.4.

[38] See chapter 8, part 8.3.3.

[39] See chapter 8, part 8.7.

the context of socio-economic rights is the reporting orders made by the Court in *Head of Department: Mpumalanga Department of Education v Hoërskool Ermelo.*[40]

Finally, the entire project of promoting law-based transformation is undermined when organs of State do not respect court orders. The High Courts have sought to respond to instances of non-compliance with court orders through a variety of mechanisms such as contempt of court orders against responsible officials, supervisory orders and punitive costs awards.[41] In *Nyathi v Member of Executive Council for Department of Health, Gauteng,*[42] the Constitutional Court confirmed the order of the North Gauteng High Court, declaring s 3 of the State Liability Act 20 of 1957 unconstitutional. It suspended the declaration of invalidity for a period of 12 months to enable Parliament to enact legislation providing for the effective enforcement of court orders.[43] This offers the potential of a renewed and more effective mechanism for ensuring compliance with court orders sounding in money. The courts must continue to strive, within their constitutional powers, to induce co-operation and compliance with their orders by public and private entities.

The recognition of socio-economic rights as justiciable rights in the Bill of Rights makes poverty and social marginalisation central issues of constitutional concern. It requires fundamental changes to South Africa's traditional legal culture which inhibits innovation and renewal in the courts' approach to constitutional interpretation and remedies. The Constitution provides a unique opportunity to reconceptualise and imagine alternatives to many of the traditional barriers to the judicial enforcement of socio-economic rights. In so doing, we can develop a legal system which is capable of responding compassionately and more effectively to socio-economic disadvantage.

Socio-economic rights litigation and adjudication patently cannot bring about the far-reaching structural changes which are required to construct the society based on social justice envisaged in the preamble of the Constitution.[44] However, constitutional adjudication can create a normative framework which stimulates and supports broad deliberation and participatory initiatives by government and civil society aimed at transforming social and economic relationships.

Constitutional adjudication of socio-economic rights claims can also continue to expose the chasm between the aspiration of law to promote justice and the embedded power relations which systematically deny justice to certain groups and classes. As Langa ACJ (as he then was) observed in *President of the RSA v Modderklip Boerdery (Pty) Ltd:*[45]

---

[40] [2009] ZACC 32. See the discussion of the Constitutional Court's judgment in chapter 9 (Postscript), part 9.2.

[41] See chapter 8, parts 8.9 and 8.10.

[42] 2008 (5) SA 94 (CC), 2008 (9) BCLR 665 (CC).

[43] See the discussion of *Nyathi* in chapter 8, part 8.9.3.

[44] As Sachs J noted in *Port Elizabeth Municipality* (note 21 above): 'The inherited injustices at the macro level will inevitably make it difficult for the courts to ensure immediate present-day equity at the micro level' (para 38).

[45] 2005 (5) SA 3 (CC), 2005 (8) BCLR 786 (CC).

> The fact that poverty and homelessness still plague many South Africans is a painful reminder of the chasm that still needs to be bridged before the constitutional ideal to establish a society based on social justice and improved quality of life for all citizens is fully achieved.[46]

The painful consciousness of this chasm should in itself spur the legal community to greater efforts in striving for just outcomes through the cases they litigate and adjudicate. If this book contributes to a more rigorous engagement with the potential of socio-economic rights to contribute to a more just society in South Africa, it will have fulfilled its objectives.

[46] Ibid para 36.

APPENDIX

Constitution of the Republic of South Africa, 1996

PREAMBLE

We, the people of South Africa,

Recognise the injustices of our past;
Honour those who suffered for justice and freedom in our land;
Respect those who have worked to build and develop our country; and
Believe that South Africa belongs to all who live in it, united in our diversity.

We therefore, through our freely elected representatives, adopt this Constitution as the supreme law of the Republic so as to —

Heal the divisions of the past and establish a society based on democratic values, social justice and fundamental human rights;
Lay the foundations for a democratic and open society in which government is based on the will of the people and every citizen is equally protected by law;
Improve the quality of life of all citizens and free the potential of each person; and
Build a united and democratic South Africa able to take its rightful place as a sovereign state in the family of nations.

May God protect our people.

Nkosi Sikelel' iAfrika. Morena boloka setjhaba sa heso.
God seën Suid-Afrika. God bless South Africa.
Mudzimu fhatutshedza Afurika. Hosi katekisa Afrika.

CHAPTER 1
FOUNDING PROVISIONS

1 Republic of South Africa

The Republic of South Africa is one, sovereign, democratic state founded on the following values:

(*a*) Human dignity, the achievement of equality and the advancement of human rights and freedoms.
(*b*) Non-racialism and non-sexism.
(*c*) Supremacy of the constitution and the rule of law.
(*d*) Universal adult suffrage, a national common voters roll, regular elections and a multi-party system of democratic government, to ensure accountability, responsiveness and openness.

2 Supremacy of Constitution

This Constitution is the supreme law of the Republic; law or conduct inconsistent with it is invalid, and the obligations imposed by it must be fulfilled.

CHAPTER 2
BILL OF RIGHTS (SS 7–39)

7 Rights

(1) This Bill of Rights is a cornerstone of democracy in South Africa. It enshrines the rights of all people in our country and affirms the democratic values of human dignity, equality and freedom.

(2) The state must respect, protect, promote and fulfil the rights in the Bill of Rights.

(3) The rights in the Bill of Rights are subject to the limitations contained or referred to in section 36, or elsewhere in the Bill.

8 Application

(1) The Bill of Rights applies to all law, and binds the legislature, the executive, the judiciary and all organs of state.

(2) A provision of the Bill of Rights binds a natural or a juristic person if, and to the extent that, it is applicable, taking into account the nature of the right and the nature of any duty imposed by the right.

(3) When applying a provision of the Bill of Rights to a natural or juristic person in terms of subsection (2), a court —

(*a*) in order to give effect to a right in the Bill, must apply, or if necessary develop, the common law to the extent that legislation does not give effect to that right; and

(*b*) may develop rules of the common law to limit the right, provided that the limitation is in accordance with section 36 (1).

(4) A juristic person is entitled to the rights in the Bill of Rights to the extent required by the nature of the rights and the nature of that juristic person.

9 Equality

(1) Everyone is equal before the law and has the right to equal protection and benefit of the law.

(2) Equality includes the full and equal enjoyment of all rights and freedoms. To promote the achievement of equality, legislative and other measures designed to protect or advance persons, or categories of persons, disadvantaged by unfair discrimination may be taken.

(3) The state may not unfairly discriminate directly or indirectly against anyone on one or more grounds, including race, gender, sex, pregnancy, marital status, ethnic or social origin, colour, sexual orientation, age, disability, religion, conscience, belief, culture, language and birth.

(4) No person may unfairly discriminate directly or indirectly against anyone on one or more grounds in terms of subsection (3). National legislation must be enacted to prevent or prohibit unfair discrimination.
(5) Discrimination on one or more of the grounds listed in subsection (3) is unfair unless it is established that the discrimination is fair.

10 Human dignity

Everyone has inherent dignity and the right to have their dignity respected and protected.

11 Life

Everyone has the right to life.

12 Freedom and security of the person

(1) Everyone has the right to freedom and security of the person, which includes the right —
   (*a*) not to be deprived of freedom arbitrarily or without just cause;
   (*b*) not to be detained without trial;
   (*c*) to be free from all forms of violence from either public or private sources;
   (*d*) not to be tortured in any way; and
   (*e*) not to be treated or punished in a cruel, inhuman or degrading way.
(2) Everyone has the right to bodily and psychological integrity, which includes the right —
   (*a*) to make decisions concerning reproduction;
   (*b*) to security in and control over their body; and
   (*c*) not to be subjected to medical or scientific experiments without their informed consent.

13 Slavery, servitude and forced labour

No one may be subjected to slavery, servitude or forced labour.

14 Privacy

Everyone has the right to privacy, which includes the right not to have —
   (*a*) their person or home searched;
   (*b*) their property searched;
   (*c*) their possessions seized; or
   (*d*) the privacy of their communications infringed.

15 Freedom of religion, belief and opinion

(1) Everyone has the right to freedom of conscience, religion, thought, belief and opinion.
(2) Religious observances may be conducted at state or state-aided institutions, provided that —
   (*a*) those observances follow rules made by the appropriate public authorities;

(*b*) they are conducted on an equitable basis; and
(*c*) attendance at them is free and voluntary.

(3) (*a*) This section does not prevent legislation recognising —
(i) marriages concluded under any tradition, or a system of religious, personal or family law; or
(ii) systems of personal and family law under any tradition, or adhered to by persons professing a particular religion.
(*b*) Recognition in terms of paragraph (*a*) must be consistent with this section and the other provisions of the Constitution.

16 Freedom of expression

(1) Everyone has the right to freedom of expression, which includes —
(*a*) freedom of the press and other media;
(*b*) freedom to receive or impart information or ideas;
(*c*) freedom of artistic creativity; and
(*d*) academic freedom and freedom of scientific research.

(2) The right in subsection (1) does not extend to —
(*a*) propaganda for war;
(*b*) incitement of imminent violence; or
(*c*) advocacy of hatred that is based on race, ethnicity, gender or religion, and that constitutes incitement to cause harm.

17 Assembly, demonstration picket and petition

Everyone has the right, peacefully and unarmed, to assemble, to demonstrate, to picket and to present petitions.

18 Freedom of association

Everyone has the right to freedom of association.

19 Political rights

(1) Every citizen is free to make political choices, which includes the right —
(*a*) to form a political party;
(*b*) to participate in the activities of, or recruit members for, a political party; and
(*c*) to campaign for a political party or cause.

(2) Every citizen has the right to free, fair and regular elections for any legislative body established in terms of the Constitution.

(3) Every adult citizen has the right —
(*a*) to vote in elections for any legislative body established in terms of the Constitution, and to do so in secret; and
(*b*) to stand for public office and, if elected, to hold office.

20 Citizenship

No citizen may be deprived of citizenship.

21 Freedom of movement and residence

(1) Everyone has the right to freedom of movement.
(2) Everyone has the right to leave the Republic.
(3) Every citizen has the right to enter, to remain in and to reside anywhere in, the Republic.
(4) Every citizen has the right to a passport.

22 Freedom of trade, occupation and profession

Every citizen has the right to choose their trade, occupation or profession freely. The practice of a trade, occupation or profession may be regulated by law.

23 Labour relations

(1) Everyone has the right to fair labour practices.
(2) Every worker has the right —
   (*a*) to form and join a trade union;
   (*b*) to participate in the activities and programmes of a trade union; and
   (*c*) to strike.
(3) Every employer has the right —
   (*a*) to form and join an employers' organisation; and
   (*b*) to participate in the activities and programmes of an employers' organisation.
(4) Every trade union and every employers' organisation has the right —
   (*a*) to determine its own administration, programmes and activities;
   (*b*) to organise; and
   (*c*) to form and join a federation.
(5) Every trade union, employers' organisation and employer has the right to engage in collective bargaining. National legislation may be enacted to regulate collective bargaining. To the extent that the legislation may limit a right in this Chapter, the limitation must comply with section 36 (1).
(6) National legislation may recognise union security arrangements contained in collective agreements. To the extent that the legislation may limit a right in this Chapter the limitation must comply with section 36 (1).

24 Environment

Everyone has the right —
   (*a*) to an environment that is not harmful to their health or well-being; and
   (*b*) to have the environment protected, for the benefit of present and future generations, through reasonable legislative and other measures that —
      (i) prevent pollution and ecological degradation;
      (ii) promote conservation; and
      (iii) secure ecologically sustainable development and use of natural resources while promoting justifiable economic and social development.

25 Property

(1) No one may be deprived of property except in terms of law of general application, and no law may permit arbitrary deprivation of property.

(2) Property may be expropriated only in terms of law of general application —

(*a*) for a public purpose or in the public interest; and

(*b*) subject to compensation, the amount of which and the time and manner of payment of which have either been agreed to by those affected or decided or approved by a court.

(3) The amount of the compensation and the time and manner of payment must be just and equitable, reflecting an equitable balance between the public interest and the interests of those affected, having regard to all relevant circumstances, including —

(*a*) the current use of the property;

(*b*) the history of the acquisition and use of the property;

(*c*) the market value of the property;

(*d*) the extent of direct state investment and subsidy in the acquisition and beneficial capital improvement of the property; and

(*e*) the purpose of the expropriation.

(4) For the purposes of this section —

(*a*) the public interest includes the nation's commitment to land reform, and to reforms to bring about equitable access to all South Africa's natural resources; and

(*b*) property is not limited to land.

(5) The state must take reasonable legislative and other measures, within its available resources, to foster conditions which enable citizens to gain access to land on an equitable basis.

(6) A person or community whose tenure of land is legally insecure as a result of past racially discriminatory laws or practices is entitled, to the extent provided by an Act of Parliament, either to tenure which is legally secure or to comparable redress.

(7) A person or community dispossessed of property after 19 June 1913 as a result of past racially discriminatory laws or practices is entitled, to the extent provided by an Act of Parliament, either to restitution of that property or to equitable redress.

(8) No provision of this section may impede the state from taking legislative and other measures to achieve land, water and related reform, in order to redress the results of past racial discrimination, provided that any departure from the provisions of this section is in accordance with the provisions of section 36 (1).

(9) Parliament must enact the legislation referred to in subsection (6).

26 Housing

(1) Everyone has the right to have access to adequate housing.

(2) The state must take reasonable legislative and other measures, within its available resources, to achieve the progressive realisation of this right.

(3) No one may be evicted from their home, or have their home demolished, without an order of court made after considering all the relevant circumstances. No legislation may permit arbitrary evictions.

27 Health care, food, water and social security

(1) Everyone has the right to have access to —

(*a*) health care services, including reproductive health care;

(*b*) sufficient food and water; and

(*c*) social security, including, if they are unable to support themselves and their dependents, appropriate social assistance.

(2) The state must take reasonable legislative and other measures, within its available resources, to achieve the progressive realisation of each of these rights.

(3) No one may be refused emergency medical treatment.

28 Children

(1) Every child has the right —

(*a*) to a name and a nationality from birth;

(*b*) to family care or parental care, or to appropriate alternative care when removed from the family environment;

(*c*) to basic nutrition, shelter, basic health care services and social services;

(*d*) to be protected from maltreatment, neglect, abuse or degradation;

(*e*) to be protected from exploitative labour practices;

(*f*) not to be required or permitted to perform work or provide services that —

(i) are inappropriate for a person of that child's age; or

(ii) place at risk the child's well-being, education, physical or mental health or spiritual, moral or social development;

(*g*) not to be detained except as a measure of last resort, in which case, in addition to the rights a child enjoys under sections 12 and 35, the child may be detained only for the shortest appropriate period of time, and has the right to be —

(i) kept separately from detained persons over the age of 18 years; and

(ii) treated in a manner, and kept in conditions, that take account of the child's age;

(*h*) to have a legal practitioner assigned to the child by the state, and at state expense, in civil proceedings affecting the child, if substantial injustice would otherwise result; and

(*i*) not to be used directly in armed conflict, and to be protected in times of armed conflict.

(2) A child's best interests are of paramount importance in every matter concerning the child.

(3) In this section «'child'» means a person under the age of 18 years.

29 Education

(1) Everyone has the right —
  (*a*) to a basic education, including adult basic education; and
  (*b*) to further education, which the state, through reasonable measures, must make progressively available and accessible.

(2) Everyone has the right to receive education in the official language or languages of their choice in public educational institutions where that education is reasonably practicable. In order to ensure the effective access to, and implementation of, this right, the state must consider all reasonable educational alternatives, including single medium institutions, taking into account —
  (*a*) equity;
  (*b*) practicability; and
  (*c*) the need to redress the results of past racially discriminatory laws and practices.

(3) Everyone has the right to establish and maintain, at their own expense, independent educational institutions that —
  (*a*) do not discriminate on the basis of race;
  (*b*) are registered with the state; and
  (*c*) maintain standards that are not inferior to standards at comparable public educational institutions.

(4) Subsection (3) does not preclude state subsidies for independent educational institutions.

30 Language and culture

Everyone has the right to use the language and to participate in the cultural life of their choice, but no one exercising these rights may do so in a manner inconsistent with any provision of the Bill of Rights.

31 Cultural, religious and linguistic communities

(1) Persons belonging to a cultural, religious or linguistic community may not be denied the right, with other members of that community —
  (*a*) to enjoy their culture, practise their religion and use their language; and
  (*b*) to form, join and maintain cultural, religious and linguistic associations and other organs of civil society.

(2) The rights in subsection (1) may not be exercised in a manner inconsistent with any provision of the Bill of Rights.

32 Access to information

(1) Everyone has the right of access to —
  (*a*) any information held by the state; and
  (*b*) any information that is held by another person and that is required for the exercise or protection of any rights.

(2) National legislation must be enacted to give effect to this right, and may provide for reasonable measures to alleviate the administrative and financial burden on the state.

33 Just administrative action

(1) Everyone has the right to administrative action that is lawful, reasonable and procedurally fair.
(2) Everyone whose rights have been adversely affected by administrative action has the right to be given written reasons.
(3) National legislation must be enacted to give effect to these rights, and must —
  (*a*) provide for the review of administrative action by a court or, where appropriate, an independent and impartial tribunal;
  (*b*) impose a duty on the state to give effect to the rights in subsections (1) and (2); and
  (*c*) promote an efficient administration.

34 Access to courts

Everyone has the right to have any dispute that can be resolved by the application of law decided in a fair public hearing before a court or, where appropriate, another independent and impartial tribunal or forum.

35 Arrested, detained and accused persons

(1) Everyone who is arrested for allegedly committing an offence has the right —
  (*a*) to remain silent;
  (*b*) to be informed promptly —
    (i) of the right to remain silent; and
    (ii) of the consequences of not remaining silent;
  (*c*) not to be compelled to make any confession or admission that could be used in evidence against that person;
  (*d*) to be brought before a court as soon as reasonably possible, but not later than —
    (i) 48 hours after the arrest; or
    (ii) the end of the first court day after the expiry of the 48 hours, if the 48 hours expire outside ordinary court hours or on a day which is not an ordinary court day;
  (*e*) at the first court appearance after being arrested, to be charged or to be informed of the reason for the detention to continue, or to be released; and
  (*f*) to be released from detention if the interests of justice permit, subject to reasonable conditions.
(2) Everyone who is detained, including every sentenced prisoner, has the right —
  (*a*) to be informed promptly of the reason for being detained;
  (*b*) to choose, and to consult with, a legal practitioner, and to be informed of this right promptly;

(*c*) to have a legal practitioner assigned to the detained person by the state and at state expense, if substantial injustice would otherwise result, and to be informed of this right promptly;
(*d*) to challenge the lawfulness of the detention in person before a court and, if the detention is unlawful, to be released;
(*e*) to conditions of detention that are consistent with human dignity, including at least exercise and the provision, at state expense, of adequate accommodation, nutrition, reading material and medical treatment; and
(*f*) to communicate with, and be visited by, that person's —
(i) spouse or partner;
(ii) next of kin;
(iii) chosen religious counsellor; and
(iv) chosen medical practitioner.

(3) Every accused person has a right to a fair trial, which includes the right —
(*a*) to be informed of the charge with sufficient detail to answer it;
(*b*) to have adequate time and facilities to prepare a defence;
(*c*) to a public trial before an ordinary court;
(*d*) to have their trial begin and conclude without unreasonable delay;
(*e*) to be present when being tried;
(*f*) to choose, and be represented by, a legal practitioner, and to be informed of this right promptly;
(*g*) to have a legal practitioner assigned to the accused person by the state and at state expense, if substantial injustice would otherwise result, and to be informed of this right promptly;
(*h*) to be presumed innocent, to remain silent, and not to testify during the proceedings;
(*i*) to adduce and challenge evidence;
(*j*) not to be compelled to give self-incriminating evidence;
(*k*) to be tried in a language that the accused person understands or, if that is not practicable, to have the proceedings interpreted in that language;
(*l*) not to be convicted for an act or omission that was not an offence under either national or international law at the time it was committed or omitted;
(*m*) not to be tried for an offence in respect of an act or omission for which that person has previously been either acquitted or convicted;
(*n*) to the benefit of the least severe of the prescribed punishments if the prescribed punishment for the offence has been changed between the time that the offence was committed and the time of sentencing; and
(*o*) of appeal to, or review by, a higher court.

(4) Whenever this section requires information to be given to a person, that information must be given in a language that the person understands.

(5) Evidence obtained in a manner that violates any right in the Bill of Rights must be excluded if the admission of that evidence would render the trial unfair or otherwise be detrimental to the administration of justice.

36 Limitation of rights

(1) The rights in the Bill of Rights may be limited only in terms of law of general application to the extent that the limitation is reasonable and justifiable in an open and democratic society based on human dignity, equality and freedom, taking into account all relevant factors, including —
  (*a*) the nature of the right;
  (*b*) the importance of the purpose of the limitation;
  (*c*) the nature and extent of the limitation;
  (*d*) the relation between the limitation and its purpose; and
  (*e*) less restrictive means to achieve the purpose.

(2) Except as provided in subsection (1) or in any other provision of the Constitution, no law may limit any right entrenched in the Bill of Rights.

37 States of emergency

(1) A state of emergency may be declared only in terms of an Act of Parliament, and only when —
  (*a*) the life of the nation is threatened by war, invasion, general insurrection, disorder, natural disaster or other public emergency; and
  (*b*) the declaration is necessary to restore peace and order.

(2) A declaration of a state of emergency, and any legislation enacted or other action taken in consequence of that declaration, may be effective only —
  (*a*) prospectively; and
  (*b*) for no more than 21 days from the date of the declaration, unless the National Assembly resolves to extend the declaration. The Assembly may extend a declaration of a state of emergency for no more than three months at a time. The first extension of the state of emergency must be by a resolution adopted with a supporting vote of a majority of the members of the Assembly. Any subsequent extension must be by a resolution adopted with a supporting vote of at least 60 per cent of the members of the Assembly. A resolution in terms of this paragraph may be adopted only following a public debate in the Assembly.

(3) Any competent court may decide on the validity of —
  (*a*) a declaration of a state of emergency;
  (*b*) any extension of a declaration of a state of emergency; or
  (*c*) any legislation enacted, or other action taken, in consequence of a declaration of a state of emergency.

(4) Any legislation enacted in consequence of a declaration of a state of emergency may derogate from the Bill of Rights only to the extent that —
  (*a*) the derogation is strictly required by the emergency; and
  (*b*) the legislation —
    (i) is consistent with the Republic's obligations under international law applicable to states of emergency;
    (ii) conforms to subsection (5); and

(iii) is published in the national {Government Gazette} as soon as reasonably possible after being enacted.

(5) No Act of Parliament that authorises a declaration of a state of emergency, and no legislation enacted or other action taken in consequence of a declaration, may permit or authorise —

(*a*) indemnifying the state, or any person, in respect of any unlawful act;

(*b*) any derogation from this section; or

(*c*) any derogation from a section mentioned in column 1 of the Table of Non-Derogable Rights, to the extent indicated opposite that section in column 3 of the Table.

Table of Non-Derogable Rights

1 *Section number*	2 *Section title*	3 *Extent to which the right is non-derogable*
9	Equality	With respect to unfair discrimination solely on the grounds of race, colour, ethnic or social origin, sex, religion or language
10	Human dignity	Entirely
11	Life	Entirely
12	Freedom and security of the person	With respect to subsections (1)(*d*) and (*e*) and (2)(*c*)
13	Slavery, servitude and forced labour	With respect to slavery and servitude
28	Children	With respect to: – subsection (1) (d) and (e); – the rights in subparagraphs (i) and (ii) of subsection (1) (g); and – subsection (1) (i) in respect of children of 15 years and younger.
35	Arrested, detained and accused persons	With respect to: – subsections (1) (a), (b) and (c) and (2) (d); – the rights in paragraphs (a) to (o) of subsection (3), excluding paragraph (d); – subsection (4); and – subsection (5) with respect to the exclusion of evidence if the admission of that evidence would render the trial unfair.

(6) Whenever anyone is detained without trial in consequence of a derogation of rights resulting from a declaration of a state of emergency, the following conditions must be observed:

(*a*) An adult family member or friend of the detainee must be contacted as soon as reasonably possible, and informed that the person has been detained.

(*b*) A notice must be published in the national *Government Gazette* within five days of the person being detained, stating the detainee's name and place of detention and referring to the emergency measure in terms of which that person has been detained.

(*c*) The detainee must be allowed to choose, and be visited at any reasonable time by, a medical practitioner.

(*d*) The detainee must be allowed to choose, and be visited at any reasonable time by, a legal representative.

(*e*) A court must review the detention as soon as reasonably possible, but no later than 10 days after the date the person was detained, and the court must release the detainee unless it is necessary to continue the detention to restore peace and order.

(*f*) A detainee who is not released in terms of a review under paragraph (*e*), or who is not released in terms of a review under this paragraph, may apply to a court for a further review of the detention at any time after 10 days have passed since the previous review, and the court must release the detainee unless it is still necessary to continue the detention to restore peace and order.

(*g*) The detainee must be allowed to appear in person before any court considering the detention, to be represented by a legal practitioner at those hearings, and to make representations against continued detention.

(*h*) The state must present written reasons to the court to justify the continued detention of the detainee, and must give a copy of those reasons to the detainee at least two days before the court reviews the detention.

(7) If a court releases a detainee, that person may not be detained again on the same grounds unless the state first shows a court good cause for re-detaining that person.

(8) Subsections (6) and (7) do not apply to persons who are not South African citizens and who are detained in consequence of an international armed conflict. Instead, the state must comply with the standards binding on the Republic under international humanitarian law in respect of the detention of such persons.

38 Enforcement of rights

Anyone listed in this section has the right to approach a competent court, alleging that a right in the Bill of Rights has been infringed or threatened, and the court may grant appropriate relief, including a declaration of rights. The persons who may approach a court are —

(*a*) anyone acting in their own interest;

(*b*) anyone acting on behalf of another person who cannot act in their own name;
(*c*) anyone acting as a member of, or in the interest of, a group or class of persons;
(*d*) anyone acting in the public interest; and
(*e*) an association acting in the interest of its members.

39 Interpretation of Bill of Rights

(1) When interpreting the Bill of Rights, a court, tribunal or forum —
  (*a*) must promote the values that underlie an open and democratic society based on human dignity, equality and freedom;
  (*b*) must consider international law; and
  (*c*) may consider foreign law.

(2) When interpreting any legislation, and when developing the common law or customary law, every court, tribunal or forum must promote the spirit, purport and objects of the Bill of Rights.

(3) The Bill of Rights does not deny the existence of any other rights or freedoms that are recognised or conferred by common law, customary law or legislation, to the extent that they are consistent with the Bill.

Abbreviations

AC	Acta Criminologica
AJ	Acta Juridica
AHRLJ	African Human Rights Law Journal
AHRLR	African Human Rights Law Reports
AJIL	American Journal of International Law
Am Univ Int Law Rev	American University International Law Review
Brook L Rev	Brooklyn Law Review
CLR	California Law Review
Cal W Int'l L J	California Western International Law Journal
CJWL	Canadian Journal of Women and the Law
Con J Int'l L	Connecticut Journal of International Law
CCR	Constitutional Court Review
Chap L Rev	Chapman Law Review
CLR	California Law Review
Colum Hum Rts L Rev	Columbia Human Rights Law Review
Conn J Int'l Law	Connecticut Journal of International Law
Const Forum	Constitutional Forum
Cornell L Rev	Cornell Law Review
DJ	De Jure
EECR	East European Constitutional Review
EHRR	European Human Rights Reports
EHRLR	European Human Rights Law Review
ESR Review	Economic and Social Rights in South Africa
Florida J of Int Law	Florida Journal of International Law
Fordham LR	Fordham Law Review
Forum Devel Stud	Forum for Developmental Studies
Geo LJ	The Georgetown Law Journal
Harvard LR	Harvard Law Review
HRLR	Human Rights Law Review
HRQ	Human Rights Quarterly
Ind LJ	Indiana Law Journal
Int J Child Rights	International Journal of Children's Rights
I Con	International Journal of Constitutional Law
Int J of Law, Policy and the Family	International Journal of Law, Policy and the Family
JoE	Journal of Education
J of Law & Soc	Journal of Law and Society

J Ment Health Policy Econ	Journal of Mental Health Policy and Economics
LDD	Law, Democracy and Development
McGill L J	McGill Law Journal
Michigan LR	Michigan LR
Michigan J of Race and Law	Michigan Journal of Race and Law
NYIL	Netherlands Yearbook of International Law
NYULR	New York University Law Review
NJHR	Nordic Journal of Human Rights
OHLJ	Osgoode Hall Law Journal
Politikon	Politikon (South African Journal of Political Studies)
PULP	Pretoria University Law Press
RCS	Review of Constitutional Studies
SA J Philos	SA Journal of Philosophy
SAJHR	South African Journal on Human Rights
SALJ	South African Law Journal
SAMJ	South African Medical Journal
SAPR/SAPL	Publiekreg/SA Public Law
SAYIL	South African Yearbook of International Law
Soc Philos Policy	Social Philosophy and Policy
Stell LR	Stellenbosch Law Review/Regstydskrif
St Louis LJ	Saint Louis University Law Journal
SUN Press	Stellenbosch University Press
Tex Int L J	Texas International Law Journal
Texas L Rev	Texas Law Review
THRHR	Tydskrif vir die Hedendaagse Romeins-Hollandse Reg/Journal of Contemporary Roman-Dutch Law
TSAR	Tydskrif vir die Suid-Afrikaanse Reg/ Journal of South African Law
UBC LR	University of British Columbia Law Review
U Pa L Rev	University of Pennsylvania Law Review
USF L Rev	University of San Francisco Law Review
Wake Forest L Rev	Wake Forest Law Review
Yale J of Law and Feminism	Yale Journal of Law and Feminism
Yale LJ	Yale Law Journal

Table of Cases

South Africa[1]

[1] References to unreported cases or cases which were not reported at the time of this manuscript being finalised are according to their neutral citation.

Canada

Germany

India

United Kingdom

United States of America

UN Human Rights Committee

African Commission on Human and Peoples' Rights

European Committee of Social Rights

European Court of Human Rights

Inter-American Court of Human Rights

Table of Constitutions and Legislation

Constitutions

Canada

Germany

India

South Africa

South African legislation

Bibliography

ABEL R L *Politics by other Means: Law in the Struggle against Apartheid, 1980–1994* (Routledge, 1995).

ADELZADEH A *South Africa Human Development Report 2003 – The Challenge of Sustainable Development in South Africa: Unlocking People's Creativity* (Oxford University Press, 2003).

AFRICAN NATIONAL CONGRESS 'Working draft of *A Bill of Rights for a Democratic South Africa*' (1991) 7 *SAJHR* 110.

ALBERTYN C 'Equality' in Cheadle H, Davis D and Haysom N (eds) *South African Constitutional Law: The Bill of Rights* (Butterworths, 2006) chapter 4.

ALBERTYN C 'Substantive equality and transformation in South Africa' (2007) 23 *SAJHR* 253.

ALBERTYN C AND GOLDBLATT B 'Facing the challenge of transformation: Difficulties in the development of an indigenous jurisprudence of equality' (1998) 14 *SAJHR* 248.

ALBERTYN C AND GOLDBLATT B 'Equality' in Woolman S, Roux T, Bishop M, Klaaren J and Stein A *Constitutional Law of South Africa* 2 ed OS (Juta & Co, 2007) chapter 35.

ALBISA C AND SCHULTZ J 'The United States: A ragged patchwork' in Langford M (ed) *Social Rights Jurisprudence: Emerging Trends in International and Comparative Law* (Cambridge University Press, 2008) chapter 12.

ALSTON P 'Out of the abyss: The challenges confronting the new UN Committee on Economic, Social and Cultural Rights' (1987) 9 *HRQ* 332.

ALSTON P AND QUINN G 'The nature and scope of states parties' obligations under the International Covenant on Economic, Social and Cultural Rights' (1987) 9 *HRQ* 156.

ANDREWS P AND ELLMAN S *The Post-Apartheid Constitution: Perspective on South Africa's Basic Law* (Ohio University Press – Witwatersrand University Press, 2001).

ARAMBULO K *Strengthening the Supervision of the International Covenant on Economic, Social and Cultural Rights: Theoretical and Procedural Aspects* (Intersentia – Hart, 1999).

ATIYAH P S AND SUMMERS R S *Form and Substance in Anglo-American Law: A Comparative Study of Legal Reasoning, Legal Theory and Legal Institutions* (Oxford University Press, 1987).

BADENHORST P J, PIENAAR J M AND MOSTERT H *Silberberg and Schoeman's The Law of Property* 5 ed (Butterworths, 2006).

BARBER A 'Fallacies of negative constitutionalism' (2007) 75 *Fordham LR* 651.

BARNARD A J 'To wonderland through the looking-glass: Conceiving a critical legal argument for contractual justice in the South African law of contract' (2006) 17 *Law and Critique* 153.

BARNARD-NAUDÉ A J 'The decision in *Hartley v Pyramid Freight (Pty) Ltd*: Justice miscarried?' (2007) 18 *Stell LR* 497.

BARNETT R E *Restoring the Lost Constitution: The Presumption of Liberty* (Princeton University Press, 2004).

BASKIN J *Striking Back: A History of COSATU* (Verso, 1991).

BATEUP C A 'The dialogic promise: Assessing the normative potential of theories of constitutional dialogue' (2005–2006) 71 *Brook L Rev* 1109.

BENHABIB S 'Toward a deliberative model of democratic legitimacy' in Benhabib S *Democracy and Difference: Contesting the Boundaries of the Political* (Princeton University Press, 1996) chapter 4.

BERGER J 'Litigating for social justice in post-apartheid South Africa: A focus on health and education' in Gauri V and Brinks D M (eds) *Courting Social Justice: Judicial Enforcement of Social and Economic Rights in the Developing World* (Cambridge University Press, 2008) chapter 2.

BERLIN I *Four Essays on Liberty* (Oxford University Press, 1969) chapter 3.

Bhana D 'The role of judicial method in the relinquishing of constitutional rights through contract' (2008) 24 *SAJHR* 300.

Bhana D and Pieterse M 'Towards a reconciliation of contract law and constitutional values: *Brisley* and *Afrox* revisited' (2005) 122 *SALJ* 865.

Bhorat H 'The South African social safety net: Past, present and future' (1995) 12 *Development Southern Africa* 595.

Bhorat H and Kanbur R 'Introduction: Poverty and well-being in post apartheid South Africa' in Bhorat H and Kanbur R (eds) *Poverty and Policy in Post-apartheid South Africa* (HSRC Press, 2006) chapter 1.

Bhorat H and Van der Westhuizen C *Economic Growth, Poverty and Inequality in South Africa: The First Decade of Democracy* (2008) 4. Available at http://www.thepresidency.gov.za/docs/reports/15year_review/social/economic_growth.pdf (accessed on 7 March 2009).

Bilchitz D 'Giving socio-economic rights teeth: The minimum core and its importance' (2002) 119 *SALJ* 484.

Bilchitz D 'Towards a reasonable approach to the minimum core: Laying the foundations for future socio-economic rights jurisprudence' (2003) 19 *SAJHR* 1.

Bilchitz D *Poverty and Fundamental Rights: The Justification and Enforcement of Socio-Economic Rights* (Oxford University Press, 2007).

Blecher M D 'Spoliation and the demolition of legal rights' (1978) 97 *SALJ* 8.

Blumberg M '*Mandament van spolie* – restoration of the *status quo ante* revisited' (1997) 60 *THRHR* 529.

Bond P and Dugard J 'The case of Johannesburg water: What really happened at the pre-paid "Parish pump"?' (2008) 12 *LDD* 1.

Bonthuys E 'Realising South African children's basic socio-economic claims against parents and the state: What courts can achieve' (2008) 22 *Int J of Law, Policy and the Family* 333.

Boshoff A 'Law as dialogic politics' in Botha H, Van der Walt A J and Van der Walt J (eds) *Rights and Democracy in a Transformative Constitution* (SUN Press, 2003) chapter 1.

Botha H 'Democracy and rights: Constitutional interpretation in a postrealist world' (2000) 63 *THRHR* 561.

Botha H 'Metaphoric reasoning and transformative constitutionalism (Part 1)' (2002) 4 TSAR 612.

Botha H 'Metaphoric reasoning and transformative constitutionalism (Part 2)' (2003) 1 *TSAR* 20.

Botha H 'Freedom and constraint in constitutional adjudication' (2004) 20 *SAJHR* 249.

Botha H, Van der Walt A J and Van der Walt J (eds) *Rights and Democracy in a Transformative Constitution* (SUN Press, 2003).

Brand D 'Disclaimers in hospital admission contracts and constitutional health rights' (2002) 3 *ESR Review* 17.

Brand D 'The minimum content of the right to food in context: A response to Rolf Künnemann' in Brand D and Russell S (eds) *Exploring the Core Content of Socio-Economic Rights: South African and International Perspectives* (Protea Book House, 2002) 99.

Brand D 'The proceduralisation of South African socio-economic rights jurisprudence or "What are socio-economic rights for?"' in Botha H, Van Der Walt A J and Van Der Walt J (eds) *Rights and Democracy in a Transformative Constitution* (SUN Press, 2003) 33–56.

Brand D 'Introduction to socio-economic rights in the South African Constitution' in Brand D and Heyns C (eds) *Socio-Economic Rights in South Africa* (PULP, 2005) chapter 1.

Brand D 'The "politics of need interpretation" and the adjudication of socio-economic rights claims in South Africa' in Van Der Walt A J *Theories of Social and Economic Justice* (SUN Press, 2005) chapter 2.

Brems E 'Indirect protection of social rights by the European Court of Human Rights' in D Barak-Erez and A M Gross (eds) *Exploring Social Rights: Between Theory and Practice* (Hart Publishing, 2007) chapter 7.

Brickhill J 'The right to a fair civil trial: The duties of lawyers and law students to act pro bono' (2005) 21 *SAJHR* 293.

Brodsky G '*Gosselin v Québec (Attorney-General)*: Autonomy with a vengeance' (2003) 15 *CJWL* 194.

BRODSKY G AND DAY S 'Beyond the social and economic rights debate: Substantive equality speaks to poverty' (2002) 14 *CJWL* 184.
BRODSKY G AND DAY S 'Denial of the means of subsistence as an equality violation' (2005) *AJ* 149.
BROWN L (ed) *The New Shorter Oxford English Dictionary* (Oxford University Press, 1993).
BROWNLIE I AND GOODWIN-GILL G S (eds) *Basic Documents on Human Rights* 4 ed (Oxford University Press, 2002).
BUDLENDER D *Women and Men in South Africa: Five Years On* (Statistics South Africa, 2002).
BUDLENDER D 'Women and poverty' (2005) 64 *Agenda* 30.
BUDLENDER D AND WOOLARD I *The Impact of the South African Child Support and Old Age Grants on Children's Schooling and Work* (International Labour Organisation, 2006).
BUDLENDER G 'Access to courts' (2004) 121 *SALJ* 339.
BUDLENDER G 'The right to alternative accommodation in forced evictions' in Squires J, Langford M and Thiele B (eds) *The Road to a Remedy: Current Issues in the Litigation of Economic, Social and Cultural Rights* (University of New South Wales Press, 2005).
BUNDY C 'Land, law and power: forced removals in historical context' in Murray C and O'Regan C (eds) *No Place to Rest: Forced Removals and the Law in South Africa* (Oxford University Press, 1990).
BURCHILL R, HARRIS D J AND OWERS A (eds) *Economic, Social and Cultural Rights: Their Implementation in United Kingdom Law* (Human Rights Law Centre University of Nottingham, 1999).
CALLAND R AND TAYLOR M 'Parliament and the socio-economic imperative – what is the role of the national legislature?' (1997) 1 *LDD* 193.
CHANOCK M *The Making of South African Legal Culture 1902–1936: Fear, Favour and Prejudice* (Cambridge University Press, 2001).
CHASKALSON M 'Stumbling towards section 28: Negotiations over the protection of property rights in the interim Constitution' (1995) 11 *SAJHR* 222.
CHEADLE H AND DAVIS D 'The application of the 1996 Constitution in the private sphere' (1997) 13 *SAJHR* 44.
CHENWI L 'Litigating socio-economic rights through *amicus briefs*: Challenges and strategies' (2009) 10 *ESR Review* 7.
CHENWI L AND LIEBENBERG S 'The constitutional protection of those facing eviction from "bad buildings"' (2008) 9 *ESR Review* 12.
CHIRWA D M 'The merits and demerits of the African Charter on the Rights and Welfare of the Child' (2002) 10 *Int J Children's Rights* 157.
CHIRWA D M 'The right to health in international law: Its implications for the obligations of state and non-state actors in ensuring access to essential medicine' (2003) 19 *SAJHR* 541.
CHIRWA D M 'Obligations of non-state actors in relation to economic, social and cultural rights under the South African constitution' (2003) 7 *Mediterranean Journal of Human Rights* 29.
CHIRWA D M 'Towards binding economic, social and cultural rights obligations of non-state actors in international and domestic law: A critical survey of emerging norms' (unpublished LLD dissertation University of Western Cape, 2005).
CHIRWA D M 'African regional human rights system: The promise of recent jurisprudence on social rights' in Langford M (ed) *Social Rights Jurisprudence: Emerging Trends in International and Comparative Law* (Cambridge University Press, 2008) chapter 17.
CHIRWA D M AND KHOZA S 'Towards enhanced citizenship and poverty eradication: A critique of *Grootboom* from a gender perspective' in Gouws A (ed) *(Un)thinking Citizenship: Feminist Debates in Contemporary South Africa* (Juta & Co, 2005) chapter 6.
CHOUDHRY S 'Globalization in search of justification: Towards a theory of comparative constitutional interpretation' (1999) 74 *Indiana LJ* 819.
CILLIERS A C, LOOTS C AND NEL H C *Herbstein and Van Winsen The Civil Practice of the High Courts and the Supreme Court of Appeal of South Africa* 5 ed (Juta & Co, 2009).
CLEMENTS L AND SIMMONS A 'European Court of Human Rights: Sympathetic unease' in Langford M (ed) *Social Rights Jurisprudence: Emerging Trends in International and Comparative*

Law (Cambridge University Press, 2008) chapter 20.
COCKRELL A 'Adjudication styles in South African private law' (1993) 56 *THRHR* 590.
COCKRELL A '"Can you paradigm?" – Another perspective on the public law/private law divide' (1993) *AJ* 227.
COCKRELL A 'Rainbow jurisprudence' (1996) 12 *SAJHR* 1.
COCKRELL A 'Private law and the bill of rights: A threshold issue of "horizontality"' in *Butterworths Bill of Rights Compendium* (Butterworths, Issue 14, May 2004) chapter 3A.
COHEN J 'The economic basis of deliberative democracy' (1989) 6 *Soc Philos Policy* 25.
COHEN J 'Procedure and substance in deliberative democracy' in Benhabib S (ed) *Democracy and Difference: Contesting the Boundaries of the Political* (Princeton University Press, 1996) chapter 5.
COLLINS P H *Black Feminist Thought: Knowledge, Consciousness and the Politics of Empowerment* (Routledge, 1990).
COMBRINCK H 'Positive state duties to protect women from violence: Recent South African developments' (1998) 20 *HRQ* 666.
CONAGHAN J 'Intersectionality and UK equality initiatives' (2007) 23 *SAJHR* 317.
COOK S AND QUIXLEY G 'Parate executie clauses: Is the debate dead?' (2004) 121 *SALJ* 719.
COOMBE R J '"Same as it ever was": Rethinking the politics of legal interpretation' (1989) 34 *McGill LJ* 603.
CORDER H AND DU PLESSIS L M *Understanding South Africa's Transitional Bill of Rights* (Juta & Co, 1994).
CORDER H, KAHANOVITZ S, MURPHY J, MURRAY C, O'REGAN C, SARKIN J, SMITH H AND STEYTLER N *A Charter for Social Justice: A Contribution to the South African Bill of Rights Debate* (Cape Town University Press, 1992).
CORNELL D 'Institutionalization of meaning, recollective imagination and the potential for transformative legal interpretation' (1988) 136 *U Pa L R* 1135.
COURTIS C 'Judicial enforcement of social rights: Perspectives from Latin America' in Gargarella R, Domingo P and Roux T (eds) *Courts and Social Transformation in New Democracies: An Institutional Voice for the Poor?* (Ashgate Press, 2006) chapter 8.
COURTIS C 'Argentina: Some promising signs' in Langford M (ed) *Social Rights Jurisprudence: Emerging Trends in International and Comparative Law* (Cambridge University Press, 2008) chapter 8.
COWEN S 'Can dignity guide South Africa's equality jurisprudence?' (2001) 17 *SAJHR* 34.
CRAVEN M 'Towards an unofficial petition procedure: A review on the role of the UN Committee on Economic, Social and Cultural Rights' in Drzewicki K, Krause C and Rosas A (eds) *Social Rights as Human Rights: A European Challenge* (Institute for Human Rights, Åbo Akademi University, 1994) chapter 6.
CRAVEN M *The International Covenant on Economic, Social and Cultural Rights* (Oxford University Press, 1995).
CRAVEN M 'Assessment of the progress on adjudication of economic, social and cultural rights' in Squires J, Langford M and Thiele B (eds) *The Road to a Remedy: Current Issues in the Litigation of Economic, Social and Cultural Rights* (University of New South Wales Press, 2005) chapter 2.
CREAMER K 'The impact of South Africa's evolving jurisprudence on children's socio-economic rights in budget analysis' (2002) Institute for Democracy in South Africa Occasional Papers. Available at http://www.idasa.org.za/gbOutputFiles.asp?WriteContent=Y&RID=721 (accessed on 22 September 2009).
CREAMER K 'The implication of socio-economic rights jurisprudence for government planning and budgeting: The case of children's socio-economic rights' (2004) 8 *LDD* 221.
CRENSHAW K 'Demarginalizing the intersection between race and sex: A black feminist critique of anti-discrimination doctrine, feminist theory, and antiracist politics' (1989) *University of Chicago Legal Forum* 139.
CURRIE I 'Judicious avoidance' (1999) 15 *SAJHR* 138.
CURRIE I *The Promotion of Administrative Justice Act: A Commentary* 2 ed (Siber Ink, 2007).
CURRIE I AND DE WAAL J *The Bill of Rights Handbook* 5 ed (Juta & Co, 2005).

DAVIES R, O'MEARA D AND DLAMINI S *The Struggle for South Africa: A Reference Guide Vol 1* (Zed Books Ltd, 1985).

DAVIS D M 'The case against the inclusion of socio-economic demands in a Bill of Rights except at directive principles' (1992) 8 *SAJHR* 475.

DAVIS D M *Democracy and Deliberation* (Juta & Co, 1999).

DAVIS D M 'Equality: The majesty of legoland jurisprudence' (1999) 116 *SALJ* 398.

DAVIS D M 'Socio-economic rights in South Africa: The record of the Constitutional Court after ten years' (2004) 5 *ESR Review* 3.

DAVIS D M 'Adjudicating the socio-economic rights in the South African Constitution: Towards "deference lite"?' (2006) 22 *SAJHR* 301.

DE FEYTER K AND GÓMEZ ISA F (eds) *Privatisation and Human Rights in the Age of Globalisation* (Intersentia, 2005).

DE LIMA LOPES J R 'Brazilian courts and social rights: A case study revisited' in Gargarella R, Domingo P Roux T (eds) *Courts and Social Transformation in New Democracies: An Institutional Voice for the Poor?* (Ashgate Press, 2006) chapter 9.

DE VILLIERS B 'The socio-economic consequences of directive principles of state policy: Limitations on fundamental rights' (1992) 8 *SAJHR* 188.

DE VILLIERS B 'Social and economic rights' in Van Wyk D, Dugard J, De Villiers B and Davis D M (eds) *Rights and Constitutionalism in the New South African Legal Order* (Juta & Co, 1994) 599.

DE VILLIERS C '*Daniels v Campbell NO* and others: The long battle of a woman married according to Muslim personal rites to acquire ownership of her home' (2003) 4 *ESR Review* 8.

DE VILLIERS N 'Social grants and the Promotion of Administrative Justice Act' (2002) 18 *SAJHR* 320.

DE VOS P 'The economic and social rights of children and South Africa's transitional Constitution' (1995) 10 *SAPL/R* 233.

DE VOS P 'Pious wishes or directly enforceable human rights: Social and economic rights in South Africa's 1996 Constitution' (1997) 13 *SAJHR* 67.

DE VOS P 'A bridge too far? History as context in the interpretation of the South African Constitution' (2001) 17 *SAJHR* 1.

DE VOS P '*Grootboom*, the right of access to housing and substantive equality as contextual fairness' (2001) 17 *SAJHR* 258.

DE WET E 'Can the social state principle in Germany guide state action in South Africa in the field of social and economic rights?' (1995) 11 *SAJHR* 30.

DE WET E 'The enforceability of socio-economic directive principles/legislative commands with special reference to Constitutional Principle XI of the South African Transitional Constitution' (1995) 112 *SALJ* 462.

DENNIS M J AND STEWART D P 'Justiciability of economic, social and cultural rights: Should there be an international complaints mechanism to adjudicate the rights to food, water, housing, and health?' (2004) 98 *AJIL* 462.

DIXON R 'Creating dialogue about socio-economic rights: Strong-form versus weak-form judicial review revisited' (2007) 5 *I Con* 391.

DU PLESSIS L M 'Legal academics and the open community of constitutional interpreters' (1996) 12 *SAJHR* 214.

DU PLESSIS L M *Re-Interpretation of Statutes* (Butterworths, 2002).

DU PLESSIS L M 'Interpretation' in Woolman S, Roux T, Bishop, M, Klaaren J and Stein A Woolman S (eds) *Constitutional Law of South Africa* 2 ed Original Service (OS) (Juta & Co, 2008) chapter 32.

DU PLESSIS L M AND CORDER H *Understanding South Africa's Transitional Bill of Rights* (Juta & Co, 1994).

DUGARD JOHN 'The judicial process, positivism and civil liberty (1971) 88 *SAJHR* 181.

DUGARD JOHN *Human Rights and the South African Legal Order* (Princeton University Press, 1978).

DUGARD JOHN *International Law: A South African Perspective* 3 ed (Juta & Co, 2005).

DUGARD JACKIE AND ROUX T 'The record of the South African Constitutional Court in providing an institutional voice for the poor: 1995–2004' in Gargarella R, Domingo P and Roux T (eds) *Courts and Social Transformation in New Democracies: An Institutional Voice for the Poor?* (Ashgate Publishing, 2006) chapter 5.

DUGARD JACKIE 'Courts and the poor in South Africa: A critique of systemic judicial failures to advance transformative justice' (2008) 24 *SAJHR* 214.

DUGARD JACKIE AND LIEBENBERG S 'Muddying the waters: The Supreme Court of Appeal's judgment in the *Mazibuko* case' (2009) 10 *ESR Review* 11.

DWORKIN R *Taking Rights Seriously* (Duckworth, 1977).

DWORKIN R 'What is Equality? Part 4: Political Equality' (1987) 22 *USF L Rev* 1.

EBADOLAHI M 'Using structural interdicts and the South African Human Rights Commission to achieve judicial enforcement of economic and social rights in South Africa' (2008) 83 *NYULR* 1565.

EBRAHIM H *The Soul of a Nation: Constitution-Making in South Africa* (Oxford University Press, 1998).

EIDE A 'Economic, social and cultural rights as human rights' in Eide A, Krause C and Rosas A (eds) *Economic, Social and Cultural Rights: A Textbook* 2 ed (Kluwer Law, 2001) chapter 1.

EIDE A, KRAUSE C AND ROSAS A (eds) *Economic, Social and Cultural Rights: A Textbook* 2 ed (Kluwer Law, 2001).

ELLMANN S 'A constitutional confluence: American "State action" law and the application of South Africa's socio-economic rights guarantees to private actors' in Andrews P and Ellman S (eds) *The Post-Apartheid Constitutions: Perspectives on South Africa's Basic Law* (Witwatersrand University Press and Ohio University Press, 2001) 444.

EMMETT T 'Disability, poverty, gender and race' in Watermeyer B, Swartz L, Lorenzo T, Schneider M and Priestley M (eds) *Disability and Social Change – A South African Agenda* (HSRC Press, 2006) 207.

EWING K D 'Social rights and constitutional law' (1999) 14 *SAPL/R* 104.

FABRE C 'Constitutionalising social rights' (1998) 6 *The Journal of Political Philosophy* 263.

FARHA L 'Committee on the Elimination of Discrimination Against Women: Women claiming economic, social and cultural rights – The CEDAW potential' in Langford M (ed) *Social Rights Jurisprudence: Emerging Trends in International and Comparative Law* (Cambridge University Press, 2008) chapter 26.

FITZPATRICK J AND SLYE R C 'Economic and social rights – South Africa – Role of international standards in interpreting and implementing constitutionally guaranteed rights' (2003) 97 *AJIL* 669.

FLEISCH B AND WOOLMAN S 'On the constitutionality of school fees: A qualified defence' (2004) 22 *Perspectives in Education* 111.

FLEISCH B AND WOOLMAN S 'On the constitutionality of single-medium public schools' (2007) 23 *SAJHR* 34.

FOSTER M *International Refugee Law and Socio-economic Rights: Refuge from Deprivation* (Cambridge University Press, 2007).

FOX L 'The meaning of home: A chimerical concept or a legal challenge?' (2002) 29 *J of Law & Soc* 580.

FOX L *Conceptualising Home – Theories, Laws and Policies* (Hart Publishing, 2007).

FRASER N 'Talking about needs: Interpretive contests as political conflicts in welfare-state societies' (1989) 99 *Ethics* 291.

FRASER N *Unruly Practices: Power, Discourse and Gender in Contemporary Social Theory* (University of Minnesota Press and Polity Press, 1989).

FRASER N 'Rethinking the public sphere: A contribution to the critique of actually existing democracy' in Calhoun C (ed) *Habermas and the Public Sphere* (The MIT Press, 1991) chapter 5.

FRASER N 'Social justice in the age of identity politics: Redistribution, recognition, and participation' in Fraser N and Honneth A *Redistribution or Recognition? A Political-Philosophical Exchange* (Verso, 2003).

FRASER N 'Reframing justice in a globalizing world' (2005) 36 *New Left Review* 1.

FRASER N 'From redistribution to recognition? Dilemmas of justice in a "postsocialist" age' in Olson K (ed) *Adding Insult to Injury: Nancy Fraser Debates her Critics* (Verso, 2008) 9.

FREDMAN S 'Providing equality: Substantive equality and the positive duty to provide' (2005) 21 *SAJHR* 163.

FREDMAN S 'Human rights transformed: Positive duties and positive rights' (2006) 3 *Public Law* 498.

FREDMAN S 'Redistribution and recognition: Reconciling inequalities' (2007) 23 *SAJHR* 214.

FREDMAN S *Human Rights Transformed: Positive Rights and Positive Duties* (Oxford University Press, 2008).

FRIEDMAN S *Building Tomorrow Today: African Workers in Trade Unions 1970–1984* (Raven Press, 1987).

FRONEMAN J C 'Legal reasoning and legal culture: Our "vision" of law' (2005) 16 *Stell LR* 3.

FRONEMAN J C 'Enforcing socio-economic rights under a transformative Constitution: The role of the courts' (2007) 8 *ESR Review* 20.

FRONEMAN J C 'The horizontal application of human rights norms' (2007) 21 *Speculum Juris* 13.

FULLER L L 'The forms and limits of adjudication' (1978) 92 *Harvard LR* 353.

GABEL P 'Symposium: A critique of rights: The phenomenology of rights-consciousness and the pact of the withdrawn selves' (1984) 62 *Texas L Rev* 1563.

GERNTHOLTZ L 'HIV testing and treatment, informed consent and AIDS orphans' (2003) 4 *ESR Review* 11.

GIESE S, MEINTJIES H, CROKE R AND CHAMBERLAIN R 'Health and social services to address the needs of orphans and other vulnerable children in the context of HIV/AIDS in South Africa: Research report and recommendations' 2003. Children's Institute and Department of Health Pretoria. Available at http://www.ci.org.za/site/frames.asp?section=publications (accessed on 27 April 2009).

GLOPPEN S 'Courts and social transformation: An analytical framework' in Gargarella R, Domingo P and Roux T (eds) *Courts and Social Transformation in New Democracies* (Ashgate Publishing Ltd, 2006) chapter 2.

GOBETTI D 'Humankind as a system: Private and public agency at the origins of modern liberalism' in Weintraub J and Kumar K (eds) *Public and Private in Thought and Practice: Perspectives on a Grand Dichotomy* (The University of Chicago Press, 1997) chapter 4.

GOLDBLATT B 'Citizenship and the right to child care' in Gouws A (ed) *(Un)thinking Citizenship: Feminist Debates in Contemporary South Africa* (Juta & Co, 2005) chapter 5.

GOLDBLATT B 'Gender and social assistance in the first decade of democracy: A case study of South Africa's child support grant' (2005) *Politikon* 239.

GOLDBLATT B AND LIEBENBERG S 'Giving money to children: The State's constitutional obligations to provide child support grants to child headed households' (2004) 20 *SAJHR* 151.

GOLDIE C 'Living in Public Space: A Human Rights Wasteland?' (unpublished PhD dissertation, University of New South Wales, Australia, 2008).

GONSALVES C, KUMAR P R AND SRIVASTAVA A K (eds) *Right to Food* 2 ed (Human Rights Law Network, 2005).

GONZALEZ E 'Venezuela: A distinct path towards social justice' in Langford M (ed) *Social Rights Jurisprudence: Emerging Trends in International and Comparative Law* (Cambridge University Press, 2008) chapter 10.

GREENAWALT K R 'The enduring significance of neutral principles' (1978) 78 *Columbia Law Review* 982.

GREENSTEIN R 'Socio-economic rights, radical democracy and power: South Africa as a case study' in Gordon N (ed) *From the Margins of Globalization: Critical Perspectives on Human Rights* (Lexington Books, 2004) chapter 4.

GUTMANN A AND THOMPSON D *Democracy and Disagreement* (Belknap Press, 1996).

HABERMAS J *Between Facts and Norms: Contributions to a Discourse Theory of Law and Democracy* (The MIT Press, 1996).

HAMILTON L 'The context and argument of *The Political Philosophy of Needs*' (2006) 25 *SA J Philos* 224.

HANDLER J F 'Constructing the political spectacle: The interpretation of entitlements, legalization and obligations in social welfare history' (1990) 56 *Brook L Rev* 899.

HANSEN J K AND SANO H 'The implications and value added of a rights-based approach' in Andreassen B A and Marks S P (eds) *Development as a Human Right – Legal, Political & Economic Dimensions* (Harvard School of Public Health and François-Xavier Bagnoud Center for Health and Human Rights, 2006) chapter 3.

HART H L A *The Concept of Law* (Oxford University Press, 1961).

HAYEK F A *The Constitution of Liberty* (The University of Chicago Press, 1960).
HAYSOM N 'Democracy, constitutionalism and the ANC's Bill of Rights for a New South Africa' (1991) 7 *SAJHR* 102.
HAYSOM N 'Constitutionalism, majoritarian democracy and socio-economic rights' (1992) 8 *SAJHR* 451.
HELEBA S 'Towards equalising the age for accessing pensions' (2007) 8 *ESR Review* 14.
HEYNS C 'Taking socio-economic rights seriously: The "domestic reporting procedure" and the role of the South African Human Rights Commission in terms of the new Constitution' (1999) *De Jure* 1.
HEYWOOD M 'Debunking "Conglomo talk": A case study of the *amicus curiae* as an instrument for advocacy, investigation and mobilization' (2001) 5 *LDD* 133.
HEYWOOD M 'Contempt or compliance? The *TAC* case after the Constitutional Court judgment' (2003) 4 *ESR Review* 7.
HEYWOOD M 'Preventing mother-to-child HIV transmission in South Africa: Background, strategies and outcomes of the Treatment Action Campaign case against the Minister of Health' (2003) 19 *SAJHR* 278.
HEYWOOD M 'Shaping, making and breaking the law in the campaign for a national HIV/AIDS Treatment Plan' in Jones P and Stokke K (eds) *Democratising Development: The Politics of Socio-Economic Rights in South Africa* (Martinus Nijhoff Publishers, 2005) chapter 8.
HEYWOOD M AND HASSIM A 'Remedying the maladies of "lesser men or women": The personal, political and constitutional imperatives for improved access to justice' (2008) 24 *SAJHR* 263.
HOEXTER C *Administrative Law in South Africa* (Juta & Co, 2007).
HUTCHINSON D 'Identity crisis: "Intersectionality", "multidimensionality", and the development of an adequate theory of subordination' (2001) 6 *Michigan J of Race and Law* 285.
HUTCHISON H B 'Non-variation clauses in contract: Any escape from the *Shifren* strait-jacket?' (2001) 118 *SALJ* 720.
ILES K 'Limiting socio-economic rights: Beyond the internal limitations clauses' (2004) 20 *SAJHR* 448.
JACKMAN M 'Constitutional contact with the disparities in the world: Poverty as a prohibited ground of discrimination under the Canadian *Charter* and human rights law.' (1994) 2 *Review RCS* 76.
JACKMAN M AND PORTER B 'Socio-economic rights under the Canadian Charter' in Langford M (ed) *Social Rights Jurisprudence: Emerging Trends in International and Comparative Law* (Cambridge University Press, 2008) chapter 11.
JEFFREY A 'The new Constitution: A triumph for liberalism? Some doubts' in Johnson R W and Welsh D with the assistance of Husemeyer L (eds) *Ironic Victory: Liberalism in Post-Liberation South Africa* (Oxford University Press, 1998) chapter 2.
KA MDUMBE F 'Socio-economic rights: *Van Biljon* versus *Soobramoney*' (1998) 13 *SAPL/R* 460.
KAGANAS F AND MURRAY C 'Law and Women's Rights in South Africa: An overview' (1994) *AJ* 1.
KENDE M S 'The South African Constitutional Court's embrace of socio-economic rights: A comparative perspective' (2003) 6 *Chap L Rev* 137.
KENDE M S 'The South African Constitutional Court's construction of socio-economic rights: A response to the critics' (2003–2004) 19 *Con J Int'l L* 617.
KENDE M S *Constitutional Rights in Two Worlds: South Africa and the United States* (Cambridge University Press, 2009).
KENNEDY D *A Critique of Adjudication {fin de siècle}* (Harvard University Press, 1997).
KHALIQ U AND CHURCHILL R 'The European Committee on Social Rights: Putting flesh on the bare bones of the European Social Charter' in Langford M (ed) *Social Rights Jurisprudence: Emerging Trends in International and Comparative Law* (Cambridge University Press, 2008) chapter 21.
KING J A 'United Kingdom: Asserting social rights in a multilayered system' in Langford M (ed) *Social Rights Jurisprudence: Emerging Trends in International and Comparative Law* (Cambridge University Press, 2008) chapter 15.
KIRSCH R 'Poor people get cancer too' (2007) 97 *SAMJ* 471.

KLAAREN J 'A remedial interpretation of the *Treatment Action Campaign* decision' (2003) 19 *SAJHR* 455.
KLAAREN J 'An institutional interpretation of socio-economic rights and judicial remedies after *TAC*' in Botha H, Van der Walt A J and Van der Walt J (eds) *Rights and Democracy in a Transformative Constitution* (SUN Press, 2003) chapter 7.
KLARE K E 'Law-making as praxis' (1979) *Telos* 123.
KLARE K E 'Legal theory and democratic reconstruction: Reflections on 1989' (1991) 25 *UBC LR* 69.
KLARE K E 'Legal culture and transformative constitutionalism' (1998) 14 *SAJHR* 146.
KLARE K E 'Legal subsidiarity and constitutional rights: A reply to André van der Walt' (2008) 1 *CCR* 129.
KLEYN D G *Die Mandament van Spolie in die Suid-Afrikaanse Reg* (unpublished LLD dissertation University of Pretoria, 1986).
KLEYN D G 'Die mandament van spolie as besitsremedie' (1986) *DJ* 1.
KOCH I E 'Dichotomies, trichotomies or waves of duties?' (2005) 5 *HRLR* 81.
KOK A AND LANGFORD M 'Water' in Woolman S, Roux T, Klaaren J, Stein A, Chaskalson M, and Bishop M (eds) *Constitutional Law of South Africa* 2 ed OS (Juta & Co, 2004) chapter 56B.
KOMMERS D *The Constitutional Jurisprudence of the Federal Republic of Germany* (Duke University Press, 1989).
KOTHARI J 'Social rights litigation in India: Developments of the last decade' in Barak-Erez D and Gross A M *Exploring Social Rights: Between Theory and Practice* (Hart Publishing, 2007) chapter 8.
KRAUSE C AND SCHEININ M 'The right not to be discriminated against: The case of social security' in Orlin T, Rosas A and Scheinin M (eds) *The Jurisprudence of Human Rights Law: A Comparative Interpretive Approach* (Åbo Akademi University Institute for Human Rights, 2000) chapter 8.
KURLAND P B 'The rise and fall of the "doctrine" of separation of powers' (1986) 85 *Michigan LR* 592.
LANGA P 'Transformative constitutionalism' (2006) 17 *Stell LR* 351.
LANGFORD M 'Hungary: Social rights or market redivivus?' in Langford M (ed) *Social Rights Jurisprudence: Emerging Trends in International and Comparative Law* (Cambridge University Press, 2008) chapter 13.
LANGFORD M AND KING J A 'Committee on Economic, Social and Cultural Rights: Past, present and future' in Langford M (ed) *Social Rights Jurisprudence: Emerging Trends in International and Comparative Law* (Cambridge University Press 2008), chapter 23.
LEHMANN K 'In defense of the Constitutional Court: Litigating socio-economic rights and the myth of the minimum core' (2006) 22 *Am Univ Int Law Rev* 163.
LENTA P 'Democracy, rights disagreements and judicial review' (2004) 20 *SAJHR* 1.
LIEBENBERG S 'Social and economic rights: A critical challenge' in Liebenberg S (ed) *The Constitution of South Africa from a Gender Perspective* (Community Law Centre in association with David Philip, 1995) chapter 7.
LIEBENBERG S 'The International Covenant on Economic, Social and Cultural Rights and its implications for South Africa' (1995) 11 *SAJHR* 359.
LIEBENBERG S 'Housing' in Davis D M, Cheadle H and Haysom N (eds) *Fundamental Rights in the Constitution: Commentary and Cases* (Juta & Co, 1997) 342.
LIEBENBERG S 'Identifying violations of socio-economic rights: The role of the South African Human Rights Commission' (1997) 1 *LDD* 161.
LIEBENBERG S 'Socio-economic rights' in Chaskalson M, Kentridge J, Klaaren J, Marcus G, Spitz D, Woolman S (eds) *Constitutional Law of South Africa* RS 3 (Juta & Co, 1998) chapter 41.
LIEBENBERG S AND PILLAY K (eds) *Socio-Economic Rights in South Africa: A Resource Book* (Community Law Centre, University of the Western Cape, 2000).
LIEBENBERG S 'The protection of economic and social rights in domestic legal systems' in Eide A, Krause C and Rosas A (eds) *Economic, Social and Cultural Rights: A Textbook* 2 ed (Martinus Nijhoff Publishers, 2001) chapter 4.
LIEBENBERG S 'Violations of socio-economic rights: The role of the South African Human Rights Commission' in Andrews

P and Ellmann S (eds) *The Post-Apartheid Constitutions: Perspectives on South Africa's Basic Law* (Witwatersrand University Press and Ohio University Press, 2001) 405.

LIEBENBERG S 'South Africa's evolving jurisprudence on socio-economic rights: An effective tool in challenging poverty' (2002) 6 *LDD* 159.

LIEBENBERG S 'The interpretation of socio-economic rights' in Woolman S, Roux T, Klaaren J, Stein A, Chaskalson M, and Bishop M (eds) *Constitutional Law of South Africa* 2 ed OS (Juta & Co, 2003) chapter 33.

LIEBENBERG S 'Taking stock: The jurisprudence on children's socio-economic rights and its implications for government policy' (2004) 5 *ESR Review* 3.

LIEBENBERG S 'The value of human dignity in interpreting socio-economic rights' (2005) 21 *SAJHR* 1 (also published in A J van der Walt (ed) *Theories of Social and Economic Justice* (SUN Press, 2005) 141).

LIEBENBERG S 'Making a difference: human rights and development – reflecting on the South African experience' in Andreassen B and Marks S P *Development as a Human Right: Legal, Political and Economic Dimensions* (Harvard School of Public Health and François-Xavier Bagnoud Center for Health and Human Rights, 2006) chapter 9.

LIEBENBERG S 'Needs, rights and transformation: Adjudicating social rights' (2006) 1 *Stell LR* 5.

LIEBENBERG S 'The judicial enforcement of social security rights in South Africa: Enhancing accountability for the basic needs of the poor' in Riedel E (ed) *Social Security as a Human Right: Drafting a General Comment on Article 9 ICESCR* (Springer, 2006) chapter 5.

LIEBENBERG S 'The application of socio-economic rights to private law' (2008) 3 *TSAR* 464.

LIEBENBERG S 'The value of freedom in interpreting socio-economic rights' in Barnard-Naudé A J, Cornell D and Du Bois F (eds) *Dignity, Freedom and the Post-Apartheid Legal Order* (Juta & Co, 2008) 149 (first published in *AJ* (2008) 149).

LIEBENBERG S AND GOLDBLATT B 'The interrelationship between equality and socio-economic rights under South Africa's transformative constitution' (2007) 23 *SAJHR* 335.

LIEBENBERG S AND PILLAY K (eds) *Socio-Economic Rights in South Africa: A Resource Book* (Community Law Centre, University of the Western Cape, 2000).

LIEBENBERG S AND O'SULLIVAN M 'South Africa's new equality legislation: A tool for advancing women's socio-economic equality?' (2001) *AJ* 70.

LOCKHAT R AND VAN NIEKERK A 'South African children: a history of adversity, violence and trauma' (2000) 5 *Ethnicity and Health* 291.

LUBBE G F 'Taking fundamental rights seriously: The Bill of Rights and its implications for the development of contract law' (2004) 121 *SALJ* 395.

LUBBE G F 'Contractual derogation and the discretion to refuse an order for specific performance' in Glover G (ed) *Essays in Honour of A J Kerr* (Butterworths, 2006) 77.

LUND C AND FLISHER A J 'Staff/bed and staff/patient ratios in South African public sector mental health services' (2002) 92 *SAMJ* 161.

LUND C AND FLISHER A J 'Community/hospital indicators in South African public sector mental health services' (2003) 6 *J Ment Health Policy Econ* 181.

MADLINGOZI T 'Post-apartheid social movements and the quest for the elusive "new" South Africa' (2007) 34 *J of Law & Soc* 77.

MADLINGOZI T 'The Constitutional Court, court watchers and the commons: A reply to Professor Michelman on constitutional dialogue, "interpretive charity" and the citizens as sangomas' (2008) 1 *CCR* 63.

MAHERY P AND PROUDLOCK P *Legal Guide to Age Thresholds for Children* 4 ed (Children's Institute, University of Cape Town and Centre for Child Law University of Pretoria, 2008).

MANDELA N R 'Address: On the occasion of the ANC's Bill of Rights Conference' in *A Bill of Rights for A Democratic South Africa: Papers and Report of a Conference Convened by the ANC Constitutional Committee, May 1991* (Centre for Development Studies, University of the Western Cape, 1991) 9.

MARAIS H *South Africa: Limits to Change – The Political Economy of Transformation* (University of Cape Town Press, 1998).

MARSHALL M H '"Wise parents do not hesitate to learn from their children": Interpreting state constitutions in an age of global jurisprudence' (2004) 79 *NYULR* 1633.

MBAZIRA C '"Appropriate, just and equitable relief" in socio-economic rights litigation: The tension between corrective and distributive forms of justice' (2008) 125 *SALJ* 71.

MBAZIRA C 'Confronting the problem of polycentricity in enforcing socio-economic rights in the South African Constitution' (2008) 23 *SAPL/R* 30.

MBAZIRA C AND SLOTH-NIELSEN J 'Incy wincy spider went climbing up again – prospects for constitutional interpretation of section 28(1)(c) in the next decade of democracy' (2007) 21 *Speculum Juris* 147.

MCLEAN K 'Housing' in Woolman S, Roux T, Bishop, M, Klaaren J and Stein A (eds) *Constitutional Law of South Africa* 2 ed OS (Juta & Co, 2006) chapter 55.

MCINTYRE D et al *SHIELD Work Package 1 Report: A Critical Analysis of the Current South African Health System* 2007 Health Economics Unit (University of Cape Town) and Centre for Health Policy (University of the Witwatersrand). Available at http://web.uct.ac.za/depts/heu/SHIELD/reports/SouthAfrica1.pdf (accessed on 7 April 2009).

MEERKOTTER A 'The impact of the HIV/AIDS epidemic on women's citizenship in South Africa' in Gouws A (ed) *(Un)thinking Citizenship: Feminist Debates in Contemporary South Africa* (Ashgate, 2005) chapter 7.

MELISH T J 'The Inter-American Commission on Human Rights: Defending social rights through case-based petitions' in Langford M (ed) *Social Rights Jurisprudence: Emerging Trends in International and Comparative Law* (Cambridge University Press, 2008) chapter 18.

MELISH T J 'The Inter-American Court of Human Rights: Beyond progressivity' in Langford M (ed) *Social Rights Jurisprudence: Emerging Trends in International and Comparative Law* (Cambridge University Press, 2008) chapter 19.

MENSCH E 'The history of mainstream legal thought' in Kairys D (ed) *The Politics of Law: A Progressive Critique* (Basic Books, 1998) chapter 1.

MICHELMAN F I 'The Supreme Court, 1968 term' (1969) 83 *Harvard LR* 7.

MICHELMAN F I 'In pursuit of constitutional welfare rights: One view of Rawls' theory of justice' (1973) 121 *U Pa L Rev* 962.

MICHELMAN F I 'Welfare rights in a constitutional democracy' (1979) 3 *Washington University Law Quarterly* 659.

MICHELMAN F I 'Law's Republic' (1988) 97 *Yale LJ* 1493.

MICHELMAN F I 'Bringing the law to life: a plea for disenchantment' (1989) 74 *Cornell L Rev* 256.

MICHELMAN F I 'The constitution, social rights, and liberal political justification' (2003) 1 *I Con* 13.

MICHELMAN F I 'The bill of rights, the common law, and the freedom-friendly state' (2003–2004) 58 *Miami Law Review* 401.

MINOW M 'Interpreting rights: An essay for Robert Cover' (1987) 96 *Yale LJ* 1860.

MINOW M *Making all the Difference: Inclusion, Exclusion and American Law* (Cornell University Press, 1990).

MOELLENDORF D 'Reasoning about resources: *Soobramoney* and the future of socio-economic rights claims' (1998) 14 *SAJHR* 327.

MOSENEKE D 'The Fourth Bram Fischer Memorial Lecture: Transformative adjudication' (2002) 18 *SAJHR* 309.

MOSENEKE D 'Transformative constitutionalism: Its implications for the law of contract' (2009) 20 *Stell LR* 3.

MUBANGIZI J C 'Public health, the South African Bill of Rights and the socio-economic polemic' (2002) 35 *TSAR* 343.

MUBANGIZI J C AND O'SHEA A 'An African Court of Human and Peoples' Rights' (1999) 24 *SAYIL* 256.

MURALIDHAR S 'India: The expectations and challenges of judicial enforcement of social rights' in Langford M (ed) *Social Rights Jurisprudence: Emerging Trends in International and Comparative Law* (Cambridge University Press, 2008) chapter 5.

MUREINIK E 'Beyond a charter of luxuries: Economic rights in the constitution' (1992) 8 *SAJHR* 464.

MUREINIK E 'A bridge to where?: Introducing the interim Bill of Rights' (1994) 10 *SAJHR* 31.

MURRAY C AND O'REGAN C (eds) *No Place to Rest: Forced Removals and the Law in South Africa* (Oxford University Press, 1990).

NAGAN W P 'International intellectual property, access to health care, and human rights: South Africa v United States' (2001–2002) 14 *Florida J of Int Law* 155.

NAUDÉ T 'Unfair contract terms legislation: The implications of why we need it for its formulation and application' (2006) 17 *Stell LR* 361.

NAUDÉ T AND LUBBE G 'Exemption clauses – A rethink occasioned by *Afrox Health Care Bpk v Strydom*' (2005) 122 *SALJ* 441.

NEDELSKY J 'Reconceiving autonomy: Sources, thoughts and possibilities' (1989) 1 *Yale J of Law and Feminism* 7.

NEDELSKY J 'Reconstructing rights as relationship' (1993) 1 *RCS* 1.

NEDELSKY J AND SCOTT C 'Constitutional dialogue' in J Bakan and D Schneiderman (eds) *Social Justice and the Constitution: Perspectives on a Social Union for Canada* (Carleton University Press, 1992) chapter 5.

NEWMAN D G 'Institutional monitoring of social and economic rights: A South African case study and a new research agenda' (2003) 19 *SAJHR* 189.

NGWENA C AND COOK R 'Rights concerning health' in Brand D and Heyns C (eds) *Socio-Economic Rights in South Africa* (PULP, 2005) chapter 4.

NHLAPO T 'African customary law in the interim Constitution' in Liebenberg S (ed) *The Constitution of South Africa from a Gender Perspective* (Community Law Centre in association with David Phillip, 1995) chapter 12.

NOLAN A 'Security of tenure from a children's rights perspective' (2006) 7 *ESR Review* 22.

NOLAN A 'Ireland: The separation of powers doctrine vs. socio-economic rights?' in Langford M (ed) *Social Rights Jurisprudence: Emerging Trends in International and Comparative Law* (Cambridge University Press, 2008) chapter 16.

NOZICK R *Anarchy, State and Utopia* (Basil Blackwell, 1974).

NUSSBAUM M C 'Capabilities, human rights, and the Universal Declaration' in Weston B H and Marks S P (eds) *The Future of International Human Rights* (Transnational Publishers Inc, 1999).

NUSSBAUM M C *Women and Human Development: The Capabilities Approach* (Cambridge University Press, 2000).

O'REGAN C 'No more forced removals: An historical analysis of The Prevention of Illegal Squatting Act' (1989) 5 *SAJHR* 361.

O'REGAN C 'From form to substance: The constitutional jurisprudence of Laurie Ackermann' in Barnard-Naudé A J, Cornell D and Du Bois F (eds) *Dignity, Freedom and the Post-Apartheid Legal Order: The Critical Jurisprudence of Laurie Ackermann* (Juta & Co, 2008) chapter 1 (first published in *AJ* (2008) *AJ* 1).

OAKES D *Illustrated History of South Africa: The Real Story* (The Reader's Digest Association South Africa (Pty) Ltd, 1988).

ODINKALU C A 'Implementing economic, social and cultural rights under the African Charter on Human and Peoples' Rights' in Evans M and Murray R (eds) *The African Charter on Human and Peoples' Rights: The System in Practice, 1986–2000* (Cambridge University Press, 2002) 178.

OLOKA-ONYANGO J 'Beyond the rhetoric: Reinvigorating the struggle for economic, social and cultural rights in Africa' (1995) 26 *Cal W Int'l L J* 1.

OMAR D 'Enforcement of Social and Economic Rights' in *A Bill of Rights for A Democratic South Africa: Papers and Report of a Conference Convened by the ANC Constitutional Committee, May 1991* (Centre for Development Studies, 1991) 106.

ONYEMELUKWE C 'Access to anti-retroviral drugs as a component of the right to health in international law: Examining the application of the right in Nigerian jurisprudence' (2007) 7 *AHRLJ* 446.

PATEL E 'The right to work' in *A Bill of Rights for A Democratic South Africa: Papers and Report of a Conference Convened by the ANC Constitutional Committee, May 1991* (Centre for Development Studies, 1991) 85.

PEARMAIN D 'Contracting for socio-economic rights: A contradiction in terms? (1)' (2006) 69 *THRHR* 287.

PEARMAIN D 'Contracting for socio-economic rights: A contradiction in terms? (2)' (2006) 69 *THRHR* 466.

PIETERSE E AND VAN DONK M 'The politics of socio-economic rights in South Africa ten years after apartheid' (2004) 5 *ESR Review* 12.
PIETERSE M 'A different shade of red: Socio-economic dimensions of the right to life in South Africa' (1999) 15 *SAJHR* 372.
PIETERSE M 'Beyond the welfare state: Globalisation of neo-liberal culture and the constitutional protection of socio-economic rights in South Africa (2003) 14 *Stell LR* 3.
PIETERSE M 'Reconstructing the private/public dichotomy? The enforcement of children's constitutional rights and care entitlements' (2003) 1 *TSAR* 1.
PIETERSE M 'Towards a useful role for section 36 of the Constitution in social rights cases? *Residents of Bon Vista Mansions v Southern Metropolitan Local Council*' (2003) 120 *SALJ* 41.
PIETERSE M 'Coming to terms with judicial enforcement of socio-economic rights' (2004) 20 *SAJHR* 383.
PIETERSE M *A Benefit-Focused Analysis of Constitutional Health Rights* 2005 (unpublished PhD dissertation University of the Witwatersrand, 2005).
PIETERSE M 'What do we mean when we talk about transformative constitutionalism?' (2005) 20 *SAPL/R* 155.
PIETERSE M 'The potential of socio-economic rights litigation for the achievement of social justice: Considering the example of access to medical care in South African prisons' (2006) 50 *Journal of African Law* 118.
PIETERSE M 'Eating socioeconomic rights: The usefulness of rights talk in alleviating social hardship revisited' (2007) 29 *HRQ* 796.
PIETERSE M 'Health care rights, resources and rationing' (2007) 124 *SALJ* 514.
PIETERSE M 'Indirect horizontal application of the right to have access to health care services' (2007) 23 *SAJHR* 157.
PIETERSE M 'On "dialogue", "translation" and "voice": A reply to Sandra Liebenberg' in Woolman S and Bishop M (eds) *Constitutional Conversations* (PULP, 2008) chapter 19.
PILLAY KAMESHNI 'Implementation of *Grootboom*: Implications for the enforcement of socio-economic rights' (2002) 6 *LDD* 255.
PILLAY KARRISHA 'The Commission for Gender Equality: What is its role?' (1998) 1 *ESR Review* 13.
PIOVESAN F 'Brazil: Impact and challenges of social rights in the courts' in Langford M (ed) *Social Rights Jurisprudence: Emerging Trends in International and Comparative Law* (Cambridge University Press, 2008) chapter 9.
PLASKET C 'Protecting the public purse: Appropriate relief and costs orders against public officials' (2000) 117 *SALJ* 151.
PLASKET C 'Administrative justice and social assistance' (2003) 120 *SALJ* 494.
POLANYI M *The Logic of Liberty: Reflections and Rejoinders* (Liberty Fund, 1951).
PORTER B 'Beyond Andrews: Substantive equality and positive obligations after *Eldridge* and *Vriend*' (1998) 9 *Const Forum* 71.
PORTER B 'The crisis of economic, social and cultural rights and strategies for addressing it' in Squires J, Langford M and Thiele B (eds) *The Road to a Remedy: Current Issues in the Litigation of Economic, Social and Cultural Rights* (University of New South Wales Press, 2005) chapter 4.
PORTER B 'The reasonableness of article 8(4) of the Optional Protocol: Adjudicating claims from the margins' (2009) 27 *NJHR* 39.
PROUDLOCK P, DUTSCHKE M, JAMIESON L, MONSON J AND SMITH C (eds) South African Child Gauge 2007/2008} 2008, Children's Institute (University of Cape Town). Available at http://www.ci.org.za/depts/ci/pubs/pdf/general/gauge2007/ChildGauge2007.pdf (accessed on 1 June 2009).
PROUVEZ N 'Committee on the Elimination of Racial Discrimination: Confronting racial discrimination and inequality in the enjoyment of economic, social and cultural rights' in Langford M (ed) *Social Rights Jurisprudence: Emerging Trends in International and Comparative Law* (Cambridge University Press, 2008) chapter 24.
QUINOT G 'An administrative law perspective on "bad building" evictions in the Johannesburg inner city: *City of Johannesburg v Rand Properties (Pty) Ltd* 2007 SCA 25 (RSA)' (2007) 1 *ESR Review* 25.
RAUTENBACH I M 'The limitation of rights and "reasonableness" in the right to just administrative action and the rights to access to adequate housing, health services and social security' (2005) 4 *TSAR* 627.

RICHTER L M AND DAWES A R L 'Child abuse in South Africa: Rights and wrongs' (2008) 17 *Child Abuse Review* 79.
ROACH K 'Constitutional, remedial, and international dialogues about rights: The Canadian experience' (2004–2005) 40 *Tex Int L J* 537.
ROACH K AND BUDLENDER G 'Mandatory relief and supervisory jurisdiction: When is it appropriate, just and equitable' (2005) 122 *SALJ* 325.
ROEDERER C 'Post-matrix legal reasoning: Horizontality and the rule of values in South African law' (2003) 19 *SAJHR* 57.
ROITHMAYR D 'Access, adequacy and equality: The constitutionality of school fee financing in public education' (2003) 19 *SAJHR* 382.
ROSA S AND DUTSCHKE M 'Child rights at the core: The use of international law in South African cases on children's socio-economic rights' (2006) 22 *SAJHR* 224.
ROSAS A AND SCHEININ M 'Implementation mechanisms and remedies' in Eide A, Krause C and Rosas A (eds) *Economic, Social and Cultural Rights: A Textbook* 2 ed (Martinus Nijhoff Publishers 2001) chapter 23.
ROSS T 'The rhetoric of poverty: Their immorality, our helplessness' (1991) 79 *Geo LJ* 1499.
ROUX T 'Legitimating transformation: Political resource allocation in the South African Constitutional Court' (2003) 10 *Democratization* 92.
ROUX T 'Continuity and change in a transforming legal order: The impact of section 26(3) of the Constitution on South African law' (2004) 121 *SALJ* 466.
ROUX T 'Pro-poor court, anti-poor outcomes: Explaining the performance of the South African Land Claims Court' (2004) 20 *SAJHR* 511 (also published in A J van der Walt (ed) *Theories of Social and Economic Justice* (SUN Press, 2005) 199.
ROUX T 'Democracy' in Woolman S, Roux T, Bishop M, Klaaren J and Stein A (eds) *Constitutional Law of South Africa* 2 ed OS (Juta & Co, 2006) chapter 10.
ROUX T 'The dignity of comparative constitutional law' in Barnard-Naudé A J, Cornell D and Du Bois F (eds) *Dignity, Freedom and the Post-Apartheid Legal Order: The Critical Jurisprudence of Laurie Ackermann* (Juta & Co, 2008) 185 (first published in (2008) *AJ* 185).
RULE P '"The time is burning": The right of adults to basic education in South Africa' (2006) 39 *JoE* 113.
SABEL C F AND SIMON W H 'Destabilization rights: How public law litigation succeeds' (2003–2004) 117 *Harvard LR* 1016.
SACHS A 'A Bill of Rights for South Africa: Areas of agreement and disagreement' (1989) 21 *Columb Hum Rts L Rev* 13.
SACHS A 'Towards a Bill of Rights in a democratic South Africa' (1990) 6 *SAJHR* 1.
SACHS A *Advancing Human Rights in South Africa* (Oxford University Press, 1992).
SACHS A 'South Africa's unconstitutional constitution: The transition from power to lawful power' (1997) 41 *St Louis LJ* 1249.
SACHS A 'The judicial enforcement of socio-economic rights: The *Grootboom* case' (2003) 56 *Current Legal Problems* 579.
SADURSKI W *Rights before Courts: A Study of Constitutional Courts in Post-Communist States of Central and Eastern Europe* (Springer, 2005) 177.
SAJÓ A 'How the rule of law killed Hungarian welfare reform' (1996) 5 *EECR* 31.
SAJÓ A 'Social rights as middle class entitlements in Hungary: The role of the Constitutional Court' in Gargarella R, Domingo P and Roux T (eds) *Courts and Social Transformation in New Democracies: An Institutional Voice for the Poor?* (Ashgate Press, 2006) chapter 4.
SCHEININ M 'Direct applicability of economic, social and cultural rights: A critique of the doctrine of self-executing treaties' in Drzewicki K, Krause C and Rosas A (eds) *Social Rights as Human Rights: A European Challenge* (Institute for Human Rights Åbo Akademi University, 1994) chapter 5.
SCHEININ M 'Economic and social rights as legal rights' in Eide A, Krause C and Rosas A (eds) *Economic, Social and Cultural Rights: A Textbook* 2 ed (Martinus Nijhoff Publishers, 2001) chapter 3.
SCHEININ M 'Human Rights Committee: Not only a committee on civil and political rights' in Langford M (ed) *Social Rights Jurisprudence: Emerging Trends in International and Comparative Law* (Cambridge University Press, 2008) chapter 25.

SCHLANGER M 'Beyond the hero judge: Institutional reform litigation as litigation' (1998–1999) 97 *Michigan LR* 1994.

SCHNEIDER E M 'The dialectic of rights and politics: Perspectives from the women's movement' (1986) 61 *NYULR* 589.

SCHWIKKARD P J 'The standard and burden of proof and evidential duties in civil trials' in Schwikkard P J and Van der Merwe S E et al *Principles of Evidence* 3 ed (Juta & Co, 2009) chapter 32.

SCOTT C 'The interdependence and permeability of human rights norms: Towards a partial fusion of the international covenants on human rights' (1989) 27 *OHLJ* 769.

SCOTT C 'Multinational enterprises and emergent jurisprudence on violations of economic, social and cultural rights' in Eide A, Krause C and Rosas A (eds) *Economic, Social and Cultural Rights: A Textbook* 2 ed (Martinus Nijhoff Publishers, 2001) chapter 32.

SCOTT C AND ALSTON P 'Adjudicating constitutional priorities in a transnational content: A comment on *Soobramoney's* legacy and *Grootboom*'s promise' (2000) 16 *SAJHR* 206.

SCOTT C AND MACKLEM P 'Constitutional ropes of sand or justiciable guarantees? Social rights in a new South African Constitution' (1992) 141 *U Pa L Rev* 1.

SCOTT S 'A private-law dinosaur's evaluation of summary execution clauses in light of the Constitution' (2007) 70 *THRHR* 289.

SEEDORF S AND SIBANDA S 'Separation of Powers' in Woolman S, Roux T, Bishop M, Klaaren J and Stein A (eds) *Constitutional Law of South Africa* 2 ed OS (Juta & Co, 2008) chapter 12.

SEEKINGS J AND NATTRASS N *Class, Race and Inequality in South Africa* (University of KwaZulu-Natal Press, 2006).

SEIDMAN L M 'Critical constitutionalism now' (2006) 75 *Fordham LR* 575.

SEN A *Poverty and Famines: An Essay on Entitlement and Deprivation* (Clarendon Press, 1981).

SEN A *Development as Freedom* (Oxford University Press, 2001).

SEN A 'Elements of a theory of human rights' (2004) 32 *Philosophy and Public Affairs* 315.

SEPÚLVEDA M 'Colombia: The Constitutional Court's role in addressing social injustice' in Langford M (ed) *Social Rights Jurisprudence: Emerging Trends in International and Comparative Law* (Cambridge University Press, 2008) chapter 7.

SETH L 'Social action litigation in India' in Liebenberg S (ed) *The Constitution of South Africa from a Gender Perspective* (Community Law Centre in association with David Philip, 1995) chapter 8.

SHANKAR S AND MEHTA P B 'Courts and socioeconomic rights in India' in Gauri V and Brinks D M (eds) *Courting Social Justice: Judicial Enforcement of Social and Economic Rights in the Developing World* (Cambridge University Press, 2008) chapter 4.

SHISANA O *Nelson Mandela/HSRC Study of HIV/AIDS* (HSRC, 2002).

SHUE H *Basic Rights: Subsistence, Affluence, and US Foreign Policy* (Princeton University Press, 1980).

SINGER J W 'Legal realism now' (1988) 76 *CLR* 465.

SLOTH-NIELSEN J 'The child's right to social services, the right to social security, and primary prevention of child abuse: Some conclusions in the aftermath of *Grootboom*' (2001) 17 *SAJHR* 210.

SLOTH-NIELSEN J 'Realising children's rights to legal representation and to be heard in judicial proceedings: An update' (2008) 24 *SAJHR* 495.

SONNEKUS J C '*Fredericks and Another v Stellenbosch Divisional Council* 1977 3 SA 113 (K)' (1978) *TSAR* 168.

SPIES G M 'Restorative justice: A way to support the healing process of a child exposed to incest' (2009) 22 *AC* 15.

SPITZ R WITH CHASKALSON M *The Politics of Transition: A Hidden History of South Africa's Negotiated Settlement* (Witwatersrand University Press, 2000).

STEINBERG C 'Can reasonableness protect the poor? A review of South Africa's socio-economic rights jurisprudence' (2006) 123 *SALJ* 264.

STEINER H J AND ALSTON P *International Rights in Context: Law, Politics, Morals* 3 ed (Oxford University Press, 2008).

STEWART L 'Interpreting and limiting the basic socio-economic rights of children in cases where they overlap with the socio-economic rights of others' (2008) 24 *SAJHR* 472.

STEYN L 'Safe as houses? Balancing a mortgagee's security interest with a homeowner's security of tenure' (2007) 11 *LDD* 101.

STEYTLER N *Constitutional Criminal Procedure* (Butterworths, 1998).

STREAK J 'Child poverty in South Africa and implications for policy: Using indicators and children's views to gain perspective' in Coetzee E and Streak J (eds) *Monitoring Child Socio-Economic Rights in South Africa: Achievements and Challenges* (IDASA, 2004) chapter 1.

SUDARSHAN R 'Courts and social transformation in India' in Gargarella R, Domingo P and Roux T (eds) *Courts and Social Transformation in New Democracies: An Institutional Voice for the Poor?* (Ashgate Press, 2006) chapter 7.

SUNSTEIN C R 'Foreword: Leaving things undecided' (1996) 110 *Harvard LR* 6.

SUNSTEIN C R 'Social and economic rights? Lessons from South Africa' (2000–2001) 11 *Const Forum* 123.

SUNSTEIN C R 'Incompletely theorized agreements in constitutional law' (2007) 74 *Social Research* 1.

SUTHERLAND P J 'Ensuring contractual fairness in consumer contracts after *Barkhuizen v Napier* 2007 5 SA 323 (CC) – part 1' (2008) 19 *Stell LR* 390.

SWART M 'Left out in the cold? Crafting constitutional remedies for the poorest of the poor' (2005) 21 *SAJHR* 215.

TAYLOR V *Social mobilisation: Lessons from the Mass Democratic Movement* (University of the Western Cape, 1997).

TEITEL R 'Transitional jurisprudence: The role of law in political transformation' (1997) 106 *Yale LJ* 2009.

TEITEL R *Transitional Justice* (Oxford University Press, 2000).

TERREBLANCE S *A History of Inequality in South Africa: 1652–2002* (University of Natal Press, 2002).

THERON J 'Employment is not what it used to be: The nature and impact of the restructuring of work in South Africa' in Webster E and Von Holdt K (eds) *Beyond the Apartheid Workplace* (University of KwaZulu-Natal Press, 2005) chapter 12.

TISSINGTON K 'Challenging inner city evictions before the Constitutional Court of South Africa: The Occupiers of 51 Olivia Road case' (2008) 5 *Housing and ESC Rights Law Quarterly* 1.

TLADI D 'One step forward, two steps back for constitutionalising the common law: *Afrox Health Care v Strydom*' (2002) 17 *SAPR/SAPL* 473.

TOEBES B C A *The Right to Health as a Human Right in International Law* (Intersentia Law Publishers, 1999).

TRENGROVE W 'Judicial remedies for violations of socio-economic rights' (1999) 1 *ESR Review* 8.

TRIBE L H *American Constitutional Law* (Foundation Press, 2000).

TUSHNET M V 'Following the rules laid down: A critique of interpretivism and neutral principles' (1983) 96 *Harvard LR* 781.

TUSHNET M V 'The possibilities of comparative constitutional law' (1999) 108 *Yale LJ* 1225.

TUSHNET M V 'New forms of judicial review and the persistence of rights- and democracy-based worries' (2003) 38 *Wake Forest L Rev* 813.

TUSHNET M V 'Social welfare rights and forms of judicial review' (2003–2004) 82 *Texas L Rev* 1895.

TUSHNET M V 'Enforcing socio-economic rights: Lessons from South Africa' (2005) 6 *ESR Review* 2 .

UNGER R M 'The critical legal studies movement' (1983) 96 *Harvard LR* 561.

UNITED NATIONS DEVELOPMENT PROGRAMME (Principal author: Taylor V) *South Africa: Transformation for Human Development* (UNDP, 2000).

VALODIA I 'Work' in Budlender D (ed) *The Women's Budget* (IDASA, 1996) 53.

VAN BUEREN G 'Alleviating poverty through the Constitutional Court' (1999) 15 *SAJHR* 52.

VAN BUEREN G 'Committee on the Rights of the Child: Overcoming inertia in this age of no alternatives' in Langford M (ed) *Social Rights Jurisprudence: Emerging Trends in International and Comparative Law* (Cambridge University Press, 2008) chapter 27.

VAN DER BERG S 'South African social security under apartheid and beyond' (1997) 14 *Development South Africa* 485.

VAN DER MERWE D The Roman-Dutch law: From virtual reality to constitutional resource' (1998) *TSAR* 1.

VAN DER WALT A J 'Tradition on trial: A critical analysis of the civil law tradition in South African property law' (1995) 11 *SAJHR* 169.

VAN DER WALT A J 'Squatting, spoliation and the new constitutional order' (1997) 60 *THRHR* 522.

VAN DER WALT A J 'Tentative urgency: Sensitivity for the paradoxes of stability and change in the social transformation decisions of the Constitutional Court' (2001) 16 *SAPRL/SAPL* 1.

VAN DER WALT A J 'Closure and openness on difference and democracy – a response to Justice Johan Froneman' (2001) 12 *Stell LR* 28.

VAN DER WALT A J 'Exclusivity of ownership, security of tenure, and eviction orders: A critical evaluation of recent case law' (2002) 18 *SAJHR* 372.

VAN DER WALT A J 'A South African reading of Frank Michelman's theory of social justice' (2004) 19 *SAPR/SAPL* 253 (also published in Botha H, Van der Walt AJ and Van der Walt J (eds) *Rights and Democracy in a Transformative Constitution* (SUN Press 2003) 163).

VAN DER WALT A J *Constitutional Property Law* (Juta & Co, 2005).

VAN DER WALT A J 'Ownership and eviction: Constitutional rights in private law' (2005) 9 *Edin LR* 32.

VAN DER WALT A J 'The State's duty to protect property owners v the State's duty to provide housing: Thoughts on the *Modderklip* Case' (2005) 21 *SAJHR* 144.

VAN DER WALT A J 'Transformative constitutionalism and the development of South African property law (part 1)' (2005) *TSAR* 655.

VAN DER WALT A J 'Legal history, legal culture and transformation in a constitutional democracy' (2006) 12 *Fundamina* 1.

VAN DER WALT A J 'Transformative constitutionalism and the development of South African property law (part 2)' (2006) *TSAR* 1.

VAN DER WALT A J 'Developing the law on unlawful squatting and spoliation' (2008) 125 *SALJ* 24.

VAN DER WALT J 'Progressive indirect application of the Bill of Rights: Towards a co-operative relation between common law and constitutional jurisprudence' (2001) 17 *SAJHR* 341.

VAN MARLE K 'Communitarian and civic republican theories' in Roederer C and Moellendorf D (eds) *Jurisprudence* (Juta & Co, 2004) chapter 16.

VAN WYK J 'The complexities of providing emergency housing assistance in South Africa' (2007) *TSAR* 35.

VAN ZYL SMIT D *South African Prison Law and Practice* (Butterworths, 1992).

VERIAVA F 'Enforcing the current laws on school fees' (2003) 4 *ESR Review* 6.

VERIAVA F 'The amended legal framework for school fees and school funding: A boon or a barrier' (2007) 23 *SAJHR* 180.

VERIAVA F AND COOMANS F 'The right to education' in Brand D and Heyns C (eds) *Socio-Economic Rights in South Africa* (PULP, 2005) chapter 2.

VIERDAG E G 'The legal nature of the rights granted by the International Covenant on Economic, Social and Cultural Rights' (1978) 9 *NYIL* 69.

VON LIERES B 'Marginalisation and citizenship in post-apartheid South Africa' in Robins S L (ed) *Limits to Liberation after Apartheid: Citizenship, Governance and Culture* (David Philip Publishers, 2005) chapter 1.

WECHSLER H 'Towards neutral principles of constitutional law' (1959) 73 *Harvard LR* 1.

WEINTRAUB J 'The theory and politics of the public/private distinction' in Weintraub J and Kumar K (eds) *Public and Private in Thought and Practice: Perspectives on a Grand Dichotomy* (The University of Chicago Press, 1997) chapter 1.

WESSON M '*Grootboom* and beyond: Reassessing the socio-economic jurisprudence of the South African Constitutional Court' (2004) 20 *SAJHR* 284.

WILLIAMS J 'Critical legal studies: The death of transcendence and the rise of the new langdells' (1987) 62 *NYULR* 429.

WILLIAMS L A 'Welfare and legal entitlements: The social roots of poverty' in Kairys D (ed) *The Politics of Law: A Progressive Critique* (Basic Books, 1998) chapter 25.

WILLIAMS L A 'Beyond labour law's parochialism: A re-envisioning of the discourse of redistribution' in Conaghan J, Fischl R M and Klare K E (eds) *Labour Law in an Era of Globalization: Transformative Practices and Possibilities* (Oxford University Press, 2002) chapter 5 (also published in A J van der Walt (ed) *Theories of Social and Economic Justice* (SUN Press, 2005) 239).

WILLIAMS L A 'Issues and challenges in addressing poverty and legal rights: A comparative United States/South African analysis' (2005) 21 *SAJHR* 436.

WILLIAMS L A 'The justiciability of water rights: *Mazibuko v City of Johannesburg*' (2009) 36 *Forum Devel Stud* 5.

WILSON S 'Out of site, out of mind: Relocation and access to schools in Sol Plaatje' (2003). Available at http://web.wits.ac.za/Academic/Centres/CALS/Education/ResearchReports.htm (accessed on 27 April 2009).

WILSON S 'Taming the Constitution: Rights and reform in the South African education system' (2004) 20 *SAJHR* 418.

WILSON S 'Litigating housing rights in Johannesburg's inner city' in C Jenkins, M du Plessis and K Govender (eds) *Law, Nation-Building and Transformation* (Intersite, forthcoming 2010).

WOODS J M 'Justiciable social rights as a critique of the liberal paradigm' (2003) 38 *Tex Int L J* 763.

WOOLMAN S 'Application' in Woolman S, Roux T, Bishop M, Klaaren J and Stein A (eds) *Constitutional Law of South Africa* OS (Juta & Co, 2005) chapter 31.

WOOLMAN S 'Defending discrimination: On the constitutionality of independent schools that promote a particular, if not comprehensive, vision of the good life' (2007) 22 *Stell LR* 31.

WOOLMAN S 'The amazing, vanishing Bill of Rights' (2007) 124 *SALJ* 762.

WOOLMAN S AND BOTHA H 'Limitations' in Woolman S, Roux T, Bishop M, Klaaren J and Stein A (eds) *Constitutional* Law *of South Africa* 2 ed OS (Juta & Co, 2006) chapter 34.

WOOLMAN S AND DAVIS D M 'The last laugh: *Du Plessis v De Klerk*, classical liberalism, creole liberalism and the application of rights under the interim and final constitution' (1996) 12 *SAJHR* 361.

WOOLMAN S AND FLEISCH B *The Constitution in the Classroom: Law and Education in South Africa 1994–2008* (PULP, 2009).

YEPES R U 'The enforcement of social rights by the Colombian Constitutional Court: Cases and debates' in R Gargarella, P Domingo and T Roux (eds) *Courts and Social Transformation in New Democracies: An Institutional Voice for the Poor?* (Ashgate Press, 2006) chapter 6.

YOUNG I M *Inclusion and Democracy* (Oxford University Press, 2000) chapter 1.

YOUNG K G 'The minimum core of economic and social rights: A concept in search of content' (2008) 33 *Yale Journal of International Law* 113.

YUSUF H O 'Oil on troubled waters: Multinational corporations and realizing human rights in the developing world, with specific reference to Nigeria' (2008) 8 *AHRLJ* 79.

ZIV N 'The social rights of people with disabilities: Reconciling care and justice' in Barak-Erez D and Gross A M (eds) *Exploring Social Rights: Between Theory and Practice* (Hart Publishing, 2007) 369.

Subject Index

www.ingramcontent.com/pod-product-compliance
Ingram Content Group UK Ltd.
Pitfield, Milton Keynes, MK11 3LW, UK
UKHW051117290926
15471UKWH00010B/1728